DRAMA
for Students

**Presenting Analysis, Context, and Criticism on
Commonly Studied Dramas**

Volume 15

David Galens, Project Editor

Foreword by Carole L. Hamilton

GALE®

THOMSON
✦
™
GALE

Detroit • New York • San Diego • San Francisco • Cleveland • New Haven, Conn. • Waterville, Maine • London • Munich

National Advisory Board

THOMSON

GALE

Drama for Students

Editor
alens

|
arie Hacht, Michelle Kazensky,
L. LaBlanc, Ira Mark Milne, Pam
r, Jennifer Smith, Daniel Toronto,
lmann

Permissions
Kim Davis, Debra Freitas

Manufacturing
Stacy Melson

Imaging and Multimedia
Lezlie Light, Kelly A. Quin, Luke Rademacher

Product Design
Pamela A. E. Galbreath, Michael Logusz

ISBN 0–7876–5253–9
ISSN 1094–9232

Printed in the United States of America
10 9 8 7 6 5 4 3 2 1

DRAMA
for Students

Table of Contents

The Study of Drama

We study drama in order to learn what meaning others have made of life, to comprehend what it takes to produce a work of art, and to glean some understanding of ourselves. Drama produces in a separate, aesthetic world, a moment of being for the audience to experience, while maintaining the detachment of a reflective observer.

Drama is a representational art, a visible and audible narrative presenting virtual, fictional characters within a virtual, fictional universe. Dramatic realizations may pretend to approximate reality or else stubbornly defy, distort, and deform reality into an artistic statement. From this separate universe that is obviously not "real life" we expect a valid reflection upon reality, yet drama never is mistaken for reality—the methods of theater are integral to its form and meaning. Theater is art, and art's appeal lies in its ability both to approximate life and to depart from it. For in intruding its distorted version of life into our consciousness, art gives us a new perspective and appreciation of life and reality. Although all aesthetic experiences perform this service, theater does it most effectively by creating a separate, cohesive universe that freely acknowledges its status as an art form.

And what is the purpose of the aesthetic universe of drama? The potential answers to such a question are nearly as many and varied as there are plays written, performed, and enjoyed. Dramatic texts can be problems posed, answers asserted, or moments portrayed. Dramas (tragedies as well as comedies) may serve strictly "to ease the anguish of a torturing hour" (as stated in William Shakespeare's *A Midsummer Night's Dream*)—to divert and entertain–or aspire to move the viewer to action with social issues. Whether to entertain or to instruct, affirm or influence, pacify or shock, dramatic art wraps us in the spell of its imaginary world for the length of the work and then dispenses us back to the real world, entertained, purged, as Aristotle said, of pity and fear, and edified—or at least weary enough to sleep peacefully.

It is commonly thought that theater, being an art of performance, must be experienced—seen—in order to be appreciated fully. However, to view a production of a dramatic text is to be limited to a single interpretation of that text—all other interpretations are for the moment closed off, inaccessible. In the process of producing a play, the director, stage designer, and performers interpret and transform the script into a work of art that always departs in some measure from the author's original conception. Novelist and critic Umberto Eco, in his *The Role of the Reader: Explorations in the Semiotics of Texts* (Indiana University Press, 1979), explained, "In short, we can say that every performance offers us a complete and satisfying version of the work, but at the same time makes it incomplete for us, because it cannot simultaneously give all the other artistic solutions which the work may admit."

Thus Laurence Olivier's coldly formal and neurotic film presentation of Shakespeare's *Hamlet* (in which he played the title character as well as directed) shows marked differences from subsequent adaptations. While Olivier's Hamlet is clearly entangled in a Freudian relationship with his mother Gertrude, he would be incapable of shushing her with the impassioned kiss that Mel Gibson's mercurial Hamlet (in director Franco Zeffirelli's 1990 film) does. Although each of performances rings true to Shakespeare's text, each is also a mutually exclusive work of art. Also important to consider are the time periods in which each of these films was produced: Olivier made his film in 1948, a time in which overt references to sexuality (especially incest) were frowned upon. Gibson and Zeffirelli made their film in a culture more relaxed and comfortable with these issues. Just as actors and directors can influence the presentation of drama, so too can the time period of the production affect what the audience will see.

A play script is an open text from which an infinity of specific realizations may be derived. Dramatic scripts that are more open to interpretive creativity (such as those of Ntozake Shange and Tomson Highway) actually require the creative improvisation of the production troupe in order to complete the text. Even the most prescriptive scripts (those of Neil Simon, Lillian Hellman, and Robert Bolt, for example), can never fully control the actualization of live performance, and circumstantial events, including the attitude and receptivity of the audience, make every performance a unique event. Thus, while it is important to view a production of a dramatic piece, if one wants to understand a drama fully it is equally important to read the original dramatic text.

The reader of a dramatic text or script is not limited by either the specific interpretation of a given production or by the unstoppable action of a moving spectacle. The reader of a dramatic text may discover the nuances of the play's language, structure, and events at their own pace. Yet studied alone, the author's blueprint for artistic production does not tell the whole story of a play's life and significance. One also needs to assess the play's critical reviews to discover how it resonated to cultural themes at the time of its debut and how the shifting tides of cultural interest have revised its interpretation and impact on audiences. And to do this, one needs to know a little about the culture of the times which produced the play as well as the author who penned it.

Drama for Students supplies this material in a useful compendium for the student of dramatic theater. Covering a range of dramatic works that span from 442 BC to the 1990s, this book focuses on significant theatrical works whose themes and form transcend the uncertainty of dramatic fads. These are plays that have proven to be both memorable and teachable. *Drama for Students* seeks to enhance appreciation of these dramatic texts by providing scholarly materials written with the secondary and college/university student in mind. It provides for each play a concise summary of the plot and characters as well as a detailed explanation of its themes. In addition, background material on the historical context of the play, its critical reception, and the author's life help the student to understand the work's position in the chronicle of dramatic history. For each play entry a new work of scholarly criticism is also included, as well as segments of other significant critical works for handy reference. A thorough bibliography provides a starting point for further research.

This series offers comprehensive educational resources for students of drama. *Drama for Students* is a vital book for dramatic interpretation and a valuable addition to any reference library.

Source: Eco, Umberto, *The Role of the Reader: Explorations in the Semiotics of Texts,* Indiana University Press, 1979.

Carole L. Hamilton
Author and Instructor of English
Cary Academy
Cary, North Carolina

Introduction

Purpose of the Book

The purpose of *Drama for Students* (*DfS*) is to provide readers with a guide to understanding, enjoying, and studying dramas by giving them easy access to information about the work. Part of Gale's "For Students" literature line, *DfS* is specifically designed to meet the curricular needs of high school and undergraduate college students and their teachers, as well as the interests of general readers and researchers considering specific plays. While each volume contains entries on "classic" dramas frequently studied in classrooms, there are also entries containing hard-to-find information on contemporary plays, including works by multicultural, international, and women playwrights.

The information covered in each entry includes an introduction to the play and the work's author; a plot summary, to help readers unravel and understand the events in a drama; descriptions of important characters, including explanation of a given character's role in the drama as well as discussion about that character's relationship to other characters in the play; analysis of important themes in the drama; and an explanation of important literary techniques and movements as they are demonstrated in the play.

In addition to this material, which helps the readers analyze the play itself, students are also provided with important information on the literary and historical background informing each work.

This includes a historical context essay, a box comparing the time or place the drama was written to modern Western culture, a critical essay, and excerpts from critical essays on the play. A unique feature of *DfS* is a specially commissioned critical essay on each drama, targeted toward the student reader.

To further aid the student in studying and enjoying each play, information on media adaptations is provided (if available), as well as reading suggestions for works of fiction and nonfiction on similar themes and topics. Classroom aids include ideas for research papers and lists of critical sources that provide additional material on each drama.

Selection Criteria

The titles for each volume of *DfS* were selected by surveying numerous sources on teaching literature and analyzing course curricula for various school districts. Some of the sources surveyed included: literature anthologies; *Reading Lists for College-Bound Students: The Books Most Recommended by America's Top Colleges*; textbooks on teaching dramas; a College Board survey of plays commonly studied in high schools; a National Council of Teachers of English (NCTE) survey of plays commonly studied in high schools; St. James Press's *International Dictionary of Theatre*; and Arthur Applebee's 1993 study *Literature in the Secondary School: Studies of Curriculum and Instruction in the United States*.

Input was also solicited from our advisory board, as well as educators from various areas. From these discussions, it was determined that each volume should have a mix of "classic" dramas (those works commonly taught in literature classes) and contemporary dramas for which information is often hard to find. Because of the interest in expanding the canon of literature, an emphasis was also placed on including works by international, multicultural, and women playwrights. Our advisory board members—educational professionals—helped pare down the list for each volume. If a work was not selected for the present volume, it was often noted as a possibility for a future volume. As always, the editor welcomes suggestions for titles to be included in future volumes.

How Each Entry Is Organized

Each entry, or chapter, in *DfS* focuses on one play. Each entry heading lists the full name of the play, the author's name, and the date of the play's publication. The following elements are contained in each entry:

- **Introduction:** a brief overview of the drama which provides information about its first appearance, its literary standing, any controversies surrounding the work, and major conflicts or themes within the work.

- **Author Biography:** this section includes basic facts about the author's life, and focuses on events and times in the author's life that inspired the drama in question.

- **Plot Summary:** a description of the major events in the play. Subheads demarcate the plays' various acts or scenes.

- **Characters:** an alphabetical listing of major characters in the play. Each character name is followed by a brief to an extensive description of the character's role in the plays, as well as discussion of the character's actions, relationships, and possible motivation.

Characters are listed alphabetically by last name. If a character is unnamed—for instance, the Stage Manager in *Our Town*—the character is listed as "The Stage Manager" and alphabetized as "Stage Manager." If a character's first name is the only one given, the name will appear alphabetically by the name. Variant names are also included for each character. Thus, the nickname "Babe" would head the listing for a character in *Crimes of the Heart,* but below that listing would

be her less-mentioned married name "Rebecca Botrelle."

- **Themes:** a thorough overview of how the major topics, themes, and issues are addressed within the play. Each theme discussed appears in a separate subhead, and is easily accessed through the boldface entries in the Subject/Theme Index.

- **Style:** this section addresses important style elements of the drama, such as setting, point of view, and narration; important literary devices used, such as imagery, foreshadowing, symbolism; and, if applicable, genres to which the work might have belonged, such as Gothicism or Romanticism. Literary terms are explained within the entry, but can also be found in the Glossary.

- **Historical Context:** this section outlines the social, political, and cultural climate *in which the author lived and the play was created.* This section may include descriptions of related historical events, pertinent aspects of daily life in the culture, and the artistic and literary sensibilities of the time in which the work was written. If the play is a historical work, information regarding the time in which the play is set is also included. Each section is broken down with helpful subheads.

- **Critical Overview:** this section provides background on the critical reputation of the play, including bannings or any other public controversies surrounding the work. For older plays, this section includes a history of how the drama was first received and how perceptions of it may have changed over the years; for more recent plays, direct quotes from early reviews may also be included.

- **Criticism:** an essay commissioned by *DfS* which specifically deals with the play and is written specifically for the student audience, as well as excerpts from previously published criticism on the work (if available).

- **Sources:** an alphabetical list of critical material used in compiling the entry, with full bibliographical information.

- **Further Reading:** an alphabetical list of other critical sources which may prove useful for the student. It includes full bibliographical information and a brief annotation.

In addition, each entry contains the following highlighted sections, set apart from the main text as sidebars:

- **Media Adaptations:** if available, a list of important film and television adaptations of the play, including source information. The list may also include such variations on the work as audio recordings, musical adaptations, and other stage interpretations.

- **Topics for Further Study:** a list of potential study questions or research topics dealing with the play. This section includes questions related to other disciplines the student may be studying, such as American history, world history, science, math, government, business, geography, economics, psychology, etc.

- **Compare and Contrast:** an "at-a-glance" comparison of the cultural and historical differences between the author's time and culture and late twentieth century or early twenty-first century Western culture. This box includes pertinent parallels between the major scientific, political, and cultural movements of the time or place the drama was written, the time or place the play was set (if a historical work), and modern Western culture. Works written after 1990 may not have this box.

- **What Do I Read Next?:** a list of works that might complement the featured play or serve as a contrast to it. This includes works by the same author and others, works of fiction and nonfiction, and works from various genres, cultures, and eras.

Other Features

DfS includes "The Study of Drama," a foreword by Carole Hamilton, an educator and author who specializes in dramatic works. This essay examines the basis for drama in societies and what drives people to study such work. The essay also discusses how *Drama for Students* can help teachers show students how to enrich their own reading/viewing experiences.

A Cumulative Author/Title Index lists the authors and titles covered in each volume of the *DfS* series.

A Cumulative Nationality/Ethnicity Index breaks down the authors and titles covered in each volume of the *DfS* series by nationality and ethnicity.

A Subject/Theme Index, specific to each volume, provides easy reference for users who may be studying a particular subject or theme rather than a single work. Significant subjects from events to broad themes are included, and the entries pointing to the specific theme discussions in each entry are indicated in **boldface**.

Each entry may include illustrations, including photo of the author, stills from stage productions, and stills from film adaptations, if available.

Citing Drama for Students

When writing papers, students who quote directly from any volume of *Drama for Students* may use the following general forms. These examples are based on MLA style; teachers may request that students adhere to a different style, so the following examples may be adapted as needed.

When citing text from *DfS* that is not attributed to a particular author (i.e., the Themes, Style, Historical Context sections, etc.), the following format should be used in the bibliography section:

"Our Town." *Drama for Students*. Eds. David Galens and Lynn Spampinato. Vol. 1. Detroit: Gale, 1998. 227–30.

When quoting the specially commissioned essay from *DfS* (usually the first piece under the "Criticism" subhead), the following format should be used:

Fiero, John. Critical Essay on "Twilight: Los Angeles, 1992." *Drama for Students*. Eds. David Galens and Lynn Spampinato. Vol. 2. Detroit: Gale, 1998. 247–49.

When quoting a journal or newspaper essay that is reprinted in a volume of *DfS*, the following form may be used:

Rich, Frank. "Theatre: A Mamet Play, *Glengarry Glen Ross*." *New York Theatre Critics' Review* Vol. 45, No. 4 (March 5, 1984), 5–7; excerpted and reprinted in *Drama for Students*, Vol. 2, eds. David Galens and Lynn Spampinato (Detroit: Gale, 1998), pp. 51–53.

When quoting material reprinted from a book that appears in a volume of *DfS*, the following form may be used:

Kerr, Walter. "*The Miracle Worker*," in *The Theatre in Spite of Itself*. Simon & Schuster, 1963. 255–57; excerpted and reprinted in *Drama for Students*, Vol. 2, eds. David Galens and Lynn Spampinato (Detroit: Gale, 1998), pp. 123–24.

We Welcome Your Suggestions

The editor of *Drama for Students* welcomes your comments and ideas. Readers who wish to suggest dramas to appear in future volumes, or who have other suggestions, are cordially invited to contact the editor. You may contact the editor via E-mail at: **ForStudentsEditors@gale.com.** Or write to the editor at:

Editor, *Drama for Students*
The Gale Group
27500 Drake Rd.
Farmington Hills, MI 48331–3535

Literary Chronology

1670: Willam Congreve is born in Bardsey (a village near Leeds), Yorkshire, England.

1700: William Congreve's *The Way of the World* is published.

1729: Willam Congreve dies.

1751: Richard Brinsley Sheridan is born on January 25 in Dublin, Ireland.

1775: Richard Brinsley Sheridan's *The Rivals* is published.

1816: Richard Brinsley Sheridan dies destitute, after being imprisoned for debt in 1813, although his wealthy friends give him an extravagant funeral.

1828: Henrik Ibsen is born on March 20 in Skien, Norway.

1890: Frances Goodrich is born in New Jersey.

1892: Archibald MacLeish is born on May 7 in Glencoe, Illinois.

1892: Henrik Ibsen's *The Master Builder* is published.

1896: Robert E. Sherwood is born in New Rochelle, New York.

1900: Albert Hackett is born in New York.

1906: Henrik Ibsen dies on May 23 in Oslo, Norway, after suffering a series of strokes.

1907: Joseph Kramm is born on September 30 in Philadelphia, Pennsylvania.

1924: James Baldwin is born on August 2 in Harlem in New York City.

1929: Howard Sackler is born on December 19 in New York City.

1933: Maureen Duffy is born on October 21 in Worthing, Sussex, England.

1933: Archibald MacLeish receives the Pulitzer Prize for poetry for *Conquistador*.

1936: Robert E. Sherwood's *Idiot's Delight* is published. Sherwood receives the Pulitzer Prize for drama.

1936: Alfred Uhry is born to an upper-middle-class German-Jewish family in Atlanta, Georgia.

1945: August Wilson is born to a white father, Frederick August Kittle, and a black mother, Daisy Wilson.

1945: Michael Cristofer is born (born Michael Procaccino) on January 28 in Trenton, New Jersey.

1947: David Mamet is born on November 30 to parents of Polish-Russian descent.

1948: David Edgar is born on February 26 in Birmingham, England.

1952: Joseph Kramm's *The Shrike* is published. Kramm receives the Pulitzer Prize for drama.

1953: Archibald MacLeish receives the Pulitzer Prize for poetry for *Collected Poems, 1917–1952*.

1955: Robert Emmet Sherwood dies of cardiac arrest.

1956: Albert Hackett and Frances Goodrich's *The Diary of Anne Frank* is published. They receive the Pulitzer Prize for drama.

1958: Archibald MacLeish's *J. B.* is published.

1959: Archibald MacLeish receives the Pulitzer Prize for drama for *J. B.*.

1967: Howard Sackler's *The Great White Hope* is published.

1969: Howard Sackler receives the Pulitzer Prize for drama for *The Great White Hope*.

1969: Maureen Duffy's *Rites* is published.

1972: James Baldwin's *One Day, When I Was Lost: A Scenario* is published.

1975: Michael Cristofer's *The Shadow Box* is published.

1976: David Mamet's *Reunion* is published.

1977: Michael Cristofer receives the Pulitzer Prize for drama for *The Shadow Box*.

1980: David Edgar's *The Life and Adventures of Nicholas Nickleby* is published.

1982: Howard Sackler dies at his home in Ibiza, Spain, leaving several plays unfinished.

1982: Archibald MacLeish dies on April 20, just three weeks before a national symposium honoring his life and work.

1984: Frances Goodrich dies from cancer on January 19 in New York.

1984: August Wilson's *Ma Rainey's Black Bottom* is published.

1984: David Mamet receives the Pulitzer Prize for drama for *Glengarry Glen Ross*.

1987: James Baldwin dies from stomach cancer on December 1 in St. Paul de Vence, France.

1987: August Wilson receives the Pulitzer Prize for drama for *Fences*.

1988: Alfred Uhry receives the Pulitzer Prize for drama for *Driving Miss Daisy*.

1995: Albert Hackett dies from pneumonia on March 16 in New York.

1996: Alfred Uhry's *The Last Night of Ballyhoo* is published.

Acknowledgments

The editors wish to thank the copyright holders of the excerpted criticism included in this volume and the permissions managers of many book and magazine publishing companies for assisting us in securing reproduction rights. We are also grateful to the staffs of the Detroit Public Library, the Library of Congress, the University of Detroit Mercy Library, Wayne State University Purdy/Kresge Library Complex, and the University of Michigan Libraries for making their resources available to us. Following is a list of the copyright holders who have granted us permission to reproduce material in this volume of *Drama for Students (DfS)*. Every effort has been made to trace copyright, but if omissions have been made, please let us know.

COPYRIGHTED MATERIALS IN *DfS*, VOLUME 15, WERE REPRODUCED FROM THE FOLLOWING PERIODICALS:

American Drama, v. 5, Spring, 1996. Reproduced by permission.—*Ball State University Forum*, Summer, 1986. Copyright (c) 1986 by Ball State University. Reproduced by permission.—*Essays in Theatre*, v. 21, November, 1983 for "Deconstructing Realism in Ibsen's *The Master Builder*," by Richard Hornby. Reproduced by permission of the author.—*New Republic*, v. 159, October 26, 1968; v. 187, August 2, 1982. Both reproduced by permission.—*Public Historian*, v. 21, Winter, 1999. Reproduced by permission.—*Theatre Journal*, v. 49, October, 1997. Reproduced by permission.—*Western Humanities Review*, v. 23, Autumn, 1969. Reproduced by permission.

COPYRIGHTED MATERIALS IN *DfS*, VOLUME 15, WERE REPRODUCED FROM THE FOLLOWING BOOKS:

Adell, Sandra. From "Speaking of Ma Rainey/ Talking about the Blues," in *May All Your Fences Have Gates: Essays on the Drama of August Wilson*. Edited by Alan Nadel. University of Iowa Press, 1994. Reproduced by permission.—Falk, Signi Lenea. From "Later Poetry and Drama," in *Archibald MacLeish*. Twayne Publishers, Inc., 1965. The Gale Group.—Innes, Christopher. From "Adapating Dickens to the Modern Eye: *Nicholas Nickleby* and *Little Dorrit*," in *Novel Images: Literature in Performance*. Edited by Peter Reynolds. Routledge, 1993. Reproduced by permission.—Kelley, Margot A. From "Life near Death: Art of Dying in Recent American Drama," in *Text and Presentation*. Edited by Karelisa Hartigan. University Press of America, 1988. Reproduced by permission.—Kimball, Sue L. From "Games People Play in Congreve's *The Way of the World*," in *A Provision of Human Nature: Essays on Fielding and Others in Honor of Miriam Austin Locke*. University of Alabama Press, 1977. Reproduced by permission.—McWilliams, James L., III. From *The Dictionary of Literary Biography,* **Volume 7:** *Twentieth-Century American Dramatists, Part 2, K–Z*. Gale Group, 1981.—Morgan, Margery. From "*The Mas-*

ter Builder," in **The International Dictionary of Theatre: Plays**. Edited by Mark Hawkins-Dady. St. James Press, 1992. The Gale Group.—Shuman, R. Baird. From "Sherwood's Universal Microcosms," in **Robert Emmet Sherwood**. College & University Press, 1964. Reproduced by permission.

PHOTOGRAPHS AND ILLUSTRATIONS APPEARING IN DfS, VOLUME 15, WERE RECEIVED FROM THE FOLLOWING SOURCES:

Baldwin, James, photograph. Archive Photos. Reproduced by permission.—Congreve, William, print. Archive Photos. Reproduced by permission.—Craig, Wendy as Mrs. Malaprop, Benjamin Whitrow, as Sir Anthony Absolute, in a scene from the 2000 theatrical production of *"The Rivals,"* by Richard Brinsley Sheridan, photograph. © Donald Cooper/Photostage. Reproduced by permission.—Cristofer, Michael, Gambier, Ohio, 1978, photograph. AP/Wide World Photos. Reproduced by permission.—*The Diary of Anne Frank,* Frances Goodrich and Albert Hackett dramatization, week of September 20, 1956 cover of *Playbill: The National Theatre Magazine,* Joseph Schildkraut, as Mr. Frank embracing Susan Strasberg, as Anne Frank, Cort Theatre, Broadway, photograph. *Playbill* ® is a registered trademark of Playbill Incorporated, N.Y.C. All rights reserved. Reproduced by permission.—Duffy, Maureen, photograph. © Jerry Bauer. Reproduced by permission.—Edgar, David, photograph by Mark Gerson. Reproduced by permission of Mark Gerson.—Engraving from the 1909 book *Sheridan: From New and Original Material,* written by Walter Sichel, Old Quin (foreground left) standing, Lord Lyttelton walking with cane, surrounded by parade crowd, North Parade turning into Pierpoint Street, Bath, England.—Gable, Clark as Henry Van, doing a card trick for small crowd, scene from the 1939 film *Idiot's Delight,* directed by Clarence Brown, photograph. The Kobal Collection. Reproduced by permission.—Goodrich, Frances, and Albert Hackett, 1956, photograph. The Corbis Collection. Reproduced by permission.—Grout, James as Sir Wilfull Witwoud ®, John Moffatt, as Witwoud, scene from the 1984 theatrical production *The Way of the World,* by William Congreve, Sir Wilfull Witwoud touching Witwoud's long wig, on stage at Theatre Royal, London, photograph. © Donald Cooper/Photostage. Reproduced by permission.—Ibsen, Henrik, photograph. © Hulton-Deutsch Collection/Corbis. Reproduced by permission.—*JB,* by Archibald MacLeish with Nan Martin, during the week of March 23, 1959 from the cover of *Playbill: The National Theatre Magazine,* Volume 3, Number 12, Anta Theatre, Broadway, photograph. *Playbill* ® is a registered trademark of Playbill Incorporated, N.Y.C. All rights reserved. Reproduced by permission.—Jones, James Earl as Jack Jefferson, in a scene from the 1970 film *The Great White Hope,* directed by Martin Ritt, photograph. The Kobal Collection. Reproduced by permission.—Kay, Lila (far left), as Mrs. Crummies, Christopher Benjamin (sitting), as Vincent Crummies, Suzanne Bertish (sitting on lap), as Fanny Squeers, Roger Rees (holding Fanny on lap), as Nicholas Nickleby, scene from the 1980–1981 theatrical production of *The Life and Adventures of Nicholas Nickleby,* written by Charles Dickens, adapted by David Edgars, photograph. © Donald Cooper/Photostage. Reproduced by permission.—*The Last Night of Ballyhoo,* by Alfred Uhry, February 1997 cover of *Playbill: The National Theatre Magazine,* Volume 97, Number 2, illustration with text and graphics, Helen Hayes Theatre, Broadway, photograph. *Playbill* ® is a registered trademark of Playbill Incorporated, N.Y.C. All rights reserved. Reproduced by permission.—Macleish, Archibald, photograph. The Library of Congress.—Mamet, David Alan, Rebecca Pidgeon, 1991, Cannes, France, photograph by Jose Goitia. AP/Wide World Photos. Reproduced by permission.—Marcell, Joseph (left), as Tick, Hugh Quarshie, as Jack Jefferson, scene from the 1987 theatrical production of *The Great White Hope,* written by Howard Sackler, photograph. © Donald Cooper/Photostage. Reproduced by permission.—*The Master Builder,* by Henrik Ibsen, March 1992 cover of *Playbill: The National Theatre Magazine,* Volume 92, Number 3, Belasco Theatre, photograph. *Playbill* ® is a registered trademark of Playbill Incorporated, N.Y.C. All rights reserved. Reproduced by permission.—Perkins, Millie (bottom center) in the title role, left to right, Joseph Schildkraut, Gusti Huber, Lou Jacobi, Richard Beymer, and Diane Baker peaking out a broken window in the film version of *The Diary of Anne Frank,* 1959, photograph. Archive Photos. Reproduced by permission.—*Reunion* by David Mamet, November 1979 cover of *Showbill,* Circle Repertory Company, Broadway, photograph. *Playbill* ® is a registered trademark of Playbill Incorporated, N.Y.C. All rights reserved. Reproduced by permission.—Rutherford, Margaret, as Lady Wishfort, wearing elaborate hat and dress, looking away from camera, from the 1953 theatrical production of *The Way of the World,* written by William Congreve, on stage at Lyric Hammersmith, London, England, photograph. © Hulton-Deutsch Collection/Corbis.

Reproduced by permission.—*The Shadow Box*, by Michael Cristofer, December 1977 cast list and cover from *Playbill: The National Theatre Magazine*, Lunt-Fontanne Theatre, Broadway, photograph. *Playbill* ® is a registered trademark of Playbill Incorporated, N.Y.C. All rights reserved. Reproduced by permission.—Sheridan, Richard Brinsley, photograph. The Library of Congress.—Sherwood, Robert, photograph. The Library of Congress.—*The Shrike*, by Joseph Kramm, week of February 11, 1952 cover of *Playbill: The National Theatre Magazine*, Cort Theatre, Broadway, photograph. *Playbill* ® is a registered trademark of Playbill Incorporated, N.Y.C. All rights reserved. Reproduced by permission.—Uhry, Alfred, photograph.

AP/Wide World Photos. Reproduced by permission.—Wilson, August, photograph. AP/Wide World Photos. Reproduced by permission.—Wood, John as Halvard Solness, Joanne Pearce, as Hilde Wangel, scene from the 1989 theatrical production of *The Master Builder*, by Henrik Ibsen, on stage at Theatre Royal, London, England, photograph. © Donald Cooper/Photostage. Reproduced by permission.—Woods-Coleman, Carol, as Ma Rainey, singing into microphone as Jacqueline de Peza, as Dussie Mae, sits and watches her, from the 1989 theatrical production of *Ma Rainey's Black Bottom*, by August Wilson, on stage at National Theatre's Cottesloe Theatre, photograph. © Donald Cooper/Photostage. Reproduced by permission.

Contributors

Bryan Aubrey: Aubrey holds a Ph.D. in English and has published many articles on twentieth-century literature. Entry on *Rites*. Original essay on *Rites*.

Cynthia Bily: Bily is an instructor of writing and literature at Adrian College. Entry on *J. B.*. Original essay on *J. B.*.

Liz Brent: Brent has a Ph.D. in American Culture, specializing in film studies, from the University of Michigan. She is a freelance writer and teaches courses on the history of American cinema. Entry on *Reunion*. Original essay on *Reunion*.

Kate Covintree: Covintree is a graduate of Randolph-Macon Women's College with a degree in English. Original essay on *The Last Night of Ballyhoo*.

Catherine Dybiec Holm: Dybiec Holm is a published writer and editor with a master's degree in natural resources. Original essay on *The Last Night of Ballyhoo*.

Curt Guyette: Guyette is a graduate from the University of Pittsburgh with a bachelor's degree in English and is a longtime journalist. Original essay on *One Day, When I Was Lost: A Scenario*.

Carole Hamilton: Hamilton is an English teacher at Cary Academy, an innovative private college preparatory school in Cary, North Carolina. Entries on *The Life and Adventures of Nicholas Nickleby* and *The Rivals*. Original essays on *The Life and Adventures of Nicholas Nickleby* and *The Rivals*.

Joyce Hart: Hart has written literary essays, books on the study of language, and a soon-to-be-published biography of Richard Wright. Entry on *One Day, When I Was Lost: A Scenario*. Original essay on *One Day, When I Was Lost: A Scenario*.

David Kelly: Kelly is an adjunct professor of English at College of Lake County and Oakton Community College in Illinois. Entry on *Idiot's Delight*. Original essay on *Idiot's Delight*.

Rena Korb: Korb has a master's degree in English literature and creative writing and has written for a wide variety of educational publishers. Entries on *The Diary of Anne Frank* and *The Last Night of Ballyhoo*. Original essays on *The Diary of Anne Frank* and *The Last Night of Ballyhoo*.

Laura Kryhoski: Kryhoski is currently working as a freelance writer. Entries on *The Great White Hope* and *The Shadow Box*. Original essays on *The Great White Hope* and *The Shadow Box*.

Melodie Monahan: Monahan operates The Inkwell Works, an editorial service, and teaches English literature at Wayne State University in

Detroit, Michigan. Original essay on *The Life and Adventures of Nicholas Nickleby*.

Kevin O'Sullivan: O'Sullivan is a writer of fiction, feature articles, and criticism. Original essay on *Reunion*.

Josh Ozersky: Ozersky is a critic, essayist, and cultural historian. Original essays on *Reunion* and *The Shrike*.

Wendy Perkins: Perkins is an instructor of twentieth-century literature and film. Entries on *The Master Builder* and *The Shrike*. Original essays on *The Master Builder* and *The Shrike*.

Chris Semansky: Semansky's essays, stories, reviews, and poems appear regularly in literary magazines and journals. Entry on *Ma Rainey's Black Bottom*. Original essay on *Ma Rainey's Black Bottom*.

Kathy Smith: Smith is an independent scholar and freelance writer. Entry on *The Way of the World*. Original essay on *The Way of the World*.

Carey Wallace: Wallace's stories, poems, and essays appear in publications around the country. Original essays on *One Day, When I Was Lost: A Scenario* and *The Shadow Box*.

The Diary of Anne Frank

FRANCES GOODRICH AND
ALBERT HACKETT

1956

The Diary of Anne Frank, the play adapted from Anne Frank's famous diary, made its theater debut in 1956. Since then, it has been reproduced countless times on stages across the country and abroad (the playscript, with extensive notes, is readily available from Dramatists Play Service). Collaborators Frances Goodrich and Albert Hackett, longtime Hollywood writers, had little experience with such a story as that of the Frank family. Previous scripts included sophisticated comedies such as *The Thin Man* or lively musicals such as *Easter Parade*. However, Goodrich and Hackett researched the play meticulously, drawing not only on Anne's diary but also on the experience of visiting Otto Frank and the attic hideout. As Evelyn Ehrlich noted in *Dictionary of Literary Biography,* Hackett in 1956 said, "We all felt we were working for a cause, not just a play."

The Diary of Anne Frank was an immediate critical and popular success, with reviewers particularly enthusiastic about Anne's spirit, optimism, and nobility. The play represented the pinnacle of Goodrich and Hackett's career. However, over the years, criticism mounted against the play for inaccurately representing Anne's own words as well as the Jewish experience of the Holocaust. Wendy Kesselman revised the script and mounted a production in 1997, but the commentary brought about by this new version of Anne's life in hiding contributes to the reader's understanding of the monumental task that faced Goodrich and Hackett in the 1950s,

as they attempted to bring together the contradictory aspects of Anne Frank.

AUTHOR BIOGRAPHY

Goodrich was born in New Jersey in 1890. After graduating from Vassar College in 1912, she went to New York where she studied for a year at the New York School of Social Work. Her first acting experience was with a Massachusetts stock company, but in 1916 she made her Broadway debut.

Hackett was born in New York in 1900, the son of professional actors. He made his stage debut when he was six years old. He performed in silent films and on stage before becoming a writer.

Goodrich and Hackett met in 1927, when both were performing with a Denver stock company. They soon began working as a writing team. The first collaborative effort was the play *Up Pops the Devil*, which opened in New York in 1930 and was made into a film the following year. Also in 1931, the couple married.

By 1932, Hollywood's MGM studio was contracting their writing services; between 1933 and 1939, they wrote thirteen films, many of them box-office successes. Their work, such as 1934's *The Thin Man* and its sequels, was characterized by its literate and sophisticated dialogue. After a brief return to New York to write plays and act, in 1941 Goodrich and Hackett signed on with Paramount but found few rewarding assignments there. In 1946, they moved to RKO to work on *It's a Wonderful Life*. In the 1940s, Goodrich and Hackett wrote several more award-winning scripts, including *Easter Parade* (1948), *Father of the Bride* (1950), and *Seven Brides for Seven Brothers* (1954).

By the 1950s, however, Goodrich and Hackett had become interested in a different sort of project: an adaptation of *The Diary of Anne Frank*. They worked on this script for two years, even meeting with Otto Frank and visiting the attic where the Franks and four other Jews hid from the Nazis. The play opened on Broadway in 1955, and it was the high point of their careers, earning a Tony Award and the Pulitzer Prize. In 1959, they adapted the play into a film, but though it was a critical success, it did not gain popularity at the box office.

Goodrich and Hackett's final film was 1962's *Five Finger Exercise*. After its failure, they returned to New York and ceased writing screenplays. Goodrich died of cancer on January 19, 1984, in New York. Hackett died of pneumonia on March 16, 1995, in New York.

PLOT SUMMARY

Act 1

The play *The Diary of Anne Frank* opens in November 1945 with Otto Frank's return to the attic rooms where he, his family, the Van Daans, and Mr. Dussell lived in hiding during the Nazi occupation of Holland. He enters the upstairs rooms carrying a rucksack. He moves slowly around the room and picks up a scarf, which he puts around his neck. As he bends down to pick up a glove, he breaks down. Hearing his cries, Miep Gies comes up the stairs, asking if he is all right and begging him not to stay up in the rooms. Mr. Frank says that he has come to say goodbye, that he is leaving Amsterdam though he doesn't yet know where he is going. As he is about to leave, Miep gives him a pile of papers that were left behind after the Gestapo came and took everyone away. Mr. Frank tells her to burn them, but Miep insists that he look at the papers. She puts Anne's diary in his hand. Mr. Frank opens the diary and begins to read the first entry, dated July 6, 1942, aloud. Gradually, Anne's voice joins his and then Mr. Frank's voice subsides. Anne describes how bad the situation got for the Jews in Holland after the German conquest. Her diary recounts the Franks' final morning at home, as they tried to make it appear they had fled the country. Instead, they went to the building where Mr. Frank had his business to go into hiding.

The next scene takes place in July 1942 in the attic where the families will hide. The Van Daans are waiting for the Franks. When they arrive, accompanied by Miep and Mr. Kraler, introductions are made between the two families; with the exception of the men, no one knows each other. After Miep and Mr. Kraler leave to get ready for work, Mr. Frank explains the rules: during the day, when the workers are downstairs, they cannot move around, speak above a whisper, or run any water. Then all of them begin to settle down and unpack their meager belongings before the workday begins. Anne tries to get acquainted with Peter and manages to find out that they attended the same school, but she immediately recognizes how shy he is. On this first day in hiding, Mr. Frank gives Anne the diary.

It is now two months later. Six o'clock has come, so everyone can move around. Anne has taken Peter's shoes, and in his attempt to get them back, they scuffle. Peter flees to his room, leaving Anne to wish that he were more fun. Dancing around the room, Anne spills milk on Mrs. Van Daan's fur coat, which causes the woman to storm angrily from the room. Mr. Van Daan follows, and Mrs. Frank warns Anne to be more courteous to their guests and reminds her that everyone is under great strain. She asks Anne to be more like Margot, who is more distant. Anne runs to her room.

Alone, Mrs. Frank and Margot begin to prepare supper. Mrs. Frank confides that she had asked Mr. Frank not to invite the Van Daans to share their hiding place, but he had insisted. At that moment, the buzzer sounds, signaling Mr. Kraler or Miep. Mr. Kraler arrives with a question: Miep's boyfriend has a Jewish friend who has no place to hide. Can Mr. Dussel stay with them for a few nights? Mr. Frank immediately tells Mr. Kraler to bring Mr. Dussel upstairs. He will share Anne's room. Mr. Frank serves cognac as a welcome. Mr. Dussel tells them what has been taking place in Amsterdam since they went into hiding. The first news is good, that people believe the Franks escaped to Switzerland. But he also tells them that hundreds of Jews are sent to death camps each day, including Anne's friends. Mr. Frank puts a stop to the conversation. Anne shows Mr. Dussel to the room they will share.

In the next scene, Anne's screams from a nightmare wake everyone up. Her parents rush into the room, but Anne sends her mother away and asks her father to stay with her. Anne tells her father that he is the only person she loves. Mr. Frank tells her that her rejection of her mother is very hurtful. Anne believes that she cannot help how she acts, but she immediately feels regretful and asks her father what is wrong with her.

It is the first night of Hanukkah, 1942. Anne has prepared presents for everyone (including the scarf Mr. Frank finds in the play's opening scene), and everyone is amazed at her ingenuity and touched by her thoughtfulness. However, the good mood is broken when Mr. Van Daan and Peter start arguing

Albert Hackett

about his cat. The argument is brought to a swift halt by a crashing sound in the offices below. Everyone immediately quiets down and takes off their shoes. While standing on a chair to extinguish the overhead light, Peter falls down. From below comes the sound of feet running. In the attic above, everyone is frightened, wondering if it is the police come to take them away. Mr. Frank goes downstairs to investigate and returns with the news that it was a thief. While he says that the danger has passed, Mr. Dussel points out that now someone knows that there are people living above the offices. To restore everyone's courage in the face of a new anxiety, Mr. Frank asks Anne to sing the Hanukkah song, and soon the rest join in.

Act 2

Act 2 opens in January 1944; the families have been in hiding close to a year and a half. Miep and Mr. Kraler have arrived with a New Year's cake. Over his wife's protests, Mr. Van Daan gives her fur coat to Miep to sell. Mr. Kraler asks Mr. Frank to come downstairs with him to go over some contracts, but Mr. Frank realizes that Mr. Kraler really wants to speak to him in private. He tells Mr. Kraler that he must say whatever he has to say in front of everyone, and so they find out that one of the workers in the office is blackmailing Mr. Kraler in exchange for his silence about the upstairs room, which he remembers as existing. Scared and angry, Anne lashes out at her mother and then runs into her room. Peter follows her, telling her that he thinks she is just fine. For the first time since they've been in hiding, Peter and Anne talk, forging a friendship.

Anne and Peter's burgeoning friendship causes tensions between their mothers; Mrs. Van Daan has been making insinuations about what is going on when Anne visits Peter in his room after dinner. Alone, Anne and Peter talk about all sorts of things, and they share their first kiss. Tensions also are growing in the cramped attic in general. One night, these tensions erupt when Mrs. Frank catches Mr. Van Daan stealing food. Mrs. Frank snaps, demanding that Mr. Van Daan leave the attic. Mr. Frank tries to calm his wife down, but she refuses to listen to reason. However, the crisis comes to an end with Miep's arrival and her welcome news that the Allied invasion of the European continent has begun.

A few weeks later finds everyone gathered in the center room, sitting tensely. The office phone downstairs rings, apparently for the third time. Mr. Dussel insists that it is a warning from Miep, who hasn't been to see them for three days. No one has come into work downstairs, either, another ominous sign. Mr. Dussel, seconded by Mr. Van Daan, begs Mr. Frank to go downstairs and answer the phone, but Mr. Frank refuses. Mr. and Mrs. Van Daan begin to argue, driving Peter into his room. Anne follows him. She is telling him about what they will do when they are free again when a car pulls up in front of the building. The outside bell rings again and again, and then comes the sound of the door being battered in. They hear heavy footsteps and another door being battered in. It is the Nazis. "For the past two years we have lived in fear," Mr. Frank says. "Now we can live in hope." They hear the door to their stairwell crash in and the sound of German voices.

The play's final scene again returns to November 1945. Mr. Kraler has joined Miep and Mr. Frank in the upstairs rooms. Mr. Frank closes Anne's diary. Mr. Kraler tells him that it was the thief who reported them. Mr. Frank tells them that Anne was happy at the concentration camp, happy to be outside in the fresh air. Of the eight who lived in the attic, Mr. Frank is the only survivor. After Auschwitz was liberated in January, Mr. Frank traveled back to Holland, learning of everyone's death along the

way. Only the day before, he had learned of Anne's death at Bergen-Belsen. Anne's voice, reading from her diary, closes the play: "In spite of everything, I still believe that people are really good at heart."

CHARACTERS

Jan Dussel

Mr. Dussel is the dentist who comes to live with the Franks and the Van Daans after they have been in hiding about two months. He is a neighbor of Miep's boyfriend, and when the Nazis begin rounding up and deporting the Jews, he has nowhere to go. Originally supposed to stay only for a few days, Mr. Dussel remains in the attic until the Gestapo take everyone away.

In his fifties and set in his ways, Mr. Dussel is difficult to get along with. He refuses to adjust to the reality of so little space shared by so many people. He also stirs up worry, for example, by making everyone fearful that the thief will report them. He also makes his dislike of Anne clear. For instance, when Mr. Van Daan says in reaction to Anne's nightmare screams, "I thought someone was murdering her," Mr. Dussel answers, "Unfortunately, no."

Anne Frank

Anne is thirteen years old when her family goes into hiding. She is a rambunctious, precocious, friendly, talkative girl. In the Franks' life in Amsterdam, Anne had many friends at school, and now, lonely in the attic, she turns to her diary as the confidante with whom she can share her thoughts. She tells her diary about her family, her past, her feelings, and her hopes for the future.

Anne's boisterousness and her determination to act as she feels and not as others believe she should pose a challenge; Mrs. Frank and the Van Daans think she should act more like a young lady, but Anne refuses to change her personality to their wishes. She rebels against societal restrictions and the values of an older generation. However, while Anne's imagination, enthusiasm, and will cannot be subdued, at times, as when Anne makes Hanukkah presents for everyone, this quality is greatly appreciated.

Although carefree on the exterior, Anne has many serious concerns that she keeps hidden. She worries about her relationship with her mother and her inability to control herself, particularly with regard to acting hurtful toward others. Another major concern is her writing; she has decided that her goal in life is to become a famous writer, but she does not know if she will be able to write well enough to "go on living even after my death." Anne also spends her time thinking about the events that have shaken the world. She knows about the concentration camps, but she still insists on believing that the world will be a better place someday. Her last words in the play are hopeful ones: "I think the world may be going through a phase, the way I was with Mother. It'll pass, maybe not for hundreds of years, but some day . . . I still believe, in spite of everything, that people are really good at heart." Anne dies in the concentration camp when she is fifteen years old.

Edith Frank

Mrs. Frank is a reserved woman, and she believes that her daughters should be the same way. Her lack of understanding regarding Anne's personality makes it impossible for the two to share a sustained emotional connection; nevertheless, she is hurt by Anne's continual rejection of her ideals and her affection. Mrs. Frank takes on the role of conciliator, trying to keep things calm in the attic; for example, she is willing that Anne should give up her one friend—Peter—to appease Mrs. Van Daan. Though she rarely argues—as Margot points out to Anne, "She can't talk back. . . . It's just not in her nature to fight back"—the night she catches Mr. Van Daan stealing food is the last straw. She adamantly demands that Mr. Van Daan leave the attic. Only Miep's arrival with good news deters her from making him leave. Mrs. Frank dies in the concentration camps.

Margot Frank

Margot, Anne's older sister, is eighteen years old when they first go into hiding. She is a reserved young woman. Margot is in every way a well-brought-up young lady. She is obedient and respectful. She does her studies with her father and helps her mother with the chores of the house. She loans her high heels to her younger sister. She rarely disagrees, but one notable exception, which shocks her mother, occurs when Margot declares, "Sometimes I wish the end would come . . . whatever it is." Margot dies in the concentration camps.

MEDIA ADAPTATIONS

- *The Diary of Anne Frank,* a film adaptation of the play, was released in 1959. It stars Millie Perkins and Shelley Winters and was directed by George Stevens. It is available on VHS and DVD.

Otto Frank

Mr. Frank and his family immigrated to Holland in the 1930s, when Adolf Hitler came into power in Germany. Mr. Frank started an import business, but the business was taken from him when the Germans conquered Holland in 1940. The family lived under increasingly repressive circumstances for a few years, but afraid of what would happen to the Jews, Mr. Frank arranged for his family to go into hiding in the attic above his former business. He invited the Van Daans as well, out of gratitude for Mr. Van Daan's help when he first arrived in Holland.

Mr. Frank is the head of the "attic" family, but he willingly shares any information regarding their safety with everyone else. His calmness and patience lead him to try to work out the difficulties that arise between members of the household. Mr. Frank is also a loving, helpful father. He teaches the girls so they do not fall behind in their studies, and he invites Peter to take part in these lessons as well. He and Anne share a special bond; Anne turns to him with her fears and nightmares, not to her mother.

Of the eight occupants in the attic, only Mr. Frank survives the concentration camps. He returns to Amsterdam in November 1945, but the memories are too painful for him, and he decides he must leave, though he doesn't yet know where he will go.

Miep Gies

Miep Gies, a Christian, is about twenty years old when the Franks go into hiding. She was a secretary in Mr. Frank's business, and now, along with Mr. Kraler, she becomes the lifeline to the attic occupants, bringing them food, other necessities, and luxuries such as books. Miep is also the person who finds and saves Anne's diary, which she gives to Mr. Frank when he returns to Amsterdam.

Kraler

Mr. Kraler, a Dutchman, worked for Mr. Frank before the Nazis took away his business. Now, Mr. Kraler runs the business. He willingly risks his life to help his friend and former employer. Either he or Miep visit the attic every day to bring food for the families. Mr. Kraler's health suffers as a result of this strain; at one point, he is hospitalized for ulcers and eventually undergoes an operation.

Peter Van Daan

Peter Van Daan is about sixteen when the families go into hiding. He is a shy, socially awkward boy with an inferiority complex. His closest friend has been his cat, whom he brings to the attic with him. As he tells Anne, he is a ''lone wolf.'' At first hostile toward Anne, eventually he realizes that she is a ''fine person,'' and the two become close friends. With Anne, Peter is able to share his private thoughts. Peter dies in the concentration camps.

Petronella Van Daan

Mrs. Van Daan is vain, flirtatious, and difficult to get along with. She has a high regard for material objects. According to her husband, it was her refusal to give up her possessions that prevented them from leaving Holland earlier and resettling in Switzerland and America. In the attic, she can be found constantly caressing the fur coat that her father once gave her. She places this coat above all else; she gets upset when her husband insists on selling it so that they can buy food and other necessities, and she doesn't spare Anne's feelings when the girl spills milk on the coat by accident. Mrs. Van Daan and her husband continually argue, but she still looks out for him, for example, by giving him the largest servings of food. Mrs. Van Daan dies in the concentration camps.

Putti Van Daan

Mr. Van Daan helped Mr. Frank when the German man first moved to Holland, which is why Mr. Frank invited the Van Daans to share their hiding place. However, Mr. Van Daan is a selfish man, and this quality introduces problems into the attic. He protests allowing Mr. Dussel to move in with them because it will mean less food for everyone else. It turns out, Mr. Van Daan has been stealing the household's food. Mr. Van Daan is also openly critical of Anne, for example, saying to her, ''Why aren't you nice and quiet like your sister Margot? Why do you have to show off all the time?'' Mr. Van Daan dies in the concentration camps.

THEMES

Repression

The Franks, the Van Daans, and Mr. Dussel are all forced into hiding by the Nazi occupation of Holland. In her diary, Anne chronicles how the Nazis began to take away the rights of the Jews. Mr. Frank lost his business. Jews could not attend schools with non-Jews, go to the movies, or ride on the streetcars. After they go into hiding, the Franks and Van Daans learn from Mr. Dussel that the Nazis have sent all the Jews in Amsterdam to concentration camps. The families' greatest hope for freedom comes from the Allied invasion of the continent, which is led by the Americans.

The rigor of living under such repressive circumstances is seen on a regular basis. The atmosphere in the cramped, crowded attic rooms grows increasingly tense. They cannot set foot aside or breathe fresh air. Anne cannot run, shout, or jump. Giving in to these natural impulses only gets her into trouble, as when she spills milk on Mrs. Van Daan's coat while dancing around the room. Anne's budding friendship with Peter is also repressed by the unnatural situation. When she wants to spend time alone with Peter, she may do so only under six sets of watchful eyes, which follow her as she crosses the room to Peter's door. The effects of such living conditions strain everyone. In act 2, scene 4, when tensions come to a head with Mrs. Frank's insistence that Mr. Van Daan quit the attic, Mr. Frank tells them, ''We don't need the Nazis to destroy us. We're doing it ourselves.''

Adolescence

Anne is a precocious thirteen-year-old when her family goes into hiding, but she becomes a

TOPICS FOR FURTHER STUDY

- Read Anne Frank's *The Diary of a Young Girl.* Compare Anne's diary describing life in the hiding place with the play adapted from this work. Then write another scene for inclusion in the play. Base your scene on an event that Anne describes and dialogue that she records, if possible.

- Conduct research on World War II. Choose any aspect that relates to *The Diary of Anne Frank,* such as the deportation of Amsterdam's Jews, the German conquest of Holland, the Allied invasion of the European continent, or the concentration camps.

- Imagine that you were directing a stage production of the play. Describe your vision of the production. What would the attic look like? What kinds of mannerisms would define the characters? Describe the types of actors you would want to play Anne and Mr. Frank.

- Create an illustration that shows the world as Anne might have seen it while she was in hiding. Illustrations may focus on the attic or anything that she learns about events in the outside world.

- Write a poem that Anne might have written about life in the concentration camp.

- Conduct research to find out how critics responded to *The Diary of Anne Frank* when it first appeared on stage in 1955, as well as how critics responded to the revamped version of the play, which was staged in 1997. How have attitudes about the play changed over the decades? How do you explain these changes?

- Find out more about Anne Frank. Write a biographical essay about her, including information about how her diary has influenced its worldwide readership.

---

young woman while living in the attic. Despite the unnatural, frightening circumstances in which she lives, Anne experiences normal adolescent problems, developments, and thrills. Like many teenagers, Anne has a difficult relationship with her mother. Anne believes that her mother does not respect her opinions and makes little effort to understand her. "Whenever I try to explain my views on life to her," Anne tells her father, "she asks me if I'm constipated." Unable to stop herself from doing so, Anne often lashes out at Mrs. Frank. Though she feels regret at causing her mother pain, it happens again and again.

Anne's relationship with Peter most clearly shows her development into young womanhood; for example, she gets dressed up to go visit him in his room at night. The two teenagers form a close friendship, causing both sets of parents to worry about its sexual nature. With Peter, Anne is able to express her innermost feelings, to the extent that she tells him that she would like to share her diary with him. Peter and Anne also share their first kiss. In her

diary, she writes about her excitement about this new relationship. "I must confess that I actually live for the next meeting. . . . Is there anything lovelier than to sit under the skylight and feel the sun on your cheeks and have a darling boy in your arms?"

Identity

During the years in hiding, Anne also searches for her own identity. In talking with Mr. Frank, she reveals her ambivalence about who she is. "I have a nicer side, Father, a sweeter, nicer side," she says. She feels that she is really two people, the "mean Anne" who comes out for everyone to see and the "good Anne" who stays hidden inside. Part of her problem in sorting out identity issues, which are quite typical of all teenagers, is that she has no one her own age to talk to. Margot is too serious, and besides, she is always good. For the majority of time, Anne discounts Peter because he is a boy. She has only her diary to turn to, and she writes, "I feel utterly confused. I am longing . . . so longing . . . for everything . . . for friends . . . for someone to talk to

. . . someone who understands . . . someone young, who feels as I do.'' Anne must draw solely on her own self to sort out these conflicting issues and feelings. While Anne explores her identity through her relationship with Peter, she also explores it through her writing. Her diary allows her to see how much she enjoys writing, and she decides to become a writer when she grows up.

STYLE

Diary

Goodrich and Hackett's play is based on Anne Frank's *The Diary of a Young Girl;* thus, it posed the challenge of creating a cohesive narrative out of a series of personal reflections. Instead of being overwhelmed by the disparate nature of diary entries, the playwrights transform the diary into a narrative vehicle. They introduce the families and the hiding place with Anne's diary entry about the day she and her family left their home. Almost every scene in the play ends with Anne's voice, reading from her diary. These excerpts serve multiple functions of reminding the audience of the play's basis, giving Anne's voice a chance to come through, and allowing the playwrights to summarize events that have taken place between the individual scenes. Anne's diary entries cover such topics as her relationship with her mother, the atmosphere within the attic, and events taking place in the outside world.

Goodrich and Hackett also incorporated within the text of the play several well-known ideas and passages from the diary. Anne exclaims to her mother, ''If we begin thinking of all the horror in the world, we're lost! We're trying to hold on to some kind of ideals . . . when everything . . . ideals, hopes . . . everything, are being destroyed!'' This speech reflects the passage from Anne's diary in which she writes, ''It's difficult in times like these: ideals, dreams and cherished hopes rise within us, only to be crushed by grim reality.'' Anne also writes in her diary of her life's goals: ''I can shake off everything if I write. But . . . and that is the great question . . . will I ever be able to write well? I want to so much. I want to go on living even after my death.'' This excerpt corresponds to Anne's entry in her diary, ''I want to go on living after my death! And therefore I am grateful to God for giving me this gift, this possibility of developing myself and writing, of expressing all that is in me!''

Narrative

The ten-scene play encompasses just over two years, spanning the period of time from July 1942, when the Franks go into hiding, to August 1944, when the Gestapo take them away. The play primarily follows a straightforward chronology, the exceptions being the first and last scenes, both of which take place in November 1945 on the day that Mr. Frank returns to the attic. These two scenes act as ''bookends'' for the play. The first scene introduces Anne, her family, her diary, and the situation that drove them into hiding. The last scene serves to conclude the drama. Miep reports that it was the thief who reported the occupancy in the attic, and Mr. Frank reports that, of the group, he is the sole survivor.

Characters

Many of the characters in the play represent archetypes more than they portray real, three-dimensional people. Mr. Frank is the sage of the group. He is kind, good, and patient. Everyone turns to him to make the final decision in any difficult situation. He also tries to put a more hopeful spin on their capture by the Gestapo: ''For the past two years we have lived in fear,'' he says. ''Now we can live in hope.'' Margot is the epitome of a good girl. She is obedient and well behaved. She helps her mother cook dinner, lends Anne her high heels, and remains unfazed by Anne's budding relationship with Peter. Mrs. Frank holds out Margot as the exemplar. Peter Van Daan is the shy boy who slowly learns to open up to a peer.

HISTORICAL CONTEXT

Post-World War I Germany

Germany in the post-World War I years experienced veritable social and economic disaster. The new Weimar Republic, created out of the desire to end the war begun under the rule of Kaiser William II, was unpopular with the German people. Many Germans both opposed a republican government and disliked their political leaders for signing the

COMPARE & CONTRAST

- **1930s and 1940s:** In 1939, the European Jewish population stands at about 10 million. However, an estimated 6 million European Jews are murdered during the Holocaust. By 1946, the total number of Jews living in Europe has fallen to about 4 million.

  Today: In 2000, the world's Jewish population is estimated at 13.2 million, of which only 1,583,000, or twelve percent, live in Europe. Most Jews live either in the United States or Israel. In most recent years, the worldwide Jewish population has risen slightly but still remains at a statistical zero-population growth.

- **1930s and 1940s:** In 1939, before the start of World War II, a reported 588,417 Jews live in Germany and 156,817 live in the Netherlands. The majority of these people die at the German concentration camps during the Holocaust.

Today: In 2000, Germany's Jewish population stands at about 60,000, and the Dutch Jewish population stands at about 30,000.

- **1930s and 1940s:** By the beginning of the 1930s, Germany's Nazi Party has 180,000 members, with supproters from all classes of society and people of all ages. Such increased support helps give the Nazi Party a majority in Germany's government in 1932. The Nazis and Adolf Hitler remain in power until 1945, when World War II ends.

1990s: The 1990s have seen a resurgence of Nazi ideology. Neo-Nazis uphold such beliefs as anti-Semitism and a hatred of foreigners. Neo-Nazi doctrine tends to draw young people in countries around the world to participate in these hate groups. In Germany, neo-Nazi youths have called for the restoration of a national Nazi regime.

---

humiliating and costly Versailles Treaty that ended World War I. For the most part, the Germans saw the Weimar Republic as a traitorous government. Germany also experienced extreme economic difficulties. Unemployment soared, and inflation rose so high that paper money derived a greater value sold as waste paper than as currency.

The Weimar Republic held on to power during its first few years, destroying several attempts at revolution, yet the many political parties that formed in the postwar years vehemently opposed the government. The National Socialist German Workers Party, reorganized as the Nazi Party in 1920, held extremely nationalistic, racist,and anticommunist views. With its promises to protect Germany from Communism, it drew the support of many wealthy business leaders and landowners.

Adolf Hitler, an early Nazi recruit, became head of the party by 1921 and led a failed uprising in Munich in 1923. While imprisoned, Hitler wrote *Mein Kampf* (*My Struggle*), in which he expressed Nazi doctrine of obtaining more land for the Ger-

man people. After his release from prison, Hitler's ideas—which included the repeal of the Versailles Treaty and the restoration of lost German territory—along with his charismatic speeches, attracted many Germans to the Nazi program. With the Great Depression, even more economically hard-hit German voters came to embrace the Nazi platform. By 1932, the Nazis held 230 seats in the Reichstag, the German legislature; however, this was not enough to give the Nazis control of the government. By January 1933, when it appeared that no other party could successfully form a government, the president of the Republic appointed Hitler chancellor. After a fire was set in the Reichstag building the following month, Hitler used his emergency powers to seize complete dictatorial control of the country.

Nazism and Anti-Semitism

Under Hitler's rule, Germany turned into a police state in which the Gestapo, a secret-police force, held wide-ranging powers to round up anyone who opposed them. Liberals, socialists, and Communists were seen as Nazi enemies. Jews, members of the so-called inferior races, also suffered severe persecution. In 1935, the Nazis instituted a series of laws against Jews, called the Nuremberg Laws, which stripped them of citizenship and forbade them from marrying Christian Germans. Jews were excluded from civil service jobs, and over time, from other professions as well. In some cities, Jews were forced to live in ghettos. In November 1938, persecution against the Jews erupted in nationwide violence. Germans set fire and otherwise damaged Jewish synagogues and Jewish-owned businesses; practically every Jewish synagogue was destroyed. By the beginning of World War II, Jews could not attend public schools, engage in some businesses, own land, associate with non-Jews, or even go to parks, libraries, or museums. They were also forced to live in ghettos. By 1941, Jews were not allowed to use the telephone and public transportation systems, and Jews over six years old were forced to prominently display the yellow Star of David on their clothing. Europe did little to help the Jews, and many Jews tried to leave the continent. From 1931 to 1941, for example, 161,262 immigrant Jews were admitted to the United States, and tens of thousands escaped to British-ruled Palestine. Some Jews also moved to other countries in Europe.

The Netherlands and World War II

At the outbreak of World War II in 1939, when the German army invaded Poland, the Dutch maintained their neutrality. However, their sympathies lay with the Allied powers, which at the time comprised only Great Britain and France. After the conquest of Poland, the German army invaded and seized Scandinavia and then turned its sights west. On May 10, 1940, German armored units invaded the Low Countries—the Netherlands, Belgium, and Luxembourg. The Netherlands fell in five days. The Dutch city of Rotterdam put up strong resistance, and even while the country's surrender was being negotiated, the German air force leveled the center of the city. The government, as well as the royal family, fled to England, where they formed a government in exile.

The Nazis established a Jewish Council to oversee all Jewish affairs. The Germans then set about separating Jews from the non-Jewish Dutch population, then confiscated Jewish property, and finally started deporting Jews to the concentration camps and work camps. A resistance movement sprang up, but the Germans retaliated against pro-

tests harshly. When dockworkers in Amsterdam went on strike to prevent the deportation of Dutch Jews, the Germans responded by executing Dutch hostages. Some Jews were able to go into hiding, but most were deported to the concentration camps. As the end of the war drew near and the Allies drew closer to Germany, the Dutch suffered from severe food shortages, and during the last months before the end of the war in May 1945, they were near famine.

CRITICAL OVERVIEW

After several years in creation, in 1956 Goodrich and Hackett's adaptation, *The Diary of Anne Frank*, opened on Broadway to immediate critical acclaim. Brooks Atkinson, theater critic for the *New York Times*, called it a "lovely, tender drama" and lauded Goodrich and Hackett for treating Anne Frank's diary "with admiration and respect." He noted that creating a play out of the diary was practically "impossible" yet asserted that Goodrich and Hackett "have absorbed the story out of the diary and related it simply." *New York Herald Tribune* reviewer Walter Kerr saw the play in a similar manner. Goodrich and Hackett, he wrote, "have fashioned a wonderfully sensitive narrative out of the real-life legacy left us by a spirited and straightforward Jewish girl." Goodrich and Hackett won several awards for *The Diary of Anne Frank*, including a Tony Award for best play of the season and the Pulitzer Prize in 1956.

Critics also strongly responded to the play's optimistic message; such optimism prevails despite the death of seven of the eight people who went into hiding. "[F]or all its pathos," Kerr declared, the play, was "as bright and shining as a banner." Greg Evans, writing for *Variety*, raved about the play as an "inspiring tribute to [the] human capacity for nobility." Nowhere was this spirit more evident, according to these critics, than in Anne herself, whom Atkinson called "unconquerable because she is in love with life and squeezes the bitterness and sweetness of every moment that comes her way."

The passage of time, however, has not been so kind to the play or its writers. Contemporary critics have tended to see the play, at best, as stilted, melodramatic, and sentimental, and at worst, as universalizing and watering down the horrors of

Millie Perkins (bottom center), as Anne Frank, in the 1959 film adaptation of The Diary of Anne Frank

Nazi oppression. More than forty years after the play's original production, in an article in *Commentary*, Molly Magid Hoagland called the play a "construct." As Hoagland noted, "As many critics have since pointed out, missing from the play were Anne's intellect, her sense of irony, her dark foreboding, her sensuality, and most of all her Jewish consciousness."

In 1997, Wendy Kesselman revised Goodrich and Hackett's original play to bring *The Diary of Anne Frank* back to Broadway. As critics turned a fresh eye to Anne's updated story, their attention returned to the 1956 version, often to its detriment. What once was seen, in the words of Walter Kerr writing for the *New York Times* in 1979, as a "10-scene structure that Frances Goodrich and Albert Hackett so carefully, so persuasively, constructed out of the unfinished memoir left by a Jewish girl in a Dutch loft," became, in the words of Markland Taylor writing for *Variety,* more "a blueprint than a fully developed play." Criticism also has been lodged against Goodrich and Hackett's characterizations, particularly in portraying Anne as an innocent, saintly girl. However, as Hoagland pointed out, some of the criticism lodged against Goodrich and Hackett can fairly be lodged against the newer

version of the play, which had the intended purpose to "repair its faults" but which still fails to present the complexity that is Anne as she presented herself in her diary.

CRITICISM

Rena Korb

Korb has a master's degree in English literature and creative writing and has written for a wide variety of educational publishers. In the following essay, Korb discusses the play's narrative structure.

Upon the initial production of *The Diary of Anne Frank*, critics commented upon the careful structure of the play. In creating the play, Goodrich and Hackett faced the challenge of adapting a personal diary, which spanned about two years' time, into narrative shape. Whereas Anne Frank's diary chronicled the day-to-day life of the families in hiding, all the while touching upon her past and her hopes for the future, the play needed to create a plot with a distinct beginning, middle, and end. Goodrich and Hackett needed to find in Anne's descriptive words

WHAT DO I READ NEXT?

- Anne Frank began to keep a diary only a short time before her family went into hiding, and she chronicled her experiences until August 4, 1944, when she and the others were taken away by the Gestapo. Otto Frank was given his daughter's diary after the war ended and the concentration camps had been liberated. At the urging of friends, he published Anne's diary in Holland in 1947. *The Diary of Anne Frank* has since become an international classic.

- *Zlata's Diary: A Child's Life in Sarajevo* (1995) is eleven-year-old Zlata Filipovic's diary describing her life in Sarajevo. Begun in 1992, before war broke out, Zlata's diary turns from daily activities to the hardships and deprivations of living under siege.

- Thomas Keneally's *Schindler's List* (1993) is a work of fiction based on the true-life story of Oskar Schindler, a German industrialist who sheltered and employed Jews in his factories to prevent their being sent to the concentration camps. Schindler's courageous actions saved more than one thousand Jews from almost certain death in the gas chambers.

- In 1944, Swedish businessman Raoul Wallenberg sheltered as many as 35,000 Hungarian Jews from the Gestapo while serving in Budapest as a Swedish diplomat. *Letters and Dispatches, 1924–1944* (1996) is a primary source account of his heroic actions.

- *A Holocaust Reader* (1976), edited by Lucy Dawidowicz, collects primary source documents surrounding the Holocaust, from Nazi legislation to Jewish eyewitness accounts.

- *Night* (1958), by Elie Wiesel, is a semiautobiographical account of a young boy's spiritual reaction to Auschwitz. Wiesel was taken from his home in Romania in 1944 and deported to Auschwitz.

- *Man's Search for Meaning* (originally published in 1959) by Viktor E. Frankl, a concentration camp survivor, explorers the psychological mechanisms by which Frankl held on to his will to live.

- *Ben's Story: Holocaust Letters with Selections from the Dutch Underground Press* (2001), written by Benjamin Leo Wessels and edited by Kees W. Boole, juxtaposes Ben's letters that document his journey from an Amsterdam ghetto to Bergen-Belsen, where he died in 1945, with reports from the Dutch underground press.

a mechanism for creating a play that depicted the growth of a pre-adolescent girl into a young woman as well as the experience of a group of people who are forced to fear for their lives every day. The fact that Goodrich and Hackett worked on this play for about two years seems to indicate that they were well aware of this challenge. Their completed play, though it can be faulted for not strictly adhering to the diary (while also adhering to some of the moral standards of the 1950s), shows a careful attention to plotting and development.

The play opens in November 1945. Hitler and the Nazis have been defeated, and the concentration camps have been liberated. Otto Frank has made his way back to Amsterdam, to the attic where he, his family, the Van Daans, and Mr. Dussel hid. As Mr. Frank moves around the room, accompanied by Miep, he touches the relics of his former life: a glove, a scarf that Anne knit for him for Hanukkah. Unbeknownst to Mr. Frank, an even more important item remains from those years in hiding—Anne's diary. As he picks it up and begins to read the first entry aloud, Anne's voice joins his and then gradually takes over. This scene introduces the key elements of any story—the who, what, where, when, why, and how. The story has been told in an abbreviated form; now it is up to the ensuing scenes to share the emotional resonance that accompanies the bare facts.

Anne's voice reading her diary and the memories that she recounts jettison the audience back to the day in July 1942 when the families first moved into their attic. Mr. Frank lays down the ground rules of their hiding, assigns everyone to a room, and gives Anne the diary. With the exception of Mr. Dussel, who joins them later, this scene introduces all of the play's characters. The audience learns that Mr. Frank has invited the Van Daans to go into hiding with them because of the immense help that Mr. Van Daan provided when he first moved to Amsterdam. This is a crucial bit of information, particularly in light of the tensions the Van Daans introduce into the living situation. Scene 2 also explains the amazingly difficult circumstances under which they must live. During the day, they cannot talk above a whisper, let alone move around their attic apartment. In Mr. Frank's giving Anne the diary (which in real life happened three weeks prior to the move), he is also contributing to the play's dramatic genesis. As Mr. Van Daan points out in the following scene, "Don't you know she puts it all down in that diary?" Anne's diary thus lays claim to its central role in the story.

Scene 3 takes place two months later. Through its depiction of a typical evening in the attic, the playwrights develop important themes and characterizations. After finishing up lessons with her father, the boisterous Anne scuffles with Peter and gets into a fray with Mrs. Van Daan. The ensuing reprimand from her mother gives the play the opportunity to explore the tenuous relationship that exists between Mrs. Frank and Anne. Mrs. Frank is displeased with Anne's behavior and unable to understand her willfulness. In Mrs. Frank's mind, Anne suffers by comparison to Margot, who is "always courteous" and dignified. The scene further develops the audience's understanding of Anne's perception of herself. Unlike her sister, who is held up to her by her mother and the Van Daans as the exemplar for young ladies, Anne is "going to be remarkable." Maybe she will be a dancer or singer, but at any rate, she will be "something wonderful." Anne's ambitions, settling on becoming a writer, will be fleshed out in later scenes.

The play also introduces the tensions that are developing between the adults. Mrs. Van Daan has begun to act with familiarity toward Mr. Frank, whom she only met a short time ago. "I don't know

THE PLAY'S FINAL WORDS, 'SHE PUTS ME TO SHAME,' ARE SPOKEN BY MR. FRANK, BUT THEY SERVE TO SUCCINCTLY ILLUSTRATE ANNE FRANK'S UNIQUE PERCEPTION, WHICH SHE WAS ABLE TO HOLD THROUGHOUT THE ORDEAL AND WHICH HER DIARY ALLOWED HER TO SHARE WITH THE WORLD."

why I didn't meet you before I met that one there [Mr. Van Daan]," she says after kissing Mr. Frank on the mouth. Her actions make Mr. Frank quite uncomfortable and set the foundation for her later gratuitous flirting. Mr. and Mrs. Van Daan also bicker in this scene—as will be their habit. In a rare moment focusing on Mrs. Frank and Margot, Mrs. Frank confides that she "told your father it wouldn't work" having the Van Daans live with them.

Another important element of the scene is the arrival of Mr. Dussel, which immediately creates more tension. In contrast to Mr. Van Daan, Mr. Frank wholeheartedly agrees to Mr. Dussel's staying with them for awhile. Mr. Dussel's arrival is crucial for another reason: he shares with the Franks and the Van Daans news about the deportation of Amsterdam's Jewish population to the concentration camps.

Scene 4 is a short scene that focuses on Anne's waking up from a nightmare and being comforted by her father. This scene is most notable for the way it explores Anne's inner anxieties and confusion and the effect her feelings have on her family. Awakened by Anne's screams, Mrs. Frank rushes to her daughter's side, but Anne sends her mother away, asking instead for her father. When Mr. Frank chastises Anne for making her mother cry, Anne responds, "Oh, Pim, I was horrible, wasn't I? And the worst of it is, I can stand off and look at myself doing it and know it's cruel and yet I can't stop doing it." The truthfulness with which Anne addresses the problem and the raw emotion displayed by Anne and her mother add poignancy to the mother-daughter relationship.

Act 2 closes with the next scene, which takes place on the first night of Hanukkah. Surprising everyone with gifts, Anne introduces the much-needed holiday spirit. In the midst of this celebration, the families hear the sound of a person in the offices below. In their haste to turn all the lights off so that whoever is below will not hear them, Peter knocks over a chair. The scene remains tense, even after the noises downstairs cease. The families worry that whoever was downstairs heard them and will report them. Only Anne's singing ''Oh, Hanukkah,'' which the rest join in on, brings back their courage.

Like scene 2, this scene has multiple purposes. On the level of character development, it shows Anne's thoughtfulness. It also adds a dramatic note to a play whose ending most of the audience will already know. Further, it ties the two halves of the play together. The thief who breaks into the office is the person who eventually reports the families' presence to the Nazis. This is a notable departure from reality, since to this day, no one knows who reported the Franks and the others. By using poetic license, the playwrights show their interest in forming the play into a more cohesive body than Anne's diary.

The final scene of act 1 also sets the tone for act 2, which opens more than a year later. Numerous changes have taken place, but none reflects the familial unit that was seen at the Hanukkah party. Anne, much to her delight, is developing into womanhood. Mr. Kraler's arrival to tell Mr. Frank of a blackmail attempt by a worker down below sets off another clash between Anne and her mother, who simply ''doesn't understand.'' After Anne runs from the room, Peter follows her. The ensuing conversation, in which Anne finally finds someone with whom she can share her conflicting feelings, leads to a friendship between the two teenagers.

By scene 2, Anne and Peter have developed a romantic friendship, much to the consternation of their mothers. The relationship between the teenagers only heightens the tension in the attic, as do the obvious signs of Anne's development into a woman, such as her wearing Margot's high heels. Anne and Peter have gotten into the habit of visiting in his room, with the door closed. When Mrs. Frank implores Anne not to ''give Mrs. Van Daan the opportunity to be unpleasant,'' Anne retorts that Mrs. Van Daan does not need any such opportunity, thus implying that she has never ceased to be unkind since they first moved into the attic. Anne and Peter's visit that day, ending in a kiss, shows important changes in each: Peter is no longer as shy, and Anne is no longer as lonely. As Anne writes in her diary, the friendship gives her something to look forward to every single day. More tellingly, she also writes of the joy of holding Peter in her arms, thus reveling in the sexual feelings that have accompanied her growing up.

Scene 3 opens with the tensions between Mrs. Frank and the Van Daans finally coming to a head. Mrs. Frank catches Mr. Van Daan stealing food and demands that he leave the attic. No coaxing by her husband can get her to change her mind. It is Miep's arrival, with the news that the Allies have begun their invasion of Europe, that turns her from this path. The attic inhabitants erupt into happiness, but even the end of the scene alludes to the coming tragedy. Though Anne first writes in her diary, ''We're all in much better spirits these days,'' her tone quickly changes:

> Wednesday, the second of July, nineteen forty-four. The invasion seems temporarily bogged down. . . . The Gestapo have found the radio that was stolen. Mr. Dussel says they'll trace it back and back to the thief, and then it's just a matter of time 'til they get to us. Everyone is low.

Scene 4 is the denouement of the play. The families tensely listen to the phone ringing below in the office and argue about answering it. Are the phone calls a message from Miep? In the midst of this fear, Anne, speaking to Peter, asserts what has since become one of the most well-known ideas of the diary:

> I know it's terrible, trying to have any faith . . . when people are doing such horrible things . . . but you know what I sometimes think? I think the world may be going through a phase. . . . I still believe, in spite of everything, that people are really good at heart.

When a police car pulls up in front of the building, everyone in the attic knows their fate.

The play's final scene brings the drama full circle; the story ends at its beginning, in November 1945. Mr. Frank, the sole survivor among the attic inhabitants, reiterates Anne's faith in humanity. The play's final words, ''She puts me to shame,'' are spoken by Mr. Frank, but they serve to succinctly illustrate Anne Frank's unique perception, which she was able to hold throughout the ordeal and which her diary allowed her to share with the world.

Source: Rena Korb, Critical Essay on *The Diary of Anne Frank,* in *Drama for Students,* The Gale Group, 2002.

Max Page

In the following essay, Page calls The Diary of Anne Frank *a "radically altered, shortened, and skewed document," and explores how and why it has been altered in stage and written versions of the work.*

"In spite of everything, I still believe that people are truly good at heart." —Anne Frank [1944]

These lines, written by fifteen-year-old Anne Frank in her "secret annex" in Amsterdam, have become some of the most famous lines uttered from the Holocaust era. They anchor the only version of *The Diary of Anne Frank* known for forty years, the Broadway play of 1955, the 1959 Hollywood movie, as well as more commonplace interpretations such as the *Cliffs Notes* version read by countless high school and college students. The lines, which many may remember reading or hearing in their youth, have come to symbolize the meaning of Anne Frank's life and death. Through these lines, the Holocaust is made endurable by the optimism of a young girl who hid for two years in an Amsterdam warehouse before being taken to Auschwitz. For if she could be optimistic about people (even, it is assumed, Nazis) then there is hope for the world in the aftermath of its greatest horror.

This is the message which countless millions of young people, as well as adults, have heard and learned in the four decades since *The Diary of Anne Frank* was first published in 1952 and subsequently translated into 56 languages. It is a message, most assumed, which originated from the diary, the "authentic" historical document. But now it is clear that what we know as *The Diary of Anne Frank* is in fact something altogether different. The diary, as written by Anne Frank, has been radically manipulated and indeed rewritten by virtually everyone who had rights to it.

This startling realization has spawned a fierce debate in the popular press. Why was the diary so transformed after its author's murder? What has the "revised" diary meant? How has it been used as a tool for understanding the Holocaust? With a new version of the 1955 play on Broadway, two books on the history of the diary, and numerous articles and reviews in major publications, the question of how the diary has fared since its author was sepa-

> THE DIARY, AS WRITTEN BY ANNE FRANK, HAS BEEN RADICALLY MANIPULATED AND INDEED REWRITTEN BY VIRTUALLY EVERYONE WHO HAD RIGHTS TO IT."

rated from her diary and killed at Bergen-Belsen, has suddenly seemed of great import. Over the past year, *The Diary of Anne Frank,* the single most widely read document of the Holocaust, has come under new, and in many ways its first, scrutiny. The fate of Anne Frank was sealed in 1944, but the fate of her diary and the historical legacy she left has suddenly exploded as an issue for intense debate.

This debate, which revolves around the interpretations of the meaning of the Holocaust, the manipulation of the past, and how historical documents are made public, poses central issues to all historians but, I would argue, especially to public historians. Why specifically should public historians be interested in this debate? I am not, after all, reviewing an exhibit or a historical documentary, or describing the Anne Frank Foundation and its museum in Amsterdam. I am not describing and critiquing a monument or a textbook or a curriculum plan for teaching the diary. One might consider the recent debate over the diary as the province of academic historians, or a debate about the uses of history in the popular press and culture. I would argue, however, that the questions raised by this debate are, or should be, at the heart of what public historians are discussing.

The issue with the Anne Frank diary is at its core a story of how a document—a primary source—made its way from a girl's handwritten journal into a best-selling book, a Broadway play, and an Academy Award-winning movie, and how it was manipulated at each stage of its move into the public arena. What the debate over Anne Frank's diary brings us back to is what is always at the heart of our profession as historians and public historians—the nature of documents of the past. In few cases can we see the perils and pitfalls of abusing the primary pieces of the past left for us as clearly as we can in the debate over this diary. For at every stage of its life in public, the document has been reinvented, by everyone from Anne Frank herself to her father, to translators, playwrights, filmmakers, school teachers, foundations, and reviewers. *The Diary of Anne Frank,* which virtually all of us read as children, adolescents, or adults, is a radically altered, shortened, and skewed document.

This, then, is a cautionary tale for our profession. It should remind us of the centrality of documents to our work, their remarkable flexibility, and their susceptibility to manipulation by well-wishers or evil-doers. The irony is that all of us who have used the diary for history classes or in the course of public history work have unwittingly perpetuated a mistaken understanding of Anne Frank and her diary. I would argue that despite the most recent revelations about the diary's manipulation, we still have not addressed the most fundamental question: How do we reclaim the meaning of a cultural icon such as Anne Frank from the forces which have reinvented her in often cynical ways? How can we, especially now, help to return the public for which we work to a fuller confrontation with this—how can I say it?—most awful of documents.

I offer these reflections and pose these dilemmas from a series of involvements in the debate. First, as a professor of a historical methods and philosophy course for new majors, I used the various documents in the debate about Anne Frank's diary to illustrate and discuss the politics of the past. As a public historian interested in the politics of memory and the manipulations of the past, I was invited to participate in an event in which the two different stage versions of a single scene were presented—one by Meyer Levin (which was never produced) and the 1955 play by Frances Goodrich and Albert Hackett. Finally, as a public historian and scholar of how Americans have used and misused the past, I have followed this mid-century tale of bringing history to the public with special fascination.

Little of this valuable debate would have taken place without a searing polemic on the subject by one of our foremost essayists, Cynthia Ozick. Indeed, the publication of her 1997 *New Yorker* article, ''Who Owns Anne Frank?'' was as much an event as the return of the play version to Broadway. Ozick's essay was built around the confluence of three new interpretations of *The Diary of Anne Frank*—the publication of two new books on the

history of the diary since it was recovered by Otto Frank from Miep Gies, one of the Dutch protectors of the Frank family, as well as the opening of the revised stage version by Wendy Kesselman.

Ozick jolted readers in part because she brought a much wider reading public the arguments made in the books by Ralph Melnick and Lawrence Graver. The books lay blame in different places and to different degrees, but each reveals the clear and extensive manipulation of the diary towards one ultimate end: the transformation of the diary into a document of consolation and uplift, a salvational historical work, which can help us find optimism in the heart of evil. Melnick is the far more critical and accusatory work (which makes it the favored interpretation by Ozick), suggesting ultimately that the softening of the Jewish themes in the Broadway play version was the product of a conspiracy, with Lillian Hellman at the center. We can dispense with the more bizarre claims—for example, Melnick's suggestion that Lillian Hellman received direct payments from Moscow to soften the ''Jewishness'' of the play—without losing the thrust of his findings: that the diary was subject not just to artistic interpretation but to calculated manipulation and censorship. Otto Frank, perhaps understandably, eliminated those passages in which Anne spoke of her sexual yearnings or of her hatred for her mother. The translator who brought the play to Germany chose to eliminate those passages of sheer hatred not only for Hitler but for Germans more generally. Goodrich and Hackett, in consultation with Hellman, eliminated most of the references to the Franks as Jews and focused instead on the story of the stirring of adolescence of Anne and her struggle for love amidst the stresses of war. In reviewing the play for the *New York Times* in 1955, Brooks Atkinson wrote that Goodrich and Hackett had wonderfully portrayed the ''shining spirit of a young girl. . . . They have not contrived anything; they have left the tool-kit outside the door of their workroom. They have absorbed the story out of the diary and related it simply.'' What the history of the diary shows, and what Ozick so fervently argued, was that there is nothing further from the truth. The story they told was a radically altered version of Anne Frank's life as told in the diary, designed to fit the needs of Broadway producers and Americans in the 1950s. It has continued to serve the needs of hundreds of thousands of teachers worldwide, who have found the diary the perfect answer to their search for an accessible, and perhaps not too depressing, work on the Holocaust.

Ozick catalogued these abuses of the document and focused especially on the elimination of "Anne's consciousness of Jewish fate or faith." To popularize the diary as an uplifting story of courage and youthful love required, Ozick argued, the removal of the specifically Jewish story that is integral to the diary. The diary was, Ozick wrote sharply, subject to "evisceration": "Evisceration, an elegy for the murdered. Evisceration by blurb and stage, by shrewdness and naiveté, by cowardice and spirituality, by forgiveness and indifference, by success and money, by vanity and rage, by principle and passion, by surrogacy and affinity. Evisceration by fame, by shame, by blame. By uplift and transcendence. By usurpation."

Ozick did not end here and thereby offer readers an opportunity to shake their heads in dismay and then quickly move on. She resisted making the simplistic call for a better, fuller interpretation of the diary. Instead, Ozick posed what is sacrilege for historians of all stripes: she suggested that Anne Frank's diary has been so manipulated that one must wonder if Miep Gies should have saved it at all. Might it have been better had the diary disappeared, or been burned, as Anne would have been had she not succumbed to typhus? As Ozick puts it, more pungently: "It may be shocking to think this (I am shocked as I think it), but one can imagine a still more salvational outcome: Anne Frank's diary burned, vanished, lost—saved from a world that made of it all things, some of them true, while floating lightly over the heavier truth of named and inhabited evil."

The thought is astonishing, and infuriating to a historian as well as to the general public. At first, this conclusion to the article seems like a form of absurd rhetorical pyrotechnic. As a historian, there is an almost visceral resistance to Ozick's suggestion: if there is anything that historians can all agree to, it is that documents of the past should be preserved so that over time society can interpret and reinterpret them. The building blocks of our endeavor are the documents from the past. But Ozick's suggestion is not lightly offered—indeed, she is shocked herself to suggest it—but seriously proposed in order to awaken us to the immensity of the diary's cynical transformation. Considering how far the manipulation of the diary has gone, and how its interpretation has been shaped by the censors and translators and playwrights and Hollywood producers, it is worth at least wondering how an important document can make its way through the minefields of popularization.

Consider one widely read "spin-off" of Anne Frank's diary: the *Cliffs Notes* to the diary, first published in 1984. The bulk of the booklet is a detailed summary of the diary, recounting the daily developments in the annex much like a soap opera digest. The main thrust of the interpretive sections of the notes follows those of the Broadway play and Hollywood movie precisely: "Above all else, Anne's feelings are ordinary and so akin to those experienced by any teenager growing up and being confronted by situations and with individuals which he or she is not yet capable of dealing with in a detached or adult way. One of the most striking features that emerges from Anne's diary is the sense of the intensity of the emotions that she experiences as an adolescent." "Essay Topics" are proposed for students: "Try to keep a diary for a week. Can you make it interesting and varied?" "What do you think makes Anne's diary interesting?" "Pretend that Anne survived the concentration camps. Write an account of what she did when she grew up." The *Cliffs Notes* version is hardly more offensive than other volumes in this plentiful series of cheat sheets. But it speaks authoritatively about a very different diary than the one we know to be Anne Frank's actual words.

Ozick wrote her article before the new Broadway play version returned to the stage but she anticipated not liking this version much more than the original play and its Academy Award-winning movie of 1959. She was not mistaken.

The common attitude in the press has been that the new play version of the diary is an improvement because it adds in some lines about Anne's sexual awakening and her conflicts with her mother and because it reintroduces the Jewish aspects in the diary. Others, such as Ben Brantley of *The New York Times,* offered greater praise. With an "uncompromising steadiness of gaze, embedded in a bleak sense of historical context," he wrote, the play is "undeniably moving." Indeed, Kesselman has gone to great lengths to make the Judaism more prominent, to make the Nazi threat seem much closer and more ominous. She has also added extensive voice-overs of lengthy passages from the diary.

But this is merely window-dressing. The 1998 play on Broadway maintains the basic structure of the earlier version and develops the same themes of adolescent awakening amidst the stresses of wartime. Those who praise the play version focus still on the progress of Anne from "self-centered girlishness to the cusp of self-aware womanhood."

And the reaction remains the expected "snuffles and sobs from the audience." (The critic Vincent Canby reports on a different reaction: at the end of the play, a woman in the row in front of him exclaimed to her companion, in shock: "You mean, she dies?") The Nazi evil is felt in booming sounds of Hitler over the radio, shadows coming in through the windows, and frightening noises in the building below as inspections bring the Franks closer to capture. The ending is pure 1950s melodrama: the SS, with very classy handguns and cocked hats, burst in while the group is enjoying a rare treat of strawberries.

The comparison that immediately came to mind was the Civil War television series by Ken and Ric Burns. This series was praised profusely for its powerful use of images from the Civil War, its stunning voice-overs by some of our finest actors, and its attempt to incorporate more than previous movies and popular Civil War histories the experience of slaves, of women, of common men on both sides. It remains, however, deeply deficient as a work of public history. For despite these efforts, there is also a nostalgic overtone to each of the thirteen episodes. The maddening repetition of the theme song, the opening sunsets over cannons, the framing of each series with military battles, and the setting of the whole series as a battle of brother against brother (white, of course), as a painful but necessary episode, now all neatly, resolved—all contribute to giving the viewer a message of nostalgia. That was a great time, the Burns brothers suggest, a time of noble fights over ideals, which is now (sadly) all gone, in the distant past. Similarly, in the play version of *The Diary of Anne Frank,* all the tweaking of scripts, the cutting and pasting, does little to restore the power of the diary or even to begin to undo the half century of manipulation.

Ozick, with the aid of Ralph Melnick's book, lines up behind the other play which was written to bring the diary to stage. Ralph Melnick most vociferously argues that had Meyer Levin, the journalist, photographer, and playwright who first urged Otto Frank to bring the diary to a wider audience, been given the job, the play version of the diary would have risen above the aspartame lessons of Hollywood's Goodrich and Hackett. In many ways, Melnick is continuing the battle Levin waged from the moment it became clear that he was to be removed from the Broadway team bringing the play to the stage. Originally favored by Otto Frank as the most able to bring Anne Frank's story to the stage, Levin was removed in favor of Frances Goodrich

and Albert Hackett by the producers, Garson Kanin and Kermit Bloomgarten. Levin countered with lawsuits, editorials, and an autobiography to defend his version and lambaste what he saw as the desecration of the diary.

Because of the success of the play and movie, Levin's version quickly slipped into oblivion. But because of Melnick's championing of Levin's cause, the Hatikvah Center in Springfield, Massachusetts sponsored a reading of two identical scenes— between Anne and Peter, the son of the other family in the annex—from the 1955 Broadway version and Levin's own rarely produced version. It was a fascinating afternoon and deeply troubling, for it showed how the diary was so effectively sapped of some of its most tragic and powerful meaning as it made its journey from private journal to public entertainment. The Goodrich and Hackett version, no one would now deny, goes as far as it can to erase the Jewish aspects of the diary and to promote a universalist message of faith and hope. "I wish you had a religion," Anne says to Peter. "I just mean some religion . . . it doesn't matter what. Just to believe in something!" Levin's version of the same scenes is substantially different. Anne is suddenly not a Levittown teenager of the 1950s but a young Jewish girl with a far darker view of the world. In Levin's version, Peter longs for the time after the war when he can leave behind his Jewish heritage and just "be one of them." Anne retorts: "But Peter. It wouldn't be honest. . . . We can never be just Netherlanders, or just English, or just French. We will always remain Jews." Whereas Goodrich and Hackett end with Anne's hopeful lines (taken out of their context in the diary) about the goodness of people, Levin's play ends with Anne gloomily reflecting (with words directly from her diary) on a world "turning into a wilderness."

The tone of Levin's play as a whole is markedly different than that of the Goodrich and Hackett version, and his script courageously addresses the Jewish themes head on. But Levin's version has its own spin, which has less to do with the diary than with his own political beliefs. Many of these speeches about being true to one's Jewish roots are based not on the diary but on Levin's own political beliefs. Although I would happily substitute Levin's version for Goodrich and Hackett's—an exaggeration of Anne's clear moral code and identification with Jewish persistence seems a lesser fault than the ethnic cleansing of Goodrich and Hackett—it hardly answers the need for truer public adaptation of the diary.

Most disturbing in all three of the play versions is that so much of them is invented. Voice-overs in the new Broadway version (horribly amplified in the theater) lead the audience to believe that the play is largely an enactment of the diary, which it could never be. The ending scene so crucial to our emotional reaction (the sobs from the audience some critics crowed about in the updated Broadway version) is, of course, not in the diary. Indeed, Anne's diary ends, on August 1, 1944, with a long entry in which she ruminates on "trying to find a way to become what I'd like to be and what I could be if . . . if only there were no other people in the world." Numerous scenes are only briefly noted in the diary, and there is virtually no dialogue. Departing from the document is necessary, of course, for transposing a historical document into another medium. But I wondered, by the end of the new Broadway play, after all that has happened to the diary, if a stage version were worth undertaking. Indeed, I wondered if a stage version, necessitating dialogue and action that is not in the diary at all, contributes to the diary's continued manipulation. For what the play version offers is a revised, perhaps improved and more honest, reflection of the diary. But Anne still becomes a symbol, mostly of an adolescent girl growing up in difficult circumstances, and less so of a Jew who will become a victim of the Holocaust.

But even this debate over what would be the true artistic rendition of the diary is somewhat misleading. What is implied is that there is a single understanding of the diary and its writer. In fact, what is striking as one rereads the diary and also the histories of the diary's life after Anne's murder, is the repeated rewriting of this document called *The Diary of Anne Frank*. It begins with Anne herself, the Jew, the adolescent girl, the German, and also, the writer. When scholars now speak of the diary they must speak about the versions: A, B, C, Definitive. Diary A is what Anne wrote in two years in hiding. Diary B is the diary with parts that she herself had begun to rewrite. One must remember that the diary—or, more accurately, its rewriting—was inspired, in part, by a 1944 radio message from Gerritt Bolkestein, a member of the Dutch government in exile, urging that Dutch citizens maintain records of war-time occupation so that evidence would be available after the war was over. Anne hoped to publish her diary—she titled this supposedly private journal "The House Behind"—and planned to go to Hollywood and become a screenwriter. In her revisions to her diary, Anne changed the names—she was Anne Aulis and, in a further revision, Anne Robin. Thus, the diary was almost a draft in progress for her, not a running series of events and observations. Diary C is what was known as *The Diary of a Young Girl* for nearly forty years; it was the edition approved by Otto Frank and it became the basis for the millions of editions published in dozens of languages, as well as the play and movie versions. The "official" version, however, is approximately one-third shorter than the diary, or diaries, that Anne had written in those two years. Only after forty years was the "definitive edition" published in 1991 that restored much of what was removed from versions A and B. (It still is, however, titled *The Diary of a Young Girl*, which was never Anne's title for it.) But even the diary we now mistakenly call the definitive version fails to show how Anne herself edited her writing—it does not show the pseudonyms she invented, nor does it show where she edited (although it includes a few passages added or edited by Anne herself). Although the definitive edition brings back into public light Anne Frank's words, in a way it is the least honest of the versions since it suggests "definitiveness" while it simply creates a new text altogether. Publishing a composite of drafts of *The Great Gatsby* as the definitive novel, for example, would hardly have pleased F. Scott Fitzgerald.

I use the analogy of a novel intentionally. What few have reckoned with in trying to come to terms with the meaning of the diary is that Anne Frank was a writer. Cynthia Ozick began her *New Yorker* piece with the surprising line that "even if she had not kept the extraordinary diary through which we know her it is likely that we would number her among the famous of this century . . . She was born to be a writer." To convey to the public the meaning of Anne Frank's diary, we must also understand that it was itself a work of public history. What we fail to understand about this document, and probably so many documents that we as public historians try to interpret, is that the documents themselves were meant to be secondary sources, works of history for the public themselves. Anne's diary was written not simply as a private journal (although she did, as any writer might, jealously protect her drafts from prying outsiders) to be kept under lock and key. She always expected that this work would be a crucial journal of the war, not just an unconscious document (I believe there are few of these, at least in the textual realm), but a conscious interpretation of the meaning of hiding, as a Jew, from Nazi Germany.

All efforts to understand Anne Frank and her unique work must contend with this fact. Indeed, by ignoring Anne's conscious development of the diary as a work of literature, we misconstrue the diary, misrepresent its author, and take inaccurate lessons that we perceive to be offered by an unconscious author.

So, how might we then, as public historians, attempt to bring *The Diary of Anne Frank* out of its textual covers and into the realm of public history? The irony of Ozick's position is that through her writing (and the publication of her writing in a prestigious magazine), the revelatory history of the diary is making its way into public light. It is difficult now for a broad segment of the reading public not to be aware that the diary has been altered repeatedly. Perhaps the complete diary can now begin to have a new career as a document of the war and of the Holocaust.

A public interpretation of Anne Frank should make one think again; it should challenge people, not just make them weep for a moment. A growing group of artists of Holocaust memorials in Germany, Israel, and the United States have recognized a simple fact of memorials: they often do as much to aid forgetting as promote active remembering. By offering readily accessible narrative forms (soldiers with guns, obelisks, grand archways), traditional memorials universalize particular tragedies in the service of advancing the politically useful feelings of nationalism, jingoism, and individual heroism. "Counter monuments" avoid these simple forms and their suspect purposes; they offer new ways of considering the costs of war and genocide. One barely glances at the American Legion—inspired Vietnam memorial of three soldiers, while one heads to the stunning black granite monument by Maya Lin. It is a monument which makes one stop and think, weep but also honor the dead, consider and remember.

But in the case of a public presentation of *The Diary of Anne Frank,* which is based on an actual historical document, a recognition of the full complexity of that document would return us to the essence of what the diary is, a continuing, writerly record of hiding by a Jewish girl who knew evil and sensed its invasion into her "Secret Annex" and who eventually was murdered by it. The philosopher Karsten Harries has written that the "ethical function" of architecture is to "represent" the act of building, that is, to make people think again about the very notion of building and the existential experience of dwelling. Just so, a public historical interpretation of the *Diary of Anne Frank* should differ

from the versions presented in the entertainment venues by promoting remembering of Anne Frank's particularity, rather than her universality, as a Jew, a young girl, a victim. A public historical interpretation may also focus on the document's life itself, its strange career since 1944, which says so much about the manipulation of history over the past half century.

One can imagine a public reading of the diary, with entries read on the anniversaries of Anne's writing of them. Or perhaps there could be parallel readings of different versions of this document, from Anne's versions A, B, and C to the Goodrich and Hackett script to Levin's version. One can also imagine a play written about the successive rewritings of the play—a play about the diary's career. In some ways, the play's life since Anne Frank was murdered could be its most lasting meaning. The diary itself has, for too long and for too many, been asked to hold the weight of meaning for the entire Holocaust. Ozick argues that the diary is "not a Holocaust document." Indeed, it has been used as the primary document for students to learn about the Holocaust precisely because the actual extermination of the Jews of Europe is, due to the nature of the document, never detailed.

Source: Max Page, "The Life and Death of a Document: Lessons from the Strange Career of *The Diary of Anne Frank,*" in *Public Historian,* Vol. 21, No. 1, Winter 1999, pp. 87–97.

Stephen Fife

In the following essay, Fife compares the unproduced script Meyer Levin wrote for The Diary of Anne Frank *to the popular version of the play written by Albert Hackett and Frances Goodrich, contending there is ample evidence that the duo plagiarized Levin's work.*

Before his recent death at age 75, Meyer Levin—author of such books as *Compulsion, The Settlers, In Search*—left the world a copy of his Ethical Will, a document that aspired to pass on to humanity "the moral values learned in a lifetime," which Levin deemed to be "as vital as worldly goods." Levin's true concern, however, turned out to be recounting the story surrounding his long "suppressed" stage version of *The Diary of Anne Frank*—a story that had obsessed him through the last thirty years of his life. And yet, despite Meyer's last literary testament, basic questions about the true authorship of the Pulitzer Prize-winning play based on Frank's diary remained unresolved at the time of his death.

Levin's association with the diary began in 1950, when he came upon the book in a French translation and was immediately convinced that he had heard "the voice from the mass graves" for which he'd been searching impatiently ever since covering the Holocaust as a war correspondent. After contacting Otto Frank and discovering that the book had still not found an American publisher, Levin volunteered his assistance on one condition: that he be allowed first crack at adapting the diary for stage and film, even though he could boast little experience in either field. Otto Frank consented to this demand (even while claiming he "couldn't see" his daughter's work as a play), and Levin went on to use his influence by helping persuade Doubleday to publish the diary, as well as by writing a glowing front-page review in *The New York Times Book Review.*

Levin's motive in all this seems not to have been greed—early on, he announced an intention of donating his proceeds to charity—but rather deeply personal and ideological, a combination of the genuine horror he felt having witnessed the liberation of Auschwitz and other death camps, and an awareness of the impact the diary could have as an indictment of Hitler and anti-Semitism. He had already written in his autobiographical memoir, *In Search* (1948), that he conceived of his artistic role as that of a link between the two great Jewish cultural centers of New York and Israel, and what better unifying force could there be than that youthfully heroic figure, Anne Frank? So it came as a blow to Levin when his adaptation of the book was rejected, first by Cheryl Crawford (owner of the original rights) and then by Kermit Bloomgarden (who had picked up her option). Soon Otto Frank himself was asking Levin to step aside in favor of a "world-famous dramatist" (Carson McCullers? Arthur Miller?); in the end Levin found himself replaced by Albert Hackett and Frances Goodrich, a non-Jewish husband-and-wife screenwriting team, who were friends of Levin's great enemy, Lillian Hellman. As if that weren't galling enough, he found their adaptation to be "the ghost of my own play," containing certain key scenes not in the book, along with whole sections of his dialogue, while omitting most of the references to Jewish issues.

Levin promptly sued Bloomgarden, the Hacketts, and Otto Frank for "plagiarism and appropriation of ideas," with the jury returning a verdict in Levin's favor, awarding him 25 percent of the royalties, or half of what the Hacketts were getting. Despite this apparent triumph, however, everything

Playbill cover from the 1956 theatrical production of The Diary of Anne Frank

went downhill for Levin from there on. First, the amount he was supposed to receive (stipulated at $50,000) was held up in appeals for so long that he eventually settled for the payment of his $15,000 legal expenses. Then his lawsuit against Anne Frank's father earned him the very damaging reputation of "litigious Levin" that would follow him throughout his career. And finally, the rights to his own adaptation—which were at the heart of the issue— were entirely removed from his possession by Otto Frank's lawyers, who threatened Levin with a countersuit if he even discussed his diary play. Levin challenged this again and again, finally going so far as to help stage a production of his play at the Israeli Soldiers Theater in 1966, which was soon shut down by Otto Frank's lawyers. This was the point at which Levin and Otto Frank were stalemated until 1981, when both men died, apparently putting an end to the issue . . . except for the legacy of doubts and questions they left behind.

Such as: did plagiary on such a bold scale really occur? Why was there so little publicity about the jury's decision? When the trial took place, the Broadway version of the diary had already enjoyed quite a long run, winning the Critics Circle Award, the Tony Award, and the Pulitzer Prize, becoming a

> "DRAMATIC LICENSE LIKE THIS MADE LEVIN FURIOUS, FOR IT SEEMED TO VIOLATE THE PLAYWRIGHT'S DUTY TO THE ORIGINAL MATERIAL, CHANGING THE DIARY FROM A SPECIFICALLY JEWISH DOCUMENT TO SOMETHING ELSE. . . ."

very successful box-office hit, and making Otto Frank into a saint overnight. And yet, as Levin never tired of pointing out later on, "not a single publication commented on the fact that for the first time in history, a Pulitzer Prize work had been judged largely the work of another." Why was this so? Why were so few people interested in what was potentially a major scandal in American letters? Why wasn't Levin's version produced as proof that it was so poor it could not be performed, and that it bore no resemblance at all to the Broadway play? And why has there been so little clarification of the issues in the years since?

One reason, of course, is the tremendous popularity that the Hackett version has enjoyed over the years, among audiences of all ages, Jews and Gentiles alike. Another reason is the extreme reverence accorded Otto Frank, whom Levin found to be as "sacrosanct" as the Broadway diary when he went on his campaign to have his own play performed. Jews especially were unreceptive to Levin, feeling that the success of the Hackett play and the subsequent veneration of Otto Frank were both marks of cultural acceptance that should not be slighted. And then there was Levin himself, whose aggressively defiant behavior could alienate even those who believed him, as he insisted on finding "conspiracies" wherever he looked. "Was I being pushed out because of my closeness to Judaism and Zionism?" he asked in the preface to his self-published play. "Was I on some peculiar form of blacklist, a McCarthyism of its own, for my Jewish views?" These charges were the more startling for being aimed at people like Hellman and Bloomgarden, themselves the victims of blacklisting—all of which earned Levin the reputation of being a Red-baiter,

on top of everything else. Even worse, they distracted people's attention from the real issues: were there enough similarities between the two plays to substantiate the plagiary charge? And was Levin's version really as good as he claimed, or was it as poor as the producers insisted—that is, did it deserve a production?

After studying the two diary scripts and comparing them with Anne Frank's book, my conclusion is that Levin has a strong case: there appears to be ample evidence that the Hacketts had access to Levin's play, either directly or through someone who was familiar with its style and emphases. Both chronicle the experiences of two Jewish families, the Franks and the van Daans, during the more than two years they spend together in a warehouse attic, hiding out from the Nazis. Both employ the same basic dramatic structure for relating that story: starting out with the families moving into the hiding place, then tracing the development of the characters through their interaction in a chronological series of episodes or scenes. Furthermore, the selection of scenes that both plays choose to present from the wealth of anecdotal material to be found in the diary is almost identical. Finally, both plays call for substantially the same stage design and performance technique: the four rooms of the hiding place are to be visible at all times, so that incidents in separate rooms can occur simultaneously, the actors' lines counterpointing each other.

Of course, all of this could be simply the result of similar creative processes at work on the same source. But this becomes harder to justify when the Hacketts start using scenes and conversations that exist in Levin's play but not in the diary. For instance, when the Jews unwittingly make their presence known to the thieves in Levin's play, it is through the singing of a Hanukkah song; an almost identical device is used in the Hackett version, yet this is not taken from Anne Frank's description. Of course, the moment is very theatrical, very effective, but why should it occur at the same point in both plays when there were so many other possibilities? There are several other uses of almost identical quotes in both plays that appear nowhere in the diary.

Certainly, though, such similarities are not like copying out a whole speech word for word, or duplicating a long scene exactly; yet they recur often enough throughout the Hackett play to make an impression. Equally striking is the pattern of differences and variations between the two plays. Levin often liked to characterize these differences by comparing two passages from the same moment in each of the works, when Anne is in Peter's room toward the end of the play, trying to convince him not to lose heart, to keep up his faith. In Levin's play, she tells him, quoting directly from Anne's words in the diary:

> Who knows, perhaps the whole world will learn from the good that is in us, and perhaps for that reason the Jews have to suffer now. Right through the ages there have been Jews, through all the ages they have had to suffer, and it has made us strong, too.

In the Hackett version, however, this same speech comes out as: "We [Jews] are not the only people that've had to suffer. There've always been people that've had to ... sometimes one race ... sometimes another."

Dramatic license like this made Levin furious, for it seemed to violate the playwright's duty to the original material, changing the diary from a specifically Jewish document to something else, which the Broadway producers called "universal." This also had the effect of assimilating Anne Frank into the general culture, a process which Levin thought responsible for creating the climate in which a Nazi Holocaust could take place. *His* diary play is all about the erosion of Jewish identity through anti-Semitism; his two families live in exile within their own country, no longer German or Dutch, yet not Jewish enough to be anything else—a problem that each of the three adolescents vows to deal with in his or her own way, according to what we've been told about them in Anne's diary. Margot, Anne's sister, is determined to become a nurse in Palestine after the war so she can look after "her own people"; Peter van Daan yearns to run away to the West Indies, where he can make lots of money and forget that he was ever a Jew; while Anne steers a middle course between them, vowing to become a Dutch journalist when the war is over, even though "we can never be just Netherlanders, or just English, or just French. We will always remain Jews."

The Broadway diary, in contrast, completely overlooks Margot Frank's Zionist tendencies, while minimizing the Jewish issue for both Peter and Anne. It concentrates instead on what it sees as the general breakdown of civilized values which gave rise to the Holocaust, viewing the Jews as unlucky scapegoats and the Nazis as representatives of man's vilest instincts. Thus, the diary comes to symbolize the generation that was wiped out in the death camps, but whose belief in mankind survived in the diary to give the Otto Franks of the world the will to go on.

This interpretation is certainly valid; it preserves the general outlines of Anne Frank's story (as well as much of its essence), and it shouldn't be too difficult to see the appeal this would have both for the Broadway producers and for Otto Frank. First of all, it condensed the horrifying and overwhelming events of the Holocaust into the easily understandable story of two loving families fighting for survival and destroyed through no fault of their own. Second, here were two non-Jewish writers, treating the Jewish characters with dignity and respect, showing them as human beings who also happened to be Jewish, thus allowing them to transcend their specific condition and become emblematic of all the people who died in the world tragedy of World War II. This was very important for Otto Frank, who wanted to spread his daughter's message of hope and belief to as many people as possible, and who wanted to provide an outlet for all the grief and suffering that Hitler had caused.

And yet this sacrificed an aspect of his daughter's spirit which was very much a part of the diary, and which persisted in asking the question: "Why the Jews? Why always the Jews?" These sections of Anne's ruminations look at the Holocaust as just one in a series of persecutions aimed against the Jewish people, and it was this side of Anne Frank that Meyer Levin was particularly interested in, since its concerns corresponded with what Levin considered to be his own "true task," his own "destiny."

Ultimately, though, Levin's enemy was not the Broadway play, it was Anne Frank's father. Otto Frank's decision to go with the Hackett play over Levin's version is understandable in both commercial and personal terms, yet why forbid performances of Levin's play altogether? Why shouldn't there be more than one interpretation of Anne Frank's diary?

Source: Stephen Fife, "Meyer Levin's Obsession," in *New Republic,* Vol. 187, No. 3524, August 2, 1982, pp. 26–30.

SOURCES

Atkinson, Brooks, "Theatre: *The Diary of Anne Frank,*" in *New York Times,* October 6, 1956.

Ehrlich, Evelyn, "Frances Goodrich and Albert Hackett," in *Dictionary of Literary Biography,* Vol. 26: *American Screenwriters,* Gale Research, 1984, pp. 129–34.

Evans, Greg, "*The Diary of Anne Frank,*" in *Variety,* Vol. 369, No. 5, December 8, 1997, p. 119.

Frank, Anne, *The Diary of a Young Girl,* edited by Otto H. Frank and Mirjam Pressler, translated by Susan Massotty, Doubleday, 1991.

Hoagland, Molly Magid, ''Anne Frank, On and Off Broadway,'' in *Commentary,* Vol. 105, No. 3, March 1998, p. 58.

Kerr, Walter, ''*Anne Frank* Shouldn't Be Anne's Play,'' in *New York Times,* January 7, 1979.

———, Review of *The Diary of Anne Frank,* in *New York Herald Tribune,* as quoted on ''Anne Frank Online,'' http://www.annefrank.com/site/af_student/study_STORY. htm (October 10, 2001).

Taylor, Markland, ''*The Diary of Anne Frank,*'' in *Variety,* Vol. 369, No. 1, November 10, 1997, p. 53.

FURTHER READING

Dawidowicz, Lucy C., *The War against the Jews: 1933–1945,* Bantam Doubleday Dell, 1991.
 This reissue edition provides a thorough history of the origins and development of the Holocaust. Dawidowicz offers a concise overview of Nazism and also delves into the daily lives of the Jews under growing anti-Semitism.

Gies, Miep, and Alison Leslie Gold, *Anne Frank Remembered: The Story of the Woman Who Helped to Hide the Frank Family,* Simon & Schuster, 1998.
 Gies recalls what it was like to shelter the Frank family and the other Jews while living under the Nazi regime.

Lindwer, Willy, *The Last Seven Months of Anne Frank,* Anchor, 1992.
 Lindwer's work covers the final months of Anne's life from the time she and the others were taken from their attic hiding place to her death in the Bergen-Belsen concentration camp.

Melnick, Ralph, *The Stolen Legacy of Anne Frank: Meyer Levin, Lillian Hellman, and the Staging of the Diary,* Yale University Press, 1997.
 Levin, a best-selling author, was instrumental in bringing Anne's story to the stage. He wrote the first adaptation of the diary, one that was faithful to Anne's entries, but Otto Frank rejected this version, instead choosing another production team who selected Goodrich and Hackett as the writers. *The Stolen Legacy* tells this story.

Muller, Melissa, *Anne Frank: The Biography,* translated by Robert Kimber and Rita Kimber, Owl Books, 1999.
 Muller's biography of Anne situates her diary within a larger historical framework.

The Great White Hope

HOWARD SACKLER
1967

The Great White Hope won three of the most important awards on Broadway—the Pulitzer Prize, the New York Drama Critics' Circle Award, and a Tony—a phenomenal achievement in the history of twentieth-century theatre. The play is based on the life of black boxer Jack Johnson. When white American fighters refused to compete with Johnson, he traveled to Australia and defeated Tommy Burns in 1908, becoming the first black Heavyweight Champion of the World. Sackler's work explores with deep consideration the consequences of Johnson's achievement in a climate of deep racial unrest.

Curiously, Sackler's original work was meant to be a musical, more lighthearted than tragic. He eventually abandoned his plans and completed the play in 1967. *The Great White Hope* opened in December of that year at the Arena Stage in Washington, D.C. Although the work is fictional, many of the events of the play, such as Jack's arrest, actually happened to Johnson at some point in his life. Thematically, the play also explores, with depth, perceptiveness, and brutal honesty, the nature of racism and racial conflict in American society. The voices of Sackler's characters, black and white, offer a colorful collage of insights. In examining the motivations of these characters, the audience gains exposure to a wide range of perspectives and, by extension, a much greater understanding of the issues surrounding them.

AUTHOR BIOGRAPHY

Howard Sackler was born on December 19, 1929, in
New York City, although he spent much of his early
childhood in Florida. He attended Brooklyn College, receiving a Bachelor of Arts degree in 1950.
He began his writing career as a poet under the
guidance of W. H. Auden. In addition to his poetry,
Sackler wrote a verse drama in the tradition of T. S.
Eliot, a one-act play titled "Uriel Acosta." In
addition to these achievements, Sackler also wrote
the screenplays "Desert Padre" (1950), "Fear and
Desire" (1953), and "Killer's Kiss" (1955) for
director Stanley Kubrick. All of these accomplishments were realized before he reached the age of
twenty-five.

Sackler also founded and became production
director for Caedmon Records, a production company engineering the recording of over two hundred
well-known plays, read by England's most respectable actors and actresses. The list of actors and
actresses includes Paul Scolfield, Sir Ralph Richardson, Rex Harrison, Margaret Leighton, Dame
Edith Evans, Claire Bloom, Albert Finney, Julie
Harris, and Jessica Tandy.

His work at Caedmon Records took him away
from the business of writing. It would not be until
1961 that Sackler would decide to put pen to paper
and write *A Few Enquiries*, a collection of four one-
act plays, as well as screenplays. Among these titles
are "The Nine O'Clock Mail" (1965) and "Mr.
Welk and Jersey Jim" (1970).

His major achievement would come in the form
of *The Great White Hope*. Sackler was intrigued by
the story of Jack Johnson, the first black Heavyweight Champion of the World. Initially, his vision
was to create a musical version of the play, but the
author soon abandoned the idea in favor of drama.
The great success of this play came with the Pulitzer Prize, the New York Drama Critics' Circle
Award, and the Antoinette Perry Award in 1969.
Sackler also received other grants and awards as a
writer, including a Rockefeller Foundation grant
(1953), a Littauer Foundation grant (1954), the
Maxwell Anderson Award (1954), and the Sergel
Award (1959).

Throughout the remainder of his career, Sackler
continued to work at Caedmon, while also continuing to direct for the stage, film, and television. Sackler died at his home in Ibiza, Spain, in
1982, leaving several plays unfinished, including
"Klondike," based on the Alaskan gold rush. While

his unfinished plays have never been produced,
other works, like *The Great White Hope*, continue to
appear in England as well as America.

PLOT SUMMARY

Act 1, Scene 1

The play opens on Brady's farm in Parchmont,
Ohio. There is a discussion between Brady, identified as "the heavyweight champion"; Fred, his
manager; Cap'n Dan, "a champion of earlier days";
Smitty, "a famous sportswriter"; and several members of the press including photographers. Goldie,
Jack Jefferson's manager, is also present. The group,
with the exception of Goldie, is encouraging Brady
to re-enter the ring in reaction to the recent performance of black athlete Jack Jefferson, who is a serious
boxing contender. Cap'n Dan pitches to Brady,
"You're the White Hope, Mr. Brady!" He shares
his fears with the heavyweight, asking how he can
let the whole country down, how he can live with a
reputation that "he wouldn't stick a fist out to teach
a loudmouth nigger, stayed home and let him be
Champion of the World."

The scene ends with a flurry of negotiations
after Brady agrees to fight Jefferson. The terms are
80–20 in favor of the promoter, the location is Reno,
as suggested by Cap'n Dan, who believes it is
necessary to avoid big towns and the likelihood of
having "every nigger and his brother jamming in
there." Goldie departs for the train, leaving Brady
to pose for photos with members of the press.

Act 1, Scene 2

The action shifts to a small gym in San Francisco, California, where Jefferson is shadowboxing
in the presence of his trainer, Tick, as Eleanor
Bachman watches. Jack and Tick are working on a
strategy for the upcoming fight when Goldie arrives.

Jack relays to Goldie that he met Eleanor on a
boat from Australia and that Eleanor is from Tacoma,
Washington. When Goldie asks Eleanor to leave
because the press is coming, Jack says, "she stay
where she is." Goldie knows he can protect Jack
from some adversaries, "guys who want to put dope
in your food there, a guy who wants to watch the
fight behind a rifle." He is not prepared to deal with
the racist backlash of those unsympathetic to Jack's
involvement with a woman outside his race.

Act 1, Scene 3

Outside the arena in Reno, the day before the fight, Jack calls out to his "homefolks" and moves to their group in the back of the room. When a member of this group of black men tells him they are rooting for him because they believe that his victory will instill in them a sense of pride, Jack responds, "Well, country boy, if you ain't there already, all the boxin' and nigger-prayin in the world ain't gonna get you there."

In a personal moment, Cap'n Dan shares with the audience his fears about a possible victory for Jack. He confides that, unlike being the world's best engineer or the world's biggest genius, to Cap'n Dan, the possibility of Jack becoming the heavyweight champion makes the world seem "darker, and different, like it's shrinking, it's all huddled down somehow."

Act 1, Scene 4

Jack is hosting the Grand Opening of the Café de Champion in Chicago and has decided to use the event to openly announce his engagement to Ellie. He is suddenly confronted by the Women's League for Temperance, whose members are protesting the opening. Jack's reaction to the crowd is to offer them chairs and refreshments outside of the café, an act that serves to disperse the crowd. The conflict is diminished by the arrival of Mrs. Bachman, Ellie's mother, who has come with an attorney to entice Ellie to leave the festivities.

Act 1, Scene 5

Cameron, district attorney for the city of Chicago, is meeting with several civic leaders and Smitty, a detective, among others, to discuss the incident outside the café, during which Clara, Jack's common-law wife, fired a shot at her "husband." As a group, they determine that Jack "personifies all that should be suppressed by law" and agree to work towards such lawful "suppression." Smitty and Cameron then proceed to interview Ellie, hoping she will say something to incriminate Jack. She repeatedly declares her love for the prizefighter. When their harassment causes Ellie's hostile departure, Cameron admits defeat, exclaiming "Nothing! Seduction, enticement, coercion, abduction, not one good berry on the bush!"

Act 1, Scene 6

Jack is arrested after he is discovered vacationing with Ellie in a cabin in Beau Rivage, Wisconsin. Federal marshals burst into the cabin with lanterns to discover the two romantically snuggled up in bed. Jack's crime is that he drove Ellie over the Wisconsin state line and "proceeded to have relations with her," apparently "illegal under the Mann Act."

Act 1, Scene 7

After his arrest, Jack visits his mother while he's out on bond. His punishment is a $20,000 fine and three years in Joliet prison. Jack tells Mrs. Jefferson that he plans to disguise himself as one of the Detroit Blue Jays, members of a Negro League who assist him in his escape out of the country. He answers his mother's objections, saying, "Ah got my turn to be Champeen of the world an Ah takin my turn! Ah stayin whut Ah am, wherever Ah has to do it! The world ain't curled up into no forty-eight states here!"

Act 2, Scene 1

The scene is London in the home office of several city officials. Jack's status as an alien is being questioned after an arrest for "using obscene language" and another for "causing a crowd to collect," among other offenses substantiated by Inspector Wainright and several other individuals present. At the completion of the meeting, Sir William, the individual overseeing the meeting, trivializes the charges. Despite Sir William's position, Jack chooses to abandon the proceedings in disgust.

Act 2, Scenes 2–3

Jack's arrival in France is celebrated, and the action quickly moves to Vel d'Hiver arena in Paris. His competition is, according to Jack, a "fifth-rate" fighter in contrast to his past experiences. Smitty appears next to Ellie as she watches the fight. The sportswriter engages Ellie with a series of probing questions about her life plans with Jack. Noticing Ellie's increasing agitation, Smitty remarks, "Living like this . . . has to burn you out . . . you're not as tough as he is, you know, you can't just go on." Jack's bloodstained appearance and shouts of "assassin" from angry spectators suddenly interrupt their conversation. The scene ends with Jack, Tick, and Ellie's hasty departure from the arena.

Act 2, Scene 4

Fred, Pop Weaver, a promoter, and Cap'n Dan are previewing film footage of what they believe to be the next "Great White Hope." They hope to strike a deal with Jack. Their plans are to drop Jack's prison sentence if he agrees to fix the fight. At first, there is some resistance from Pop and Fred; both object to the illegal activity. To Cap'n Dan, Jack's freedom is a small price to pay for a "white" victory, something that eventually all can agree on. The success of blacks in American society, that is, Jack, is threatening to men like Mr. Dixon, who enters into the discussion claiming, "we cannot allow the image of this man to go on impressing and exciting these people [blacks]."

Act 2, Scene 5

In his search for work, Jack is unsuccessful in Germany. According to Ragosy, Jack "will not divert" or get any attention unless he fights. Goldie offers up information concerning a possible fight in Chicago, stating that "Fred's got this kid" who wants to fight Jack. The profits involve "10 G's guaranteed" and a reduced prison sentence of six months for Jack. When Jack objects, Goldie, seeing the futility of the situation, tells Jack he will be returning to the States.

Act 2, Scene 6

The scene shifts to Cabaret Ragosy in Budapest. It appears that Ragosy finally has convinced Jack, Ellie, and Tick to act in a dramatic performance based on *Uncle Tom's Cabin*. They must stop the show after the crowd becomes more hostile, booing them off the stage.

Act 2, Scene 7

In the train station in Belgrade, Jack, Ellie, and Tick meet up with Smitty, who relays to them that Jack's mother is ill. He then offers Jack the chance to fight in the States, which Jack immediately refuses. When Smitty responds, asking, "What is it," is it that he wants to "stay the champ and keep the belt a bit longer," Jack replies, "Champ don mean piss-all ta me man. Ah bin it, all dat champ jive been beat clear outta me."

Act 3, Scene 1

The scene is a funeral procession on a street in Chicago, given for Jack's mother. Tensions in the crowd heighten as Clara soulfully speaks of the dead woman's tribulations. When Goldie expresses his sympathy, Clara responds, "you an dat white b——an de whole pack a ya—come on ovah to de box here, sugah, see how good y'all nail de lid down." Her statements provoke the crowd's anger towards Goldie, and there is great confusion as violence erupts and fists and billy clubs fly.

Act 3, Scene 2

Back in Pop's office in New York, Pop, Smitty, and Cap'n Dan are heatedly discussing Jack Jefferson. The group speculates on how best they can defame Jack, and they come up with an idea to manipulate his future, to bribe his trainers to abandon him, and to bribe officials so there are no exhibition matches or competitions open to Jack. The goal is to entice Jack to return to the States to fight their most promising young fighter, their "Great White Hope." Says Cap'n Dan, "we're gonna squeeze that dinge so . . . hard soon a fix is gonna look like a hayride to him!"

Act 3, Scene 3

Jack has switched training locations to a disused barn in Juarez, Mexico. "Well, you kin work wid da heavy ones, time bein. Bettah fo ya, anyhow," replies Tick, when Jack says he's going to sell his boxing gloves for cash. Everyone involved in Jack's training must catch the train, leaving Ellie and Jack alone to talk.

"Jack, it's slow poison here, there's nothing else to wait for, just more of it, you've had enough—please, you're being paralyzed," pleads a discouraged Ellie. Jack responds that it is Ellie who is dragging him down and that, for him, refusing to give in is a matter of self-respect. Angrily responding to a lack of support, Jack asks Ellie to "get out." Ellie begs him to reconsider only to be met with a hurl of insults. He blames Ellie for his failure, stating, "evvy time you pushes up dat pinch-up face in fronna me, Ah sees where it done got me."

Ellie exits, and Jack finds himself in the company of Goldie, El Jefe, Dixon, and another government agent. The agent answers Jack's protests, stating, "it is perfectly legal" to "request cooperation of the parties in charge" in Mexico in an effort to apprehend him. At that moment, Jack learns of Ellie's suicide, her body presented to him "mudsmeared and dripping." When Goldie asks Jack how he can help, Jack cries, "Set dat . . . fight up!"

Act 3, Scene 4

Jack's black supporters spiritedly rally around him in the streets somewhere in the United States.

Act 3, Scene 5

The final scene of the play takes place at Oriente race track, Havana. Jack has been sparring in the ring with a young white fighter for ten rounds. To the wonderment of Pop and Smitty, Jack refuses to go down, even after Smitty says he has "given the high sign two rounds ago." Ultimately, Jack is defeated in the final round. When he is repeatedly asked why he has lost the fight, Jack replies, "Ah ain't got dem reallies from de Year One . . . An if you got'm, step right down and say em," resigning to a state of racial inferiority.

CHARACTERS

Eleanor Bachman

Eleanor (Ellie) is Jack's white girlfriend and love interest. After meeting Jack on a boat returning from Australia, she follows Jack to San Francisco rather than returning to her home in Tacoma, Washington. She is good-natured and supportive but not a bit naïve about interracial relations. Ellie is aware of the challenges Jack faces as a black man and is fiercely protective of him. Volunteering to be interviewed by Cameron, Ellie tells him her reasons for participating, saying, "I wanted to head off any notions you have of getting at him through me."

Contrary to the opinions of those opposing her relationship with Jack, Ellie truly loves him and has no desire other than to be with him. She suffers the scrutiny and judgment of others, only to face disbelief and disrespect rather than support and acceptance. At one point during her interview with Cameron, she is driven to tears, pleading, "why can't they leave us alone, what's the difference?"

Mrs. Bachman

Mrs. Bachman's objective is to get her daughter out of arm's reach of Jack. Although she appears infrequently during the course of the play, she surfaces to deliver an important dramatic monologue. Her speech is revealing—it helps the audience to understand her motivations concerning Ellie as well as those of other characters in the play. Her fear, her ingrained loathing for what she calls blackness, is described by association, "the black hole and the black pit, what's burned or stained or cursed or hideous, poison and spite and the waste from your body and the horrors crawling up into your mind."

MEDIA ADAPTATIONS

- *The Great White Hope* was made into a movie in 1970 by Twentieth Century Fox.

Brady

Brady is the former Heavyweight Champion of the World and a possible contender chosen to win the title back from Jack.

Cameron

The district attorney for Chicago, Cameron is behind the efforts of Cap'n Dan and others, but for professional reasons rather than personal ones. He indicates this in a conversation about Jack, stating, "You know . . . if a good White Hope showed up and beat him it would take the edge off this." It would certainly take the edge off Cameron, who recognizes that revoking the fighter's privileges or charging him with a dozen misdemeanors would not help because "they want [Jack's] head on a plate."

Clara

Clara is a former lover of Jack's who has surfaced in his life to rekindle their relationship. Although she claims to be his common-law wife and that Jack is dishonoring her, Jack has a different story to tell. Clara does not deny Jack's accusations— that she left him for a pimp named Willie or that she sold off his clothes, ring, and silver brushes. She is determined to win Jack back, which can be witnessed in her saying, "you ain't closing up the book so easy, Daddy."

Clara cannot be silenced. The mistrust and jealousy she harbors for Ellie has become a personal crusade against her. To Clara, Jack is at Ellie's disposal. Ellie maintains Jack in her life simply for the purpose of her own amusement. Clara's anger towards Ellie is really a vehicle for social commentary. Ellie is, as Clara sees it, the force behind her oppression, merely on the basis of her color. Clara believes Ellie to be a catalyst for Jack's arrest and Mrs. Jefferson's death.

Cap'n Dan

He is described simply as a champion of earlier days. Cap'n Dan is the main force behind the group of white fighters, sportswriters, and promoters who would like to see Jack lose his title. He expends a great deal of energy and effort to make his dream a reality. For Cap'n Dan, Jack's victory is a threat not only to his social status and his reputation as a fighter but also to his white lifestyle. He sees Jack, and black citizens in general, as inferior. Jack's status as champion is more than a victory; it is an affront, an attack on his core belief system. Says Cap'n Dan:

> I hold up his hand, and suddenly a nigger is Champion of the world. Now you'll say, Oh, that's only your title in sports—no, it's more. Admit it. And more than if one got to be world's best engineer, or smartest politician, or number one opera singer, or world's biggest genius at making things from peanuts.

Jack's victory has a profound effect on Cap'n Dan precisely because he feels a sense not only of superiority but of entitlement as a white individual. The idea that a black man attained the same success and status as Cap'n Dan is a threat to him. He has, in a sense, failed to live up to the white standard he has imposed on himself and to a belief system that says he is better than any black male, regardless of talent or ability.

Dixon

Offering his expertise as a federal agent, Dixon provides professional support in assisting the district attorney of Chicago in his apprehension of Jack. He suggests the use of the Mann Act, which leads to Jack's successful arrest.

Dixon also has a personal interest in seeing Jack brought to justice after he flees the country. In a meeting with Cap'n Dan and others, he states "When a man beats us out like this, we—the law, that is—suffer in prestige, and that's pretty serious." And like Cap'n Dan, Dixon believes that he cannot "allow the image of this man" to impress and excite "millions of ignorant Negroes, rapidly massing together."

Ellie

See Eleanor Bachman

Goldie

He serves as Jack's manager as well as his friend. Goldie is aware of the challenges Jack faces as a black fighter and is very supportive and protec-

tive of Jack. When negotiating the terms for Jack's fight with a promoter, Goldie is quick to point out the inequity of the situation, saying, "my Jackie would fight for a nickel, tomorrow. But it wouldn't look nice for you to take advantage, so you'll offer me low as you can get away with and I'll say OK."

Goldie is also a father figure to Jack. When he finds out that Jack is seeing a white woman, he says in dismay, "Last night in my head it's like a voice—Dumbbell, go home quick, somethin's goin on with him!" This statement is followed by a stern lecture not only about the dangers of being a black man dating a white woman but also about those inherent in just being a black heavyweight champion. The audience comes to see Goldie not only as a manager but as a family member and friend when he chooses to support Jack in his flight from justice and then participates in Mrs. Jefferson's funeral on Jack's behalf.

Jack Jefferson

Jack is more than a heavyweight fighter; he is a top-notch athlete, fiercely devoted to his sport. Jack is also unwilling to succumb to the demands society places upon him, both as a black man and as a black athlete. Despite Goldie's repeated warnings that dating a white woman would hurt his career, Jack insists on announcing his engagement to Ellie publicly, at the grand opening of a café in Chicago.

His fighting ability is also challenged strictly on the basis of his color. Cap'n Dan and others insist Jack defend his title on their terms, hoping he will eventually lose. Jack, however, does not feel an obligation to Cap'n Dan, nor does he give in to the harassment and enormous pressure put on him by white society. Jack refutes any pressure or suggestion from the group, stating, "Ah got my turn to be Champeen of the World an Ah takin my turn! Ah stayin whut Ah am, wherever Ah has to do it!"

This defiance is characteristic of Jack's behavior throughout the work. He repeatedly insists on maintaining personal autonomy and self-respect among whites and blacks alike, even if it means risking incarceration or his own life. Jack will go to any extreme to preserve his identity, becoming a fugitive on the move for almost the entire play.

Mrs. Jefferson

Jack's ailing mother is a troubled, God-fearing woman who deeply loves her son, despite his shortcomings. She also feels a sense of responsibility for what is happening to her son, pleading, "Lawd fogive me not beatin on him young enough or hurtin him bad enough to learn him after, cause ah seen this day comin.'' Mrs. Jefferson does not blame Ellie for Jack's troubles, nor does she question Ellie's affections for her son. When Clara attacks Ellie, Mrs. Jefferson defends her, replying, ''could be she do love him, Clara.'' More important, her death serves to heighten racial tensions among the black characters of the play who blame Jack's arrest for her death.

Pastor

The audience is introduced to the activities of the pastor as he interacts with Mrs. Jefferson. He is a mediator attempting to soothe tense, racially charged moments with church rhetoric. He provides opportunities for social commentary from Scipio, Clara, and others. When the pastor tries to calm the angry crowd during Mrs. Jefferson's funeral, Scipio responds sarcastically, ''Dass right, chillun, suffer nice an easy—school em on it, boss!'' Scipio's comments eventually insight a riot. For Scipio and others, the church represents another part of white culture that has been imposed on blacks to subdue them.

Ragosy

Ragosy is the Hungarian impresario who encourages Jack to give up any ideas he may have of fighting in Germany to join his Cabaret. The engagement is short-lived, however, when Jack and Ellie's performance ends abruptly after a disastrous reception.

Scipio

A street philosopher, Scipio appears during several moments in the course of the play to illuminate or explain the nature of the white institutionalization he and others of his race have been subjected to. His perspectives amplify the sentiments of those African Americans who are no longer content to ''just get along,'' to be passive as well as complacent in the context of a society controlled by whites.

Smitty

The famous sportswriter seems always to be lurking in the shadows of Jack's life. At the opening of the play, he is a witness to the fight between Jack and Clara and is one of the first people to learn of Jack and Ellie's relationship. He is also behind the scenes, privy to the efforts of Cap'n Dan and others to dethrone Jack as World Heavyweight Champion.

At every turn in the play, Smitty is present, asking questions of Ellie, Jack, Cap'n Dan, and others. His probing interviews also function to give the audience a different perspective into the motivations of many of the characters. At a railway station in Belgrade, Smitty attempts to advise Jack, urging him to surrender and return to the United States to defend his title. He tells Jack that he'd ''rather have [the fight] straight,'' if he ''weren't so good.'' This comment betrays Smitty's true feelings, and as the play wears on, the audience discovers that Smitty is not just an ambitious journalist, but an informant for Cap'n Dan.

Tick

Loyal to Jack as his trainer, Tick never really leaves his side throughout the play. He is a silent man. More than a trainer, he is a steady, trustworthy, and supportive companion to Jack.

Pop Weaver

The promoter from New York behind the Havana fight, Pop Weaver works with allies Cap'n Dan and Fred to plan Jack's defeat by introducing some young raw white talent. When he learns the fight will be fixed, he is quick to offer up his objections. Eventually, he agrees to go along with the plans stating, ''We'll balance it out on the one after this. Everything back on the gold standard, right?''

THEMES

Racism and Racial Conflict

The Great White Hope is a title reflective of the racism and racial conflict present throughout the work. There is an air of superiority, a notion among several white characters in the novel that they are better than their black neighbors. The rights and privileges of black members of such a society are defined by white interpretation. Cap'n Dan feels that Jack's status as a boxer is wrong and should be corrected. He says at the outset of the play that Jack has no right to think he can be a champion. This notion is reflected in Cap'n Dan's statement when he asks Smitty:

> How're you going to like it when the whole ... country says Brady let us down, he wouldn't stick a fist out to teach a loudmouth nigger, stayed home and let him be Champion of the World?

Blacks themselves also define their place in step with white perceptions. A black man, only

TOPICS FOR FURTHER STUDY

- Compare the structure of Sackler's play to a Shakespearean play of your choosing. In what ways do both works mirror or match each other structurally? Thematically?

- Study the life story of Jack Johnson. Take note of any differences between Sackler's work of fiction and the reality of the events that touched Johnson's life. Does the author's representation at all compromise the play?

- Consider Joseph Conrad's *Heart of Darkness* in light of the white characters in the play. How do the feelings of characters like Mrs. Bachman and Cap'n Dan compare with the overall mood of Conrad's work?

- Choose a historical figure, event, or aspect of the play and investigate the significance of it. Explain how that figure, event, or aspect had an impact on society during the time in which the play takes place, as well as the author's time.

---

identified as "Negro," comments on the threat Jack poses to the community, stating, "For the Negro today, the opportunity to earn a dollar in a factory should appear to be worth infinitely more than the opportunity of spending that dollar in emulation of Mr. Jack Jefferson."

Racial conflict is an outgrowth of these prevailing white attitudes represented throughout the work. In one scene, Clara uses Mrs. Jefferson's funeral as a forum for protest. She singles out Goldie to express her outrage at whites. When the preacher condones her behavior, one of the participants exclaims, "Shame on me, shame on alla us, for BEIN de oppressed, an bein it, an bein it!" This comment and others move the crowd to engage in a violent struggle, black against white.

Black Identity

The spirit of those behind Jack in his quest for victory is guided by their need to foster some sense of identity. Sackler captures this spirit in the voices of his black characters, using them to comment on the cultural oppression of black America for the sake of white ideals. Such ideals have meant involuntary conformity, assuming a position of inferiority, and a loss of cultural identity for black Americans.

Some characters see championing the white culture as a means of earning their respect. To Jack's black supporters, his victory represents not only a triumph for the entire black race but also a chance for them to redeem themselves as individuals.

Jack has a different response to the question of black identity. He sees a characteristically undesirable mentality, a "cullud" mentality, among his supporters. Jack demonstrates this idea when he expresses to the group that he doesn't have to earn or prove his need for self-respect because he already has it. When a young man states, "Ah be proud to be a cullud man tomorrow," Jack replies, "Well, country boy, if you ain't there already, all the boxin and nigger-prayin in the world ain't gonna get you there." He refutes the belief that his victory represents one for his race, further maintaining that such beliefs constitute "cullud" thinking, beliefs that ultimately limit, rather than foster, achievement. If one thinks "cullud," then all one will ever do is live inside the box, that is, be "cullud."

Scipio sympathizes with Jack's views on identity, perhaps more profoundly, stating in his monologue that it's "time again to make us a big new wise proud dark man's world." He sees freedom from oppression in regaining self-respect, as well as self-love, by celebrating his own heritage. "Learn brothers, learn! Ee-gyp!! Tambuctoo!! Ethiopya!! Red'n goldin cities older den Jeruslem."

Interracial Relationships

The issue of interracial relations is a prominent theme within the context of the play. Time and time again, blacks and whites alike challenge Jack and Ellie's relationship. The controversy begins immediately when Jack is asked to hide his white girlfriend from the unsympathetic eyes of the press. Ignoring Goldie's requests, Jack asks:

> Whut Ah s'pose to do! Stash her in a iddy biddy hole someplace in niggertown an go sneakin over there twelve o'clock at night, carry her roun with me inside a box like a pet bunny rabbit or somethin?

Ellie has to endure the intense scrutiny of others concerning her relationship with Jack. In the

Chicago district attorney's office, her feelings for Jack are repeatedly questioned during an increasingly probing, intensely personal interview. Cameron insists at several points with Ellie that she is lonely, unhappy somehow, in an attempt to explain what he infers is an "unnatural" relationship. He has an agenda. Like other characters, he cannot accept Ellie's affection for Jack—to him, her feelings aren't just impossible; they aren't right. Cameron's ideas only mirror the sentiments of other characters in the play whose belief systems are challenged by Jack and Ellie's relationship.

When Jack goes to jail for taking Ellie across the Wisconsin state line, Clara is quick to offer her opinion. She blames the situation on Ellie and is ready to "smoke her out." What Clara recognizes is Jack's liability in the affair. When Ellie and Jack are caught together, it is Jack who suffers the arrest rather than his white girlfriend. She questions Ellie's claim to love Jack when her presence repeatedly compromises his life.

Free Will and Determinism

The catalyst for Jack's troubles is his demand for autonomy and self-respect as a black man in a racially unjust environment. His insistence on crossing the boundaries of what is socially acceptable to realize personal achievement is a futile endeavor in the context of the racist society of which he is a part. While Jack is struggling to achieve his own personal goals as an athlete, the white power structure is trying to tear him down. Specifically, there are whites that would like to see him lose his title less for an appreciation of boxing than for their own supremacist satisfactions. Goldie is the first to warn Jack he's in over his head in dating a white woman, stating, "a white girl, Jack, what, do I have to spell it on the wall for you, you wanna drive them crazy, you don't wanna hear what happens."

Instead of earning the respect of his contemporaries for being a great athlete, he is pursued by them as if his talents are criminal. About to be arrested, Jack questions the credibility of being apprehended outside of his own country. The agent is quick to answer, offering, "It is perfectly legal once we've ascertained where a wanted man is, to request cooperation of the parties in charge there." The reality of Jack's life is that no matter where he travels to escape the limitations imposed on him by white society, whether Canada or Europe, he can never truly realize freedom and autonomy as a black man.

Foreshadowing

Elements in the plot that create expectation or help to explain later developments are represented in dramatic monologue. These moments occur in boldface within the text of the play, functioning either as part of a larger dialogue or within a dramatic monologue. When the press discovers that Ellie is dating Jack, for example, Goldie turns to the audience mid-dialogue and says, "if it gets out, God knows what could happen." The warning to the audience proves true later in the play, when Jack is arrested for taking Ellie on a weekend getaway.

Mrs. Bachman's dramatic monologue also foreshadows the tragic events of the play's climax. White, pained, and haggard, she appears to the audience later in the play to express her sorrow over her daughter's involvement with Jack. She sends the audience a warning, stating, "I know what Black means . . . wait until it is your every other thought, like it is theirs, like it is mine. Wait until it touches your own flesh and blood." Her monologue is prophetic because her daughter Ellie's involvement with Jack ultimately causes Ellie to kill herself. To Mrs. Bachman, the very idea of what it means to be touched by "blackness" brings up all kinds of horrifying associations.

Dramatic Monologue

Many of the secondary characters give a speech to the audience during the course of the work. These monologues, in addition to foreshadowing upcoming events, provide the audience with insight into personal motivations for a character's actions. Cap'n Dan's motivations to defame Jack, while shortsighted, are not fueled by ill intent. In a dramatic monologue, he reveals his fear about Jack's success, exclaiming, "I really have the feeling it's the biggest calamity to hit this country since the San Francisco earthquake." To him, Jack's victory, if unchallenged, will cast a dark shadow across the world. Cap'n Dan fears the kind of change that will bring equality, a force he admits he can't even understand.

Other monologues serve as insight into the motivations of those oppressed. Scipio's role is a perfect example of dramatic monologue used to illuminate the black perspective. Addressing the woeful singing in response to Jack's arrest, Scipio takes the moment to address the audience. In a moving monologue, he condones the spirit of passivity plaguing the black man in America. Scipio states:

> Oh mebbe you done school youself away frum White Jesus—but how long you evah turn you heart away frum white! How you lookin, how you movin, how you wishin an figgering—how white you wanna be, that whut Ah askin!''

Scipio's speech offers a perspective not unlike Jack's. Like Jack, he advocates that the black man regain his identity, find his self-respect by exploring his roots and taking pride in his heritage as a person of color. He makes a compelling point as well: ''Five hundrid million of us not all together, not matchin up to em, dat what harmin us!''

Point of View

The work is operating in the third person omniscient point of view. This claim is substantiated particularly by the use of dramatic monologue that often provides insight into the motivations or feelings of many characters of the play, as opposed to being relevant only to those actions of the speaker. Not only does it predict a character's movements, but this insight also draws the audience in, giving them a variety of perspectives from various characters of various races. Scipio's monologue, for example, is a deeper exploration into Jack's views of what it means to operate as a ''cullud'' rather than as an individual. Statements made by Jack, which came off as callous or harsh, now take on a nobler meaning in light of Scipio's remarks.

Other insights change or transform perceptions of a character's motivations completely. Clara, for example, is presented as someone spurned by love and driven simply by jealousy, after Jack rejects her for a white woman. During Clara's monologue, she pleads to the audience, ''drag him on down. Oh won'tya, fo me an mah momma an evvy black-ass woman he turn his back on, for evvy gal wid a man longside dreamin him a piece a what he got.'' Clara's dialogue is revealing. She is no longer simply a crazy, money-grubbing ex-girlfriend. The audience sees Clara's deeper motivations. She is a victim, seeing herself as one of many black women rejected by men of her own race who seek to aspire to white values, men who voluntarily put the love and support of those black women behind them for the sake of personal gain.

Rising Action

The rising action is marked by the overseas travels of Ellie and Jack. The change in the tenor of the plot begins when Jack encounters some trouble in England and chooses to walk away from further conflict. This conflict only increases, however, as Jack and Ellie move from country to country, putting a strain on their already fraying relationship. Finally, at the moment before his arrest, Jack tells a pleading Ellie to leave him be.

The climax, or the turning point in the plot where the action is at its greatest intensity, occurs during Jack's arrest. Up until this moment, he is resistant to offer himself to the authorities. When Ellie's mud-smeared and dripping body is presented to Jack, he surrenders to the authorities, realizing, ''what Ah done to ya, what you done, honey, honey, whut dey done to us.'' This single event is a turning point in the play. Jack recognizes the futility of his actions, implicit or obvious in his willingness to fight in Havana.

Colloquialism/Colloquial Speech

Colloquial or informal speech patterns give life to the voices of black characters appearing throughout the work. Words such as ''dat,'' ''cullud,'' and ''dere'' are just a few examples of the use of colloquial language to differentiate characters by race.

HISTORICAL CONTEXT

Jack Johnson, Heavyweight Champion of the World

The Great White Hope is a work of fiction based on a historical figure, a black American prizefighter named John Arthur ''Jack'' Johnson. Not unlike Sackler's fictional Jack Jefferson, Johnson aggravated white America by refusing to behave in a passive, submissive fashion expected of blacks at that time. In 1908, he traveled to Sidney, Australia, to fight and defeat Tommy Burns and became the first black Heavyweight Champion of the World. Public outrage and disbelief over the victory were catalysts for the match between former champ Jim Jeffries, ''The Great White Hope,'' and Johnson. On July 4, 1910, Johnson defeated Jeffries after fifteen rounds.

Johnson later married two white women in the years following the victory. He was also arrested in the company of his white fiancée in 1912 in accordance with the Mann Act. He escaped incarceration, fleeing to Canada and Europe, where he continued his career as a fighter. Havana led to a fixed fight with Jess Willard in exchange for Johnson's free-

COMPARE
&
CONTRAST

- **1902:** Joseph Conrad's *Heart of Darkness* is published, a story about a dangerous riverboat journey into the heart of the Congo in search of a missing white fur trader.

  Today: A television show called *Survivor* airs for the first time, pitting teams of contestants against each other in perilous, jungle-like conditions for one million dollars in prize money.

- **1908:** Jack Johnson defeats Tommy Burns in fourteen rounds to become the first black heavyweight boxing champion of the world.

  Today: Laila Ali, daughter of Muhammad Ali, fights Jacqui Frazier-Lyde, daughter of Joe Frazier, in the boxing ring. After a seven-round slugfest, Ali is declared the winner.

- **1965:** Lyndon Baines Johnson passes the Voting

Rights Act of 1965 to protect the right to vote of all citizens "without distinction of race, color, or previous condition of servitude. . . . "

  Today: Thousands of liberal voters in Dade County, Florida, cry foul to the use of hard-to-understand or faulty ballots during the U.S. presidential election, claiming their vote did not "count."

- **1965:** The country goes through a wave of social reform as Lyndon Baines Johnson increases spending to create Medicare and Medicaid as well as the Higher Education Act, among other programs.

  Today: George Bush announces a large tax cut, distributing surplus revenue among all Americans in the form of a tax refund.

---

dom. Although he did lose after twenty-six rounds, his charges were never dropped. An eventual surrender led to a year in Leavenworth, Kansas, in 1920. After his release, Johnson worked for carnivals and as a vaudeville performer.

LBJ's "Great Society"

The era leading up to the publication of Sackler's work was a time characterized by great social conflict and upheaval. After John F. Kennedy's death, a grieving nation was left to struggle with civil rights issues and the Vietnam War. Lyndon B. Johnson assumed the role of president of the United States, fully committed to JFK's liberal program of social reform in an effort to meet such challenges.

Johnson had a vision of what he called a "Great Society," and he was determined to realize this goal through liberal social policy. This vision led to several social programs, including the creation of Medicare in 1965, to assist citizens over sixty-five pay for medical treatment, as well as Medicaid, to help welfare recipients meet medical costs. Educational policy was also enacted in the creation of the

Elementary and Secondary Education Act and the Higher Education Act. As a result of such policy, government funding was provided so that poorer students would realize an education reserved traditionally for the middle class. The "War on Poverty," as Johnson called it, also resulted in additional social policy and the creation of community programs like the Job Corps, Project Head Start, and the Food Stamps program.

Racial Unrest

Racial and ethnic tensions blemished the character of American life during the 1960s. This tension was mirrored in the passage of the Civil Rights Act in 1964. The legislation forbade segregation and discrimination in public accommodations such as restaurants, nightclubs, hotels, and theaters. Critical citizens, blacks and whites alike, believed morality could not be legislated. Optimistic citizens believed that such legislation was a step toward rectifying the inequities of the past based on the legacy of slavery.

White society did not realize or adopt a spirit of cooperation with their black neighbors. Urban areas suffered the sting of white flight, the mass exodus of whites to suburban areas. Urban blacks felt betrayed by such movement. This migration hurt the life-styles of those blacks that had become dependent on white businesses to employ them, as well as to support their neighborhoods by providing goods and services at reasonable prices. The result of this flight amounted to greater urban decay and the rise of the inner cities or ghettos.

The enactment of the Civil Rights Act was not an end to violence perpetrated against blacks as a result of racial tension and unrest. After countless acts of terror perpetrated by white segregationists, the Southern Christian Leadership Conference, or SCLC, staged a march from Selma, Alabama, to Montgomery, the state capital, on March 7, 1965. The marchers never made it to their destination but instead were attacked by police, succumbing either to the sting of tear gas or the blow of a billy club. James Reeb, a northern white minister active in the Civil Rights movement, was also murdered that Sunday evening by white segregationists. The day went down in history as "Bloody Sunday," prompting LBJ to pass the Voting Rights Act of 1965, which protected black America's right to vote.

Vietnam

Johnson was determined to move forward with the Vietnam conflict. He proved this with the enactment of the Gulf of Tonkin Resolution. The report of two U.S. destroyers in the Gulf of Tonkin provided the opportunity for Johnson to satisfy his desire to expand the war effort. In reality, only one destroyer, the Maddox, had actually been attacked in error as South Vietnamese attempted to seize the northern coast of Vietnam. At this point Johnson chose to gradually escalate the war effort with a vision of eventual occupation. This approach only served to prolong the conflict: however many troops LBJ sent, however much ground he managed to gain, was only lost to the Viet Cong, outsmarted by their political infiltration and military strategy.

CRITICAL OVERVIEW

Perhaps it is fitting that Howard Sackler achieved such high acclaim with the success of *The Great White Hope*. Critics were quite impressed when the young playwright produced his treatise on racial hatred, characterizing the plot as a rather fast-moving, yet smoothly flowing entity as it seamlessly

transitions from one scene to the next. The work is crafted in the tradition of a great Shakespearean play, the text written in flowing verse, the main character firmly grounded, central to all of the action swirling around him. Every event in the play either directly or indirectly relates to Jack's life. In *Western Humanities Review,* Marion Trousdale comments on this centrality, calling it "irreducibly dramatic." States Trousdale, "[the play] did what Aristotle said a play should do, and what few playwrights know how to do—it imitated an action by means of an action." Therefore, the critic adds, the play has a "histrionic heart."

While many readily accept such glowing comparisons, John Simon, critic for the *Hudson Review,* has a different perspective on the play. He responds to Sackler's work, stating, "How nice if Sackler, who had the good sense to use Shakespeare and Brecht as his models, had come up with something worthy of them." He continues, claiming that Sackler's writing is functional rather than fantastic, simply "overambitious middlebrow stuff."

Sackler's work also betrays a penchant or preference for the historical. His sense of history lies at the thematic core of most of the author's works. Such structure lends itself to a certain dynamism, in setting, in characterization and dialog, as well as in mood, traits which are viewed as functioning to strengthen the work as a whole. Trousdale offers that the performers are also "noisy and loud and unabashedly theatrical," which serves to strengthen the play, and are simply an "outward form of the 'invisible currents that rule our lives.'" Structurally the play follows the classical model. But in consideration of dimension, space, and a certain dynamism inherent in the work, the play clearly takes on a modern feel.

Later works by Sackler, although not having as profound an impact on his career, mirror the poetry and sheer artistry to some degree that many have admired in *The Great White Hope*. More recent efforts, such as "Goodbye Fidel," inspire the same feelings of passion and excitement as does his Pulitzer Prize-winner.

CRITICISM

Laura Kryhoski

Kryhoski is currently working as a freelance writer. In this essay, Kryhoski considers Sackler's

*use of contrasts as well as his historical considera-
tion of the work.*

The Great White Hope is a story of contrasts, of
black versus white, or the dark versus the light. Two
of Sackler's white characters, Cap'n Dan and Mrs.
Bachman, use these contrasts in their own dramatic
monologues to express their feelings about Jack
Jefferson. Their feelings are a function of their own
ignorance. For these characters, their ignorance
serves as an impetus or as a reason for exercising
racism. It is these voices, of both Cap'n Dan and
Mrs. Bachman, that Sackler employs to illuminate
belief systems fueling racism. Through both voices,
the author is able to capture, with amazing historical
accuracy, the current of prejudice running through
white America at the turn of the nineteenth century.

Cap'n Dan describes Jack Jefferson in terms of
darkness. In the beginning of the play, he reveals his
feelings about Jack's victory on a personal level,
stating, "it feels like the world's got a shadow over
it." He goes on to explain a "darker, different,
shrinking," world, that it's "all huddled up somehow." For Cap'n Dan the world, as he has come to
understand it, is getting smaller and becoming increasingly unfamiliar to him. Further, he admits
feelings of powerlessness, even to the point of
intimidation, and these feelings are preventing him
from any sort of protest or retaliation. He expresses
these sentiments as if dark clouds are rolling in over
his life, "You want to holler, what's he doin up
there, but you can't because you know . . . that
shadow's on you, and you can feel that smile." As
curious a proposition as it seems, one man, Jack
Jefferson, has the ability to turn Cap'n Dan's life
upside down.

His monologue betrays uneasiness rooted in a
struggle to preserve identity. The darkness permeat-
ing Cap'n Dan's psyche can be explained simply by
the words "darker, different, shrinking." A black
fighter, for the first time in the history of the sport,
has earned a title reserved only for white males.
Cap'n Dan feels the world is "shrinking" or "all
huddled-up somehow"; he feels intimidated because he too is a former champion. The victory
attacks his value system, one embracing a belief in
white superiority. On a more personal level, Jack's
victory raises questions about Cap'n Dan's own
abilities. The world "shrinks" as black men intrude
gradually on Cap'n Dan's world, the world of the
professional white boxer.

*James Earl Jones, as Jack Jefferson, in
a scene from the 1970 film adaptation of*
The Great White Hope, *directed by
Martin Ritt*

"I know what Black means," exclaims Mrs.
Bachman, and for dramatic effect Sackler stages a
blackout before she appears to the audience. Stepping out into the light of the stage, she expresses
great despair over her daughter's choice of love
interests. "Blackness" sets off something in Mrs.
Bachman's heart. She shares her negative, heartfelt
associations with blackness: "pitch black, black as
dirt, the black hole and the black pit, what's burned
or stained or cursed or hideous, poison and spite and
waste from your body and the horrors crawling up
into your mind." Her feeling is that God, if responsible for a meeting of the races, black and white,
used the opportunity as an expression of hate rather
than one of love.

These descriptions form a rather curious collection of sentiments about what it means for Mrs.
Bachman to be in the presence of someone "black"—
this is what she "knows." For her, black is unclean
and filthy but, curiously, involves spite and waste
from her own mind and body. It is as if in the
meeting of the races, she has somehow been exposed to some horrible contaminant. More curiously, she concedes or surrenders to the possible

WHAT DO I READ NEXT?

- *Dreaming in Color, Living in Black and White: Our Own Stories of Growing Up Black in White America,* by Laurel Holiday (2000), is a collection of stories of young black Americans' experiences in a racist society.

- *Hurricane: The Miraculous Journey of Rubin Carter,* by James S. Hirsch (2001), is the story of a black prizefighter who spends years in jail for a crime that he did not commit.

- In *W. E. B. DuBois: The Fight for Equality and the American Century, 1919–1963* (2000), David Levering Lewis recounts the words and life of one of the most prominent leaders of the black community in the twentieth century.

- *Want My Sheperd: Poems* is a collection of poetry published by Howard Sackler in 1954.

---

reactions of the audience, sharing with them an understanding that her thinking may be flawed. To say that she "knows what black means" outside of the context of her daughter's involvement is to say that she is just as, if not more, concerned about how Jack's presence in her life will impact herself as her daughter. Again, as with Cap'n Dan, Mrs. Bachman feels a sense of encroachment or intrusion upon her world, that somehow her life has been violated merely by Jack's presence. One could also infer that her comments betray her real fears—she is quick to deny or submerge any feelings of guilt or remorse she has concerning the legacy of slavery and her responsibility to a disenfranchised black America.

Sackler draws on the feelings expressed by both Cap'n Dan and Mrs. Bachman to convey with historical accuracy the social climate of the early 1900s, the backdrop for his play. What characterizes America at that time, what has been characterized as a "key theme" during this time period, is the desire to live life against nature. Historian Dr. Alan Axelrod, in his *Complete Idiot's Guide to Twentieth Century History,* expands on the idea, stating that the theme is identifiable "in the work of Freud (who sought to illuminate the dark places of the mind)" and also "in the electric light of Edison (who sought to illuminate dark places, period)." He also points to the influences of imperialists in Great Britain, who wished to bring the "light" of civilization to such "dark places" as Asia and Africa. Joseph Conrad's novel, aptly titled *Heart of Darkness,*

touched on the same theme. Published in 1902, the novel was the product of Conrad's travels to the Congo, a target of imperialism for King Leopold II of Belgium. The protagonist or leading character of the story, Marlow, travels deep into the Congo (the heart of darkness) on a riverboat in search of a missing white trader, Kurtz—eventually becoming part of the darkness. Adopting the role of chieftain, Kurtz decorates the outside of his hut with the skulls of his adversaries.

Axelrod's ideas are evidenced in the dialogue of the play. Cap'n Dan, for instance, believing Jack's victory is a "calamity," adds, "Oh, I don't think all the darkies'll go crazy, try to take us over, rape and all that." The statement is riddled with negative associations directed towards blacks. In his off-handed comment, Cap'n Dan shares his impressions of black America. He characterizes blacks as being savage, uncivilized, and hard to control. During the course of the play these concerns of possible retaliatory acts of savagery are consistently raised by Cap'n Dan and other white males closely associated with his plan to upset Jack's boxing career. Calling blacks "darkies" serves to reinforce the idea of the black fighter casting a dark shadow over Cap'n Dan's life. The question for Cap'n Dan, then, becomes one of far greater significance—if it is possible for an uncivilized, savage individual to achieve what he has achieved, how valid or important is such a title?

The use of dark and light is not only apparent in the dialogue of characters like Cap'n Dan and Mrs. Bachman, but such contrast is also used for dramatic purposes. Both characters appear after a blackout occurring during the play; both figures come into the light to reveal their inner feelings to the audience, truths driving the action of the work. Consequently, the substance of such heartfelt, personal monologues enlightens the audience. Clara also comes into the light to reveal what she believes to be true about the relationship between Jack and Ellie. Ceremoniously holding up an excrement- and blood-stained garment to the light, she cries out for justice in the death of Mrs. Jefferson, believing that Jack's affair with Ellie has killed her, also hoping it will kill him.

Sackler's play on contrasts is a natural consequence of the work's subject matter. To experience Sackler's play, even by today's standards, involves facing the often jolting perspectives of America, black and white, to understand the shades of racial conflict present within the work. The conclusion Sackler reaches in *The Great White Hope* is perhaps best expressed by Joseph Conrad's narrator Marlow, who believed that the "conquest of the earth, which mostly means the taking it away from those who have a different complexion or slightly flatter noses than ourselves, is not a pretty thing when you look into it."

Source: Laura Kryhoski, Critical Essay on *The Great White Hope,* in *Drama for Students,* The Gale Group, 2002.

Marion Trousdale

In the following review-essay, Trousdale provides an overview of the initial productions of The Great White Hope, *examining the play's "profound histrionic sensibility."*

The theatre's name like its shape is as self-defining and as functional as the new apartment buildings surrounding it in Washington's Southwest are meant to be. It calls itself Arena Stage, and it is octagonal without as within to provide seats for the spectators who, arena-fashion, both enclose and participate as audience in the performance that takes place below. It was here in winter 1967 under the direction of Edwin Sherin that Howard Sackler's *The Great White Hope* was first staged. The play later opened in New York, under the same director and with almost the same cast, where its success story by now is well-known. In their reviews of October, 1968, *Life* magazine and the *New Yorker* agreed that the play is spectacular and a hit: to *Life* its dramatic

> TO EXPERIENCE SACKLER'S PLAY, EVEN BY TODAY'S STANDARDS, INVOLVES FACING THE OFTEN JOLTING PERSPECTIVES OF AMERICA, BLACK AND WHITE, TO UNDERSTAND THE SHADES OF RACIAL CONFLICT PRESENT WITHIN THE WORK."

sensationalism is a virtue; its anonymous review remarked that the play is startingly contemporary, a "visceral interpretation" of "the tragic and gaudy life of the first black heavyweight champion, Jack Johnson." And as evidence Pete Hamill, New Yorker fashion, accompanied Muhammad Ali to the Alvin Theatre and watched him watch the play. "Hey," Hamill says Ali said, "This play is about me! Take out the interracial love stuff and Jack Johnson is the original me!" The *New Yorker*'s Edith Oliver does not deny the play's contemporaneity; she calls it a highly effective tract. But she complains that the play's "tumultuous, irresistible avalanche" of action that "hurls itself from the stage" is a kind of theatrical *trompe d'oeil.* Behind the "deafening and bedazzling blows in the face," she remarks, lies a work of little literary merit, an "oddly insubstantial affair."

Both reactions say more about the New York version than they do about the play as played at Arena Stage. In New York Sherin by reducing Sackler's text has made the play more brash, more arrogant, more "militant"; like the stage on which it is performed it now has only one dimension, that of its "message," and that message extends beyond the play's hero, whom Sackler calls Jack Jefferson, to include not only Muhammad Ali but the play's star as well, James Earl Jones. At the end of the ecstatic curtain calls he walks toward the audience and, pulling the blood-soaked rag from around his neck, drops it defiantly on a nude stage. Edith Oliver's description is both damning and accurate: she calls the play a "sad, cautionary tale of a good black man betrayed by a handful of evil Negro-hating white men," and she remarks that because "the play's heart is so evidently in the right place

> SACKLER PRESENTS HIS STORY BY A SERIES OF SCENES SUGGESTIVE OF BRECHT, AND THE DIFFICULTIES OF A BROADWAY PRODUCTION CAN BE SEEN EVEN FROM THE PROGRAM."

and because we wish our hearts to be in the right place as well, we allow the play to take away our judgment along with our breath." Such criticism, if true, must serve as last rites for anything that purports to be more than spectrally dramatic. Other things might have been said of the play in Washington; it ran for some three and a half hours and Clive Barnes, among others, found it a sprawling chronicle. But it was not a tract, nor do I think tract an accurate tag for Sackler's text. The play is filled with a kind of ticker tape immediacy and hence popular in the worst sense of the word, and what is popular in it—its race message—has been exploited with box office success in New York. But as played at length in Washington's Arena the action of the play was not didactic. Rather it was irreducibly dramatic. It did what Aristotle said a play should do, and what few playwrights know how to do—it imitated an action by means of an action. The play had, in short, an histrionic heart.

Both the Washington success and the New York failure say a great deal about the nature of theatre. But of the two the Washington achievement is the more notable, if only for its suggestion of an idea of theatre that renders the American experience in a viable dramatic form. The quest for such a theatre, as for the "great American novel," seems omnipresent; it is too much to say that Sackler has discovered it. But in *The Great White Hope* he has formed at least a partial mirror at the center of our culture, and at "the center of the life and awareness of the community." The phrase is Francis Fergusson's; he is describing what he calls the symbolic stage of the Elizabethans. As he notes such a mirror is rarely formed. More recently Peter Brook has joined in the conscious search, although he, like Fergusson, seems to feel that such a theatre is possible only in a more ceremonious age. The

artist in an age in which tradition has vanished, he remarks, "imitates the outer form of ceremonies, pagan or baroque, adding his own trappings. Unfortunately the result is rarely convincing." If Sackler has in his text managed in Brook's words to "capture in his art the invisible currents that rule our lives," then his achievement is worth examining in detail. It may tell us something about the nature of ritual and about the nature of that mirror a player holds up when he plays on a stage.

The plot is quite obviously the corruptible center of Sackler's play. As *Life* indicates, his story loosely follows the life and times of Jack Johnson, called by Sackler Jack Jefferson, who in 1908 by defeating an Australian, became the first Negro heavyweight champion of the world. The phrase "white hope" came to mean any possible white fighter who might beat Johnson and carry on his shoulders the hopes of the white race. The play begins with the first white hope, Frank Brady, ignominiously defeated in the third scene. It ends with the second white hope, the Kid, who defeats Jefferson in a fair fight that was meant to be fixed. Thus Sackler has taken as his hero not only, in the play's language, a dinge, but an initially successful dinge whose position as black champion wins him all of the culturally induced, cliche-ridden reactions, both black and white, to a black man's making it in a white man's world. At the beginning he is triumphant, at the end defeated. Therein lies the shape of the cautionary tale.

What keeps such a fable from being text for a sermon and makes of it instead an imitation of an action is in part its form, and it may well be that this particular form can not be made to work effectively on a traditional stage. Sackler presents his story by a series of scenes suggestive of Brecht, and the difficulties of a Broadway production can be seen even from the program. In Washington the three acts had respectively seven, eight, and five scenes, and a straight listing of place suggests the disembodied geographical sense of an airline official: Parchment, Ohio; San Francisco; Reno; Chicago; Beau Rivage, Wisconsin; then on to the Home Office in London, Le Havre, Paris, New York, Berlin, a cabaret in Budapest, a Belgrade railway station; then back once more to Chicago and on to New York and Juarez, Mexico, to end finally at the Oriente Racetrack in Havana where the hero loses his heavyweight championship to the all-American Kid. The word act, is, in fact, a misnomer. Theatrically the fabric of the play depends upon the uninterrupted sequence of these scenes that occur in rapid, almost kaleidoscopic succession to create the play's irrefutable surface of dramatic tension. Sackler's virtuosity can be seen in the way in which they vary greatly one from the other in texture, in pace, in composition; but they are also highly stylized, having about them in some respects the sharply edged lines of burlesque. It is yet another indictment of the New York version that Edith Oliver should have remarked of Jane Alexander as Jefferson's white mistress that "unlike most of the other characters . . . she has the advantage of being seen to alter radically," and that the rest of the huge cast consisted of stereotypes, as though she were criticizing the reality-making apparatus of the play.

I give one extended example of the play's composition from the middle of the first act: After Jefferson has beaten Brady, the first "white hope," and celebrated by opening a Café de Champion on Wabash Avenue in Chicago, there is a scene set in the District Attorney's office in which some of the establishment's reactions to Jefferson both as champion and as Negro acting champion are dramatically realized. The scene begins with a group of the morally militant demanding the hero's arrest for the flagrantly immoral act of sleeping with a white girl; it ends with the District Attorney himself diffidently leading this same white girl, Eleanor Bachman, into a frank avowal of amorous pleasure with Jefferson in the hope of trapping her into an admission of unnatural acts. The reflectors of the action in this instance include the so-called civic leaders, a distinguished looking "Uncle Tom," a Federal agent, the District Attorney and the white girl herself; what they reflect are the personal and social nuances of a black man sleeping with a white girl. The scene is followed by a bed somewhere with the two lovers, one black and one white, talking of swimming and making love. Ellie imagines lying in the sun until she has become very dark and then appearing with Jefferson as a different woman whom no one would notice. But with that comic book sense of caricature of himself Jefferson tells her it wouldn't work. "Evvybody know ah gone off cullud women," he tells her. "Ah has, too," he adds, "'cept for ma momma," and he sits up in bed, his black bare chest shining, and grins at her and then around at the audience with what a reporter earlier in the play has described as his big banjo smile. Jefferson is playing the music-hall Negro for his sweetheart, for the audience, and for himself and relishing every minute of it. The love-making ends abruptly as a group of "Keystone Cops" arrive to arrest the fighter

under the Mann Act for illicit relations. The scene, as any scene must, advances the plot. But more interestingly it reflects from yet a different angle the same underlying action as the previous scene. Neither the meeting in the district attorney's office nor the love-making is presented in realistic terms. Rather what is created by a seemingly haphazard cascade of vignettes is a highly structured pattern of dramatic action; it is this that keeps the play, at least in its shape, from being yet one more thinly masked polemic about race. It is possible, in fact, to say of the play's structure what Fergusson said of *Hamlet;* he was attempting to determine what it meant to imitate an action, and he observed that in *Hamlet* "the moral and metaphysical scene of the drama is presented only as one character after another sees it and reflects it; and the action of the drama as a whole is presented only as each character in turn actualizes it in his story and according to his lights."

Scenes, alone, of course, do not make a play, and Sackler's episodic structure which has offended some critics might be seen only as tiresomely derivative were it not for what I can only inadequately term his profound ludic sense. Joan Littlewood once remarked that theatre ought to be like a circus or a fair which takes over a town and everybody comes and dances in the street. *The Great White Hope* is that kind of theatre. To watch it as played out in the heart of the audience at Arena was to participate in a kind of communal celebration that must have been commonplace in Elizabethan England but is rare on our stage. For some critics such a celebration can only mean a condemnation of the play, for it is in its way a condemnation of the ways and means that as a community we celebrate. The performers are noisy and loud and unabashedly theatrical like the cheer leaders at a local football game. But therein lies the play's strength. It is the outward form of the "invisible currents that rule our lives" that Sackler has uncovered. He has discovered the emblematic nature of our rituals, such as they are, and his large cast celebrates them with an audience who participates in the performance. As they are public rites, not private, an audience is necessary. And so the audience becomes an integral part of the play.

The structural importance of obviously public ceremonies can be seen again from a list of scenes. On three different occasions newspaper reporters formally interview a famous boxer. The play's ceremonies include as well a formal police arrest, an organized protest march, a prayer meeting, a funeral and three fights. These fights, the play's essential ''act,'' are all seen from the wings where the onstage public's participation in the ceremony of the match is the mirror by means of which the match is shown. The last one ends with a flagwaving crowd spilling out onto the stage where the blare of trumpets and the chalk-faced victor on their shoulders create the ironic ambiance for the jubilant, ragged formation of their victory parade. There are lesser rituals as well—the blackfaced minstrel amusing a white crowd before the first fight; the black betting scenes before the last; the training sessions; a business meeting in a sports promoter's office— that invite by their style the word caricature. In a play that uses as vehicle public forms, neither slapstick nor melodrama are ever far from the surface, and the importance of this essential banality can be seen in the individual characters as well as in the public rites. It is not that the characters are stereotypes by default; rather they are stereotypes by design. It is as public performers in social pageants that they are important. The dramatic force of the play comes not from its realistic apprehension of psychological complexity but from the ways in which social cliches are used to reflect the complexity of that experience which they both structure and obscure. Both the cliches of character and the cliches of language by means of which American experience is known—both a kind of social posturing—become on stage ironic devices that reveal rather than conceal. And in this revelation, as in the celebration, the audience exists at the center of the play.

The use of verbal cliche as an ironic device can be seen most obviously in the kind of speech that Cap'n Dan makes in Pop Weaver's office when they are trying to convince one of their party, Fred, of the necessity of fixing the fight. He remarks:

> I don't have to make anybody no speech here
> about how good I feel working something crooked!
> None of us like it—*we wouldn't be the men we are
> if we did, or be where we are! I know it's lousy!*

The italicized portion is spoken directly to the audience, and brings a laugh, as it was meant to do. The audience understands the language and is quite aware of the moral duplicity. They sit as judge. But more often Sackler manages a collusion of audience and actors in that kind of social posturing against which the force of the play moves. Dixon, the federal agent, for instance, at the end of this scene addresses the audience directly, remarking that they seem to be indignant at what has just taken place, and he advises them, ''Give it some thought, next

time you're alone on the streets late at night.'' Scipio, the juju man, preaches at the few of his kind whom he claims to see ''out there''; ''How much white you wanna be?'' Clara, Jefferson's commonlaw black wife, sees them as the enemy. ''Who set him runnin,'' she asks, ''Who put de mark on him? Dem,'' she says, at Arena, looking up, ''dem, dem, dem.'' By means of such direct address Sackler makes of his playing space literally an arena in which the spectators are the true center of the play's contests. Like the spectators on stage who watch the fights, they are used as reflectors of the stage action. They both celebrate and, like the onstage performers, are judged. But the extent to which the play's profound ludic sense is inseparable from its use of social myth can best be seen in Sackler's handling of his hero. Jefferson, as the other characters in the play, defines himself by means of cultural cliches, but unlike the other characters he uses these cliches to show what he is not. In essence he stages his own rituals, and they are the basis more often than not of a kind of racial pun. When a reporter remarks that Jefferson's only worry seems to be when in the fight to take Brady, Jefferson replies,

> Yeah, an dat take some thinkin, man!
> If Ah lets it go too long in dere,
> juss sorta blockin an keepin him offa me,
> then evvybody say, ''Now ain't dat one shif'less
>   nigger,
> why dey always so lazy?'' An if Ah chop him down
>   quick,
> third or fourth roun, all at once then dey holler,
> ''No, t'aint fair,
> dat po 'man up dere fightin a gorilla.'

The same kind of idiom structures the sequence in which he changes places with one of the Detroit Bluejays in order to jump bail. Mrs. Jefferson worries that he will be caught, but with great deliberateness he first removes his jacket to reveal a raspberry-colored shirt and then he stands by the window where the police will be able to see him. When his stand-in begins to peel off his jacket and jersey, Jefferson says wryly,

> He look mighty fine, ole Rude here, don' he!
> Not pretty is me, but he near is big
> an just a half shade blacker an—
> Oh, mercy, he got dat shirt on too!

and as he puts on Rudy's cap and jacket he adds, ''You hear that sayin how all niggers look alike!'' When it suits his purpose he plays the white man's ''nigger'' and the black man's, but the key word is *plays*. ''But you, Jack Jefferson,'' one of the reporters says before the first fight, ''Are you the Black

Hope?'' ''Well,'' he replies laconically, ''Ah'm black and Ah'm hopin.'' It is the same thing that he says just before jumping bail. ''Ah stayin whut Ah am, wherever Ah has to do it'.''

What he *is* ultimately defines the dramatic nature of Sackler's play. In the most obvious sense he is an American pop hero. Plot drips off of him as it drips off of Raskolnikov, only the violence is American violence and it pours out like sweat from every pore. Like some roaring Western his story bounds from crisis to crisis with each more soul-crushing than the last. Apprehended while making love with his white girl, given the maximum penalty under the Mann Act, kept from fighting a decent match in England, in France, in Germany because he is a dinge, he is reduced to acting out Uncle Tom's Cabin with a vaudeville troupe in Budapest and betrayed finally in Juarez, Mexico, by the local gun-toting chief who hands him over to the American authorities. As his trainer Tick remarks, he turns mean as a red hyenna and as stinking, and before his arrest he lashes out at Ellie with all of the rage of injustice behind him. In a scene that drives her to suicide he identifies her, now ugly with slum squalor, with his own ''white'' misery. It is melodrama purely and simply, the melodrama of Jack Armstrong, of Little Orphan Annie, of Helen Trent. But if it sometimes veers toward bathos, still the center holds. It holds because our rituals, aided by Elizabethan scene technique, ironically reflect the complexity of the situation they attempt to structure. Jefferson in the simplest terms is a black man who is wronged. But in his own terms he is a man who is black and who is wronged and wrongs in turn. The fragmented social images of his situation are presented as scene follows scene: in one a white man in blackface amuses a white crowd by pretending to read a sermon over the hopefully defeated Jefferson; in another a piously sedate Negro preacher prays with the hero's mother; in a third the juju man preaches at the audience, ''So all you black flies, you light down together an hum pretty please to white man's Jesus.'' Cap'n Dan near the end of the play says of Jefferson: ''We're gonna squeeze that dinge so goddam hard soon a fix is gonna look like a hayride to him,'' damning the establishment. But his words echo the prayer of Jefferson's black commonlaw wife: ''Drag him on down. Oh won'tya, fo me an mah momma an evvy black-ass woman he turn his back on,'' she says, ''offa dat high horse an on down de whole long mud-track in fronna him . . . limpin an slippin an shrinkin an creepin an sinkin right in.'' The cliches of our culture appear on stage

as mimetic action and as mimetic action they reflect, to use Fergusson's language, ''from several angles and with extraordinary directness the moral and metaphysical scene of the play.''

It is this profound histrionic sensibility which makes *The Great White Hope,* even in its failures, an important play. It distinguishes it, in the first instance, from other recent plays which appear to use a similar technique. I am thinking particularly of the Peter Brook production of Peter Weiss' *Marat/ Sade* where again an almost bewildering variety of dramatic actions makes the play, in Brook's words, dense in experience. But the word dramatic here is accurate only in its attention-creating sense. Weiss's actions are dramatic, even melodramatic. The central action in which insane people act out a play has a Brueghelesque grotesqueness about it that can be both jangling and theatrically effective. Brook claims that Weiss forces us to ''relate opposites and face contradictions. He leaves us raw.'' Possibly. Certainly the play is well got-up by a playwright well-versed in the liberal dialogue and in contemporary theatre. As Brook points out Brecht, Beckett, Genet all play their part. Hence Roux can say at the end of Act I, ''Woe to the man who is different,'' and the Herald can announce to the audience that it is a play, ''not actual history,'' that ''our end which might seem prearranged/ could be delayed or even changed.'' But this theatrical self-consciousness is not basically histrionic, and the result is dialectic rather than mimetic. Weiss searches for meaning. He does not imitate an action. Sackler, too, draws heavily upon culture, but it is the popular culture that for better or worse is in our bones. His sources are those artifacts on which we were weaned: comic books, soap operas, Westerns, the Saturday afternoon baseball games, the cheer leaders, the American Legion, Ovaltine. By means of these Sackler has found a way to take the violence that lies at the center of our culture and make it theatrically viable on stage. Brook in his explicit search for ritual has most recently staged Seneca's *Oedipus* at the National Theatre in London. With an anonymous chorus beating gilded bongo boxes, a seven-foot phallus, and rock 'n roll revels he tries to artificially recreate that sense of ritual which he feels the theatre has lost. His production seems only to demonstrate what he himself says in *The Empty Space:* ritual cannot be artificially staged. But he is wrong in his belief that true rituals are no longer at our disposal. Rather, as Sackler seems to show, ritual as a pattern of feeling continues to structure our society and, once perceived, can still provide an authentic means of dramatic action. As Fergusson suggests, it underlies the verbal. As a pattern of feeling ritual remains the primary source of theatre as a mimetic art.

The extent of the New York betrayal is most apparent in the last scene. Down and out as any depression bum, squeezed to his last self-assertive act under the threat of extradition and with the still dripping corpse of his drowned sweetheart stretched out on the table before him, Jefferson has agreed at last to the fixed match with the Kid, only to refuse to throw it once he is in the ring. In the last scene we see him re-enter to face the press, a blood-smeared hero, his mouth swollen to balloon proportions. They want to know why he was beaten, and in a mumbled roar he answers, "He beat me, dassall. Ah juss din have it." It is the voice of Jack Jefferson, prize fighter, beaten at last on his own terms when his own terms are no longer enough. It is the voice as well of the first white hope and of Cap'n Dan and of the fight fans who just before have reported on the fight's progress by a series of sportcaster-like commentaries from a ladder where one of them can see the fight off stage. "Christ, the nigger's all over him, pile-driven, whalin at him" is followed by "The coon's given ground," "Smell him out Kid," and finally, "The nigger can't do it, he's hitten but he's outa juice! He's punched out." He is, of course, punched out. That's what Jefferson himself says. And what saves him dramatically is that he says it not with that corrupting twang of self pity that Jones in New York has allowed into the play but with that histrionic sense of complexity that keeps him from seeing himself as the Black Hope. There is no literalness to this play and there is no "message." Rather Sackler exploits all of the verbal and visual nuances the subject of black and white in America has to offer to hammer out its identity. Like his hero he refuses to simplify, and he makes that refusal dramatically feasible. In so doing he seems to have found again at least fragments of that mirror with which Hamlet's players showed the very age and body of the time its form and pressure. Therein lies the great hope of this play.

Source: Marion Trousdale, "Ritual Theatre: *The Great White Hope*," in *Western Humanities Review,* Vol 23, No. 14, Autumn 1969, pp. 295–303.

Richard Gilman

In the following review excerpt, Gilman praises The Great White Hope *for, among other things, its energy and message, but feels that in the end the work lacks "final authority."*

Howard Sackler's *The Great White Hope* is so pertinently addressed to our present concerns, makes such intelligent use of so many stage resources, possesses such fine energy in places and offers so many superior moments that I wish I could embrace it wholeheartedly and not feel, as I do, that something central hasn't been accomplished, something remains below the mark. The mark I have in mind is that line which nobody can or would want to fix with precision but that is there anyway, separating the plausible and welcome from the conclusive and inimitable. This play about the first Negro heavyweight champion, Jack Johnson, is distinguished, in other words, by everything except final authority, unassailable rightness.

Sackler has taken a history and a legend and animated one while revising the other. I remember the legend from the time in my boyhood when I became interested in boxing: Johnson was a great fighter but a dissolute character who ostentatiously surrounded himself with white women, lived high, fell abjectly and imposed on the black race a profligate image it took Joe Louis' clean, "inspiring" one 20 years later to cancel. A famous photograph stands out: Johnson in a huge polo coat, fedora tipped back, big cigar jutting out, his arms around two blond showgirl types, his black moon face glistening. I think it was taken on shipboard, which contributed to my thinking of Johnson as the oddest kind of man of the world. Jack Johnson did indeed like to live well, and may have overcome it in the kind of excessiveness sudden wealth can bring about, but the decisive truth—and it's the informing one of Sackler's play—was that he was significant, in his day and in our imaginations now, as a victim, a man whose reality was almost wholly shaped by external pressures. His flamboyance was at least partly a slap at the whites who bitterly resented his being champion, his wanderings were the outcome of his having been blacklisted in America, his predilection for white women must have had a large element of defiance in it. He stood at a point in our national experience when a black man was a dramatic and not a typical figure if he defied mores and broke stereotypes.

The play begins with Johnson (or Jack Jefferson, as he's for some reason renamed; why not stay with the evocative archives?) challenging for the heavyweight title in 1908 (he is to win it later that year) and ends with his defeat in Havana by Jess Willard in 1915. During those seven years he is relentlessly ground down, squeezed into the tightest physical and moral corners. The fact that a black

Joseph Marcell, as Tick, and Hugh Quarshie, as Jack Jefferson, in the 1987 theatrical production of The Great White Hope, *performed at the Mermaid Theatre in London*

man has won the championship inspires an almost mystical horror in whites. ''It feels like the world's got a shadow across it,'' an ex-champion who is instrumental in the machinations against Johnson says: ''Everything's—no joke intended—kind of darker, and different, like it's shrinking, it's all huddled down somehow, and you with it, you want to holler 'What's he doin' up there'. . . ''

He has made a public liaison with a white girl, and this is the first ground on which he is cut down. Arrested on a trumped-up charge of violating the Mann Act, Johnson is sentenced to three years in prison, but slips out, flees with the girl to Canada, then England. There bigots and prudes prevent him from fighting; he goes to France, then Germany, Hungary, Yugoslavia, finding it harder and harder to get matches, being reduced to exhibitions, then to nightclub appearances, turning more and more resentful, violent and determined to hold out.

Going to Mexico, he trains in a barn in Juarez for the fight he insists they have to give him. But ''they'' are implacable; what they offer him is a fight on one condition—that he throw it. For their search for a ''white hope'' has turned up nobody they can feel confident about against Johnson, even

in his present slack shape. At last, nearly penniless, harassed from every side, his girl a suicide after a violent quarrel with him, Johnson agrees to the fix. The fight with Willard ends with the white hope's ambiguous victory; the question remains whether or not Johnson actually threw the fight, though the play implies that at the last moment he refused and went down to a bloody defeat by a man he could in even reasonable shape have easily beaten.

In taking hold of these events Sackler moves throughout to establish a two-fold dramatic actuality: that of Johnson's own beleaguered, far from simple being and that of American racial consciousness and bad dream, for which he is both instigator and innocent occasion. The material calls unmistakably for some sort of ''epic'' treatment, but Sackler's choices aren't fully assured or in coherence with each other. Wavering among Brecht, topical revue and a sort of historical pageantry for his main structural lines, he has also to try to make space and atmosphere for his protagonist's private experiences. The failure quite to bring this off is responsible, I think, for the curious intermittent sagging of our interest, a curious thing because so much of the time we're being vigorously and adroitly solicited

SACKLER HAS TAKEN A HISTORY AND A LEGEND AND ANIMATED ONE WHILE REVISING THE OTHER."

and because the raw stuff of the drama is so high in natural energy.

Separating the play's three acts and twenty-odd scenes by blackouts, bridging them aurally with musical passages that are sometimes enormously effective—ominous drums and cymbals, violent brasses—and trying always to maintain a nervous, quick-footed, *contemporary* pace, the direction by Edward Sherin nevertheless frequently has an effect of occlusion: too much is being done to too much material, a superfluity of possibility from time to time stops us in our enthusiasm. One example of what I mean is this: a gnarled, Tiresias-like Negro appears sporadically to deliver prophetic, and anachronistic and barely relevant, tirades against black involvement with American values: "How much white you up to? How white you wanna be?" Another is this: the funeral of Johnson's mother, a minor matter at best, becomes a full-scale independent production, full of "colorful" black rhythms and gestures; it seemed to me to be there for the sake of that picturesqueness and also for the purpose of getting-it-all-in. Finally, having the characters periodically address the audience (in which Sherin simply follows the text's direction) is a Brechtian device that lacks Brecht's intellectual and aesthetic reasons for using it.

Beyond this, there is the problem of Sackler's language. A case could be made for its doing the job, for its adequacy and general appropriateness. Yet if this is true, and I think it is, if Sackler seldom over-writes (a line like this is rare: "Time again to make us a big new wise proud dark man's world") it remains true, too, that he's done very little more than the job; he hasn't lifted this splendid material into any kind of irrefutable new statement. The point has nothing to do with a failure to be sufficiently "literary" but simply with Sacklers inhibitions (as I see them) in the face of history, which seems to demand restraint, a colloquialism designed to protect its "human" quality by adhering to the

cliches and inadequacies of actual speech. But history is only ransomed by speech other than its own, by amazing utterance, and Sackler's gifts are clearly not for that.

. . . Any number of moments stay in memory: Johnson thigh-slappingly answering the questions of newsmen about his popularity among blacks:

"Man, ah ain't runnin' for Congress! Ah ain't fightin' for no race, ain't redeemin' nobody! My momma tole me Mr. Lincoln done that—ain't that why you shot him?"

The champion reduced to playing Uncle Tom in a Hungarian nightclub, standing in mysterious silence and slowly taking off his grey frizzly wig while the audience covers him with execrations. Johnson mourning his dead lover: "Honey, baby, please, sugar, no!—whut Ah—whut Ah—whut Ah—baby, what Ah done to yo, whut you done, honey, honey, whut dey done to us. . ." The end of the Willard fight and of the play, Johnson standing with a towel swathing his puffed and bloody face and saying, "Come on Chillun, let em pass by" as the winner, even more terribly marked, is carried on men's shoulders in a triumphal procession so painful, ironic and ill-begotten as to constitute the emblem of a disaster. . .

Moved directly by Johnson-Jefferson who is really *there*, really suffering and being shamefully whittled down, we lose sight of history—the present in preparation—which remains, for all the epic dramaturgy, outside the play's hold on the inevitable, so that we have constantly to be reminded of it by hints and references to the present day—unsafe streets, black power, and so on.

What this means is that for Johnson to have been what he was, to have had happen to him what did, and for us to be what we are now are never reconciled or merged dramatically, which is what I meant at the beginning of this review by the play's ultimate lack of impregnable authority. And this accounts, I think, for the reaction, which has made itself apparent, to *The Great White Hope* as a splendid liberal occasion, an opportunity for self-congratulation on the part of whites, a species of theatrical *Nat Turner* in which we look back and see how we done them wrong. The play is more than that, but it does contain the materials for its own misreading.

Source: Richard Gilman, "Not Quite Heavyweight," in *New Republic,* Vol. 159, No. 17, October 26, 1968, pp. 36–39.

SOURCES

Axelrod, Alan, *The Complete Idiot's Guide to Twentieth Century History,* Alpha Books, 1999, pp. 377–94.

Contemporary Dramatists, 5th ed., St. James Press, 1993.

Crinkley, Richmond, in *National Review,* December 17, 1968, pp. 1282–83.

Hungerford, Robert W., "Howard Sackler," in *Dictionary of Literary Biography,* Vol. 7: *Twentieth-Century American Dramatists,* Gale Research, 1981.

Kerr, Walter, in *New York Times,* October 13, 1968.

Sackler, Howard, *The Great White Hope,* Dial, 1968.

Simon, John, *Hudson Review,* Winter 1968–1969, pp. 707–10.

Trousdale, Marion, "Ritual Theatre: *The Great White Hope,*" in *Western Humanities Review,* Autumn 1969, pp. 295–303.

Wetzsteon, Ross, "Review of *The Great White Hope,*" in *Village Voice,* October 10, 1968, pp. 45–46.

FURTHER READING

Funke, Lewis, *Playwrights Talk about Writing: 12 Interviews with Lewis Funke,* Dramatic Publishing, 1975.
  This collection contains an interview with Howard Sackler and other notable authors.

Gottfried, Martin, "Introduction," in *A Few Inquiries,* Dial, 1970.
  This prefaces *A Few Inquiries* and provides, through critical analysis, additional insight into the collection of plays.

Sackler, Howard, *A Few Inquiries,* Dial, 1970.
  This is a collection of one-act plays by Sackler, including "Sarah," "The Nine O'Clock Mail," "Mr. Welk and Jersey Jim," and "Skippy."

Trousdale, Marion, "Ritual Theatre: *The Great White Hope,*" in *Western Humanities Review,* Autumn 1969, pp. 295–303.
  This book is a thorough exploration into and examination of the structure and integrity of Sackler's work.

Idiot's Delight

ROBERT E. SHERWOOD

1936

Robert E. Sherwood's *Idiot's Delight* takes place at a resort in the Italian Alps at an undetermined time, soon before the start of World War II. In the play, passengers on a train bound for Switzerland are prevented from leaving the country because war is going to break out. Tensions are high, as nobody, including the local authorities, knows which country or countries will attack which. The interesting characters who are detained at the hotel include a German doctor who is close to finding a cure for cancer; a British couple on their honeymoon; a French Communist who is returning from an international labor conference; a mysterious Russian countess and her companion, an arms merchant who has inside knowledge about when the fighting will begin; and a company of American showgirls, led by a manager who is a seasoned show business professional and confidence man.

The situation described in the play is fictional—Sherwood describes World War II starting with Italian planes bombing Paris, though in fact the war did not begin until three years after the play was produced, with Germany's invasion of Poland. Still, the situation that he concocted for this play puts audiences right into the difficult situation in Europe in the thirties, when war really was expected at any moment. The play also includes performances of singing and dancing and a plot line about long-lost lovers reuniting at the final moments of their lives. Sherwood won his first Pulitzer Prize for drama for *Idiot's Delight* in 1936.

AUTHOR BIOGRAPHY

Robert Emmet Sherwood was born in New Rochelle, New York, in 1896. His writing career began early, when at age seven he edited a magazine called *Children's Life*. His mother was an artist and illustrator, and she encouraged his writing throughout his whole life.

After graduating from Milton Academy in Massachusetts in 1914, Sherwood entered Harvard, where he became editor of the internationally famous humor magazine *Harvard Lampoon*. His college career was cut short when he went to fight in World War I with the Canadian Black Watch. His service in the war was to have a lasting effect on Sherwood's writing: most of his plays, like *Idiot's Delight*, reflect a sense of the horrors of warfare and its devastating effects on community.

Returning from Europe in 1919, Sherwood secured a job as drama critic for *Vanity Fair* magazine. There, he became associated with some of the greatest humorists of his time, who met regularly for lunch at the Algonquin Hotel in New York City. The famed Algonquin Round Table group included, along with Sherwood, Dorothy Parker, Robert Benchley, George S. Kaufman, and Heywood Broun. In 1924, he became editor-in-chief of *Life*.

Sherwood's career as a playwright was successful from the start. His first play, *The Road to Ruin*, about Hannibal crossing the Alps to attack Rome, received both critical and popular support, allowing Sherwood to give up his magazine work and concentrate entirely on writing for the stage. Other important plays from his early period include *Waterloo Bridge* (1929), *Reunion in Vienna* (1931), and *The Petrified Forest* (1935). The film version of the last, starring Bette Davis, Leslie Howard, and Humphrey Bogart, is considered a classic of American cinema.

Idiot's Delight opened on Broadway at the Shubert Theater in 1936 and ran for three hundred performances. It received the Pulitzer Prize for drama that year. Sherwood's next play, *Abe Lincoln in Illinois*, also won the Pulitzer, in 1939. He was to win a third Pulitzer for drama, in 1941, for *There Shall Be No Night*.

In 1940, Sherwood reversed his earlier opposition to war and joined a group that supported America's entry into World War II, which was already going on in Europe. As a member of the Committee to Aid America by Defending the Allies, he spent $42,000 of his own money to take out

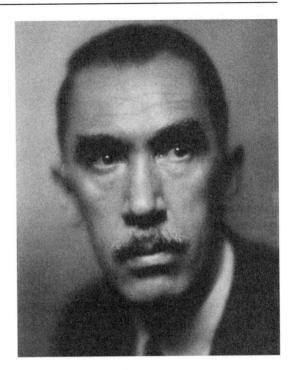

Robert Sherwood

newspaper ads calling on America to 'Stop Hitler Now!' His political action was noticed, and he was hired as a speechwriter for President Franklin D. Roosevelt. During the war, from 1941 to 1944, he ran the overseas branch of the Office of War Information, with a staff of eighteen people under him and a budget of $20 to $30 million dollars. After the war he received a fourth Pulitzer for his 1948 biography *Roosevelt and Hopkins*, about the president and his closest advisor. He wrote two more plays, but the postwar world showed little interest in his dramatic themes, and they closed quickly. Sherwood died in 1955 of cardiac arrest.

PLOT SUMMARY

Act 1

Idiot's Delight takes place at the cocktail lounge of the fictional Hotel Monte Gabriele in the Italian Alps near the borders of Austria, Switzerland, and Bavaria. Next to the hotel is an airfield for Italian bomber planes. It is set in a time before the beginning of World War II when the inevitability of the coming war was on everyone's mind. Act 1 begins with Donald Navadel, an American expert who has been hired by the hotel to attract tourists to Monte Gabriele for winter sports, entering the lounge. He notices that there are no guests and tells the orchestra to take a break. Pittaluga, the hotel manager, enters, angry that Don has overstepped his authority. Captain Locicero, the commander of the Italian headquarters, comes in and explains that the air field at Monte Gabriele will be important when war begins, although he does not know specifically who the enemy will be.

The train that is supposed to pass through on its way to Geneva is detained at Monte Gabriele because the border has been closed. Disgruntled passengers filter into and out of the lounge, in their attempts to book rooms: Dr. Waldersee, Mr. and Mrs. Cherry, and a troupe of showgirls, led by their manager, Harry Van. The doctor is German, but he needs to get to Austria to continue his experiments, which he is sure will yield a cure for cancer. The Cherrys, a British couple, were married days before in Florence. Quillery enters and sits down at the bar to have a drink with Harry. He explains that though he was born in France, he does not think of himself as having any nationality at all, identifying himself as a laborer. Quillery tells Harry that he is a pacifist, that peace will prevail. Harry responds that he once had an insight, while on cocaine, that everyone is addicted to something: ''false beliefs—false fears—false enthusiasms.''

Quillery races out when he hears some Italian soldiers in the bar say that the war has begun. Dumptsy, the bellhop, strikes up a discussion with Harry, explaining the local political situation: Monte Gabriele was part of Austria up to the end of World War I. With the Treaty of Versailles in 1919, the mountain was transferred to Italy and renamed. Citizens had to learn the new language, and gravestones were erased and rewritten in Italian.

Irene enters, followed soon by her companion, Achille Weber. They assure the people there that there will be no war. Harry is fascinated with her and, when she leaves, starts playing the Russian folk tune ''Kak Stranna,'' unaware that he associates it with Irene. They see bomber planes leaving from the air field, and there are rumors of war between Italy and France, but nothing is confirmed.

Act 2

Scene 1 takes place that evening. The hotel staff says that they can get no news of any war on the radio. Quillery enters and says that Weber, who is a major arms dealer, will know if there is going to be a war or not. He and Dr. Waldersee argue about the way that the Nazi party runs Germany; then he argues with Cherry because the English are too comfortable and wealthy to fight.

Harry enters after Quillery and the Cherrys leave and expresses interest in Irene. He also suggests that his girls can put on their show at the lounge that night to help ease the mounting tension.

Irene and Weber enter, and secretly he tells her that the planes that left the airfield were off to bomb Paris. When he leaves, she tells the Cherrys a story about being a countess, part of the Romanoff family, and being chased out of Russia by Bolsheviks, only to be saved by English soldiers. At the end of the scene, she admits to Mrs. Cherry that she has seen Harry Van perform before.

In scene 2, Captain Locicero reports that he cannot get any news on the radio about whether or not there is a war. He leaves when some of the bomber planes return to the airfield, and Weber and Irene speak frankly with one another, professing their disdain for the people who will be killed in the war. Weber senses that Irene is going soft, becoming a little too sarcastic about the wholesale slaughter of people. Harry Van's troupe gives a show, which is interrupted when Quillery comes in and announces that Paris has been bombed. Harry tries to calm him, but Quillery becomes enraged with a patriotic fury, shouting at the Italians in the bar, telling them that France, England, and America will stand up together against them, although Mr. Cherry and Harry, representing the latter two, apologize for his outburst. The scene ends with Quillery, who previously said that he was a citizen of no country, being dragged away shouting, ''Vive la France!'' (Long live France!).

Scene 3 takes place later that night. Irene tells Harry another one of her made-up stories about how she escaped from Russia during the revolution. As she goes on to describe what a well-respected man Weber is, he stares at her, trying to place her. The subject turns to her career, and, mentioning that he once worked a mind-reading act, Harry remembers a young redheaded Russian girl named Irene with whom he'd had a one-night stand in Omaha, Nebraska. It dawns on him that this Irene is that girl, although she denies it.

Act 3

The following afternoon, Captain Locicero announces that he has received permission from the government to let most of the people from the train leave and cross the border. Harry announces to his girls that the act will be better when they get to Geneva if he does not sing or dance. Don comes in and announces that he is leaving the hotel, too— going back to California—in part because he was in town earlier in the day when Quillery was executed before a firing squad. Mrs. Cherry reflects on how her husband will probably join the war and might end up bombing Venice, where they were married days earlier. When the captain tells the Cherrys that their passports have been released by a technicality— that the approval for them to leave came just seventeen minutes before Britain declared war on France— Mrs. Cherry repeats Quillery's damnation of the Italians, while her husband tries to quiet her. Dr. Waldersee says that he is giving up his cancer research and returning to Germany, even though it will probably mean that he will be put to work making chemical weapons.

Irene's passport is not approved, but the captain is willing to let her go because she is with Weber. Weber says that he will not be responsible for her, leaving Captain Locicero no choice but to detain her. Harry stays with her until the last minute, with his girls and Don calling him to the train. As he leaves, she tells him that it actually was she who spent a night with him in the hotel in Omaha, and to prove it she tells him that the room they were in was room 974. A few minutes after the train leaves, Harry comes back and tells her that he will leave with her the next day, that he will take her on as a partner and teach her the secret of the mind-reading act that he had promised to teach her in Omaha. As French bombs start dropping on and around the air field, in retaliation for the previous day's raid, Harry is at the piano playing Wagner's "Ride of the Valkyries," but Irene asks if he knows any hymns. The play ends with bombs exploding and both of them singing "Onward, Christian Soldiers."

CHARACTERS

Auguste

Auguste is an employee of the Hotel Monte Gabriel.

Mr. Jimmy Cherry

A painter who has been in Australia painting a mural for the government, Cherry was married just a few days earlier in Venice. He is an Englishman, and when war is declared, he is enthusiastic to fight,

MEDIA ADAPTATIONS

- *Idiot's Delight* was adapted as a film in 1939, starring Clark Gable, Norma Shearer, and Burgess Meredith. Robert E. Sherwood adapted the screenplay from his own drama. Directed by Clarence Brown, released by MGM, the 1991 video is available from MGM/UA Home Video.

- In 1983, legendary lyricist Alan Jay Learner did a musical adaptation of the play called *Dance a Little Closer*. Charles Strouse did the music. This version closed after one performance. A 1987 compact disc of the music by the original Broadway cast is available from Topaz Entertainment Inc. and Theaterland Productions.

but he also goes out of his way to be cordial to the German doctor and Italian commander who will soon be his enemies.

Mrs. Cherry

Recently married to an artist, Mrs. Cherry works at a store named Fortnum's, as she says, "wearing a smock, and disgracing my family." After hearing the news that Quillery has been executed for speaking out against the Italians, she becomes angry enough to face the same kind of punishment: "Don't call *me* your friend," she tells Captain Locicero, "because I say what Quillery said—damn you—damn your whole country of mad dogs for having started this horror." Her husband calms her and gets her to apologize before they leave.

Edna Creesh

Edna is one of the girls in Harry Van's troupe.

Dumptsy

The forty-ish bellboy of the resort, Dumptsy has lived in that area since it was a province of Austria. It was ceded to the Italians at the end of the First World War, and overnight Dumptsy and his family became Italian citizens. Explaining this to

Harry, he laughs and says, "But it doesn't make much difference who your masters are. When you get used to them, they are all the same." In the last scene, he appears in an Italian army uniform, having been drafted into service.

Bebe Gould

Bebe is one of the girls in Harry Van's troupe.

Irene

She pronounces her name "Ear-ray-na," which is one reason that Harry Van does not recognize her as the girl he once knew named Irene. She presents herself as a member of the Russian royal family, the Romanoffs, who were exiled from the country when the Communists took over in 1917. Her story about escaping from Russia changes, depending on whom she is talking to. Sometimes she says that she rode a sled across the ice, pursued by Bolshevik attackers; at another time she is on a raft at sea, rescued by English soldiers. In the end she confesses to Harry that she is not a Romanoff but that her real origin is still left a mystery. Irene likes to give the impression that she is an important personage, as evinced by the way she drops the name of the Maharajah of Rajpipla when she first arrives, referring to him with the familiar name "Pip."

Irene is traveling with Achille Weber. They are not married, and the implication is that she is his mistress. When they are alone, she is quite ruthless and graphic about imaging the carnage that the war will bring. Her description is so gruesome that it tips Weber off to the idea that the young British honeymooners might have "touched a tender spot."

Since she has traveled around the world throughout her life, Irene has no definite nationality, only a passport issued by the League of Nations. After Italy declares war, it no longer recognizes the League of Nations. Captain Locicero is willing to let Irene leave the country without a valid passport, as a companion of Achille Weber, but he refuses to take responsibility for her.

Harry Van says that he recognizes Irene as a member of a traveling Russian troupe who played at a theater in Omaha with him in 1925: he was working in a mind-reading act and the Russian girl came to his room to learn how his act worked and they spent the night together. At first, Irene denies any knowledge of it, but when she has been abandoned by Weber and Harry is leaving, she tells him that she remembers the exact room number they were in that night. He returns to her and says that he will teach her the secret of the mind-reading act and that together they can tour with his dancing girls. She chooses the exotic name "Namora" as her stage name, but the French start bombing Mount Gabriele just as the play ends.

Shirley Laughlin

Something of a lieutenant to Harry Van, Shirley is the member of "Les Blondes" that Harry speaks to most often. She is the one who oversteps Harry's authority to show Beulah how to do the "Maxie Ford" dance step. When Harry decides to stop performing with the troupe, he gives Shirley his singing part, which, along with her natural assertiveness, implies that she will be their leader when he leaves them.

Captain Locicero

As commander of the Italian headquarters, the captain's must detain all of the passengers from the train before they can leave the country, as war is being declared. He is civil and courteous to all, even though they are citizens of countries that have become Italy's enemies. When Weber leaves Irene to face death, the captain detains her, as is his duty, apologizing to her, but he does not blame Weber, showing himself to be concerned and responsible.

Francine Merle

Francine is one of the girls in Harry Van's troupe.

Elaine Messiger

Elaine is one of the girls in Harry Van's troupe.

Donald Navadel

Donald is the hotel's social director. An American, he was hired away from another resort in the hope that he would attract other Americans to come there. He is discontented because no guests come to the resort, but he is unwilling to leave before his contract is up in March. After the war starts, he does decide to leave Italy and return to California after seeing Quillery shot.

Orchestra Leader

When the play opens, the orchestra is playing to an empty room, and Donald Navadel gives the orchestra leader permission to stop playing.

Pittaluga

The proprietor of the Hotel Monte Gabriele, Pittaluga feels that Don Navadel is too presumptuous in giving orders around the hotel and invites Navadel to break his contract and quit.

Quillery

A labor organizer from France who is returning from an international Labor Congress in Zagreb, Yugoslavia, when the train is stopped at Monte Gabriele. He does not acknowledge any nationality. ''Perhaps if I had raised pigs,'' he explains, referring to his family's business, ''I should have been a Frenchman, as they were. But I went to work in a factory—and machinery is international.'' Later, however, after receiving word that Paris has been bombed, Quillery becomes enraged at the Italians in the hotel, shouting at them, ''Down with Fascism!'' He identifies himself as a French citizen. When he is executed, he dies like a patriot, shouting, ''Long live France!''

Signor Rossi

Signor Rossi is only mentioned twice and only speaks in Italian. He is a consumptive. Before medical advances, people used to go to resorts like Monte Gabriele to treat consumption, which is known today as tuberculosis. The resort was once a sanatorium for treating consumptives, but, as Dumptsy explains, ''the Fascists—they don't like to admit that anyone can get sick.''

Signora Rossi

Signora Rossi walks through with Signor Rossi, speaking with him in Italian.

Beulah Tremoyne

Beulah is one of the girls in Harry Van's troupe, ''Les Blondes.''

Harry Van

After an inconspicuous entrance, Harry turns out to be the play's main character. He is the manager of a troupe of singing and dancing girls and is responsible for their physical and moral well-being. Harry has a long history in show business. At one time, he sold a patent medicine remedy that was supposed to cure cancer, among other things. He was a ''stooge'' in a vaudeville act with ''Zuleika, the Mind Reader,'' in the Midwest. He has played piano accompaniment to silent movies. He has been a drug addict, taking cocaine ''during a stage in my career when luck was bad and confusion prevailed.'' And he has toured Europe with his girls.

Harry is an outgoing person, willing to agree with any perspective. As he sits at the piano in the lounge, different characters come by and talk with him, telling him their stories. He is intelligent, which he explains as being a result of having been an encyclopedia salesman in college: he ended up buying a set of encyclopedias and reading them while on the road. Another reason he gets along with people so well is that he likes just about everyone. As he explains, ''All my life . . . I've been selling phony goods to people of meager intelligence and great faith. You'd think that would make me contemptuous of the human race, wouldn't you? But—on the contrary—it has given *me* faith.''

He is interested in Irene from the moment that she comes in, but it is not until he is in the middle of a conversation that he recognizes her as a red-headed girl from another act in vaudeville. He lured her up to his room one night, at the Governor Bryan Hotel in Omaha in the fall of 1925, promising to teach her how the mind-reading trick worked, and they slept together, but they went separate ways soon after. Irene denies having known him.

When Irene is abandoned to stay in Monte Gabriele, Harry is hesitant to leave her, but at the last minute she admits that it was she in Omaha. He leaves but then returns after the train has left, touched that their night together so long ago meant so much that she remembered the room number. When bombs start dropping on the Hotel Monte Gabriele, Harry keeps playing the piano and drinking champagne, being brave in the face of death.

Dr. Waldersee

Dr. Waldersee is very anxious to get out of Monte Gabriele and get to Zurich, Switzerland. He is German, but he is working on a cure for cancer, completing the work of a Dane named Fibiger. If he stays in Germany during the war, he knows that he will be forced to work on chemicals for warfare, to kill instead of cure people. When the war starts, though, the doctor becomes so disillusioned with mankind that he decides to return to Germany and be just as much of a bloodthirsty maniac as everyone else.

Achille Weber

Weber is the only truly sinister person in the play. He is an arms dealer, and Sherwood strongly implies that it is men like him, not the politicians or the citizens of the nations involved, who are responsible for war. In public, he hardly speaks, but in private he tells Irene that the planes from Monte Gabriele are headed for Paris, which is news that not even the local authorities know. When she suggests that his sister might be in Paris, he snaps that they are in Montbeliard, indicating that he has known about this raid long enough to check on the safety of his family members.

Alone, Irene congratulates Weber on "all of this wonderful death and destruction." He neither accepts her praise nor is horrified by it but responds in an even more frightening way: he takes her emotionalism to be a sign that she has "turned commonplace." Before the bombing, the Italian authorities say that they cannot allow Irene to leave alone but that, out of respect for Weber, they will let him take her with him, and he refuses, leaving her to die.

THEMES

Love

Although the situation of *Idiot's Delight* revolves around the political situation in Europe, the play is ultimately a love story, with two lovers who spent a night together ten years earlier realizing that they are still in love. The years have changed both Harry and Irene, to such an extent that they do not recognize each other immediately. From their very first meeting, Harry does not know who Irene is, confused by her changed hair color and her strongly Russian pronunciation of her name; still, he is fascinated with her and shows excessive interest in her relationship with Weber. It is not until act 2, scene 3, that they have some time alone together, and Harry explains that she reminds him of the redheaded girl he knew in Omaha. "I was crazy about her," he tells Irene. "She was womanhood at its most desirable—and most unreliable." Even when he is certain that "Eye-ray-na" is the "Irene" that he once knew, she does not acknowledge having met him before. The audience knows that she is lying, that she earlier told Mr. Cherry that she had seen him perform before.

The casual approach that these two lovers have toward one another melts away in the face of death. When Irene is left at the hotel, probably to die in an air raid, she tells Harry that she remembers him from Omaha and gives the number of the room they stayed in. The fact that she remembers such an irrelevant detail after so many years is an indication

of how much their affair meant to her. Harry gives up his life to be with her, facing the expected bombing raid because she did remember. He does nothing to deny it when Irene says, "All these years—you've been surrounded by blondes—and you've loved only me!" In the end, Irene, who had denied knowing him, tells Harry that she has loved him ever since that night they spent together. Together, in love, they face death.

Fatalism

The characters in this play all know that war is coming and that it will affect their lives. At first, they each come onto the stage expressing their urgent need to get out of the war zone before the fighting begins. When it has been confirmed that bombs have been dropped on Paris, though, they all realize that their lives are going to be subject to circumstances beyond their control.

The mildest case is Donald Navadel. Early in the play, he expresses his wish to stay at the Hotel Monte Gabriele through the end of his contract, but he also had good reason for wanting to leave. In the end, after he has seen Quillery executed, he knows that Italy will not be a decent place to live any more, and so he knows he must leave.

Dumptsy accepts the unpleasant fact that he must fight for the Italian army, even though he does not think of himself as an Italian. By the same token, Mr. Cherry and his wife know that he must fight for England, even if it means dropping bombs on the beautiful country where they chose to celebrate their wedding just days earlier.

When Irene is left behind by Weber, she does not complain, accepting it as just the kind of fate that befalls a woman like her. Harry accepts that Irene is his fate, and he returns to the hotel, even though the odds are good that he will die there, in order to be by her side.

The most extremely fatalistic character is Dr. Waldersee. Early in the play he is full of hope, determined that political events cannot be allowed to stop him in his search for a cancer cure. After the bombs start falling, though, and he sees the pacifist Quillery turn into a raging nationalist, the doctor realizes that his efforts to cure people are futile in a world bound to destroy itself with war. "Why should I save people who don't want to be saved," he asks, "—so they can go out and exterminate each other? Obscene maniacs!" With such a fatalistic view of humanity, he returns to Germany to work on developing chemical weapons.

TOPICS FOR FURTHER STUDY

- Write a short play that shows what happened to some of the characters from this play: the Cherrys, for example, or Dr. Waldersee or Don Navadel or Harry and Irene, if they survive the bombing.

- Examine what has become of the countries of this region since World War II. Which have been broken up? Which areas have become part of different nations?

- Dr. Waldersee abandons his cancer research to return to Germany during the war. Research what sort of projects a biochemist may have been put to work on during Hitler's Nazi regime.

- Harry Van promises to show Irene how to do the mind-reading trick that he once did with Zuleika. Find some information about how such vaudeville acts were accomplished and try to perform this trick with your class.

- Signor and Signora Rossi are barely mentioned in this play, but Sherwood must have had some reason for including them. Find some descriptions of tuberculosis sanatoriums in the early twentieth century and explain why you think he wanted to include this aspect in the play.

- Sherwood dedicated this play to Alfred Lunt and Joan Fontaine, who played the key parts in the Broadway production. Research their careers and explain how the information about the actors has changed your perception of the play.

- In this play, everyone knows that there is going to be a war soon, but there is no real reason for the coming war except that the munitions manufacturers want it. Explain when, if ever, you think it is right for a country to go to war.

War

This play presents a rare case in which war is actually used as a theme more than as a plot point. Although every action in the play revolves around the coming war, there is really little involvement in the war until the very end. The guests are stranded at the hotel because of the rumor that war is coming, and as they talk in the first half of the play, the idea of war is very abstract and theoretical. When, in the middle scene of the middle act, confirmation comes that the war has begun, the personalities of all those gathered begin to change. The Cherrys, for example, who came to Monte Gabriele oblivious to anything but their love for each other, realize that they will soon be separated under life-or-death circumstances, and they both become short-tempered. The doctor changes from thoughts of life to thoughts of killing. Quillery quits identifying himself as a worker and instead sees himself as a Frenchman. Weber carefully scrutinizes his companion, Irene, for any weakness or sensitivity about killing, and she in fact does become more aware of the brutality of war once it becomes real and is no longer theoretical. Only Harry seems able to retain a stable personality once war becomes a fact of their lives. He continues to joke and play lighthearted songs. His long career of trying to cheat people has left him immune to shock about human depravity. War does not stir fear, pity, or anger in him. What it does is make Irene vulnerable, so that, faced with no future, she opens up to Harry, who, in turn, places himself in danger of falling bombs.

Patriotism

Sherwood seems to be making the point in this play that, given extreme circumstances, almost anyone will become patriotic. The most obvious examples are Quillery and Dr. Waldersee. Early in *Idiot's Delight*, Quillery refuses to call himself a Frenchman. He identifies the French with pig farmers, as his father was, while he sees himself as belonging to a new breed of industrial workers. If he has any political affiliation at all, it is with Communist party leader Nikolai Lenin, the leader of the Russian Revolution. After the assault on Paris, however, Quillery identifies himself as a Frenchman. He seals his own doom by cursing the Italians for what they have done to his country, and he goes to his death shouting patriotic slogans. Dr. Waldersee falls into patriotism as a negative reaction to the war. He loses hope in saving the world from cancer, and, hopeless, he realizes that he is at heart a German citizen.

Sherwood makes his case for patriotism most clearly when he has his characters called by their nationalities, as Quillery is confronting the members of the Italian army. The scene works because it is consistent with the characters of Harry and Mr. Cherry to try to intervene in the barroom scuffle, and Quillery draws attention to the symbolic union by calling them by the names of their respective countries: ''You see, we stand together! France—England—America! Allies!'' The patriotism of the moment is deflated when Harry tries to distance himself from the equation, using Quillery's technique sarcastically, shouting, ''Shut up, France!'' He is trying in vain to save Quillery from being punished for his patriotic enthusiasm, more concerned with the human before him than in nationalistic posturing.

STYLE

Polemic

A polemic is an argument for or against one side of a controversy. Artists are very seldom successful when they engage in polemics in their works, because doing so usually means the work is guided by the lesson that the artist wants to teach rather than by artistic principles.

Idiot's Delight is a work by a pacifist, and it espouses pacifist ideas, but the ideas are not forced into the work. There is enough diversity in the characters for Sherwood to address the issues that he wants to with a sense that they would naturally come up among these characters in this situation. For example, the German munitions dealer, Weber, is clearly the villain of the piece, and Sherwood underscores his villainy by making him cold and merciless, willing to double-cross his lover and leave her to die. Still, it is not Weber who talks joyously about destruction, but Irene, giving her impression of the sort of gruesome talk she thinks he might appreciate. Weber himself is quiet about what he thinks. This serves to make him a chilling charac-

ter, but it also saves the drama from having to oversell his viciousness. He does not even openly accuse Irene when he suspects that she is too sentimental to be trusted but instead gives her his argument in favor of the poison gas business, saying that the people who buy from him deserve what they get. If Sherwood had gotten carried away with his polemics, this character would have been much more unconvincingly despicable.

The same holds true for the hero and heroine of this work. Harry and Irene are both flawed individuals, both accustomed to taking advantage of people through lying. Sherwood does not try to make angels of them but instead trusts audiences to recognize that their observations about the war are true even though their personal lives have been based on falsehood. No other characters feel the effect of the war as much as these two, and they are only able to bear the horror of the final shelling because they have each other. Even though they have the insight to see the world as Sherwood wants to present it, they are not made to seem unbelievably righteous.

Setting

There are two aspects of this play's setting that make it the perfect place to show off the ideas that it deals with. The first is the geographic location in the Italian Alps. Several times, characters point out the fact that one can see four countries from the hotel: Italy, Switzerland, Austria, and Bavaria. This point is significant because it reflects the diversity of the people who are passing through Monte Gabriele. There is an inherent tension in a border town during wartime, with enemies of the government trying to escape and the government trying to restrain them so that they cannot return to their homelands to aid the fight. That tension is real enough along a single border, but it is especially pronounced when several countries with different allegiances come together.

The specific setting of the play is the lobby of a hotel that was once a sanatorium for tuberculosis sufferers but that has lately been trying to attract a recreational crowd. Hoping to emphasize winter sports, the management has hired an American social director, but his good spirit is wasted on the people who are forced to stay at the Hotel Monte Gabriele against their wills. A hotel is a good setting for showing off an international cast of characters: it is a public place, and so it is likely that any of them could show up there. It is also generally a relaxed vacation spot, an expectation that helps to highlight their tension about being detained.

Mood

Sherwood manages to keep audiences interested in the events onstage by playing two conflicting moods off each other. As a drama set in the first days of the war, *Idiot's Delight* has elements of deadly seriousness about it. Subjects such as curing cancer, nerve gas, and execution serve as reminders of just how terrible the world can be. On the other hand, there are many light elements presented. The girls from ''Les Blondes'' never seem to grasp the dire circumstances surrounding them, and audiences can laugh at their shallow perception. Don Navadal's argument against his employer, Pittaluga, is funny because neither of them is serious enough about their disagreements to fire the other or quit. To add to the lighthearted aspects, Sherwood includes a time in the middle of the play when audiences can temporarily forget the important issues being discussed by watching a show-within-a-show, with singing and dancing that has no more purpose than pure entertainment. The mix of these two moods, serious and whimsical, prevents audience members from becoming too complacent or making assumptions about what the play has to say to them.

HISTORICAL CONTEXT

Fascism in Italy

During World War I, Italy was a part of the Allied forces, which included Britain, France, Russia, and the United States. They were gathered against the Central powers, which included Germany, Austria-Hungary, Turkey, and Bulgaria. When the Allies won, the Treaty of Versailles decided upon a reorganization of territories that were held by the defeated countries. In *Idiot's Delight*, Monte Gabriele is in an area of the Alps that had been part of Austria but that was ceded to Italy by the Treaty of Versailles.

At the end of the war, the Italian political system was in disarray. Socialists, Communists, and Fascists all tried to gain control of the country. Fascism was a new form of political system, supported by armed bands of nationalists. The Italian term, *fascio,* which refers to a bundle of axe-headed rods that symbolized the ancient Roman Republic, had been used in Italy as early as the 1870s to describe the new radical organizations that sprang up around the country. As World War I ended, these separate bands gathered together as a unified national party called *Fascio di Combattimento.* This new party promoted action, modernism, and a strong sense of national identity. At its onset, the Fascist Party was primarily a left-wing organization.

Within three years of the party's formation, Benito Mussolini had worked his way up within its ranks to become the country's premier, and almost immediately he began cutting off democratic means of political change, so that by 1925 he ruled Italy as a dictator. The Fascist Party under Mussolini became increasingly right wing, so that its primary objectives were to keep order and to control Italy at any cost. Fascists invented the term ''totalitarianism'' to describe their goal of keeping total control on all aspects of life.

In 1935 and 1936, Italy fought a war to annex Ethiopia (which Harry refers to in act 1 when he says, ''You mean—that business in Africa?''). After their success, Adolph Hitler sought out Mussolini to make an alliance. When World War II began in 1939, Italy was unprepared, and the social cost in lives and money made the people turn against Fascism. Mussolini was driven from power in 1943, though he and a small band of Fascists were supported by Hitler in northern Italy as the Italian Socialist Republic, which waged a civil war against the rest of the country. In the meantime, the new democratic Italian government changed sides during the war and fought against Germany. In the final days of the war, Mussolini tried to escape to Switzerland, but he was caught by the Italian government and executed.

The Start of World War II

In this play, an armed conflict begins, which the characters recognize to be the start of a second world war. In reality, though, World War II did not begin until 1939, four years after *Idiot's Delight* was written. During that time, the tensions were so obvious to an observer of international affairs like Sherwood that another war of global proportions seemed inevitable.

The causes of World War II grew out of the way that the world was left when the Treaty of Versailles was signed in 1919. The treaty marked the end of the most terrible, widespread international conflict the world had ever known, with thirty-two countries eventually involved. Germany was the most prominent nation on the losing side of that conflict, and the treaty extracted a heavy price, both to punish and to make sure that Germany would not have the means to assemble a powerful

COMPARE
&
CONTRAST

- **1936:** The world is in the middle of a global economic depression, which started with the stock market crash of October 1929.

  Today: After record-breaking economic growth in the 1990s, supported by the spread of personal computers and the Internet, the world economy is softening into recession.

- **1936:** News of events in other countries comes from those countries on short-wave radios.

  Today: People all over the world are connected to the latest developments. Television news stations have bureaus all over the world, and many people get constant news updates via the Internet.

- **1936:** The Great Purge begins in the Soviet Union. Over the next two years, 8 to 10 million people are murdered by Stalin's government.

  Today: Ten years after the fall of Communism, Russia is struggling to create a viable, stable economy based on capitalist principles.

- **1936:** The Japanese government is taken over in a mutiny by young army officers who established a military dictatorship, tilting Japan toward its eventual alliance with Germany and Italy.

  Today: Japan is one of the world's great economic superpowers, with a government of elected officials that answers to the will of the people.

- **1936:** A group of female performers traveling in a foreign country need a man to manage them and to chaperone them so that men would not take advantage of their naïveté.

  Today: Old stereotypes have been broken, and women in most countries are respected enough to be able to travel without a male chaperone.

- **1936:** There is fear that hostility between the world's superpowers could lead to years of conflict between ground troops.

  Today: Most of the world's powerful countries have nuclear capabilities and are willing to try hard to settle disagreements diplomatically without resorting to nuclear weapons.

---

army again. In addition to forfeiting millions of dollars in money, ships, livestock, and natural resources, it had to give up much of the land that it had acquired as a result of the war. All of these losses caused great economic hardship in Germany, especially when a worldwide depression began in the 1930s. Inflation in Germany reached triple digits, making the money earned from working worth less by the time it was spent.

In their misery, the Germans sought out a strong leader who felt that the treaty had been unfair and was willing to fight about it. In 1933, they elected Adolph Hitler, a charismatic candidate who made Germans feel good about themselves by promoting military strength and by playing off racial prejudices. After being elected chancellor, Hitler turned the government into a dictatorship and began a program of military aggression.

Other countries were also unhappy with the Treaty of Versailles. France and England were left in the uncomfortable position of having to rebuild their own economies after the war and to enforce the treaty as best as they could. Instead of staying with the wartime coalition, the United States began a new program of isolationism after the war, which meant political isolation from the rest of the world. Italy, which had been aligned with the winning Allied powers, felt that they had not received a proper share of the land that was divided up by the treaty: when Mussolini rose to power in the 1930s, he began a program of armed aggression, starting with the Ethiopian campaign in 1935. The Japanese military also created a dictatorship that was reaching out to conquer other nations.

When the play was written, the international situation was clearly volatile, changing weekly, but the world war that Sherwood anticipated still did not happen. Germany, Italy, and Japan signed treaties in 1936 and 1937, and each continued to conquer smaller countries. Reluctant to become involved in another terrible conflict like World War I, France and England accepted Germany's moves, even though they broke the Treaty of Versailles. When Germany annexed Czechoslovakia in 1938, threatening Poland; Britain and France signed a pact promising Poland's defense. After Stalin agreed to leave Germany alone, which meant that Hitler would not have to defend the country's east border, Germany invaded Poland in 1929, and France and Great Britain declared war soon after. Eventually, most of the countries in the world were involved in the conflict.

CRITICAL OVERVIEW

Idiot's Delight was a hit when it first appeared on Broadway in 1936. The play appeared at a time when Robert E. Sherwood's career was at its creative and popular peak, and its stars, Alfred Lunt and his wife, Lynn Fontanne, were two of the most popular Broadway stars of the 1930s and 1940s. Sherwood had come naturally to writing for the stage, having been a drama critic and film critic and having closely associated with such successful Broadway writers as George S. Kaufman and Marc Connelly as a part of the social group that gathered regularly at the Algonquin Hotel in New York City throughout the 1920s. Sherwood's first professional play, *The Road to Rome*, a clever version of the story of Hannibal's assault on Rome, was a smash hit in 1927, establishing Sherwood as a talented, reliable playwright and giving him the chance to leave his position as literary editor for *Life* magazine. After that, Sherwood's name became a constant and familiar sight on Broadway marquees with a string of clever social comedies and love stories, each alluding in one way or another to the horrors of war.

The 1935 drama *The Petrified Forest* was the first to show Sherwood at his philosophical, serious best, and it anticipated the structure that was to appear again in his later work, *Idiot's Delight*. In it, a group of strangers passing through a Nevada gas station are detained and threatened by a sinister presence, an escaped gangster. In *Modern American Playwrights,* Jean Gould refers to an anonymous critic of the time who accused Sherwood of "perpetuating hokum of the highest type on the American public." Gould also includes a reply by Burnes Mantle, who praised the playwright as "a melodramatist who, in place of pretending to despise the hokum of our theatre, boldly embraces it with noble purpose and to fine effect." Gould goes on to add her own thoughts about the subject: "Hokum or no, *The Petrified Forest* was chilling melodrama bordering on true tragedy, and was an overnight success when it appeared on Broadway in early January, 1935."

If *The Petrified Forest* prepared audiences to accept Sherwood as a serious, committed playwright of ideas, it was *Idiot's Delight* that fulfilled that promise. The play had the commercial elements that made the clever comedies of Sherwood's earlier career appeal to the masses, including songs and music and romance, performed by the ever-popular Lunts. Sherwood himself recorded his responses to reviews of the play in his diary, as noted in John Mason Brown's biography *The Worlds of Robert E. Sherwood—Mirror to His Times, 1896–1939*:

> Mar. 25. Read Notices. First I read was Atkinson's in the *Times* & it was lukewarm. The others seemed not much better. Disappointed. Anderson's in the *Eve. Journal* was marvelous, & so was Lockridge's in *The Sun.* General opinion was that all notices were superlatively good for box-office—but except for the last two mentioned they're far from satisfying me.... why do they deliberately close their ears to everything of importance that is said in a comedy? You'd think it was a crime to state unpleasant truths in an entertaining way.

In spite of Sherwood's disappointment and perhaps owing to the worsening of the conditions in Europe that he predicted in *Idiot's Delight*, the play grew in critical esteem during its run. He was rewarded for daring to state "unpleasant truths" with the Pulitzer Prize for drama for that year. He also won the Pulitzer for his next play, *Abe Lincoln in Illinois*, which showed the president's growth from a pacifist in the 1840s to the commander in chief of the Union Army in the 1860s. Sherwood's third Pulitzer was for the next play in succession, *There Shall Be No Night*, a pro-war play that served to fulfill the doubts about pacifism that began showing themselves in *The Petrified Forest*.

During World War II, Sherwood worked for the government, and after the war he found that his award-winning plays held no more interest than dated newspapers. Though his craftsmanship has never been questioned, his artistry has never been overtly praised either. Without being able to relate *Idiot's Delight* to current events, audiences can only see it as a slick piece of antiwar propaganda. Sher-

A scene from the 1939 film adaptation of Idiot's Delight, *featuring Clark Gable, as Henry Van*

wood's plays have continually appeared in anthologies of best-loved plays because they capture a particularly ambivalent aspect of the American culture, but they seldom appear in anthologies of best-written plays.

CRITICISM

David Kelly

Kelly is an adjunct professor of English at the College of Lake County and Oakton Community College in Illinois. In this essay, Kelly examines how the two American characters in Idiot's Delight *can be used to understand Robert Sherwood's pacifist ideals.*

Robert Sherwood's play *Idiot's Delight*, set at the brink of an imagined world war, features characters from all over the Western world, representing an array of perspectives. They tend toward stereotype, but Sherwood usually manages to humanize each role. The German doctor, Waldersee, is a good example: stern and nationalistic, he originally bucks the tired generalization during Hitler's reign that

Germans were soulless barbarians, with his hope to improve the world by defeating cancer. By the end, though, under the pressure of the war, he becomes the barbarian stereotype and returns to his homeland to produce nerve gas instead. Mr. and Mrs. Cherry are as gung-ho about duty as cartoon British people tended to be, but Sherwood softens some of the brittleness of their stereotype by making their love deep and fresh and by having Jimmy Cherry be an artist. As Mrs. Cherry puts it, "We're both independent," and even thinking that they are spares them from being stereotypical Brits. The Frenchman is hotheaded; the Austrian is resigned; and the Russian woman is mysteriously superior: all of these stretch beyond the functions of their particular characters to stand as representatives of their governments' attitudes toward war.

With this pattern established, it seems unnecessarily repetitive that the play has two American men, especially when it could so easily have made the social manager of the Hotel Monte Gabrielle a representative of another European nation. Apparently, Harry Van does not tell audiences all that Sherwood thinks they need to know about America's position in the international situation of the time. Since there are, in fact, two Americans, it

WHAT DO I READ NEXT?

- Sherwood's play *The Petrified Forest* has a similar structure and similar themes to *Idiot's Delight:* a mismatched assemblage of travelers is trapped together in a bus station in the West by a desperate gunman, whose violence threatens to destroy the social ideals of an intellectual pacifist. The play was first published in 1935 and is currently available from Dramatist's Play Service, published in 1998.

- Those interested in Sherwood's life will want to read James R. Gaines's *Wit's End: Days and Nights of the Algonquin Round Table,* about the legendary social group that Sherwood shared with Dorothy Parker, George S. Kaufman, and other literary figures of the twenties and thirties. This book, considered the best on the subject, was published in 1977 by Harcourt Brace Jovanovich.

- During World War II, Sherwood worked for the administration of President Franklin D. Roosevelt. His 1949 Pulitzer Prize–winning biography, *Roosevelt and Hopkins,* about the president's relationship with controversial aid Harry Hopkins, has just been re-released in paperback in December 2001 by Enigma Books.

- Playwright Maxwell Anderson's name is often linked with Sherwood's; they both wrote at the same time and covered similar topics, often incorporating the war into their works. Anderson's *Winterset* was produced the same year as *Idiot's Delight* and won the New York Drama Critics' Circle Award that year. It is an experimental play written in verse about a young man out to clear the name of his father, who was executed. Dramatist's Play Service published a new version in 1998.

- John Mason Brown is recognized as the preeminent Sherwood biographer. He has two books about Sherwood. *The Worlds of Robert E. Sherwood, Mirror to His Times,* published by Harper & Row in 1962, covers the playwright's development up to the start of World War II in 1939. *The Ordeal of a Playwright: Robert E. Sherwood and the Challenge of War,* published by Harper & Row in 1970, is about the war years and includes the text of Sherwood's Pulitzer Prize–winning play *There Shall Be No Night.*

---

seems a safe bet that examining the contrast between them will reveal more of the author's intent than one could see if there were just one.

The essence of this play, as with all of Sherwood's pre–World War II writing, is his basic assumption that war is an avoidable mistake that humanity commits again and again, but does not need to. In the "Postscript" to the original publication, Sherwood explains why he does not think war is inevitable, but why, nonetheless, it will probably go on: "I believe," he writes, "that the world is populated largely by decent people, and decent people don't want war." The problem decent people face is that "they are deluded by their exploiters, who are members of the indecent minority." In the play, both Harry and Don are decent people, but

only one seems ripe for exploitation. The defense that Sherwood offers against becoming ''intoxicated by the synthetic spirit of patriotism'' is to face the fear-mongering political leaders with ''calmness, courage, and ridicule.'' Harry Van is a model of these qualities, and one senses that, if he were to survive the air raid that comes at the final curtain, he would be immune to the allure of war. Donald Navadel, on the other hand, presents the audience with just the sort of qualities that the purveyors of war can exploit.

Don is the first character that audiences get to know in *Idiot's Delight*. In the stage directions at the beginning of the play, he is described as ''a rather precious, youngish American, suitably costumed for winter sports by Saks Fifth Avenue.'' These

> HIS FAITH IS THE SOURCE OF THE 'COOLNESS, COURAGE AND RIDICULE' THAT SHERWOOD PRESCRIBES, KEEPING HARRY DETACHED FROM THE MOUNTING FEAR AND ANGER THAT DRAWS THE OTHERS, AND THEIR RESPECTIVE NATIONS, TO WAR."

facts present Don as an interesting enough character, given his situation. He is a classic "fish out of water" character—a wealthy, young American in the thick of Europe's twisted political situation at a time when Americans were particularly notorious for their ability to ignore the rest of the world's troubles. The situation Don is in at the opening curtain could keep an audience's attention throughout *a* whole play, but not this play. It turns out, after opening on him, that the play is not about Don at all.

It is worth noting, given the fact that he is on stage so little during the play, that Sherwood supplies Donald Navadel with a compelling back-story and a distinct personality. He draws viewers' attention in the play's first few minutes, and then he virtually disappears. When he is there, though, he is loud and aggressive, not at all the image of the successful sportsman that his Saks Fifth Avenue "costume" would belie. "I'm fed to the teeth, personally," he tells his employer, Pittaluga, after telling the band to "Get out!" and ordering Dumptsy "Do as you're told!" Without the impending danger of war behind them, his sharp comments might seem to be the cries of a young man of promise who was hired away from a thriving situation to be stuck in a dead-end job. Within the context of war, though, his lack of composure identifies him as a part of the system that keeps international conflict alive.

Don is prey for the purveyors of war because he takes himself seriously. His pride is wounded because he does not like the situation he works in and he feels that someone must be to blame. He immodestly refers to his own career as "conspicuously successful"; by contrast, he calls the place where he works an "obscure tavern" and "a deadly,

boring dump." His indignation is the kind that drives people to wars to defend their national honor; his anger is exactly the kind of fuel that the world expected to ignite in Europe in 1936.

Harry Van, on the other hand, exudes the kind of self-control that Sherwood clearly admired. He is not presented as having a superior personality, as a model of the sort of person who could eventually lead the world to peace. He seems like an ordinary, slightly bright man, who has been made wise by the circumstances of his life, so that he takes nothing for granted. Sherwood introduces Harry as an "American vaudevillian promoter, press agent, book-agent, crooner, hoofer, barker or shill, who has undertaken all sorts of jobs in his time, all of them capitalizing on his power of salesmanship and none of them entirely honest." In the course of the play, Harry describes a few of his former careers, ranging from the dangerously dishonest selling of useless medicine to the winking dishonesty of participating in a phony mind-reading act to the self-dishonesty of playing background music for silent films when he is actually an accomplished classical performer.

It is Harry's dishonesty that makes him able to accept human weakness. He is capable of falling in love with Irene, the only character in the play more insincere than himself. He is, in fact, able to put up with the foibles and pretentions and self-deceit of anyone he meets at the Hotel Monte Gabriele. Audiences come to know the background stories of these characters because Harry Van is always there, ready to let them talk without passing judgment. As Mrs. Cherry tells him at the start of act 2, "I can't tell you what a relief it is to have you here in this hotel."

In his later scenes, it is even more obvious that Don Navadel, the professional winter sportsman, is too intolerant to stand up to the social forces leading toward war. This becomes particularly clear in the scenes that Don and Harry share, where their different temperaments can be easily compared. When Achille Weber, the arms manufacturer, has been introduced, Don is dead serious and "impressed," whereas Harry hardly notices the impressive man because he is fascinated with the mysterious woman, Irene. In an earlier scene, Don is particularly impatient with Harry: "It may be difficult for you to understand, Mr. Van," he tells the man who is fifteen or twenty years his senior, "but we happen to be on the brink of a frightful calamity." Harry responds blithely that the Italians would not start a worldwide conflict because they are "far too romantic.'' When Harry brings up the idea of putting on a show at the hotel, he works his way into it by asking Don his job description, likening it to ''a sort of Y. M. C. A. secretary''; Don's reactions in this conversation grow from ''impatient'' to ''simply furious,'' according to the stage directions.

Harry Van is, because of his optimism, a model for the virtues that Sherwood believes are needed to resist the temptations of war—as he outlines in an often-quoted speech. In taking advantage of ''suckers,'' he has experienced their faith: ''Faith in peace on earth and good will to men—and faith that 'Muma,' 'Muma' the three-legged girl, really has got three legs.'' Instead of making him more cynical, humanity's ability to constantly come up with more faith has given Harry his own sort of faith— ''It has made me sure that no matter how much the meek may be bulldozed or gypped they *will* eventually inherit the earth.'' His faith is the source of the ''coolness, courage and ridicule'' that Sherwood prescribes, keeping Harry detached from the mounting fear and anger that draws the others, and their respective nations, to war.

The differences between the two Americans in this play become clearest at the end. Don concludes his employment at the Hotel Monte Gabriele with the line, ''What a relief it is to be out of this foul place!,'' as he launches into a description of the Frenchman's execution. After that, he passes through the play to show a devotion to punctuality. ''Four o'clock. Correct!'' he answers when Harry asks the train departure time, and later Don appears, shouts, ''We can't wait another instant!,'' and goes. Harry leaves the security of a train to Geneva and steps right into the war zone, fully aware of what he faces. Don is anxious to get on the move; Harry, staying with danger all around him, is calm.

Source: David Kelly, Critical essay on *Idiot's Delight*, in *Drama for Students*, The Gale Group, 2002.

R. Baird Shuman

In the following essay excerpt, Shuman explores the anti-war sentiment in Idiot's Delight *and how Sherwood renders the message in the play.*

Maxwell Anderson and Laurence Stallings wrote *What Price Glory?* in 1924 and concluded it with the words, ''What a lot of goddam fools it takes to make a war.'' Twelve years later, when news of the Spanish Civil War and of the Italian invasion of Ethiopia occupied the headlines, and when Hitler was rattling his saber ominously over his neighbors

in eastern Europe, Robert Sherwood presented audiences with *Idiot's Delight* which reflected the growing anti-war sentiment in the United States in the mid-1930's. Sherwood's message is somewhat different from that of Anderson and Stallings. In the postscript to his play he writes, ''. . . let me express here the conviction that those who shrug and say, 'War is inevitable,' are false prophets. I believe that the world is populated largely by decent people, and decent people don't want war. Nor do they make war. They fight and die, to be sure—but that is because they have been deluded by their exploiters, who are members of the indecent minority.'' This sentiment represents a mellowing from the attitude expressed implicitly in *The Petrified Forest* in the characterization of the blood-thirsty Legionnaires, who have ''fought to make the world safe for democracy,'' who love to shoot and kill, and who care little whether they are shooting at the just or the unjust.

It is clear that the sentiment in *Idiot's Delight* is that human conflict is largely the fault of those who make it possible, in this specific case, the munitions manufacturer, Achilles Weber. His Russian mistress, Irene, realizes this fact; and, when war finally erupts, she cries out to Weber: ''All this great, wonderful death and destruction, everywhere. And you promoted it!'' But Weber, who whimsically declines to take all the credit, retorts: ''. . . But don't forget to do honor to Him—up there—who put fear into man. I am the humble instrument of His divine will.'' And again Weber declines to accept the full responsibility for his part in bringing about conflict when he asks Irene, ''. . . who are the greater criminals—those who sell the instruments of death, or those who buy them, and use them?'' The question of responsibility, of course, is the compelling question of the age, and it recurs in such works as Clifford Odets' *Golden Boy,* Arthur Miller's *All My Sons,* Paul Green's *Johnson Johnson,* Maxwell Anderson's *Winterset,* and a host of other plays of the 1930's and '40's. By shifting responsibility, the foul deed can be done, yet everyone involved can be exonerated. The ''indecent minority'' is a minority of faceless buck-passers.

One of the major points of *Idiot's Delight* had been made ten years earlier in *The Road to Rome,* when Amytis deflated Hannibal after he had stated that he had been motivated in his conquests by the voice of his god, Ba-al, and she had replied: ''That wasn't the voice of Ba-al, Hannibal. That was the voice of the shopkeepers of Carthage, who are afraid that Rome will interfere with their trade. . . .

IT IS CLEAR THAT THE SENTIMENT IN *IDIOT'S DELIGHT* IS THAT HUMAN CONFLICT IS LARGELY THE FAULT OF THOSE WHO MAKE IT POSSIBLE, IN THIS SPECIFIC CASE, THE MUNITIONS MANUFACTURER, ACHILLES WEBER."

Hatred, greed, envy, and the passionate desire for revenge—those are the high ideals that inspire you soldiers, Roman and Carthaginian alike." In *Idiot's Delight*, Ba-al is dead, and the ancient god of the Hebrews has been reduced to a "... poor, lonely old soul. Sitting up in heaven, with nothing to do, but play solitaire. Poor, dear God. Playing Idiot's Delight. The game that never means anything, and never ends." This is the God of a skeptical age, and this is life in Spenglerian terms or in terms of the philosophy of T. S. Eliot in *The Waste Land* or in *The Hollow Men,* where life *does* end, but with a whimper rather than a bang.

Harold Clurman has called the sentiment which led Sherwood to write *Idiot's Delight* cogent. He has very astutely and perceptively noted that the play "... echoes the American fear of and profound estrangement from the facts of European intrigue which led to war," and he supports this contention by reminding readers that Sherwood's French pacifist, Quillery, is cast as a Radical-Socialist who venerated Lenin; but, in reality, the Radical-Socialists of pre-war France were the small businessmen who hated Lenin. But Clurman praises the play for giving "... us an inkling of the moral climate in our country" during this period of crisis. Clurman also makes the point that during this time "... the attitude of our dramatists, generally speaking, was fundamentally moral rather than, as some are now inclined to believe, political."

This, of course, is a disputed point, and Casper H. Nannes presents a case for *Idiot's Delight* as political drama in *Politics in the American Drama,* in which he claims, quite validly, that Sherwood's anti-war bias reached its peak in *Idiot's Delight.*" Actually Sherwood's stand in regard to war is much easier to understand and to accept as a moral rather

than as a political stand. Surely the attitude which he is working toward in *Abe Lincoln in Illinois* and which he finally achieves in his propagandistic *There Shall Be No Night* is a moral stand. The fact that both of these plays are closer temporally to audiences than was a play such as *The Road to Rome* can easily mislead them into seeing the more immediate political implications of what Sherwood is saying than the moral implications. However, it is clear, especially in the case of *There Shall Be No Night*, that had the play been fundamentally political rather than moral, Sherwood could not in good conscience have rewritten it in 1943 and changed the nationality of the chief contending parties in the action from Finnish to Greek. And those critics who castigated him for "dumping the Finns" were obviously insensitive to the underlying purpose of this play, and perhaps of all of his plays which dealt with the problem of war.

Sherwood managed to put more tension into *Idiot's Delight* than he was able to achieve in many of his other plays. The uncertainty that the people assembled in the Italian *pensione* will be permitted to cross the border into Switzerland pervades the play and causes the characters to show tension in their various ways. The tension is enhanced by the sounding of air raid sirens, and it reaches a peak with the execution of Quillery. However, John Mason Brown understates a very important point when he writes that "The tension in Europe added to the tension of *Idiot's Delight*." The play capitalized on this tension increasingly at every performance. It opened in New York two days after Italy had invaded Ethiopia; it opened in London less than a week after Hitler's forces had marched into Austria. It played amid constant international tensions, and even its most successful revival came in 1951 at a time when an undeclared war was being fought at great cost of human life in Korea.

Sherwood had to exercise considerable control to make *Idiot's Delight* as serious a play as he did. More than any other Sherwood drama, this play has a message. It was written with great intensity, indeed with such great intensity that its author wrote on one occasion until well past midnight, went to bed, but couldn't stand not knowing the outcome of the second act; so he arose again at three and continued writing until dawn. The play, which was written and presented to the Lunts in a period of two weeks, was not entirely ready for Broadway in its original form. Sherwood had once said, "The trouble with me is that I start off with a big message and end with nothing but good entertainment," and

Idiot's Delight is an especially apt case in point. At one of the early rehearsals, Lawrence Langner pointed out that the play seemed too light for its very serious content. This was a thoughtful observation for at this point, as Langner notes, the play "... had drifted perilously between the delightful story of a group of chorus girls lost in Italy, and the more serious implications of the oncoming war."

Lynn Fontanne, as well as Alfred Lunt and Robert Sherwood, agreed with Langner's analysis; and, after considerable pondering, Miss Fontanne suggested that Sherwood write into the play a significant scene for her—she played Irene—and Achilles Weber, the munitions baron. Sherwood did so, and the play took on a more serious tone, even though this increased seriousness was attained through means which did not detract from the play's initial humor and pleasing pace. Also, the irony of the play was increased by this change; and, through the increased irony, Weber's personality was projected more fully to the audience. His unchivalrous abandonment of Irene, an abandonment to almost certain death, is directly attributable to the fact that Irene expresses pacifist sentiments. The munitions manufacturer will tolerate no threat to his commercial interests in the form of such sentiments; by abandoning Irene, he shows himself unmistakably to be a man with no fundamental loyalties. One might compare Weber to Robert Murray in *Small War on Murray Hill;* Murray shows similar tendencies, although his personality in Sherwood's later play is just sketched in, whereas Achilles Weber is a more fully realized character in *Idiot's Delight.*

The microcosm which Sherwood creates in *Idiot's Delight* is suggestive of a diminutive *Magic Mountain,* translated into American terms. The characterization is of the utmost importance in Sherwood's play, just as it is in Mann's novel, for each character is a broad representative of a specific *Weltanschauung;* each speaks for a large class.

Harry Van is the prototypical "hoofer" and is virtually a master of ceremonies in the play. He represents American views much more fully than does the other male American in the play, Don Navadel. Van has a marked feeling of loyalty to his girls, but he also has a feeling of loyalty to Irene, the phony Russian countess, because he is convinced that he spent the night with her once in Kansas City, but even more so because she apparently remembers that they spent the night together and has some sentiment about it. Harry is the peacemaker, but this writer feels—with Grenville Vernon who reviewed

the play for *Commonweal*—that Harry is artistically false. His chief function in much of the play is that of pace-setter. Harry denounces war, but he never really presents any significant arguments for doing so. He is statically pacifistic in his presentation. Further, his heroic action in coming back to the *pensione* to die with Irene is not convincing. He has not, like Alan Squier, shown a death wish. His death does not lead to anything greater. He is representative of meaningless action, as is the French pacifist, Quillery.

Harry Van's philosophy is never really expressed clearly. The closest he comes to expressing any sort of idealogical stand is in the first act when he says to Dr. Waldersee, "All my life ... I've been selling phoney goods to people of meagre intelligence and great faith. You'd think that would make me contemptuous of the human race, wouldn't you? But—on the contrary—it has given *me* faith. It has made me sure that no matter how much the meek may be bulldozed or gypped they *will* eventually inherit the earth." The thinking in this passage is so confused and inconsistent that one can scarcely generalize about Harry's philosophy from it; yet this is typical of Harry's more serious utterances.

Quillery is often somewhat less than convincing in much the same way that Harry Van is. Having attempted to be a citizen of the world, Quillery very suddenly becomes a Frenchman again when war is declared. He is opinionated and dogmatic, but very insecure psychologically. He has fuzzy notions of how to bring about a better world, and he becomes an immature social boor when he begins to expand his hazy theories. He feels that the strongest force in the world is "... the mature intelligence of the workers of the world! There is one antidote for war—Revolution!"

Quillery is used to point the finger unquestionably at Achilles Weber. Having reached a frenzied state of anti-war sentiment, he tells Cherry, the Englishman, that Weber "... can give you all the war news. Because he *made* it... He has been organizing the arms industry. Munitions. To kill French babies. And English babies." In the following scene, Irene is to become even more graphic in describing the horror of what Weber is making possible when she speaks of what the war will be like: A young woman "... lying in a cellar that has been wrecked by an air raid, and her firm young breasts are all mixed up with the bowels of a dismembered policeman, and the embryo from her womb is splattered against the face of a dead bishop.'' As Irene's pacifism grows, it seems that she would be more appealing to Quillery than to Harry Van; and Sherwood might indeed have added credibility to the play had he spared Quillery rather than having him executed by the Fascisti. Had Quillery returned to the *pensione* to remain with Irene, the action would have been as convincing as was Boze's action in *The Petrified Forest* when he risked his life and grabbed Mantee's gun.

In many respects Quillery is suggestive of Boze. He is utterly lacking in objectivity and is very egocentric. He is a master of the hollow insult, as Boze was. His speech to Dr. Waldersee exemplifies this quality: ''The eminent Dr. Hugo Waldersee. A wearer of the sacred swastika. Down with the Communists! Off with their heads! So that the world may be safe for the Nazi murderers.'' He then turns on the British couple, the Cherrys, and insults them by saying, ''And now we hear the voice of England! The great, well-fed, pious hypocrite! The grabber— the exploiter—the immaculate butcher! It was *you* forced this war, because miserable little Italy dared to drag its black shirt across your trail of Empire.''

Despite this tirade, Quillery tells the Italian officers later in the same scene that ''England and France are fighting for the hopes of mankind.'' He then launches into the fanatical diatribe which costs him his life. He shouts, ''Down with Fascism! Abbasso Fascismo!''. He is placed under arrest by the Italians, who have very little choice but to do this, and he shouts, ''Call out the firing squad! Shoot me dead! But do not think you can silence the truth that's in me.'' These are brave, stirring words; but they are those of a person who has regressed to adolescence and whose idealism leads to nothing but death without meaning. The role is well depicted and, in itself, is credible. However, the play as a whole would have gained in credibility had Quillery been permitted to live and to fall in love with Irene. The reunion of the pathological patriot with the pathological liar would have been much more satisfying than was the reunion of the good-natured Harry Van with Irene.

The Cherrys are brought into the play for two reasons. In the first place, they represent the effect of war upon young love—always an appealing theme. But in a broader sense, they represent the English stand in regard to war. They are restrained and calm. They do not like what is going on, but they do not explode into action as might the more volatile French, represented by Quillery. In this regard, Harry Van represents his country, the United States. He shepherds his girls to the frontier, but he returns for personal reasons to stay with Irene. His involvement in the war is unofficial, but morality leads him to take a stand, even though the bases of this morality are personal and private.

Dr. Waldersee, of course, represents the dilemma of the scientist who is essentially dedicated to something far larger than nationalism, but whose blood tie with his country is great enough to divert him from his scientific pursuits for the benefit of mankind to scientific pursuits which will be quite the opposite. In reality, Dr. Waldersee is faced with the same sort of moral dilemma which faced Dr. Valkonen in *There Shall Be No Night,* and the solution of the conflict, on a moral level at least, is similar in both cases.

Idiot's Delight amazed audiences because Sherwood not only had foreseen the broad outlines of history, but also had dealt with specifics which were in time to be borne out by developments in international politics. The play continued to have a very definite appeal through the early years of the war; and, when it was revived in 1951, audiences were again to be much in awe of Sherwood's ability to prognosticate with such accuracy.

The areas in which *Idiot's Delight* appealed to audiences are as diverse as the areas in which *The Road to Rome* made its appeal. Grenville Vernon, writing a second review of the play six weeks after he had first reviewed it, felt that it ''. . . is not all of one piece. It is perhaps even too shrewdly made for popular appeal. It is in its entirety neither comedy, melodrama, musical comedy nor propaganda play. It is by turns all of these . . . there are those who would have wished [Sherwood] had stuck a little closer to artistic unity.''

The play's most severe structural flaw is obviously the ending. Bombs are falling, Harry and Irene are in the *pensione,* certainly doomed. Harry has been playing ''The Ride of the Walküries.'' Irene asks him if he knows any hymns, and in jazz time he begins to play ''Onward, Christian Soldiers.'' The irony of this is almost too heavy handed; and, for every critic who agreed with *Newsweek's* critic in calling the ending ''a stirring bit of theatre,'' there were dozens who felt, like Grenville Vernon, that it was ''hokum of a peculiarly annoying kind.'' Sherwood's intention to represent in *Idiot's Delight* ''. . . a compound of bland pessimism and desperate optimism, of chaos and jazz,'' is achieved in his ending; but the method to achieve it is so jarringly melodramatic that the impact is all but lost.

In *Idiot's Delight*, Sherwood's out-and-out pacifism is replaced by pessimism. Joseph Wood Krutch has noted that the author's main contention in this play is that "... men are too emotional and too childish to carry to a successful issue any plan for abolishing war." This is the first step away from the pacifism of Sherwood's earlier works. In *Idiot's Delight*, the author has not turned his back on pacifism, but he is not hopeful that men will be pacific. The thinking in this play leads directly into *Abe Lincoln in Illinois* and reaches its final culmination in *There Shall Be No Night* with its "Yes, but ..." attitude.

Source: R. Baird Shuman, "Sherwood's Universal Microcosms," in *Robert Emmet Sherwood,* College & University Press, 1964, pp. 52–74.

SOURCES

Brown, John Mason, "Postscript," in *Idiot's Delight,* Charles Schribner's Sons, 1936, pp. 189–90.

———, *The Worlds of Robert E. Sherwood: Mirror to His Times, 1906–1939,* Harper & Row, 1962, p. 341.

Gould, Jean, "Robert Sherwood," in *Modern American Playwrights,* Dodd, Mead & Company, 1966, p. 107.

FURTHER READING

Auchincloss, Louis, "Robert E. Sherwood," in *The Man behind the Book: Literary Profiles,* Houghton Mifflin Company, 1996, pp. 192–98.
Auchincloss's brief overview of Sherwood's life is a good starting point for students.

Meserve, Walter J., *Robert E. Sherwood: Reluctant Moralist,* Pegasus Press, 1970.
Meserve focuses on Sherwood's hopes and fears for humanity, centering his book around the playwright's shift from pacifist to supporter of American involvement in war.

Morgan, Philip, *Italian Fascism, 1919–1945,* St. Martin's Press, 1995.
The last half of this study deals with the situation in Italy after 1933 and serves as clear and readable overview of the background of this play's politics.

Moses, Montrose J., "Robert E. Sherwood," in *Dramas of Modernism and Their Forerunners,* D.C. Heath and Company, 1941.
This introduction to *Idiot's Delight,* in an anthology published while Sherwood was at the height of his career, views his work as a more sustained and coherent body than contemporary critics usually do.

J. B.

ARCHIBALD MACLEISH

1958

J. B., published in 1958, is a play in verse based on the biblical story of Job. It represents Archibald MacLeish's responses to the horrors he saw during two world wars, including the Holocaust and the bombings of Hiroshima and Nagasaki. The author explains in the foreword to the acting edition of his play that turning to the Bible for a framework seems sensible ''when you are dealing with questions too large for you which, nevertheless, will not leave you alone.'' *J. B.* tells the story of a twentieth-century American banker-millionaire whom God commands be stripped of his family and his wealth but who refuses to turn his back on God. MacLeish wondered how modern people could retain hope and keep on living with all the suffering in the world and offered this play as an answer. J. B. learns that there is no justice in the world, that happiness and suffering are not deserved, and that people can still choose to love each other and live.

MacLeish had been earning his living as a poet for fifty years before this, his third verse play, was published. Shortly after the publication of the book, the play was produced on Broadway and underwent substantial revisions. There are, therefore, two versions of the play available for readers: the original book published by Houghton Mifflin and the acting script available from Samuel French. Both were published in 1958, and neither has ever gone out of print. *J. B.* won the Pulitzer Prize for drama in 1959 (MacLeish's third Pulitzer), as well as the Tony Award for best play. More important, the play

sparked a national conversation about the nature of God, the nature of hope, and the role of the artist in society.

AUTHOR BIOGRAPHY

Archibald MacLeish was born in Glencoe, Illinois, on May 7, 1892. His father was a successful businessman, and his mother had been a college instructor; they saw to it that MacLeish was well educated. He attended public schools in Glencoe, and at the age of fifteen he was sent to a college preparatory academy in Connecticut. He began college studies at Yale in 1911.

Before college, MacLeish had been only an average student. At Yale, however, he began writing poetry and fiction for the literary magazine, excelled in water polo and football, earned high grades, and was elected to the Phi Beta Kappa honorary society. After graduation in 1915, he entered Harvard Law School, hoping that a career in law would give him a way to bring order out of chaos, just as poetry did. He married Ada Hitchcock in 1916; served briefly in the army; published his first book of poetry, *Tower of Ivory*, in 1917; and graduated first in his law school class in 1919. He taught government at Harvard for a short time and then worked as an attorney in Boston, but never lost his devotion to writing poetry.

In 1923, MacLeish moved with his family to Paris, determined to become a serious poet. During this period, many important American and European writers were living in Paris, and MacLeish became friendly with them, determined to learn from them. He taught himself Italian, so he could study the work of the fourteenth-century poet Dante Alighieri, and he studied the history of English poetry as well. These five years transformed his work, giving him a mature style that pleased both him and the critics. When he returned home, he was able to earn a living as a writer and to buy a small farm in Massachusetts where he and Ada lived together until his death.

His will to bring order and harmony to human existence informed MacLeish's career for the next sixty years. He published more than fifty books of poetry, drama, and essays, but he also accepted positions as the Librarian of Congress, Assistant Secretary of State, and part of the U.S. Delegation to the United Nations that established the United Nations Educational, Scientific and Cultural Organiza-

Archibald MacLeish

tion (UNESCO). He believed that the poet's duty was to address contemporary social concerns and to ask important questions. His distress at the bombings of Dresden, London, and Hiroshima led him to wonder how humans could respond with hope to such suffering. He posed this question in the 1958 play, *J. B.*, a retelling of the biblical story of Job, which brought MacLeish several awards and his largest financial success.

Over his career, MacLeish won three Pulitzer Prizes, the National Book Award, a Tony Award, an Academy Award for best screenplay, and nearly two dozen honorary degrees. In 1977, he received the Presidential Medal of Freedom. He died on April 20, 1982, just three weeks before a national symposium honoring his life and work.

PLOT SUMMARY

Prologue

The first characters to appear on stage in *J. B.* are Mr. Zuss and Nickles, a balloon seller and a popcorn seller in a run-down circus. They approach and then mount a sideshow stage in the corner of a circus tent to play out the story of Job from the

Bible, with the stage as Heaven, the ground as Earth, and the lights as the stars. Zuss (whose name sounds like "Zeus," the god of Greek mythology) will play God. From the beginning, he is as arrogant as one might expect a man who believes he is right for the role to be, and he is indignant at the idea that Job would dare to demand justice.

Nickles, on the other hand, understands Job's suffering and does not accept that God would cause that suffering just to prove his authority and power. Nickles sings a song that includes the play's central paradox: "If God is God He is not good, / If God is good, He is not God." Nickles, whose name is a variation of "Old Nick," a slang term for the devil, will play Satan. As the two men point out, there is always someone to play Job.

Zuss and Nickles don masks that they find in a pile of costumes. The Godmask is white, with closed eyes, showing his indifference. The Satanmask is dark, with open eyes, because "Satan sees." They review their lines, which will come from the King James Bible. When the lights go down for the play to begin, a Distant Voice speaks the first line: "Whence comest thou?" It is not Zuss who speaks but, apparently, God. Zuss and Nickles take over, and the lights dim.

Scene 1

As scene 1 begins, the raised stage where Zuss and Nickels stand is in darkness, while gathered around a table in the light are the wealthy banker J. B., his wife Sarah, and their five children. They are a wealthy New England family, celebrating Thanksgiving. Sarah would like the children to be more thankful for the bounty they enjoy. She believes that there is a kind of bargain with God: "If we do our part He does His." Our "part" is to thank God; if we forget God, He will punish. J. B. believes that God has chosen him for success and that his duty is to appreciate the gift, to enjoy his life.

Scene 2

The focus shifts again to Zuss and Nickles, whose first impulse is to belittle J. B.'s acting ability. Still, he is their "pigeon," the man who will play Job. Nickles believes that once J. B. is stripped of his wealth, as Job was, he will lose his piety, but Zuss insists that J. B. will praise God no matter how much he suffers. Why then, asks Nickles, must Job be made to suffer at all? If God knows Job will pass the test, then why administer the test? Because, Zuss answers, Job needs to see God clearly. The two

actors put their masks on and speak lines from the Bible. Satan challenges God to a bet: he will take everything away from Job, to demonstrate that even an upright man will curse God if pushed hard enough. God accepts.

Scene 3

Six or seven years have passed. Two drunken soldiers come to J. B.'s house, comrades in arms of David, J. B.'s oldest son. In a bumbling fashion, they reveal that David has been killed—not heroically in the war but accidentally and stupidly by his own men after the hostilities. As Sarah tries to understand that God has really taken her son, J. B. denies that David is really dead. Nickles encourages them to challenge God, but they do not hear him.

Scene 4

On the sidewalk, two reporters talk to a "Girl," a young woman perhaps in her twenties. They persuade her to approach a couple who will come by soon and to catch their attention so they will be facing the camera when the reporters tell them that two of their children have died in a car accident. The couple, of course, are J. B. and Sarah. The dead teenagers are their children, Mary and Jonathan, killed by a drunk driver when their car crashed into a viaduct. Sarah despairs and asks why God would do this. Nickles, who is visible, grins appreciatively. But J. B. insists that they cannot "Take the good and not the evil." He tries to embrace Sarah, but she flinches.

Scene 5

J. B. and Sarah talk to two men. The biblical story includes two messengers, and here they are played by police officers. Rebecca, the youngest child, is missing. J. B. did not call the police right away because he imagined that he could find her by himself. Sarah explains bitterly, "We believe in our luck in this house!" The luck again is bad, however. Rebecca has been raped and murdered by a teenaged drug user. "The Lord giveth," J. B. says, "The Lord taketh away." But he does not say the end of the line, which Nickels, Zuss, and the audience are expecting: "Blessed be the name of the Lord."

Scene 6

Two messengers enter carrying Sarah. She has been rescued from a collapsed building after a bombing destroyed a whole city block. J. B.'s bank is destroyed, and his last remaining child, Ruth, is dead. J. B. urges Sarah not to despair, urges her to say with him, ''The Lord giveth. The Lord taketh away.'' While Sarah shouts, ''Kills! Kills! Kills! Kills!'' J. B. completes the famous line, ''Blessed be the name of the Lord.''

Scene 7

Zuss and Nickles discuss J. B. Zuss is pleased with J. B.'s responses so far, but Nickles is disgusted. Although they are playing out a story that both know well, Nickles believes that this time the story will end differently, that J. B. will stop praising God once he experiences physical pain himself. When their argument delays the progress of the story, the Distant Voice begins to speak God's lines. Zuss and Nickles understand that they are to continue.

Scene 8

J. B. lies on a table, clothed only in rags, with Sarah, also in rags, by his side weeping. An atomic blast has killed thousands, and J. B. is wounded. Women standing nearby comment on the sores covering J. B.'s body and on how far the two have fallen. Sarah is bitter and angry, but J. B. is puzzled. He knows there must be a reason for God's punishment, but he cannot fathom what the reason is. Nickles observes that if J. B. knew the reason—if he knew that God was making the innocent J. B. suffer simply to demonstrate His own power—J. B. would despair. Sarah cannot accept J. B.'s theory that the family has deserved this suffering. She turns her back on J. B., urging him to ''curse God and die,'' and she runs out to kill herself. Now completely alone, J. B. begs God to ''Show me my guilt.'' Nickles sneers at Zuss.

Scene 9

In the biblical story, three comforters come to Job to scold him for questioning God and to ''justify the ways of God to man.'' Here, the three comforters are Zophar, a Catholic priest, Eliphaz, a psychiatrist, and Bildad, a Marxist. The three spout empty rhetoric and jargon to explain J. B.'s suffering, and they only add to J. B.'s despair. Finally, J. B. cries out, ''God, my God, my God, answer me!'' In response, the Distant Voice speaks God's words from the Bible, asserting his power and authority, demanding that J. B./Job repent for daring to ask questions of God. J. B. does, also speaking a line from the Bible, ''I abhor myself and repent.''

Scene 10

Nickles acknowledges that Zuss has won the bet, but Zuss is uneasy with his victory. He sees that

for Job to forgive God is a sign of Job's goodness and strength, not God's. He loses all enthusiasm for playing his role and starts to climb down from the stage, but Nickles reminds him that there is one more scene to play. In the biblical story, God restores everything Job has lost. Nickles is sure that this time J. B./Job will refuse God's offering, that he will not risk losing everything again. To make sure, he goes to J. B., tells him God's plan, and begs him to kill himself instead. But J. B. hears someone at the door and goes to meet his future.

Scene 11

Typically, in a play-within-a-play, the outer play ''frames'' the other, taking the first and last words. But J. B. and Sarah have the last scene to themselves, without the commentary of Nickles and Zuss. Sarah sits on the doorstep, holding a forsythia branch in bloom. She discovered it on her way to drown herself in the river, found hope in it, and came back to J. B. She explains to her husband, ''You wanted justice and there was none—/ Only love.'' People will not find illumination or love from God, but in their own hearts. Sarah and J. B. embrace and then set to work tidying up the stage.

CHARACTERS

Bildad

Bildad is one of the three comforters who come to reassure J. B. in scene 9, after J. B. has lost everything. Spouting jargon-filled clichés, Bildad explains J. B.'s suffering from a Marxist viewpoint, posing an economic answer to J. B.'s problems. J. B. should not wallow in guilt, he claims, because ''Guilt is a sociological accident.''

David

Thirteen years old at the start of the play, David is the oldest son of J. B. and Sarah. As a young man, David becomes a soldier. He survives the war only to be accidentally killed by his own comrades before he can return home.

Distant Voice

At two points in the play, while Zuss and Nickles are arguing in their roles as God and Satan, another voice from offstage is heard speaking lines attributed to God in the King James Bible. In the list of characters, the voice is named The Distant Voice. As MacLeish himself explained several times, the

MEDIA ADAPTATIONS

- A recording of *J. B.,* performed by some of the actors from the Broadway production, was issued by RCA Victor (LD6075) as a record album around 1960. It has not been reissued on compact disc or audio cassette.

voice belongs to God himself, another character in the play.

Eliphaz

Eliphaz is one of the three comforters who come to reassure J. B. in scene 9, after J. B. has lost everything. Wearing a white doctor's coat and lecturing like a pompous professor, he speaks for psychiatry, claiming that "Guilt is a / Psychophenomenal situation." His words offer no comfort.

J. B.

J. B. is a perfect and upright man, a successful New England banker, a millionaire, blessed with a loving wife, five children, and a comfortable life. There is no question about his standing for the biblical character Job; his wife Sarah calls him "Job" when she addresses him directly. J. B. is grateful for all he has, but unlike Sarah he does not see the need to express his thanks directly to God; he believes that it is enough to fully appreciate what he has been given. He feels that he is essentially lucky and that all will turn out well in the end. As he suffers each subsequent loss, J. B. insistently thanks God, as Sarah grows increasingly angry. Even after he has lost his family, his wealth, and his physical well-being, J. B. refuses to turn away from God. It is his refusal to "curse God" that finally pushes Sarah to leave him. But J. B.'s optimism is rewarded: God restores everything J. B. has lost and more. The central question of the play comes down to this: knowing he could run the risk of losing them again, how can J. B. accept the new gifts? How can he choose life in a world with no justice?

Jonathan

Jonathan, the younger son of J. B. and Sarah, is three years younger than David. He and his sister Mary are killed by a teenage drunk driver in scene 4.

Mary

Mary is the oldest daughter of J. B. and Sarah. When the play opens, she is twelve years old, a year younger than David. She and her brother Jonathan are killed by a teenage drunk driver in scene 4.

Nickles

Nickles is an old, has-been actor, now reduced to selling popcorn in a derelict circus. As the play begins, he and Mr. Zuss enter the circus tent, find some old masks in a pile of costumes, and take on the roles of God and Satan from the biblical story of Job. Nickles will play Satan (his name is a play on the name "old Nick," a seventeenth-century slang term for the devil) in the play-within-the-play. Nickles's mask is dark, with wide eyes. Unlike Zuss, who plays God, Nickles has some sympathy for Job and bitterness about man's willingness to accept suffering for God's sake. He challenges Zuss to a bet, wagering that if Job were stripped of everything he values, he would curse God. They select J. B. to play Job, and the play-within-the-play begins.

As J. B. loses his children one by one, Nickles/Satan sneers at Zuss/God and his cruel way of showing J. B. his power. Nickles is witty and intelligent, and some critics have said he represents MacLeish in finding humans more worthy of admiration than God. Whereas Zuss is indifferent to J. B.'s suffering, Nickles feels pity. Challenging God and his majesty, Nickles speaks the most frequently quoted lines from the play: "If God is God He is not good, / If God is good He is not God." But when Ruth and twenty thousand others are killed in a bombing and J. B. still praises God, Nickles's feelings turn to disgust. Knowing that at the end of the story God will restore all of J. B.'s treasures, Nickles speaks to J. B. and suggests he kill himself instead. In his last speech, Nickles proclaims violently, "Job won't take it! Job won't touch it!" But he does.

Rebecca

Rebecca, the youngest child of J. B. and Sarah, is only six years old at the beginning of the play. In scene 5 she is raped and murdered by a nineteen-year-old drug user and left in an alley clutching her toy parasol.

Ruth

Ruth, the middle daughter of J. B. and Sarah, is eight years old when the play begins. The last of the children to die, she is killed in the bombing in scene 6 that kills thousands.

Sarah

Sarah is J. B.'s wife of many years and the mother of his five children. Her name is an invention of MacLeish's; Job's wife is not named in the Bible. She is, according to the stage directions, "a fine woman with a laughing, pretty face but a firm mouth and careful eyes, all New England." When the family first appears, sharing a Thanksgiving feast, Sarah insists that they all stop and thank God for all they have. But when her innocent children are killed one by one, it is she who demands that Job "curse God and die." When he will not, she leaves him, heading to the river to drown herself. She returns in the last scene, having found hope and comfort in a forsythia branch blooming at the river's edge. She has learned that there is no justice but there is love.

Zophar

Zophar is one of the three comforters who come to reassure J. B. in scene 9, after J. B. has lost everything. Wearing a tattered clerical collar, Zophar claims that "Guilt is a deceptive secret," that man is inherently evil, and that J. B.'s suffering is more than deserved. He represents the empty comfort of religion, specifically of the Catholic Church.

Mr. Zuss

Mr. Zuss, like Nickles, is an old man, an actor who has fallen on hard times and now sells balloons at the circus. He and Nickles are the first characters on stage. They enter the circus tent, find a sideshow stage, and agree to take on the characters of God and Satan in a play-within-a-play, the biblical story of Job. Mr. Zuss, whose name carries echoes of "Zeus" or "Deus," will play the role of God, wearing a white mask whose closed eyes betray no expression. He accepts a wager from Nickles/Satan: he will allow Satan to destroy everything J. B. values, and J. B. will continue to praise God. Zuss and Nickles agree that J. B. is a "perfect and upright man," that he has done nothing to deserve his destruction. Zuss believes that this relationship between God and man is proper and that for man to challenge God or seek justice from him is inappropriate.

Throughout the story of J. B./Job, Zuss and Nickles argue about J. B.'s responses. To the pompous and arrogant Zuss, it is merely fitting that J. B. should continually praise and thank him, even as J. B.'s suffering increases. When thousands are killed in an explosion and J. B. is still grateful to God, Zuss is pleased whereas Nickles is disgusted. Both men know how the story will turn out, but Nickles continually rails against what he knows will happen, whereas Zuss placidly watches the story unfold.

THEMES

Hopelessness and Despair

The world of *J. B.* is a frightening world. In the beginning of the play, J. B. and his family are healthy and wealthy, happy and loving. J. B.'s children have never known suffering or deprivation; as J. B. tells Sarah, the world seems to them "New and born and fresh and wonderful." J. B. himself trusts his "luck" because it comes from God. He is safe in his knowledge that God is "just. He'll never change."

But without warning—and without cause—J. B.'s luck does change. His children are killed in particularly senseless ways: David by accident, by his own men when the war is over; Mary and Jonathan by a drunken teenaged driver; Rebecca by a teenager on drugs; Ruth in a bombing. J. B. himself is injured in an atomic blast, and his body is covered with radiation burns. There is no sense to it all, and that is the point. The world is so violent and frightening that even blameless people will be driven to despair. The surprising thing is not that Sarah eventually loses all hope, but that J. B. does not.

The hopelessness and senselessness of the world is first decried by Nickles, who speaks bitterly to Zuss, comparing the world to a "dung heap" and a "cesspool." Remembering the bombed-out cities of World War II, he says, "There never could have been so many / Suffered more for less." Throughout the play, Nickles badgers Zuss about suffering in the world and mocks humans like J. B. for thinking God cares about their suffering. The masks that Nickles and Zuss wear emphasize their relationship to human pain: Zuss's Godmask has blind eyes, but Nickles's Satanmask has open eyes, and, as Nickles says, "Those eyes *see.*" In the end, J. B. is not

TOPICS FOR FURTHER STUDY

- Research the theories of communism, socialism and Marxism. What do these groups believe about the ways societies function and should function? What do they believe about individual freedoms and responsibilities?

- The decade after World War II was a time of prosperity for many people and a time of increased poverty for others. Who profits financially from a war? Whose economic stability is threatened? Explain why this is the case.

- The use of masks for theatre and for religious practices is a tradition that reaches far back in time and all around the world. Research the ways in which masks are used in African, Native American, and other cultures to represent and to communicate with God.

- Read and research the biblical Book of Job. What is the origin of the story? When and where was it written? What questions do biblical scholars ask about the Prologue and the Epilogue? Do they agree in regard to the central idea, or question, of the book?

---

driven to despair, but Nickles is. Nickles comes to believe that the best thing for J. B. to do would be to commit suicide, to refuse to live in the world God has given him. For many readers, this hopelessness is the central theme of the play. It is not until the last scene that the reader has any reason to see anything more promising in the play.

Justice versus Love

MacLeish himself spoke publicly and wrote about *J. B.* several times, and he was always clear as to what he believed his play was "about" (although, as the poet who created the famous lines "A poem should not mean / But be," he discussed themes with some reluctance). When he addressed the cast of a college production of the play in 1976, he stated, "The play is not a struggle between God and J. B." The central question of the play, accord-

ing to the author, is "the question of the justification of the injustice of the Universe."

This theme is played out in the characters of J. B. and Sarah. From the beginning, J. B. believes that he is lucky and blessed because he has earned God's favor—that his bounty is a form of justice. When his children are taken away from him violently, one by one, he looks for reasons for his suffering. Although Nickles and Zuss (Satan and God) agree that J. B. is an innocent man who has done nothing to deserve his punishment, J. B. can think only in terms of justice, and so he concludes that he and the children must have sinned. Sarah rejects justice as the reason for their trials. In scene 8, she begs J. B. not to "betray" the children by calling them sinners: "I will not / Let you sacrifice their deaths / To make injustice justice and God good!" When J. B. refuses to listen, she leaves him.

When Sarah returns in scene 11, it is because she has learned that the world, and the humans who love in it, are reason enough to live. She explains to J. B., "You wanted justice, didn't you? / There isn't any. There's the world." She left him, she says, because "I loved you. / I couldn't help you any more. / You wanted justice and there was none—/ Only love."

When MacLeish took *J. B.* to Broadway, he and the director Elia Kazan agreed that for the play to work on stage, J. B. should be the one to settle the conflict between justice and love in the end. In the acting edition, therefore, the last scene was rewritten to give J. B. most of Sarah's final lines and to expand on them. In both versions, it is clear that God does not love humans, and He does not act out of justice or injustice. He simply is. It is humans who have the capacity for love. In a world where blessings and sufferings can not be earned or deserved, people must love each other, or despair.

STYLE

Allusion

When a writer refers to a well-known character or story from the past, either from fiction or nonfiction, that writer is said to be using an allusion. This device works as a kind of shorthand, enabling a writer to convey a lot of information quickly and without explanation, because the reader can be assumed to bring knowledge about and responses to the things alluded to. Clearly, MacLeish's play is at least in part a retelling of the biblical story of Job. There are several parallels between the two stories. The name ''J. B.'' echoes the name ''Job.'' What is more, Sarah, Nickles, and Zuss all sometimes call him by the name Job. The names of J. B.'s comforters in scene 9, Eliphaz, Zophar, and Bildad, are the names of the three comforters in the Biblical story. Although Sarah and the children are not named in the Bible, MacLeish has chosen Biblical names for each of them. The overall story, with the wager between God and Satan and the systematic destruction of all of J. B.'s possessions, echoes the story of Job. Some of the lines are direct quotations from the King James Version of the Bible.

MacLeish—and his characters Zuss and Nickles—expects that the audience is already familiar with the biblical story. When the two circus vendors arrive on the scene, Zuss indicates the stage area and comments, ''That's where Job sits—at the table. / God and Satan lean above.'' Nickles does not ask Zuss who or what he is talking about; he knows the story and knows that the audience knows. In fact, a bit later in scene 1, Nickles summarizes the torments that Job suffered and that J. B. is about to suffer: ''God has killed his sons, his daughters, / Stolen his camels, oxen, sheep, / Everything he has.'' Apparently, MacLeish not only does not mind that his audience knows what is going to happen to J. B.; he insists upon it.

Throughout the play, Zuss and Nickles refer to what is about to happen and occasionally speak directly to the characters to urge them to play—or not to play—their roles as written. When Rebecca's body is found, J. B. tries to utter one of the most well-known lines from the Job story. He is able to get most of the words out (''The Lord giveth . . . the Lord taketh away!''), but even with Zuss's urging he cannot overcome his grief and finish the line (''Blessed be the name of the Lord''). This scene works only if the audience knows the words and knows how the line is supposed to end. The point is not to tell the story, but to retell it and to comment on it, to point out that this story is reenacted over and over again.

Verse

Although he wrote plays and essays and even a screenplay, MacLeish is primarily known as a poet, and he devoted much of his life to studying poetry. *J. B.* is written entirely in verse, which was a common form for English drama in earlier centuries (many of Shakespeare's play, for example, are written in iambic pentameter verse) but extremely rare in the 1950s. When the play did well on Broadway, critics marveled that a play in verse could find an audience. *J. B.* is written in unrhymed four-stress lines without strict meter. In a conversation with college students cast for a production of the play, published as ''MacLeish Speaks to the Players,'' the author explains that ''those four syllables are accented . . . by the sense of the words; if you read the words to *mean,* they will take their right emphasis.''

The effect of the four stresses is subtle at best; it is possible to read the dialogue without paying attention to the sound, and many readers of the text will not hear the rhythm. But when the play is performed, the four-stress line creates an undercurrent that works emotionally on the audience. For MacLeish, this undercurrent was grounded in an essential difference between poetry and prose and between myth and history. In an interview in *Horizon* magazine, he explained that while history is true at a particular place and time, stories like the story of Job are mythical, ''true at any place and time: true then and therefore true forever; true forever and therefore true then.'' Chronological time, therefore, is less important than ''always'' in a drama based on myth, and '''always' exists in poetry rather than prose.''

For secular readers and audiences of the early twenty-first century, drama in verse may seem as exotic as the language of the King James Bible. The language and the four-stress line serve to elevate the drama, to place it in a not-quite-familiar place and time. While the trials J. B. and his family suffer are brutally recognizable even today, the poetry of the lines achieves MacLeish's purpose: it prevents the audience from sinking into familiarity, from seeing J. B.'s story as the story of one individual man.

HISTORICAL CONTEXT

World War II

With the development of new technologies, World War II saw more civilian casualties than any previous war. Bombs from the air could deliver more destructive power than single bullets from a rifle, but they did not kill only soldiers, nor were they intended to. Nickles comments in scene 1 that ''Millions and millions of mankind'' have been ''Burned, crushed, broken, mutilated,'' and he par-

COMPARE
&
CONTRAST

- **1940s:** Major cities in Europe and Japan suffer thousands of casualties in bombings during World War II.

  1950s: Americans live in fear of a nuclear attack.

  2001: Terrorists flying hijacked airplanes crash into the World Trade Center in New York City, into the Pentagon Building in Washington, D.C., and into the ground at another crash site, killing or wounding over 3,000 people. It is the first time the United States has suffered a large number of civilian casualties from attackers from outside the country.

- **1940s:** CBS demonstrates color television in New York City, and WNBT, the first regularly operating television station, debuts in New York with an estimated 10,000 viewers.

  1950s: Some 29 million American homes have television—approximately one in five. Most people still get their news from newspapers.

  Today: Nearly every American home has at least one television, and most have two or more. With twenty-four-hour news channels and the ability to broadcast live from any location, television is the source most Americans turn to for news.

- **1940s:** During World War II, with the United States and the Soviet Union as wartime allies, membership in the American Communist Party reaches an all-time high of 75,000.

  1950s: Communists are hated and feared throughout the United States. Senator Joseph McCarthy investigates alleged Communist activity within the United States and is denounced as a witch-hunter. The fear of a Communist takeover of Vietnam and then the rest of Asia involves the United States in Vietnam.

  Today: The American Communist Party is small, and Communism has lost much of its influence on world politics.

- **1950s:** The United States, the U.S.S.R., and Great Britain have the capability of detonating atomic bombs. Americans build bomb shelters in their homes and practice safety measures to take if a bomb is dropped on them.

  Today: Although more than a dozen nations have nuclear weapons, including several "rogue nations" with unstable, unpredictable governments, Americans largely disregard the threat of nuclear attack.

---

ticularly mentions those who died because they were "Sleeping the wrong night wrong city—/ London, Dresden, Hiroshima." These three cities stand for the thousands of innocent civilians who died on both sides of the war.

London, the capital city of England, was bombed by the Nazis for fifty-eight consecutive days in 1940 and less frequently for the following six months, in the series of raids known as the Blitz. Nearly a third of the city was brought to ruins, and nearly 30,000 Londoners were killed. Dresden was one of the most beautiful cities in Germany, a center for art and culture. In February 1945, six square miles of its downtown were destroyed by Allied bombing, re-

sulting in the deaths of between 35,000 and 135,000 people in two days. Six months later, on August 6, 1945, the first atomic bomb was dropped on the city of Hiroshima, Japan, killing almost 150,000 people.

When World War II ended in 1945, the misery did not end for people who had lived through it, particularly for people who lived in the areas that had been hardest hit by the bombing. MacLeish got the idea for *J. B.* in the late 1940s, when he visited a London suburb that had been nearly flattened by Nazi bombing. There, he met families who had been bombed in one town, moved away, and had been bombed in the new place. Many had lost relatives and friends. The senselessness of their suffering and the increasing human capacity to inflict more suffering troubled him and eventually led to *J. B.*

Cold War

Contrary to the common, nostalgic view that the 1950s was a time of unbroken happiness and prosperity, many people suffered greatly, both inside and outside the United States. World War II had just ended, and many people had lost loved ones and property. The extent of the horrors of the Holocaust was gradually becoming known. In short, the world seemed to many people like a place where suffering and evil were not only possible but present, and without measure.

The Cold War, with the threat of nuclear annihilation, was constantly in the back of many Americans' minds. The term ''Cold War'' referred to the idea that the United States and the Union of Soviet Socialist Republics (USSR) were waging a political and economic battle (not a ''hot'' war with weapons) for influence in the world. As the two ''superpowers'' gained political strength, each also increased its capacity to engage in an armed conflict if necessary. The resulting arms race, in which each side eventually created enough nuclear weapons to destroy the entire planet, left people on both sides of the Cold War feeling not safer but more anxious. Even young people were exposed to the climate of fear. School children were trained to ''duck and cover'' in the event of an atomic bomb threat. As horrible as the destruction caused by World War II had been, the next major war threatened to leave even more misery in its wake.

Renaissance of the Verse Play

Most students are aware that Shakespeare wrote plays in iambic pentameter lines but have come to expect modern drama to be written in simple, conversational language. Some writers have felt, as the poet T. S. Eliot did in the 1930s, that the conventional language of everyday speech is not grand enough to raise important questions. Eliot decided to try to revive the verse play, producing a half dozen dramas in verse including *Murder in the Cathedral* (1935), an historical play about the assassination of the Archbishop of Canterbury in the twelfth century; and *The Cocktail Party* (1950), a combination of drawing room conversation and incantation. Audiences and critics were curious but not enamored of the form. Eliot's plays were profound and thoughtful, but often they were not good drama. *Murder in the Cathedral,* his first verse play, is generally considered his best.

In the late 1940s and early 1950s, other playwrights attempted verse drama. The British playwright Christopher Fry wrote and directed eight plays in verse. Some, including *A Sleep of Prisoners* (1951), were serious, based on religious themes; the verse supported a mystical, ponderous tone. These plays were well regarded by the critics and compared favorably with the earlier work of Eliot. Audiences much preferred Fry's comedies, including *The Lady's Not for Burning* (1948), in which the verse was a vehicle for wit, wordplay, and surprising rhythm. Fry's comedies were the first modern verse plays to be both critical and popular successes. Significantly, Fry was a playwright and director, not a poet, when he turned to this form.

MacLeish was taking a chance when he wrote *J. B.* in verse. He had written two minor radio plays in verse, and he had written hundreds of poems, but he did not have much experience as a playwright. Still, he felt as Eliot and Fry and others before him that the question he was addressing was too large and important to be expressed in prose. When he took the play to Broadway, his director Elia Kazan supervised months of revision because the play as written did not work dramatically. Everyone was surprised that the new version of the play turned out so well; it was assumed that a play based on the Bible and written in verse would draw only a small intellectual audience. Instead, *J. B.* enjoyed a long run on Broadway, won two major awards, and made a lot of money.

It was not the beginning of a trend. Verse plays continue to appear occasionally, but none has matched the success of *J. B.* Even this play, which was a staple of college theatre companies through the 1960s and 1970s, has rarely been performed since.

CRITICAL OVERVIEW

J. B. was something of a sensation in its time, especially because of MacLeish's audacity and deftness in attempting to write verse drama for a modern audience. The play was published as a book months before it was ever performed, and so its first reviewers were readers, not members of an audience. Because MacLeish was well known as a poet, his play in verse received more critical attention in the major newspapers and magazines than it might have otherwise. The poet John Ciardi, in a review titled ''Birth of a Classic,'' written for the *Saturday Review of Literature,* called the play ''great poetry, great drama, and . . . great stagecraft.'' Other critics were more modest in their praise but were largely favorable. After its first production, at Yale University in 1958, the play was selected for the World's Fair at Brussels.

The substantially revised Broadway version of *J. B.* was widely reviewed and much discussed in bars and coffeehouses. The morning after the opening, MacLeish appeared on the *Today* show to talk about the play, and open forums were held after some of the early performances so that religious scholars could debate theology with the playwright. The play won the Pulitzer Prize for drama in 1959 (MacLeish's third Pulitzer), as well as the Tony Award for best play. It had a long run on the British stage and was translated and performed in other European countries as well. Until the early 1980s, the play was frequently performed at colleges and universities, and the book form of the play became MacLeish's best-selling work.

Criticism of the play can be divided roughly into two types: criticism (often negative) that speaks to MacLeish's religious views, reflecting on his treatment and understanding of the biblical story, and criticism (often positive) that speaks to the play as art and reflects on the author's handling of character or language or on the differences between the book and the acting edition of the play. Typical of the first type is "J. B., Wrong Answer to the Problem of Evil,'' written by Martin D'Arcy for *Catholic World.* D'Arcy acknowledges that *J. B.* is "good theater,'' but he concludes that it is bad theology because "In the solution which MacLeish offers, no reference is made to immortality nor to the Christian Cross.'' The conflict is summed up neatly in the title of Preston R. Gledhill's analysis in *Brigham Young University Studies:* "J. B.: Successful Theatre versus 'Godless' Theology.'' Several of these critics have quarreled with MacLeish's interpretation of the Job story, believing that in his retelling he has a duty to be completely faithful to his original source. But in a 1974 article in *Studies in Religion/Sciences Religieuses,* Elizabeth Bieman bemoans "the chasm which separates the humane vision of MacLeish's play from the conservative theology'' and describes several ways in which "MacLeish opens the door to profound mystery.''

Another body of criticism is willing to meet MacLeish on his own terms. They approach the play with the expectation that the author has used the story of Job as a framework for his own work and accept that any variations he may create in his version are conscious choices, not failings to understand. As explained by Thomas E. Porter in *Myth and Modern America Drama,* MacLeish "cannot simply retell the Job story in modern terms. He has to reshape his source so that the message he finds there is translated into dramatic terms for the audience.'' Shannon O. Campbell, who admires MacLeish's adaptation, explicates the differences between the two versions of the story, attributing the variations to the different cultural settings, in *English Journal.* Marion Montgomery, in the journal *Modern Drama,* closely examines the four-stress line and how MacLeish varies the lines to demonstrate character and emotional states. She concludes that much of the verse is effective but that the play overall is not.

The character of J. B. is a subject for discussion. Early audiences surprised MacLeish by finding J. B. unlikable. Daniel Berrigan, in a review for *America,* comments that J. B. is not "marked by depth of character, skill and command in giving point to thought''; rather, he is "a rather simple overdrawn Main Street Type, so pale as to be invisible at noon.'' To Porter, however, J. B. is "the humanist hero, a responsible free agent.''

CRITICISM

Cynthia Bily

Bily is an instructor of writing and literature at Adrian College. In this essay, Bily asks whether the United States in the beginning of the twenty-first century is sadly ripe for a revival of J. B.

Although some pieces of literature feel timeless, like Homer's *Odyssey* or some of the plays of Shakespeare, other perfectly fine works are products of a specific time and place and belong so strongly to that setting that they languish when their time is past. A cursory look at lists of winners of the Pulitzer Prizes or the National Book Awards reveals many works that have stood the test of time: novels and poetry that are still in print, plays that are still performed. Pearl S. Buck's *The Good Earth,* which won the 1932 Pulitzer Prize for fiction; Edward Arlington Robinson's *Collected Poems,* winner of the 1922 Pulitzer Prize for poetry; Ralph Ellison's *Invisible Man,* winner of the 1953 National Book Award for fiction; *A Streetcar Named Desire,* by Tennessee Williams, the 1948 winner of the Pulitzer Prize for drama. Other names have disappeared from our collective awareness, known to scholars but not frequently sought out by readers and directors: the poets Alan Dugan and Leonora Speyer, the novelists J. F. Powers and Julia Peterkin, the plays *Miss Lulu Bett* and *Craig's Wife*.

Archibald MacLeish's play *J. B.* has seemed, for at least two decades, like one of the forgotten works, destined to be read occasionally in English classes but overlooked by serious scholars and producers. A search of the *Modern Language Association Bibliography* database turns up only two articles about the play in the 1980s and none since. Although the play enjoyed a long run on Broadway in 1958 and 1959 and twenty years as a staple of college theatre companies, it has been infrequently performed since MacLeish's death in 1982.

Ten years after the Broadway opening, when the reviewers were done with the play and the literary critics took over, *J. B.* was hailed as a play of its own time. Murray Roston included *J. B.* in his discussion of *Biblical Drama in England* and explained why the Bible was a sensible source for MacLeish: "In the mid-twentieth century, the obliteration of Hiroshima provided the most glaring modern instance of such indiscriminate slaughter, the Bible had reached the nadir of its sanctity, and the time was ripe for a new surge of interest in its themes, and particularly in the Jobian quest translated into modern terms." In 1970, Sy Kahn located the play squarely in the 1950s, when "writers reverberated to the impact of the events of World War II and especially to the accumulating evidence of Nazi persecution and extermination programs, and these events sharpened the points of the old, excruciating questions." He concluded that *J. B.* was "a play right for MacLeish, right for a post-war and war-fearing world, right for America in mid-century." More recently, in 1982, Richard Calhoun looked back on the play and its reception, commenting that "In my view MacLeish intended to give his audience an American version of *Job* appropriate for the 1950s, a decade not as blandly idyllic as that popular TV series *Happy Days* made it appear. This was a time of a cold war that became a small but fierce hot war in Korea. It was a decade of suspicion and of communist witch-hunting. . . . *J. B.* was written at a time for serious questions about the human costs of mid-twentieth-century destruction and whether under such conditions it was possible to have a belief in life."

Calhoun's use of the past tense is telling. Over the next twenty years, the world underwent drastic

Playbill cover from the 1959 theatrical production of J. B.

changes, socially and politically. The Berlin Wall came down, and the Cold War came to an end. Wars were fought far away, "cleanly," with precision missiles that in theory hit only their targets. Americans enjoyed a strong economy and peace at home. Although membership in Bible-based organized churches was growing, the United States was determined to maintain a separation of church and state and was growing increasingly uneasy with professions of faith and references to the Bible in public.

How could one best approach *J. B.* in the new century, when things seemed to be going so well. What would North American students understand about J. B.'s suffering and his need to make sense of it? What would they know of World War II or of living in a climate of fear and suspicion? What would they make of Nickles's bitterness and anger or of J. B.'s search for justice? The answers to these questions came when the events of September 11, 2001, made *J. B.* horribly relevant again.

The play centers on the character of J. B., a good, decent, upright man. He is wealthy and part of a loving family; he has been blessed by God, and he is grateful to God. He is also largely unaware of the lives of other less fortunate people, although neither

WHAT DO I READ NEXT?

- MacLeish draws heavily on the Book of Job, part of the Old Testament, for the basic plot and some of his characters' names. The italicized lines in the printed version of *J. B.,* spoken by Nickles, Zuss, and others, are quoted from the King James Version, first published in 1611.

- *Collected Poems, 1917–1952* (1952) was MacLeish's second Pulitzer Prize–winning book. The poems in this volume demonstrate MacLeish's range, from public to personal voice and from political to intimate themes.

- In *Songs for Eve* (1954), MacLeish draws on the biblical story of Adam and Eve's Fall and their eviction from the Garden of Eden, as he draws on the story of Job for *J. B.* Here, Eve is glad to have left Eden because the knowledge of mortality makes her feel more alive.

- The script for the play, as it was performed on Broadway in 1958, is available as *J. B.: A Play in Verse,* published by Samuel French, Inc. MacLeish and the director Elia Kazan collaborated on several substantive changes to make the play more effective dramatically and to resolve philosophical issues that Kazan felt were troublesome in MacLeish's original book.

- In the novel *The Red Badge of Courage* (1895), Stephen Crane's protagonist, Henry Fleming, sees horror and destruction as a soldier in the American Civil War and comes to wonder how God can allow such evil to exist.

Zuss nor Nickles blames him for this. J. B. appreciates what he has been given and enjoys it fully, but there is no sense that he is aware that on a chilly Thanksgiving Day there are people outside sleeping on a grate. MacLeish was said to have been taken aback when some critics pointed out that they found the man J. B. unlikable, self-satisfied. Nickles cannot stop thinking about:

> Millions and millions of mankind /
> Burned, crushed, broken, mutilated, /
> Slaughtered, and for what? For thinking! /
> For walking around the world in the wrong /
> Skin, the wrong-shaped noses, eyelids: /
> Sleeping the wrong night wrong city— /
> London, Dresden, Hiroshima. /
> There never could have been so many /
> Suffered more for less.

Why is J. B. oblivious?

One reason *J. B.* languished for several years is that it has not seemed urgent. Like J. B., Americans (at least that portion of the population that attends plays) have been largely protected from catastrophe. London, Dresden, and Hiroshima were long ago. More recent suffering in Cambodia and Rwanda and Bangladesh was far away. MacLeish's original

audiences were afraid, but audiences in the 1990s were not.

Of course, suffering does reach J. B. He loses his children one by one, the last in a bombing. This is the event that pushes Sarah over the brink into despair. She was one of those who were pulled from the wreckage. Someone "heard her underneath a wall / Calling" the name of her last daughter, Ruth, who died in the explosion. When he wrote the images, MacLeish was remembering what he had heard of the Blitz, but today's readers will picture the countless scenes, played over and over on TV, of people pulled from the wreckage, living or dead, in Oklahoma City, in New York City, in Washington, D.C. Nickles predicts that when J. B. suffers as Sarah has, not just seeing her children killed but herself physically injured, when J. B.'s body "hurts him—once / Pain has penned him in," he will despair and reject God.

Sarah rejects J. B. when he will not curse God. She leaves him and goes "Among the ashes. / All there is now of the town is ashes. / Mountains of ashes. / Shattered glass. / Glittering cliffs of glass all shattered." Nickles is disgusted by J. B. when he actually *thanks* God for his punishment. In the end, J. B. chooses life, though he does not know how he will live it, and it is Sarah who shows him how.

The tensions in the United States today make Americans ready, in a way that they have not been for twenty years, to contemplate the questions so large that MacLeish could not stop asking them. When people suffer, when they die, when they are afraid, how can they go on? When the forces that act on them are beyond their comprehension, how can they support each other? If the answers to these essential questions are not found in psychiatry or politics or religion, where are they? Why don't we all follow Nickles's advice and take a rope, or take "a window for a door?" Is MacLeish's answer, that there is no justice but there is love, sufficient?

These questions had people talking all night in 1958, arguing in the newspapers, shouting out comments in the theatre. Complacency put the questions to bed for awhile, but many of them are being voiced again, on talk shows, on the twenty-four-hour news channels, in church services and coffeeshops. The *Doonesbury* cartoon by Gary Trudeau that ran in newspapers on October 5, 2001, had Boopsie asking, "What kind of God allows such terrible suffering and death?" When *J. B.* was new, critics and reviewers argued over MacLeish's answers to big questions. With the North American corner of the world in turmoil, the old questions seem new again.

It will remain the work of historians, sociologists, political scientists, and religious scholars to sort out who was innocent and who was guilty on the day of the terrorist attacks in New York and Washington, D.C., and all the days leading up to it, and all the days after. As J. B. does, a person or a country might cry out for justice, but there is none. Sarah learns about justice and explains to J. B., "Cry for justice and the stars / Will stare until your eyes sting. Weep, / Enormous winds will thrash the water." In a way that the Americans have recently been reminded, the world is a big place full of ungovernable forces, security is fragile, and innocent people do suffer. As Zuss says at the beginning of *J. B.*, "there's always / Someone playing Job."

Source: Cynthia Bily, Critical Essay on *J. B.,* in *Drama for Students,* The Gale Group, 2002.

James L. McWilliams III

In the following essay excerpt, McWilliams discusses MacLeish's play and its resemblance to the Book of Job.

> IN THE END, J. B. CHOOSES LIFE, THOUGH HE DOES NOT KNOW HOW HE WILL LIVE IT, AND IT IS SARAH WHO SHOWS HIM HOW."

Commercially and critically, MacLeish earned the great bulk of his reputation as playwright with *J. B.* Originally staged by the Yale School of Drama in April 1958, *J. B.* played at the Brussels World's Fair in September and opened at the ANTA Theatre in New York on 11 December 1958. After a run of 364 performances, the play closed on 24 October 1959. In published form, *J. B.* was a best-seller and translated into many foreign languages. Later productions were mounted in many nations including England, France, Egypt, Israel, and Mexico.

Essentially the Book of Job transplanted into the twentieth century, *J. B.* asks how man, with dignity and hope, can love and serve a god who allows so much evil to exist in the world. The action unfolds under a giant circus tent, recreating the universe-as-big-top analogy earlier seen in MacLeish's own poem "The End of the World." As a play-within-a-play, *J. B.* begins with the entrance of two ragtag gentlemen named Mr. Zuss and Nickles. The pair discover and don masks of God and Satan, thus setting the inner play into motion. For the rest of the play Zuss and Nickles each fulfill a dual role, one deified and one human. Together they act as a Greek chorus, both taking part in and commenting upon the action of the play, Zuss as orthodox believer and Nickles as rebellious cynic.

When we first see Job's modern counterpart, J. B., he is celebrating Thanksgiving with his wife and children. Prosperous and happy, J. B. is overflowing with love of God. Then, the senseless misfortunes begin. One son is killed overseas in an absurd accident following the Armistice. One daughter is brutally raped and murdered by a sexual psychopath. Two other children die in a gruesome automobile accident. The last child perishes when J. B.'s bank is bombed. In each case, the news is borne to J. B. by callous messengers—drunken soldiers, photographers with glaring flashbulbs, raincoated policemen, and steel-helmeted civil defense officers. J. B. himself is stricken with boils and, with his wife Sarah, left the pitiful survivor of an atomic blast. Sarah, however, soon leaves, urging J. B. to denounce God and surrender life. As the first half of the play comes to a close, J. B., wounded and bewildered, cries out: "Show me my guilt, O God!" God responds with agonizing silence.

In the second half comes the parade of comforters, giving no comfort at all. Bildad expounds Marxist jargon about collective humanity. Eliphaz, a Freudian psychiatrist, talks about guilt as an illusion. Finally, Zophar, a theologian, argues that guilt is an inevitable part of being human. J. B. rejects panaceas of all the comforters but finds the words of Zophar most cruel because they imply a gamester-God who creates sin to punish sin. With nothing left to do, J. B. simply restates his faith and trust in God. This time God answers, in the form of a distant, disembodied voice over the public address system. But to J. B.'s surprise, God speaks only to question him and rebuke him for his presumptuousness in trying to instruct the Lord. In MacLeish's words, J. B. "has not been answered at all—he has merely been silenced." Humbled by God's chiding, J. B. repents. Not long after, Sarah returns to him out of love and together they resolve to begin a new world.

This was the version of *J. B.* staged at Yale University. Before the play reached New York, however, it underwent a significant metamorphosis, mostly at the behest of director Elia Kazan. The multiscene structure of the original gave way to a more conventional two-act form. Zuss and Nickles, segregated from the J. B. scenes in the Yale version, were more fully incorporated into the total action of the play. Most significant, especially in terms of later critical opinion, was the addition of what Kazan called a recognition scene, in which J. B. rejects both complacent ignorance and cynicism in facing the ills of the world. Instead, he finds hope and salvation inside himself, inside the human heart, saying to his wife: "The candles in the church are out. / The lights have gone out in the sky! / Blow on the coal of the heart / And we'll see by and by. . . ." From a solid majority of the critics, *J. B.* harvested high praise. John Gassner called it an "exalted work of the dramatic and poetic imagination in a generally commonplace theatre." John Ciardi of the *Saturday Review* called it "great poetry, great drama, and . . . great stagecraft" and added, "the poetry and the drama are organically one." Dudley Fitts, mixing prophecy with praise, wrote: "A passionate work, composed with great art . . . a signal contribution to the small body of modern poetic drama, and it may very well turn out to be an enduring one."

Citing the emotional power of the play, Samuel Terrien of the *Christian Century* observed that even "the most blase audience submits to the spell in an almost unbearable experience of empathy." Finally, Brooks Atkinson, writing for the *New York Times,* said: "It portrays in vibrant verse the spiritual dilemma of the twentieth century."

Transforming a familiar story, however, invites comparison with the original, and here the critics butted heads. In the view of Henry Hewes, *J. B.* "adds precious little to what has already been said more beautifully in the Bible." In a more orthodox vein, another spokesman for *Christian Century* concluded: "While Mr. MacLeish's drama is a brilliant recreation of the story of Job, the character of J. B. is completely foreign to that of the hero who speaks in the biblical poem." Joseph Wood Krutch disagreed with both of these critics, saying: "MacLeish's interpretation is strong and interesting, neither merely repeating what the biblical drama says nor perverting it into something else."

Without doubt, the religious implications of the recognition scene in *J. B.* stirred the greatest controversy and inspired the most biting detractions. Scores of critics, religious and secular, agreed with Martin D'Arcy of *Catholic World* that "evil cannot be solved within us; help and grace must come from outside, from a God." As Brooks Atkinson added, "a declaration of individual independence from God differs from cursing God only in degree, and it weakens the force of the purity of J. B.'s character." Henry Van Dusen alone came to MacLeish's defense in the matter of religious doctrine, arguing in Christian Century after the detractors had spoken: "If MacLeish has recourse to human integrity and human love for the answer to J. B.'s need, it is, again, because the biblical Job offers him nothing beyond obeisance before an arbitrary and heartless Cosmic Power." All critics concurred on one final point: *J. B.* was a genuine rarity—a commercially successful religious verse play.

Source: James L. McWilliams III, "Archibald MacLeish," in *Dictionary of Literary Biography,* Vol. 7: *Twentieth-Century American Dramatists, Part 2: K–Z,* Gale Research, 1981, pp. 58–61.

Signi Lenea Falk

In the following essay excerpt, Falk examines J. B. *within the context of the morality play, focusing on similarities between it and the story of Job in the Bible.*

Writing in 1955, MacLeish rejected T. S. Eliot's statement that no play should be written in verse if prose were ''dramatically adequate.'' He answered Eliot by saying that prose is adequate for an illusion of the actual; but, if the dramatist is concerned with the ''illusion of the real,'' then he is concerned with ''the illusion which dramatic poetry can pursue.'' He gave as examples ''the illusion of Oedipus apart from the plot,'' or ''the metaphor of Prospero's island,'' or ''Yeats' Purgatory,'' or *Hamlet* which offers ''a perception of the nature of the human heart.'' Only poetry creates an illusion which can foster an understanding by the mind, by the emotions, and by the senses—that is, by the whole being.

In the undergraduate verse in *Tower of Ivory* (1917) MacLeish was concerned with man's interpretation of God and with the meaning of human experience. In the early poetic drama *Nobodaddy* (1925), he reflected an interest in Blake's attitudes toward conventional religion and morality. In that early play the serpent tempted Adam to raise questions and to use his power of reason. This same voice, more fully developed in Cain, made him ask what kind of God demands sacrifice of the trusting and destroys the innocent. The sonnet ''End of the World'' as well as parts of *Einstein* (1926) and *The Hamlet of A. MacLeish* (1928), also questioned the place of man in an indifferent universe. Another kind of callousness—a human kind of indifference—was reflected by the Announcer to the suffering of the village inhabitants in *Air Raid* (1939). The pattern of thought to be found in these earlier poems and plays is more fully developed in the play about the modern Job.

MacLeish compounded problems for himself when he set out to recast the Old Testament poem into a modern drama. The Book of Job is one of the most controversial in the Bible. The text itself raises innumerable problems. Because of the nature of the contestants, man against God and Satan, there can be no real dramatic conflict. The extended arguments between Job and the three comforters, which consume the major part of the Bible story, are not material for drama. After the terrible sufferings of Job, his restoration at the end negates any possibility of the poem as tragedy in the usual sense of the term.

MacLeish turned to the Book of Job to raise questions about the nature of a God who would consent without cause to the destruction of a good man, the killing of all his children, and the infliction of physical suffering upon him. MacLeish seems

> " MACLEISH TURNED TO THE BOOK OF JOB TO RAISE QUESTIONS ABOUT THE NATURE OF A GOD WHO WOULD CONSENT WITHOUT CAUSE TO THE DESTRUCTION OF A GOOD MAN, THE KILLING OF ALL HIS CHILDREN, AND THE INFLICTION OF PHYSICAL SUFFERING UPON HIM."

to be raising questions whether this concept of God—the God of the Old Testament, the God of Vengeance—belongs to a world in which Germans murdered millions of Jews in gas chambers and Americans destroyed Japanese at Hiroshima and Nagasaki. ''Good'' Germans and ''good'' Americans, indifferent about their own guilt, obviously need to find another image of God, and of goodness, one that incorporates love with a sense of responsibility, one that can unite a compassion for others with a concern for the individual spirit. MacLeish, as he has asked other poets to do, seems to be casting off a metaphor that belongs to the past and to be seeking a new metaphor for our own time.

As the framework for *J. B.* MacLeish returned to the image he used in the early sonnet, ''The End of the World'', in which man's life is likened to a circus performance, his universe indifferent and meaningless. *J. B.* is very much like a morality play. It also a play within a play: two broken-down, ham-actors—one wearing the God mask, the other the Satan mask—observe and comment upon the lives and misfortunes of an American family. The stage is bare except for a low platform on which J. B.'s family act out their story; the stage level represents the earth upon which Satan walks to and fro, and an elevation to the right suggests heaven. During the first part of the play, a huge circus tent covers the acting area. It is like the protection of a friendly universe, or perhaps the inherited beliefs about a friendly universe. During the last part of the play, this tent disappears; its absence gives the effect of exposing J. B. completely to indifference and meaninglessness. Scattered around the stage are what seem to be vestments of several times and churches. Even the God mask and the Satan mask,

Mr. Zuss and Mr. Nickles, seem to be relics of the past, to be parodies of man's sometime religious experience.

Mr. Zuss is an imposing, deep-voiced man of "magnificent deliberation" suitable to play a God who never laughs, who sees nothing wrong with the arrangement of the world. Nickles says that the "blank, beautiful, expressionless mask with eyes lidded like the eyes of the mask in Michelangelo's Night" belongs to God and the Creator of animals. He says God fumbled Job when He gave him a mind, made him grateful, and made him think "there should be justice somewhere." When Mr. Zuss answers that "Demanding justice of God" is rank irreverence, Nickles retorts that God's reasons are for animals, not for men.

Nickles, who plays "the opposite," traditionally called Father of Lies, but whom Zuss sneeringly describes as "the honest, disillusioned man," feels sympathy for J. B., a man given the light of reason but deprived of the answers. When Mr. Zuss indifferently observes that there is always someone playing Job, Nickles agrees; but he is appalled by the frequency:

> There must be
> Thousands! What's that got to do with it?
> Thousands—not with camels either:
> Millions and millions of mankind
> Burned, crushed, broken, mutilated,
> Slaughtered, and for what? For thinking!
> For walking round the world in the wrong
> Skin, the wrong-shaped noses, eyelids:
> Sleeping the wrong night wrong city—
> London, Dresden, Hiroshima.
> There never could have been so many
> Suffered more for less.

In answer to Mr. Zuss's indifference, Nickles reiterates that Job is everywhere.

Nickles' mask is dark in contrast to Zuss's white one, and it is open-eyed: *"The eyes, though wrinkled with laughter, seem to stare and the mouth is drawn down in agonized disgust."* According to Zuss, it is the traditional image of evil, or of spitefulness, an echo from "some subterranean memory probably." Nickles answers that it is not an expression of evil, but of disgust: "Look at those lips: they've tasted something / Bitter as a broth of blood." Zuss's mask has a look of "cold complacence"; Nickles', one of pity. When Zuss rebukes Nickles for laughing, for being irreverent to God, Nickles retorts that, having seen, he cannot laugh. Having seen the world, he says, "I know what Hell is now—to *see.* / Consciousness of consciousness."

Nickles repeats that it is not the little Freudian insights but the sickening rape of innocence that

> Satan *sees.*
> He sees the parked car by the plane tree.
> He sees behind the fusty door,
> Beneath the rug, those almost children
> Struggling on the awkward seat—
> Every impossible delighted dream
> She's ever had of loveliness, of wonder,
> Spilled with her garters to the filthy floor.
> Absurd despair! Ridiculous agony!
> What has any man to laugh at!

For Zuss, the Job story is a simple scene; and, unaware of Nickles' perception of the suffering involved, he directs him to play his part. These two old actors, modifications of Good and Evil, are not only rivals for supremacy but for domination over this rich American banker, the current Job.

J. B., the twentieth-century Job, is a New England millionaire who with his attractive wife Sarah and their five children—David, thirteen; Mary, twelve; Jonathon, ten; Ruth, eight; Rebecca, six— celebrate an abundant, happy Thanksgiving. The euphoric J. B. has ridden the crest of good luck; his business, his family, and his friends seem never to have created any problems. Sarah, nagged by a conscience that demands verbalized thanks and humility before God, expresses the simple, conventional faith that, if man does his part, God will not forget. J. B., intuitive like his children, glories in the grace of God. He never doubted that God was on his side. Sarah's God, who punishes and rewards, is just; but she fears her "happiness impending like a danger." The spirit of this opening scene is one of innocence, goodness, and optimism; no chastening experience has ever made this banker question the meaning of his life.

Zuss and Nickles recognize this J. B. as their pigeon, the good man to be tested to prove a point— "the victim of a spinning joke," as Nickles calls it. From their point of view, he is a lousy actor. They spar over concepts of piety among the poor and among the rich. When Zuss asserts that "God will show him what God *is* . . . Infinite mind in midge of matter!" Nickles caustically asks why J. B. must suffer. "To praise!" answers Zuss. Nickles deplores man's credulity, his certainty that he "Is born into the bright delusion / Beauty and loving-kindness care for him." When he rejects the concept that suffering teaches, Zuss asserts that man can best see God from the ash heap. Nickles answers that "A human / Face would shame the mouth that said that!"

They put on their masks and in "magnified and hollow voices" repeat the Biblical wager over "*A perfect and upright man, one / That fearest God and escheweth evil!*" Satan mask taunts his rival with the proposition that this good man, deprived of all his good fortune, would rise and curse him. The God mask, furious, "his arm thrown out in a gesture of contemptuous commitment," gives his man over to the Satan mask: "*All that he hath is in thy power!*" Suddenly the Distant Voice prompts the faltering actor to finish his lines: "*Only / Upon himself / Put not forth thy hand!*"

Messengers appropriate to each tragedy report to the parents what has happened, and both the ham-actors and the audience watch their reactions. These several tragedies are reported without emotion; the repeatedly senseless destruction of innocence makes the bargain between the God and the Satan masks increasingly horrible. Sarah rebels, as she does in the Biblical story, against this ruthlessness; but J. B. does not question God's plan. The vividly described deaths of the children make the yea-saying of J. B. difficult to accept and account for some of the questions about the characterization.

In the first of these scenes two drunken, foul-mouthed soldiers, welcomed by J. B. and Sarah as David's friends, bumble words about the war's end, an unaccountable order given, the absence of "the right length of lumber." Nickles, watching the stunned parents and hearing J. B. assuring himself that it couldn't happen to him and his wife, jeers at this "pigeon's" credulity: "Couldn't it? Suppose it did though: / What would the world be made of then?"

In the next scene the two messengers are newsmen with camera and notebook, and with them is a girl, the society editor, who protests, "I wish I was home in bed with a good / Boy or something. I don't like it." Her part is to keep the parents talking until "a flash bulb / Smacks them naked in the face— / It's horrible!" The newsman, indifferent to the suffering of the parents, only thinks of his chance for a prize story:

How do I get the
Look a mother's face has maybe
Once in a lifetime: just before
Her mouth knows, when her eyes are knowing?

The second newsman makes the report: four kids in a car—two of them J. B.'s son and daughter, Jonathon and Mary—the drunk kid was driving seventy or seventy-five. Sarah, moving like a sleepwalker, asks, "Why did He do it to them? / What had they done to Him—those children ... What had *we* done?" J. B. answers that they have to take the evil with the good: "It doesn't mean there / *Is* no good!" Nickles prompts, "Doesn't it?" Sarah rejects J. B.'s certainty.

Nickles taunts Zuss about the way "a perfect and upright man" learns God's purpose for him. Zuss indifferently observes, "He can't act and you know it." Nickles, the Satan mask, which wears a look of pity, answers the God mask: "He doesn't have to act. He suffers. / It's an old role—played like a mouth-organ." Cynically, he remarks that what Job needs to see is "That bloody drum-stick striking; / See Who lets it strike the drum!"

In the scene that follows, the messengers are two policemen making their early morning report. They identify the youngest of the four children, Rebecca, as the little girl dressed in white, with red shoes and a red toy umbrella; they puzzle over the enigma of why the potter worked equally in worthies and monsters. One policeman finally blurts out the story to the parents: just past midnight they stumbled upon a big nineteen-year-old, "Hopped to the eyes and scared." They ordered him to take them to "it." Their suspicions were justified when they found the little girl's body. As J. B., holding the child's red parasol, speaks brokenly, "The Lord giveth ... the Lord taketh away," the two masks argue over their "pigeon." Zuss asks why he won't act; Nickles answers that he isn't playing, "He's where we all are—in our suffering. / Only ... (*Nickles turns savagely on Mr. Zuss.*) Now he knows its Name!"

In the next catastrophe the messengers in steel helmets and brassards return with Sarah, who had been looking for her lost child, Ruth, in the bombed ruins. J. B.'s millions, the bank, the whole block are gone; only a floor remains. Still believing that he shares desperation with God, he tries to make Sarah repeat after him, his certainty, "The Lord giveth—" She rebels and shrieks, "Takes! / Kills! Kills! Kills! Kills!" J. B. answers, "Blessed be the name of the Lord."

Mr. Zuss preens over the yea-saying of J. B., but Nickles is disgusted over man's insensitivity to others' suffering; to Nickles it is indecent to be thankful when twenty thousand have been suffocated in a bombed-out town. He resents the hideous, senseless deaths of the children: "And all with God's consent!—foreknowledge!— / And he blesses God!" God, not content with this victory—according to Nickles—overreaches himself to demand "the proof of pain." When Mr. Zuss chants the equation that man's will is God's peace, Nickles retorts, "Will is rule: surrender is surrender. / You *make* your peace; you don't give in to it." Nickles seems to cling to the belief that, when man is himself trapped in pain, he will learn to "Spit the dirty world out—spit." Nickles insists that, "when his suffering is *him*," he will not praise. As they put on their masks for the next test, the old Biblical words flood over them. The Distant Voice repeats the lines, concluding

> And still he holdeth fast his integrity . . .
> Although thou movedst me against him
> To destroy him . . .
> without cause . . .

The God-shadow raises its arm again *"in the formal gesture of contemptuous commitment"* and intones the words: "Behold he is in thine hand . . . but . . . Save his life!"

When the modern J. B. is revealed as the one pitiful survivor of an atomic blast, Nickles cackles to Zuss that, as usual, he has blundered: "Tumbled a whole city down / To blister one man's skin with agony." A few women and a girl sarcastically comment on the sufferings of the rich they have known only through news pictures and review without feeling the catastrophes. J. B., though raising questions about the blindness, the meaninglessness of what has happened, clings to the belief that God is just, that he himself is guilty. Sarah says that, if God demands deception, she will not buy quiet with her children's innocence:

> They are
> Dead and they were innocent: I will not
> Let you sacrifice their deaths
> To make injustice justice and God good!

When in her anguish she urges J. B. to "curse God and die" and then leaves him, he insists, "We have no choice but to be guilty. / God is unthinkable if we are innocent." When in his agony he prays to God to show him his guilt, Nickles caustically prompts Zuss to bring on the cold comforters "Who justify the ways of God to / Job by making Job responsible."

The major part of the Biblical poem is the extended dialogue with the three comforters; the modern playwright, by involving the audience in the violent deaths of the children, increased the difficulties of maintaining dramatic tension in the latter part of the play. He must try to give dramatic form to philosophical material: ideas about guilt and innocence, about suffering and responsibility, about the relationship between man and the forces of good and evil. MacLeish adapted the three comforters

into approximations of three phases of modern society: Zophar, a fat priest; Eliphaz, a lean psychiatrist in a dirty interne's jacket; and Bildad, a Marxist, a thick short man in a ragged windbreaker.

They present three different opinions on the question of guilt. To Marxist Bildad the suffering of one is not significant because what matters is not justice for one man but justice for humanity. History is not concerned with the guilt of one man: "Guilt is a sociological accident: / Wrong class—wrong century—" To Eliphaz, the psychiatrist, "Guilt is a / Psychophenomenal situation— / An illusion, a disease, a sickness": All men are victims of their own guilt even though they may be ignorant of it. J. B. rejects this idea of "an irresponsible ignorance" as the cause of his suffering, for he needs to know that he "earned the need to suffer."

Zophar, the priest, says the guilt idea is necessary to man's quality as a human being, otherwise he would vanish as do the animals: "our souls accept / Eternities of reparation." When J. B. wants to be shown his guilt, Zophar elaborates upon the "deceptive secret" of guilt that may have been "conceived in infancy." J. B. tells the priest that, until he knows the reasons for his suffering, even until death he will not violate his integrity. Zophar cynically answers that J. B.'s sin was to be born a man; to be a man is to have a will and a heart that is evil, both "Corrupted with its foul imagining." J. B. rejects the priest's answer as the most cruel of the three because it makes God "the miscreator of mankind."

Still hoping for some justification for his suffering, J. B. repeats his trust in God. The Distant Voice, the Voice out of the Whirlwind, poses a series of questions to J. B. concerning the powers of God and the wonders of His creation; the Distant Voice for the second time rebukes J. B. for trying to instruct God; and the third time, again in a series of questions, the Distant Voice rebukes man for his presumptuousness: *"Wilt thou disannul my judgment? . . . Wilt thou condemn / Me that thou mayest be righteous? / Hast thou an arm like God? Or canst thou / Thunder with a voice like Him?"* J. B. humbly concedes the omnipotence of God, confesses to having spoken without knowledge, abhors himself and repents.

In the original version of the play, in the scene following this "repentance," Zuss uncomfortably asks Nickles how J. B. voiced his repentance, and whether he did it for God or for himself. A scene very important in the development of the experience of Job is thus presented second-hand. At the end of this scene, in very few lines and very briefly, J. B. rejects Nickles' suggestion of self-annihilation. This affirmation of life is followed by the return of Sarah and by a brief lyrical expression of human love. In this original version there is no scene in which J. B. is made to reveal what he has learned from experience, a scene very much needed in the play and one necessary for the interpretation which MacLeish gives to the Job legend. This so-called "recognition scene" was developed during the rehearsals and was substituted for the original and weaker one.

In the Broadway version J. B., thinking over the magnificent words of God about his own right hand and its power to save him, lifts to his face the scrofulous hand. Zuss, as if he were prompting his suffering victim in order to encourage him in the belief that only in the fear of God lies true repentance and his only comfort, hears J. B. repeat the vow that he abhors himself and repents. Nickles, sickened by what he calls a forced repentance because God threw at J. B. the whole creation, rages that J. B. has forgotten what happened to his little children. In his disgust over the choice that God offered, he thinks it dubious triumph that J. B. swallowed the world rather than rejecting it. Zuss petulantly asks whether or not God is to be forgiven. Nickles with supreme insolence asks, "Isn't he?"

As Nickles turns away, Zuss reminds him of the final scene in the Bible poem no matter who plays Job. He accuses his cynical opposite of not having the stamina to finish his part in the play. Nickles replies that the restoration illustrates God's mercy to man who never asked to be born. He refuses to believe that J. B. will begin all over again, risk again "all that filth and blood and / Fury . . ." The acting version portrays more clearly J. B.'s resolution. As he brings himself to his feet, his voice strong and firm, J. B. asks:

> Must I be
> Dumb because my mouth is mortal?—
> Blind because my eyes will one day
> Close forever? Is that my wickedness—
> That I am weak?

The two masks are stunned by what they hear, incredulous that J. B. should ask if his breathing should be forgiven. Nickles, sensing an advantage, answers, "Not this generation, Mister." Professing to be not the Father but the Friend, he tries to impress upon J. B. that death is not the worst alternative; the worst is having to relive all the senseless suffering. He reminds him of the millions who refused the second chance, who found a con-

venient means to end it all. None of those, says Nickles, knew what J. B. does: "Job's truth." Desperately Nickles tries to negate God's gift by saying that Job would rather take the filthiest kind of death than live his suffering life all over again.

When J. B. rejects Nickles, Zuss is triumphant. Zuss then restates the position implied by the Distant Voice that there is no resolution to the problem of "unintelligible suffering" but submission to the divine will. But J. B. also sternly rejects this pattern of submissive acceptance:

> I will not
> Duck my head again to thunder—
> That bullwhip cracking at my ears!—although
> He kills me with it. I must know.

When Mr. Zuss, astonished over what he has heard, repeats his theme that there is no peace except in obedience, J. B. defiantly answers both the Satan and the God masks: "I'll find a foothold somewhere *knowing.*" He vows he will not laugh at life's filthy farce nor weep among the obedient and the meek, "protesting / Nothing, questioning nothing, asking / Nothing but to rise again and / bow!"

In the final scene Sarah, who had told her husband to "curse God and die," returns to J. B. because of her love for him. These stricken people, whose experience has shown that they are alone in an indifferent universe and that they can be sure only of their human love for each other, determine to begin their lives again. Depending not on the kind of a God who will destroy children for no reason, nor on churches where the candles have gone out, they will continue to seek the answers—to know. This conviction is stated by J. B. at the close of the play:

> The one thing certain in this hurtful world
> Is love's inevitable heartbreak.
> What's the future but the past to come
> Over and over, love and loss,
> What's loved most lost most.

In the final lines J. B. expresses the human capacity for suffering and, in spite of the inexplicable, the strength to continue to live and to love:

> And yet again and yet again
> In doubt, in dread, in ignorance, unanswered,
> Over and over, with the dark before,
> The dark behind it . . . and still live . . . still love.

MacLeish explained that he saw in the Job poem a relation to our own time, a time of "inexplicable sufferings" when millions were destroyed because of their race or because they lived in a certain city. He suggests that God delivered Job into Satan's hands "Because God had need of the suffering of Job." In the struggle between God and Satan,

"God stakes his supremacy as God upon man's fortitude and love." It is man alone who can prove that man loves God; only man, by his persistence, can overcome Satan, of the kingdom of death, and love God, of the kingdom of life. Without man's love, God is only a creator. It is in man's love, says MacLeish, that God exists and triumphs; in man's love that life is beautiful; in man's love that the world's injustice is resolved. "Our labor always, like Job's, is to learn through suffering to love—to love even that which lets us suffer."

The religious implications in *J. B.* aroused considerable controversy. Charles A. Fenton commented on the original production at Yale: "The notion that the individual is superior to God—is not critically palatable to the institutionalized." Tom F. Driver, after the Broadway production, described the play as suffering "from a sort of theological schizophrenia" because it began on what he thought a high religious plane and ended on a purely Humanistic one. Theodore A. Webb, who disagreed with Driver, said that MacLeish began the play on a Humanistic level when he depicted broken-down "ham-actors" as gods. Samuel Terrien wrote that "The Joban poet deals with the problem of faith in an evil world, while the author of *J. B.* presents modern man's reaction to the problem of evil without the category of faith in a loving God." He described Job as almost "an incarnation of an anti-God," but he also thought of him as an emasculated, piously conventional victim of fate who rarely rises above an intellectual stupor. Henry P. Van Dusen took issue with both Driver and Terrien. He considered the three comforters to be a brilliant and sound translation into the realities of our time. He did not find, as did Terrien, "an intelligent, eternal and gracious Power" in a God whose last words begin, "Who is this that darkeneth counsel by words without knowledge?" Richard Hayes summarized the varied opinions expressed for and against the play and added his own reservations: "cultural piety demands each year its raw meat of sustenance." Reinhold Niebuhr praised MacLeish's honest statement of the problem and his ingenuity in adapting the ancient poem to modern times. He felt that the emphasis on meaningless suffering led to the neglect of the more searching question in the Book of Job about the meaning of life and thus the "message" to contemporary man: for instance, the paradox of man's capacity to discover nuclear energy and his lack of wisdom in its use. Niebuhr pointed out that MacLeish does provide two answers to modern man: he repeats the voice out of the

"Whirlwind" contrasting the greatness of God's creation and man's limitations; he also states his "courageous acceptance and affirmation of life with a modern romantic emphasis on love."

J. B., published by Houghton Mifflin, March, 1958, was first produced by the Yale School of Drama on April 22, 1958; during the summer it was taken on tour to the World's Fair at Brussels and to other European capitals. The very favorable review by Brooks Atkinson of the Yale performance led to the Broadway production which opened on December 11, 1958. During the rehearsal period Mrs. Elia Kazan made one of the most perceptive comments on the play when she said that the first act had "tremendous identification" in the scenes of suffering; it had action and interaction of people that had "a forward sweep." She felt that in the second act there was too much argument, too much philosophy; the events were not dramatically developed; there was "a long presentation, statement of a point of view, followed by a comment or brief rejection." During the New York production she had reservations about the production's becoming too theatrical.

Brooks Atkinson said that MacLeish had written "an epic of mankind" and he anticipated a long life for the play. He said that the playwright was not a solemn poet, and that much of the writing, particularly in the characters of God and Satan, was pungent and earthy. Some of the verse, he felt, was too compact for theater, and some of the scenes were begun in the middle. He also noted that the dignity, gravity, and simplicity of the King James Version was hard to match in modern poetry. He called *J. B.* impressive "in its valiant affirmation at the end," a play worthy of our time. MacLeish "has imposed his own sense of order on the chaos of the world."

Source: Signi Lenea Falk, "Later Poetry and Drama," in *Archibald MacLeish,* Twayne Publishers, Inc., 1965, pp. 118–50.

SOURCES

Berrigan, Daniel, "Job in Suburbia," in *America,* Vol. 100, October 4, 1958, p. 13.

Bieman, Elizabeth, "Faithful to the Bible in Its Fashion: MacLeish's *J. B.,*" in *Studies in Religion/Sciences Religieuses,* Vol. 4, 1974, pp. 25, 27.

Calhoun, Richard, "Archibald MacLeish's *J. B.*: Religious Humanism in the 80s," in *The Proceedings of the Archibald MacLeish Symposium May 7–8, 1982,* edited by Bernard A.

Drabeck, Helen E. Ellis, and Seymour Rudin, University Press of America, 1988, pp. 79–80.

Campbell, Shannon O., "*The Book of Job* and MacLeish's *J. B.*: A Cultural Comparison," in *English Journal,* Vol. 61, May 1972, pp. 653–57.

Ciardi, John, "Birth of a Classic," in *Saturday Review of Literature,* Vol. 41, March 8, 1958, p. 48.

D'Arcy, Martin, "*J. B.,* Wrong Answer to the Problem of Evil," in *Catholic World,* Vol. 190, November 1959, p. 82.

Gledhill, Preston R., "*J. B.:* Successful Theatre versus 'Godless' Theology," in *Brigham Young University Studies,* Vol. 3, December 1961, pp. 9–14.

Kahn, Sy, "The Games God Plays with Man: A Discussion of *J. B.,*" in *The Fifties: Fiction, Poetry, Drama,* edited by Warren French, Everett/Edwards, 1970, pp. 250, 255.

MacLeish, Archibald, Foreword to *J. B.,* Samuel French, 1958, p. 6.

———, "MacLeish Speaks to the Players," in *Pembroke Magazine,* Vol. 7, 1976, pp. 80, 82, 83.

———, "On Being a Poet in the Theatre," in *Horizon,* Vol. 12, January 1960, p. 50.

Montgomery, Marion, "On First Looking into Archibald MacLeish's Play in Verse, *J. B.,*" in *Modern Drama,* Vol. 2, December 1959, pp. 231–42.

Porter, Thomas E., *Myth and Modern American Drama,* Wayne State University Press, 1969, pp. 82, 96.

Roston, Murray, *Biblical Drama in England: From the Middle Ages to the Present Day,* Northwestern University Press, 1968, p. 309.

Trudeau, Gary, *Doonesbury,* Universal Press Syndicate, October 5, 2001.

FURTHER READING

Donaldson, Scott, in collaboration with R. H. Winnick, *Archibald MacLeish: An American Life,* Houghton Mifflin, 1992.

In this definitive biography of MacLeish, the discussion of *J. B.* presents MacLeish's reasons for writing the play and describes his writing and revising process as he moved from written script to performance.

Drabeck, Bernard A., and Helen E. Ellis, eds., *Archibald MacLeish: Reflections,* University of Massachusetts Press, 1986.

Arranged in a question-and-answer format, this book was pieced together from several interviews MacLeish granted during the last years of his life. MacLeish considered this book the autobiography of his professional life. His discussion of *J. B.* focuses on the differences between the published and the performed versions of the play.

Ellis, Helen E., Bernard A. Drabeck, and Margaret E. C. Howland, *Archibald MacLeish: A Selectively Annotated Bibliography,* Scarecrow Press, 1995.

With more than twenty-three hundred entries and two indices, this book is an excellent starting-place for locating books, articles, and reviews by and about the author. The book also includes a brief biography and a chronology of significant dates in MacLeish's life.

Falk, Signi Lenea, *Archibald MacLeish,* Twayne, 1965.

In an analysis of the first half century of MacLeish's career, Falk demonstrates how MacLeish's poetry grew out of and then away from the poetry of other important modern poets and how all of his writing came to demonstrate his convictions about a writer's responsibilities to address the political and social world. The book includes a thirteen-page close reading of *J. B.*

Gassner, John, *Theatre at the Crossroads: Plays and Playwrights of the Mid-Century American Stage,* Holt, Rinehard and Winston, 1960.

After an analysis that leads toward generalities about the plays produced in New York from the end of World War II through the 1950s, Gassner examines dozens of individual plays. His analysis of *J. B.* focuses on the differences between the Yale and the Broadway productions.

The Last Night of Ballyhoo

ALFRED UHRY

1996

In his second play, *The Last Night of Ballyhoo*, Alfred Uhry explores the lives of Jewish southerners, a society that he introduced to the American theater-going public with his Pulitzer Prize-winning play, *Driving Miss Daisy*. The setting and plot of *The Last Night of Ballyhoo* developed from stories Uhry heard growing up in a southern Jewish family, as well as his own experiences. As he told Don Shewey from *American Theatre,* "I went to one of the last Ballyhoos there was, when I was 16—it was like a German-Jewish debutante ball." However, Uhry also had a keen desire to explore Jewish identity, including prejudice inflicted on Jews by other Jews. Uhry combined these two interests to create the privileged world of the Levy/Freitag families. They live in a large home on one of Atlanta's finest streets. They belong to an elite country club. Their children may attend prestigious private universities. All these trappings and conveniences of wealth, however, cannot change the fact that they are Jews who live in an overwhelmingly Christian society. The prejudice that they experience as a result of their religion does not deter them from embracing mainstream southern society or from replicating this discrimination within their own culture; German-Jews such as the Levys and Freitags look down on "the other kind" of Jews— Eastern European Jews. While *The Last Night of Ballyhoo* deftly explores this anti-Semitism, Uhry also intersperses his serious message with sparkling banter, comedic non sequiturs, and hilarious charac-

ters and characterization. *The Last Night of Bally-hoo* was first produced at the Atlanta Olympic Games in 1996 and went to Broadway the following year; its playscript is available from Theatre Communications Group.

AUTHOR BIOGRAPHY

Alfred Uhry was born in 1936 to an upper-middle-class German-Jewish family in Atlanta, Georgia. His father was a furniture designer and artist, and his mother was a social worker. He attended Brown University in Rhode Island, graduating with a degree in English in 1958.

Uhry had worked on varsity shows at Brown with Robert Waldman; Uhry wrote the script and lyrics, and Waldman wrote the music. After college, Uhry moved to New York to begin his career in show business, where he continued to collaborate with Waldman. Their musical, *The Robber Bridegroom* (1975), was based on a novella by southern writer Eudora Welty. Uhry wrote the script and the song lyrics. The play was a surprise hit off-Broadway and moved to Broadway for the 1976–1977 season. It earned Uhry a Tony Award nomination and a Drama Desk nomination.

Uhry continued to work on other musicals, but these projects were unsuccessful, either closing on opening night, or soon thereafter, or never opening at all. Uhry began to write comedy scripts for television shows and lyrics for commercials and also taught English and drama at a New York high school. In 1984, as Uhry was struggling to get a musical about Al Capone off the ground, the idea came to him to write a play instead.

The characters in *Driving Miss Daisy* (1987) are based on people that Uhry knew growing up, including his grandmother and her African-American chauffeur. *Driving Miss Daisy*, Uhry's first play, was an instant success, running for three years in New York. Uhry won a Pulitzer Prize in 1988 for it. Uhry also wrote the adaptation for the film version of this work.

After his surprise hit, Uhry was approached by the Olympic Games' Cultural Olympiad to produce a play for the 1996 Olympic Games that would be held in Atlanta. He revisited Atlanta's Jewish milieu that he knew so well to create his story about intra-ethnic prejudice. *The Last Night of Ballyhoo* went on to win Uhry another Tony Award. In 1998,

he wrote the book for the musical *Parade*, which played at Lincoln Center in New York. It also had anti-Semitism as a central focus.

Uhry lives in New York, where he is active in the Dramatists Guild. He also has served as an advisor to the Guild's Young Playwrights Festival.

PLOT SUMMARY

Act 1

The Last Night of Ballyhoo opens in the living room of the Freitag/Levy home, where Lala is decorating a Christmas tree. It is 1939 in Atlanta, Georgia, the afternoon of the premiere of *Gone With the Wind*. Boo comes into the room and starts talking to Lala about calling Peachy Weil to get a date for Ballyhoo, which is now less than two weeks away. Boo ruins Lala's good mood, and she goes rushing from the room. Boo is worried because Lala is unmarried and unpopular. Reba confesses that Sunny does not have a date for Ballyhoo either. While the sisters-in-law are talking about their children, Adolph arrives home. He tells the women he has invited Joe Farkas, a new employee, home for supper. When Joe arrives, Boo gets annoyed that she has not been told that he is working for the family company. The women retire to the kitchen, and Lala comes downstairs. She suggests that Joe attend the movie premiere with her that evening.

After dinner, conversation shifts to Joe's family and whether he will go home for Christmas. Joe explains that his family doesn't celebrate Christmas but he will be going home for Pesach, or Passover. The Levys don't celebrate Passover. They went to Passover one year when Lala was in fifth grade, and Lala remembers it as boring. She is more interested in finding out whether Joe will be in town for Ballyhoo. They explain Ballyhoo to Joe: it is a social party that young Jewish people from all over the South attend. Then Lala again suggests that Joe and she go downtown, but Joe says he must go home since he has to catch a train early the next morning. After he leaves and Lala has gone upstairs, Boo turns to her brother and says, ''Adolph, that kike you hired had no manners.''

The next scene opens five days later aboard a southern-bound train. Sunny is in a sleeping compartment reading a book when Joe knocks on the door. Adolph had asked him to check in on Sunny to see if she needed anything. Sunny and Joe get into a

Alfred Uhry

conversation that ends in his asking her to go to Ballyhoo with him.

The next scene returns to the Freitag house. It is the morning that Sunny's train is due to arrive, and Adolph plans on meeting her. While he waits for Reba to get dressed, he comments that he is disturbed about Adolf Hitler's attack on Poland. Boo thinks he should be concerned with his own family instead, and then she complains that Adolph favors Sunny. Adolph reminds her that Sunny's father took care of them all after their father died. Boo also complains because she never got to work in the family business even though she got better math

grades in school than either of her brothers. After Adolph and Reba have left, the phone rings. It is Peachy Weil calling for Lala. Peachy is coming to Atlanta the day after Christmas, but he does not ask Lala to Ballyhoo. Boo picks up the phone to call Peachy's aunt and set things straight.

That night, Sunny and Adolph are playing cards, and Reba is sitting nearby, knitting. A conversation develops about a local girl who went crazy after going to teachers' college. Sunny never heard about this story, and Reba confesses it's because the girl was "the other kind." Sunny doesn't understand what her mother means, and Reba explains that the phrase refers to Jews who are from Eastern Europe instead of Germany, like them. Reba and Adolph claim that "the other kind" can be identified by their appearance.

Boo and Lala return from seeing *Gone With the Wind,* which Lala thinks is a masterpiece. Then Joe comes to the door, bringing some figures for Adolph. Adolph insists that Joe have some coffee, and Lala goes to the kitchen to make it. Alone with Sunny, Joe asks her if she and her family are really Jewish. Sunny insists that she always just wanted to be like everyone else, but Joe thinks that she is. To show he is wrong, Sunny tells him about the summer when she was going into the seventh grade and she was at the Venetian Club Pool with her friends. A man came by the pool and called out her name and then told her that Jews were not allowed to swim in the club pool. Joe then asks Sunny out for a date and leaves shortly thereafter. When Lala finds out that Joe has asked Sunny to Ballyhoo, she gets angry and calls Joe aggressive. Lala and Sunny argue about who gets more attention in the family, and Lala says that Sunny is a hypocrite because she is going to Ballyhoo even though she claims she doesn't care about going. Lala points out that she will be going to Ballyhoo with someone who belongs there—"a Louisiana Weil"—whereas Sunny will be going with "a New York Yid."

Act 2

Act 2 opens the next day. Lala and Boo are arguing because Lala refuses to call Peachy. Lala eventually calls, but Peachy has already left for Atlanta. Boo calls the cook and asks her to check if Peachy's tuxedo is in his closet. When they find out it is not, Lala and Boo take this as positive proof that Peachy is going to take Lala to Ballyhoo. They go shopping for a new dress. That night, Lala models her new dress, which is an unbecoming hoop skirt. Sunny and Joe come in from their date. He dances with Lala but manages to step on her dress and tear it. Boo and Lala go upstairs to fix the dress. Adolph gives Joe tickets to Ballyhoo; he gets them free because he is a past president of the club, which is restricted to wealthy Jews. Joe leaves, and Sunny and Adolph talk about love.

The next scene takes place on Christmas Day. The presents have been opened. Peachy Weil comes over, and he and Lala exchange impertinent quips, but eventually he officially invites her to Ballyhoo. The next evening finds Peachy and Joe awaiting their dates. The talk turns to war in Europe, but it is

clear that Peachy cares little about the events there. The couples depart for Ballyhoo.

At Ballyhoo, while Sunny and Lala are in the ladies' room, Joe learns from Peachy that the Standard Club, which hosts the dance, is a closed club. "The other kind" of Jews attend the Progressive Club; the Standard Club is only for German Jews. However, Joe shouldn't be worried about being treated poorly, since Adolph once was a president of the club. Furious, Joe leaves the party, leaving Sunny to wonder what happened. She gets a ride home from a friend. However, Joe comes by the house later. He and Sunny angrily discuss why he left Ballyhoo. He doesn't think she should have taken him to a club that discriminates against Jews, and Sunny retorts that she didn't think it would make a difference; according to Sunny, the Standard Club is nothing at all like the Venetian Club. The fight escalates with Joe accusing Sunny of speaking "Jew hater talk." The two part. Then the doorbell rings. It is Lala. Peachy has proposed, and she and Boo are thrilled.

The final scene takes place one week later on a train approaching Wilmington, Delaware. Sunny is in her sleeping compartment when there is a knock on her door. It is Joe. At first he claims he is on the train because he is in the area for work and, besides, Adolph asked him to check up on her. However, he later admits that he drove all the way to the train just to see her. Sunny says that Joe's "Jew hater talk" can't be true because it would be as if she hated herself. She apologizes for taking him to Ballyhoo. Joe and Sunny confess to missing each other and end up kissing and crying. The train is about to depart, so Joe must leave. Sunny is sad, but Joe tells her that they have the whole future ahead of them and to "think of something really good, and we'll just make it happen." What Sunny thinks of is dinner at her home in Atlanta, with Adolph, Boo, Reba, Lala, and Peachy already seated. Sunny and Joe join them, and Sunny lights the Sabbath candles and says the blessing.

CHARACTERS

Joe Farkas

Joe Farkas is a Brooklyn Jew who has moved to the South to work for Adolph at the bedding company. Joe never went to college, but according to Sunny, he is "very bright." Proud of his heritage,

Joe is surprised to meet a family with no real sense of Jewish identity. Unlike the majority of the characters in the play, Joe manifests concern for the Jews in Europe, not simply because he has relatives there but because he feels a bond with his co-religionists. Joe is extremely sensitive to the prejudice that the Levys hold toward him—and any Eastern European Jews. When he finds out that the Standard Club does not allow his "kind" of Jew to belong, he leaves the dance and Sunny. He also accuses Sunny of "Jew hater talk." However, he comes to regret his hard words and effects a reconciliation with her.

Adolph Freitag

The bachelor Adolph Freitag, who lives with the two widows, runs the family's bedding business that was first started by their oldest brother, Sunny's father, who is now dead. Of the older members of the family, Adolph is the only one who demonstrates any real recognition of the world outside of the Atlanta Jewish community; for instance, he shows concern over the situation in Europe, particularly with regard to the Jewish population. He enjoys a special bond with Sunny, a closeness not replicated with the airheaded Lala, and is pleased at the developing relationship between her and Joe. Despite these positive qualities, Adolph is not immune to the social snobbishness that afflicts his family; for example, he is a past president of the restricted Standard Club.

Reba Freitag

Reba Freitag, the widow of Boo and Adolph's brother, shares a house with the two of them. Generally seen knitting, Reba is far more easygoing than her sister-in-law, but she also is a little vague. The play's character notes describe her as "not quite in synch with everybody else."

Sunny Freitag

Sunny Freitag is Reba's twenty-year-old daughter. She is the opposite of her cousin Lala, with her cheerful disposition, blond hair, and intellectual curiosity. Despite her so-called Aryan features, Sunny has been the victim of prejudice: when she was a teenager, she was kicked out of a private swimming pool in front of all her classmates. This experience has made her grow up feeling different from all her friends. She has returned from Wellesley, where she is majoring in sociology, for the Christmas holidays. Sunny is unique in her family. More open-minded, she has never even heard the phrase "the

other kind" and cannot fathom what it means. Although she disparages Atlanta's Jewish social scene, she agrees to attend Ballyhoo with Joe. She grows increasingly fond of him in a short period of time, yet her deception in not telling him that the Standard Club is restricted threatens their burgeoning relationship. In the resulting fight, when she explains to Joe that she regards them as "equals," Sunny reveals that she has been touched by the social snobbery that is so pervasive among her family. Unlike her family, however, Sunny comes to comprehend the inherent irrationality of disliking Jewish people simply because they come from Eastern Europe or New York or wherever, for she realizes that would be like hating herself. By the end of the play, having reconciled with Joe, she demonstrates a clear and real interest in exploring her religious and cultural background. Thus, Sunny, who previously believed that religion didn't matter in today's world, shows that she has undergone a major transformation.

Boo Levy

Beulah "Boo" Levy is a widowed southern matron. She and Lala live in the family home with her brother-in-law and sister-in-law. Worried that the unpopular and socially awkward Lala will never marry, her greatest concern seems to be getting Lala a date for Ballyhoo. She willfully tries to ignore the fact that Lala is unpopular because of personality issues, and she insists that Lala make use of the family's social standing to win suitors. When Lala resists, Boo resorts to bullying, browbeating, and dominating tactics. Her methods pay off. Boo forces Lala to call Peachy Weil and makes her attend Ballyhoo, but by the end of the play, Peachy has proposed to Lala.

Boo holds social standing above all else. She is ecstatic about Lala's engagement to Peachy—even though he makes no effort to conceal his offensive, boorish behavior—simply because he is a member of one of the South's most well-regarded Jewish families. By contrast, she dislikes Joe Farkas because of his family background; she even calls him a "kike." Like the rest of her family, Boo believes that German Jews, such as themselves, are superior to Eastern European Jews, such as Joe.

Lala Levy

Beulah "Lala" Levy is Boo's socially awkward twentyish-year-old daughter. Having left college before finishing the first semester because she did not get pledged to the good Jewish sorority, Lala lives at home and seems to do very little with herself. She is prone to flights of fantasy. For instance, with the Atlanta movie premiere of *Gone With the Wind,* Lala declares herself an author. However, like her mother, her foremost desire is to obtain a date for Ballyhoo. When she first meets Joe, she sets her sight on him, but he prefers Sunny. This partiality unleashes Lala's long-standing jealousy of her prettier, smarter, less stereotypically Jewish cousin. Lala thinks that Sunny has always gotten all the attention in the family. However, once Peachy asks her to attend Ballyhoo with him, she immediately feels superior to Sunny because she has a date with a member of one the South's best Jewish families, whereas Sunny's date is a "Yid." Like her mother, Lala exalts their social position and looks down on people not of their milieu. Thus, Lala is delighted by Peachy's proposal, despite the utter lack of romance or emotion involved.

Peachy
See Sylvan Weil

Sylvan Weil

Sylvan "Peachy" Weil hails from a good Jewish family in Lake Charles, Louisiana. He has come to Atlanta with his family, and Lala and Boo have their eyes set on him as a Ballyhoo date. He is uncouth, socially inappropriate, and either completely unaware or disinterested in the offenses he inflicts on others, particularly Joe. Despite these glaring faults, Lala is delighted with his marriage proposal.

THEMES

Social Standing

Social standing plays an important role in Boo's world. Her family numbers among the best Jewish families in Atlanta. Adolph is a past president of the restricted Standard Club, and their family home is the only Jewish household on Habersham Road. Boo wants her daughter to associate only with the right kind of Jews. For instance, she disparages the sorority bid because "Nobody but *the other kind* belong to A E Phi." She encourages Lala to try to become popular, insisting, "Your place in society sits there waiting for you, and you do nothing about it." The importance of social standing eventually allows even the socially awkward Lala to make a good marriage. Peachy Weil, himself uncouth and

TOPICS FOR FURTHER STUDY

- Do you think the final scene of the family's Sabbath dinner is fantasy or reality? Explain your answer.

- Find out more information about American-Jewish reactions to the persecutions of European Jews. What efforts did American Jews make to help European Jews? What additional efforts do you think they might have made?

- Investigate other forms of racism that took place in the South in 1930s, such as discrimination against African Americans.

- Write a journal entry, as if you were Joe, explaining how you feel about the Levy/Freitag family.

- Find out more about Jewish life in the 1930s. Compare Jewish life in the South to Jewish life in the North. Are the characters in *The Last Night of Ballyhoo* accurate reflections of their time period?

- Do you think the play is more comedic or more serious? Do you think the use of comedy is an effective tool for putting forth important social issues? Explain your answer.

offensive, proposes to Lala. Because he is from one of the finest Jewish families in the South, Boo is ecstatic. Similarly, Peachy's father approves of his son's engagement to Lala because he and his wife know "what they're getting here, all the way back on both sides."

Other members of the family are also affected by the concept of social standing. While Lala disparages her mother's class presumptions, she is not above using their status to impress Joe, making sure that he knows that their address is "about the best" in town. When she gets upset because Joe prefers Sunny to her, she lashes out at Sunny, telling her that Joe is just a "New York Yid," whereas she will be going to Ballyhoo with someone who belongs there—"a Louisiana Weil." Sunny's education also reflects her background—it is not a coincidence that she is majoring in sociology at the elite, private Wellesley College. There she reads books with socialist leanings like Upton Sinclair's *The Profits of Religion,* which, according to Joe, glorifies the "unwashed masses and the beauty of the working class."

Assimilation

The Levys, Freitags, and Weils represent those families who emigrated from Europe generations ago and assimilated to the United States fairly quickly. Assimilation is a common practice for immigrants, and for many cultures, success is indicated by integration into mainstream society. Unlike the newer Jewish immigrants, both the Levy and Weil families claim an extended southern lineage. Peachy's family has been in Louisiana for one hundred and fifty years, and they have no relatives remaining in Europe. This family history contributes to their status as the "Finest family in the South!" The Levys and Freitags also have an extended southern lineage. Boo takes great pride in the fact that great grandma's cousin Clemmie was the "first white child born in Atlanta." The assimilation of the Levy/Freitag family is apparent in Boo's claims to connections and birthright. However, the assimilation process also poses social and personal problems. Does the family's birthright give them claim to inferior status in southern society, or does it give them claim to a religious heritage that dates back more than two thousand years?

Though the characters believe that being as much like their Christian southern neighbors as possible represents the pinnacle of success, assimilation does not always bring positive transformations. As Stefan Kanfer points out in the *New Leader,* one of the undercurrents of the play is "Sunny's feelings of rootlessness—her antecedents make the coed too foreign for WASP acceptance, yet she knows nothing about the traditions or lore of Judaica." The assimilation of Jewish families who have been in the United States for a long period of time also leads them to look down on the newer immigrants, who tend to be those from Eastern Europe, contributing to the divisions that exist between these two groups.

War and Anti-Semitism

The war in Europe provides a backdrop to the play. Although European events are only mentioned in passing, they are relevant because World War II has become a symbol of rampant anti-Semitism. Adolf Hitler brought his anti-Semitic feelings to the forefront of Germany's social policy in the 1930s, and with Germany's conquest of other European countries, Hitler was able to spread his message (often already in existence among other European populations) and murder about two-thirds of Europe's Jewish population. Among the Levy/Freitag household, however, with the exception of Adolph, no one pays attention to events in Europe. At one point, Adolph verbalizes his concern over Hitler's attack on Poland, and Boo's response is that he should be concerned for his family instead. On the night of Ballyhoo, the topic of the war comes up among Peachy, Joe, and Adolph. Peachy's only response to Joe's worry about his relatives in Poland and Russia is the flippant, "Let's hope they can dodge bullets." In 1939, many Americans were still hoping that the United States could keep out of the European conflict, and Peachy's feeling about the matter—that it is Europe's problem and Europeans should figure it out themselves—is reflective of popular opinion at that time. It would seem that the Levys and Freitags would be more sensitive to the persecution of their fellow Jews in Europe, but they have internalized the anti-Semitism of the society that surrounds them to such an extent that they subconsciously inflict it on their fellow brethren in Europe.

STYLE

Ending

The ending of *The Last Night of Ballyhoo* remains ambiguous. Does the family's Sabbath dinner represent Sunny's fantasy of the future, or does it represent a future that has become realized? The scene is so brief that it is impossible to formulate an accurate answer to this question. However, whether the scene is fantasy or reality, it does highlight the direction in which at least one member of the family is headed; for Sunny, the future clearly holds a new interest in Judaism. With Joe's help, Sunny will try to steer her family to learn more about their religious and cultural heritage.

Comedy

The Last Night of Ballyhoo is a comedy. Many of the characters indulge in deadpan banter and one-liners. When Lala emerges dressed in a hoop skirt like Scarlett O'Hara wears in *Gone With the Wind,* Adolph calls her Scarlett O'Goldberg. To explain why he never married, Adolph tells Sunny that he fell in love with a girl he saw on the streetcar every day. She was the love of his life because "I never saw her for more than twenty minutes at a time, and I had no dealings with her whatsoever." The characters also evoke humorous images of unfortunate people. Boo foresees Lala's future if she doesn't get married soon: she will be keeping house for eighty-five cats and getting arrested for running down the street wrapper. Reba counsels Lala against going on a date with Ferdie Nachman because "his father picked his nose during his own wedding ceremony." Reba's statement that higher education can lead to insanity is one of the funniest non sequiturs (a statement that does not follow logically from anything previously said). Reba recalls the story of Viola Feigenbaum, the "least hideous" of seven hideous sisters. Viola, being the smartest, attended teacher training school but then went crazy on the train, taking off all her clothes and running up and down the coach.

Setting

The play is set in Atlanta in 1939, a location that is particularly relevant because the South was rife with prejudice. In the 1930s (and for several decades thereafter), white society significantly discriminated against African Americans. They were segregated at schools and restaurants, on buses and in train stations, and into their own communities; African Americans lived a separate life from white southerners. While Jewish southerners are not excluded nearly to that extent, they too are excluded from certain institutions, such as the Venetian Club. By setting the play in the South, Uhry is able to subtly remind the audience of the South's long-standing history of prejudice. In such an environment, intra-ethnic prejudice is more likely to develop.

HISTORICAL CONTEXT

The Great Depression

The United States spent the 1930s in the midst of the Great Depression. This global economic recession was the worst depression in American history. Thousands of banks closed, leaving their customers with lost savings. Unemployment jumped dramatically, from just less than four percent in 1929 when the depression began; it reached its height in 1933, when about twenty-five percent of the U.S. population was out of work. By the late 1930s, many families had begun to feel some eco-

nomic relief, but the depression did not end until the United States entered World War II in 1941.

Popular Culture in the 1930s

Americans turned to the movies as a way of forgetting their problems during the Great Depression. *Gone With the Wind,* based on a novel by Margaret Mitchell, became the most popular film of the decade. Comedies and musicals were also popular. However, some filmmakers illustrated social issues. *Sullivan's Travels* depicted the hobo life, and *Mr. Deeds Goes to Town* criticized the wealthy.

Literature of the 1930s often reflected a new wave of realism. Books like John Steinbeck's *The Grapes of Wrath* portrayed the hard life of migrant farm workers as they traveled to California in search of a better life. Richard Wright's *Native Son* reflected a young African-American man's bitter experiences in a racist world.

Theater of the 1930s saw a shift throughout the course of the decade. At the beginning of the 1930s, many plays dealt with the country's labor and class struggles, while some plays, like Lillian Hellman's *The Little Foxes,* attacked upper-class greed. By the late 1930s, however, the most popular plays celebrated traditional American values, such as Thornton Wilder's *Our Town.*

World War II

War broke out in Europe in 1939. Adolf Hitler had already annexed Austria and Czechoslovakia to the Third Reich, and on the morning of September 1, 1939, Hitler announced the annexation of Danzig, a Polish port city with a large German population. At the same time, Germany began a massive attack on Poland. Nazi troops and tanks entered the country by land, while the air force bombed from above. With this act of aggression, Hitler broke the pact that he had made in 1938 with Great Britain and France, promising to make no more claims on territory in Europe. Within forty-eight hours of the German attack, Britain and France had declared war on Germany. However, they took no military action to turn back the German assault, and Poland was easily subdued, surrendering on September 17.

In western Europe, France and Britain began mobilizing for a war, but little military action took place. Newspapers began to speak of a "phony war" in the region, but this terminology proved invalid on April 9, 1940, with Germany's invasion of Denmark and Norway. Both countries quickly fell to the German onslaught and remained under

COMPARE & CONTRAST

- **1930s:** Over 100,000 German Jews enter the United States between 1933 and 1939, but many, many more Jews are denied entry because of existing quota laws. Most of these Jews will die in Nazi concentration camps.

  Today: Between 1991 and 1998, 54,900 Germans immigrate to the United States. During this same period, another 371,658 immigrants are admitted as permanent residents under existing refugee acts.

- **1930s:** In 1939, almost all of Europe is involved in World War II. However, the United States still remains out of the war, although it provides Great Britain with military supplies.

  Today: In 2001, in response to a terrorist attack, the United States launches its war on terrorism. In October, the United States begins bombing raids on terrorist training camps and other military targets in Afghanistan, which is believed to shelter the terrorists responsible for the attacks on the United States. The United States has the backing of NATO in this assault.

- **1930s:** The most popular film of the decade is 1939's *Gone with the Wind,* a technicolor epic. For years, the film is the leader in box office receipts.

  Today: *Titanic,* made in 1997, is one of the most popular films of the 1990s. It grosses more than $600 million, giving it the all-time number one box office ranking.

- **1930s:** Americans entertain themselves by going to the movies, listening to radio programs, listening to music, and reading. Clark Gable, who stars in *Gone with the Wind,* is a leading heartthrob.

  Today: In addition to attending movies, watching television, and listening to music, many Americans find entertainment on the World Wide Web. On the Web, people can download music and movies, communicate via email, make purchases, read magazines, and conduct any number of other activities.

German occupation until the end of the war in 1945. Hitler next turned his sights westward, invading the Low Countries in rapid succession. By June 1940, even France had fallen; Britain stood alone to face the Nazi menace.

U.S. Involvement in World War II

Throughout the 1930s, the United States had expressed its determination to remain neutral in future wars. Though some people believed that the Nazis posed a threat to the whole of civilization, most Americans did not think the United States should concern itself with Europe's war. The United States did revise the Neutrality Act in 1939 to allow American firms to sell munitions to Great Britain. After the fall of France, American sympathy for Britain increased, and President Franklin D. Roosevelt, convinced that the United States would be drawn into the war eventually, transferred fifty old American naval destroyers to Britain in 1940. Congress also passed the first national draft law to be adopted by the country during peacetime. By early 1941, the United States was selling war materials to Britain on credit, and by that autumn the U.S. Navy was involved in an undeclared war with German submarines. On December 7, 1941, Japan, which was allied with Germany and Italy, attacked a U.S. naval base at Pearl Harbor, Hawaii, and the United States officially joined the war on the side of the Allies.

CRITICAL OVERVIEW

The Last Night of Ballyhoo was originally commissioned by the Alliance Theatre Company for presentation at Atlanta's 1996 Olympic Arts Festival. It immediately drew an appreciative audience, including Michael Sommers, who introduced the play to the American Theater Critics Association (ACTA) prize-awarding committee. According to Sommers, *The Last Night of Ballyhoo* was full of "tasty regional talk, seriocomic situations, and well-crafted realistic form." *The Last Night of Ballyhoo* went on to win an ACTA citation as an outstanding new play.

In 1997, *The Last Night of Ballyhoo* opened on Broadway, and the majority of theater critics responded as favorably as earlier audiences had. Greg Evans called it a "winning new play" in *Variety* and made special note of the "wonderfully crafted script." Richard Zoglin pointed out in *Time,* "Uhry juggles a lot of elements with no evident strain, creating a believable family that seems both quirky and emblematic." Edward J. Mattimoe wrote in *America* of the drama's pathos, calling it a "human comedy," one that ends in both laughter and tears. *The Last Night of Ballyhoo* won a Tony Award for the best play of the 1997 season.

Uhry had first come to national attention ten years earlier, with his prize-winning *Driving Miss Daisy. The Last Night of Ballyhoo* bore certain resemblance to the earlier play; it too was set in Atlanta among upper-class Jews. *The Last Night of Ballyhoo* also reunited crucial members of *Driving Miss Daisy*—playwright, actor, and director—so it is not surprising that *The Last Night of Ballyhoo* would be compared to its predecessor. Like the earlier play, wrote Don Shewey in *American Theatre,* "it operates by stealth, adopting a disarmingly conventional form to tell a story we haven't quite heard before." Evans agreed that, with its "abundant humor" and "laugh-provoking dialogue," *The Last Night of Ballyhoo* was "a more than worthy successor" to *Driving Miss Daisy.* To Zoglin, *The Last Night of Ballyhoo* was actually superior, "richer, more textured than the rather schematic Miss Daisy."

Critics also responded to what Sommers called "the dark central issue the play so winningly illuminates": the treacherous place of Jews within a Christian society. According to Zoglin's analysis, the Levy and Freitag family is forced into a "tricky dance of assimilation and accommodation." Because of their religious background, the family experiences discrimination, yet they also discriminate against those Jews they deem to be of lower quality. Mattimoe noted, "[T]here are enough unsettling comments about Jewish people—made by Jewish people—to show that any ethnic group, once put

Playbill cover from The Last Night of Ballyhoo, *performed at the Helen Hayes Theatre in 1997*

down absorbs some of the negativity themselves." More than one critic commented on the audience's shocked response to Boo Levy's use of the word "kike." This very real discomfort reflects the unsettling facts of discrimination. Yet, as Shewey wrote, "Part of the triumph of *The Last Night of Ballyhoo* is that Uhry allows ethical dilemmas and class tensions to arise without turning his characters into stick figures or the drama into a predetermined 'issue' play."

CRITICISM

Rena Korb

Korb has a master's degree in English literature and creative writing and has written for a wide variety of educational publishers. In the following essay, Korb discusses the anti-Semitism felt by the Jewish family in Uhry's play.

Uhry's *The Last Night of Ballyhoo* is a humorous play that still raises a serious social issue: anti-Semitism inflicted by Jews. Although the Levy/

WHAT DO I READ NEXT?

- Uhry's *Driving Miss Daisy* (1987) is the play that rocketed the author to success. Uhry won the Pulitzer Prize for this play about a southern Jewish matron's decades-long relationship with her African-American chauffeur.

- Lanford Wilson's play *Talley's Folly* (1980) is set in the South in the 1940s. It tells of the courtship of a Protestant woman by her persistent Jewish suitor.

- Many critics have compared *The Last Night of Ballyhoo* to Tennessee Williams's play *The Glass Menagerie* (1944). One of Williams's finest dramas, this play revolves around a down-and-out St. Louis family. In hopes of finding a husband

for her painfully shy daughter, Amanda encourages her son to bring "gentlemen callers" home to his sister, but her plans backfire.

- Wendy Wasserstein's play *The Sisters Rosenswieg* (1992) deals with issues of self-hatred among expatriate Jewish New Yorkers. The sisters are three Brooklyn-born women who gather to celebrate one sister's birthday and end up confronting their past and future.

- Southern writer Eudora Welty's novel *Delta Wedding* (1946) focuses on the relationships between members of a plantation family gathered for a wedding in 1923.

Freitag family lives in a society in which Jews are discriminated against on a regular basis and although they personally have experienced prejudicial treatment because of their Jewish faith, they persistently regard "the other kind" of Jews—those who do not descend from German Jewry—as socially inferior. Like their friends, the Nachmans, Strausses, and Lillienthals, they see nothing wrong with their behavior, nor do they ever equate their prejudicial treatment of others with the discrimination that is wrought upon themselves. Indeed, their greatest efforts are seen, not in attempting to thwart discrimination but in imitating their Christian neighbors. Through their negative reaction to their Eastern European brethren as well as their own embrace of Christian traditions over Jewish ones, the family demonstrates marked anti-Semitic characteristics. This issue is compellingly explored against the hardly mentioned but ever-present backdrop of the events leading up to the European Holocaust, thus serving as a chilling reminder of the pervasive and dangerous effects of anti-Semitism, or prejudice in whatever form it chooses to take.

The play opens with a scene that sets the family's glorification of Christianity over Judaism: Lala is decorating the family Christmas tree. The

fact that she is "surrounded by cardboard boxes of ornaments" clearly shows that a Christmas tree is a family tradition in the Levy/Freitag home. Boo, however, is unhappy with Lala's adorning the tree with a Christmas star. As she chastises her daughter, "Jewish Christmas trees don't have stars." A star would be as bad as setting up a manger scene on their lawn; both decorations would make people think "we're a bunch of Jewish fools pretending we're Christians." Irony abounds in this scene. First, although Boo, supported by Reba, insists that Christmas is an American holiday, on par with Valentine's Day or Halloween, it is a celebration of the birth of Jesus Christ. Second, and more notably, Boo and Reba and all of their upper-class Jewish milieu actively and eagerly take on the trappings of their Christian neighbors. They imitate the social activities of the Christians, from forming their own country club to creating a closed membership list at those clubs. As Sunny tells Joe, "Ballyhoo is asinine. . . . a lot of dressed up Jews dancing around wishing they could kiss their elbows and turn into Episcopalians."

Despite the pretensions that the upper-class Jews make to society, they are bitterly aware of what they lack. Lala succinctly sums up their status in this important first scene. "Guess what, Mama? We're Jews. We have no place in society," she says. Boo concedes that maybe the Levys and Freitags are "not right up there at the tip top with the best set of Christians, but we come mighty close." The fact that the family is the only Jewish household on Habersham Road supports Boo's assertion, but no one stops to analyze the dysfunction inherent in this situation; not only has the Levy/Freitag family chosen to live amidst people who do not regard them as equal, but the family also can make no claims to actually belonging amidst these people because even they think they are actually inferior.

For the most part, however, the Levy/Freitag family does their best at overlooking their self-perceived inadequacies resulting from their Judaism. December 25 finds them in a living room strewn with the remains of ribbons, wrapping paper, and gift boxes. In stark contrast to this celebration is their ignorance of and disinterest in Passover, an important Jewish holiday. When Joe mentions this holiday, Boo has to remind her daughter of "[T]hat time we went to the Seder supper with one of Daddy's business acquaintances. . . . You were in the sixth grade." Lala's remembrance of this holy occasion, however, centers on spilling red wine and being terribly bored by "all the ish-kabibble."

The family feels drawn to Christian traditions despite the fact that they have experienced very real instances of discrimination. For example, the only reason Ballyhoo even takes place is that southern Jews were denied entrance to the private country clubs. More telling and more personal, however, is Sunny's recollection of being discriminated against the summer she was going into seventh grade. At the Venetian Club Pool with her best friend, Sunny's name was called out by a man who "said I had to get out of the water." She tells Joe, "And Vennie Alice asked him why and he said Jews weren't allowed to swim in the Venetian pool. And all the kids got very quiet and none of them would look at me." The reaction to this discrimination also provides insight into the relationship between the Jews and their Christian friends. Sunny recalls how Vennie's mother called up her mother and apologized, and she and Vennie "stayed friends—sort of. Neither of us ever mentioned it again, but it was always there." Sunny's recollection shows that while southern society prefers to pretend that such discriminatory treatment does not happen, they are aware of these instances as well as the inherent validity behind them; after all, no one protests such rules or such humiliations. Like the rest of her community, Sunny, who always

> MANY THEATER CRITICS COMMENTED ON THE SURPRISED GASP THAT BOO'S WORDS, WHICH CLOSE THE SECOND SCENE OF ACT I, DREW FROM THE AUDIENCE: 'ADOLPH, THAT KIKE YOU HIRED HAS NO MANNERS.'"

wanted "to be like everybody else," accepts that being Jewish and being Christian are distinct from each other. Interestingly, Joe agrees with her but for a very dissimilar reason; where he comes from, in Brooklyn, Jews are proud of being Jews.

More disturbing than the glorification of Christianity, however, is the Jews' imitation of Christian behavior to such an extent that they, too, have created their own social echelon. In their class system, Jews like themselves—from German background—are at the top, whereas Jews who do not come from a German background, or Jews "east of the Elbe," the river that separated Germany from Czechoslovakia, are seen as vastly inferior. Joe's entry into their lives sets off this alarming and perhaps unexpected prejudice. Many theater critics commented on the surprised gasp that Boo's words, which close the second scene of act I, drew from the audience: "Adolph, that kike you hired has no manners."

To Boo and her Jewish set, Joe is simply one of "the other kind." Although Jews of Eastern European ancestry are different from German-descended Jews, no one really specifies in what way. Reba claims that a person can identify them merely by the "way they look," but despite her foolish words, when Sunny tells her mother of the Ballyhoo date with Joe, Reba refers to him as "that good-looking boy who works for Adolph" and is pleased. Ironically, the whole family recognizes that Lala looks more like "the other kind" than the good kind of Jew; Lala herself regards her physical characteristics in comparison to the blond, Aryan-featured Sunny as proof that God prefers her cousin. "Look at my hair! Look at my skin! Look at my eyes! Listen to my voice!" she exclaims to Sunny. "I try, and I try, and no matter what I do it shows, and there's just nothing I can do about it.'' Physically then, Lala is like Joe: "too Jewish."

The family is forced to deal with their anti-Semitism on the night of Ballyhoo. The insensitive Peachy lets Joe know that the Standard Club is restricted. By rights, people like Joe, "where you people went. . . . The Other Kind. . . . Russian. Orthodox,'' go to the Progressive Club. The Standard Club is historically limited to German Jews, although they have started to let in a few non-German Jews, "but they try to only take ones that are toilet trained." The argument that Joe and Sunny have as a result of this revelation is the most pointed discussion of Jewish anti-Semitism in the play. Despite her experience of being discriminated against because of her Judaism, it never occurred to Sunny that Joe would not want to be at a place that would discriminate against him because of his particular Jewish background. When Sunny tells him that the discrimination practiced by the Standard is not the same as the discrimination that was perpetrated against her by the Venetian Club, that in fact she regards herself and Joe as "equals," Joe becomes extremely offended. Then Sunny tells him how embarrassed she felt at his impolite behavior of leaving her alone at the dance. She says, "How could you know any better?" which Joe interprets as Sunny saying that he could not possibly know any better because "the other kind" of Jew lacks the manners that the genteel German Jews possess. "Jew hater talk, . . .'' he lashes out. "I been hearing that garbage all my life, but damned if I thought I'd ever hear it coming out of a Jewish girl."

As Edward J. Mattimoe wrote in *America,* this anti-Semitism inflicted by Jews "show[s] that any ethnic group, once put down, absorbs some of the negativity into themselves." The Jewish self-hatred plays out against the muted backdrop of the events in Europe. By December 1939, German Jews, living under the Third Reich, had already been deprived of their citizenship and segregated from Aryan society, and they had experienced numerous physical assaults in attacks on their person and in the destruction of their businesses and synagogues. As Don Shewey writes in *American Theatre,* "It's a mark of Uhry's skilful understatement that, without a word being spoken, the audience is agonizingly aware that on the other side of the Atlantic, Hitler's 'final solution' is making a mockery of distinctions between German Jews and 'the other kind.'" The historical knowledge of the losses the Holocaust inflicted upon the Jewish population renders Sunny's

belief that Hitler is an "aberration" painfully and terrifyingly naïve.

The Last Night of Ballyhoo ends with the challenge it presents to the family to reject this ethnic negativity and stop turning on each other and, instead, to recognize the fallacy of Jewish anti-Semitism. They must embrace themselves as they are, with Jewish warts and all, and come to the recognition that being Jewish does not make them inferior, no matter what their Christian counterparts might think. The final image the play presents shows a future in which Sunny, at the very least, has come to learn about and value her Jewish heritage.

Source: Rena Korb, Critical Essay on *The Last Night of Ballyhoo,* in *Drama for Students,* The Gale Group, 2002.

Catherine Dybiec Holm

Dybiec Holm is a published writer and editor with a master's degree in natural resources. In this essay, Dybiec Holm discusses multiple sources of tension in Uhry's story that make it so effective.

In all storytelling, including drama, tension is a necessary element that makes the story interesting. Tension can be created by conflicts that characters need to overcome or by obstacles that their environment presents to these characters. In Alfred Uhry's *The Last Night of Ballyhoo*, tensions abound, creating layers of nuances and dilemmas. These make for an interesting play and quickly let one know that this story goes far beyond the surface.

The primary source of tension in this play is the characters' shame and denial of their own Jewish religion. But Uhry takes an already interesting premise and adds additional twists. The characters live in the South and are a minority in Atlanta, a predominantly Christian community. It is 1939, and Hitler is in power across the ocean. Jews in this community label each other in a racist fashion; German-American Jews feel that they are superior to Eastern European-American Jews.

Uhry's loosely knit, extended family of characters knows little about their Jewish heritage and chooses not to pursue it. So desperate are these people to fit in with the rest of Atlanta's non-Jewish population that the Freitag/Levy family puts up a Christmas tree every year, though no evidence of menorah candles (to celebrate Hanukkah) is found in the house. Boo, a character completely concerned with presenting the right appearance to society, justifies the presence of their Christmas tree without a star by making it clear to her daughter Lala that

"Jewish Christmas trees don't have stars." Boo walks a fine tightrope between realizing she is not a Christian and not wanting to seems too Jewish:

> Boo: If you have a star on the tree, you might as well go . . . buy a manger scene and stick it in the front year.
> Lala: I'd like that.
> Boo: Fine. Then everybody that drives down Habersham Road will think we're a bunch of Jewish fools pretending we're Christian.

Both Boo and Lala emphasize that their presence on Habersham Road is significant, since it's the most upscale street in town and they are the only Jews on it (the other Jewish family lives "at the tacky end of the street where it doesn't count").

Boo is so concerned with appearances that she expends great energy to make sure that Lala doesn't foul up and make the rest of the family look bad. She berates Lala for getting rejected by a college sorority, but Uhry never loses sight of the opportunity to show the audience the strange tightrope that these Southern Jews walk:

> Boo: You keep making the same mistakes over and over! Your place in society sits there waiting for you and you do nothing about it.
> Lala: Guess what, Mama? We're Jews. We have no place in society.
> Boo: We most certainly do! Maybe not right up there at the tip-top with the best set of Christians, but we come mighty close. After all, your great-grandma's Cousin Clemmie was—
> Boo and Lala: The first white child born in Atlanta!

Even the superficial and immature Lala has a sense for what their community really thinks about Jews. Much later, Lala again shows evidence of shame and self-hate when she compares her looks with Sunny's:

> Lala: Oh come on, Sunny. You've always gotten the attention. Even from God!
> Sunny: What?
> Lala: He didn't give you one Jewish feature and look at me!
> Sunny: That's absurd.
> Lala: Look at my hair! Look at my skin! Look at my eyes! Listen to my voice! I try and try and no matter what I do it shows and there's just nothing I can do about it.

For Lala, her looks are the ultimate stamp of disgrace, something that cannot be disguised or hidden, something she is stuck with.

In scenes like these, Uhry plays with tension. The obsession that Lala and Boo have with appearances and societal mores is paired (and sometimes overshadowed) by the larger tension that these Jews are never completely accepted by society around

AMAZINGLY, UHRY ACCOMPLISHES THE BALANCE OF COMEDY AND SERIOUSNESS, OF SUBTLETY AND DIRECTNESS, ALL WITHIN THE LAYERS OF TENSION THAT THIS STORY ENCOMPASSES."

them. For example, both Lala and Boo are determined to find Lala a date for Ballyhoo, a prestigious holiday dance for Atlanta's well-off, young Jews. But even the prestige of Ballyhoo is dampened with the knowledge that the local Christian population has their own holiday party, and Jews are not invited. Adolph and Joe discuss the Standard Club, the country club where Ballyhoo will be held:

> Joe: Sounds pretty spiffy.
> Adolph: I wouldn't say that.
> Joe: Jews only?
> Adolph: You bet.
> Joe: No Christians allowed?
> Adolph: Technically, but the truth is none of 'em would wanna come anyway. They've got clubs of their own, which they won't let us near.

Then, in the next line of dialog, Joe gets his first hint of discrimination between Jews, though he does not learn the details until later:

> Joe: So this is where all the Jews go.
> Adolph: Oh no. We're restricted too.
> Joe: What do you mean?

With some discomfort, Adolph explains that only wealthy Jews get into this club. It is much later that Joe learns the real reason: the club is open to German-American Jews and closed to American Jews of Eastern European descent. It is yet another layer of tension that Uhry weaves into this play.

With the introduction of Joe Farkas, the Jew from New York, Uhry places further illumination on the Freitag/Levy family's shame and denial of their own heritage. Joe, a practicing Jew from a community where people are proud of their heritage, is a perfect foil for the denial and ignorance of people like Boo and Lala. Even the well-educated Sunny (who is a foil herself for the less-sophisticated Lala) knows very little about her Jewish traditions. But she knows enough to see that she does not fit in. And Sunny reveals, inadvertently, that she has some discomfort with the dysfunctional tightrope her family walks regarding their religious beliefs.

> Joe: Are you people really Jewish?
> Sunny: 'Fraid so. A hundred percent back—on both sides.
> Joe: 'Fraid so?
> Sunny: Oh, you know what I mean.
> Joe: Yeah. You mean you're afraid you're Jewish.
> Sunny: No. Of course not. That's just an expression.
> Joe: Ok. What do you mean?
> Sunny: I don't think I mean anything. It was just something to say. Can we please talk about something else?

Joe's initial comment is also telling; these Jews are so unlike the Jews whom he lives among that he questions whether they are really Jewish.

Uhry also uses Joe to vocalize things Jewish, such as common Yiddish words like *klutz* or the Yiddish word for William (Velvel). It's even more telling that the Freitag/Levy family usually does not know what the Yiddish words mean. Joe is also able to elaborate on traditions of which the family is either ignorant or disdainful, including Passover:

> Lala: You have to sit through one of those boring things every single year? One night of all that ish-kabibble was enough to last me the rest of my life.
> Boo: Now, Lala. Be tolerant.
> Joe: I sit through two every year. First night at Aunt Sadie's. Second night at home.
> Lala: Poor baby!
> Joe: Are you kidding? I wouldn't miss either of 'em for anything in the world.

Not lost in the exchange is the irony of Boo telling Lala, a Jew, to be tolerant of Jewish customs. These Jews truly want to separate themselves from anything Jewish.

Shamed by their own Jewishness, the Freitag/Levy family holds onto the hope that as German-American Jews, they are at least superior to other Eastern-European American Jews. When Joe reveals his lineage ("Russia, Poland, Hungary. My family came from everywhere"), Boo takes an immediate dislike to him. In one of the most explosive and loaded moments in the play, Joe dodges taking Lala to a movie. After he leaves, Boo says, "Adolph, that kike you hired has no manners."

Because Sunny is more aware and educated than the self-centered Lala, it makes sense that Sunny will, in the course of this play, honestly confront her own discomfort and puzzlement with the family shame. Sunny even has a hurtful story of discrimination from her own past that she shares with Joe. But Lala's ignorance provides the perfect opportunity for Uhry to introduce another character to demonstrate the tension of self-hatred and denial that is so present in this play. Peachy Weil provides an excellent foil: he's the opposite of Joe; he's ashamed of his Jewishness (but vehemently proud to be a German-American Jew rather than an Eastern European one); he's rich, of old southern money, and extremely concerned with appearances. Uhry makes Peachy's obnoxious and ignorant persona obvious from the start. Here, Peachy not so subtly alludes to his alleged superiority as a German-American Jew, while making some pretty heartless statements:

> Joe: Howza' war news, Mr. A?
> Adolph: Not so good.
> Joe: Yeah, I got relatives over there.
> Adolph: Poland?
> Joe: Uuh-hunh. And Russia.
> Adolph: Well. Let's hope for the best.
> Joe: Yep.
> Peachy: Let's hope they can dodge bullets.
> Joe: Excuse me?
> Peachy: Hey! Easy there, bud! None of this mess is my fault. It ain't even my problem.
> Joe: That right?
> Peachy: You bet. It's Europe's problem and they gotta solve it on their own. Right, Adolph?
> Adolph: I'd say that depends on where your family is.
> Peachy: Well, mine's been in Louisiana for a hundred and fifty years.

At times, Uhry's characters touch upon subjects that could be considered feminist or gender role issues. These create interesting minor tensions of their own, though not as important to the story as some of the other contrasts that have been presented. Still, these moments serve to further compare the difference between Joe's background and the Freitag/Levy family. Boo, for example, seems surprised and none too pleased when Joe informs her that he can cook and do dishes. However, when Sunny later mentions that she makes coffee in her dorm room all the time, Lala snipes, "I can imagine what that must taste like!" It is as if Lala is determined to hang on to something that she might be able to do better than Sunny, even if it is traditional "women's work." It is a credit to Uhry's talent as a writer that he manages to keep the tone of the play both light and serious at the same time, amidst the sniping that takes place in this family.

The Last Night of Ballyhoo is a complex play with many opportunities for tension and for the exploration of troubling subjects. Despite this, the story manages to maintain a simultaneous mood of comedy. Don Shewey of *American Theatre* describes the play as edging "toward a sitcom formula without falling into it." Amazingly, Uhry accomplishes the balance of comedy and seriousness, of subtlety and directness, all within the layers of tension that this story encompasses.

Source: Catherine Dybiec Holm, Critical Essay on *The Last Night of Ballyhoo,* in *Drama for Students,* The Gale Group, 2002.

Kate Covintree

Covintree is a graduate of Randolph-Macon Woman's College, with a degree in English. In this essay, Covintree discusses the impact of southern culture on Jewish identity for the characters in Uhry's play.

To be southern or to be Jewish in 1939 is to be part of a specific community with principles, ceremonies, language, attitude, and actions that represent and reinforce the culture. To be southern *and* Jewish is to be a part of a unique community that Alfred Uhry focuses on in his play *The Last Night of Ballyhoo.* Though the play primarily takes place in the house of Adolph Freitag, it coincides with two major events—the opening of the movie *Gone With the Wind* and Hitler's rise to power—that stand like bookends at either side of the story and its characters. These events and the characters' reaction to them reflect the struggle for allegiance this family must find. Are they true to their southern upbringing or their Jewish religion? This family is both southern and Jewish, and they stand in the midst of both cultures. As Tony Horwitz states in his book *Confederates in the Attic,* "[i]t was the honor-bound code of the Old South. One's people before one's principles." For Jews in the South, the statement is compounded: who are the people, Jews or southerners, and which are the principles, orthodoxy or upbringing? The answer to this question for a southern Jew could completely alter his or her life. In *The Last Night of Ballyhoo,* Uhry argues that the Freitag family has misunderstood their priorities and improperly answered this question. These southern Jews have currently chosen the South before their Jewishness, but when introduced to Joe Farkas, the Freitags are forced to examine their southernness and their Jewishness.

For years, the Freitags and Levys have lived together as southerners. Since the deaths of Adolph and Boo's brother and then Boo's husband, Adolph has shared his home with his sister, Beulah, his sister-in-law, Reba, and their daughters, Lala and

> EVEN ONE OF THE MOST SACRED OF JEWISH HOLIDAYS AND THE BASIC LANGUAGE THAT SURROUNDS IT ARE FOREIGN TO THE FREITAGS."

Sunny, respectively. Like others of southern high society, Beulah Levy goes by her nickname, Boo, Adolph is a past president of the club, and they can trace their bloodline to "the first white child born in Atlanta."

Lala Levy is a typical southern girl. She and her mother, Boo, are constantly worrying about keeping up appearances in the city of Atlanta. From the very first pages of the play, Lala's two main concerns appear to be seeing the new movie *Gone With the Wind* and finding an appropriate escort to the social event of the season, Ballyhoo. Boo is constantly pressuring her to make acceptable choices and to rise to her place in society. She is embarrassed at her daughter's choice to leave college after the disgrace of not getting into the right sorority. She vigorously works to ensure a date to Ballyhoo for Lala and to marry her off to someone acceptable and appropriate.

As German Jews, Boo and Lala clearly see themselves as superior to "the other kind" of Jews, the Orthodox Jews from Eastern Europe. But Lala, as with the rest of her family, is keenly aware of how being Jewish means that there are those in society superior to her. Nothing will ever make her completely acceptable in southern Christian society. The family struggles with being a part of the Jewish upper class, knowing they will never be a part of the Christian upper class. Adolph is past president of the Standard Club, a Jewish club, just as restrictive but started because Jews were not allowed in the other clubs. Lala has been raised with southern culture at the forefront, but she cannot reconcile the fact that her looks will always proclaim her as Jewish:

> Look at my hair! Look at my skin! Look at my eyes! Listen to my voice! I try and I try and no matter what I do it shows and there's just nothing I can do about it.

Lala blames her Jewish features for her inability to get a date to Ballyhoo and perhaps for her social failures at college.

As Sunny tells Joe, she and her family are a part of a class of "dressed up Jews ... wishing they could kiss their elbows and turn into Episcopalians." Perhaps this is why there is a Christmas tree in the Freitag home, a lifetime tradition for Sunny, a tradition that Boo justifies by comparing it to a Halloween decoration and banning the star. Perhaps, like other southern Jews of the time, their meals are not completely kosher, their weenie-roasters not strict about using all-beef hot dogs. Tony Horwitz gives an example in his book *Confederates in the Attic* of one such restaurant that fuses Jewish and southern culture: "Gershon Weinberg's Real Pork Barbeque."

This desire to be something else also explains Lala's obsession with *Gone With the Wind*, a Hollywood movie that focuses on the survival of plantation owners following Emancipation near the end of the Civil War. In his book *Confederates in the Attic*, Horwitz argues that the movie "had done more to keep the Civil War alive, and to mold its memory, than any history book or event since Appomattox." Though Jews went back as far as the Civil War, the movie clearly omits this. When Lala talks of writing a related story, she wants to name the plantation "something elegant and pure and real Protestant." She chooses the name of her own street, not because her own Jewish family lives there but because it is a street that primarily belongs to "half the membership of the Junior League!"

It could be assumed that the Freitags and Levys are a family of Reform Jews, but they are so far reformed that they seem removed from the real Jewish center of this culture. As Uhry himself confesses to Alex Witchel in the *New York Times* article "Remembering Prejudice, of a Different Sort," this family is "ashamed of being Jewish," and there is "an ignorance, a hole where the Judaism should be." It is not enough that there is a Christmas tree in their house, but none of the family members even knows what time of year Passover occurs. The Freitags do not know the Hebrew name for it, Pesach. They respond to the mere mention of the holiday as if it has nothing to do with their heritage, calling the seder meal "interesting" (Boo) and "boring" (Lala) and referring to the Hebrew prayers as "all of that ish-kabibble." Even one of the most sacred of Jewish holidays and the basic language that surrounds it are foreign to the Freitags.

When Joe Farkas enters the home of this family, he is entering a Jewish home that is southern first and Jewish much further down the line. Of course, Joe is a part of "the other kind," an Orthodox Jew raised in New York on food from the "Old Country," who "think[s] being Jewish means being Jewish." He finds this type of southern Jewish home completely unbelievable and questions its very validity. Boo feels no conflict of loyalty in treating him poorly, even calling him a "kike," as she believes that Eastern European Jews are also lower-class Jews. Of course, Joe's desire to pay for Ballyhoo and Adolph's response to the exchange briefly suggest that Boo's assumption of class is inaccurate. Still, Boo, Lala, and Peachy see no conflict in mistreating Joe because he is more Jewish than they are.

Within this family, Joe withstands hurts like the ones Sunny admits to, hurts of which she herself is afraid. Though Adolph, Reba, and Sunny treat him with general kindness, it is still clear they are unfamiliar with his type of Jewishness and are not always able to prepare him for hurtful situations. Sunny has had her own experience with being the victim of unreasonable prejudice, when she was pulled out of a country club pool as a child for being Jewish. Even though Sunny tells Joe this story, she does not forewarn him about the possible attitudes and assumptions held by those at the Standard Club for Ballyhoo. When he comes to pick her up, he is not wearing a tuxedo and does not have a corsage. He is also unaware of the restrictive attitude of the club, and so Sunny unintentionally puts Joe in a situation that is just as insulting and humiliating as her own childhood experience with prejudice was.

In addition to this personal insult, Joe is appalled that these socialite Jews barely seem aware of the rising situation with Hitler in Europe. Peachy sees no connection between himself and the Jews in Europe. With the audience's knowledge of the Holocaust, it almost becomes unreal that these Jewish characters think nothing of insulting other Jews nor of remaining ignorant to the injustices caused by the Hitler regime. In a time when southern society is so careful to separate types of Jewish people, there is a German government putting all Jews into one community, one that cannot tolerate any type of Jew.

Adolph and Sunny are perhaps the only people in their family even slightly aware of what it might really mean to be Jewish and its universal connection. Sunny is a stellar student, reading forward thinkers like Upton Sinclair, yet she remains removed from these ideas, never claiming any of them personally. She is guided by her southern culture and upbringing and has many prejudices to overcome and much to learn about what it really means to be Jewish. Her romantic relationship with Joe forces her to a private off-stage epiphany during which she must reassess the questions of who are her people, what are her principles, and how do these two things share company?

Sunny's answers to these questions comprise the final scene of the play. Though the scene could be argued either as fantasy or reality, it clearly answers the question of southern/Jewish loyalty for her, for Joe, for the rest of the cast, and for the audience. Sunny's ideal wish, her ''something good,'' is her answer—a shared Sabbath with her family, a moment when community is formed through the deep bond of the Jewish religion. Through Sunny, Uhry has also answered this question, scripting every character to speak in Hebrew. Uhry ends the play with simple stage directions, ''the candles shine,'' closing the play with this vision of hope and religious devotion and making his point and his position clear.

Source: Kate Covintree, Critical Essay on *The Last Night of Ballyhoo,* in *Drama for Students,* The Gale Group, 2002.

SOURCES

Evans, Greg, ''*The Last Night of Ballyhoo,*'' in *Variety,* Vol. 366, No. 5, March 3, 1997, p. 77.

Horwitz, Tony, ''Georgia: Gone with the Window,'' in *Confederates in the Attic: Dispatches from the Unfinished Civil War,* Pantheon Books, 1998.

———, ''Mississippi: The MiniéBall Pregnancy,'' in *Confederates in the Attic: Dispatches from the Unfinished Civil War,* Pantheon Books, 1998.

———, ''Tennessee: At the Foote of the Master,'' in *Confederates in the Attic: Dispatches from the Unfinished Civil War,* Pantheon Books, 1998.

Kanfer, Stefan, ''*The Last Night of Ballyhoo,*'' in *New Leader,* Vol. 80, No. 4, March 10, 1997, p. 22.

Mattimoe, Edward J., ''*The Last Night of Ballyhoo,*'' in *America,* Vol. 176, No. 10, March 29, 1997, p. 24.

Richards, Gary, ''Scripting Scarlett O'Goldberg: Margaret Mitchell, Tennessee Williams, and the Production of Southern Jewishness in *The Last Night of Ballyhoo,*'' in *Southern Quarterly,* Vol. 39, No. 4, Summer 2001, pp. 5–16.

Shewey, Don, ''Ballyhoo and Daisy, Too: Between the Lines with Alfred Uhry and Dana Ivey,'' in *American Theatre,* Vol. 14, No. 4, April 1997, p. 24.

Uhry, Alfred, *The Last Night of Ballyhoo,* Theater Communications Group, 1997.

Zoglin, Richard, ''*The Last Night of Ballyhoo,*'' in *Time,* Vol. 149, No. 11, March 17, 1997, p. 68.

FURTHER READING

Arad, Gulie Ne'eman, *America, Its Jews, and the Rise of Nazism,* Indiana University Press, 2000.
   Israeli historian Arad discusses American Jewry and their lack of significant reaction to the Nazi crisis in Europe.

Freedman, Samuel, *Jew vs. Jew: The Struggle for the Soul of American Jewry,* Touchstone, 2000.
   Freedman explores how relationships among American Jews have changed in the latter half of the twentieth century and offers suggestions on how American Jews can unite.

Hayward, Dave, ''*Ballyhoo* and Brotherly Love: Alfred Uhry's Olympic Premiere,'' in *Back State,* Vol. 37, No. 34, August 23, 1996, p. 39.
   Hayward and Uhry discuss the genesis of *The Last Night of Ballyhoo.*

Sterritt, David, ''A Voice for Themes Other Entertainers Have Left Behind,'' in *Christian Science Monitor,* July 29, 1996.
   Uhry talks about the family in *The Last Night of Ballyhoo,* their prejudices, and his own interest in exploring his religion in his writing.

Witchel, Alex, ''Remembering Prejudice, of a Different Sort,'' in *New York Times,* February 23, 1997, sec. 2, p. H5.
   Witchel explores class divisions among Jews as depicted in *The Last Night of Ballyhoo.*

The Life and Adventures of Nicholas Nickleby

DAVID EDGAR

1980

When it appeared on the London stage in 1980, David Edgar's *Nicholas Nickleby* became the longest play ever produced, and when it moved to a lavish production in New York for the eight-and-one-half hour theater endurance test (viewed either in one marathon sitting or in two long evenings), it boasted the most expensive theatre ticket price ever set, at $100 each. Edgar found himself identifying more and more with the Dickensian spirit of being ''generously angry'' as he worked on *Nicholas Nickleby*. This is a play that takes the social consciousness of the original Dickens novel to new dimensions, where audiences can be reminded of the need for social reform, as well as uplifted by the play's message. Edgar sees three avenues of success in his production: ''First, it looks at adaptations in a new way. It says that a group of people with a strong view about the world can take a work of art and frame it and transform it in a way that makes the adaptation one not *of* the original work of art but *about* the original work of art. Point two . . . it's accessible; it's not obscure. . . . [And] the third point is that it was . . . on the side of the underdog for the entirety of its not inconsiderable length.'' The play combines Dickensian social realism with modern theatrical spectacle and genuine heart.

AUTHOR BIOGRAPHY

David Edgar was born in Birmingham, England, on February 26, 1948. His father, Barrie Edgar, was a television producer, and his mother had been an actress. Birmingham's proximity to Shakespeare's birthplace, Stratford-Upon-Avon meant that David saw numerous productions of Shakespeare plays as he grew up. He attended Oundle School, a liberal private school north of London, where he acted in and directed plays and discovered his passion for socialist politics. He went on to earn his bachelor of arts in drama from Manchester University, in 1969. Edgar briefly held a position as a journalist while beginning his career as a playwright. During and after college, he wrote and acted in numerous plays, and by 1973 he had produced his first television play, *The Eagle Has Landed.* As Edgar's socialist sentiments grew, he helped to found the Theatre Writer's Union (1975) and produced primarily *agit-prop* plays, simple pieces with a socialist agenda. These plays most often ran in small theaters to little notice, and ultimately Edgar decided, as he explained in an interview with biographer Elizabeth Swain, that he needed the arena of the larger theater with its capacity for spectacle in order to convey complex "political questions which concern the relationship between historical events and the perceptions of the people who are passing through them." His chance came when his antifascist, antiracist play *Destiny* moved to the Aldwych Theatre in the fashionable West End theater district of London. Edgar's political insight was recognized, and he was courted by left-wing newspapers to write political essays.

Edgar soon established a parallel career as a political essayist and speaker, one that he continues to nourish alongside his prolific career as a playwright. Contacts with the prestigious Royal Shakespeare Company and a commission to produce Charles Dickens's *Nicholas Nickleby,* led to the 1980 production of his most successful work to date, *The Life and Adventures of Nicholas Nickleby.* Before beginning to write his adaptation of the Dickens novel, Edgar met with directors Trevor Nunn and John Caird and a group of forty-five of the main actors over a period of five weeks, reading the Dickens novel together and discussing how to stage the play. The resulting eight-and-a-half-hour production fulfilled Edgar's goal for theatrical spectacle with a political message. Edgar was especially pleased when a reviewer likened him to Balzac, a French novelist known for epic novels that portrayed nineteenth-century society with all of its

David Edgar

problems. Like Balzac, the reviewer said, Edgar "seems to be a secretary for our times." Edgar responded, "That defined rather more precisely than I'd ever defined before, what I'd like to be. I'd like to be a secretary for the times through which I am living. I'm an unreconstructed social realist, nineteenth-century social realist—or becoming one." David Edgar currently chairs the masters program in playwriting at Birmingham University.

PLOT SUMMARY

Part 1, Act 1

The Life and Adventures of Nicholas Nickleby briefly outlines the reasons that Nicholas Nickleby, his sister Kate, and their mother travel to London—because of the father's death—and then portrays a town meeting wherein a large muffin company ousts private "muffin boys" through a ruse of guaranteeing lower muffin prices to help the poor. Surveying the selling of the new company's stock is Nicholas's parsimonious uncle, Ralph Nickleby, to whom the now-destitute relatives turn for assistance. Ralph places Nicholas as an assistant in Dotheboys Hall, a Yorkshire boarding school, and

Kate in a milliner's shop, coldly splitting them apart. Kate and Mrs. Nickleby move out of their temporary lodgings with the kind portrait artist, Miss La Creevy, and into one of Ralph's sparsely furnished rental homes. Nicholas is skeptical of the one-eyed schoolmaster, Mr. Wackford Squeers, with his appalling lack of knowledge and his gruff treatment of the charges, most of whom are illegitimate or disfigured. Nevertheless, Nicholas dares not question his employer until Squeers starts to beat Smike, a severely limited student whom Nicholas has befriended. In a fit of rage, Nicholas strikes Squeers, and Smike is able to make a getaway. Then Nicholas, too, departs, and Mrs. Squeers tends to her husband. Nicholas runs into John Browdie, a neighbor engaged to a friend of Squeers's daughter Fanny. John gives Nicholas a bear hug for beating the schoolmaster. Smike and Nicholas take the road back to London. Fanny writes a letter to Ralph Nickleby condemning Nicholas as having ruthlessly attacked both of her parents. In the meantime, Kate has been taken in by Madame Mantalini and her crew of milliners. Because she is young and pretty, Kate works with Miss Knag in the shop itself, awkwardly helping rich, spoiled, young women try on hats. Miss Knag befriends the young newcomer.

Part 1, Act 2

Newman Noggs, secretary to Ralph Nickleby, reads Fanny's letter and then goes to visit his downstairs neighbors, the Kenwigs. This family has three daughters and an infant named Lillyvick, named after Mrs. Kenwigs' uncle, a water-rate collector. Mrs. Kenwigs is obviously expecting another child. The family panders to Uncle Lillyvick, for he holds the key to their salvation, if he chooses to leave his inheritance to their girls, which will provide them with a reliable means of subsistence. Nicholas visits Noggs and tells him about his encounter with Squeers and then searches for new employment, temporarily acting as French tutor to the Kenwigs children. His mother does not know whether to believe her son or Ralph about Nicholas's attack of Squeers. However, Kate, who has by now replaced Miss Knag in the milliner's shop and incited her jealousy, has complete faith in her brother. He and his sister embrace, and he leaves with Smike for Portsmouth to find some means of supporting them all. Along the road, they meet the Crummles theatrical family, headed by Mr. Vincent Crummles and featuring the Crummles sons and daughter, otherwise known as the Infant Phenomenon, a girl of fifteen who has been playing a ten-year-old for at

least five years. Nicholas signs on to write a new piece for the company, for a weekly rate of one pound, and ends up playing Romeo, while Smike joins the troupe as the Apothecary. In the audience, Uncle Lillyvick falls in love with the actress Miss Petowker, and they marry, leaving the Kenwigs without a benefactor.

Madame Mantalini's business is about to be foreclosed, due to her husband's profligate ways. When she visits Ralph Nickleby for help, she discovers her husband trying to cash in some outstanding accounts he has stolen from her. She announces her intention to separate from him and says that she has taken steps to put the shop into Miss Knag's hands, a clever way to keep the shop from devolving to her husband, since a married woman cannot own property. Miss Knag now employs Madame as manager, and Mr. Mantolini is left in the cold. It is revealed that Ralph Nickleby had engineered the foreclosure and then stood ready to advance the money to salvage the shop, at a profitable rate of interest. With Miss Knag in charge, however, Nickleby's backing will no longer be needed, but Kate is fired.

The poisoning scene of *Romeo and Juliet,* beginning with the line, ''Who calls so loud?'' is played in tandem with the revelation that Ralph has arranged to have Kate act as hostess for a party at his house, where he will entertain several gentlemen with whom he does business. Smike's line, ''My poverty and not my will consents'' takes on added significance when applied to the juxtaposed scene of Kate having to fulfill her uncle's request despite her misgivings. She soon discovers that she is the evening's entertainment, when Sir Mulberry Hawk tries to seduce her. Ralph sees her to a carriage and realizes the terrible mistake he has made. He admonishes Hawk, but the latter aptly points out that Nickleby would have turned a blind eye had Lord Frederick Verisopht fancied the girl. In the meantime, Nicholas and Smike participate in a fantastically modified happy ending to *Romeo and Juliet,* in which, miraculously, almost everyone survives.

Part 2, Act 1

The second half of the play begins with a brief summary through narration of the events of part I and introduces a new plot line: a love interest for Nicholas. First, however, Kate briefly holds a position as a lady's companion and once again has to fight off the unwelcome advances of Hawk, as she accompanies her mistress to the opera. When Kate takes her complaint to her uncle, he asks her to endure the advances a little longer, until they find "another entertainment," in order not to spoil his relationship with them. She is horrified, but Noggs gives her the empathy she needs and sends for Nicholas. Nicholas heads for London the moment he gets the news, bringing Smike. Coincidentally, the pair arrives in a London coffeehouse only to overhear Hawk and Verisopht talking about Kate. A fight ensues, and Nicholas nearly kills Hawk with a horsewhip. The next day, Nicholas meets the charitable Mr. Charles and Mr. Ned Cheeryble, who enlist Nicholas to help a young, destitute girl, Madeline Bray, whose ailing father has squandered the family fortune. Nicholas has already met her when he goes to confront Nickleby for mistreating his sister, and he is in love. In the meantime, Smike has been caught by Squeers, while wandering around London. Squeers locks him up, but John Browdie, in town on his wedding trip, frees the hapless boy.

Part 2, Act 2

In a coffee room, Nicholas thanks Browdie for saving Smike and meets the Cheeryble's amiable nephew, Frank Cheeryble, who will fall in love with Kate. Nicholas then visits the Kenwigs, whose latest child has arrived. Nicholas breaks the "good" news that Uncle Lillyvick has married an actress, which prompts resentment from Mr. Kenwigs for his "defrauded, swindled infants." Nicholas tells Noggs of his love for Madeline Bray, and Noggs very soon discovers a way to help both Nicholas and Madeline, when he overhears Ralph Nickleby plotting with Arthur Gride, an avaricious old moneylender, to forgive Bray's debts if he gives up his daughter to marry Gride. Nickleby stands to profit in the transaction because Gride has promised to leave his inheritance to Ralph. Noggs urges Nicholas to marry Madeline quickly, to save her from this fate, and Nicholas manages to do so, in the typical boy-gets-girl subplot, with an eleventh-hour appearance at her wedding. Things are looking up for everyone, as Kate and Frank fall in love and the Kenwigs welcome Uncle Lillyvick back to the fold, his erstwhile wife having eloped once again, this time with an itinerant actor. Everyone's fortune seems secure now, although Smike dies, seemingly of his unrequited love for Kate, in a heart-wrenching reprise of his apothecary scene. The bad guys get their due, too, for Squeers is arrested, Hawk shoots his former friend Verisopht and runs off to France, and Ralph commits suicide after learning that Smike is the son he thought he had sent away to the country years ago. Everyone is celebrating Christmas in the usual

Dickens fashion, but Edgar adds a somber note to the story in the form of a new Smike, who shivers outside of their warm circle. As the curtain falls, Nicholas picks up and holds the boy in his arms.

CHARACTERS

Madeline Bray

Madeline Bray, the beautiful, proud, and intelligent daughter of Walter Bray, nearly submits to her father's request to marry the much older, lecherous Arthur Gride so that her ailing father might have the peace of mind of knowing his daughter will have a home after he dies. She had sought the help of the Cheeryble brothers and does not know it is they who have sent Nicholas Nickleby to her to make the small purchases that are keeping her finances afloat. Madeline keeps her attraction to Nicholas Nickleby to herself, hoping that by accepting the arranged marriage to Gride, she can ensure that her father dies happy. He dies before the wedding's conclusion, which is interrupted by Nicholas, whom she eventually marries. In the meantime, she inherits twelve thousand pounds upon her marriage.

Walter Bray

At the end of a dissolute life and hopelessly in debt to Ralph Nickleby, Walter arranges to marry his daughter off to a lecherous old miser, Arthur Gride, in a deal orchestrated by Ralph. Tyrannical and miserable, Walter, at the last moment of his life, regrets his betrayal of his only daughter and closes his eyes so that he will not see the wedding, which does not take place, due to Nicholas Nickleby's interference.

John Browdie

John is a simple Yorkshireman with a thick brogue, whom Nicholas meets during his brief stay at Dotheboys Hall. John assists Nicholas's escape, after the latter strikes Mr. Squeers for his mistreatment of the boys at Dotheboys. John marries Tilda Price, and they travel together to London on their honeymoon, where John once again helps Nicholas, this time to free Smike from Mr. Squeers.

Charles Cheeryble

A philanthropist whose "kindheartedness" and "good-humour" "light up his jolly old face," Charles and his brother act as benefactors to Madeline Bray, and they leave their business to Nicholas after

MEDIA ADAPTATIONS

- The Royal Shakespeare Company production was filmed for television in 1982 and is available on video tape in a boxed set consisting of nine 60-minute tapes.

- Two BBC productions of Dickens's *The Life and Adventures of Nicholas Nickleby* have been produced, one by Vincent Tilsey in 1957 and one in 1968 by Hugh Leonard. Saxon Lucas and D. Corr produced a "pop opera" called *Smike* for BBC television in 1973. None of these came close to the power and spectacle of the David Edgar production.

- Also available on video is the 1947 film directed by Alberto Cavalcanti for Ealing Studios (screenplay by John Dighton), starring Cedric Hardwicke, but it, too, is not as powerful as the televised Royal Shakespeare Company production.

---

they retire, just in time to set him up financially for his marriage to Madeline. Of the two brothers, Charles is more confident and outgoing; he does the planning of their benevolent enterprises.

Edwin Cheeryble

Brother to Charles, Ned participates in their secret dealings to raise people out of poverty and misery and to spread good will. Ned is eager and agreeable, and he willingly implements the generous plans Charles devises.

Frank Cheeryble

The nephew to the Cheeryble brothers, Frank comes to London from Wales, just in time to fall in love with and marry Kate Nickleby. Frank is as good-natured and kindhearted as his generous uncles.

Mrs. Crummles

The boisterous and good-natured wife of Vincent Crummles, Mrs. Crummles welcomes Nicho-

las to the world of the itinerant theatrical troupe. She embraces the world of illusions of the stage and of life.

Ninetta Crummles

See Infant Phenomenon

Mr. Vincent Crummles

The father and manager of the theatrical Crummles family and parent of The Infant Phenomenon, Vincent hires Nicholas to play the part of Romeo in a much-revised version of that play, in which the two lovers miraculously survive their suicide attempts. He also pays Nicholas to produce other lighthearted theatrical fare.

Arthur Gride

A lecherous old miser, about seventy-five years old, who works out a deal with Ralph Nickleby in return for an arranged marriage to Madeline Bray, many years his junior. The basis of his scheme is his illicitly gained knowledge that Madeline will inherit a small fortune upon her marriage. His deaf maid, Peg Sliderskew, steals a document that proves his guilt, in retribution for his intention to marry and leave her (Peg) without a means of living.

Mrs. Grudden

A kindly old soul, Mrs. Grudden is the piano player and extra player with the Crummles theatrical troupe.

Sir Mulberry Hawk

An aristocratic young man, he spends his time gambling and drinking with Lord Verisopht. They meet Kate Nickleby at the home of Mrs. Witterly, where Kate serves as the lady's companion. Hawk tries to seduce Kate, and when she rebuffs him, he tries to take her by force. When Nicholas hears Hawk making rude remarks about Kate and then refusing to identify himself, he beats Hawk nearly senseless with a horsewhip. Hawk swears vengeance. Hawk is thoroughly bad; he and Verisopht have been taking advantage of other gamblers, but their alliance does not prevent Hawk from trying to cheat Verisopht as well. He shoots Verisopht in a duel and escapes to France.

The Infant Phenomenon

This is the stage name of Ninetta Crummles, a child of about fifteen who has been playing the part of a ten-year-old for five years. She is the hope and pride of the theatrical Crummles family.

Morleena Kenwigs

Morleena fawns over her uncle Lillyvick, hoping to encourage his willingness to act as her family's benefactor. She screams in horror when she learns that he has married and then fawns over him again when he announces that his marriage has failed.

Mr. Kenwigs

Mr. Kenwigs is the head of the family downstairs from Newman Noggs. His is a generous family who frequently invites the bachelor to dine with them. He has a rather large family—his seventh child, Lillyvick, is born during the play—but he hopes for a marriage between his wife's rich uncle, Mr. Lillyvick, and his daughter Morleena to cement their livelihood. When Kenwigs learns that the uncle has eloped with an actress, he despairs and expresses his distaste for the older man, but all is repaired when the uncle announces that his marriage has fallen apart because the actress eloped again with an actor.

Mrs. Susan Kenwigs

Mrs. Kenwigs is a hearty woman from a "genteel family," who takes things in stride better than her husband does.

Miss Knag

Miss Knag presides over the milliner's shop belonging to Madame Mantalini. At first, she shows Kate Nicholas the ropes when the latter comes to work for them. But when it becomes apparent that Kate's youth and beauty make her a more attractive storekeeper, she hates her rival. When Mr. Mantalini's spendthrift ways cause the business to go bankrupt, Miss Knag buys it from Ralph Nickleby.

Miss La Creevy

Miss La Creevy is a self-proclaimed artist, a painter of miniatures, with whom Kate and Mrs. Nickleby take lodgings when they arrive in London. Her optimism helps them overcome their fears, but Ralph Nickleby quickly forces the pair to move to more humble lodgings.

Mr. Lillyvick

Uncle to Susan Kenwigs, Mr. Lillyvick has saved up a small fortune as a "collector of water rates." He falls in love with the actress Miss Petowker, follows her to Portsmouth, and marries her. However, she runs off with another actor, and he returns to London, to the great relief of the Kenwigs family, who hopes to inherit his money when he dies.

Mr. Alfred Mantalini

Mr. Mantalini is an oily profligate and womanizer, who embezzles money from his wife's milliner's shop to support his spendthrift lifestyle. His catchphrase "demned" and its various interpretations reveals his attempt at sounding like an aristocrat. He calls himself the "demdest villain ever lived" when his wife discovers he has taken several unpaid bills to Ralph Nickleby to cash in.

Madam Mantalini

The owner of a fashionable milliner's shop in London, Mrs. Mantalini fails to see through her husband's fawning flattery, even when she catches him stealing money from her store. After he has driven her to bankruptcy with his wasteful spending, she surprises him by throwing him out and announcing that she has had the foresight to sell the business to Miss Knag and will serve as manager of the shop instead of owner.

Ned

See See Edwin Cheeyble

Kate Nickleby

Nicholas's sweet and demure seventeen-year-old sister innocently takes on one menial job after another, in hopes of earning enough to keep herself and her mother out of the poorhouse and away from the clutches of her avaricious uncle, Ralph Nickleby. Kate first works in Mrs. Mantalini's millinery and then serves as hostess at a dinner party for her uncle, where Sir Mulberry Hawk makes unwelcome advances. Kate inspires love from the socially damaged Smike, but he never reveals his feelings to her. She never loses faith that her brother eventually will save her from destitution. She and Nicholas vow never to marry for money, but when Frank Cheeryble insists that he loves her, she demurs happily.

Mrs. Nickleby

Mrs. Nickleby is based loosely on Charles Dickens's own mother. She is a garrulous woman whose talk meanders in a desultory manner, and she clings to an illusory gentility, despite her bleak surroundings, for she has never had a knack for recognizing reality. When an insane neighbor tosses vegetables into her garden as a form of courtship, she takes his advances seriously and never realizes his limitations. Her disconnection with reality makes it possible for her to sail through her family's misery with no ill effect on herself.

Nicholas Nickleby

The spirited hero of the story, Nicholas fights villainy and corruption with a ferocity that seems out of character with the mild-mannered hero often found in Victorian novels. Dickens defended his characterization of Nicholas as a natural, not an idealized, young man, saying in the Preface to his 1848 edition, ''If Nicholas be not always found to be blameless or agreeable, he is not always intended to appear so. He is a young man of an impetuous temper and of little or no experience; and I saw no reason why such a hero should be lifted out of nature.''

He accepts a position as tutor at Dotheboys Hall, even though it requires separating from his mother and sister, so that he can begin to earn his way in the world. At first he ignores the mistreatment of the young, deformed, and unwanted charges, but eventually he rebels and strikes Mr. Squeers, the schoolmaster, and leaves, taking young Smike, a mentally retarded child, with him. Nicholas then begins his adventure in earnest, taking a position in the theatre as an actor and playwright and returning to London when he hears that his sister needs him to defend her honor against Sir Mulberry Hawk.

The benevolent Cheeryble brothers take him in, and with their guidance he is able to save his mother and sister, as well as Smike, and to discredit his uncle Ralph and his cohorts. After falling in love with Madeline Bray, who has sought the financial help of the Cheerybles, he frets over how to win her and only succeeds in doing so after Newman Noggs, Ralph's disgruntled assistant, encourages him and gives him information about her upcoming marriage to Gride. Nicholas often seems unable to act decisively without the guidance of older, wiser characters such as Noggs, the Cheerybles, and John Browdie. Eventually, he marries Madeline and plans to raise a big family in the country near his old family home.

Ralph Nickleby

Ralph Nickleby is a conniving and avaricious Scrooge type of character. He does not welcome his sister-in-law, niece, and nephew when they come to him for aid after his brother dies. To get Nicholas out of the way, he sends him to Dotheboys Hall, to work for his erstwhile partner in crime, Mr. Squeers. Rather than truly help his relatives to find their way

in the city, a setting in which they feel unsure and out of place, Ralph only pushes them into situations that are dangerous for them and potentially profitable for him. Thus, he parades his niece to a profligate aristocrat, Sir Mulberry Hawk, simply to cement a business relationship. However, he does not account for the spirit that Nicholas shows in saving Smike and rescuing both Kate and Madeline. Through Nicholas's efforts, Smike is revealed to be Ralph's son from a distant love relationship that withered long ago in Ralph's past. When Ralph learns of this, he hangs himself in remorse, thus demonstrating that he had a heart after all.

Newman Noggs

Noggs is Ralph's clerk, a middle-aged man with the face and habits of an alcoholic. Noggs was from a good family, but through a dissolute lifestyle, he had lost his money when Ralph took him in. Watching Nickleby's criminal schemes has driven him to continued drinking, and he wrings his hands constantly in frustration. On one occasion he punches an imaginary Ralph Nickleby in the air to vent his anger. Noggs hides in a closet and overhears Ralph and Gride plotting to trade Madeline for releasing Mr. Bray's debts. Even through his drunken state, Noggs is horrified, and this latest act of villainy on Ralph Nickleby's part pushes him to action. Noggs becomes a kind of father to Nicholas as he girds the young man to overturn the plan and marry Madeline himself.

Miss Petowker

Miss Petowker is an itinerant actress who entices Mr. Lillyvick to marry her and then runs off with another man.

Tilda Price

Tilda (short for Matilda) Price is a friend of Fanny Squeers. Tilda tries to push Nicholas and Fanny together, but Nicholas takes no interest in her. Tilda marries John Browdie, and Fanny accompanies them on their wedding trip to London.

Peg Sliderskew

The ugly, deaf maidservant of Arthur Gride, Peg steals the documents about Madeline's inheritance so that Gride will not marry Madeline and thus leave Peg out in the cold. She gets caught, but the satisfaction of having spoiled Gride's plans compensates for her misery.

Smike

Smike is the son of Ralph Nickleby from an early marriage whom he has all but forgotten. Ralph had put the child into the care of Brooker, who dropped the boy off at Dotheboys Hall. Ironically, then, Ralph contributes to the mistreatment of his own child, through his dealings with the schoolmaster, Mr. Squeers. Smike is badly fed, badly treated, and badly clothed, and years of neglect and abuse have stunted his mental and physical health. Nicholas takes Smike away from Dotheboys Hall and cares for him until Squeers recaptures the boy, simply to cause harm to Nicholas. John Browdie helps Nicholas get Smike back. Smike silently worships Kate, and he dies of pining for her. Kate and Nicholas attend him in his last moments and bury him under a tree in their old homestead.

Mr. Snawley

Snawley is an associate of Ralph Nickleby who poses as Smike's father but confesses.

Fanny Squeers

The daughter of Mr. Squeers, Fanny has hopes of wooing Nicholas Nickleby, but these are quickly squelched, and she spends the rest of the play hating him.

Mrs. Squeers

Mrs. Squeers collaborates with her husband to keep the Dotheboys Hall schoolboys too weak to complain about their care or education. She administers a weekly dose of ''brimstone'' to dull their appetites. She riffles through the children's mail, removing anything of value, and she skimps on Nicholas's portions of food, as she does the children's. Despite their sordid surroundings, she laughs and flirts gaily with her ''Squeery dearie.''

Mr. Wackford Squeers

A one-eyed, ugly ogre, Mr. Squeers is the hateful master of Dotheboys Hall. Dickens based him on an actual schoolmaster who had been sued for his mistreatment of school children. He cares more about the well-being of his cows and pigs than that of the children, whose fevers and illnesses he punishes as acts of insubordination. Squeers dishes out stingy and inadequate meals and beats the children for minor and imagined misdemeanors, seeming to enjoy hurting them. When he tries to beat the hapless Smike, Nicholas beats Squeers

instead and runs off with the boy. Squeers is one of Ralph Nickleby's partners, so he comes to London to help retrieve the papers stolen by Peg Sliderskew. There he chances upon Smike and locks the boy in a closet. When all is exposed, Squeers goes to prison.

Young Wackford Squeers

The fat, spoiled son of Mr. and Mrs. Squeers, the young Squeers eats well while the rest of the boys are nearly starved.

Lord Frederick Verisopht

A dashing and dissolute young aristocrat who whiles away idle hours gambling and drinking with Sir Mulberry Hawk. Verisopht, too, is smitten with Kate, but he has the good breeding to withdraw when she does not encourage him. In fact, Verisopht attempts to foil Hawk's designs on her, thus instigating a duel, in which he is shot and killed by his former friend.

THEMES

Money

Ralph Nickleby is a prototype for Ebeneezer Scrooge, the covetous miser of *A Christmas Carol*. Having himself lived the life of a poor child forced to work in a shoe blackening company at a young age, Dickens was fascinated by the power and influence of money, with its potential to push bad men to the point of irretrievable corruption and evil. The nineteenth century was a period obsessed with money and ways to make it, as capitalism hit its stride. Investment opportunities existed throughout the burgeoning British Empire—both legitimate and not. Dickens's novel appealed to a wide public, fascinated with the amassing of wealth that bought status and power. And, regardless of their own financial status, they could join in approbation of his avaricious villains and their rapacious manner of swindling their fellow citizens. Money concerns lie at the heart of almost every problem in *Nicholas Nickleby*, from the break-up of the Mantalinis to Kate's vulnerability to Sir Mulberry Hawk. Daughters and unwanted children are particularly at risk when a family cannot provide for them, and avaricious people like Ralph profit from the innocence of others. Dickens seems to be saying that families

TOPICS FOR FURTHER STUDY

- Dickens's novel *Nicholas Nickleby* ends happily, with the siblings' marriages. Why does Edgar change the ending to show a second Smike?

- How did the fact that, in nineteenth-century Britain, married women could not own property affect their life choices?

- Does Nicholas's fractious personality detract from his character? Explain your point of view.

- What is the role of money in this play?

must overcome the obstacle of poverty in order for the society to be a moral one.

School Reform

Dickens, a reformist who targeted many of the social inequities of Victorian England, originally intended his serially published novel *The Life and Adventures of Nicholas Nickleby* (1838–1839) to attract attention to the abuses being committed in schools for cast-off children in the Yorkshire area. He had gathered information about the problem by interviewing several Yorkshire schools, in the guise of someone wanting to board his children at one of them. He was appalled by the conditions of the children and of the license taken by their schoolmasters. Dickens said that Squeers and Dotheboys Hall were, as Dickens reported in his 1848 Preface, "faint and feeble pictures of an existing reality, purposely subdued and kept down lest they should be deemed impossible." With no government funding, the schools relied on collecting school fees from the neglecting parents themselves and on contributions from the few benefactors who might have some interest in the well-being of unwanted children, many of whom were illegitimate or physically deformed. It was a cottage industry that attracted the worst sort, those willing to line their pockets by skimming the tuition of unfortunate and unsponsored children. Ten years after its original publication in monthly serial form, Dickens took credit for reducing the number of Yorkshire schools

in the Preface to the 1848 edition of *The Life and Adventures of Nicholas Nickleby.*

Some sort of education was needed for poor children, so Dickens also worked toward establishing a public school system for this purpose. His efforts were gratified with the establishment in 1844 of the Ragged School Union, a program for running schools for poor children in London and other crowded cities. Dickens later praised this program in several issues of his weekly news magazine, *Household Words.*

The Change of Heart

The change of heart is a common theme in the novels of Charles Dickens. In fact, the moment of climax usually involves the complete transformation of a formerly wicked character who has had a sudden epiphany about his own evil actions. The stages of this transformation are symbolically outlined in his work *A Christmas Carol.* Ebeneezer Scrooge undergoes three realizations: 1) that he has lost his connection to other people, 2) that he is causing suffering to others, and 3) that his heart will be assessed after his death. In *A Christmas Carol,* the three stages are marshalled in by the Ghosts of Christmas Past, Present, and Future. His connections to his deceased sister and to his fiancée remind him of the power of love, seeing the suffering he has caused the Marley family reminds him of his mistakes, and seeing his own gravestone causes him to reflect upon his day of reckoning. With these three crucial stages accomplished, Scrooge experiences a transformation from an embittered and selfish miser to a paragon of generosity and kindness. In *The Life and Adventures of Nicholas Nickleby,* written five years before *A Christmas Carol,* Ralph Nickleby undergoes the same three realizations, although his transformation is temporary and aborted by suicide. First, Ralph Nickleby feels an echo of human connection when he looks into Kate's eyes and sees her resemblance to his dead brother. This connection allows him to see the pain he has caused her through exposing her to Hawk's unwelcome advances. He gets a second dose of guilt when he learns that Smike is the son he had sent away years ago; this knowledge puts a new face on his abuse of Smike as a means to punish his nephew Nicholas. With these two realizations, Ralph can no longer distance himself from the suffering he has caused to others. In a soliloquy, Ralph weighs his life decisions in the scales of judgment and finds himself wanting. He muses about the man he might have become, had he raised Smike himself, and then realizes that the boy has been taught to hate his very name instead. Because he feels condemned by the hatred of his son, he cannot imagine redemption, and so he kills himself.

Edgar retains the first two aspects of the change of heart in his adaptation of the Dickens novel, although he leaves out Dickens's episode of Ralph taking a walk through a cemetery, which reminds him of a man who committed suicide. This episode contains the seeds of the graveyard scene conducted by the Ghost of Christmas Future in *A Christmas Carol*. In the original Dickens story, Ralph, calling on the Devil for help, commits suicide as a final act of violence against Nicholas and his friends, as a way to "spurn their mercy and compassion." Edgar's version is closer to the redemptive change of heart that would become the hallmark of Dickens's novels. In Edgar's play, Ralph experiences his judgment day as he envisions the father he might have become and realizes that he has caused his son to hate his very name. Despairing of redemption, even though the angelic brothers Cheeryble are trying to contact him, Ralph mutters, "Cast out. And homeless. Me," and hangs himself. In Edgar's adaptation, the audience is painfully aware of the change of heart that Ralph is unable to experience.

STYLE

Filmic Staging

Edgar perfected several forms of theatrical presentation that resemble filmic methods, such as the "zoom lens" effect, scenic cuts, and superimposed scenes. Through a combination of stage arrangement, lighting, and juxtaposition, *Nicholas Nickleby* simulates film, as when separate episodes are displayed simultaneously, indicating that actions are occurring in separate parts of London at the same time. Often, these juxtapositions underscore a thematic connection as well. For example, in one scene Noggs overhears Ralph plotting with Arthur Gride to split Madeline's inheritance in return for arranging her to marry Gride, while Mr. Charles and Mr. Ned Cheeryble arrange for Nicholas to help extract the same girl from poverty. In this case, the benevolence of the Cheerbyles, who seek to give their money away, is contrasted with Ralph's grasping for money that he obtains through the most nefarious means. A shift in lighting and sound transfers attention from one group to the other, while keeping both situations in the mind and eye of the audience. The contrast becomes more intense and obvious because of this juxtaposition. In another scene, Nicholas and Smike practice their lines from *Romeo and Juliet* while Ralph ruthlessly withdraws his investment from two businessmen, ruining their business, and Mrs. Nickleby informs Kate that she must dine with her uncle that night. Smike's line, "My poverty and not my will consents," referring to the starving apothecary's decision to sell poison to Romeo, takes on added significance when applied to Kate's necessity to follow her uncle's command to dine with him, again, out of destitution. David Edgar termed this kind of double entendre "referential irony," which is a form of dramatic irony in that the audience understands more than the characters do, such that words expressed innocently take on a secondary importance. Any double entendre refers to a second meaning, but in Edgar's juxtapositions, the second context involves a deeper meaning expressly because of its application to that other context, which is enhanced by the interweaving effect of the two story lines.

The Influence of Epic Theater

Following Bertold Brecht's concept of "epic theater," theater designed to disrupt the spell of theatrical illusion and turn the spectator into a judge who retains the sense of watching a dramatic performance, Edgar draws attention to the play *as a play*. One of these methods is self-referential narration, in which an actor steps out of character to deliver an aside to the audience, commenting on the action. This happens frequently in *Nicholas Nickleby*. Various characters step "out front" to present summary narration, an effect that reminds the audience that the original source of the work was a novel, since the narration comprises segments of Dickens's own writing. In addition, some of the characters, especially Nicholas himself, speak of themselves in the third person, again drawing attention to the artificial construct of the play. The purpose of such disruption for Brecht was to awaken the audience to the social ills portrayed by the play by discouraging the passivity of watching for entertainment, generating instead a kind of "complex seeing" so that, while following the action of the plot, the viewer also judges how and why the playwright is presenting this spectacle. David Edgar acknowledged the influence that Brechtian theater has had on his works, calling Brecht's legacy "part of the air we breathe." Before undertaking *Nicholas Nickleby*, Edgar had written a number of "agit-prop" plays, social reformist plays that were produced in small theaters. But, recognizing the limitations of agitprop, he decided to stage theatrical "spectacles" that would more aptly portray the workings of society itself and then present complex social issues to a wider audience. *Nicholas Nickleby* portrays a number of important social themes. In an interview with theater critic Elizabeth Swain, Edgar identifies some of them, calling the play a "show which is highly ambivalent about riches, highly antagonistic towards moneymaking, in favor of schoolboys against schoolmasters, in favor of employees against employers, in many respects, in favor of actors against directors, in favor of women against men, and servants against masters." Many of these themes appear in the Dickens original, yet Edgar wants to cast some doubt on Dickens's moralizing. Edgar uses the art of "disillusion" to problematize the hopefulness of Dickens's story. Edgar explains, "One of the absolute reasons that we wanted to preserve the distance between the adaptation and the original work is to say, actually we think Dickens is being a bit optimistic." By using Brechtian theatrical methods, disrupting the viewer's engagement in the plot so that the themes are portrayed in bold relief, *Nickleby* becomes both entertainment and instruction. Unlike Brecht, however, whose works attracted only a small coterie of Brecht fans, Edgar sought and found a larger audience, which he accomplished by producing an epic play, a spectacle consisting of over one hundred and thirty parts, with hundreds of costumes and wigs, a lavish and costly production. Edgar considered this break from Brechtian tradition worth it, discovering that his work could be "popular and serious and social at the same time."

HISTORICAL CONTEXT

Industrial Revolution

During what is commonly termed the "Industrial Revolution," England witnessed the explosion of capitalism in the economy of the British Empire. Adam Smith had published his *Wealth of Nations* in 1776, but it took nearly a hundred years for what he called the "invisible hand" of individuals pursuing their own self-interest for their accumulating wealth to have an appreciable effect on the British economy and thus on the everyday lives of individual Britons. By the time Dickens was writing, mills, factories, and workshops had sprung into being in every major city, attracting menial laborers from the agricultural environs to the cities, where they hoped

to earn a better livelihood. As Dickens chronicled, for the majority of workers, such hopes went most dismally unmet. It was the factory owners and managers who profited from Smith's capitalist ideas, while the average working man, woman, and child suffered in ways they could not have suffered on the farm. Social reformists such as Dickens promoted schools and workhouses to aid workers in bettering their lives, while the parliament attempted to legislate humanitarian conditions. Gradually, conditions improved, and women gained a measure of autonomy when they were able to earn wages as an alternative to marrying.

Women in Victorian England

The women's suffrage movement, attempting to gain the right to vote for women, had its beginnings in the Victorian era, specifically after 1867. However, the prevalent image of the "Home Goddess" (Dickens's term) prevailed; the "Home Goddess" was the dainty woman of the house, who through compliant sweetness managed the household and did not interfere with her husband's world. This image coexisted with the predominant ideology that women were intellectually inferior to men. They were valued not for their intellect but for their efficiency in the "separate sphere" of the household and for maintaining decorum under any circumstance. Thus Kate Nickleby cannot assertively confront Sir Mulberry Hawk for accosting her but must plead with her uncle to protect her, and she serves as an idealized mother figure and angelic supporter for both Smike and her brother Nicholas. Women had few political or economic rights: a woman could not vote or initiate a divorce or get a formal education; and property and children belonged to the husband. It would not be until after World War I, when women were needed to fill the gap left by men fighting and dying in the trenches, that they would win the vote (1918), and another ten years would pass before they achieved full political equality.

Social Reform

The nineteenth century saw a series of legislation aimed at ameliorating social problems resulting from the Industrial Revolution and its accompanying migration of low-wage workers to the cities. The Poor Law of 1834 canceled the government dole for the poor and relegated them to separate workhouses for men, women, and children. The intention was to force poor people to become independent and for the father of a family to provide for

COMPARE & CONTRAST

- **Early Nineteenth Century:** It is nearly impossible for people born into poverty to escape it, although the growth of cities and factory jobs lures many to attempt to work their way out of destitution. The lack of employment regulations puts men, women, and children into dangerous jobs, where they literally risk life and limb. The Poor Law of 1834 cancels a policy of governmental handouts to the poor, so they are forced into unhealthy and inhumane workhouses run by the state.

  1980: The social consciousness of Great Britain has resulted in a substantially socialist government that subsidizes business and provides social services. However, the recent election of Margaret Thatcher as prime minister (1979) introduces an era of increased privatization of social services, thus returning England to a more capitalistic economy.

  Today: Despite the movement away from socialism of the 1980s, Britain continues to offer comprehensive social services to the poor, although this system is being challenged by a tremendous influx of low-income immigrants seeking the safety of England's egalitarian political climate.

- **Early Nineteenth Century:** Only boys from wealthy families can count on getting an advanced education that will open the door to economic independence. Women cannot obtain the education they need to achieve economic independence, for only a handful of schools cater to them, and even in those schools the curricula does not teach them what they need to learn to find practical careers. Women and young girls are educated in the home in the art of household

management, and only occasionally in classic literature.

  1980: After the feminist movement of the 1960s, the number of women nearly equals the number of men in universities, which had remained predominantly male despite the fact that women had achieved political equality after World War I and had been allowed to enter the universities to obtain an education equal to that available to men.

  Today: Equitable public education is available for children of all socioeconomic groups. However, the growing number of non-English-speaking immigrants presents challenges to school systems to offer this group equal access to society through equal education.

- **Early Nineteenth Century:** Illegitimate children are looked upon as bearing the sins of the parents who conceive them. Unwanted by society, these individuals are usually unable to extricate themselves from poverty and either enter a life of crime or of wandering from one place to another. The Yorkshire schools take advantage of parents of illegitimate children by offering an out-of-the-way location with "no vacations" to embarrass the parents as they attempt to get on with their lives.

  1980: The stamp of illegitimacy no longer carries the stigma it did in the nineteenth century, and the number of unwanted children is diminishing, thanks to the birth control pill.

  Today: A child's legitimacy is no longer an issue of social condemnation in most liberal, first world nations. However, fundamentalist groups in second and third world nations continue to punish offenders and their offspring.

his wife and children, but conditions in the workhouses bred disease, fatigue, and accidents, and the law required wives, too, to enter the workhouse when their husbands could not provide for them;

thus poor families usually were unable to break out of the poverty cycle. The Marriage Act of 1836 made it easier for the poor to acquire legal married status, another measure aimed at fostering responsibility in poor families. The Matrimonial Causes Act of 1857 made divorce easier (it had been a "privilege" of the rich), but although a man could divorce his wife for adultery, women could only initiate a divorce under the most heinous of conditions—adultery was not enough. Two Factory Acts (1842, 1847) reduced working hours and prevented women and children from working in mines. The Matrimonial Property Acts (1870, 1882) conferred a woman's right to control her own property. Two Reform Bills (1833, 1867) expanded the electorate to include wider representation in the House of Commons.

Charles Dickens was a parliamentary reporter during a time of considerable transformation in the spirit of social responsibility in Britain. He also wrote for the newspapers that sprang into being to feed a public hungry for information about the changing policies of the government. Caught up in the general movement toward greater social responsibility, Dickens both recorded and inspired social reform in England.

CRITICAL OVERVIEW

The original story of Nicholas Nickleby was produced in serial form and printed in twenty monthly parts. It was so popular that Dickens had to issue a proclamation threatening "summary and terrible reprisal" for those who might publish the story under another name. It was his most popular novel to date, and it sold 50,000 copies in short order. When Dickens became even more popular, he performed readings from *Nickleby,* to audiences that "roared" with approval.

Edgar was by no means the first playwright to stage an adaptation of the Dickens novel. In fact, Dickens himself attended the first dramatization, adapted by Edward Stirling and produced by Frederick Yates in London at the Adelphi Theatre in 1838. The production ran for over one hundred performances, and Dickens deemed it "admirably done in every respect." Another production, by William Moncrieff in 1839, did not earn his approval because it revealed information that had not yet come out in Dickens's serialized story of Nicholas—that Smike was Ralph's son. For this breach, Dickens retaliated in a subsequent serial

issue: in chapter 48, Dickens attacks dramatists who transcribe a work from one medium or language to another with little change and then take credit (and profit) for the result. David Edgar, adapting the Dickens piece a century and a half later, himself felt criticized for taking the "easy way" of adaptation. In a 1980 article for the *Times* (as quoted in *Plays from the Contemporary British Theater*), Edgar wrote, "I met the full force of the prejudice that has always existed against the transformation of literature from one medium to another. My work, I was told, had ceased to be 'original.' It was assumed that I was only doing it for the money, or that I was 'marking time' while I developed a 'proper idea.'" Edgar wants his work to be judged as a real play, and his contemporary critics have done just that.

David Edgar worked closely with two talented directors, Trevor Nunn and John Caird, as well as forty-five members of the cast of the original Royal Shakespeare Company production in developing the script for the dramatic version of *The Life and Adventures of Nicholas Nickleby*. The group read the novel together and then rehearsed it scene by scene, with Edgar writing and rewriting the play as the ideas evolved among a rather disparate group of talented artists, including actors, directors, and writer. As Edgar acknowledged, it was a collaborative effort: "It's not a personal statement; it's Dickens having been passed through a filter of 45 people and written down by me." The production ran at the Aldwych Theatre for six weeks, followed in 1981 with two equally successful runs of six weeks each, with audiences often giving fifteen-minute standing ovations. The play won the Society of West End Theatres award for best play, even though the London reviews generally were mixed. Michael Billington of the *Guardian* questioned the judiciousness of adapting a Dickens novel, commenting, "the RSC has come up with a perverse and needless triumph: a great deal of skill and imagination has been expended on the creation of something that gains only marginally, if at all, from being seen rather than read. Undeniably this *Nicholas Nickleby* has been done well. My question is: should it have been done at all?" Some reviewers found the play desultory and over-long, while Bernard Levin of the *Sunday Times* proclaimed that London had never seen anything "so richly joyous. . . . life-enhancing, yea-saying and fecund, so. . . . Dickensian." The New York Broadway production ran for fourteen weeks and won the Antoinette Perry ("Tony") Award and the New York Drama Critics' Circle

A scene from the 1980 theatrical production of The Life and Adventures of Nicholas Nickleby, *written by Charles Dickens and adapted by David Edgar*

award for best play in 1982. The production was filmed for television in 1983 by director Jim Goddard and produced by Colin Callender. This made-for-television version boasts Peter Ustinov as host, but *Time* reviewer Richard Corliss complained that the filming left the viewer feeling as though he has just seen ''a pageant through a peephole'' because television cannot reproduce the spectacle of the stage. Nevertheless, the televised version of *The Life and Adventures of Nicholas Nickleby* won an Emmy Award nomination from the Academy of Television Arts and Sciences in 1983. Although the Edgar version seemed to ''belong'' to the Royal Shakespeare Company of London, the Great Lakes Shakespeare Company of Cleveland, Ohio, produced a very successful show in 1982. A 1985 revival by the Royal Shakespeare Company (with a different cast) once again demanded top ticket prices of one hundred dollars and once again convinced audiences, according to a *Time* review by William A. Henry III in 1986, that ''Nickleby may be the most jubilant and thrilling experience to be had in a theater.'' Expensive and exhausting both to produce and to watch, *The Life and Adventures of Nicholas Nickleby* nonetheless stands as a triumph of socially uplifting theater.

CRITICISM

Carole Hamilton

Hamilton is an English teacher at Cary Academy, an innovative private college preparatory school in Cary, North Carolina. In this essay, Hamilton examines the effect of financial difficulties on Victorian families as represented in Edgar's adaptation of the Charles Dickens novel, The Life and Adventures of Nicholas Nickleby.

Charles Dickens grew up in a family with eight children, a family that continually struggled to make ends meet. At the age of twelve, he had to work in a shoe blacking factory while his father served time in debtor's prison. Not surprisingly, Charles Dickens shared the Victorian fascination with money: with ways of getting it and how money problems affected family relationships. The original title of *The Life and Adventures of Nicholas Nickleby* emphasizes these two concerns, for it continued, ''Containing a Faithful Account of the Fortunes, Misfortunes, Uprisings, Downfallings and Complete Career of the Nickleby Family, edited by 'Boz.''' The inclusion of the word ''family'' is significant, as is the pun of the family name that

WHAT DO I READ NEXT?

- The original Dickens novel, a meandering behemoth, follows the pattern of the picaresque tale and seems to be based on Tobias Smollett's picaresque novels, *The Adventures of Roderick Random* (1748) and *The Adventures of Peregrine Pickle* (1751), both of which Dickens read during his childhood. All of Dickens's novels discuss social reform of one kind or another, but two of them in particular consider the plight of poor children: *Hard Times* (1845) and *Oliver Twist* (1837–1839).

- Like Dickens, David Edgar writes plays of social reform. Notable among his works are *Mary Barnes* (1977), about an unusual experimental psychiatric treatment of a schizophrenic woman, and *The Jail Diary of Albie Sachs* (1966), the story of a Jewish South African lawyer imprisoned for defending opponents of apartheid.

suggests that the family sought their living "nickel by nickel." Furthermore, the title words such as "uprisings" and "downfallings" cast the family history in the terms of a financial stock. Clearly, Dickens equated family fortune with financial fortune, and his readers enthusiastically followed the ups and downs of the Nickleby family fortune as each of the twenty serialized chapters appeared in monthly installments. Although the novel was not one of his best-structured works, being a rambling series of disconnected episodes, its desultoriness suits the theme of financial ups and downs. Like stock investments, the fad of Victorian financiers, the Nickleby family quest for fortune takes many twists and turns and often succeeds by mere chance. Dickens records a society as it makes a transition from the clarity and predictability of inherited fortune to becoming a society in which fortunes can be made but with little or no predictability other than that the blind pursuit of fortune destroys families. He does this by portraying a series of families and the various harms that come to them as they put financial gain above the sanctity of the family.

One of the worst effects of the pursuit of money on the family unit portrayed by *The Life and Adventures of Nicholas Nickleby* is separation. When Nicholas departs from his mother and sister for remote Yorkshire to take a post as assistant at a boys' school, he leaves them unprotected, and Kate becomes vulnerable to the unwanted attentions of Sir Mulberry Hawk. Nicholas himself moves from a

healthy, natural family situation to the hodge-podge of miserable, unwanted children and their cruel guardians that constitute the "family" of Dotheboys Hall. The contrast lies at the heart of the Victorian social problem—that the nuclear family was being threatened and could not be replaced. In addition, Nicholas's peregrinations do not bring him the wealth he seeks. He never obtains financial security until he returns to his family, takes up again his role of protector of the women, and generates another family tie, that of marrying the heiress Madeline Bray.

The Kenwigs family demonstrates the interpersonal strains that financial worries cause in families. The Kenwigs are a warm, loving family, with the virtue of hospitality that they naturally extend to Nicholas. They rejoice at the birth of a fifth child, even though it means another mouth to feed. However, their worries about their daughters preoccupy them so much that it distorts their relationship with the one relative who might offer them a secure future. The Kenwigs patronize Uncle Lillyvick in the hope that he will confer his inheritance on their daughters. They urge their pretty daughter Morleena to kiss him and jump to attention at his frequent criticisms. Instead of Uncle Lillyvick enjoying the respect due to him as an elderly relation, the family bends to mollify his every whim. In effect, their obsequiousness has turned him into a peevish and miserable person. Through the portrayal of the Kenwigs, Dickens demonstrates how family power relationships are distorted by need. They experience the height of family betrayal, in Victorian terms, when he elopes with an actress. And they enjoy the classic Victorian happy ending—a reunited, financially secure family—when he returns and promises, "I shall settle on your children all these moneys I once planned to leave them in my will."

The Bray family demonstrates the worst-case family scenario, in which a father "sells" his daughter into marriage. Walter Bray has squandered his fortune through his dissolute lifestyle, yet his innocent daughter Madeline still reveres him, true to the Victorian ideal of the all-suffering daughter and woman. She willingly goes along with his arrangement to marry Arthur Gride, a lecherous old man of seventy-five. Nicholas identifies her decision as a contest between family and money, and he warns her that "the most degraded poverty is better than the misery you'd undergo as wife to such a man as this." Her misguided resolve stems from the hope that her act will release her father "not from this place, but from the jaws of death," for poverty is killing his will to live. Like the impoverished apothecary who is forced by his own poverty to consent to sell poison to Romeo, Madeline is forced by poverty to consent to an unhappy marriage. She fails to realize that money alone cannot repair the damage that poverty has caused, and she fails to realize that her desperation would have desecrated her new "family," thus extending the cycle of misery, had Nicholas not saved her.

Dickens also portrays families that manage to evade the effects of financial insolvency, at least for a time. The theatrical Crummles family is, as Lillyvick exclaims at the wedding they host for him, "chock full of blessings and phenomena." The Crummleses are generous to Nicholas, paying him one pound a week to act and write scripts for them, and welcoming to anyone who joins their path. Their instant acceptance of Smike is one of the most heartwarming events in the play. They feed, clothe, and employ a child who had been undernourished, beaten, and misused by the Squeers. In more ways than this, the Crummles family is the antithesis of the Squeer "family." The Crummles family, too, is a hodge-podge: the Crummles entourage includes a myriad of actors they have picked up during their travels. But in the Crummles "family," each member has his or her own skill or talent, and each is welcome at the expansive dinner table, even though the Crummleses live hand-to-mouth as they travel from one theatrical engagement to another. But, like the revised happy endings they tack onto every dramatic piece they perform, they are living in a

> "ONE OF THE WORST EFFECTS OF THE PURSUIT OF MONEY ON THE FAMILY UNIT PORTRAYED BY *THE LIFE AND ADVENTURES OF NICHOLAS NICKLEBY* IS SEPARATION."

fantasy world that has little relevancy to real life. It is they who seal the vows between Lillyvick and Miss Petowker, and it is they who harbor the actor she runs away with, leaving Lillyvick hurt and alone. They flaunt the rules of conventional social institutions. They cannot even accept the maturation of their "infant phenomenon," a girl of fifteen who has been playing the role of a ten-year-old for more than five years. Nicholas finds solace for a time at the breast of this family, but while he acts the part of Romeo, his sister is being stalked by the vile Sir Mulberry Hawk. Her situation is compared to that of Juliet, when her parents announce her arranged marriage, while she is secretly in love with Romeo.

Edgar emphasizes the parallels by having the players enact the *Romeo and Juliet* scene all around Kate, and the lines meant for Juliet take on an ironic double meaning when applied to Kate. The apothecary's line, "Who calls so loud?" initiates the only moment in the play that Ralph exhibits true familial concern, for it is spoken just as he looks at Kate's hair, rumpled during her escape from Hawk. Noggs narrates, "And Ralph Nickleby, who was proof against all appeals of blood and kindred—who was steeled against every tale of sorrow and distress— staggered while he looked, and reeled back into the house, as a man who had seen a spirit from a world beyond the grave." The line from *Romeo and Juliet,* "who calls so loud?" seems to imply a calling to conscience for Ralph, who momentarily experiences a family bond. It also calls to Nicholas, who has been living in a fantasy world, separated from his sister, who clearly needs his presence to protect her. In the beginning of Act 2, Mr. Crummles admits that he thinks his family should settle down, for, as he points out, "we're not immortal." His words lead Nicholas to feel a pang of worry about his mother and sister. He has been brought back down to earth, and, as he tells Smike, he rues "the time we have spent dallying here." Perhaps Dickens is expressing his own guilt for having indulged himself in playwriting while he was at Wellington House Academy, soon after his father's release from debtor's prison. He was to be forced to leave school when his family once again fell on hard times. Autobiographical connections aside, including the Crummles family in *Nicholas Nickleby* demonstrates that the idealized family is little more than a fantasy, one that Nicholas ultimately rejects in favor of taking responsibility for his mother and sister.

To further emphasize the mistake of delusional fantasy, Dickens presents the mismatched couple of Mr. and Mrs. Mantalini. Mr. Mantalini hides his peccadilloes behind a mask of insincerity that reaches comic proportions as he calls his wife everything from a ''rose in a demd flowerpot'' to ''juice of pine-apple.'' For years he has been frittering away the money his wife earns from her milliner's shop, as the workers and Miss Knag all realize. However, Mrs. Mantalini continually forgives him, taken in by his ridiculous remonstrances of undying love and his lame, staged ''attempts'' to kill himself. It is only when creditors begin the process of foreclosure—when money problems prevail—that she assesses the situation realistically and separates from him. However, Mrs. Mantalini shows great financial astuteness; she has taken the precaution of signing over the shop to Miss Knag so that it will not revert to him, since the Victorian marriage laws proscribed married women from owning property themselves. Through the portrayal of the Mantalinis, Dickens condemns this policy and demonstrates that granting too much power to dissolute husbands licenses profligacy and destroys the foundation of a marriage. A better model is one that evenhandedly distributes power and does not impinge the woman's freedom to find a new mate when her husband proves unsuitable.

Ironically, the proper familial spirit is portrayed in *The Life and Adventures of Nicholas Nickleby* not by a family but by a pair of brothers, the Cheerybles. The need for true ''Brotherhood'' is underscored by the fact that the book opens and closes with two very different sets of brothers. Dickens suggests that the antithetical Nickleby brothers, Ralph and Godfrey, who pursue separate life paths, should have behaved like Ned and Charles Cheeryble, who act like twins and who cooperate to earn money and also care enough about others to share their riches. The brothers Cheeryble ''adopt'' Madeline and rescue her, with the assistance of Nicholas as a go-between. Like the Crummles, the brothers accept their fellow humans as they are and

offer brotherly love and fatherly help. They even produce a husband for Kate, in the form of their nephew Frank. In contrast, Ralph Nickleby fails in every familial role: he refuses aid to his brother's family and attempts to destroy Nicholas for defying him, which essentially is to say that Ralph hates Nicholas for valuing family above money. Ralph's worst anti-family acts are to ''sell'' his niece to cement a business relationship and to give up his own child without a moment of remorse until after the child is dead. All of his failed family relationships stem from avarice, for money holds the place in his values system that family should hold. Nicholas, through the ''Uprisings and Downfallings'' of his ''life and adventures,'' discovers that his family means more to him than fortune, and he feels unable to marry Madeline, for fear that she might think her wealth attracted him. Of course, his virtue is rewarded both with marriage and money. The play also demonstrates that when families break apart to pursue financial security at the price of family stability, these fissures form cracks in the larger family of society, but that upholding family and brotherly love brings its own form of prosperity.

Source: Carole Hamilton, Critical Essay on *The Life and Adventures of Nicholas Nickleby,* in *Drama for Students,* The Gale Group, 2002.

Melodie Monahan

Monahan operates The Inkwell Works, an editorial service, and teaches English literature at Wayne State University in Detroit, Michigan. In this essay, Monahan places David Edgar's adaptation of the Charles Dickens novel in its historical context and explains its stage success in terms of production techniques Edgar devised to translate the novel's Victorian insights to the 1970s English stage.

The first inkling of an English stage production of Dickens occurred to director Trevor Nunn when he visited the Soviet Union in 1977 and realized the Gorky Theater was engaged in transforming *The Pickwick Papers* into drama. Nunn discovered, in fact, that stage productions of Dickens were commonly done in the Soviet Union. Two years later, in England, Nunn, along with codirector John Caird, began to pool ideas for a similar venture. The hope was to create a play that presented on stage the whole of a Charles Dickens novel. The novel of choice was *The Life and Adventures of Nicholas Nickleby.* There was only one choice for the playwright: the socialist, activist, and extraordinarily prolific David Edgar, who had just completed two adaptations, *Mary Barnes* and *The Jail Diary of*

Albie Sachs (both written in 1978). These works, along with Edgar's known fascination for agitprop technique, suggested that his approach would resonate naturally with the social justice theme in Charles Dickens's novel.

Staging Dickens's work was not a new idea, however. In fact, during the novelist's life, many adaptations of his plays were produced, and existing copyright laws did not protect his work from these truncated reproductions. What made the present idea unique was the aspiration to present the entire novel on the stage, to leave out nothing. The play was ultimately performed in two parts by The Royal Shakespeare Company at the Aldwych Theatre in London in 1980, entailing thirty-nine actors playing 123 speaking parts in ninety-five scenes, lasting eight and a half hours. Reviewing the play for the London *Sunday Times,* Bernard Levin wrote:

> This production . . . is a tribute to England's greatest writer of prose and of the teeming world he conjured up . . . It is a celebration of love and justice that is true to the spirit of Dickens' belief that those are the fulcrums on which the universe is moved.

This essay introduces readers to some of the bridge-making strategies David Edgar used to bring Dickens to the stage and connect his nineteenth-century text to the 1970s world of English theatergoers.

If not immediately upon its opening, then immediately after Levin's positive review, Edgar's play was an extraordinary success. It had two more runs in England, from November 13, 1980, to January 3, 1981, and again from April 23 to June 20, 1981, and then the play had a fourteen-week run in New York City, opening September 23, 1981. It played in Cleveland, in Chicago, and then, on December 10, 1983, it opened in Sidney, Australia. David Edgar's *Nicholas Nickleby* was a phenomenon, a unique stage experience, both contemporary and Victorian, both socialistic and sentimental. The play won awards both in England and in the United States. It was, moreover, a perfect vehicle for some of the deeply held dramatic and ethical convictions of the man who reconceived it.

In his interview with Elizabeth Swain, included in her book *David Edgar: Playwright and Politician* (1986), Edgar pointed out that his parents conceived him just two doors up the street from the address at which Charles Dickens (1812–1870) wrote *Nicholas Nickleby.* This coincidence seemed in line with other affinities between the playwright and novelist. Born 112 years after the novel's composition and

> DAVID EDGAR'S *NICHOLAS NICKLEBY* WAS A PHENOMENON, A UNIQUE STAGE EXPERIENCE, BOTH CONTEMPORARY AND VICTORIAN, BOTH SOCIALISTIC AND SENTIMENTAL.''

coming of age in the turbulent protest-driven 1960s, Edgar developed his own brand of Dickensian outrage at human cruelty, and as of 2001 he has written over sixty pieces, many of which were carefully researched and designed to foreground individuals caught in historical events. Like Dickens, Edgar wrote in social protest, casting a spotlight on injustice, abuse, and oppression. Like Dickens in Victorian England, Edgar in the England of the 1970s and 1980s tried to change public consciousness by exposing what people may well not have seen on their own. The two adaptations Edgar wrote for the stage immediately preceding *Nicholas Nickleby* are examples.

The play *Mary Barnes* is a stage adaptation of the psychological case history, *Mary Barnes: Two Accounts of a Journey Through Madness,* which was co-authored by the schizophrenic and successful painter, Mary Barnes, and her doctor, Joseph Berke. The play, like the book, dramatizes the apparent cure of Barnes who was treated at Kingsley Hall (1965–1970), following the nurturing guidelines of R. D. Laing, while it criticizes conventional shock treatment therapy. The second adaptation by Edgar brought to the stage Albie Sachs's account of his imprisonment in South Africa, *The Jail Diary of Albie Sachs.* A Jewish lawyer who defended opponents of apartheid, Sachs was held in solitary confinement for three years without ever being charged with a crime. In each of these cases, Edgar turned the spotlight on an important individual and social issue.

As a socialist, Edgar also brought to the production of *Nicholas Nickleby* his fascination with the early 1970s technique called agitprop. The term itself, according to Swain, derives from the Soviet idea that agitation and propaganda are effective forms of shaping public opinion. Agitprop technique can be used in various ways, but the part Edgar used entails presenting a significant problem to an audience and inviting the audience to participate. The point is to engage the audience in protest, to reveal a social evil, an oppression, or injustice, and to invite viewers to react. One scene in *Nicholas Nickleby* illustrates this technique.

In Edgar's play, an early scene shows a meeting of the United Metropolitan Improved Hot Muffin and Crumpet Baking and Punctual Delivery Company. In the production of the Edgar's play, some actors integrate the audience, object loudly to the on-stage action, and encourage members of the audience to join them as they throw muffins onto the stage in protest. The top hats on stage are capitalists, moneymakers, who exploit their workers and the starving street people. By inference, the people in the audience become the exploited ones who protest the meeting. Thus, the play begins with this dramatic display of an idea, economic exploitation, and it invites an interaction of challenge and protest by aligning the audience with the underdogs.

Another important topic for the novel and the play is the abusive proprietary schools in nineteenth-century Yorkshire. Like Edgar, Dickens researched his subjects before he dramatized them in his writings. Charles Dickens began as a journalist, and like a journalist preparing a story, he investigated the Yorkshire boys' schools, the originals upon which his Dotheboys Hall is based. In the Author's Preface to the novel, Dickens explains how he pretended to be a gentleman looking for such a school in order to get a firsthand impression of what they were like. The Preface also explains that while Dickens was intent on ''calling public attention to the system'' that perpetrated ''atrocities'' far worse than any depicted in the novel, he also acknowledges that these schools had been severely reduced by lawsuits brought against them.

The character of Smike, the handicapped, supposedly mentally retarded boy whom Nicholas befriends at the school and later discovers to be his cousin, the abandoned son of Ralph Nickleby, has a crucial role in arousing sympathy for the dispossessed and rejected and for asserting the human connection and social responsibility that these writers valued. Smike is the one who clarifies for Dickens's readers and for Edgar's audience the poignancy of the outcast. In part 1, act 1, scene 13, Smike says he was with his friend Dorker when Dorker died. Smike says: ''I was with him at the end, he asked for me. Who will I ask for? Who?''

While Nicholas does not yet understand the magnitude of Smike's isolation, Smike is drawing attention to the fact that when he dies, he will have no one in the world to ask for. As if to explain further to Nicholas, Smike continues: ''O-U-T-C-A-S-T. A noun. Substantive. Person cast out or rejected. Abject. And forsaken. Homeless. Me.''

For much of the play, Nicholas's main concern is making enough money to support himself, his widowed mother, and his unmarried sister Kate. But he takes upon himself Smike, takes up his cause immediately in his decision to beat the sadistic Squeers who runs the school, and in the staging, Nicholas literally carries Smike on his back as they escape. That Smike turns out to be the cousin of Nicholas fulfills, on the literal level, an important thematic point: across class and other hierarchies, human beings are connected, are related, are responsible for one another. Additionally, the central refusal of Uncle Ralph to help Nicholas is seriously qualified when it becomes clear that Ralph earlier refused to care for his own son. In all, the revelation of abuse and injustice is intended to call readers and playgoers to a higher vision, one of brotherhood and shared responsibility.

The production uses two devices that allow Edgar to compress large amounts of text and emphasize meaning through juxtaposition: one is narration, either imbedded in the dialogue or delivered like a chorus refrain, and the other is a manner of open staging that allows one scene to melt into another without conventional breaks. The play's dialogue includes narrative passages rendered in the third person. These summarize action and intention, much as Dickens might have written them. Then, too, Edgar devised a platform for moving furniture up or down stage; thus, scenes could ''fade out'' without really ending, since, as the room withdraws to the back of the stage space, actors may continue to appear to play out the scene that space defines. Similarly, actors could by their costumes and actions create a sense of place, which can envelope and then be superimposed upon a previous scene. These two techniques, narration and what might be called scene blending, allowed Edgar to compress quickly and highlight meaning in the meandering epic plot of Dickens's novel. In each of these techniques, Edgar takes the opportunity to render new interpretation through rearrangement and juxtaposition. One example may serve as illustration.

The Crummles theatrical troupe's production of *Romeo and Juliet,* a happy-ending adaptation by

Nicholas, employs Smike in the role of the apothecary. Dickens and Edgar manipulate the Elizabethan play-within-the-play device for thematic purposes. Smike's lines include the question, "Who calls so loud?" (part 1, act 2, scene 16), which echoes his earlier question to Nicholas when they are still at Dotheboys Hall. Moreover, Edgar has the presentation of the tragedy alternate with a London scene in which Ralph Nickleby experiences a rare sense of human feeling while he hands his niece, Kate, into her carriage. The Crummles actors engulf Ralph and Kate, act around them. So as Ralph is pondering Kate, Edgar's audience watches Smike (Ralph's abandoned son) call out. The juxtaposition of the scenes extends the idea of tragedy from the Shakespeare play to the Nickleby plot, as it parallels Smike's vulnerability with Kate's. The ideas that money can disrupt familial ties, that love can connect people across barriers, and that disconnection or connecting across those barriers can extract great cost are thematic for Shakespeare's play, for Dickens, for Edgar. In Edgar's play, these thematic issues are underscored again when Smike dies, a scene in which the apothecary lines are used another way, this time to suggest that Smike hears a call from Heaven.

Narration summarizes and interprets. In the London scene with Ralph and Kate, which co-occurs with the Shakespeare production, Edgar has Ralph's secretary, Newman Noggs, step forward to describe Ralph's reaction to having these human feelings. Noggs states: "And Ralph Nickleby, who was proof against all appeals of blood and kindred—who was steeled against every tale of sorrow and distress—staggered while he looked, and reeled back into the house, as a man who had seen a spirit from a world beyond the grave." Like scene directions in a play, like the prose description a novelist uses, Noggs's words suggest that Ralph has seen a ghost, and they also point to an important, albeit sentimental, idea: even the most hardened person can feel, is capable of moments when point of view shifts and the previously sustained balance with which he holds himself erect becomes precariously endangered.

In his interview with Swain, David Edgar said the novel *Nicholas Nickleby* is about "a time in which industrialization is breaking down old hierarchies and barriers but is leaving people open and naked and uncertain about how they relate one to another." Edgar conveys this uncertainty at the end of the play in which, amid a generally happy conclusion, Nicholas spies another child abandoned in the snow, a new Smike. Against the backdrop of family singing, Nicholas picks up the boy and walks toward the audience with a piercing look in his eye. It is as though in the staging David Edgar has allowed for a happy ending (although it may be "pasted on," as Nicholas's ending of *Romeo and Juliet* is), while at the same moment he arranges the happy ending to be upstaged by a challenge about human responsibility in the face of continued suffering. In an effort to describe his role as playwright, David Edgar told Swain, "I'd like to be a secretary for the times through which I'm living." In doing so, he purposefully joins hands with Dickens, across genres and across the centuries.

Source: Melodie Monahan, Critical Essay on *The Life and Adventures of Nicholas Nickleby,* in *Drama for Students,* The Gale Group, 2002.

Christopher Innes

In the following essay excerpt, Innes examines a contemporary staging of Nicholas Nickleby *by David Edgar to identify challenges that the play poses for modern theater, and Edgar's solutions to those challenges.*

Perhaps the main reason for the immense popularity of *Nicholas Nickleby* as dramatic material is the theatrical nature of one extended section, in which Nicholas joins up with the Crummles's acting troupe. Originally this was a satirical attack on a well-known actor-manager and his much promoted daughter, who—incredibly—performed Shylock at the incongruous age of 8 just a year before Dickens embarked on the novel. Yet the exaggerated display of Victorian coarse acting makes wonderful farce. It is also a form of metatheatre. Heightening the artifice of stage performance by self-parody has been a traditional comic technique. But this has gained a particular contemporary relevance: exposing the mechanics of stage-business by presenting the whole drama as a play or dealing with characters who are actors, expresses a doubleness of vision and self-referentiality that has become one of the defining qualities of post-modernism. In addition, it is the basis of Bertolt Brecht's dramaturgy, which has had a widespread influence on the younger generation of British playwrights, including David Edgar.

A conventional example of the exploitation of such theatrical elements is provided by a 1969 dramatization at the Glasgow Citizens Theatre. 'Faced with the apparently insoluble problem of editing . . . the rich, shapeless mass of the novel' the adapters used the Crummles's scenes as a frame,

> IN EDGAR'S VIEW THERE WERE STRONG PARALLELS BETWEEN THE SOCIAL CONTEXTS OF THE 1830S AND THE PRESENT, BOTH BEING PERIODS IN WHICH RAPID TECHNOLOGICAL CHANGE AND THE DISAPPEARANCE OF EARLIER MORAL STANDARDS UNDER THE PRESSURE OF CAPITALIST EXPANSION RESULTED IN THE EXACERBATION OF INEQUALITY AND INJUSTICE."

through which the story could be accommodated to the stage:

Like so many authors tackling their first play or novel, Nicholas's answer [to the demand that he write a script] is to make it strictly autobiographical. The Crummles Company, unaware of the involvement of the two principals in the events of the real life story, play it out with gusto for a miserly speculator whom they hope will discharge their debts.

However, distancing the action like this defused any possible social criticism, reducing the story to the level of a comically anachronistic acting display.

By contrast, Edgar's version emphasized the political immediacy of Dickens's material by making the production itself a prism, with the overt theatricality giving a multiple perspective to every scene. The whole cast of 49 actors was present on stage throughout the action: interjecting commentary, visibly supplying sound effects, and (above all) observing the scenes. As Edgar put it, the central concept of the adaptation was 'that the acting company were in collective possession of an entire story, which they were then to tell to the audience'; and their silent reactions conditioned the audience's response as they stood 'watching their story unfold'. Passages of narration that linked the episodes were spoken by the onlookers as a group, with the lines divided among them; apart from Nicholas and his sister, each of the actors played multiple parts; and they continually stepped out of their roles to narrate the characters' feelings about themselves or

others in third-person description. They also formed the 'scenery': grouping to represent the stage-coach in which Nicholas and Smike returned to London, lining up in different configurations across the stage as the walls of various houses that Ralph Nickleby visits, or coalescing into the dark cloud of guilt and retribution that hangs over him, dogging his heels on his final flight through the streets. Thus every aspect of the performance consciously emphasized theatrical pretence, making the medium of expression as much the subject of the drama as the story itself.

Although superficially similar to Brechtian dramaturgy—in the actor stepping out of character, the objective third-person narration, the avoidance of illusion—the result was very different. The world created, being a purely human one, was psychological, symbolic, an imaginary projection. It was also shown as conditional, rather than presented as a fixed reality, by the concept of the play as a communal product. So that the actors

—who knew how it was to end—were expressing a huge collective 'wouldn't it be good if' aspiration, as they watched and told the unfolding events. This distancing device, which in Brecht is supposed to clear the mind of emotion, had in our case the effect of directing and deepening the audience's own visceral longing for Ralph's vision of the world to be disproved.

This emotional response was intensified by the physical involvement of the audience in the action. The cast entered through the spectators at the beginning of each performance, and the two-tier set extended out into the auditorium. Built out of a rough wooden scaffolding—specifically an acting-space, rather than scenery, requiring spectators to participate imaginatively by visualizing the various settings—the upper level ran all the way around the front of the mezzanine. The chase-scenes in each half of the play took place above the heads and in the middle of the audience. Compounding this, Edgar shifted the focus of the story from Dickens's hero to the pitiful Smike, the abused boy Nicholas rescues from the inhuman Yorkshire school.

Like the part of Oliver Twist, the role of Smike had traditionally been played by women to bring out the pathos of Dickens's characterization (a practice that continued up until the 1920s). In the novel Smike is described as starving, dispirited and simpleminded, his only physical impairment being a slight lameness. In order to deny Dickensian sentimentality, Edgar exaggerated his disabilities. Smike became an infantile schizophrenic, crippled almost to the point of paralysis. Although some critics felt that the bravura performance of the role (David Threlfall in the first production) unbalanced the whole dramatization, the effect was central to Edgar's thematic intentions Smike literally embodied the deforming effects of an unjust society. The audience's initial revulsion at his grotesquely distorted and drooling figure, which associated them subliminally with the oppressors, intensified their reactions as the action revealed the victim's real humanity. Emotions evoked for the individual were thus almost automatically turned against the system responsible for his condition. Hence the spontaneous nightly applause at the point when Nicholas takes revenge on the sadistic schoolmaster, which—unusually for the theatre—signalled approval for the action, rather than appreciation of the performer.

In Edgar's view there were strong parallels between the social contexts of the 1830s and the present, both being periods in which rapid technological change and the disappearance of earlier moral standards under the pressure of capitalist expansion resulted in the exacerbation of inequality and injustice. At the same time (quoting Marx) he rejected the type of solution espoused by Dickens, whose novel incorporated an essential affirmation of existing conditions in its exuberance, and proposed idealized personal charity, innocence and the unexpected inheritance of a modest fortune (concealed by villains) as sufficient for reform. Thus Edgar's adaptation was designed as 'a play about Dickens that criticized his form of social morality, rather than a straight dramatization of the novel'.

This was expressed through subtle changes to Dickens's story, even though in general Edgar's script is remarkably faithful to the novel. Through extensive doubling, practically all Dickens's figures appear, so that the list of characters includes over 120 named parts, plus various groups (and the anonymous populace of London). Although compressed, the dialogue and much of the linking narrative is produced verbatim; and the substance of Dickens's major passages of commentary is included, as well as most of his characters' main speeches. At the same time, the eponymous Cheeryble twins—paragons of charity that even Dickens's contemporaries had criticized as incredible, despite his pointing to their real-life analogues—were downplayed, as was the folly of Nicholas's mother (omitting the comic madman next door, with whom she imagines herself in love). As a result, over two-thirds of the performance time was devoted to the first half of the novel, thus focusing on the more general depictions of inhumanity and

corruption in the book—plus the theatrical parody of the Crummles Company—and de-emphasizing the positive pole of Dickens's story. Some scenes, spread out over several installments, were reorganized into continuous units to facilitate the flow of the action. Others, separated in the novel, were interwoven in counterpoint to underline the social criticism; and this was extended by the most significant of Edgar's additions.

These additions were the drawing of political morals from the story, the inclusion of a travestied *Romeo and Juliet* as performed by the Crummles, and the final image of Nicholas holding out a 'new Smike' to the audience. What Nicholas and Kate explicitly learn from their experiences in Edgar's version is the universal corruption and destructiveness of money, declaring that even the kindest and noblest souls are inevitably 'tainted' by its touch. The conclusions of both halves reinforce this by underlining the illusory nature of Dickens's utopian solution. Transforming *Romeo and Juliet* into a travesty in which everyone but Tybalt turns out to be alive after all and Viola is imported from *Twelfth Night* as a substitute bride for Juliet's arranged husband (echoing the worst excesses of eighteenth-century treatments of Shakespeare) provides a graphic image of the spuriousness of happy endings. Similarly, the conventional image of social renewal in the marriages that crown the novel is undercut by presenting the happy couples as a sentimentalized Christmas-card tableau. Along with these false images, the audience is challenged to take action. The first half of the play closes in a parody of a patriotic Victorian Afterpiece (Mrs Crummles as Britannia) with the injunction:

> England, arise:
> Join in the chorus!
> It is a new-made song you should be singing . . .
> See each one do what he can

while the 'New Smike' cradled in Nicholas's arms is intended 'as a reminder that for every Smike you save there are still thousands out there, in the cold'.

What marks Edgar's version of *Nicholas Nickleby* out from previous adaptations is partly the way such political relevance is achieved through exploiting the dramatic form itself, keeping the audience constantly aware of theatrical conventions. The presence—and consciousness—of modern-day actors, as interpreters of a 150-year-old story, simultaneously intensified the audience's emotional involvement and gave a critical perspective on the action. On a still more obvious level, what makes this dramatization unique is the way Edgar's use of overt theatricality enabled the complete novel to be staged in its entirety, although doing so still required eight-and-a-half hours playing time, so that the story was divided into two distinct halves. Exactly the same qualities characterize Christine Edzard's treatment of *Little Dorrit,* but with cinematic elements substituted for the theatricality.

Source: Christopher Innes, ''Adapting Dickens to the Modern Eye: *Nicholas Nickleby* and *Little Dorrit,*'' in *Novel Images: Literature in Performance,* edited by Peter Reynolds, Routledge, Inc., 1993, pp. 64–79.

SOURCES

Asquith, Ros, ''A Dickens of a Play,'' Review, in *Time Out,* June 20, 1980.

Billington, Michael, ''A Triumph of Perversity,'' Review, in *Guardian,* June 23, 1980.

Corliss, Richard, ''The Life and Adventures of Nicholas Nickleby,'' Review of the televised production, in *Time,* Vol. 121, January 10, 1983, p. 62.

Davis, Paul, *Charles Dickens A to Z,* Facts on File, Inc., 1998, p. 265.

Dickens, Charles. ''Author's Preface,'' in *Nicholas Nickleby,* Everyman's Library, 1970, p. xvii.

———, *The Life and Adventures of Nicholas Nickleby,* 1839, reprint, Oxford University Press, 1957, pp. xviii & xix.

Edgar, David, *The Life and Adventures of Nicholas Nickleby,* in *Plays from the Contemporary British Theater,* edited by Brooks McNamara, Penguin, 1992.

Henry, William A., III, ''*The Life and Adventures of Nicholas Nickleby,*'' Review, in *Time,* Vol. 128, July 14, 1986, p. 68.

Levin, Bernard, ''The Truth about Dickens in Nine Joyous Hours,'' in *Sunday Times* (London), July 8, 1980, p. 40.

Schlicke, Paul, ''Nicholas Nickleby,'' in the *Oxford Reader's Companion to Dickens,* Oxford University Press, 1999, p. 404.

Swain, Elizabeth, *David Edgar: Playwright and Politician,* Peter Lang Publishing, 1986, pp. 65, 145, 221, 263, 268, 277, 330–31, 335, 336.

FURTHER READING

Brockett, Oscar Gross, *Century of Innovation: A History of European and American Theatre and Drama Since the Late Nineteenth Century,* Allyn and Bacon, 1991.
    This book provides a thematic overview of theatrical movements that have shaped modern theater.

Dickens, Charles, *The Life and Adventures of Nicholas Nickleby,* 1839, reprint, Oxford University Press, 1957.
    This is the original Nicholas Nickleby novel by Dickens.

Edgar, David, ed., *Playwrights on Playwriting,* State of Play Series, Faber and Faber Limited, 1999.
    This anthology of essays on playwriting contains an introduction by the volume editor, David Edgar.

Matthew, Colin, ed., *The Nineteenth Century: The British Isles: 1815–1901,* Oxford University Press, 2000.
    This book of essays by leading historians covers the economy, politics, society, gender, religious, and artistic world of nineteenth-century Britain.

Painter, Susan, *Edgar, The Playwright,* Methuen, 1996.
    A study of Edgar's works, this book includes a chronology of his life and production dates as well as some photos.

Price, Martin, ed., *Dickens: A Collection of Critical Essays,* Prentice-Hall, 1967.
    This collection of essays, mostly focusing on one or another of Dickens's novels, includes an essay by Dickens Scholar Barbara Hardy entitled ''Change of Heart in Dickens' Novels.''

Rubin, Leon, *The Nicholas Nickleby Story: The Making of the Historic Royal Shakespeare Company Production,* Heinemann, 1981.
    This book is a documentary of the first production of the play, including photos.

Swain, Elizabeth, *David Edgar, Playwright and Politician,* Peter Lang Publishing, 1986.
    Swain examines the way in which, as she sees it, Edgar's political plays of the 1970s portray British history, post–World War II.

Tucker, Herbert, ed., *A Companion to Victorian Literature,* Polity Press, 1999.
    The book is comprised of a collection of essays by recent Victorian scholars.

Williams, Raymond, *Culture and Society 1780–1851,* 1958, reprint, Columbia University Press, 1983.
    This readable scholarly work on the literary and social history of industrialized Britain poses the hypothesis that culture became a commodity during this time.

Ma Rainey's Black Bottom

AUGUST WILSON

1984

August Wilson's *Ma Rainey's Black Bottom*, his first play in a ten-play cycle, each chronicling a decade in the African-American experience, was first performed at the Yale Repertory Theater in 1984, though Wilson began writing the play in 1976, after listening to the blues for more than a decade. Set in a Chicago recording studio in 1927, the two-act drama tells the story of a recording session with blues legend Ma Rainey, her band members, and the white producer and agent who made themselves wealthy through Rainey's recordings. The play explores race relations between blacks and whites in 1920s America and the African-American search for identity. The title comes from the song of the same name, which is at the heart of a major conflict in the play. Of particular note is Wilson's character, Levee, who literally embodies the aspirations and disappointments of black males during this era and, arguably, today. Wilson pits Levee against Rainey, the band members, and the whites, examining various stripes of inter- and intra-racial conflict.

Partly inspired by the plays of Amiri Baraka, who warned black writers to keep their characters faithful to the black experience, Wilson finished the first version of the play in 1981 and had it accepted by the Eugene O'Neill Theater Center's National Playwrights Conference in the summer of 1982. In 1985, the play opened on Broadway at the Cort Theater, and it subsequently captured a slew of awards including the New York Drama Critics'

Circle Award for best American play. *Ma Rainey's Black Bottom* is considered Wilson's first major play and helped to cement his reputation as an important American playwright.

AUTHOR BIOGRAPHY

Born in 1945 to a white father, Frederick August Kittle, and a black mother, Daisy Wilson, August Wilson grew up in Pittsburgh, Pennsylvania. A voracious reader who credits his mother for his love of language, Wilson dropped out of school in the ninth grade, educating himself at libraries. In 1962, Wilson enlisted in the U.S. Army but was discharged a year later. In 1965, he decided to become a writer, buying his first typewriter for twenty dollars. In 1968, he helped to found Pittsburgh's Black Horizons on the Hill Theater, with the goal of "politicizing the community." Wilson was heavily involved with the Civil Rights movement during this time and described himself as a "Black Nationalist." After he moved to St. Paul, Minnesota, in 1978, Wilson's career began to gather steam. Following the oft-given advice to write what you know, Wilson created characters that spoke like people he knew in black neighborhoods of Pittsburgh.

In 1980, the Playwright's Center in Minneapolis accepted his play, *Jitney*, a drama set in a Pittsburgh taxi station, and in 1982 the prestigious Eugene O'Neill Center accepted *Ma Rainey's Black Bottom*. The success of this play helped catapult Wilson into the national limelight. *Ma Rainey's Black Bottom* received the New York Drama Critics' Circle Award for best play and an Antoinette Perry ("Tony") Award nomination from the League of New York Theatres and Producers. Wilson's next effort, *Fences*, was even more successful, garnering an Outstanding Play Award from the American Theatre Critics, a Drama Desk Outstanding New Play Award, a New York Drama Critics' Circle Best Play Award, a Pulitzer Prize for drama, a Tony Award for best play, and a Best Broadway play award from the Outer Critics Circle. The latest installment in Wilson's ambitious plan to write a ten-play cycle—each dealing with a decade in Black American history—is *King Hedley II*, which opened in 2001 on Broadway. Set during 1985 in Pittsburgh's Hill District, *King Hedley II* explores the relationship between an ex-convict struggling to understand his life and the impoverished community in which he lives. Wilson continues to write and to speak out, from his home in Seattle, Washington, for the creation of and the funding for black theaters.

PLOT SUMMARY

Act 1

Ma Rainey's Black Bottom opens in a Chicago recording studio in early March 1927. Rainey has taken a break from touring to record some songs for Sturdyvant's studio. As the lights come up, Sturdyvant is warning Irvin that he will not put up with any of Ma Rainey's "shenanigans." Sturdyvant characterizes Rainey as a prima donna, someone who expects the world to do her bidding. Irvin's assurances that Rainey will show up on time do not sound convincing, however, and the more Sturdyvant warns Irvin that he won't put up with Rainey's attitude, the more prepared the audience becomes for an inevitable conflict when she does appear.

Cutler and the band appear shortly, and Levee shows up carrying his new shoes, which he paid for in part with money he won from Cutler the night before playing craps, a dice game. Levee's new Florsheim shoes represent a shift in musical taste from blues to jazz and swing, a change that Sturdyvant wants to exploit, at least initially, when he tells Irvin to have the band record Levee's version of "Ma Rainey's Black Bottom."

The bulk of act 1 is comprised of bantering between and among band players, with Levee arguing with almost everyone. The stories the band members tell and the subjects of their arguments both reveal their respective characters and outline a particular struggle blacks historically have had with whites.

One of these struggles is exemplified when Rainey finally makes her entrance, along with Sylvester, Dussey Mae, and a policeman, who threatens to arrest her for assaulting a cab driver after the group attempted to leave an automobile accident they were in. Wilson's scenarios are universal enough to appeal to a racially diverse audience and to create empathy for dilemmas specific to blacks. The struggle for financial control of goods made by black labor is evident, for example, in the way in which Rainey responds to Irvin and the way in which Sturdyvant pressures Irvin. Act 1 ends with Levee, the youngest band member, telling the story of his mother's rape and his father's murder at the hands of white men. The important thing to remember about the action in this act isn't what happens, but the emotional effect racial conflict has on how band members interact with one another, as well as with whites.

Act 2

In this act, Rainey asserts her prerogative in having Sylvester do the introduction to "Ma Rainey's Black Bottom," even though band members and Irvin think it's a bad idea because of his stuttering. Rainey's insistence, however, symbolizes the duty she feels in giving powerless blacks a voice, both literally and figuratively. This demand—and her refusal to sing unless she has a Coca-Cola—illustrates almost stereotypical behavior of prima donna celebrities. However, Rainey's motivation for behaving this way is more closely related to her desire to let her white producer and agent know that they cannot take advantage of black people in general and her in particular. Various characters, including Rainey, give speeches about white exploitation and mistreatment of blacks throughout the act. Levee, who Sturdyvant had promised could record some of his own songs, is humiliated by the producer, who now tells him that his music isn't what people want. Enraged at a system that has squelched his creative powers, at a people who have shamed and exploited him, and at a man who has lied to him, Levee stabs Toledo. He does so, not because Toledo stepped on his shoe, but because Toledo was unfortunate enough to be in the vicinity just after Sturdyvant's exchange with Levee. By offering no transcendence or resolution at the end of the play, Wilson figuratively "sticks it" to his audience as well, reminding them that the plight of African Americans remains the same.

CHARACTERS

Sylvester Brown

Ma introduces Sylvester as her nephew. He is young and built like an "Arkansas fullback," and he stutters. He was the driver during the car accident, but Ma absolves him of blame. Ma insists that he introduce her song, "Ma Rainey's Black Bottom," even though he stutters. Critics have raised

August Wilson

the possibility that perhaps Sylvester is Ma's lover, rather than her nephew, and that Sylvester's sniping with Dussie Mae reflects competition for her affection and attention.

Cutler

Cutler is the guitar and trombone player and leader of the instrumentalists. He is in his mid-fifties and, Wilson writes, "has all the qualities of a loner except the introspection." He plays the music straight, with no embellishment. During the session, he smokes reefer (marijuana). Cutler's story about Reverend Gates being humiliated by a gang of white men illustrates his attitude that black men have to do what's necessary to survive.

Dussie Mae

Dussie Mae is Ma Rainey's beautiful girl (her lover). She is a "young, dark-skinned woman whose greatest asset is the sensual energy which seems to flow from her." Dussie Mae wears a fur jacket and a tight-fitting yellow dress. She is deferent to Ma Rainey, but when she is alone with Levee, she kisses him and tells him that she'll be his woman when (if) he gets his band together.

MEDIA
ADAPTATIONS

- In *August Wilson: A Conversation with August Wilson,* Wilson describes his role as passing down the practical and spiritual wisdom of the African-American community in his plays and writings. He discusses the influence of black traditions like storytelling and blues music on his plays. The video, 22 minutes long, is part of the series, *In Black and White: Six Profiles of African American Authors,* and can be purchased from California Newsreel, 149 Ninth St., San Francisco, CA 94103.

- The Classic Blues label released *The Essential Ma Rainey* in 2001, a collection of Rainey's most popular songs.

- In 1988–1989, *August Wilson, Playwright* was filmed by City University Television in association with the Center for Advanced Study in Theater Arts and the Harold Clurman Endowment.

Irvin

Irvin is Ma Rainey's white agent who is "a tall, fleshy man who prides himself on his knowledge of blacks and his ability to deal with them." Most of his energy is spent placating Ma Rainey and Sturdyvant. He solves Ma's issue with the policeman by bribing him to make it go away. Although he seems comfortable communicating with the band and with Ma Rainey, he is chiefly motivated by money.

Levee

Levee is the talented, temperamental trumpet player, and, in his early thirties, the youngest player in the band. He prides himself on his appearance, especially his shoes, which he bought with money won from Cutler at craps. Levee wants to put a band together and record his own songs, and he tells other band members that Sturdyvant said he would help him do this. Levee's version of "Ma Rainey's Black Bottom" is faster, more of a swing song than a blues

number. Levee is frustrated and bitter and argues with all of the band members; he also attempts to seduce Dussie Mae. Like the other band members, Levee has a story about his past that illuminates his present relationships with both blacks and whites. When he was a child, he witnessed his mother being raped by a gang of white men. He tried to stop the men but was seriously injured after being struck with a knife by one of the men. His father subsequently sold their farm to one of the men who raped his wife, settled his family in another town, and then returned for vengeance. He killed four of the men before being killed himself. Levee's anger reaches a fevered pitch at the end of the play, when Sturdyvant won't let him record the songs he previously told him he could. Levee winds up stabbing Toledo, killing him, after Toledo steps on his shoe.

Policeman

The policeman is the third white man in the play. He enters with Ma Rainey, Sylvester, and Dussie Mae and engages in a shouting match with them to tell Irvin the story of Ma's automobile accident. Eventually, he is satisfied that Rainey is "as important as she says she is" and takes money from Irvin to forget the incident and not take Ma to jail.

Ma Rainey

Wilson's Ma Rainey is based on the historical Ma Rainey, widely considered to be the Mother of the Blues because of her influence on other female blues singers. Born Gertrude Pridgett in Columbus, Georgia, in 1886 to parents who were minstrel performers, Rainey first appeared onstage in 1900. She toured with William "Pa" Rainey, a minstrel song and dance man whom she married in 1904, and with groups such as Tolliver's Circus and Musical Extravaganza. Rainey signed a recording contract with the "race division" of Paramount Records in 1923, when she was thirty-eight years old. Her recording career ended in 1928, after she had recorded some one hundred songs, many of them classics today. Rainey is rumored to have coached a young Bessie Smith in singing the blues, and she played with jazz musicians such as Louis Armstrong, Tommy Ladnier, Coleman Hawkins, and Buster Bailey. Rainey died in 1939.

In Wilson's play, Rainey is the bandleader and has the final say in recording decisions. Rainey has no illusions about her relationship with her agent, Irvin, or Sturdyvant, the producer, recognizing that they cater to her only because she can make them money. She tells Cutler, the bandleader: "They don't care nothing about me. All they want is my voice. Well, I done learned that, and they gonna treat me like I want to be treated no matter how much it hurt them." Rainey's petty demands, however, often make her appear as a prima donna. She won't sing without her Coca-Cola, for example, and she insists on having her "nephew," Sylvester, a stutterer, do the introduction to one of her songs. Rainey recognizes the band members for what they are. She praises Slow Drag's bass playing and warns Levee numerous times to behave himself, before she finally fires him. Rainey travels with both Sylvester, whom she calls her "nephew," and her lover, Dussie Mae.

Slow Drag

In his mid-fifties, Slow Drag is the slow moving but talented bass player. Like Cutler, he is a professional who is focused on his music, always giving each take his best effort. Slow Drag's name stems from an incident in which he slow danced with a woman in an endurance contest for money. Critic Mary Bogumil writes that Slow Drag's playing "reflects the fundamental rhythmic, harmonic, and melodic nuances found in African music. His style of play could be characterized as an Americanized version of the African."

Mel Sturdyvant

Sturdyvant is the overworked white owner of the recording studio and Ma Rainey's producer, a penny-pinching tightwad concerned exclusively with money. Uncomfortable dealing with black performers, Sturdyvant communicates primarily with and through Irvin. Sturdyvant repeatedly tells Irvin throughout the play that he is responsible for Ma Rainey, saying, "She's your responsibility. I'm not putting up with any Royal Highness . . . Queen of the Blues bull——!" Representing white exploitation of black labor, Sturdyvant promises Levee throughout the play that he will be able to record his own music, but at the end of the play he changes his mind, telling him that his songs aren't what people want. Sturdyvant offers to buy Levee's songs from him for five dollars a piece, acting as if he's doing Levee a favor. The reason for his change of mind is

unclear. Maybe he feels uncomfortable backing Levee against Ma, or maybe he's just more comfortable with the established rather than the new.

Toledo

Toledo is the literate piano player and the most reflective of the band members. As a musician "in control of his instrument, he understands and recognizes that its limitations are an extension of himself." Kim Pereira writes, "To Toledo, style is indistinguishable from content; it is a manifestation in the artist's fidelity to the main musical idea or theme, whatever his improvisations." Toledo discusses abstract concepts such as racial memory and the plight of the black man, but he frequently misapplies his knowledge. When he attempts to make a philosophical point through storytelling, Levee takes him literally rather than figuratively.

Toledo has lost his wife and children to divorce, telling band members that his wife left him for the church. At the end of the play, Levee kills Toledo instead of Sturdyvant, the person who had wronged him the most.

THEMES

Power

The dramatic question in the play is whether the band will complete the recording session despite conflicts among various band members and the power struggles between Rainey and Sturdyvant. The battle of wills between Rainey and Sturdyvant echoes the historical battle between capitalists and workers; only in this case, Rainey holds on to the goods (i.e., her music) that she produces until she gets what she wants from the white producer. It is only after her demands are met and she and her band members are paid that Rainey signs off on the contract. The power struggle between Levee and the other band members over whose version of "Ma Rainey's Black Bottom" is recorded reflects a generational conflict defined by different attitudes towards music. Rainey and the band represent the older generation, preferring to play the song as they always have. Levee, the youngest band mem-

TOPICS FOR FURTHER STUDY

- Characterize the communication among the band members, Ma Rainey and her entourage, and Irvin and Sturdyvant. If you were a counselor for this group, charged with helping its members gain insight into the ways in which they communicate, what issues would you explore and what changes in behavior would you suggest?

- Ma Rainey suggests that white people do not really understand the blues, that only blacks can truly relate to the blues. Do you agree with this thinking? Why or why not?

- Compare Ma Rainey as a feminist figure to a feminist figure of today. Before starting, be sure to research the role of women, particularly black women in America in the 1920s.

- Each of Ma Rainey's band members has a story to tell that embodies something representative of the black experience. Write a story that you believe is representative of the experience(s) of your gender, race, or ethnicity.

- Research the recording industry of the 1920s in the United States, paying particular attention to how working conditions for blacks and whites differed. Present your findings to your class.

- Compare white acceptance of hip-hop or rap music today with white acceptance of the blues in the 1920s. Note differences and similarities.

- Write lyrics for a blues song using any of the following subjects: lost love, infidelity, parent-child conflict, work, or disappointment. If you are musically inclined, put your lyrics to a song and perform it for your class.

- With at least three other classmates, listen to Ma Rainey's album, *Ma Rainey's Black Bottom.* Then write an essay detailing the emotional effect the music had on you. How do your responses compare with the responses of other members in your group?

- Research the kinds of music popular in the United States during the 1920s. Report to your class any connections you see between the music and the region of popularity of various kinds of music.

- Argue for or against the play being read as a tragedy.

- With at least five other classmates, write a third act for the play and perform it for your class. Assign one member of your group to explain the choices you made.

---

ber, represents the new order, preferring a more improvisatory, jazz-like version of the song.

The Great Migration

In American history, 1915 to 1960 is often referred to as the Great Migration, to signify the millions of blacks who moved from the agricultural South to the industrialized North in search of work and a better way of life. The band members and Ma Rainey herself were part of this migration, and the music industry represented for them the hope for a more prosperous future. Finding work, however, especially in an environment rife with racism, was

difficult, and the blues was a way through which blacks expressed their disappointment and struggle.

Black Identity

The band members engage in a process of self-definition through their storytelling and their interactions among themselves and with Sturdyvant and Irvin. Each band member's story tells readers something about him while also forming a theme of the blues. Toledo defines himself through his ability to read (he is the only literate band member) and through his failed relationships with women. Levee defines himself through his appearance, of which his shoes are a central symbol, through his womanizing, and through his musical differences with other band members. His story about the brutalization of his mother and the murder of his father at the hands of whites also provides insight into Levee's argumentative nature and rage. Cutler's story is a familiar story for most blacks, in theme if not in plot: appeasing white power to survive.

Structure

Wilson's play observes the three unities, criteria devised during the Renaissance and based roughly on Aristotle's theory of drama in his *Poetics*. These criteria include the unities of time, action, and place. The action of plays embodying them takes place during a single day and in a single place, and the plot clearly details the causal relationships between characters and action. Although *Ma Rainey's Black Bottom* takes place over the course of a few hours in a Chicago recording studio, thereby adhering to the unities of time and place, and although one event follows another in a more or less causal order, there is not a whole lot that happens in the play. Most of the story consists of talk, frequently a character telling a story. In this way, the characters' speech and what it says about their relationships with one another is more important than what happens, the plot. This is fairly standard fare for modern drama, which tends to be character driven in nature and more intent on delivering a single emotional impression than in detailing events.

The play also has elements of a modern tragedy, insofar as Levee's downfall is his inability to control his pride and his rage. However, the play does not fit the conventional definition of tragedy, in that Levee is neither a courageous figure nor one who behaves in a particularly dignified manner.

Verisimilitude

Wilson's play achieves verisimilitude—the illusion of reality—through observing the unities of time and place but also through his use of vernacular dialogue. That is, his characters talk using the rhythms, speech patterns, vocabulary, and phrasing that black urban Americans of the 1920s used. This technique, which Wilson has honed to perfection over his career, helps the audience suspend their disbelief and empathize with the characters.

HISTORICAL CONTEXT

Harlem Renaissance

In 1927, when Wilson's play takes place, the Harlem Renaissance was in full swing. Black pride manifested itself across the country in art and politics. In poetry, Langston Hughes, Sterling Brown, and James Weldon Johnson wrote in black vernacular, using the rhythms of the blues and spirituals in their verse. Johnson's 1927 poetry collection, *God's Trombone: Seven Negro Folk Sermons,* one of the more popular works of the era, used the speech patterns of an old black preacher to capture the heart of the black idiom. Novelist Claude McKay detailed the life of working class blacks in *Home to Harlem,* and Jean Toomer told the story of poor southern blacks in her novel, *Cane.* Georgia-born, Ma Rainey and blues and jazz artists such as Louis Armstrong, Bessie Smith, and Ethel Waters signed contracts with recording studios such as Paramount Records to cut albums to be sold in cities like Chicago, New York, and Birmingham, which had a burgeoning market of urban blacks. Frank Day, writing in his book, *August Wilson* notes, ''Ironically, many of these records were cut in Chicago . . . where they sold badly, until Bessie Smith refined the gut-bucket approach evolved by Ma.'' Harlem speakeasies such as the Cotton Club, which served only whites, became a symbol of the erotic and the exotic appeal of the ''New Negro.'' The influence of the blues showed up in the visual arts as well, as hot colors and improvisatory compositions dominated the work of painters such as Archibald J. Motley Jr. and Aaron Douglas, whose genre portraits of Harlem nightlife embodied the excitement and passion of the times. In his essay on the art of the Harlem Renaissance, ''Modern Tones,'' Paul Gilroy notes the different responses to black music:

> There was a sharp divergence between those who emphasized that black music was a folk form in

COMPARE
&
CONTRAST

- **1920s:** Through live performances and recordings, Ma Rainey, Bessie Smith, and Louis Armstrong help to popularize blues and jazz as distinctive forms of black music.

  1980s: The black group Sugarhill Gang inaugurates the history of hip-hop with their single "Rapper's Delight," a multi-platinum seller and radio hit. From the Sugarhill Gang come the works of Grandmaster Flash and the Furious Five. In the early 1980s, this group take the lead from the Gang and developed rap, integrating the sounds of a live disc jockey scratching on wax on their albums.

  Today: Hip-hop and rap music, though originating from black performers, are widely embraced by white audiences and practiced by white performers such as Eminem.

- **1920s:** The Ford Motor Company introduces the Model T and produces their 15 millionth Model A.

  1980s: Worldwide earnings at Ford reach an all-time high of $5.3 billion in 1988, the highest to-date for any automotive company.

  Today: Ford opens new plants in Portugal, Poland, Brazil, India, and Russia.

- **1920s:** Oscar De Priest, the first black congressman from the North, is elected in Chicago's First District.

  1980s: Black civil rights leader Jesse Jackson runs twice in the Democratic presidential primary, finishing third in 1984 and second in 1988.

  Today: Colin Powell is the first black man appointed as United States Secretary of State.

transition towards varieties of high cultural expression that could demonstrate the overall worth of the race and others who saw it instead as a sophisticated urban and cosmopolitan phenomenon of an inescapably modernist type.

While white intellectuals theorized black music, the black community asserted their political strength. In the South, black students at Fisk University protested policies of the school's white president, staging campus strikes. In the North, Oscar De Priest won election to Chicago's First District, becoming the first black congressman ever elected from the North. By the end of the decade, blacks held one quarter of the postal service jobs in Chicago. These events contributed both to a heightened black race consciousness and to the belief that social change was possible.

1980s

Wilson's play opened in 1984, towards the end of Ronald Reagan's first term as president of the United States. That year, Jesse Jackson, the fire-brand Baptist minister and civil rights leader, finished third in the Democratic Party's presidential nomination. Though Jackson didn't win the nomination, he did help black reformer, Harold Washington, win the Chicago mayoralty. Jackson spoke out against Reagan's policies, both foreign and domestic, repeatedly during the 1980s, arguing that they were unfair to minorities and women. In 1987, seeking to consolidate his constituency, he formed the National Rainbow Coalition and announced his candidacy for the Democratic presidential nomination once again. Though Jackson failed to win the nomination, he did win five state primaries and finish second in the delegate count. Such a showing once and for all proved the might of the black voter in national politics.

CRITICAL OVERVIEW

Reviews of *Ma Rainey's Black Bottom* were mixed when it debuted in 1984. Writing for *Women's*

Wear Daily, Howard Kissel notes the freshness of the dialogue and says the cast is "excellent." *New York Times* reviewer, Frank Rich notes that Wilson is a find for American theater and lauds the production by the Yale Repertory Theater. Those finding fault with the play include the *New York Post*'s John Simon, who complained about the play's weak structure, saying that, as a play it is only "intermittently drama." Edwin Wilson, writing for the *Wall Street Journal,* agrees, noting that the play is long on theme and short on plot. Wilson writes, "Polemics don't make a play." Academics have also paid attention to the play. Kim Pereira, for example, in *August Wilson and the African-American Odyssey,* examines the themes of separation, migration, and spiritual reunion in the play and the significance of African folklore. Joan Herrington, in *i ain't sorry for nothin' i done,* argues that although critics have found problems with the play's "bifurcated focus" on white men and black men, "[a]udiences seem to have found the bifurcation an apt and powerful metaphor for the inequities of the segregated world Wilson was portraying."

CRITICISM

Chris Semansky

Semansky's essays, stories, reviews, and poems appear regularly in literary magazines and journals. In this essay, Semansky considers the blues as a mode of communication in Wilson's play.

In his preface to the play, Wilson writes this about the blues: "It is hard to define this music. Suffice it to say that it is music that breathes and touches. That connects. That is in itself a way of being separate and distinct from any other." By positioning the blues as a form of communication, Wilson underscores his desire that the audience watch the play as they would listen to the blues, for its emotional impact, rather than its plot. Although Wilson tells us how the blues work, he doesn't tell us what they are.

Historically, the word *blues* emerged from black American folk music. It denotes both a form of music and a melancholic state of mind as, for example, when someone feels depressed and says, "I've got the blues." Formally, the blues are comprised of eight-, twelve-, and thirty-two-bar harmonic progressions that form the foundation for improvisation. The vocal style of the blues derives from the southern work songs of blacks, and by the

turn of the twentieth century it was typically comprised of three-line stanzas. When blacks began migrating north in the 1920s, singers such as Bessie Smith, Ma Rainey, and Sara Martin brought the blues with them. These singers cultivated their fan base through live performances in traveling vaudeville shows. By the 1940s–and with significant urban influences–the blues developed into rhythm-and-blues, which singers such as Muddy Waters helped to popularize. The rhythm-and-blues, in turn, had and continues to have, their own influence on rock-and-roll, as seen in the music of bands such as the Rolling Stones.

Wilson's play, however, is more closely related to the state of mind the blues embodies and the way in which it acts as a kind of glue, bonding the characters to one another. The stories of the band members themselves can be considered blues, for they encapsulate the hopes, dreams, and disappointments of their tellers, as well as of black people as a whole. Critic Mary Bogumil writes this about the blues: "If a struggle can be inherited, the blues is inherited, for the blues functions as the documentation of those who experience that struggle. It is an inherent tradition in the African American culture." Those struggles are documented in the characters' stories, which are themselves reflected in the songs. Here, for example, are the first two stanzas from "Hear Me Talking to You," which Slow Drag sings during the band's rehearsal in act I:

> Rambling man makes no change in me
> I'm gonna ramble back to my used-to-be
> Ah, you hear me talking to you
> I don't bite my tongue
> You wants to be my man
> You got to fetch it with you when you come.
> Eve and Adam in the garden taking a chance
> Adam didn't take time to get his pants
> Ah, you hear me talking to you
> I don't bite my tongue
> You wants to be my man
> You got to fetch it with you when you come.

This song, about a woman's love for her man in spite of his wandering ways, speaks to the values of endurance and forgiveness, values cultivated by blacks who have survived and flourished in a society that has exploited and then scorned them. Wilson's Ma Rainey speaks to the inability of whites to understand the blues and, hence, the black experience:

> White folks don't understand about the blues. They hear it come out but they don't know how it got there. They don't understand that's life's way of talking. You don't sing to feel better. You sing cause there's a way of understanding life. . . . The blues help you get out of bed in the morning. You get up knowing you

A scene from the 1989 theatrical production of Ma Rainey's Black Bottom, *featuring Carol Woods-Coleman, as Ma Rainey*

ain't alone. There's something else in the world. Something's been added by that song. This be an empty world without the blues. I take that emptiness and try to fill it up with something.

Ma's pointing to white ignorance of the origin and cause of the blues underscores white people's essential indifference to the black struggle. This stance is illustrated by Sturdyvant and Irvin's behavior. The former is so uncomfortable being around Ma and the band that he has Irvin communicate most of his desires. The latter treats Ma and the band as unruly children he is obligated to appease to win their cooperation in the studio. Despite the bickering and arguing among band members, they all share the common history of white oppression. Their stories, like their music, transcend particulars and allegorize their struggle. Each recognizes himself in the story of another. For example, when Cutler is telling the story of Reverend Gates, who is humiliated by white men who force him to dance while ripping his crucifix from his neck and tearing up his Bible, Toledo stops him, saying, ''You don't even have to tell me no more. I know the facts of it. I done heard the same story a hundred times.''

That ''same story'' in which Toledo sees his own experience echoed is emotionally enacted in the performance of the blues. Interestingly, Wilson originally had only five members in his script. Joan Herrington writes that he added the band members after listening to blues recordings of male singers. Herrington quotes Wilson: ''I suddenly realized there were four musicians there, waiting in the band room. In them, I found the key to the play—the divisions, the tensions, the meaning of their lives.'' The addition of Levee as a tragic character allows Wilson to develop the familiar story of black response to white exploitation. Levee believes he is competing with Ma in attempting to curry favor with Sturdyvant and Irvin to get his version of ''Ma Rainey's Black Bottom'' recorded and have his songs produced. But in Levee's behavior, Wilson shows that blacks' strategy, historically, of appeasing white power is no longer effective, or at least no longer morally tenable. The only way to get ''white respect,'' as Levee calls it, is to withhold something that whites want: in Ma's case, it's her music and her signature on the release forms. It is only by controlling these that she is able to record her own version of the song and have Sylvester paid separately and not from her own pocket.

Continuing to appease white power, Wilson suggests, will only result in intra-racial conflict and

WHAT DO I READ NEXT?

- Holly Hill's essay, "Black Theater into the Mainstream," which appeared in Bruce King's collection of essays, *Contemporary American Theater,* examines tensions among blacks in Wilson's plays.

- After opening on Broadway in 1987, Wilson's play *Fences* won a Pulitzer Prize, a Tony Award, a New York Drama Critics' Circle Award, an American Theater Critics' Association Award, a Drama Desk Award, and the Outer Critics' Circle Award. *Fences* explores the relationships between husband and wife, father and son, two lovers and two friends.

- Wilson's play, *Joe Turner's Come and Gone,* tells the story of Harold Loomis who, while searching for his wife in Pittsburgh, is haunted by the memory of being illegally enslaved by bounty hunter Joe Thomas in 1917. The play opened at the Yale Repertory Theatre in late 1986 and won the New York Drama Critics' Circle Award.

- Carla McDonough's intriguing book, *Staging Masculinity: Male Identity in Contemporary American Drama* (1997), provides a sociological reading of Wilson's plays, focusing on the subjects of crime, guns, and work among his urban black male characters.

---

a diminution of one's own self-worth. If, instead of internalizing his despair and rage at Sturdyvant and taking it out on Toledo, Levee had enlisted the band and Rainey in his cause, perhaps there could have been success for everyone. But Levee's fate was written in his character, as he had neither the emotional restraint nor the insight into his own desires to do battle with the forces arrayed against him. African-American men today suffer a similar fate, as many of them, lacking adequate education and opportunity and stigmatized by society at large, do battle with one another rather than against a common adversary. For Wilson, it is the heritage of Levee's struggle that forms the basis of the blues in contemporary America.

Source: Chris Semansky, Critical Essay on *Ma Rainey's Black Bottom,* in *Drama for Students,* The Gale Group, 2002.

Harry J. Elam

In the following essay, Elam studies how Wilson uses blues music to treat themes related to the African-American experience in Ma Rainey's Black Bottom.

> Somewhere along the way it dawned on me that I was writing one play for each decade. Once I became conscious of that, I realized I was trying to focus on what I felt were the important issues confronting Black Americans for that decade, so ultimately they could stand as a record of Black experience over the past hundred years presented in the form of dramatic literature. What you end up with is a kind of review, or reexamination of history . . . The importance of history to me is simply to find out who you are and where you've been. It becomes doubly important if someone else has been writing your history. I think Blacks in America need to re-examine their time spent here to see the choices that were made as a people. ("An Interview with August Wilson")

As indicated in the quote above, August Wilson's dramaturgical project is to review African American history in the twentieth century by writing a play for each decade. He re-creates and re-evaluates the choices that blacks have made in the past by refracting them through the lens of the present. Wilson focuses on the experiences and daily lives of ordinary black people within particular socio-historical circumstances. Carefully situating each play at critical junctures in African American history, Wilson explores the pain and perseverance, the determination and dignity in these black lives. He has now written plays for the 1910s, 1920s, 1930s, 1950s, 1960s, and 1970s. Viewed together, these plays represent a decidedly proactive dramaturgy

❝ WILSON'S PLAY . . . IS MORE CLOSELY RELATED TO THE STATE OF MIND THE BLUES EMBODIES, AND THE WAY IN WHICH IT ACTS AS A KIND OF GLUE, BONDING THE CHARACTERS TO ONE ANOTHER."

that not only reflects on the past but intends to empower the African American present and future.

Implicitly and explicitly, within his dramaturgy Wilson desires to recuperate the African in African American experiences. Wilson's plays talk to each other, repeating, revising, building upon narrative tropes. Images and concepts that are developed in one play are extended and re-imagined in subsequent plays. A significant element in this process is Wilson's reconsideration of African American spirituality and faith. Dissatisfied with the relationship African Americans have historically shared with Christianity, Wilson works to establish a syncretic African and African American based theology. At the center of this typology is music, in particular the blues. According to Wilson, the discovery of one's blues song is critical to reintegrating African Americans with their African, spiritual and cultural roots. Repeatedly in his plays, Wilson imagines black people in a liminal space, displaced and disconnected from their history, their individual identity and in search of spiritual resurrection and sociopolitical re-connection. They search for and are in need of their blues song.

Ma Rainey's Black Bottom, Wilson's first critically acclaimed play and the most musical of his plays to date, establishes a foundation for Wilson's blues theology that he articulates further with each of his later plays. In *Ma Rainey*, the significance of finding one's cultural and spiritual regeneration through the blues song plays out principally through the conflicting views of the title character, Ma Rainey, and the spirited young trumpet player, Levee, the pivotal character, who fails to understand his relationship to the music and never realizes his blues song. Ma Rainey, on the other hand, recognizes that the blues can become both a self accentuating song and a declaration of the collective, cul-

tural memory of African Americans. Wilson's dramatic canon extends and expands on this exploration of this blues theology. In fact, close readings of his more recent plays provide insight into the early manifestations of Wilson's blues project revealed in *Ma Rainey*. Accordingly, in this essay, I will discuss the significance of Wilson's blues theology or ''bluesology'' in *Ma Rainey*, by reading this play on and through an understanding of his subsequent plays.

Historically the blues have not only been a site for black cultural production, but a space for critical inquiry and considerable theoretical speculation as well. Ralph Ellison argues that the blues have the power of ''transcendence;'' the blues can transcend ''those conditions created within the Negro community by the denial of social justice'' (*Shadow and Act*). The fact that blues can act as a transcendent, oppositional location has brought both critics and artists to this space. In the 1960s, Amiri Baraka theorized that the emergence of the blues in slavery times marked ''the beginning of the American Negro'' (*Blues People*); the point where blacks ceased to be Africans and became consciously African Americans. Houston A. Baker, expanding and revising Baraka, sees the blues as the foundation for African American vernacular culture and as a critical element in his vernacular theory for African American literary criticism. He imagines himself as a ''critique-as-blues singer'' analyzing African American literary texts with an '' invitation to inventive play'' (*Blues, Ideology*). More recently, black feminist critics such as Hortense Spillers and Hazel Carby have recuperated the early blues and black women blues singers as examples of black feminist self-assertion. In this theoretical context, Wilson's play emerges at a fertile text in which to examine the agency of the legendary black female blues singer Gertrude Pridgett ''Ma'' Rainey, to explore blues theories in practice and to observe what Paul Carter Harrison refers to as Wilson's ''blues poetics''(''August Wilson's Blues Poetics'').

Wilson discovered the blues in 1965 while listening to an old recording of Bessie Smith's ''Nobody in Town Can Bake a Sweet Jellyroll Like Mine.'' This recording transformed his life and his cultural ideology. The blues not only became a guiding force in his writing but the foundation he found for African American expressive culture and for what he believes is a distinctly African American way of being''.

I saw the blues as a cultural response of a nonliterate people whose history and culture were rooted in the oral tradition. The response to a world that was not of their making, in which the idea of themselves as a people of imminent worth that believed their recent history was continually assaulted ... In such an environment, the blues was a flag bearer of self-definition ... It was a spiritual conduit that gave spontaneous expression to the spirit that was locked in combat and devising new strategies for engaging life and enlarging itself. (*Three Plays by August Wilson*)

According to Wilson, then, the cultural, social, political and spiritual all interact within the blues. Forged in and from the economics of slavery as a method of mediating the pains and dehumanization of that experience, the blues are purposefully duplicitous, containing a matrix of meanings. The blues are built upon the complexities and contradictions that comprise African American life. In *Ma Rainey*, Ma reminds her band leader and guitar player, Cutler, "The blues always been here." Houston A. Baker, Jr, similarly calls the blues "an economically determined and uniquely black 'already-said'" (*Blues, Ideology*). The blues for Wilson continue to offer a methodology for negotiating the difficult spaces of African American existence and achieving African American survival.

In *Ma Rainey*, as in Wilson's subsequent works, the dominant culture seeks to suppress, to control and to commodify the black blues song. *Ma Rainey* opens with two white characters: Ma Rainey's manager, Irvin, and Sturdyvant, the recording studio owner and a producer of "race records," on the stage. Together Irvin and Sturdyvant strategize on their plan for the recording session and for capturing Ma Rainey's blues voice. Sturdyvant reminds Irvin, "I just want to get her in here . . . record the songs on the list. . . and get her out. Just like clock work, huh?" Wilson juxtaposes Irvin and Sturdyvant's plan to commercialize Ma Rainey's blues song with Ma's own resolve to protect the integrity of herself and her music. Ma testifies to Wilson's contention that the blues are a uniquely black voice that whites desire, but cannot understand, "White folks don't understand about the blues. They hear it come out, but they don't know how it got there.

Throughout his historical cycle of plays, Wilson replays this theme, as whites repeatedly attempt to seize or possess black music, the black blues song. Early in *The Piano Lesson*, when the protagonist, Boy Willie, inquires about potential buyers for the family's heirloom, a carved piano, his uncle Doaker tells him that there is a white man going around trying to buy up black people's musical instruments. Even more significantly, the ghost of the

> IN *MA RAINEY,* AS IN WILSON'S SUBSEQUENT WORKS, THE DOMINANT CULTURE SEEKS TO SUPPRESS, TO CONTROL AND TO COMMODIFY THE BLACK BLUES SONG."

recently deceased white southern land owner, Sutter, materializes in the Pittsburgh home of Doaker and Boy Willie's sister, Berniece, in an effort to reclaim the family's piano, the symbol of their African American struggle and survival. In *Joe Turner's Come and Gone*, the brooding central figure in the play, Herald Loomis, has lost his identity and his place in the world after being incarcerated by Joe Turner. The title character, Joe Turner, is an absent presence in the play. Mythologized in an old blues song, Joe Turne(y)r, the brother of a former Governor of Tennessee, kept black men in servitude for seven years. These indentured black men functioned as a personal chain gang performing menial labor throughout the state. Through the action of the play *Joe Turner*, Wilson reveals that Joe Turner imprisoned Herald Loomis and these other black men in an effort to capture their song. In Wilson's plays, music and song act as metaphors for African American identity, spirit and soul. Through the invisible presence and symbolic activities of off-stage white characters, Wilson suggests that the dominant culture has continually sought to subjugate African American humanity and suppress the power and ability of African Americans to sing their song.

This musical metaphor has considerable contemporary significance. It reflects on the ways black cultural expression has been commercialized and exploited in today's mediatized culture. The raw, hard edge and social critique of black urban rap music, for example, has been commodified and softened to sell everything from soft drinks to hamburgers. In addition, Ma Rainey's obstinacy in the face of white hegemony parallels Wilson's own struggle against co-optation as a black artist and his desire to maintain his creative integrity and autonomy. Wilson's fierce resolve not to allow the film version of *Fences* to go forward without a black director evidences his determination to protect his agency as a black artist.

Wilson's blues theology privileges the blues musician. He posits the blues musician as a potentially powerful site of black resistive agency. Too often, however, the musicians do not realize the power that they possess. As with any gift or power, the power of the blues musician exacts certain costs and expectations from the ones to whom it is given. Lyons in *Fences,* Jeremy in *Joe Turner's Come and Gone*, and Wining Boy in *The Piano Lesson*, all represent blues musicians who have not recognized the spiritual force of the blues song and the cultural responsibility inherent in their ability to play the blues. As a result they are exploited for their music and fall victim to those who wish to control their spirit and song. The band members in *Ma Rainey*, similarly, do not realize the power and privilege of their music, their blues voice. Toledo, the piano player, chastises his fellow band members, "You lucky they [white people] let you be an entertainer. They ain't got to accept your way of entertaining. You lucky and don't even know it." Still it is on and through these musicians that Wilson positions himself as blues musician improvising on a theme (*Blues, Ideology*).

One theme that Wilson continually improvises on in his work is the struggle for African Americans to find connections, to reorient and re-establish themselves after the disorienting and dislocating experiences of the Middle Passage, slavery and the northern migrations. Yet, Wilson's blues improvisations not only infuse the content of his plays, but his form and structure as well. Ralph Ellison calls the blues a unique combination of the tragic and the comic, of poetry and ritual (*Shadow and Act*). The structure of *Ma Rainey* embodies this blues formula. The events that transpire—from Sylvester's stuttering rendition of the introduction to the recorded version of "Ma Rainey's Black Bottom" to Toledo's unfortunate death—combine the comic and the tragic, the poetic and the ritualistic. *Ma Rainey* plays out as an extended series of blues riffs providing each of the members of the band the opportunity to solo. Wilson sets the band interaction in the band room downstairs and separated from the recording studio above. The band room represents what Houston A. Baker terms a "blues matrix" (*Blues, Ideology*). Baker envisions the blues matrix is a "point of ceaseless input and output, a web of intersecting", crisscrossing impulses always in productive transit" (*Blues, Ideology*). For Baker the prototypical site of the blues matrix is a railroad

crossing, "the juncture of multidirectionality," a place "betwixt and between" (*Blues, Ideology*). Situated at the blues matrix, the blues singer through blues song transcends spatial and socio-historical limitations. Positioned at the blues matrix, the blues singer is empowered with unlimited and ending possibilities. The band room as blues matrix is equally a site of power and potential. The band room is a space of unfinished business, where the band must rehearse its songs for the recording sessions. It is a metaphorical space where the band members enact rituals and tales of survival that replicate the patterns of black experiences in America. Like Seth's boarding house in *Joe Turner's Come and Gone*, the band room is a liminal space; a space that people pass through; a space where the band must await the arrival of Ma Rainey. The liminality of the space is subconsciously recognized by Levee, who comments upon entering into the room, "Damn! They done changed things around. Don't never leave well enough alone . . . That door! Nigger, you see that Door? That's what I'm talking about. That door wasn't here before." The liminality of the band room makes it a location of great creative and destructive force. Within the storytelling riffs of the band members and the tragic demise of Toledo, both the creative and destructive potential of liminality are realized in Ma Rainey's band room.

> Down in the band room, the band members engage in a series of vernacular games, the dozens, and signifyin'. All are extensions of the blues, variations on a blues theme. Wilson adds, through the voice of Toledo, that these forms of blues games are also examples of African retentions. When the bass player, Slow Drag, signifies on Cutler in order to extract a reefer from him, Toledo explains that what he has performed is an "African conceptualization": That's what you call an African conceptualization. That's when you name the gods or call on the ancestors to achieve whatever your desires are.

Correspondingly, in the climactic moment of *The Piano Lesson*, Wilson extends this blues riff and the concept of African conceptualizations through the actions of the character, Berniece. When Berniece sits at the piano to play, she employs an African conceptualization. Just as Toledo suggests in *Ma Rainey*, her song at the piano calls on the power of her ancestor to exorcise the ghost of the white land owner, Sutter, and to save her brother Boy Willie.

Toledo's declarations of the need for African Americans to recognize their connections to Africa represent an important element of Wilson's blues theology. Wilson believes that in order for African Americans to be able to sing their own song, to feel truly liberated in the American context, they must rediscover their ''Africanness''. ''One of the things I'm trying to say in my writing is that we can never begin to make a contribution to the society except as Africans'' (*In Their Own Words*). Toledo, accordingly, reprimands the band and himself for not being an ''African'' and for being ''imitation white men.'' In later plays, such as *The Piano Lesson*, Wilson further delineates the connections he sees between African cultural roots and contemporary African American identity. In *Joe Turner's Come and Gone*, Bynum's rituals of pigeons and blood, his story of the shiny man, as well as Herald Loomis' cleansing himself with his blood are all rooted in Yoruba religious practices and cosmology. Wilson's bluesology builds on African traditions adapting them to an African American context. In fact, Wilson's valorization of music and the blues musician parallels the position that Wole Soyinka establishes for music in Yoruba cultural expression. According to Soyinka,

> The European concept of music does not fully illuminate the relationship of music to ritual and drama among the Yoruba . . . The nature of Yoruba music is intensively the nature of its language and poetry, highly charged, symbolic, myth-embryonic . . . The true tragic [Yoruban] music, unearths cosmic uncertainties which pervade human existence, reveals the power of creation, but above all creates a harrowing sense of omni-directional vastness where the creative Intelligence resides and prompts the soul to futile exploration (''The Fourth Stage'').

For Soyinka, music in Yoruba tragedy transcends the physical world and particularized meanings. Music expresses the cosmic, the spiritual, the meta-physical. Similarly, the blues are an integral component of Wilson's dramaturgy. They express and embody the African American soul. The blues inform both the content and form of Wilson's work enabling the spirituality and mythopoetic power of the works to emerge.

To further the blues mood in *Ma Rainey*, Wilson composes his blues musician characters to correspond with the instruments which they play. Slow Drag, the bass player, maintains the bass line in the play. He is a slow and deliberate voice who reinforces the action around him. Cutler, the band leader and guitar player, strikes a practical tone. He is not one to improvise but has the power to embellish a theme, as when he tells the involved story of Reverend Gates. Toledo, the piano player, is the only member of the group who can read. He is a philosopher who engages in monologues and story telling riffs that are analogous to virtuoso, improvised

piano solos. Toledo preaches a doctrine of Afrocentric nationalism. ''As long as the colored man look to white folks to put a crown on what he say. . . as long as he looks to white folks for approval . . . then he ain't never gonna find out who he is and what he's about.'' Toledo agitates for black nationalist consciousness. In the plays of the Black Arts Movement of the 1960s and 1970s, Toledo would have been the most prominent voice in the play. Toledo's voice in Wilson's drama, however, is muted. He is part of the ensemble, one instrument blending with the other blues sounds emanating from the blues matrix band room.

Still, in Wilson's bluesology, as in the 1960s and 1970s platforms of black cultural nationalism, the cultural and the spiritual are inextricably connected to the political. Wilson advocates and agitates for African American social consciousness and black nationalistic self-determination through his art. Accordingly, Toledo instructs the band members as to their status as products of the economics of slavery. These are lessons that Wilson wants all African Americans to understand. In his powerful, poetic and humorous analogy of a stew, Toledo explains that African Americans are historical leftovers. ''See we's the leftover. The colored man is the leftovers. Now what the colored man gonna do with himself? That's what we waiting to find out. But first we gotta know we the leftovers.'' For Wilson, African American advancement can only come after African Americans recognize their leftover status, appreciate the legacies and lessons of slavery and realize and express their Africanness. In *Ma Rainey* unfortunately, Toledo's words do not activate an increased social awareness in the brash young trumpeter, Levee, nor in the other band members.

Levee, the youngest member of the band presents himself with a boldness that the others lack. His self-importance is both stubborn naivete and camouflage. Levee desires to fit in with the band, to be accepted, to achieve within a world that devalues African American spirit and accomplishment. Like a trumpet, Levee blares onto the stage. According to Wilson, ''With the trumpet you have to force yourself out through the horn. Half-consciously I tried to make Levee's voice a trumpet. . .Levee is a brassy voice'' (*In Their Own Words*). Levee with his brassy voice represents the forces of modernity in conflict with tradition. Significantly, Wilson has set the play in 1927, at a time when the country blues of Ma Rainey were fading in the taste of the black consuming public and being replaced by the more upbeat, danceable blues of Bessie Smith and the jazz sounds emerging from urban cities. Levee symbolizes this modern, urban blues landscape. Paul Carter Harrison writes that Levee's very name signifies, "possible kinship with the new music soundings of jazz being created along the Mississippi levees of New Orleans during the period" ("August Wilson's Blues Poetics"). Levee rejects and ridicules the "jugband" circus style songs of Ma Rainey. He desires to play music that makes people move and that he can "lay down in the peoples lap." Yet, Levee does not recognize nor understand that his new urban blues sound and jazz beats are deeply indebted to earlier African and African American sounds and socio-cultural traditions. One of the most significant and repeated messages in Wilson's historical project is that modernity cannot erase but must embrace tradition, that the past constantly and continually impacts on the present.

Tragically individualistic, Levee speaks of personal ownership and individual achievement. He wants to play "his" music, write "his" songs and form "his" band. He is unable to heed Toledo's warning to embrace communality and to think collectively:

> It ain't just me, fool! It's everybody! What you think. . .I'm gonna solve the colored man's problems by myself? I said, we. You understand that? We. That's every living colored man in the world got to do his share.

Levee does not think in terms of "we", but rather, isolates and alienates himself from the other band members and systems of African American communal empowerment. Rejecting communality, Levee believes that he is on a mission to sing his song. Yet, he does not understand the technologies of capitalism and white racism which constrict him and prevent such self-actualization.

> Levee does, however, have a profound aversion to black peoples' unquestioning acceptance of and devotion to the doctrine of Christianity. Waving a knife at Cutler and at the heavens, Levee decries Christ's lack of action in protecting his mother from being gang raped by a group of white men. He berates the traditionally Christian Cutler, "God don't pay niggers no mind. In fact . . . God hate niggers! Hate them with all the fury in his heart. Jesus don't love you nigger! Jesus hate your black ass!"

Levee feels betrayed by the inability of a Christian god to act proactively on behalf of black people. He finds Christianity severely insufficient in meeting the spiritual and practical needs of black people. Wilson similarly comments on the impotence of

Christianity in African American lives in his later plays. At the end of *Joe Turner's Come and Gone*, Herald Loomis, wielding a knife like Levee, bemoans the ineffectiveness of Christianity in his life. Ironically, Joe Turner captured Herald Loomis when he had stopped to preach the Christian gospel to some men who were gambling on a Memphis street corner. In *Piano Lesson*, Christianity again fails. Avery, called upon to perform a Christian ritual of exorcism to rid the house of Sutter's ghosts, loses his resolve when confronted with the powerful spiritual forces present within the house. The picture Wilson paints in these plays is of a Christianity that has not provided blacks with tangible support in the struggle for liberation.

Consequently, Wilson in his bluesology formulates alternative syncretic strategies for African American spirituality. In the final moment of *Fences*, Gabriel Maxson performs an atavistic dance that unites him with his African origins, his blues spirit and serves to open the gates of heaven for his recently deceased brother Troy to enter. At the conclusion of *Joe Turner's Come and Gone*, Harald Loomis subverts the traditional Christian ritual of blood letting in which Christ died for our sins. Loomis, instead, bleeds for himself. He cuts himself with his knife and then, in Yoruba fashion, cleanses himself with the blood. Through this symbolic process, Herald Loomis re-discovers his identity and his ability to sing his blues song. Berniece, after witnessing Avery's aborted exorcism in *The Piano Lesson*, turns to an African conceptualization and calls for the intervention of her ancestors. Her actions not only save her brother, but also bring spiritual redemption to herself and her family. Significantly, all these moments infuse the Christian with the African, and transpire on and through music.

Despite his protest against the inaction of Christ and the racism of Christianity, Levee has not yet found a recourse in the syncretic spirituality of the blues. Instead he turns to the devil. He is quite literally willing to sell his soul to the devil. Interestingly, the notions of the "devil" within *Ma Rainey* implicitly resurrect the black nationalist rhetoric of the 1960s and 1970s which referred to members of the dominant culture as "white devils". In *Ma Rainey*, the "white devil" to whom Levee is willing to sell his soul is Sturdyvant. Levee gives Sturdyvant his songs and expects that Sturdyvant will help him to form his own band. Levee naively believes that Sturdyvant will protect and serve his interests. Levee, however, is betrayed and undone by these actions, as Sturdyvant only desires to exploit him. Levee's deal with the devil signals his demise. Tragically, Levee disavows African American community and allows his music, his song to be commodified and controlled by Sturdyvant.

Levee believes that his interactions with Sturdyvant build upon lessons he learned from his father on how to "deal with the white man." At the end of the play's first act, Levee tells of his father's act of retribution against the white men who gang raped his wife, Levee's mother. Levee explains that his father, Memphis Green, "acted like he done accepted the facts of what happened," while he gathered the names of the white men involved. Memphis even smiled in the face of one of these white men and sold that white man his farm. Later, after he had sold the land and moved his family, Memphis returned and managed to kill four of his wife's attackers before he himself was killed. Memphis' actions unite the power of the trickster with that of the revolutionary. Duplicitously, Memphis had smiled in the face of a white man who had wronged him and his family deeply, all the while plotting his revenge. Present in Memphis' response to his wife's rapists is the inherent irony of the blues. In effect, his performance is analogous to that of Baker's blues musician at the crossroads. Memphis, through his actions, negotiates and transcends the excruciating pain of his African American experience. Interestingly, in *Two Trains Running*, Wilson again features a character named Memphis who has also been abused and run off his land by a group of white men. Much like the earlier Memphis, this Memphis, a restaurant owner in *Two Trains Running*, has unfinished business that he must settle. After a conversation with Aunt Esther—a woman who, at over three hundred and twenty years of age, is as old as the black presence in America—Memphis reconnects with his past and discovers his blues voice and the power to sing it. At the end of the play, he will return south to reclaim his land.

Levee in *Ma Rainey*, however, misinterprets his father's legacy. While his father plotted revenge with cunning duplicity, Levee approaches Sturdyvant with romantic naivete. Levee defers to Sturdyvant because he believes that Sturdyvant has the power to make him a band leader and a star. Levee does not recognize the authority of black people over the blues song. Cutler attempts to explain this reality to Levee citing Ma as an example: "The white man don't care nothing about Ma. The colored folks made Ma a star. White folks don't care nothing about who she is. . .what kind of music she make." Levee does not listen to Cutler's explanation. Unlike

his father, Memphis, Levee allows his blues voice to be bought and controlled by the mechanisms of institutionalized racism. Memphis sells his land but maintains his power of self determination, his soul. Levee, on the other hand, internalizes his oppression and becomes both a victim and a victimizer.

Wilson establishes Levee's status as victim with his first entrance onto the stage. Levee enters the band room later than the rest of the band members because he has been delayed buying shoes. The shoes function as a symbol of his internalized oppression. Levee's sense of respect and identity are constructed around his sense of acquisition and property rather than an internal sense of self-worth and pride in his blues voice. This notion of "respect" being tied to external, material items is repeatedly played out on contemporary urban streets, where black young men battle fiercely with each other and without any recognition of their blues voices. Young black men kill each other over tennis shoes and issues of respect. Such battles for respect evidence the ultimate lack of respect for the black self. In his autobiographic memoir, *Make Me Want to Holler* Nathan McCall writes of this battle for respect:

> For as long as I can remember, black folks have had a serious thing about respect. I guess it's because white people disrespected them so blatantly for so long that blacks viciously protected what little morsel of self respect they had left . . . It's still that way today. Young dudes nowadays call it "dissin'." They'll kill a nigger for dissin' them. Won't touch a white person, but they'll kill a brother in a heartbeat over a perceived slight. The irony was that white folks constantly disrespected us in ways unseen and seen, and we tolerated it. (*Makes Me Want to Holler*)

Levee, as victim, suffers from a similarly impoverished self-image. When Sturdyvant exploits him for his songs, he is further diminished. Levee then encounters the ultimate frustration that many blacks experience under white oppression. At that moment, Levee the victim turns victimizer. His internalization of his oppression constricts him from acting out against Sturdyvant. Instead, he strikes out with fury against Toledo for the disrespect of stepping on his shoes. As Wilson explains, Levee transfers his "aggression to the wrong target" (*In Their Own Words*). The result reinforces the tragic implications of black-on-black violence: the senseless, self-destructive loss of black lives.

In contrast to Levee, Ma Rainey, the title character, realizes her blues song and understands her relationship to the music. Ma Rainey recognizes the power of the music to move through her. "You don't sing to feel better... You sing 'cause it's a way of understanding life. Ma explains that singing the blues is not simply therapy but rather an engagement with a complex and enabling force that acts to understand and even to transform and to transcend life. Ma, unlike Levee, perceives her blues voice as a source of identity, collective African American empowerment and self-actualization. Her late entrance into the play is juxtaposed against Levee's tardy appearance in the band room. Levee is late because he falls victim to the seductive authority of American capitalism. Ma's tardiness is also due to her victimization. She, however, finds herself the victim of institutionalized racism when she refuses to be commodified. Ma struggles against the efforts of the policeman, who accosts her after a traffic incident, to treat her as just another "nigger". Repeatedly and insistently Ma shouts to her manager Irvin, as she enters the studio accompanied by the arresting officer, "Tell him who I am"! With her late, chaotic entrance, well into the play's first act, Wilson focuses the spectators' attention on Ma and further establishes her importance.

Ma remains a fiercely independent woman throughout the action of the play. Her interaction with all the men in the play is analogous to Baker's reading of the blues musician at the crossroads; she situates herself inventively and uses the resources she has at her disposal to control and mediate the world around her. Ma demonstrates a practical understanding of the material hierarchy of the record industry and her place within it. Recognizing that the purpose of the recording session is to record her voice and her music, Ma does not allow herself to be objectified but uses her position as a desired musical commodity to legitimize her authority. She reminds Irvin, "What band? The band work for me! I say what goes!" After the recording session, Ma exercises her blues voice in one final act of defiance. She leaves the studio without signing the release forms that legally grant Irvin and Sturdyvant control over her recorded music. Through this act, she asserts the power of blues singer to transcend and overcome material limitations. She retains her artistic autonomy and rebuts the usurpations of others who wish to claim her song. Wilson maintains,

> The music [blues] is ours [African Americans], since it contains our soul, so to speak—it contains all our ideas and responses to the world. We need it to help us claim the African-ness and we would be a stronger people for it. It's presently in the hands of someone else who sits over it as custodian, without even allowing us its source. (*In Their Own Words*)

While Ma confronts the desires of the dominant culture to control and suppress her blues voice, she also must struggle against the patriarchal hegemony that seeks to commodify and objectify her as a woman. Ma must negotiate systems of oppression not only as an African American but as a woman. Interestingly, in *Ma Rainey*, Wilson uses his black male characters, rather than the white ones, to reveal attitudes of sexism and male privilege. In their band room bonding rituals and verbal games, the band members speak of women only as sexual objects. At one point Cutler admonishes Levee, "Slow Drag don't need you to find him no p——y. He can take care of himself." Ma is well aware of the objectification of women as well as the exploitation of African American musicians. In fact, at one moment she uses the image of black woman-as-sexual property to emphasize her position as expendable commodity with the dominant culture's musical economy: "As soon as they [white folks] get my voice down on them recording machines, then it's just like if I'd be some whore and they roll over and put their pants on."

In Wilson's character Ma Rainey, as well as in the real persona of the legendary blues singer Gertrude Pridgett "Ma" Rainey, issues of race and gender interact. The legendary blues singer Gertrude Pridgett "Ma" Rainey continually and purposefully challenged the limits placed on women. Through her music and its lyrical content, her public performances and stylistic flair, Ma Rainey developed an image that contradicted conventional representations of black female sexuality. By traditional standards of western beauty, Ma Rainey would have been perceived as an ugly woman. Yet, her body in performance signified not the limitations of stereotypes but the possibilities of self-definition. Ma Rainey became known for her flamboyance. She adorned herself in lavish gowns and extravagant gold jewelry. Through her performance the image of the heavy-set black woman as mammy figure was subverted and transformed into a symbol of sexuality and style. Her performance revealed traditional western beauty standards to be a socially constructed means of oppressing black women. Since the horrors and inequities endured by slave women on the plantation, the American patriarchal system has denied or misrepresented black women's sexuality. Historically, mainstream American culture limited black female sexuality to two stereotypical images—the wanton black whore and the asexual black mammy. In *Sex and Racism in America* Calvin Hernton argues that in American public discourse black woman disappear as legitimate subjects of female sexuality. Michelle Russell posits the blues and black female blues singers as important historical sources of black women's sexual empowerment. Russell writes that the blues

> are the expression of a particular social process by which poor black women have commented on all the major theoretical, practical and political questions facing us and have created a mass audience who listens to what we say in that form (''Slave Codes and Liner Notes'').

Through the activity of singing the blues, Black women such as Ma Rainey positively acknowledged and represented black women's sexuality. Ma Rainey's songs displayed an earthy and forthright, crude and sassy sensuality. As she asserted control over the content and form of her songs, she equally declared control over her own sexuality. ''She is in the moment of performance the primary subject of her own being. Her sexuality is precisely the physical expression of the highest self-regard and, often, the sheer pleasure she takes in her own powers'' (''Interstices: A Small Drama of Words''). Present always in Ma Rainey's performance of her music was the concept of the black woman as empowered subject.

In her personal sex life as well as in her music and on stage performances, Ma Rainey refused to conform to traditional gender expectations. She was a bisexual with acknowledged lesbian relationships. According to Harrison, ''Rainey's and Bessie Smith's episodes with women lovers are indicative of the independent stance they and other blues singers took on issues of personal choice'' (*Black Pearls*). Her lesbianism and the public knowledge of it further testified to Ma Rainey's personal revolt against male hegemony and her ability to survive outside male domination and societal norms.

Paradoxically, while Ma Rainey's own activities in life attempted to subvert the male dominated, heterosexual status quo, the events of Wilson's play appear to uphold it. Decidedly more overt than the physical exchanges between Ma and Dussie Mae, her younger lesbian or bi-sexual companion, is the sexual embrace shared by Dussie Mae and the young rebellious trumpet player, Levee. Protected by the privacy of the downstairs band room, they exchange a passionate kiss. Their stolen embrace emphasizes Levee's fateful defiance of Ma's authority. Significantly, Dussie Mae jeopardizes her financially stable—Ma has supplied her with money and clothing—but non-traditional lesbian relationship with Ma Rainey for an extremely tenuous but

conventional heterosexual affair with Levee. Implicit is the message that relationships with men are more valuable.

Ma, a woman, is not the primary subject of Wilson's *Ma Rainey*. Although placing Ma Rainey's entrance late in the first act draws the audience's attention to her, it also provides Wilson with the time to establish interest and involvement in the lives of the band members who await Ma Rainey's arrival. The construction of the set further emphasizes the collective voice of the band, while silencing the presence and power of Ma Rainey. Ma Rainey remains above, on the surface, in the Recording Studio. In the band room below, the domain of the men, the drama simmers. In the stories and conflicts of these men, she is powerless. Significantly, Levee's murder of Toledo occurs after Ma has gathered her entourage and left the recording studio. Just as she does not determine the action at the outset of the play, she does not determine its conclusion. The play does not end with Ma's defiant exit from the recording studio, but escalates into tragedy in the band room below. Despite her assertions of her blues voice and her powers of self-determination, Ma remains outside of the discourse of men and the decisive action of the play. While Gertrude Pridgett's own life and blues music represent examples of black women's sexual agency and strategies of feminist empowerment, black female sexuality and the politics of gender are neither the subjects of Wilson's play nor the focus of his bluesology. As evidenced in *Ma Rainey*, Wilson's bluesology is both a racialized and gendered ideology and practice.

The ending of *Ma Rainey* is a complex and confounding blues moment. It stands in stark contrast to endings of Wilson's later dramas in which characters reach moments of spiritual fulfillment, acknowledge their relationships to the African American past, and perform actions of self-actualization, self-determination and communion. Present in the final scene is the ironic anguish of the blues wail. Levee's stabbing of Toledo, like all acts of black-on-black violence, strikes out against African American collectivity and cultural unity. The murder of Toledo represents a performance of tragic, unfulfilled promise, a loss of the black self that must be reclaimed through the triumph of the blues voice. The death of Toledo stands as a lesson that African Americans must learn from and that Wilson will build upon in his later plays. In African American life and Wilson's historical project of African American cultural expression, African Americans can and must overcome by acknowledging their blues voice and learning to sing their own blues song.

Source: Harry J. Elam, "*Ma Rainey's Black Bottom:* Singing Wilson's Blues," in *American Drama,* Vol. 5, No. 1, Spring 1996, pp. 76–99.

Sandra Adell

In the following essay, Adell provides background on the real Ma Rainey, and explores the theme of blues music as release from oppression in Ma Rainey's Black Bottom.

> I've traveled 'Til I'm tired
> And I ain't satisfied
> I've traveled 'til I'm tired
> And I ain't satisfied
> If I don't find my sweet man
> I'll ramble 'til I die
> Ah Lawdy Lawd Lawd Lawdy
> Lawd Lawdy Lawd lawd Lawd
> Ah Lawdy Lawd lawd lawdy
> Lawd lawdy lawd lawd lawd
> Lawd lawdy Lawd Lawd Lawd
> Lawd Lawdy lawd lawd lawd
> —"Slow Drivin' Moan" by
> Gertrude (Ma) Rainey
> Oh Ma Rainey
> Sing yo' song;
> Now you's back
> Whah you belong,
> Git way inside us,
> Keep us strong.
> —Sterling Brown

August Wilson's drama receives its strongest impulses from what Houston Baker has called the "blues matrix"—that metaphorical space where down-home folk like Boy Willie, Wining Boy, and Doaker in *The Piano Lesson,* Bynum in *Joe Turner's Come and Gone,* and Madame Ma Rainey in *Ma Rainey's Black Bottom* all reside. Each of these characters serves as a kind of repository for a musical tradition that Wilson considers crucial to the development of the historical perspective he needs in order to write. In a 1989 interview with Bill Moyers, Wilson explained why the blues are so important for his work:

> The blues are important primarily because they contain the cultural responses of blacks in America to the situation that they find themselves in. Contained in the blues is a philosophical system at work. You get the ideas and attitudes of the people as part of the oral tradition. This is a way of passing along information. If you're going to tell someone a story, and if you want to keep information alive, you have to make it memorable so that the person hearing it will go tell someone else. This is how it stays alive. The music provides you an emotional reference for the information, and it is sanctioned by the community in the sense that if someone sings the song, other people sing the song. They keep it alive because they sanction the information that it contains.

Like the blues singer, Wilson keeps *his* story alive by improvising on a theme: the theme of displaced Southern black people struggling to survive in a hostile Northern urban environment. Wilson makes his story memorable by elaborating a philosophical system in which music becomes the metaphysical activity par excellence. Music is tied to understanding in a most primordial way, one that evades any logical explanation. This is the point Ma Rainey makes when she complains to Cutler about how badly white folks have misunderstood what it means to sing the blues:

> White folks don't understand about the blues. They hear it come out, but they don't know how it got there. They don't understand that's life's way of talking. You don't sing to feel better. You sing 'cause that's a way of understanding life.

It is also a way of securing for one's *self* a temporary reprieve from the forces of oppression with which each of Wilson's characters must always contend. And it is through the figure of Ma Rainey that Wilson most strongly articulates the possibility for grounding this kind of self-possession in the rituals and soulful rhythms of those low-down dirty gut-bucket blues.

Ma Rainey's Black Bottom is the first of what August Wilson has referred to as a "cycle of history plays," which he hopes will "stand as a record of Black experience over the past hundred years." Set in a Chicago recording studio in 1927, this two-act play attempts to explore, among other things, the tensions arising out of a conflict between a traditional vaudeville-based down-home blues aesthetic and a new, more fast-paced and urbane style of the blues. It also presents a powerful and persuasive image of the woman who was called the Mother of the Blues.

Gertrude "Ma" Rainey was born on April 26, 1886, in Columbus, Georgia. According to one source, she made her theater debut in 1900 in a talent show called "The Bunch of Blackberries." Four years later she married William "Pa" Rainey with whom she spent many years traveling and performing on the Southern minstrel and vaudeville show circuit. By the 1920s when she began to record for Paramount records, she had already become the most popular female down-home blues singer in the country. For the folk down home and the down-home folk up North, Ma Rainey represented the epitome of black female wealth, power, and sensuality. She had her own group of musicians, a spectacular wardrobe, and for a while, her own touring bus. She also had a strong voice that could project her raunchy lyrics, without the aid of a megaphone, over the music and the noise of the crowds who regularly attended her blues performances.

An important feature of Ma Rainey's performances was a large cardboard replica of a Victrola, from which she emerged, extravagantly attired in a sequined gown and a necklace made of twenty-dollar gold pieces, singing her big recorded hit, ''Moonshine Blues.'' This part of her stage performance most certainly must have symbolized for Ma Rainey's audiences her great success as a recording star, but in *Ma Rainey's Black Bottom* it becomes, at least implicitly, the technical instrument that detaches the down-home blues singer from the domain of the blues tradition. The Victrola makes it possible for Ma Rainey's voice to be heard in places other than the great circus tents where she usually performs. One no longer has to *be there* to experience Ma Rainey coming out of the Victrola; all one needs is a phonograph record. The phonograph record reproduces the sound of Ma Rainey singing the blues and, to borrow a phrase from Walter Benjamin, it ''enables the original to meet the beholder halfway.'' What it cannot reproduce is what Benjamin, in ''The Work of Art in the Age of Mechanical Reproduction,'' refers to as the ''aura'' or the presence, in space and time, that guarantees an object—be it a painting, a choral performance, or a staged performance—its uniqueness and singularity.

According to Benjamin, the ''aura'' of a work of art is what ''withers'' in the age of mechanical reproduction:

> That which withers in the age of mechanical reproduction is the aura of the work of art. This is a symptomatic process whose significance points beyond the realm of art. One might generalize by saying: the technique of reproduction detaches the reproduced object from the domain of tradition. By making many reproductions it substitutes a plurality of copies for a unique existence. And in permitting the reproduction to meet the beholder or listener in his own particular situation, it reactivates the object reproduced. These two processes lead to a tremendous shattering of tradition which is the obverse of the contemporary crisis and renewal of mankind. Both processes are intimately connected with the contemporary mass movements. Their most powerful agent is the film. Its social significance, particularly in its most positive form, is inconceivable without its destructive, cathartic aspect, that is, the liquidation of the traditional value of the cultural heritage.

> ''LIKE THE BLUES SINGER, WILSON KEEPS *HIS* STORY ALIVE BY IMPROVISING ON A THEME: THE THEME OF DISPLACED SOUTHERN BLACK PEOPLE STRUGGLING TO SURVIVE IN A HOSTILE NORTHERN URBAN ENVIRONMENT.''

One might also generalize by saying that the second most powerful agent is the phonograph record. Like the film, the phonograph record is designed for its own reproducibility and marketability rather than for the transmission of the ''traditional value of the cultural heritage.'' In that sense, the phonograph record, like the film, does indeed lead to a ''tremendous shattering of tradition.'' What Benjamin argues in his essay and what August Wilson dramatizes in *Ma Rainey's Black Bottom* is that the age of mechanical reproduction reduces everything within the aesthetic domain to a simple matter of supply and demand. And by the time Ma Rainey is scheduled to record her ''Black Bottom Blues,'' that demand, especially among her loyal displaced downhome fans, has already translated into enormous profits for the two white entrepreneurs, Irvin and Sturdyvant, who control the techniques of reproduction and the ''recording machines.'' What they cannot control—and this becomes obvious during the first moments of the play—is Ma Rainey, upon whose cooperation those enormous profits necessarily rely.

Ma Rainey does not cooperate with Irvin and Sturdyvant. Fully aware of the extent to which she is being exploited, Ma Rainey uses her exploitation to her advantage whenever she can. To cite just one example, although she does not deliberately disrupt Irvin and Sturdyvant's plan to run the recording session ''just like clockwork,'' when she finally arrives at the studio she takes advantage of the commotion caused by the automobile accident that detained her to gain the upper hand. Ignoring Irvin's remarks about her tardiness, Ma Rainey insists that he talk to the policeman who is trying to arrest her for hitting a taxi driver and set him straight about who she is:

Ma Rainey: Tell the men [*sic*] who he's messing with!

Policeman: Do you know this lady?

Ma Rainey: Just tell the man who I am! That's all you gotta do.

Policeman: Lady, will you let me talk, huh?

Ma Rainey: Tell the man who I am!

Irvin: Wait a minute . . . wait a minute! Let me handle it. Ma, will you let me handle it?

Ma Rainey: Tell him who he's messing with!

Irvin: Okay! Okay! Give me a chance! Officer, this is one of our recording artists . . . Ma Rainey.

Ma Rainey: Madame Rainey! Get it straight! Madame Rainey! Talking about taking me to jail!

Unintimidated by the threat of arrest, Ma Rainey refuses to "await her verb," as Hortense Spillers might put it. Ma Rainey does not ask, "Who am I?" Ma Rainey demands instead that the world be informed about who she *is*—a social *and* sexual subject who, as the drama unfolds, continuously challenges the presumed authority of the white men and the black men who make up her immediate environment. She is, as blues singer, what Spillers calls "a metaphor of commanding female sexuality . . . who celebrates, chides, embraces, inquires into, *controls* her womanhood through the eloquence of form that she both makes use of and brings into being" (emphasis added). That control, however, is negotiable. For Ma Rainey, it has an exchange value, particularly insofar as her managers are concerned. She exchanges the rights to her voice for a right that is denied most other blacks, including her musicians: the right to be treated as she wants to be treated. But, as she makes clear to Cutler, her lead musician, she has no illusions about the limits of that control. Ma Rainey knows that she gets her way because she has something that Irvin and Sturdyvant want—her voice. She knows that Irvin and Sturdyvant lack any real commitment to her, her music, or the blues tradition and that they will put up with her only as long as it is profitable for them to record her songs.

> They don't care nothing about me. All they want is my voice. Well, I done learned that, and they gonna treat me like I want to be treated no matter how much it hurt them. They back there now call me all kinds of names . . . calling me everything but a child of god. But they can't do nothing else. They ain't got what they wanted yet. As soon as they get my voice down on them recording machines, then it's just like if I'd be some whore and they roll over and put their pants on. Ain't got no use for me then.

This is what the trumpet player Levee fails to comprehend when he talks about leaving Ma Rainey and getting his own band together and making records for Irvin and Sturdyvant. Levee wants to be like Ma Rainey. He believes that the white men respect her and that all he has to do to make them respect him is to turn over a good profit. Yet unlike Ma Rainey, who knows that it was black people and not white people who made her a star, Levee relies on Irvin and Sturdyvant to give him his break. Ma Rainey, on the other hand, has learned, after long years of performing on the Southern circuit, how to manipulate the powers that be. She has also learned to place a higher value on the blues tradition and all that it implies than on its technical innovations and mechanical reproduction. For example, when Irvin balks about not having enough time to let her stuttering nephew Sylvester record the lead-in lines to her "Black Bottom Blues," Ma Rainey does not hesitate to remind him that this recording session is something she does not need to do. She can easily return to her Southern tour, where over the years she has cultivated large numbers of loyal fans:

> If you wanna make a record, you gonna find time. I ain't playing with you, Irvin. I can walk out of here and go back to my tour. I got plenty fans. I don't need to go through all of this. Just go and get the boy a microphone.

Ma Rainey doesn't need to go through the performance-inhibiting ordeal of a recording session because she remains solidly grounded in the tradition out of which her music evolved. Her *contract* is not with Irvin and Sturdyvant; it is with the people, the down-home folk who identify most closely with her brand of the blues. Her "Black Bottom" belongs to them, and she refuses to give it up to anyone else unless she gets something in return. As the last line of her "Moonshine Blues" goes, "You got to fetch it with you when you come." And when Irvin comes out of the control booth after the recording session with Sturdyvant's crooked deal to pay Sylvester with part of the money he owes her, Ma Rainey sends Irvin right back to fetch the boy's pay, then makes him and Sturdyvant beg her to sign the release forms.

Sturdyvant: Hey, Ma . . . come on, sign the forms, huh?

Irvin: Ma; . . . come on now.

Ma Rainey: Get your coat, Sylvester. Irvin, where's my car?

Irvin: It's right out front, Ma. Here . . . I got the keys right here. Come on, sign the forms, huh?

Ma Rainey: Irvin, give me my car keys!

Irvin: Sure, Ma . . . just sign the forms, huh!

(He gives her the keys, expecting a trade-off.)

Ma Rainey: Send them to my address and I'll get around to them.

Irvin: Come on, Ma . . . I took care of everything, right? I straightened everything out.

Ma Rainey signs. Just before she makes her exit she signs, but by that time she has gotten everything she can out of Irvin and Sturdyvant and their recording machines, including the satisfaction of making them put everything on hold, of making them wait.

Ma Rainey's Black Bottom is structured around the *act* of waiting and its consequences for her four black musicians, for whom waiting seems to be a condition of their being: waiting to play a halfway decent gig; waiting to get paid, in cash, when they do play a gig; waiting to have just one mo' good time; waiting for a good woman to help ease their trouble-in-mind; waiting for Ma Rainey to sing her "Black Bottom Blues."

Sandra Shannon has commented on how the act of waiting is crucial for establishing the tensions that culminate in Levee's murderous act at the end of the play. In "The Long Wait: August Wilson's *Ma Rainey's Black Bottom,*" Shannon argues that Wilson makes us all wait for Ma Rainey in order to focus more closely on the musicians as they wait for Ma Rainey to arrive:

> Capitalizing on the knowledge that both the reader and the viewer subconsciously expect the sassy blues singer to grace the stage at any moment, Wilson manages to upstage her entrance by focusing instead upon seemingly trivial conversations among her band members. Not only does Wilson make the rehearsal group wait for Ma Rainey, but he strategically places the audience on hold as well. Subconsciously they experience, in some measure, the frustration of waiting and its accompanying effects upon the cast. As a result of the delay, what they learn about the various idiosyncrasies of the troubled group serves as a context for understanding their motives when they are finally in the company of Ma Rainey.

What we learn is that each of the musicians has a story to tell, and that embedded in these stories are clues to why they interact with each other the way they do. We also learn that, with the exception of Levee, each of the musicians is strongly committed to doing things Ma Rainey's way. As Cutler and Slow Drag remind the rebellious Levee, who insists on doing things Irvin and Sturdyvant's way, when it comes to her music or her *self,* what Irvin and Sturdyvant want doesn't matter: Ma Rainey will always have the final say.

Cutler: Levee, the sooner you understand it ain't what you say, or what Mr. Irvin say . . . it's what Ma say that counts.

Slow Drag: Don't nobody say when it come to Ma. She's gonna do what she wants to do. Ma says what happens with her.

Levee: Hell, the man's the one putting out the record! He's gonna put out what he wanna put out!

Slow Drag: He's gonna put out what Ma want him to put out!

Consequently, although Wilson does indeed manage to upstage her entrance, his strategy does not close off the possibility of rendering Ma Rainey powerfully present even in her absence. In fact, her *presence* causes everyone, and especially Sturdyvant, a great deal of anxiety long before she arrives on the scene.

Sturdyvant would rather not deal with blacks under any circumstances and finds it particularly irritating to have to put up with one who comports herself as if she were a queen. As he helps Irvin test the studio's sound equipment for the one o'clock recording session, Sturdyvant continually reminds Irvin that it is his responsibility to keep Ma Rainey in line.

Sturdyvant: She's your responsibility. I'm not putting up with any Royal Highness . . . Queen of the Blues [bull—]!

Irvin: Mother of the Blues, Mel. Mother of the Blues.

Sturdyvant: I don't care what she calls herself. I'm not putting up with it. I just want to get her in here . . . record those songs on that list . . . and get her out. Just like clockwork, huh?

Irvin: Like clockwork, Mel. You just stay out of the way and let me handle it.

And for the most part, Sturdyvant does stay out of the way, in the control booth, while Irvin tries to handle a situation that, from the moment the musicians arrive without Ma Rainey, becomes increasingly chaotic. There is confusion about the songs the group is supposed to record. Irvin hands Cutler, who can't even read, a list that is different from the one Ma Rainey told him they would be recording. According to Toledo, the only member of the group who can read, Irvin's list includes four songs instead of six and one of them is Bessie Smith's version of "Moonshine Blues." It also includes Levee's *and* Ma Rainey's versions of "Black Bottom Blues." To further complicate matters, Levee refuses to rehearse the music on the list because he feels that it is outdated and requires a different kind of band, a jug band. This leads to a heated discussion about whether or not this style of music can be called art.

> *Levee:* You ain't gotta rehearse that . . . ain't nothing but old jug-band music. They need one of them jug bands for this.
>
> *Slow Drag:* Don't make me no difference. Long as we get paid.
>
> *Levee:* That ain't what I'm talking about, nigger. I'm talking about art!
>
> *Slow Drag:* What's drawing got to do with it?
>
> *Levee:* Where you get this nigger from, Cutler? He sound like one of the Alabama niggers.
>
> *Cutler:* Slow Drag's all right. It's you talking all that weird [sh—] about art. Just play the piece, nigger. You wanna be one of them . . . what you call . . . virtuoso or something, you in the wrong place. You ain't no Buddy Bolden or King Oliver . . . you just an old trumpet player come a dime a dozen. Talking about art.

But it is about art. It's about an art that is being divested of its Being, for the three-and-a-half-minute mechanically reproduced sound of the blues will always lack the presence, in time and space, of the "unique existence" that assures its authenticity. What is at stake, especially for the folk down home, is not just a musical style but a way of being, a way of understanding, defining, and improvising upon a world from which the Christian God had disappeared long before those white men *waited* 'til Levee's daddy went to Natchez to buy that seed and fertilizer and then came to Levee's daddy's house when Levee wasn't nothin' but about eight years old and had to do with his mama "any way they wanted" and Levee tried to save her *'cause God couldn't since he was already dead* and one of those white men cut him so bad that his mama had to carry him two miles to keep him from dying too and his daddy came back and acted like didn't nothin' happen and even sold his land to one of those white men and then moved out of that county and *waited* and then went back and got four of them before the other four or five got him.

> *Hear me talkin' now people. I'm talkin' about the BLUES!*

Levee's got the blues! Levee's got the blues so bad that he thinks he learned from his father's example how to handle the white man. When Cutler and Slow Drag criticize him for the way he "yessirs" Sturdyvant, and Toledo accuses him of being "spooked up with the white man" like everyone else, Levee tries to defend himself by insisting that his daddy's actions taught him what to do:

> I seen my daddy go up and grin in this cracker's face . . . smile in his face and sell him his land. All the while he's planning how he's gonna get him and what he's gonna do to him. That taught me how to handle them. So you all just back up and leave Levee alone about the white man. I can smile and say yessir to whoever I please. I got time coming to me. You all just leave Levee alone about the white man.

What Levee forgets is that his daddy did not smile and yessir the white man in order to get something from him. He did it in order to do something to him, and he carried his plan out to the bitter end. A true warrior, Memphis Green learned how to do what his son cannot. He learned how to live with his "head in the lion's mouth," as the enigmatic grandfather in Ralph Ellison's *Invisible Man* puts it. He did what the grandfather advised Ellison's protagonist's father to do. He overcame 'em with yeses, undermined 'em with grins, and agreed 'em to death and destruction before they destroyed him. What Memphis Green didn't do was what the grandfather in *Invisible Man* insisted in his dying breath that *his* son must do: "Learn it to the younguns." Memphis Green couldn't learn it to his "youngun": his time ran out just a bit too soon. Consequently, Levee lets his personal ambition dictate how to do battle with his oppressors. In so doing, he reverses his father's smile-and-sell strategy and substitutes compliance for subversiveness. Levee believes that all he has to do to make his way to the top of an industry already dominated by the immutable figure of the Mother of the Blues is yessir and smile and sell Sturdyvant a few of his songs. His strategy fails. Sturdyvant agrees to buy Levee's compositions—for five dollars apiece—but refuses to let him record them because he doesn't "think they'd sell like Ma's records." When Levee objects, Sturdyvant shoves five dollars in his pocket for the song he's already given him. And as Sturdyvant leaves the room, he lets the door slam in Levee's face. This makes Levee *mad.* However, instead of confronting the real enemy, Levee displaces his anger and resentment—first onto Cutler, who tries to persuade him, through his story of Reverend Gates, not to expect respect from white men, and then onto Toledo, who makes the mistake of stepping on one of his brand-new shoes.

Cutler's story is a familiar one, one that Toledo insists isn't worth telling since it has already been told "a hundred times." A black preacher takes a train to visit a sick relative and ends up, through no fault of his own, in a no-(black)man's-land surrounded by a group of white men who have nothing better to do than terrorize and humiliate him. What

Cutler tries to make Levee see is that it is foolish for a black person to expect to be respected by people who won't even respect a "man of God" if he happens to be black. But all Cutler succeeds in doing is making Levee even *madder* than he already is. As far as Levee is concerned, Cutler's story is proof enough that this God that Cutler is so fond of is "a white man's God" who "don't pay niggers no mind. In fact . . . God hate niggers! Hate them with all the fury in his heart." As Levee's own fury intensifies, so do his blasphemous attacks on God. This in turn provokes a bloody battle between the two men. Toledo and Slow Drag break it up just as Levee pulls a knife on Cutler and dares "Cutler's God" to come and save him:

> Cutler's God! Come on and save this nigger! Come on and save him like you did my mama! Save him like you did my mama! I heard her when she called you! I heard her when she said, "Lord, have mercy! Jesus, help me! Please, God, have mercy on me, Lord Jesus, help me!" And did you turn your back? Did you turn your back, [motherf—r]? Did you turn your back? (Levee *becomes so caught up in his dialogue with God that he forgets about* Cutler *and begins to stab upward in the air, trying to reach God.*) Come on! Come on and turn your back on me! Turn your back on me! Come on! Where is you? Come on and turn your back on me! Turn your back on me, [motherf—r]! I'll cut your heart out! Come on, turn your back on me! Come on! What's the matter? Where is you? Come on and turn your back on me! Come on, what you scared of? Turn your back on me! Come on! Coward, [motherf—r]!

Cutler's God can't come. Cutler's God is the Christian God, and that God had already been pronounced dead by another *madman*, Nietzsche's madman who, in *The Gay Science,* went running around the marketplace with his lit lantern looking for Him. When the people in the marketplace laughed at him for seeking a God they had long ago ceased to believe in, Nietzsche's madman proclaimed his death and said that *we* have killed him: "God is dead. God remains dead. And we have killed him. How shall we, the murderers of all murderers, comfort ourselves? What was holiest and most powerful of all that the world has yet owned has bled to death under our *knives*" (emphasis added). The bloody knives of unbelief killed God once. Now Levee is trying to conjure him up in order to make him bleed all over again. The difference is that this time the potential murderer "of all murderers" is not an unbeliever. Levee believes in God as much as Cutler does. What Levee has lost faith in is the idea of God as the "holiest and most powerful of all that the world has yet owned." In that sense, Levee stands in the shadow of Nietzsche's most "uncanny guest," nihilism, or what Martin Heidegger in "The Word of Nietzsche: 'God is Dead'" calls, after Nietzsche, the ongoing historical event of the "devaluing of the highest values up to now."

Heidegger defines the highest values as the suprasensory world, which is subsumed under the name God, and the true, the good, and the beautiful. These values

> are already devaluing themselves through the emerging of the insight that the ideal world is not and is never to be realized within the real world. The obligatory character of the highest values begins to totter. The question arises: Of what avail are these highest values if they do not simultaneously render secure the warrant and the ways and means for a realization of the goals posited in them?

For the nihilist these values are of no avail once their "obligatory character" and their authority begin to totter. That does not imply that in the face of this "tottering of the dominion of prior values," the world falls into decline and decay. The world remains, but it lacks the essential something that must occupy the authoritative realm which is preserved despite the fact that God is absent from it. As Heidegger explains,

> if God in the sense of the Christian god has disappeared from his authoritative position in the suprasensory world, then this authoritative place itself is still always preserved, even though as that which has become empty. The now-empty authoritative realm of the suprasensory and the ideal world can still be adhered to. What is more, the empty place demands to be occupied anew and to have the god now vanished from it replaced by something else.

August Wilson's Ma Rainey also recognizes the importance of replacing that now-empty realm with something else. However, unlike Toledo, who in the first act suggests that the gods be reconceptualized and named according to African traditions, Ma Rainey turns away from the theological altogether. Using the idiom of the blues tradition, Ma Rainey explains to Cutler and Toledo how her music helps to fill that space:

> *Ma Rainey:* The blues help you get out of bed in the morning. You get up knowing you ain't alone. There's something else in the world. Something's been added by that song. This be an empty world without the blues. I take that emptiness and try to fill it up with something.
>
> *Toledo:* You fill it up with something the people can't be without, Ma. That's why they call you the Mother of the Blues. You fill up that emptiness in a way ain't nobody ever thought of doing before. And now they can't be without it.

Ma Rainey: I ain't started the blues way of singing. The blues always been there.

Cutler: In the church sometimes you find that way of singing. They got blues in the church.

Ma Rainey: They say I started it . . . but I didn't. I just helped it out. Filled up that empty space a little bit. That's all.

The blues is what excites the will-to-power of those beings who would otherwise lack the power to will beyond the narrow and racially defined spheres of their existence. In the absence of the God of Christianity, the blues is what *em*-powers them to seek their truth in a "dimension of happening" that transcends the value-laden realities of the everyday. Ma Rainey's *truth* is her song transformed into a communal act. In that sense, she has much in common with Dionysius whom Nietzsche, in *The Birth of Tragedy,* credits with having broken the "spell of individuation" that governs the artistic energies of the Apollonian, or the plastic arts, and opening the way for the symbolic expression of what he feels is at the heart of all human experience: the tragic. Nietzsche writes that while Dionysian art "wishes to convince us of the eternal joy of existence," it urges us to seek it "not in phenomena, but behind them" in order to recognize, without fear, that

> all that comes into being must be ready for a sorrowful end; we are forced to look into the terrors of the individual existence—yet we are not to become rigid with fear: a metaphysical comfort tears us momentarily from the bustle of the changing figures. We are really for a brief moment primordial being itself, feeling its raging desire for existence and joy in existence; the struggle, the pain, the destruction of phenomena; now appear necessary to us, in view of the excess of countless forms of existence which force and push one another into life, in view of the exuberant fertility of the universal will. We are pierced by the maddening sting of these pains just when we have become, as it were, one with the infinite primordial joy in existence, and when we anticipate, in Dionysian ecstasy, the indestructibility and eternity of this joy. In spite of fear and pity, we are the happy living beings, not as individuals, but as the *one* living being, with whose creative joy we are united.

What Nietzsche had in mind when he developed his concepts of the Apollonian and the Dionysian was tragedy as it is manifest in the works of Richard Wagner. But he could just as easily have been talking about the blues. For the spirit of Dionysius is transfigured onto Ma Rainey, whose music celebrates and mourns—many of her songs are called "moans"—one of the most tragic cultures of the modern age. Furthermore, Ma Rainey's music is valued only insofar as it links her with her

people in a communal "bond of kinship" signaled by her name. Levee breaks out of that bond and separates himself from his immediate "kin" when, in the second act, he deliberately provokes Ma Rainey until she fires him just before she leaves.

Afterwards, while the musicians wait in the bandroom for Sturdyvant to pay them their twenty-five dollars each, Slow Drag offers to show Levee a card trick just "to be nice." Levee refuses Slow Drag's friendly gesture, thus further alienating himself from the group. Toledo plays the game instead and pulls the six of diamonds, which, in the end, proves to be his unlucky card. After having "done been through life" and "made [his] marks," Toledo ends up the target of Levee's terribly misguided "warrior spirit."

August Wilson has described the "warrior spirit" as a refusal to accept the limitations of a racist society and a "willingness to battle, even to death" the forces that threaten existence in a real and immediate way. He feels that throughout the play Levee is guided by the "warrior spirit" despite the fact that he progresses toward the wrong target. Toledo posed no threat to Levee. If anything, Toledo simply forced him to confront his own ignorance about music and about what it means to be a struggling musician in a business that is being controlled by white men. He also showed him how little he understands "the basic understanding of everything." But *Ma Rainey's Black Bottom* is very much in the tragic mode. And tragedy demands that someone be sacrificed. Tragedy insists that someone must die.

Source: Sandra Adell, "Speaking of Ma Rainey/Talking about the Blues," in *May All Your Fences Have Gates: Essays on the Drama of August Wilson,* edited by Alan Nadel, University of Iowa Press, 1994, pp. 51–66.

SOURCES

Bogumil, Mary, *Understanding August Wilson,* University of South Carolina Press, 1999, pp. 15–33.

Day, Frank, *August Wilson,* Twayne, 1999, pp. 39–54.

Gilroy, Paul, "Modern Tones," in *Rhapsodies in Black: Art of the Harlem Renaissance,* edited by Richard J. Powell, University of California Press, 1997.

Herrington, Joan, *i ain't sorry for nothing i done,* Limelight Editions, 1998, pp. 41–51.

Kissel, Howard, Review of *Ma Rainey's Black Bottom,* in *Women's Wear Daily,* October 12, 1984.

Pereira, Kim, *August Wilson and the African-American Odyssey,* University of Illinois Press, 1995.

Rich, Frank, Review of *Ma Rainey's Black Bottom,* in *New York Times,* April 11, 1984, 1C.

Simon, John, "Black Bottom, Black Sheep," in *New York Post,* October 22, 1984, p. 95.

Wilson, August, *Three Plays,* University of Pittsburgh Press, 1991.

Wilson, Edwin, "On Broadway: *Ma Rainey,*" in *Wall Street Journal,* October 16, 1984.

FURTHER READING

Baker, Houston A., Jr., *Modernism and the Harlem Renaissance,* The University of Chicago Press, 1987.
    Baker argues that the Harlem Renaissance predates the 1920s and that its influence is still echoed in a broad spectrum of twentieth-century African-American arts.

Lieb, Sandra R., *Mother of the Blues: A Study of Ma Rainey,* University of Massachusetts Press, 1983.
    This biography is a good resource for those who want to learn more about Ma Rainey. It is well researched and contains numerous anecdotes about the singer and her circle of friends and business associates.

Nadel, Alan, ed., *May All Your Fences Have Gates: Essays on the Drama of August Wilson,* University of Iowa Press, 1994.
    Nadel collects useful critical essays on the role of issues such as gender, history, art, politics, and race in Wilson's plays.

Shafer, Yvonne, *August Wilson: A Research and Production Sourcebook,* Greenwood Press, 1998.
    In this indispensable book, Shafer surveys Wilson's life and work, summarizing his plays and providing critical overviews on them. Shafer also includes an exhaustive bibliography.

Shannon, Sandra, *The Dramatic Vision of August Wilson,* Howard University Press, 1995.
    Shannon details the development of Wilson's aesthetic sensibility. Her study also includes an interview with Wilson, in which he discusses his dramatic vision.

The Master Builder

HENRIK IBSEN

1892

Initially, the response to Henrik Ibsen's *The Master Builder* (*Bygmester Solness* in Norwegian) was mixed. The play received overwhelming praise when it was published in Scandinavia in 1892, but the demands it placed on actors made it difficult to stage, and as a result, the early performances of the play were criticized. As the actors and audience became accustomed to the play's innovative technique, however, audiences began to applaud Ibsen's creative mix of realism and expressionism in his compelling portrait of a middle-aged architect who assesses his obsessive drive to succeed.

The Master Builder chronicles the career and personal relationships of Halvard Solness, a man who has not let anything stand in the way of his rampant ambition. As he struggles with the destructive consequences of his monomaniacal pursuit and his growing fear that he has lost his creative powers, a mysterious young woman appears. She will help Solness gain a glimpse of his former robust self as she leads him to his tragic fate. In *The Master Builder*, Ibsen paints an intriguing portrait of one man's consuming desire for success.

AUTHOR BIOGRAPHY

Henrik Ibsen was born on March 20, 1828, in Skien, Norway, to Knud (a businessman) and Marichen (Altenburg) Ibsen. His wealthy family was thrown into poverty in 1834 when his father lost his store. As a result, Ibsen was forced to leave school at age fifteen and accept a position as a pharmacist's assistant. The humiliation his family suffered as they sold off most of their property to pay off debts became a dynamic in his later plays, especially in *A Doll House* (1879) and *John Gabriel Borkman* (1896). Fire, which was a constant threat to Skien's wooden shacks, was another subject in some of his plays, including *Ghosts* (1881) and *The Master Builder* (1892).

In the early 1850s, Ibsen attended Christiania University in what is now Oslo and began writing poetry. In 1850, he wrote his first play, *Catiline*, but it did not appear on the stage for several years. Soon after completing the play, he began a stint as stage manager for the Norwegian Theater in Bergen, where he was required to write and stage a play each year. These plays were not well received; however, they helped Ibsen fine-tune his dramatic skills. The plays explored the intricacies of human behavior against the backdrop of a repressive society, a theme that would reemerge in his later work. His fears that he was illegitimate, coupled with the birth of his own illegitimate child, surfaced in his characters, including Dina Dorf in *Pillars of Society* (1887), Regine in *Ghosts*, and Hedvig in *The Wild Duck* (1884).

In 1864, Ibsen left Norway after suffering severe mental stress brought on from overwork. Assisted by government grants and scholarships, he traveled through Italy and Germany for the next few decades, continuing his playwriting, which became increasingly well received. By the production of *Master Builder* in 1892, Ibsen's reputation as one of the world's leading dramatists was cemented. Although he never completed his degree at Christiania University, he was awarded an honorary degree from the University of Uppsala in 1877. After suffering a series of strokes, Ibsen died on May 23, 1906, in Oslo, Norway.

PLOT SUMMARY

Act 1

The play opens in a workroom in Halvard Solness's house where his assistant, Knut Brovik, and his son Ragnar are working on blueprints, and Kaja Fosli is tending the books. Knut, who is having difficulty breathing, declares, "I can't go on much

Henrik Ibsen

longer," noting that his health is quickly deteriorating. His son shows great concern over his father's condition. Knut refuses to go home and rest until he has tried to convince Solness to recognize his son's drafting abilities and to allow him to head a project. Solness, however, insists that Ragnar is not yet talented enough to work independently. Knut admits that Ragnar drew up plans for one of Solness's clients who considered them new and modern, an assessment that angers Solness.

Solness accuses Kaja of being behind Knut's request, so that she and Ragnar could marry. Kaja, however, insists she has had no part in it, although Ragnar and her uncle have been pressuring her to marry soon. She admits that she has fallen deeply in love with Solness. The master builder pretends to return her affections in an effort to make sure she, and thus Ragnar, does not leave.

During a visit, Dr. Herdal, the family doctor, tells Solness that his wife, Aline, suspects that he has feelings for Kaja. Solness admits that Kaja has fallen in love with him but insists that he wants her to stay only to keep Ragnar, whose work is valuable to him. He recognizes the fact that he is exploiting her but claims that he cannot prevent it. When Dr. Herdal suggests he tell his wife that he is not in love with Kaja, he declines, admitting that he wants his wife to think badly of him, finding "a kind of beneficial self-torment" in letting her think that he is guilty. Solness expresses his fear that he may be losing his mind.

The doctor admits that Solness has had a lot of bad luck, beginning with the burning down of Aline's family home, where they used to live. He notes that the builder began as a poor country boy and now he is at the top of his profession. Solness expresses a Faustian dread that he will have to pay for his good fortune. He is certain that the young will cause great changes, which will make him obsolete.

Hilda, a young woman dressed in hiking clothes and "shining with happiness," appears at the Solness home. She explains that Aline had invited her to visit after the two met at a mountain lodge last summer. Her true motive, however, begins to emerge when she reminds Solness that ten years ago, when she was twelve, she had met him when he built a tower on the church in her hometown. The doctor tells Solness that he must be able to predict the future since youth has indeed come knocking at his door.

As Hilda describes the moment when Solness climbed to the top of the tower during a wreathing ceremony, she admits that he became a thrilling, godlike figure to her. She then reminds him that when he came back to her family home that evening after the celebration, he called her his princess. He insisted that he would come back in ten years and buy a kingdom for her, and then kissed her several times. She declares that it has been ten years to the day, and she has come to claim her kingdom. Solness cannot remember the incident but thinks he might have willed it to happen.

Solness admits to her that he does not build church towers any longer, only homes "for human beings," but he has built a new home with a tower for himself. After telling her of his present discontent, he notes how happy it makes him to talk to her.

Act 2

Later that day, Solness promises Aline that they will be happier when they move into the new house, but she notes that the house is not important to her. She has never recovered from the loss of her parents' home and the death of their two children, for which she blames herself.

Solness explains the past to Hilda, telling her that after the fire, Aline was so despondent that she

could not properly nurse her babies and she refused to let anyone else care for them. They died as a result. After the fire, he subdivided the land on which it had stood, and built homes that were quite lucrative for him. After the death of his sons, he could not build another church, only homes.

Solness admits that he knew there was a crack in the chimney in their old house but did not fix it, knowing a fire would allow him to build on the land. The fire broke out in a closet, though, not the chimney. Solness suspects that he has special powers; when he desires something, he gets it, which proves, he claims, that he is one of the chosen. Yet he blames himself for the children's death and Aline's condition.

Hilda convinces Solness to write some encouraging words on Ragnar's drawings, since his father is dying. He is convinced that change is coming and retribution is inescapable. When Hilda shares her vision of him placing a wreath on a high church tower, he asks her what she wants from him, and she replies, "her kingdom." Later, Solness tells Kaja that he will not be needing her or Ragnar's services any longer. When Aline discovers his plan to place the wreath on the tower of their new home, she fears for his safety, but Hilda urges him on.

Act 3

That evening on the veranda, Aline shares her pain with Hilda and her guilt over the death of her children. She then expresses her hope that they can be friends. Hilda is moved by her talk with Aline and tells Solness that she should leave. However, when Solness admits that he no longer cares about his craft, Hilda tries to convince him that he should not be held back by guilt. She implores him to build a castle with a high tower. He agrees to construct a real castle in the air with solid foundations.

Ragnar arrives with the wreath and announces that his father is in a coma and never was able to read Solness's comments on his work. When he claims Solness will be too afraid to climb the tower, Hilda professes her love and confidence in the master builder. Later, Aline expresses her fears that Solness will become dizzy and will fall.

Before he climbs the scaffolding, Solness tells Hilda that he is afraid of retribution. Yet, he reiterates his promise to build a castle for them. He claims that he will climb the tower so that he can talk to God and tell him he will build a beautiful castle "together with a princess that I love."

Ragnar and his friends come to watch Solness, sure that he will not have the courage to climb up the tower. He does, however, and Hilda declares him "great and free again." She sees him struggling on the tower with someone. He waves, then falls with some planks and splintered wood. Refusing to acknowledge the fact that he is dead, Hilda fixes her vision on the tower, crying with wild intensity "my—my master builder!"

CHARACTERS

Knut Brovik

Formerly an architect, Knut Brovik is now an assistant to Solness. At the beginning of the play, his deteriorating health prompts him to confront Solness over the lack of support Solness has shown Ragnar. He admits that his confidence in his son has been shaken by the fact that Solness has never appreciated his son's work. Calling on the little strength he has left, Knut demands that Solness evaluate and appreciate Ragnar's drawings. Solness responds too late, however, and Knut falls into a coma before he reads his employer's comments.

Ragnar Brovik

Knut's son Ragnar works as a draftsman for Solness. He appears stooped in the play, which reflects his inability to stand up to his boss and demand recognition. When his resentment over Solness's refusal to recognize his talent prompts him to confront the older man, he quickly backs down when he is told his drawings are worthless. Yet, he becomes for Solness the symbol of youth—everything of which Solness is afraid.

Ragnar's lack of perception surfaces when he determines that Solness has not allowed his father or himself any measure of independence because Solness wanted to keep Kaja close to him. His bitterness emerges in the final scene when he comes to the celebration of Solness's new home so that he can see his employer fail in his attempt to climb the tower. Ragnar notes "how horrible" Solness's fall is, yet his final words in the scene reinforce his employer's failure.

Kaja Fosli

Kaja works as Solness's bookkeeper. She has fallen desperately in love with him, even though she is engaged to Ragnar. Ibsen never develops her character, using her, for the most part, as reinforcement of Solness's power and status.

Dr. Herdal

Dr. Herdal serves as the family doctor and advisor. He councils Solness about his wife's condition and offers her comfort and support.

Aline Solness

Aline Solness, Halvard's wife, has become barren physically and emotionally, due to the tragedies that she has experienced. When her parents' home and everything in it went up in flames, Aline could not get over the loss of her possessions and mementos. The mental and emotional strain that resulted prevented her from adequately nursing her babies, and her stubbornness caused her to refuse anyone's help. She admits that she did not have the strength of character to endure the fire, and she determines that she was punished for this through the death of her children.

The sense of duty she displayed regarding the nursing of her children has been magnified during the ensuing years. Her daily activities center on her duties to others. When Hilda appears at the house with few possessions, Aline promptly buys her enough items to make her feel comfortable. Yet, when Hilda thanks her, Aline responds that it was her duty to take care of her guest, removing all sense of spontaneity or real connection. She treats her husband in the same manner. She tells Hilda that it is "her duty to give into him." She reveals her estrangement from him when she leaves the room each time he walks in.

She appears to take no pleasure in her tasks or her interactions with others, especially her husband. Haggard and depressed, Aline dresses in black, as if she were in perpetual mourning. She does however, show openness to Hilda toward the end of the play, when the young woman takes the time to talk to her about the past. Halvard suggests that his wife had the potential for living a life of fulfillment, noting that she had a talent for "building up the small souls of children," but that potential was destroyed by the death of their boys.

Halvard Solness

Master builder Halvard Solness is a forceful, ambitious man, used to getting his own way. He has become successful through his drive to be the best in his field and through his ruthlessness. Knut Brovik insists that Solness's ambition caused him to "cut the ground out from under'' all in his way. Solness himself admits that he beat Brovik down and broke his spirit. He refuses to let Ragnar become independent, claiming that he will ''never give ground'' over to the young. His determination to keep Ragnar from succeeding springs from his fear that if the younger man gets a chance, he will ''hammer [him] to the ground'' and break him the same way he broke Ragnar's father.

Solness tries to justify his ambition in his explanation of his initial goals. He tells Hilda that his dream was to build churches as monuments to God, determining that this activity would be the noblest thing he could do with his life. Yet, somehow, his plans went awry. He explains, ''I built those poor country churches in so honest and warm and fervent a spirit that ... He should have been pleased with me,'' but for some reason, He was not. As a result, Solness insists, God ''turned the troll in me loose to stuff its pockets, put devils in me,'' which turned his ambition toward more selfish ends.

Solness feels that the house burning is evidence of God's displeasure, and that God took his children to prevent him from becoming attached to anything except his mission. He claims that his life has been ruined as a result. Yet, he also blames himself for his and his wife's tragic fate. He feels that he owes a debt to Aline since his desire to parcel the land on which her parents' home stood caused his ''troll'' to burn down the house and so ''suck all the lifeblood out of her.''

His spirit and confidence in himself returns, however, with Hilda's arrival. She refocuses his attention on his craft when she begs him to build the two of them a ''castle in the air.'' She also reinvigorates him through her obvious sexual desire for him, which allows him to feel youthful and thus powerful again.

Hilda Wangel

Hilda is a mysterious young woman who comes to stay with the Solnesses after Aline invites her for a visit. The two had met at a mountain lodge the previous summer. Hilda's real motive for the visit, however, is to seduce Solness and to convince him to fulfill his promise to build a castle for her, which he had made ten years earlier when she was twelve. He made such an impression on the young Hilda that she has become obsessed with the man she envisions as a god.

In her middle-class Victorian world, Hilda tries to absolve herself of responsibility for her desires,

which threaten to break up a marriage. She insists that like Solness, she too has a ''troll'' and ''devils'' inside of her that have driven her to him. Solness admits that when these internal forces gain strength, ''we have to give in—whether we want to or not.'' This sense of Hilda's possession by uncontrollable forces is reinforced by Solness's description of her as a ''little devil in white,'' screaming his name as he climbed up the tower in her hometown.

Periodically, though, Hilda's concern for others overrides her obsession with Solness. She insists that Solness find some words of praise for Ragnar's drawings to help ease his father's mind as he approaches death. Also, she shows compassion for Aline as the older woman describes her tragic life. At one point, Hilda is so overcome with sympathy for her that she tells Solness that she plans to leave. However, when Solness admits that he no longer cares about his work, she becomes incensed at the thought that anything would interfere with his artistry, and so her passion for him reasserts itself. When he falls from the tower at the end of the play, she cannot accept his fate, refusing to take her eyes off the heights he has attained.

THEMES

Self-Deception

Solness is aware of the suffering he has caused others, especially his wife, during his self-serving rise to power. In an effort to cope with the harsh consequences of this unchecked ambition, he tries to convince himself that he has not been completely responsible for his actions. He struggles to persuade others, as well as himself, that he is beset by internal devils, ''players'' that impose his will on others, without his consent. Solness insists that all he has to do is think of something he desires and immediately with no instruction from him, his devils carry out the deed. For example, the first time he meets Kaja, he thinks that he would like her to work in his office so Ragnar ''would stay put too.'' As he is telling this story to Dr. Herdal, he swears he ''didn't breathe a word'' of these thoughts to anyone, but the next day, Kaja came back to the office, acting as if he had already given her the job. As a result of these thoughts, Solness admits to the doctor that he fears that he is going mad.

Hilda reinforces this self-deception when she insists that she also has a troll inside of her and that the trolls in each of them have brought them together. By absolving them of the responsibility of their desire for each other and their plans to run off together, Hilda tries to assuage their guilt over destroying Solness's marriage and abandoning Aline.

Age versus Youth

As Solness struggles to cope with the consequences of his actions, he becomes obsessed with the idea that he is losing his creative edge. This obsession is compounded when Brovik tells him that Ragnar has drawn up blueprints for a young couple who have applauded his "new modern" ideas. Solness admits to Dr. Herdal that he harbors "a terrible fear" that an inevitable change is coming, heralded by the young, and as a result, he will become obsolete.

In an effort to stop this process, he tries to break Ragnar's spirit and confidence in his abilities by refusing to allow him to work independently on a project. Solness cannot overcome his consuming fear even when Ragnar's father, with his dying wish, begs him for a word of praise for his son.

Rejuvenation

Rejuvenation comes in the form of Hilda, a young woman who sparks Solness's waning creativity and sexuality. When Hilda first comes to the house, Solness admits that he is no longer interested in building homes, for no one appreciates his work. When Hilda tells him that the sight of him climbing the tower in her hometown was "wonderfully thrilling" and "lovely," and reminds him that he kissed her several times that evening, his pride in his work reemerges along with his sense of sexual prowess. After Hilda expresses unwavering confidence that he can again build and climb magnificent towers, he admits, "all these years I've been going around tormented by . . . a search for something—some old experience I thought I'd forgotten." She helps him remember the passion and creativity of his youth and instills in him the belief that he can regain his old powers. Hilda convinces him that he can carry her off to a magnificent castle in the air that he will build for the two of them. As a result, he admits to her, "you are the one person I've needed the most."

What Hilda helps him recapture during these musings is youth, the very thing that he thought would usurp his power and position. Solness, however, is ultimately unable to retain his sense of rejuvenation, and as his old fear of failure returns, he falls off the tower to his death.

TOPICS FOR FURTHER STUDY

- How would you stage the last scene of the play? Consider how you would show Solness climbing up and falling from the tower. How would you direct Hilda in this scene?

- Read Ibsen's *A Doll House* and compare the theme of power to that of *The Master Builder*.

- Research the causes and consequences of an overweening sense of ambition. What kind of counseling could Solness have received that might have helped change his behavior?

- Investigate the class structure of Norwegian society at the end of the previous century. How difficult was it for those of the lower classes to become financially successful?

STYLE

Realism and Expressionism

Ibsen combines elements of realism and expressionism in the play. Most of Ibsen's plays can be grouped into the realist movement, the dominant literary form in the latter part of the nineteenth century. In *The Master Builder*, however, Ibsen experiments with expressionism, a new movement that was coming into vogue. Realist and expressionist techniques merge in his characterizations. As Ibsen charts the rise and fall of master builder Halvard Solness, he takes a close look at cause-and-effect relationships. As in most realist works, the main character in Ibsen's play faces a moral choice, in this case whether or not to allow his ambition to run unchecked. When he decides that he will let nothing thwart his dream of rising to the top of his profession, he must face the destructive consequences. Ibsen presents a realistic depiction of the pain Solness's choice has caused not only his wife but also, ultimately, himself.

Ibsen's expressionistic techniques emerge in Solness's insistence that he has devils and trolls that enforce his will. When Solness claims that these devils were responsible for the burning of his home and Kaja's decision to seek employment with him, Ibsen suggests they are manifestations of Solness's own guilt. Ibsen also employs expressionism in his depiction of Hilda, who reenergizes Solness's creative spark and thus his confidence in himself, which provides him with the will to climb the tower again. Her mysterious arrival, just at the moment Solness needs to rejuvenate his creative energies, coupled with her unexplainable obsession for him, suggests that she may be a fantasy figure.

Symbolism

The dominant symbol in the play is the tower that Solness climbs on two occasions, a phallic structure that suggests his authority and sexuality. Hilda watches transfixed both times as he climbs the vertical edifices to the top, thrilled at the power and courage he displays as he rises high above the town. Her active observance of Solness's physical prowess causes her to become obsessed with him, so much so that she is willing to break up his marriage to the long-suffering Aline.

HISTORICAL CONTEXT

Realism

In the late nineteenth century, playwrights turned away from what they considered the artificiality of melodrama to a focus on the commonplace in the context of everyday contemporary life. They rejected the flat characterizations and unmotivated violent action typical of melodrama. Their work, along with much of the experimental fiction written during that period, adopted the tenets of realism, a new literary movement that took a serious look at believable characters and their sometimes problematic interactions with society.

To accomplish this goal, realistic drama focuses on the commonplace and eliminates the unlikely coincidences and excessive emotionalism of melodrama. Dramatists like Henrik Ibsen discard traditional sentimental theatrical forms as they chronicle the strengths and weaknesses of ordinary people confronting difficult social problems, like the restrictive conventions nineteenth-century women suffered. Writers who embraced realism use settings and props that reflect their characters' daily lives and realistic dialogue that replicates natural speech patterns.

Anna-Marie Taylor, in her overview on Ibsen for the *Reference Guide to World Literature,* comments that the author's realism centered on middle-class manners. She argues that his plays effectively deflated "bourgeois self-confidence" as they suggested that the "cosiest and best furnished of drawing rooms could harbour grim secrets, dissatisfaction, and despair." The exposure of deception and restrictions became a main focus of his social dramas, especially *A Doll House* and *Pillars of Society.* Later, when his plays became more experimental, Ibsen incorporated realistic techniques into a more symbolic structure.

Expressionism

Dramatists during the early decades of the twentieth century also adopted the techniques of another new literary movement. expressionism eschewed the realists' attention to verisimilitude and instead employed experimental methods that tried to objectify the inner experiences of human beings. Influenced by the theories of Freud, playwrights like August Strindberg used nonrealistic devices that distorted and sometimes oversimplified human actions in order to explore the depths of the human mind.

Ibsen's long career reflected the shifting styles of the theatre at the end of the nineteenth century that would continue into the twentieth. His early social dramas were realistic depictions of the interactions between family members and between men and women. In the later part of the decade, he experimented with more symbolic forms of drama, most notably in *The Master Builder* and *When We Dead Awaken.* In the former play, the action is centered on the consciousness of the central character. Often viewers are not certain whether Solness's life becomes a construct of his dreams and desires, especially his relationship with Hilda, who becomes a muse figure in the play.

CRITICAL OVERVIEW

When *The Master Builder* (*Bygmester Solness* in Norwegian) was published in Scandinavia in 1892, the public response was greater than for any other Ibsen play since *A Doll House.* Henrik Jaeger praises the structure of the play in *Dagbladet,* writing that it becomes "a dialogue" between Solness and Hilde "so powerful and brilliant that it is more gripping than the most exciting 'scene.'" Christian

COMPARE & CONTRAST

- **1890s:** In the latter part of the nineteenth century, realism becomes the dominant literary movement in the Western world. In the last decade of the century, symbolism and naturalism emerge as important new movements.

  Today: Musicals, like *The Producers,* and reality based plays, like *Rent,* dominate Broadway.

- **1890s:** The Klondike gold rush begins in 1896 in northwest Canada. News of the discovery of gold there prompts thousands to rush to the area, hoping to strike it rich.

  Today: Eastern nations criticize what they see as rampant materialism in the Western world.

- **1890s:** Samuel Clemens dubs this decade "The Gilded Age," due, in large part, to the industrialization of the West. During this period, a handful of large industries gain control of the economy in the United States. Those industrialists who profited saw their fortunes grow at a rapid rate, while the working class suffered with low wages and dangerous working conditions.

  Today: Public awareness of major companies exploiting foreign workers has grown. Many fear that the current push for economic globalization will reinforce the imbalances between the rich and the poor.

Brinckmann, in his review in *Nyt Tidsskrift,* applauds the way "despair resounds like jubilation and madness sounds like wisdom" in the play.

Some reviewers, however, criticized what they considered obscure subject matter. George Göthe, in *Nordisk Tidskrift,* insists that the play presents "precious and pretentious abstract grandiloquencies." He notes that solving riddles can "be amusing," but "when the riddles are so complex that one suspects that even the riddler himself does not really know the answer, the game ceases to be amusing."

The response to the initial stage performances of the play, which opened simultaneously in Berlin and Trondhjem, Norway in 1893, however, was mostly negative, due to its intricate structure, which placed heavy demands on the actors. Reviews of a later staging in London included one in the *Daily Telegraph* that claimed that in the play, "dense mist enshrouds characters, words, actions, and motives." A writer for the *Saturday Review* called it "a distracting jumble of incoherent elements" and argued that "there is no story" and "the characters are impossible." Appreciation of the play, though, has grown since its first productions. Most critics now consider *The Master Builder* to be one of

Ibsen's finest, echoing Edvard Brandes's assessment in *Politiken* that the play blends "supreme craftsmanship" and "characteristic profundity."

CRITICISM

Wendy Perkins

Perkins is an instructor of twentieth-century literature and film. In this essay, Perkins examines Ibsen's adaptation of the Faust myth in Ibsen's play.

The story of a man who sells his soul to the devil so that he can gain knowledge, power, and riches can be traced back to the beginning of Christianity. This tale has been told under various names until the Renaissance, when it became known as the Faust myth. A German history of Dr. Faustus, the first known written account of the legend, inspired Christopher Marlowe's celebrated version, *Dr. Faustus* (1604). Since Marlowe's play, the story has appeared in various forms including Goethe's *Faust* (1808). In *The Master Builder,* Ibsen creates his own version of the myth as he weaves it into the thematic fabric of his play. Through the tragic Faustian tale of architect Halvard Solness, Ibsen

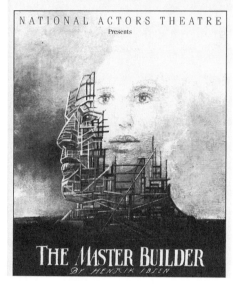

Playbill cover from the theatrical production of The Master Builder, *performed at the Belasco Theatre in 1992*

explores the nature and devastating consequences of unchecked ambition.

In Marlowe's version of the Faust myth, the central character embarks on a quest for knowledge—in this case medical knowledge—so that he may "heap up gold" but also so that he can "make men to live eternally." His monomaniacal pursuit of knowledge prompts him to enter into a pact with the devil, which fulfills his ambitions to acquire this godlike power. Ultimately, however, Faustus's arrogance is punished when he must give up his soul at the end of the play and suffer eternal damnation.

In *Master Builder*, Ibsen's central character, Halvard Solness, has been driven by overweening ambition to gain the position of "master builder." He was able to achieve this acclaim after his in-law's home, in which he and his wife were living, burned to the ground, affording him the opportunity to subdivide the land and build on it. Initially, he had built country churches with a fervent spirit, but his ambitions turned him toward more selfish ends.

Solness believes that he willed the fire, aided by a personal troll and devils, "helpers and servers" whom he calls on incessantly to help him realize his ambitions. As a result, Solness has achieved a godlike status in his position as master builder, reinforced by the adoration of two young women: his bookkeeper Kaja, and Hilda, the mysterious guest who comes to stay with him and his wife. His superior position is symbolized when he climbs the church tower in Hilda's hometown to place a celebration wreath at the top. It was then that Hilda fell in love with him, explaining how "wonderfully thrilling" it was for her to stand below, looking up and seeing "the master builder himself."

In his ruthless climb to the top, he has ignored the needs of others, especially his wife, whose despair over losing her parent's home led to the death of their two sons. Although he never imagined the tragic effects his ambition would have on Aline, he has been more pitiless with his employees. In an effort to guard his supremacy, he has "broken" Brovik, his assistant, and impeded his son's development, fearing the young man will eventually surpass him. He also cruelly manipulates Kaja's feelings for him, in an effort to keep Ragnar in his place.

As Faust must eventually relinquish his soul in payment for his success, so too must Solness, although the master builder has suffered during his entire climb to the top of his profession. He feels a great sense of guilt over the loss of his sons, which he directly attributes to his desire for power and position. This guilt is compounded by his acknowledgement that Aline's despair stems from her inability to cope with the loss of their children. He admits that the devilish powers within him have "sucked all the lifeblood out of her," that she is now emotionally dead, and so he has been "chained to the dead." As a result, there is "never a touch of sun, not the least glimmer of light" in their home.

In her introduction to Marlowe's *Doctor Faustus,* Sylvan Barnet discusses the problem of ambition in the play. She notes that while his "ideals are corrupted . . . they reveal an abundance of energy that makes Faustus indisputably greater . . . than any of the other mortals in the play." The same can be said of Solness, who has risen to greater heights, as symbolized by his climb to the top of the tower, than has any other architect. He has been a commanding and dominant presence to those who come into his circle, cementing his reputation as master builder. Yet, at the beginning of the play, his position at the top has become undermined.

WHAT DO I READ NEXT?

- *A Doll House* (1879), Ibsen's most celebrated play, uses the realist techniques to study the life of a woman repressed by the tenets of her society.

- *Dr. Faustus* (1604) is playwright Christopher Marlowe's rendition of the Faustian legend.

- *When We Dead Awaken* (1899), Ibsen's last play, presents an expressionistic view of the intricacies of the human mind and personality.

- *History of the Theatre* (1998), by Franklin J. Hildy and Oscar Gross Brockett, presents a comprehensive view of theatre through history, including an examination of different types of drama.

Solness's guilt and growing fear that he is losing his artistic abilities, and so will soon be overtaken by the young, paralyzes him to the point where he does not want to build any more. His lack of confidence in himself prevents him from recognizing the value of Ragnar's work and causes him to deny the younger man's request to build a home from his own "new, modern" plans.

Hilda's adoration, however, gives him new confidence in his artistic abilities and his manhood. Her appreciation of his artistry, coupled with her obvious sexual attraction toward him, prompts her insistence that he carry her away and build them a castle in the air. In his guilt and despondency, Solness opens himself up to Hilda and accepts her fantasized image of him. As a result, she convinces him to again climb to the highest heights where she insists he belongs, this time to decorate the tower of his new home.

A consideration of Solness's ultimate fate raises similar questions to that in the Faust myth. Barnet notes that Marlowe's Faustus is responsible for the choices he makes, but those choices have been influenced by "a hostile cosmos that entraps him." Barnet suggests the devils in his cosmos may be "not so much independent external creatures as they are aspects of himself, symbols perhaps of his pride." In a similar way, Ibsen complicates the vision of Solness's responsibility for his fate. Solness explains that his initial goal was to build "poor country churches in so honest and warm and fervent a spirit" that God would be pleased with him. However, he claims, he instead earned God's dis-

pleasure and as a result, He caused his house to burn and his children's death, so that Solness would not attach himself emotionally to anything except his work. When he climbed up the tower in Hilda's hometown, successfully suppressing his fear of heights, he determined that he would be an independent creator, in his own realm. At that point, he swore that he would no longer build churches, but instead "homes for humans." Yet, the achievement of his artistic goals resulted in the shattering of his personal life.

Solness insists that God has been aided in his plan to control and to punish him by influencing the "troll" and "devils" within him. He claims that God "turned the troll in me loose to stuff its pockets." When Kaja appeared to read his mind as he was thinking that she should work for him, he determines that the "players" within him carried out his will and prompted her to ask for a position. Hilda confirms the existence of these internal devils when she insists that the trolls within each of them have brought them together.

Throughout the play, Ibsen suggests that the devils within Solness are most likely manifestations of the same pride that controlled Faust. Yet the final scene adds a note of ambiguity. At the end of the play, Solness's fears that the younger generation will cause his downfall are realized in an ironic sense. He is destroyed not through the jealousy of the young, but through the worship of a young woman who encourages him to climb the tower one more time. After Solness moves up the side of the tower attached to his house, Hilda watches from

> SOLNESS INSISTS THAT GOD HAS BEEN AIDED IN HIS PLAN TO CONTROL AND TO PUNISH HIM BY INFLUENCING THE 'TROLL' AND 'DEVILS' WITHIN HIM."

below. When he reaches the top, she insists that she sees someone up there struggling with him. Seconds later, he falls, along with "some planks and splintered wood," suggesting the possibility that as with Faust, devils have come to demand the payment of his soul.

The final scene of the play reinforces the complex image Ibsen has created of his protagonist. As the others look at his broken body lying on the ground in a heap, Hilda keeps her steady gaze on the tower and on her vision of Solness as the master builder. Through this portrait of the driven architect in *The Master Builder*, Ibsen reinvents the Faustian myth of a magnificent, powerful man who is celebrated yet ultimately destroyed by the corruption of his ambitious vision.

Source: Wendy Perkins, Critical Essay on *The Master Builder*, in *Drama for Students,* The Gale Group, 2002.

Margery Morgan

In the following essay, the author gives a good overview of Ibsen's play The Master Builder.

Two different kinds of play are interlinked in *The Master Builder*. The first introduced is a naturalistic social drama concerning a successful, middle-aged man's attempt to block the path of a potential younger rival (Ragnar Brøvik), whose father he himself displaced; working on the susceptible nature of Ragnar's finacée, Kaia, Master-Builder Solness has created an infatuation with himself which will keep both young people, and Old Brøvik, working in his office. Still within Act I, a drama of the inner life—of fantasy, obsession, and neurosis—begins with the arrival of youth personified in Hilde Wangel and ousts the first level of the play from the centre of attention. The disturbing strangeness of the work as a whole springs from Ibsen's maintaining and interrelating the two dramatic modes to the end, so that Solness's inner renewal allows him to

release Ragnar, and his death by falling from a tower suggests a multiplicity of meanings.

A direct reflection of Strindberg's *The Father* appears in Solness's suspicion that his wife, Aline, and Dr. Herdal believe him to be insane. The Swedish playwright's example had undoubtedly encouraged Ibsen to tread more boldly in dramatic territory represented in all his plays after *The Wild Duck* (1884). This advance involves recognition that the human mind operates in stranger ways than the limited, naturalistic view that rationality admits, and that human motivation and action can have a mythic dimension. He uses the technique of intimate duologues, as developed in his social plays (especially *Ghosts*), as a method of tracing the influence of the past in the present, to explore the secret mind and the innermost nature of human relationships. One school of critics, clinging to the tenets of naturalism, interprets the play as a study in mental abnormality: Solness, Aline, and Hilde in turn qualify for the madhouse. It is more rewarding to move with the play into a more imaginatively conceived understanding of reality, not choosing between alternatives, but reaching out to encompass divergent views.

Ibsen is careful to locate Hilde in the social world: both Dr. Herdal (the confidant) and Mrs. Solness remember meeting her before, in mundane situations; it is Solness who does not recall her. She has a history outside the play: the younger daughter of Dr. Wangel of Lysanger, in *The Lady from the Sea,* has put on years and arrived unexpectedly at the Solness house, come like the devil cheerfully on cue. To all the other characters she appears an attractive, lively, unconventional young woman, spontaneously friendly, if self-willed; to Solness, in their long solitudes *à deux,* she is an enchanting inquisitor who draws out of him all his hidden fears, desires, and sense of guilt, opens the prison of his everyday life and gives him hope. He is not troubled to verify or reject the story she tells him of their earlier meeting and her reason for seeking him out. Its fairytale quality insulated them from actuality in a world of the imagination and provides a language of metaphor in which they can talk freely. An emotionally adult woman, Hilde uses her fantasy from the past as an erotic challenge to Solness which he finds irresistible.

Although each of the three main characters recalls memories, the past that they reveal is ambiguous and unstable, as they do not verify each other's accounts. This is not the past as historical fact, but the fiction they each construct to live by. Ibsen has left it open to the actress playing Hilde to allow the character an awareness of the process that neither Solness nor Aline shares. The oddity of a mature young woman claiming a childish hero-worship of the Master Builder, and clinging to a pubertal fantasy of how, ten years before to the day, he chose her as his future princess, may be simply piquant. Solness, who spares scarcely a thought for the ruthlessness with which he treated Knut Brøvik in the pursuit of his own ambitions, and less for having failed to give his wife a love through which she might have blossomed as a woman, has attached his sense of guilt to the burning down of her home which he knows, rationally, he did not cause. Aline's is the most horrifying displacement: grieving, not for the babies who died, but for her dolls and her own lost childhood. The obsessional symbols may have a deeper truth to tell.

An unnatural arresting of time emerges as one of the play's themes through its repetition within each of the main characters: Hilde's fixation on the day, ten years ago, when Solness climbed the church tower at Lysanger; Aline, who has grown old without growing up; and Solness, intent on resisting the process of change whereby men pass from youth to age and others take over from them. The "out-of-time" quality of the duologues is entirely apt. It is also a condition of contemplation in which the play's poetic reach can be explored. As a psychological drama, *The Master Builder* testifies to the symbolic and superstitious modes of thinking sophisticated human beings still employ alongside the scientific and rational, and which poets utilise most deliberately. It is a kind of poets' thinking that passes between Solness and Hilde, and it forces its way through into the action at the end of the play.

From the play's first appearance it has been regarded as partly autobiographical, the various phases of Solness's career as a builder corresponding to the major changes in Ibsen's dramatic style from the great philosophical plays in verse onwards. Yet it has also taken its place among the supreme modern tragedies. The obvious, phallic symbolism is subsumed in the traditional tragic symbolism of the rise and fall of overweening ambition. Hilde's recollection of the master builder, high in the air, challenging some invisible power and triumphing, is matched both by Solness's terrified thought that he has called down fire from heaven and by his response to the lure of the impossible: building a new house for Aline and himself, unhappy though they are together, with three nurseries, though they

neither have nor can expect to have any children, giving it a tower, and siting it vertiginously on the edge of a quarry, even though he has lost his head for heights. An impression of more than human stature attaches itself to the fault-ridden human figure, and the philosophical ideas are not far away: Aline has nothing to live by but the categorical imperative of duty, to which Ibsen opposes *livsglede* (the joy of living); and Solness, in going beyond his nature to achieve the impossible, takes on the quality of the Nietzschean vision of man becoming superhuman. Hilde, who has goaded him out of mere idealistic dreaming (building castles in the air) and waves Aline's shawl at him in ecstasy, may be seen as his destroyer. But the Solness who takes the wreath to climb the tower is a better man than we have seen earlier in the play. He may not know that he is going to his death, but he is ready for it. The achievement is real.

Source: Margery Morgan, *"The Master Builder,"* in *International Dictionary of Theatre–1: Plays,* edited by Mark Hawkins-Dady, St. James Press, 1992, pp. 493–94.

Richard Hornby

In the following essay, Hornby examines The Master Builder *as a "point of departure" from the realist dramas of Ibsen's middle period to a combination of realism and romanticism that anticipated such twentieth-century movements as surrealism and expressionism.*

It has long been known that Ibsen's late plays—*The Master Builder, Little Ejolf, John Gabriel Borkman,* and *When We Dead Awaken*—represent a departure from the famous realistic plays of his middle period. Even Bernard Shaw, who had been obsessively concerned with Ibsen the moralist, described Ibsen as now having "completed the task of warning the world against its idols and anti-idols," and instead having written "tragedies of the dead." But more than this, the late plays demonstrate Ibsen's greatness, both as a significant (though independent) figure in the Symbolist movement of the 1890s, and as a significant precursor of twentieth-century literary movements. In his late plays Ibsen anticipates such twentieth-century concerns as the function of the artist, the use of personal experience in literature, and the importance of the inner life of both the conscious and the unconscious mind.

The Master Builder, published in 1892, shows all these concerns. Its hero is an artist, Halvard Solness, a successful architect (or "master builder,"

John Wood and Joanne Pearce in the 1989 theatrical production of The Master Builder, *performed at the Theatre Royal in London*

as he prefers). Perfection of the work seems to have blocked perfection of the life; his artistic success has coincided with contempt for his clients, ruthlessness toward his associates, the loss of his children, the mental breakdown of his wife. He is restless, alienated, and afraid of being superseded by younger architects. Into his life comes a strange, alluring, naive young woman, who seems to know his deepest secrets, and who claims to have had a near-sexual affair with him ten years before, when she had been little more than a child. In contrast to the drab, realistic world in which he works, she talks of trolls and magic kingdoms and harps in the air, fascinating him and ultimately leading him to destruction.

Solness's psychological problems—a fear of growing artistic and sexual impotence, and a fascination with a young girl—reflect those of Ibsen himself at the time the play was written. *The Master Builder* is Ibsen's most personal play. Indeed, it has become common for critics to compare the details of the play with the pattern of Ibsen's career as a playwright: Solness began by designing churches, then shifted to houses, and now designs houses with steeples; Ibsen, at the time the play was written, had gone through three similar phases, first writing

Romantic plays, then realistic plays, and finally realistic plays with Romantic overtones like *The Master Builder* itself. The shift in style in *The Master Builder* is not truly a reversion to Romanticism, however; the play instead looks forward to the work of the Surrealists and Expressionists of our century, in its exploration of inner psychological states.

The realistic plays of Ibsen's middle period were far more than simplistic problem plays taking moralistic stands on social issues. Nevertheless, they did follow standard realistic conventions, which, I shall attempt to show, provide a point of departure for the pivotal late play, *The Master Builder*. In *A Doll House* (1879), for example, we find ordinary, middle-class characters inhabiting a mundane, realistic world. The setting is an ordinary bourgeois living room. The characters' concerns are work, family, love, money. The action arises from conflicts between characters rather than within individual ones; Nora has forged a note to get money to treat her sick husband, Torvald Helmer, but this caused her no inner anguish—if anything, she is proud of it. Her problems arise when the loan shark, Krogstad, discovers the forgery and uses it to blackmail her. She fears being exposed (because she thinks that her husband will take the blame onto himself and go to prison), but she still feels no guilt.

All the information needed to drive the plot forward in *A Doll House*, as in Ibsen's other realistic plays, is provided by an extraordinary amount of exposition, necessitated by the late point of attack of the plot—in *A Doll House*, long after the forgery, after the husband's recovery, and just as the note is at last about to be paid off. A convention of this kind of realistic exposition is that it is always presented to the audience as *factual*; even though Nora has always cheerfully lied whenever it was necessary to cover up her scheme, when she explains it all to her confidant, Mrs. Linde, we take her every word for truth. This truth never comes into question, and is always perfectly clear. The play moves toward a climax in which Nora's husband is exposed as a hypocrite (instead of taking on the blame himself, as she had always expected he would, he plots a coverup), and in which Nora herself, bitterly disappointed in Helmer and seeing her whole life in a new light, leaves him to cast out on her own. It is a powerfully dramatic conclusion, but it is not in any sense a psychological one.

Although Ibsen's later realistic plays, such as *Rosmersholm* or *Hedda Gabler*, are decidely psychological, the psychology still exists within the same framework of realistic convention. The exposition, again, is presented as clear, uncontradictory truth. Thus when Rebecca West, in her famous speech, describes how she drove Rosmer's wife mad, it comes out in a blunt, straightforward manner:

I wanted Beata out of here, one way or another. But even so, I never dreamed it could happen. With every step ahead that I gambled on, it was as if something inside me cried out: "No further! Not one step further!" And yet I *couldn't* stop. I *had* to try for a tiny bit more. Just the least little bit. And then again—and always again—until it happened. That's the way these things *do* happen.

Rebecca is describing her own psychological turmoil, but her tone is clinical, as detached as a doctor describing a patient. Her conclusion—"That's the way these things *do* happen"—is a profound insight, but again, is meant to be taken as straight truth by the audience, as is her whole speech. The audience may well be shocked by Rebecca's compulsion, but they experience no disorientation themselves. The psychology here is vivid, pitiable, even terrifying, but definitely *understood*. It is still realistic, in the sense of being clear and comprehensible.

The Master Builder, however, is in fact a "deconstruction" of realism. Using conventions

> "SOLNESS'S PSYCHOLOGICAL PROBLEMS—A FEAR OF GROWING ARTISTIC AND SEXUAL IMPOTENCE, AND A FASCINATION WITH A YOUNG GIRL—REFLECT THOSE OF IBSEN HIMSELF AT THE TIME THE PLAY WAS WRITTEN."

that would have been familiar to late nineteenth-century audiences, Ibsen first creates apparently realistic characters in a realistic situation. Gradually, however, he moves into his hero's mind, to an inner world of unconscious desires and exotic symbolism. Written at the time of Freud's early work, the play anticipates much of Freud's theory, exposing the existence of the unconscious mind, the significance of dreams and mistakes, the ambivalence of emotion, and the unconscious belief in the omnipotence of thought. Nineteenth and twentieth-century techniques are thus combined in the play, which represents a major turning point in the history of dramatic literature.

The play opens in Solness's "plainly furnished workroom," immediately establishing a realistic, mundane atmosphere for the audience. Solness's two assistants, Knut Brovik and his son Ragnar, are seated, busy with blueprints and calculations, while a young bookkeeper, Kaja Fosli, stands at her ledger. We are in the everyday world of work. Solness enters, and in a brief aside with the girl, Kaja, reveals that they are intimate. There follows a scene between Solness and Knut Brovik. Brovik is ill, and probably dying; he is concerned that his son be given a commission, to establish his career as an independent architect. Unaware of Solness's relationship with Kaja, Brovik speaks of his son wanting to marry her. Solness is callous toward Brovik, and frightened of giving up a commission to a younger man.

Thus, all the materials for a realistic problem play are here: the realistic setting with a workaday atmosphere, the sexual hypocrisy, the problems of aging and loss of power. The audience would expect that young Ragnar would ultimately triumph, winning a commission and the girl, while, Solness would either die or somehow become reconciled to his loss. The audience would also expect to draw moral conclusions about the nature and abuses of power, the importance of kindness and fidelity, the limits of individualism. Instead, the trio of Brovik, Ragnar, and Kaja turn out to be relatively unimportant in the play. After a few brief scenes, Ibsen introduces a *raisoneur,* in the character of Dr. Herdal; in his scene with Solness, a major incident warns us that we are in for a very different experience from the realistic power struggle that we expected.

Dr. Herdal tries to get Solness to see that he really is very well established, with nothing to fear from young Ragnar, but Solness is vehement. "The change is coming," he insists. "Someday youth will come here, knocking at the door—", when lo and behold, there actually is a knock at the door, and youth does enter, in the person of Hilda Wangel, a girl whom Solness had met ten years earlier. The moment is one of the great *coups de théâtre* in the history of drama, grotesque, funny, shocking—and awkward. (It has often been ridiculed.) What critics have not recognized is that the literal representation of a metaphor, such as this one, is something that Freud was noticing, around the time the play was written, as a common element in dreams. In *The Interpretation of Dreams,* published in 1900, Freud was to give many examples, such as the dream of a horse frolicking in a field of the finest oats being an obvious manifestation of the expression, "feeling one's oats." Expressionist playwrights, in the early decades of twentieth century, were often to use the concrete manifestation of aphorisms as a device for inducing shock and laughter; Ibsen uses it for the same purpose here, starting his deconstruction of the realistic atmosphere and action that he had so carefully established.

The scene with Hilda at first seems realistic, however. She is no imaginary construct of Solness's, but a real flesh-and-blood girl, the daughter of a public health officer (a position of social responsibility, perhaps echoing Ibsen's own *An Enemy of the People*). Even Dr. Herdal has met her before, and recognizes her now. She has real bodily needs, too: she mentions that her underwear needs to be washed, that "they're real grimy." The grimy underwear represents Ibsen's sly evocation of naturalism, the extreme form of realism that depicted man in purely physical, animal terms. The audience seems to find itself on familiar ground once again.

The familiarity is an illusion, however, Dr. Herdal soon exits, leaving Solness and Hilda alone. Gradually, without a seam showing, the tenor of the scene changes. Grimy reality melts away, to be replaced by something like a dream. Hilda describes the occasion of their first meeting, when she was a girl of twelve or thirteen. Solness had built a church tower in her town, and dedicated it by climbing to the top and hanging a wreath on the weather vane. In the late twentieth century, we hardly need to be told the sexual symbolism of climbing a tower, but to the audience of the time it would have seemed evocative and disturbing. More important, however, is what follows: Hilda says that she and Solness met afterwards, alone, and that he first promised that he would come back in ten years, carry her off "like a troll," and buy her a kingdom. Then, she says, he held her in his arms, bent her back, and kissed her— "many times." Solness is shocked and dazed, first denying the incident, then saying, "I must have willed it. Wished it. Desired it. And so—Doesn't that make sense? Oh all right, for God's sake—so I did the thing too!" We have again left the external world of realism for the inner, dream world of Expressionism.

This passage is extraordinary in its anticipation of Freud's theory of "the omnipotence of thought." The infant cannot distinguish between dreams and reality, between wishing a thing and doing it. As adults, we continue to equate thought and reality in our unconscious minds, which is why we can feel guilty for something that we never did, but only wished. Here Solness cannot remember whether he actually kissed Hilda or not, but he realizes that he *wanted* to, which in his unconscious mind is equivalent to having done it. As for Hilda, she no longer seems the real live girl with the dirty underwear she was earlier. She has shifted to a mythic plane, describing herself as a princess and Solness as a troll, and demanding that he come up with the promised kingdom. Troll, princess, and enchanted kingdom show an obvious connection with the Symbolist movement, but we never leave the real world entirely. Ibsen's purpose is not so much to evoke a magical, poetic vision as it is to explore, very precisely, his hero's unconscious mind. Hilda now appears to be a fantasy, a projection of Solness's desires and fears.

The second act begins the following morning; Hilda has spent the night at Solness's house. She says that she dreamed the night before of falling over "a terribly high, steep cliff." As in Freud, her dream seems charged with significance; it also foreshadows Solness's own fall at the end of the play. In addition, however, it signals another deconstruction of realism to Expressionism. As in the first act, there is another long scene between her and Solness. He tells of a disastrous fire that consumed the house in which he and his wife lived early in their marriage. The fire helped make Solness's reputation; he was then able to subdivide the land and build houses on it, which established him as an architect. As a result of the fire, however, Solness's two children died. Here again we have the basis for a realistic struggle of career versus family (a distinct echo of the great neoclassical theme of honor versus love), but the details are odd: the children did not die in the fire itself, but rather because of Mrs. Solness having taken sick from the strain, which affected her milk. Instead of the kind of simple, surface causality that we would expect in a realistic play, the causality here is strangely oblique, as if some inner, unseen mechanism were operating. The information that follows is even stranger: it turns out that Solness had noticed a crack in the chimney of the house, long before the fire, and neglected to fix it. He sensed, even then, that if the house were to burn down, he would be given a wonderful opportunity to advance his career. Here, we might think, is the kernel of the play, the original sin. Solness's neglect— a "Freudian slip," fulfilling his wish to get rid of the house—brought him fame and fortune, but cost him his children. "What price glory?" But then, in another bizarre and cunning stroke, Ibsen destroys our standard reaction. Solness says that "It's been proved without a shadow of a doubt that the fire broke out in a clothes closet, in quite another part of the house." It seems that Solness had nothing to do with starting the fire at all!

Yet once again, Solness believes that his inner state at the time represented true reality. In a key speech, he reflects on the power of wishes:

> Don't you believe with me, Hilda, that there are certain special, chosen people who have a gift and power and capacity to *wish* something, *desire* something, *will* something—so insistently and so—so inevitably—that at last it *has* to be theirs? Don't you believe that?

This is omnipotence of thought once again, which Solness is coming to think of as an actual reality. Such omnipotence is found elsewhere in the play. For example, Solness says that he has got Kaja to come to work in his office simply by wishing it one day; then, "in the late evening, . . . she came by to see me again, acting as if we'd already struck a bargain." But Ibsen in the long run is not so crude as to suggest that thought is literally omnipotent; all the things wished for could have occurred by accident, or in this case, by Kaja's sensitivity to nuances of expression and attitude in Solness. Ibsen's focus is instead on Solness's confusion and fear with regard to his inner life, on his awareness that it *might* have powers far beyond his conscious understanding, and on his guilt for the immoral desires that seem to come true. Freud maintained that unfulfilled desires actually make us feel more guilty than fulfilled ones; the undischarged psychic energy of the desire turns inward, against the self. This is the case with Solness. He is not at all guilt-ridden about his sexual affair with Kaja, but feels extremely guilty about his desires for Hilda, even though they were never actually consummated. In the same vein, Solness's wife, Aline, feels more upset about the loss of her collection of dolls in the fire than about the loss of her two sons; her imaginary love for the dolls is more real to her than her ostensibly real love for her flesh-and-blood children. The pattern in the play is always that a character's inner life is paramount; the outer, realistic world, while genuine enough (Ibsen is no solipsist), is not the world in which one actually *lives*.

Ibsen continues his exploration of the inner life in his depiction of Solness's death. Solness, afraid of heights, no longer climbs towers to plant celebratory wreaths on them. Nonetheless, Hilda demands that he climb the tower on his latest building. Solness's acrophobia is distinctly ambivalent, in keeping with Freud's theory that strong conscious feelings of revulsion against something are always accompanied by equally strong unconscious feelings of desire for it. Solness unconsciously seems to yearn to climb and fall, just as he unconsciously wanted sex with the forbidden Hilda. In the end, it is the power of thought that again seems the catalyst: Hilda wishes his climb, twice saying, "I *will* see it!" At the ultimate moment, she excitedly snatches a white shawl and waves it at Solness, shouting from below to him high on the tower, "Hurray for master builder Solness!," causing Solness to plunge to his death. Again, the exact nature of causality is ambiguous: did Solness fall because Hilda distracted him by shouting and waving, or because she *willed* him to fall? Is Hilda a real girl with an obsessive neurosis, who destroys Solness by palpable methods, or a witch, troll, a projection of Solness's own fantasies, who destroys him by the power of the unconscious mind? The greatness of the play is that it explores the boundary between outer and an inner reality, deconstructing the former to bring us to the latter. At the final curtain, the audience is as confused and frightened as Solness, confronted with the power of the unconscious mind, and unable to determine its extent or its meaning. They have entered the twentieth century.

Source: Richard Hornby, "Deconstructing Realism in Ibsen's *The Master Builder*," in *Essays in Theatre,* Vol. 21, No. 1, November 1983, pp. 34–40.

SOURCES

Barnet, Sylvan, "Introduction," in *Doctor Faustus,* by Christopher Marlowe, Signet, 1969, pp. vii–xix.

Brandes, Edvard, Review of *The Master Builder,* in *Politiken,* December 22, 1892.

Brinckmann, Christian, Review of *The Master Builder,* in *Nyt Tidsskrift,* 1892–1893, pp. 272–81.

Göthe, George, Review of *The Master Builder,* in *Nordisk Tidskrift,* 1893, pp. 153–57.

Jaeger, Henrik, Review of *The Master Builder,* in *Dagbladet,* December 27, 1892.

Review of *The Master Builder,* in *Daily Telegraph,* February 1892.

Review of *The Master Builder,* in *Saturday Review,* February 1892.

Taylor, Anna-Marie, "*The Master Builder:* Overview," in *Reference Guide to World Literature,* 2d ed., St. James Press, 1995.

FURTHER READING

Bentley, Eric, *The Playwright As Thinker,* Harcourt Brace, 1987.
  This study examines the philosophical point of view in Ibsen's works.

Egan, Michael, *Ibsen: The Critical Heritage,* Routledge, 1972.
  Egan traces the history of the critical response to Ibsen's plays.

Haugen, Einar, *Ibsen's Drama,* University of Minnesota Press, 1979.
  Haugen engages in a comprehensive examination of the themes and structure of Ibsen's plays, including *The Master Builder.*

Meyer, Michael, *Ibsen: A Biography,* Doubleday, 1971.
  Meyer presents a thoughtful analysis of Ibsen's life, tracing "his development as a man and as a writer" and offering an assessment of his work, "both intrinsically and historically." He also discusses Ibsen's impact on the theatre.

One Day, When I Was Lost: A Scenario

James Baldwin's screenplay *One Day, When I Was Lost: A Scenario* was adapted from Alex Haley's *Autobiography of Malcolm X* (1965). Although *One Day, When I Was Lost: A Scenario* was written as a movie script, it has never been produced solely on its own merits. *One Day, When I Was Lost: A Scenario* came closest to being realized on the screen in the documentaries *Malcolm X* (1972), co-written by Baldwin and Arnold Perl and the re-written version by Spike Lee, *Malcolm X* (1992).

Malcolm X had been a friend and hero of Baldwin's, so it was with relish that Baldwin immersed himself in Haley's *Malcolm X* in his attempts to extrapolate a dramatic representation. At first, the script was supposed to have been written as a stage play in conjunction with Haley and Elia Kazan, a famous Broadway director. However, before the writing had begun, Columbia Pictures bought the movie rights of Haley's book and asked Baldwin if he would be interested in writing the screenplay.

Although urged by friends and family not to accept the Hollywood offer, Baldwin, who had always wanted to write a script for a movie and who also believed that he owed it to the memory of Malcolm X to write it, decided in Columbia's favor. He would regret his decision, as the movie studio's demands for changes in his script would frustrate his creative spirit and his sense of loyalty to his friend, Malcolm.

JAMES BALDWIN

1972

Baldwin's belief that Hollywood was ready for a truthful encounter with the facts of Malcolm X's life was soon diminished. One of Baldwin's strongest battles with the studio was fought over the starring role in the film. At one point, Columbia supposedly went so far as to suggest a white actor, who would be, according to Baldwin's biographer, David Leeming, "darkened up a bit" to portray the character of Malcolm X. After repeated communications from Columbia suggesting revisions in his script, Baldwin proclaimed that he would write it in his own words or not at all. In reaction, Columbia sent another writer, Arnold Perl, to collaborate with Baldwin. Baldwin resented this, believing that only he could be true to Malcolm X's story.

Adding to his depression and anger with Columbia was the assassination of Martin Luther King, Jr., which occurred in the middle of Baldwin's attempts to write the script. Shortly after King's assassination, Leeming states, Baldwin "took an overdose of sleeping pills." Upon recovering, Baldwin abandoned the dream of a Hollywood movie. Baldwin went on to finish *One Day, When I Was Lost: A Scenario* which was published in text form only.

AUTHOR BIOGRAPHY

James Baldwin, author of the screenplay *One Day, When I Was Lost: A Scenario*, was also a preacher, novelist, essayist, screenwriter, playwright, and freedom fighter. He was born in Harlem in New York City on August 2, 1924. During the 1960s, at the peak of his political activism and his literary influence, he was considered, writes John Stevenson for the *Boston Book Review,* "a prophet of the decade's black liberation struggle."

Baldwin not only aided the Civil Rights Movement by helping with the voter registration crusade in Jackson, Mississippi, he was also one of the most widely read authors during that decade, influencing both white and black audiences. Baldwin considered Martin Luther King, Jr. a friend. Like King, Baldwin had a dream for those turbulent but inspiring times. He was fueled by a vision that the 1960s were the most opportune time for all the races in America to come together. Toward this aspiration, he wrote numerous essays, trying to define the problems that had kept his dream from materializing. Because of his inspired vision, he also became a

great admirer of Malcolm X, despite the fact that Malcolm's radical views sometimes ran contrary to Baldwin's beliefs.

Baldwin's hopes, if not dashed, were definitely tempered when the fight for civil rights became more militant in the black community and deflated by the assassinations of King and Malcolm. Baldwin, from the age of fourteen until he turned seventeen, fervently believed that the problems of racism began within the heart and soul of oneself. That's why, when a fit of rage burst from him one day, an outburst that could have cost a life, Baldwin decided to leave the States and permanently established himself in Europe. There he felt more accepted and could view American culture more objectively. In Europe, Baldwin found that racial, as well as homosexual, lines were not so radically defined.

Baldwin's personal anger began at an early age and resulted in his leaving the home of his mother, Emma Berdis Jones, and his stepfather, David Baldwin, when he was seventeen. Emma was distracted by a household full of children. Baldwin's stepfather, who suffered from a mental disorder, was often abusive. After leaving home and while working at poorly paid, menial jobs, Baldwin continued to cultivate his love of reading and writing. He eventually sought out Richard Wright, an author whom Baldwin highly respected. Both were self-educated. Wright encouraged the young Baldwin and helped Baldwin win a Eugene Saxton Fellowship, an acknowledgement that was to foster the beginning of Baldwin's professional writing career.

Although Baldwin's first attempts at fiction were turned down by many different publishers, his published book reviews and essays eventually gained him respect as a serious and skilled writer.

Through the continuing support of Wright, Baldwin's writing improved. While living in Paris, he finished his first and most successful novel, *Go Tell It on the Mountain* (1953), a recounting of his experiences as a youthful preacher. In 1956, Baldwin published his second novel, *Giovanni's Room*, a story in which he explores issues of his homosexuality. Baldwin would go on to write several more novels, two somewhat successful plays, the movie script based on *The Autobiography of Malcolm X*, and several respected collections of essays. The critic Stevenson claimed of Baldwin, "for a few years in the early 1960s he lit up the cultural landscape like a bolt from the heavens."

On December 1, 1987, Baldwin died of stomach cancer at the age of sixty-three in St. Paul de Vence, France.

James Baldwin

PLOT SUMMARY

Part 1

One Day, When I Was Lost: A Scenario opens in a parking garage, in New York City, with a man (Malcolm X) walking toward, and finally getting into, a car. When the man starts the car, the radio comes on with an announcement that Malcolm X will be speaking at the Audubon Ballroom that evening. The camera then shifts to the side-view mirror and an image of a fire and hooded men on horseback is seen. A young mulatto, pregnant woman tries to run away from the men on horseback, while a male voice shouts: "Our homeland is in Africa!" Next scene in the mirror is a "beaten, one-eyed black man," who is lying on the tracks of an oncoming streetcar.

The scene then jumps to another time. Malcolm X is in Africa, being welcomed by an enthusiastic crowd. An African ruler gives Malcolm a new name: Omowale, which means, "the son who has returned." Another quick scene shows Malcolm receiving yet another name: El Hajj Malik El Shabazz, his Muslim name. Then a shot to a family Bible in which is inscribed a fourth name: Malcolm Little.

There is another flashback in the side-view mirror. This time it is a dance hall in which Malcolm, who was then referred to as "Red," is dancing with Laura, a young black woman. Another quick flashback shows Malcolm with a white woman, Sophia. They are in bed. There is a third quick flashback scene in which Malcolm is in jail, fighting, with the crowd calling him Satan.

A more detailed flashback shows Louise and Earl Little, Malcolm's parents. Louise is pregnant. Earl, a preacher, talks about the movement of black people back to Africa to establish their own nation. In quick succession, the hooded men on horses threaten the Littles, smashing all the windows of their house. Action moves forward. Malcolm is a young child, watching with his brothers and his parents as their house burns down. Also watching from a distance is a group of firemen who have not attempted to put the fire out.

Another scene has Malcolm on a beach, walking with Laura. Malcolm tells Laura that for them to be together, he would have to kidnap her, because her parents want her to marry someone respectable. The flashbacks continue, switching back and forth from Laura and Malcolm to Malcolm's parents. In one scene, Malcolm's mother attempts to collect on her husband's life insurance policy, which is denied her. The insurance agent insists that Earl Little committed suicide. Earl's body was found on the streetcar tracks. Louise loses her job, and then her children are taken away by a welfare agent. Next, Louise is shown in an asylum.

Malcolm is now in a foster home. He does well in school and is elected president of his class; but when he asks a counselor about becoming a lawyer, the counselor, Mr. Ostrovski, tells him that "colored people" shouldn't aspire to jobs they'll never have. With a jump in time, Malcolm is in Boston, learning how to be a good "darky" to win big tips, as he and his friend Shorty work as porters in the men's restroom of a fancy hotel. Shorty attempts to citify Malcolm, helping him to buy clothes and showing him how to straighten his hair. Malcolm works at various, menial jobs.

Another scene shows Malcolm in a bar in New York, where he meets West Indian Archie, a man old enough to be Malcolm's father. Archie takes an interest in teaching Malcolm the way of the streets. Archie is a numbers runner, a person who takes bets on certain numbers, an early and illegal form of a lottery.

In a later scene in another bar, Malcolm runs into Laura who is with a white man named Daniel. Laura has grown up, gained confidence. She and Malcolm talk briefly before the scene changes and Malcolm is with Sophia. The scene switches again, this time to Malcolm and Archie laughing at how Malcolm pretended to be crazy to avoid the draft.

Scenes move quickly again: Malcolm selling drugs, stealing, acting as a pimp. Malcolm is then shown out celebrating. He's won big money on the numbers. Later, Archie questions the legitimacy of Malcolm's win and accuses Malcolm of cheating. Archie threatens to kill Malcolm, so he and Shorty move back to Boston. Shorty, Sophia, and Malcolm pull off several big burglaries and eventually are caught and sent to jail.

Part 2

Malcolm is in prison, where he meets Luther, an older man who takes Malcolm into his care. He encourages Malcolm to control his anger, to take better care of his health, and to read. He tells Malcolm that white people want black people to fight against one another, want black people to use their fists instead of their brains. He also asks Malcolm why he wants to straighten his hair. Does he think that makes him white? He encourages Malcolm to be proud that he is black. Malcolm comes to trust Luther. He starts eating better, stops putting chemicals on his hair, and reads every book he finds in the library. He signs up for correspondence courses. Luther tells Malcolm that God is black and that white men are the devil.

After much indoctrination, Luther tells Malcolm that he has written to "the Leader" about Malcolm, and that Malcolm should expect to receive a letter from him soon. Later, Malcolm practices his writing skills by responding to the Leader's correspondence. Shortly after, Luther leaves jail, a free man. Soon to follow him is Malcolm.

Part 3

Malcolm meets Sidney, Luther's son. Sidney is trying to start a newspaper for the Black Muslims. Luther asks Malcolm to help Sidney in this effort. Once, when they are out on the streets of Harlem delivering the newspaper, Malcolm goes to Archie's

apartment only to find the man suffering from memory loss and doing very poorly.

At this point, there is a scene that introduces Betty, who is teaching a class. Luther introduces her to Malcolm. This scene is short and immediately breaks away to a street scene in which two black men are fighting. White policemen arrive, and when the crowd tries to manage the fight for themselves, telling the policemen that they are not needed, one of the policemen hits a Muslim man across the head. Sidney is there and immediately runs across the street to telephone Malcolm. The next scene takes place in front of the police station where Malcolm controls a group of Muslims who refuse to leave until they have seen the Muslim minister who was hit over the head. The Muslims win their case and because of their insistence that the Muslim minister be taken to the hospital, the man's life is saved. The incident is broadcast in the news, giving Malcolm credit, placing media focus on him.

Malcolm runs into Laura again. This time she looks haggard and old. She's become a drug junkie under the influence of her white boyfriend who has since deserted her. Malcolm tries to convert her to Islam, but he is unsuccessful. Laura says it is too late.

Malcolm and Betty are married. There are several brief scenes of Malcolm talking to the press, while intermittent shots portray racial bigotry and Civil Rights activities. Malcolm's popularity is growing.

Sidney is shown talking on the phone to his father. He does not like what his father is telling him. Sidney defends Malcolm but is disillusioned by the time he hangs up the phone. Next, in another scene, Betty softly complains that Malcolm is spending too much time away from his family. She is also growing suspicious about Luther and the Muslim movement. She wonders why all the papers carry stories about Malcolm except the paper that Sidney and Malcolm created, the Black Muslim newspaper. She questions Malcolm about Luther. Malcolm is oblivious of any dissention. He tries to convince Betty not to worry.

Betty is not convinced by Malcolm's lack of concern. She goes to Sidney in the next scene to confront him. He admits that he has heard some talk in the movement that could be defined as jealousy over Malcolm's popularity. Betty tells Sidney that she's heard people say that Malcolm is a danger to the movement and that he should be expelled.

The news that President Kennedy has been shot is acknowledged. The dictum goes out that no Black Muslim should make an official comment about the incident. In the next scene, Malcolm is answering questions from the press. He talks about the assassination, calling it "a terrible kind of justice." In the following scene, Luther is angry with Malcolm for having broken the rule of silence. This is yet another example that Malcolm is not working within the dictates of the Leader, or Honorable Messenger. Malcolm, as punishment, is told he cannot speak publicly for ninety days. In the next scene, Sidney tells Malcolm that he was told to place a bomb in Malcolm's car.

Malcolm confronts Luther and has his suspicions confirmed. Luther is ambitious. He is not as passionate as Malcolm about saving the people. Luther is more hypocritical about his faith. After meeting with Luther, Malcolm tells Betty that he is going to start his own branch of the Muslim faith. Sidney joins him.

Malcolm travels to Mecca. Up until that time, Malcolm had preached hatred of white people. But in Mecca, he befriends people of all races and sees people from all over the world coming together. He returns to the United States a changed man with a new vision. Sidney hears that Malcolm now loves white people, and he thinks that Malcolm has sold out. Sidney turns to armed robbery to support himself since leaving both his father and Malcolm. He eventually is sentenced to prison. Malcolm visits him there.

Malcolm is at home with Betty when a Molotov cocktail crashes through the window, setting the house on fire. Malcolm calls the fire department, but the truck never comes. The next scene returns to where the script started, the day that Malcolm is to speak at Audubon Ballroom. After telephoning Betty and asking her to attend, he is shown standing on the stage as a volley of bullets hit him.

CHARACTERS

Archie

West Indian Archie is an older man who takes Malcolm under his wing and teaches him how to make a living running numbers, an early (and illegal) form of the contemporary lottery system. Archie thinks of Malcolm as his son. However, when Malcolm claims that he has a winning number, and

MEDIA ADAPTATIONS

- Spike Lee directed, co-produced, wrote, and starred (as Shorty) in the 1992 Warner Brothers film *Malcolm X* that was loosely based on Baldwin's screenplay.

- *Brother Minister* (1995), directed by Jack Baxter and narrated by Roscoe Lee Brown, is a seven-part video inquiry into the assassination of Malcolm X.

- In 1993, Black Audio Film Collective produced John Akomfrah's *Seven Songs for Malcolm X,* a filmed homage to this Black Muslim leader. The video includes an interview with Betty Shabazz and Spike Lee.

- *Malcolm X—Make It Plain* was produced by PBS Video in 1994. It is an extensive look at Malcolm X's life.

- The collaborative work between James Baldwin and Arnold Perl was produced in 1972 and called *Malcolm X.* This is a video documentary staring Ossie Davis and narrated by James Earl Jones.

Archie has to pay him a large sum of money, Archie accuses Malcolm of cheating. In Archie's mind, this means that he must kill Malcolm to save face. Because of this, Malcolm leaves New York City and organizes a ring of thieves, which eventually leads him to a prison term.

There is one more scene with Archie later in the script. He is much older and is losing his memory. Although he remembers Malcolm, he cannot recall what happened to force Malcolm to leave New York City.

Honorable Messenger

Although this character never appears in the story, he is often referred to as the head of the Black Muslim Movement, the Nation of Islam. He sends letters to Malcolm while Malcolm is in prison. He dictates most of the circumstances of Malcolm's life once Malcolm is out of jail. It is suggested that the

Honorable Messenger arranges that Malcolm be assassinated.

Laura

Laura is one of Malcolm's first loves. She is a young black woman, living in Boston, who in the beginning of the script represents innocence. Malcolm thinks she is too young and inexperienced for him. He leaves her for Sophia. Later, Malcolm runs into Laura at a bar in New York City. She is with a white man, who eventually leads her to drugs. Toward the end of the script, Laura is a drug junkie when Malcolm meets her again. He tries to convert her to Islam, but Laura says it is too late. Laura always tells Malcolm that he is smart enough to become whatever he wants to be.

The Leader

See Honorable Messenger

Earl Little

Earl is Malcolm X's father. He is a preacher living in the rural South. He preaches the philosophy of Marcus Garvey, a nationalist who believed that all African Americans should move back to Africa and create a new nation. The Ku Klux Klan continually harassed Earl. He eventually moves his family to the North. However, due to his outspokenness, his home is burned to the ground, and he is allegedly beaten and killed.

Louise Little

Louise is Malcolm's mother. She is a light-skinned woman who wishes she had darker skin because she hates what the white people around her are like. She is pregnant with Malcolm when she insists that her husband move the family to the North. She is tired of the children living in fear of the Ku Klux Klan. Upon her husband's death, the insurance company refuses to pay off the life insurance premium. Because of an inability to provide for her children, they are taken away from her. Louise has a mental breakdown and ends up in an asylum.

Malcolm Little

See Malcolm X

Luther

Luther is another father figure to Malcolm. They first meet in prison. Luther guides Malcolm, helping him to temper his anger, then encouraging him to become educated. Luther converts Malcolm to Islam. Luther is a high official in the Black Muslim Movement. He encourages, and is supportive of, Malcolm until Malcolm becomes too popular. Then Luther becomes jealous of him. It is suggested that Luther may have been the one who, under the dictates of the Honorable Messenger, plotted Malcolm's death. Luther is the father of Sidney, and it is through Sidney that Malcolm discovers Luther's disloyalty to him. Luther's hypocrisy is exposed in the end. He is unfaithful to his wife and is a seeker of power rather than a seeker of truth that he had initially claimed.

Malcolm X

Malcolm X is the main character of this screenplay, a character who is based, sometimes loosely, on a real person. Malcolm was born in the rural South, and as an adult he lives in New York and Boston. He is a country boy who learns the ways of the city through the examples of pimps and number runners. When he graduates to petty theft and then burglary, he is caught and sent to jail. In jail, he meets Luther, who converts him to Islam.

Both an intelligent and passionate man, Malcolm, through his presence and ability to instill enthusiasm of new ideas into those around him, quickly gains power. He embarks on a national tour, converting thousands of disenfranchised African Americans to Islam.

As his personal appeal and power increase, so does the jealousy of the leaders of the Black Muslim Movement. Malcolm becomes so impassioned about his beliefs that he often speaks his thoughts rather than foster the beliefs of the Black Muslims, as dictated by the ruling clerics. In an attempt to control him, stories about him are removed from the Black Muslim newspaper. Later, the leaders force him into silence. Finally, he is told that people in the Movement have placed threats on his life. When he learns of this, he breaks away from the main branch of the Nation of Islam and starts his own mosque. In the end, he is assassinated by alleged members of the Black Muslims as he is giving a speech, with his wife and children looking on.

Omowale

See Malcolm X

Mr. Ostrovski

Mr. Ostrovski is Malcolm's school counselor. When Malcolm goes to Mr. Ostrovski to ask how he might enter college to study law, Mr. Ostrovski tells Malcolm that because he is black, he should not expect to be a lawyer. This causes Malcolm to lose all interest in attending college and shortly after, he leaves with Shorty to move to Boston.

Betty Shabazz

Betty becomes Malcolm's wife. She is teaching at the mosque when he meets her. Luther blesses their marriage. Betty is extremely supportive of Malcolm. She worries about his being away from home so much. Later, she becomes suspicious of Luther's jealousy of Malcolm, and she warns her husband. When Malcolm travels to Mecca and comes home a changed man, she understands him better than any one else can. She tells him that it is hard for the people to accept his changes because they have not witnessed the things that he has experienced. Malcolm changes his mind, at the last minute, and invites her to hear the speech he planned to deliver at the Audubon Ballroom the day that he is assassinated.

El Hajj Malik El Shabazz

See Malcolm X

Shorty

Shorty is a friend of Malcolm's. Malcolm meets him while he is still in high school. Shorty is a little older than Malcolm, and when he meets him, Shorty is a pimp. Malcolm becomes disillusioned with New York, and Shorty takes him to Boston. Shorty teaches him how to be a good "darky," to get bigger tips from white people. Shorty also takes Malcolm to the barbershop to have his hair chemically straightened. Later, Shorty works with Malcolm in a series of big-time burglaries. He ends up in jail at the same time that Malcolm is sentenced.

Sidney

Sidney is the son of Luther. He befriends Malcolm, who helps him expand the circulation of the Black Muslim newspaper. When Malcolm becomes too popular, Luther orders Sidney to stop publishing stories about Malcolm in the newspaper. Luther is concerned that Malcolm is getting too much coverage already. Sidney respects his father's wishes, although he does not agree with them. Eventually, Sidney is told to place a bomb in Malcolm's car. Sidney cannot go this far. He defies whomever it was who gave this order. (It is not clear if it was Luther.) When Malcolm decides to start his own branch of the Black Muslim religion, Sidney leaves

his father and goes with him. After Malcolm travels to Mecca, Sidney believes that Malcolm has sold out to white society when Malcolm declares that black people should not hate white people. Sidney then leaves Malcolm's new mosque and ends up in jail when he turns to burglary. Malcolm visits him in prison, then goes to Luther in support of Sidney.

Sophia

Sophia is a white woman who loves Malcolm. She is sophisticated and well off financially. She does not love Malcolm enough to marry him, but she does become involved in his ring of thieves, casing the homes of wealthy people, telling Malcolm where their money is kept and how to get inside. Sophia ends up being sentenced to jail at the same time that Malcolm is.

Mrs. Swerlin

Mrs. Swerlin is Malcolm's foster parent. She runs a home for orphaned children and for children who are taken from their parents. She sees promise in Malcolm and encourages his studies. However, one of the final conversations that Malcolm overhears betrays Mrs. Swerlin's prejudices.

West Indian Archie

See Archie

THEMES

Alienation

Baldwin's screenplay *One Day, When I Was Lost: A Scenario* begins with the theme of alienation. Earl Little, Malcolm X's father, is a preacher who is alienated from white society. Earl fully believes in the philosophy of Marcus Garvey: the only way that black people can successfully find their freedom is to come together, pool their resources, and move back to Africa to begin a new nation. After Earl's death, Malcolm's mother, Louise, becomes alienated from life and suffers a mental breakdown upon the loss of her children.

Malcolm graduates from high school. Despite the fact that he has done well in school, he is alienated from furthering his education because of the comments of his counselor. The counselor tells Malcolm that he has expectations that far exceed the

TOPICS FOR FURTHER STUDY

- James Baldwin's *One Day, When I Was Lost: A Scenario* is based on Alex Haley's *The Autobiography of Malcolm X*. Read Haley's book and write a paper on the similarities and the differences between these two works. What liberties did Baldwin take? What characters did he change? Did these changes strengthen or weaken Baldwin's work in your estimation?

- Baldwin worked with Columbia Pictures for a while, in an attempt to turn *One Day, When I was Lost: A Scenario* into a movie. Columbia became impatient with him and asked Arnold Perl to collaborate with Baldwin. The two men worked on a script together that was later produced as the documentary *Malcolm X*. Find a video copy of this film (or substitute Spike Lee's later film by the same name, which was loosely based on Baldwin's work) and compare it to *One Day, When I Was Lost*. Which did you find more powerful? Make a presentation to your class about the cinematographic techniques employed in Baldwin's work and those later used in the documentary (or the film). Which do you think was the most creative? Which told a better

story? Which made you empathize more with Malcolm X?

- Research the history and development of the Black Muslims. What was their approach to improving the lives of African Americans? What was their role in the Civil Rights Movement? How did they affect African Americans? What was their connection, if any, to Martin Luther King, Jr.? The Black Panthers? Write a paper about your findings.

- Baldwin wrote fiction and plays. However, it was his nonfiction collections of essays that earned him the reputation of a prophet. Read his *Fire Next Time* (1963) in which he predicted that American race relations were in danger of becoming violent. Then, research the riots that occurred throughout the late 1960s. Write a paper about your findings. Do you think that Baldwin correctly identified the causes of those riots? Had people heeded his warnings, do you think the riots could have been avoided? Conclude with your thoughts about the future of race relations in the United States. Have they improved? Or do conditions continue to exist that could cause future riots?

---

limits of his race. Later, in prison, Luther preaches a philosophy held by the Black Muslim Movement that praises the benefits of African Americans alienating themselves from white people. Then, in the course of Malcolm's rise in the Movement, Luther and the other leaders alienate themselves from Malcolm, believing that he has gained too much power.

Malcolm, because he is so outspoken about his belief that black people should arm themselves to protect their homes and families from white attacks, alienates himself from the white media and the white portion of American society. Finally, when Malcolm returns from Mecca where he witnesses the benefits of all races working together, he alienates himself from many of his followers because

they think his radical transition is a sign that he has sold out to white society.

Crime

There are many different types of crimes that are perpetrated during the course of this screenplay. Some are petty; some are lethal. Some go unsolved; others are ignored. Only a few are brought to justice. First there are the crimes of the Ku Klux Klan in harassing the Little family by breaking the windows in their house, striking fear in Louise Little and her children, and demanding that Earl Little stop preaching about uniting the black people in his community. When the Littles move to the North, their house burns while fireman look on, making no effort to smother the flames. Earl is later found dead, having been run over by a trolley car. His death is deemed a suicide even though the back of his head had been bashed in with a blunt instrument. The insurance company then refuses to pay the premium that Earl had struggled to keep up to date, leaving Louise Little with no financial means of keeping her children. Because she cannot feed her children, they are taken away from her. Some of these are not crimes against a specific law but crimes against humanity and decent morality.

Malcolm tires of the menial jobs he must take that force him to swallow his pride and kowtow to whites who look down upon him. In an effort to improve his financial situation and remove himself from the dealings of white people, Malcolm learns to run numbers, an illegal lottery system that once thrived in many large cities, especially among the inner-city poor. He also learns to deal drugs and commit petty thievery. He is never caught as long as he keeps his crimes on a small scale. However, once he moves to Boston and organizes a group that steals money and valuables from the wealthy people in Boston's upper society, Malcolm is caught and sent to prison.

The screenplay also covers the assassination of John F. Kennedy, president of the United States. Crime also occurs in the scene with Sidney, during which he admits to knowing how to tie a bomb to Malcolm's car and blowing it up, implying he has done this before. Finally, Malcolm is shot to death at the close of the play.

Prejudice

Prejudice comes in many forms in this screenplay. Rampant prejudice exists in the minds of the Ku Klux Klan. Louise Little, a light-skinned woman, loses her job after her husband is murdered; her employer discovers through the news coverage that Louise is not white. More subtle prejudice follows Malcolm through high school when his counselor dashes Malcolm's hopes of ever becoming a lawyer based on Malcolm's race. Malcolm also overhears prejudiced statements coming from his foster mother, who refers to black people as ''niggers,'' a prejudice that she had previously hidden from him.

When Malcolm moves to Boston, Shorty teaches him how to be a good ''darky.'' This means that if Malcolm learns to act like white people want African Americans to act, he'll earn bigger tips. There is reverse prejudice when Malcolm converts to Islam. He is taught to hate white people. When he writes the Honorable Messenger, Malcolm states: ''I see how the devil is the white man.'' He believes that by harboring this hate and understanding it, he will cure all the evils in his life. When he gets out of prison, he uses his newly discovered prejudice to preach a hatred of all white society. However, when he goes to Mecca, he thinks he was wrong. He sees a society in which racial prejudice appears to be nonexistent. His followers do not easily understand his new conversion in thought. It was much easier for them to comprehend prejudice and hate, concepts they'd grown used to.

Search for Identity

To be black in Malcolm's time meant to be impoverished, to be different, and to be excluded. Therefore, many black people believed that the whiter they looked, dressed, or acted, the more successful they would be. Baldwin brings this theme into the play in different ways. First there is the discussion between Laura and Malcolm. Malcolm implies that Laura's family tries very hard to be white. Malcolm ridicules the way Laura's people dress and take on airs, relating to white people in every manner available to them.

There is another dialogue between Malcolm and Shorty in which Shorty claims that women are crazy for Malcolm because he is light skinned. There was a time when prejudice within the African-American community existed: the lighter a person's skin was, the higher the value they received in black society. This led to darker skinned people trying to bleach their skin. It also became a common practice of both men and women to chemically straighten their hair to make it look more like white people's.

Luther makes Malcolm look at himself, makes Malcolm see how he is trying to be white. Luther instills in Malcolm a pride of being who he is, a black man. This was also one of the overall themes in the Black Muslim Movement that made it so popular—giving African Americans a reason to be proud to be black.

STYLE

Flashback

Through the continual use of flashback, Baldwin fills in the history of Malcolm X's life as Malcolm drives his car from a parking lot in New

York City to the Audubon Ballroom on the day of his assassination. In the first few lines of the opening scene of *One Day, When I Was Lost: A Scenario*, Baldwin uses the side-view mirror of Malcolm X's car to flashback to historical scenes in Malcolm's life. As the screen fills with fire, Baldwin takes the audience to the threatening image of hooded men on horseback, destroying a home and scaring a pregnant woman, who turns out to be Malcolm's mother.

As Malcolm drives along the city streets, this flashback process continues as certain images, such as the ''cupola, at the topmost height of a New York building,'' stir memories in Malcolm's mind. Without warning, the audience is taken to Africa, Omaha, Milwaukee, Boston, and New York. Some of these flashbacks are very brief—a few descriptive lines, a couple exchanges of dialogue. Some of the flashbacks are repeated to fill in more details. Some of them are so extended they take up whole scenes. The audience forgets they are flashbacks until Baldwin quickly brings them back to the present. The flashbacks do not appear in any specific chronological order.

In essence, the whole screenplay covers only one day (as suggested by the title). The flashback concept is an adaptation of the theory that right before people die, their lives flash before them. Baldwin's use of flashback, as Malcolm drives toward his death, elongates that process, slowing down Malcolm's drive across town to give the audience a comprehensive look at the circumstances that lead to Malcolm's assassination.

Foreshadowing

Baldwin often intersperses short scenes of Malcolm X's father's life into the story of Malcolm's evolution as a national figure. By doing this, he foreshadows incidents and circumstances that will shortly mark Malcolm's life. For instance, Earl Little, Malcolm's father, was a preacher who tried to organize African-American people. Earl's message was considered very controversial, especially by white people. Earl also believed that African Americans would find answers to their problems in Africa. Because of his beliefs, Earl's house was set afire. While watching the house burn, Earl counts his children to make sure they are all safe. Although the fire truck appears, no one attempts to stop the fire. In the end, Earl is killed.

Each one of these events is played out in Malcolm's life. Malcolm also becomes a preacher, reaches out to his African roots, watches his house burn while counting his children, and is, in the end, murdered.

Stream of Consciousness

Stream of consciousness is a technique that is used by novelists in an attempt to mimic the flow of impressions, thoughts, and feelings as they pass through a character's mind. Baldwin uses this style cinematically by presenting images as Malcolm X might be viewing them in the present moment, then quickly shifting to a new set of impressions. For instance, in the beginning of *One Day, When I Was Lost: A Scenario*, while Malcolm is driving down a New York City street, he ''watches a very attractive blond girl striding along the avenue.'' From this real image in the present time, Baldwin then presents a quick flashback scene, as if Malcolm were remembering it. From watching the blond girl, Malcolm is reminded of Sophia, a blond woman he used to know. In the flashback scene, Malcolm is making love to her.

Immediately following the brief love-making scene, Baldwin rapidly imposes another image, as if Malcolm's mind were following a string of thought (or stream of consciousness) that takes him from the memory of making love to Sophia to a fight scene in prison. Since Sophia was involved in the crime that eventually led to Malcolm's imprisonment, Baldwin surmises that Malcolm's mind might have naturally made that leap, flowing from one memory to another interconnected one. As the play progresses, so do Malcolm's thoughts, leaping from one scene to another, sometimes only connected by the thinnest of filaments. As the audience is drawn more deeply into the story, the stream of consciousness becomes more complex as Baldwin slowly works his way deeper into Malcolm's life and then slowly back to the present moment of the play.

HISTORICAL CONTEXT

Universal Negro Improvement Association

In 1918, in Liberty Hall in the Harlem district of New York City, Marcus Garvey created the U.S. headquarters of the Universal Negro Improvement Association (UNIA). Garvey, born in Jamaica and a world traveler before situating himself and his organization in the States, believed that as long as black people remained in a minority they would never gain freedom. He preached the merits of black

COMPARE & CONTRAST

- **1940s:** Although interracial marriages occur in the United States during this decade, a statistical record is not made of them. The exception is the occasional famous marriage, such as the black novelist Richard Wright who marries Ellen Poplar, a white woman, in 1941. Twenty-nine out of the forty-eight states consider interracial marriage a crime.

  1960s: Nineteen states continue to observe their laws against interracial marriages. However, there are 51,000 interracial marriages recorded in the United States.

  Today: Over twelve percent of the African-American population is involved in interracial marriages, with recorded marriages standing at over 300,000. Although specific records are not kept, it is estimated that one in every twenty children under the age of five is the product of interracial parents. This does not include African Americans who may have a white grandparent or great-grandparent.

- **1940s:** Ten percent of the African-American population receives a high school diploma, compared to twenty-five percent of the white population. Two percent of African Americans graduate from college compared to five percent of whites.

  1960s: Twenty percent of the African-American population receives a high school diploma compared to forty-five percent of the white population. Four percent of African Americans graduate from college compared to eight percent of whites.

  Today: Sixty-five percent of the African-American population receives a high school diploma compared to seventy-five percent of the white population. Twelve percent of African Americans graduate from college compared to twenty-three percent of whites.

- **1940s:** African Americans in the arts include Charlie Parker, Duke Ellington, and Ella Fitzgerald in the field of music. Richard Wright's *Black Boy* becomes a bestseller. Marginal movie roles are played by Lena Horne (*Stormy Weather*), Hattie McDaniel, and Butterfly McQueen (both in *Gone with the Wind*).

  1960s: During this decade, black artists enjoy commercial success. In music, singers such as the Supremes, Gladys Knight and the Pips, James Brown, Jimi Hendrix, and Aretha Franklin influence new standards in popular music. In literature, books by James Baldwin, Maya Angelou, and Ralph Ellison win popular acclaim. Lorraine Hansberry's play *Raisin in the Sun* wins awards, and Sidney Poitier becomes a familiar and popular face in the movies.

  1990s: George Walker wins the 1996 Pulitzer Prize for his classical music composition, ''Lilacs,'' a milestone for black musicians. In 1993, novelist Toni Morrison wins the Nobel Prize in literature. In film, movie-maker Julie Dash wins the 1992 Sundance Film Festival's first prize in cinematography for her *Daughters of the Dust*.

  Today: Halle Berry receives the Oscar for best actress in a leading role in *Monster's Ball* (the first African American to win this award in the seventy-four-year history of the Academy Awards), Denzel Washington receives the Oscar for best actor in a leading role in *Training Day* (the second African American to win this award, following Sidney Poitier for *Lilies of the Field* in 1963), and Sidney Poitier receives an Oscar for lifetime achievement.

people coming together to create their own nation. To promote his beliefs, he established the *Negro World,* a newspaper that attracted the attention and eventual membership of over eight million people at the height of his nationalist movement.

Garvey rejected all concepts of integration and in its place, he promoted self-sufficiency and racial pride among all black people of the world. Toward this end, he raised money and created a shipping line entirely owned and run by black people. His vision was to promote international trade among all black nations. He also encouraged African Americans to move to Liberia, an African country originally established (in 1821) to support freed slaves. Garvey is also credited with creating the red, black, and green flag that symbolized black power.

In 1925, Garvey's shipping line suffered economic losses and Garvey was convicted of mail fraud. He was sentenced to jail but released two years later and deported to Jamaica. Although he tried to continue his movement, his separation from the masses of his followers in the United States diminished his influence. In retrospect, he has been called one of the most influential black leaders of the 1920s. Garvey was named the first national hero of Jamaica and is considered the impetus for both the Rastafarian movement in Jamaica as well as the development of the Nation of Islam (the Black Muslims) in the States.

Black Muslim Movement

In 1930, a man by the name of Wali Farad had a loose organization of followers of the Islamic faith. When Farad mysteriously disappeared in 1934, Elijah Mohammad took over the leadership of the group, which became known as the Black Muslims. Elijah moved the headquarters from Detroit to Chicago and spread his concepts of nationalism to communities of poor black people and those in prison. Elijah believed that African Americans would never attain freedom in the United States unless they created an autonomous state of their own.

Elijah's group of followers numbered only about eight thousand until the 1950s and 1960s when Malcolm X's charismatic and inspiring speeches began to attract a wider audience of devotees. However, tension grew between Malcolm and Elijah, forcing Malcolm to break away and create his own branch of Islam. Malcolm's assassination caused great dissention in the Movement, and upon Elijah's death in 1975, his (Elijah) son Wallace D. Mohammad, in an attempt to de-radicalize the or-

ganization, created the American Muslim Mission, which was open to anyone regardless of race.

The more militant and nationalistic faction of the Black Muslims refused to follow the softer tone of Wallace's leadership and in 1977, Louis Farrakhan broke away from the newly formed American Muslim Mission to create his own organization. Farrakhan's group favors the old philosophy of Elijah Mohammad, that of racial segregation.

Civil Rights Movement

The Civil Rights Movement in the United States had several leaders but none as popular as Malcolm X and Martin Luther King, Jr. Whereas both men fought against racial prejudice and did so from a religious philosophy, the two leaders progressed down different roads, which came surprisingly close to one another in the end.

Malcolm X grew up in poverty and in the midst of crime. He found religion, as well as a self-education, while serving a prison sentence. His religious beliefs proclaimed a strict segregationist policy as he preached a hatred of all white people. Martin Luther King, Jr., on the other hand, grew up in a middle-class family and received a full institutional education through a doctorate's degree. King preached non-violence and believed in a fully integrated society.

Although Malcolm and King were contemporaries, the only time that they met was during the debates in Congress over the Civil Rights Bill in 1964. King and the National Association for the Advancement of Colored People (NAACP) considered Malcolm too radical for the good of the Civil Rights Movement. Malcolm X, meantime, believed that King was too heavily influenced by the white people who supplied financial resources to the NAACP. However, toward the ends of their lives, Malcolm, upon his visit to Mecca, began to understand the merits of integration. King, tired of the slow progress of the leaders of the black southern churches, was considered too radical by his fellow ministers. Malcolm and King had a planned second meeting, scheduled two days after Malcolm's assassination.

CRITICAL OVERVIEW

Baldwin's *One Day, When I Was Lost: A Scenario* was published as a screenplay in text form but was never produced as a movie. In a collaborated form, co-written by Arnold Perl, a similar screenplay was produced as a documentary in 1972. Also, in 1995, Spike Lee very loosely based his famous adaptation, *Malcolm X,* on Baldwin's screenplay. However, since the play was only published as text, it has received very little critical attention.

Patsy Brewington Perry's article "One Day, When I was Lost, Baldwin's Unfulfilled Obligation" is an exception. The title of her essay foreshadows her attitudes about Baldwin's dramatic adaptation of Alex Haley's *The Autobiography of Malcolm X,* as well as Baldwin's own obligation to write truthfully and fairly about his friend Malcolm. Perry concludes that Baldwin fell short of the duty and trust that Baldwin claimed. "Does Baldwin fulfill his obligation, or does 'lost' of the title refer more aptly to Baldwin's purpose than to his subject, Malcolm?" She believes that Baldwin, who believed that he would undertake the project as a writer and not an interpreter of Malcolm's life, did just the opposite.

Perry states, "Baldwin undermines Malcolm's complex nature" by eliminating important details of his life, adding characters that did not really exist, and combining other characters into one simple figure. One of Baldwin's more damaging omissions, according to Perry, is Malcolm's "interracial, international, and political perspectives" that would eventually lead to "Malcolm's crowning achievement—his work to internationalize the struggle for human rights." Perry goes on to write that Baldwin's "single-minded efforts toward developing the theme of violence" completely obliterates "the positive spirit of *The Autobiography*" as well as Malcolm's reversal of philosophy at the end of his life toward ending violence.

Fred L. Standley, in his "Introduction" to his collection, *Critical Essays on James Baldwin,* writes that Baldwin's screenplay "was not particularly well-received; in fact one respondent labeled it 'no substitute for the original.'" Most critics agree that Baldwin's strength was not in writing dramatic pieces either for the stage or the screen. His most potent voice was heard first in his essays and second in his fiction. Tom F. Driver, in talking about Baldwin's role as a dramatist in general, writes in his essay "The Review That Was Too True to be Published," that the characters in Baldwin's plays are often portrayed as stereotypes, a criticism that many reviewers comment on. However, Driver does not see this as a fault but rather he believes that

Baldwin does this on purpose. He compares Baldwin to the great German dramatist, Bertolt Brecht.

> Though Baldwin is no Brecht, the temper of his play is Brechtian . . . in that it uses what people will think are stereotypes for the deliberate purpose of challenging received ideas. It asks us to reconsider whether the 'stereotypes' may not be nearer the truth than the theory that explains them away.

In other words, Driver believes that Baldwin's plays, on the whole, tend to challenge the status quo.

Although specific reviews of Baldwin's *One Day, When I Was Lost: A Scenario* are hard to find, his writing has been praised for its clarity, articulation, passion, and prophetic understanding of human nature and the race situation in the United States. He has been deemed the most significant and influential writer of the turbulent 1960s. His voice was often tempered with an undertone of love that would inspire the more militant movement of African-American writers who followed him; the writers involved in what would be later referred to as the Black Arts Movement.

CRITICISM

Joyce Hart

Hart has written literary essays, books on the study of language, and a soon-to-be-published biography of Richard Wright. In this essay, Hart examines Baldwin's portrayal of Malcolm X's search for a father figure in the screenplay.

Despite the fact that James Baldwin stated that he felt it was his duty to write the screenplay *One Day, When I Was Lost: A Scenario* as a writer and not an interpreter of Malcolm X's life, when the screenplay is compared to Alex Haley's *Autobiography of Malcolm X* (from which it was adapted), it is easy to point out incidents of Baldwin's use of poetic license. For this reason, this essay will examine Baldwin's screenplay not as a biography of Malcolm X but as a work of dramatic fiction, a work of Baldwin's creative intelligence.

Shortly after the opening moments of his screenplay, Baldwin develops a flashback to a scene of Malcolm X's father. This same scene, or a slight variation, is woven throughout the play, emphasizing the influence of Earl Little, Malcolm's father, on his son. The use of flashback is a creative device that cinematically demonstrates that Earl is forever pres-

WHAT DO I READ NEXT?

- To gain a deeper understanding of Malcolm X's life, read *The Autobiography of Malcolm X* (1965). This was written in collaboration with Alex Haley and fills in more details and truth in this charismatic and controversial man's life.

- James Baldwin's *Another Country* (1962) is set in New York's Greenwich Village, Harlem, and France. It is a searing tale that captures the emotions and the sensuality of relationships stripped of definitions of gender and race during the 1970s.

- *Go Tell It on the Mountain* (1953) is Baldwin's first and most popular book of fiction. The story follows one day in the life of a fourteen-year-old boy, who recounts the harsh realities of his past.

- Baldwin wrote two successful plays. *The Amen Corner: A Play* (1968) is a play about family. Margaret Alexander must face her estranged husband, a jazz musician, when he suddenly returns home because he is dying. Margaret must not only bridge the gap between herself and her husband, but between her son and his father. She must also bridge the different roles she plays between her home and her church. This is an emotional and inspiring work. Baldwin's other play, *Blues for Mr. Charlie* (1964), takes place in a small Southern town and opens with the murder of a black man. Unflinchingly, Baldwin portrays the agonizing pain and fear that most African Americans had to face in growing up in the South, especially in the 1950s.

- Baldwin's second book, *Giovanni's Room* (1956), was very controversial for its time. It tells the story of a young man David, struggling with his sexuality, torn between his love for his fiancé and a male Italian bartender. The setting is Paris during the 1950s. When David's fiancé returns from Spain to find out that he has had an affair with a man, his life spins out of control.

- *The Autobiography of Martin Luther King, Jr.* (2001) was edited by Clayborne Carson, a noted historian, who researched all of King's essays, notes, letters, speeches, and sermons to write this book. By reading about King's life, one gains not only a fuller understanding of the times and struggles that faced the nation during the 1960s but also a more balanced look at the Civil Rights Movement. King and Malcolm X were contemporaries, but they were often on opposite sides.

- For a feminine point of view of what it's like to be black in America, read Ntozake Shange's *for colored girls who have considered suicide when the rainbow is enuf* (1977), which was produced as a play on Broadway and won the Obie award. The play is really a long poem, written in dialogue form in which spirituality, rage, fear, love, female sexuality, and cultural roots are discussed.

---

ent in Malcolm's life in spite of the fact that he died when Malcolm was quite young. The flashback also acts as a window into Malcolm's mind, making it appear as if the audience could see into Malcolm's thoughts.

By continually referring back to Earl, Baldwin also creates an obvious theme—an almost mythological search for a father figure. Since the screenplay is written more like a work of fiction than as a documentary, it is not known whether this quest for the father is a reflection of Baldwin's own deep psychological need or is a passion that Baldwin perceived in the real life of Malcolm. It is not crucial to know the reason why Baldwin established this theme but rather to use the theme in order to grasp a more complex meaning of the play.

In Baldwin's script, two developments occur. First, he has events in Malcolm's life that appear to mimic, or mirror, his father's life; and second, he has Malcolm experience significant encounters with adult men who want to take Malcolm under their wing as a father figure might do. In reference to the first development, Baldwin's supposition is that a boy who never knew his father might foster a sense of void as he is growing up. Subconsciously, that young child, in an attempt to define who his father was, might take upon himself to live out parts of the father's life as he remembers it, or as his mother might have related it to him in the form of stories. To this end, Baldwin inserts numerous flashbacks of Earl being harassed by the Ku Klux Klan. The Klan is angry with him because he preaches the philosophy of Marcus Garvey, the leader of the so-called Back to Africa Movement. This aspect of Earl's life mirrors Malcolm's life as a preacher of the Nation of Islam, which also causes Malcolm to be harassed because he also believes in creating a separate nation for African Americans. Whereas Earl is harassed by the KKK, Malcolm is harassed by the white press and eventually by the leaders of the Black Muslims.

Another incident that the father and son share is the fire that destroys their homes, and the firefighters who, in the father's case, stand by and watch the house burn down; and in the son's situation, never show up. The third, more dramatic similarity is the fact that both men are murdered for their beliefs.

The parallels between the two men's lives are interesting, but it is the creation of the father figures in Baldwin's script that is more fascinating, because by following the development of Malcolm's supposed search for a father, as Baldwin dramatizes it, the reader can surmise that Malcolm might have fully realized the answers he was seeking.

The first substitute father that Malcolm finds, or more literally, who finds Malcolm, is Archie. Baldwin even spells out the relationship by having Archie refer to Malcolm, upon first seeing him, as being about the same age that Archie's son would be. Archie feels sorry for Malcolm, who is obviously dressed as a man newly arrived to the city from the country would be. Archie immediately (and somewhat unnaturally, given the short span of time between their initial meeting and Archie's summation) senses Malcolm's potential and takes him into his care. He teaches Malcolm how to make a living in the city without having to humble himself to white people. Under Archie's directions, Malcolm becomes more street-wise and more independent. He becomes so good, as a matter of fact, that he eventually challenges Archie, something that a

> BALDWIN BRINGS HIS SCRIPT TO A CLOSE BY ENDING MALCOLM'S SEARCH. MALCOLM IS NO LONGER A BOY. HE HAS FULLY TAKEN ON THE PATERNAL ROLE. THE FATHER OF MALCOLM'S QUEST NOW RESIDES WITHIN HIM."

son might do in order to progress from the role of a child to that of an adult.

The challenge, although somewhat convoluted, reflects the psychological relationship between a father and a son. Malcolm beats Archie at his own game, that of numbers running. Archie, as the father figure, can't believe that his so-called son could have done that without cheating. This incident marks a turning point in their relationship; and the son must leave home. Much later, Malcolm returns home to see Archie, who shows not only signs of physical old age but also of mental deterioration. This vindicates Malcolm, demonstrating that he did not cheat Archie, that he was a good son. Instead, it was Archie's loss of memory that led to Archie's downfall. Malcolm visits Archie as a son might visit a father in a nursing home, caring enough to take the time to see the old man, but not so devoted as to offer much assistance.

At the turning point of Archie and Malcolm's relationship, although he has outgrown Archie and must leave home, Malcolm is not yet fully mature. Almost as soon as he leaves Archie's side, Malcolm gets into trouble with the law and is sent to prison. He still has lessons to learn. In prison, however, another older man is attracted to Malcolm. This time it is Luther who takes Malcolm to heart. Luther, like Archie, immediately sees Malcolm's potential. He senses that underneath Malcolm's immature anger is a man crying out for direction. Luther's direction is to get Malcolm to embrace his identity as a black man, to encourage him to read, and to guide him toward spirituality. Luther also teaches Malcolm to focus and intensify his dislike of white people. It is through the discipline that Luther teaches Malcolm that Malcolm finds his way out of prison. It is also through Luther's direction that Malcolm leaves prison as a better-educated man. When Malcolm is released, he goes directly to Luther's home.

Malcolm learns about Islam under Luther's tutelage, much as he learned about petty crime under Archie's instructions. Once again, he advances so quickly and so successfully that he challenges his new father figure, Luther. Like Archie before him, Luther is uneasy with Malcolm's achievements and contrives a showdown with him. Like Archie's confrontation, Luther's challenge threatens Malcolm's life.

Malcolm must again conclude that it is time to leave the home of the father. He cannot live under Luther's house rules. So he strikes out on his own. First, he establishes his own mosque, separate from his so-called father's. This is much like a son going out into the world and finding his own job, his own identity. Instead of having to bow to the dictates of his father, he can now create his own rules. Malcolm uncovers the weaknesses and hypocrisies of Luther, much as a son, when he grows up, sometimes sees the frailties of his father. However, despite the fact that Malcolm leaves Luther, he continues to be influenced by him. He continues to preach the same philosophy that he has learned under Luther's guidance. Although Malcolm is growing up, he is not yet fully mature.

Malcolm experiences a new conversion. During his pilgrimage to Mecca, he witnesses the world, especially the Middle Eastern world of Islam. He sees people through much different lenses than the ones that Luther had given him. When Malcolm travels to Africa and the Middle East, he hears Muslims preach a love of mankind regardless of race. At this point, he senses that the hate that the Black Muslims inspire is no more progressive than the hate that white Americans practice through their racial bigotry. With this new realization, Malcolm reflects on the influence of all the fathers who have raised him. He questions Earl's allegiance to Marcus Garvey's philosophy of Nationalism. He rids himself of Archie's con games and petty criminal attitude. More significantly, he examines the underlying premise of the Nation of Islam, the viewpoint that Luther had taught him.

By the time Malcolm returns to the United States, he has begun to create a belief system of his own. He has also all but freed himself from all his fathers' influences and is starting to realize a new identity, one that he has put together on his own. Now he can go forward unheeded. As Baldwin has him say, in an attempt to explain to his wife the dramatic changes in his outlook, ''I'm trying to turn a corner.''

Having attained new insights into himself and the beliefs that drive him, Malcolm faces Luther one more time, much as he had faced Archie upon being released from jail. During their confrontation, Luther, in essence, tells Malcolm that he is a dreamer. Luther says that Malcolm has lost his way because he wants to change the world, wants to change people. Luther, on the other hand, believes that people are more like him: they don't want to be changed. Malcolm listens to Luther but remains strong in his newfound beliefs. He knows that Luther is wrong. If Malcolm can change, he knows that anyone can change. ''I don't believe you,'' he says to Luther. ''I know better. Like I know I'm better than you—I know people are better than that.'' This cuts the remaining strings between Malcolm and Luther and marks the full maturation of the son.

In the last segments of the play, Baldwin shows a new development in Malcolm's psychology. Baldwin has Malcolm appear with his children. First, there is the scene in which Malcolm's house is fire bombed. After running out of the house, Malcolm has his wife count the children. This scene is a reflection of a previous one, which showed the fire that Malcolm experienced as a child. In the prior incident, Malcolm's father also asked Malcolm's mother to count the children, as they watched their house burn down. Then, in the final scenes of the script, Baldwin has Malcolm call his wife and ask her to come with their children to hear him make his speech at the Audubon Ballroom, the day of his assassination. With these two scenes, Malcolm has become the father. Baldwin brings his script to a close by ending Malcolm's search. Malcolm is no longer a boy. He has fully taken on the paternal role. The father of Malcolm's quest now resides within him.

Source: Joyce Hart, Critical Essay on *One Day, When I Was Lost: A Scenario,* in *Drama for Students,* The Gale Group, 2002.

Carey Wallace

Wallace's stories, poems, and essays appear in publications around the country. In this essay, Wallace considers Baldwin's use of names and naming to chart the way in which Malcolm X's identity, both public and private, shifted over the course of his life.

Satan. Homeboy. Red. El Hajj Malik El Shabazz. Malcolm Little. Malcolm X.

Over the course of his short, dramatic life, the man most commonly known as Malcolm X was known by many names and went through as many changes. He was a class president and a drug dealer, a thief and a prisoner, a minister, an agitator, a peacemaker—and with each new identity, he seemed to take a new name. In *One Day, When I Was Lost: A Scenario*, James Baldwin's screen adaptation of Alex Haley's landmark *Autobiography of Malcolm X*, Baldwin plays with these names and the larger question of naming, to understand and chart the course of Malcolm X's transformations, both in the public eye, and in his very personal life.

In the opening pages of *One Day, When I Was Lost: A Scenario*, Malcolm begins the reverie that frames the retelling of his life with the line "So many names." In the scene that immediately follows, the reader is confronted with one of the central naming issues of the screenplay: the fact that, for much of the action, the character Baldwin refers to as Malcolm is called something else by the other members of the cast. In this case, that name is "Red"—a nickname given to Malcolm by his young black friends, called out to him over the dance floor of a black dance hall in which Malcolm escapes the all-white school he attends by day. In the next scene, Malcolm names himself for his white girlfriend, asking, "What you going to tell your white boy about your black boy? Your fine black stud? Your nigger?" But in her world, she tells him, he'll remain nameless, saying "I am not going to speak about you at all." Baldwin introduces one final name for Malcolm before he ends the montage: Satan, given to Malcolm by his guards and fellow inmates in prison, in reference to his violent tendencies. In closing, Malcolm's voice-over repeats again, "So many names."

In this montage, and throughout the play, others will assign Malcolm different names, and he himself will announce various changes. But Malcolm's names are not the only ones Baldwin engages. Baldwin is concerned with questions of naming, and identity, on a larger scale. He uses Malcolm's search for a true name to describe and understand two races, and a nation, in search of identity.

Baldwin's concern with issues of identity is first hinted at in the very next scene, a memory from Malcolm's childhood. Louise, Malcolm's mother, stands on the front porch, barring her door to a pack of KKK riders. Baldwin describes her as "nearly as white as they are," adding that this "lends her a very particular bitterness and a contemptuous au-

"WHAT IS FUNDAMENTAL ABOUT A PERSON, GOOD OR BAD, REMAINS THE SAME—AND IS TIED UP IN A PERSON'S TRUE NAME."

thority." Louise, whom the riders refer to as a "half-white [b——]," throws into relief the issue of what makes a person "black" or "white." In appearance, she is very much like the men she is defending her children against, a fact that she doesn't let them forget, telling them that "I might be your daughter, for all you know . . . or your sister . . ."

In reality, she is "blacker" than the members of her race who might prize her light skin, saying later that she hates even the part of herself that is white, "every drop of that white rapist's blood that's in my veins!" She also drops one of Baldwin's first statements on the theme of true identity, when she calls one of the riders by name, saying "You can veil your face, but you can't hide your voice, Mr. Joel. I know every one of you." Change as much of the exteriors as you like, Louise claims. What is fundamental about a person, good or bad, remains the same—and is tied up in a person's true name.

Baldwin quickly expands on Louise's statement that, regardless of name, the fundamentals of identity don't change. In the following scenes, Baldwin explores the way naming both reveals and obscures the reality, not just of an individual's identity, but of the true nature of the entire world. When Malcolm's father, Earl, meets his death on the railroad tracks, after being badly beaten by the same whites who harassed his wife earlier, the white-owned insurance company names the death a "suicide." Again, Louise renames reality for what it is, asking, "How a man going to beat in the back of his own skull?"

His father's death and mother's institutionalization leave Malcolm in the hands of the state, where he is, for the first time, directly confronted with the dissonance between the harsh realities of his life and the way in which the authorities play with names to obscure the truth. "You lucky," a white official tells Malcolm on the drive to the home that will replace his own. "This ain't the reform school. This is just a nice private home.'' In the same conversation, another official attempts to rename Malcolm's mother's sickness, telling Malcolm that Louise is ''just tired,'' and that ''she'll be all right.'' Interestingly, Malcolm's stony silence elicits the only grain of truth from either official. Uncomfortable with the long pause, the second official finally admits, ''Okay. It's rough.''

On arriving at the home of his well-meaning foster mother, Malcolm is confronted with another case in which the named truth conflicts sharply with reality. ''This is Malcolm,'' Mrs. Swerlin says, introducing him. ''He's just like all the rest of us.'' For Malcolm, whose father died because of the difference in skin color between Malcolm and his foster ''brothers,'' that lie would be impossible to forget. And it would be impossible for the white world to truly forget it, either. Despite the fact that Malcolm excels at his school, even becoming class president, when he confides in a favorite teacher that he'd like to be a lawyer, the teacher informs him that he'll never achieve that ambition, and that he should look for work he can do with his hands.

Disillusioned, Malcolm turns to the company of his black friend, Shorty, who teaches Malcolm to use the names the white world has given to them against it. For the time being, Malcolm accepts Shorty's assertion that his teeth, revealed in an insincere, subservient grin, are worth ''more than a college education,'' and sets about acting the profitable caricature of a ''happy darky.'' Shorty, who has always been insistent on Malcolm's identity as a black man, calls Malcolm ''homeboy,'' and Malcolm gives himself another, new name, the first in a what will become a long string: ''Detroit Red.'' But he almost always stays a step removed from the name he's given himself, telling customers and friends that ''People call me Red,'' rather than ''I'm Red,'' or ''My name's Red.''

This change of name allows Malcolm to play with other details of his identity, like his age. ''Honey,'' a woman at the dance hall tells Malcolm, ''I know you ain't twenty-two, like you claim. But you sure is big for your age.'' Malcolm's namings of himself, interestingly, are not the complete fabrications of the white world, but somehow reflect a larger truth. He may not be twenty-two, but the 'lie' does, in some ways, more accurately reflect his true identity than his actual age. Even as a teenager, Malcolm is both more physically mature, and has more life experience than other boys his age.

But when Malcolm starts dating Laura, his first love, he begins again to try to name things for what they are, telling her ''I'm not nice at all. . . . Maybe everything I ever told you was a lie.'' But, like his mother, Laura insists that she can see through names to true identity, responding that she knows him, and that he's ''smart, and distinguished,'' and ''nice.'' Laura retains this ability to see through to Malcolm's true identity for much of the play. Years later, when his identity as Detroit Red is fully solidified, and far darker than when they first met, Malcolm and Laura meet again, and she immediately identifies him by a name no one else has spoken for years: ''Malcolm. Malcolm Little.''

But although Laura still recognizes him as the star-student she knew as a young girl, ''Red's'' lifestyle leads into an almost inevitable downward spiral, and Malcolm lands in prison. There, he's given another name, ''Satan,'' in reference to his violent tendencies. Despite the demonic nickname, it is in prison that Malcolm finds salvation, which, interestingly, comes partly through a name. Luther, a fellow inmate and disciple of the Nation of Islam, approaches Malcolm and calls him ''Red.'' ''How'd you know my name?'' Malcolm asks, and then adds, ''You the first person ever to call me by my name . . . in this joint.'' Touched, Malcolm becomes friends with Luther, who eventually learns his ''true name,'' Malcolm, and begins to call him by it.

Malcolm quickly becomes a disciple of Islam. Studying scripture, he runs across the story of history's most famous name change—Saul, who became Paul after his dramatic conversion to Christianity. As Malcolm undergoes a similarly profound transformation, both prisoners and authorities are baffled. But none of them know his name. ''What's wrong with Satan?'' the prisoners ask. ''What's the matter with you, boy?'' the prison doctor inquires. But since they never knew any of his real names, they can't understand the current transformation.

In fact, for the first time, things seem to be going right for Malcolm, a fact that Baldwin again marks by the use of his name. When Malcolm makes it out of prison and joins the Nation of Islam, for the first time in his life someone asks him for permission to use his name. Malcolm grants the permission to Luther's son Sidney graciously, but negotiating the tangled web of names in his past is not so easy. Shorty still calls Malcolm ''Homeboy,'' and writes his conversion off as a new hustle. Archie, a buddy from his life of crime, will never know Malcolm as anyone other than "Red." And Malcolm himself seems to know that even his given name doesn't quite fit the new man he's become. As he grows in power as a leader in the nation of Islam, he drops his last name, replacing it with an "X"—a protest against the "white rapist" who gave his family it's name, but also a gesture that suggests that someday a truer name may replace the spot X marks.

As a leader in the nation of Islam, Malcolm begins to more boldly play with names and naming to create and reveal identity. During a peaceful standoff outside a police station where another leader is being held, a captain tries to push Malcolm back into the facelessness the white world has forced on the black race, calling Malcolm "Mac," as if his name and identity are not really worth knowing. But with the Nation of Islam at his back, Malcolm is free to correct him. Interestingly, he does not entrust the policeman with his true name, but tells him only that he's wrong in his assumptions: "My name ain't Mac." Malcolm then retaliates with a name of his own, calling the policeman a "dog," and then revising that statement, saying that the captain doesn't even share the identity of a dog, that "a dog wouldn't do this."

But even strict adherence to the Nation of Islam doesn't seem to be a perfect path for Malcolm, who, through all the public work and organizational intrigues, is still searching for his own, personal truth, a sense of his true identity—his real name. As the organization he's served begins to implode around him, Malcolm makes the traditional Muslim pilgrimage to Mecca, discovering a world he'd never dreamed of, where white, black, yellow, and brown worship together in seeming peace. And there he is also given a new name: "El Hajj Malik El Shabazz," or "the son who has come home."

When Malcolm does return home, though, the world that has always misnamed him, and missed his true identity, is still a step behind. He's won a victory of sorts in that America has accepted Malcolm X, the most recent name he'd chosen. Reporters, guards, and colleagues still refer to him as "Malcolm," "Mr. X," and "Malcolm X." But El Hajj Malik El Shabazz is already a step beyond them, struggling, as he says, with the fact that every time he tries to turn a corner "the old Malcolm X stands there, barring the way." Only his wife, who adopts the name "Betty Shabazz," seems to grasp the significance of Malcolm's Mecca-driven shift in vision.

In the end, his enemies' perception of "the old Malcolm X" leads to Malcolm's famous assassination. But it may be in death that he finds his true identity. Malcolm, Homeboy, Red, Satan—throughout his life, the character Baldwin calls "Malcolm" has answered to, and chosen, many names. But he is imbued from childhood with his mother's insistence that what is fundamental about a person never changes, Malcolm continually reached for his true identity, and for the accompanying name. The inscription on his grave reads, "El Hajj Malik El Shabazz." And in that, Baldwin seems to suggest, the great man found his true nature, and his true name.

Source: Carey Wallace, Critical Essay on *One Day, When I Was Lost: A Scenario,* in *Drama for Students,* The Gale Group, 2002.

Curt Guyette

Guyette is a graduate from the University of Pittsburgh with a bachelor's degree in English and is a longtime journalist. In this essay, Guyette talks about racism and the spiritual journey made by Malcolm X.

The purpose of the novelist, James Baldwin explained in a 1962 *New York Times Book Review* essay, "involves attempting to tell as much of the truth as one can bear, and then a little more." His "scenario" based on Alex Haley's *The Autobiography Of Malcolm X* achieves that goal, revealing one extraordinary man's remarkable journey through the dark heart of American racism. Although based on a true story, it contains all the hallmarks of epic fiction, with the hero overcoming tremendous hardship to reach the promised land of enlightenment.

It is not surprising that Baldwin found inspiration in the story of Malcolm, whose struggle against bigotry propelled him along a journey of self-discovery similar to that found in much of the author's other work. As Louis H. Pratt notes in his book, *James Baldwin:* "Malcolm X, like the characters that abound in Baldwin's fiction, is a man in search of himself." Baldwin uses the title of the screenplay itself to suggest that this journey of Malcolm's is being viewed from the perspective of someone who has finally found his way: "One day when I *was* lost." That concept of looking backward is reinforced in the scenario's first few lines, which offer a glimpse of events through a car's sideview mirror "that fills the screen." Malcolm has already arrived. But before it is even completely clear exactly where he is, flashes of the racial hatred

" . . . LIKE ANY NUMBER OF OTHER PROPHETS, HIS RETURN TO SPREAD A NEW WORD IN A LAND NOT YET FULLY READY TO HEAR IT LEADS TO BOTH TRAGEDY AND, ULTIMATELY, TRIUMPH."

that set him to wandering in a sort of wilderness begin to appear.

While still in the womb, Malcolm Little was subjected to the kind of terror frequently experienced by African Americans during much of the twentieth century. In a chilling scene, Baldwin depicts white-hooded horsemen smashing windows, a pregnant young Louise Little flinching as they stampede past. This is the America of Malcolm Little's boyhood. And by the time he is a teenager, his father—an outspoken proponent of black nationalism—is dead, his skull crushed by a bigot's hammer and his still breathing body tossed on the tracks of an on-coming trolley. It is an image that haunts Malcolm throughout his life.

This is the kind of hard truth Baldwin said the writer must tell, no matter how painful. It's the kind of truth that shaped the direction of Malcolm's life. Also tragic is that fate of Malcolm's mother, who, unable to carry on without the courageous husband she loved and respected, is locked away in an insane asylum. That, too, leaves Malcolm with an image that will continue to haunt him. After running afoul of the law, he catches what appears to be a break and is placed in the care of a kindly white woman, who says she loves Malcolm like a son. But, during what should be one of his happiest moments—the day a judge comes to say it's been determined Malcolm has "reformed" himself and become an upright young man, he overhears a conversation that leaves another deep emotional scar. This woman, too, reveals herself to be yet another racist.

Despite these setbacks, Malcolm's natural intelligence and outgoing personality allow him to prevail. He earns top grades in school, and is elected class president. Like his fellow students, he has vision of a bright future, but when he approaches a trusted guidance counselor, the man quashes Mal-

colm's dreams of pursuing a career in law, saying that's not an option for a black boy. His dreams crushed, Malcolm Little disappears.

The person who emerges in his place is a street hustler who goes by the nickname "Red." It is, as the character Malcolm notes, one of many names he would adopt throughout his life, each one serving as a milepost marking a different point in his life's journey. Red is an abandonment of all of young Malcolm's highest ideals and aspirations. This person is a womanizer, hard-drinker, thief and drug user who's clever enough to avoid the draft and stay one step ahead of the law—for a while. Despite a growing hatred of whites, he has no real pride in being black. This is evidenced by his willingness to undergo the near-torturous process of using lye treatments to have his hair "conked," or straightened.

By the end of the scenario's first act, a debauched Red has run out of fast talk and clever ploys, and has nothing more to look forward to than spending the foreseeable future behind bars on robbery charges. It is in prison, where his violent ways earn him the new nickname of "Satan," that Malcolm experiences what Pratt describes as the first of two "epiphanies." He meets a fellow inmate named Luther, who takes a liking to young Malcolm and begins trying to convert him to a black nationalist form of Islam that demonizes whites. Pointing to Malcolm's conked hair, Luther asserts, "You go to all that trouble and all that pain and sweat and put all that poison in your hair, what for? Because you ashamed of being black and you want to be white." Luther keeps working on Malcolm, convincing him to give up cigarettes, alcohol, and pork, all the while preaching his brand of Islam: "You don't even know who you are. You don't even know, the white devil has hidden it from you." By the time Luther is released, Malcolm is a convert. He's no longer Satan; he's become Malcolm X, the slave-name Little discarded in favor of a mark that represents his stolen heritage.

When he's finally set free, Malcolm finds a home with Luther and his fellow followers in the Nation of Islam. Once again, his intelligence propels him, and he advances quickly, taking charge of the sect's newspaper to spread its views to masses of African Americans. That sense of purpose and fulfillment carry over into the start of the third act, which finds Malcolm as happy as he's ever been. He's leading a morally upright life, providing meaning to his life by committing himself to a cause he totally believes in. He's also fallen in love and married an attractive, intelligent woman named Betty, a fellow church member. They have children, and his success grows.

Malcolm's combination of natural charisma and intense belief pay off in a way he never imagined, with thousands of people turning out to hear him speak. The church's militancy inspires followers fed-up with the second-class treatment suffered by African Americans, and Malcolm's angry speeches and fiery, no-compromise writings promise change by any means necessary.

But there's a downside to this success: before long, his mentor Luther and the church's leader grow jealous. Betty sees trouble brewing, but Malcolm refuses to heed her warnings. Then he is told of a murder plot. As hard as it is for him to believe, the people at the top levels of the church he wholeheartedly committed himself to want him dead. That threat, coupled with a desire to visit the birthplace of Islam, compel Malcolm to make a pilgrimage to Mecca. It is there, seeing masses of Muslims representing all races, that he experiences what Pratt describes as a second epiphany. In a letter to Betty he writes, "I have never before seen true and sincere brotherhood practiced by all colors together, irrespective of their color." "True Islam," he adds, "has shown me that a blanket indictment of all white people is as wrong as when whites make blanket indictments against blacks. Yes, I have been convinced that some American whites do want to help cure the rampant racism which is on the path to destroying this country."

Writes Pratt: "Here in the Muslim world, Malcolm witnesses the true fellowship and goodwill of men of all races and color, and his enlightenment is developed and reined into a state of perception." Alex Haley, in *The Autobiography of Malcolm X*, also notes the profound effect of the experience, noting that Malcolm came to realize that "both races . . . had the obligation, the responsibility, of helping to correct America's human problem."

Like a loop, Baldwin's screenplay takes readers full circle. As it comes to the end, it returns to where the story began, with Malcolm looking into the rear-view mirror of his car as it pulls up to the Harlem ballroom where he is scheduled to speak. He has arrived home once again, but now he's preaching a message altered by the experiences of his pilgrimage. And, like any number of other prophets, his return to spread a new word in a land not yet fully ready to hear it leads to both tragedy and, ultimately, triumph. He no longer believed in

the essential message of the church that he'd devoted himself to, and it's leaders feared his popularity would drain away followers and resources. Just as he looked across America and saw few white people willing to look with honesty at the terrible hardships their racism has caused, he also realized that his former allies weren't prepared to accept the broader vision he now wanted to share. As he told a friend, "Maybe, you know, there are never very many people, no matter what their color, who are dedicated to change."

This marked the completion of a long spiritual journey. Through hardship and loss, degradation and suffering, he'd made the passage from darkness into the light of understanding. And with that knowledge, he was ready to go out anew and create a better America. His wife and children sat in the audience, joining the packed house in that Harlem ballroom. But instead of hearing Malcolm X speak, they saw black men rise up, draw their guns, and shoot him dead. And that is the tragedy of his life. Like his father before him, he was taken far too soon. The triumph is found in the words of his wife, Betty. Baldwin closes out his screenplay by having her say to everyone all the same thing she always told Malcolm as he prepared to leave on a trip: "You are present when you are away."

His message, like his spirit, has become eternal.

Source: Curt Guyette, Critical Essay on *One Day, When I Was Lost: A Scenario,* in *Drama for Students,* The Gale Group, 2002.

SOURCES

Baldwin, James, "As Much Truth As One Can Bear," in *New York Times Book Review,* January 14, 1962, p. 14.

Driver, Tom F., "The Review That Was Too True to Be Published," in *Negro Digest,* Vol. 13, 1964, pp. 34–40.

Leeming, David, *Baldwin: A Biography,* Alfred A. Knopf, 1994.

Perry, Patsy Brewington, "*One Day, When I Was Lost,* Baldwin's Unfulfilled Obligation," in *James Baldwin, A Critical Evaluation,* edited by Therman B. O'Daniel, Howard University Press, 1977, pp. 213–27.

Pratt, Louis H., "The Darkness Within," in *James Baldwin,* G. K. Hall & Co., 1978, pp. 98, 100.

Standley, Fred L., and Nancy V. Burt, "Introduction," in *Critical Essays on James Baldwin,* G. K. Hall & Co., 1988.

Stevenson, John, "James Baldwin: An Appreciation," in *Boston Book Review,* December 1995.

X, Malcolm, with the assistance of Alex Haley, *The Autobiography of Malcolm X,* Grove Press, 1966, p. 456.

FURTHER READING

Brown, Jamie Foster, ed., *Betty Shabazz: A Sisterfriends' Tribute in Words and Pictures,* Simon & Schuster, 1998.
   Malcolm X's wife, Betty Shabazz, was left with the task of raising six children after her husband's death. She was a strong woman and is remembered by friends and colleagues in this tribute to her life. Betty died tragically in 1997 from burns suffered in a fire set by her grandson.

Campbell, James, *Talking at the Gates: A Life of James Baldwin,* Viking, 1991.
   Campbell provides an insightful look into the life and the significance of the times of James Baldwin.

Cleaver, Eldridge, *Soul on Ice,* Cape, 1969.
   Cleaver spent much of his youth in jail. While there, he educated himself and wrote his memoirs. Once released, he became a follower of Malcolm X and the Nation of Islam. After Malcolm's assassination, Cleaver joined the Black Panthers. He eventually escaped the United States and lived abroad. Upon returning, he went through a religious transformation and conversion to Christianity, recording his changes in another book called, *Soul on Fire* (1978).

Foner, Philip S., *The Black Panthers Speak,* Da Capo Press, 1995.
   The Civil Rights Movement was a time of varying philosophies and tactics. Malcolm X was not the only radical voice during those times. This book presents a history of the Black Panther movement, their philosophy of separatism, their court battles, and what they stood for.

Lincoln, C. Eric, *The Black Muslims in America,* Africa World Press Inc., 1994.
   This is a sociological study that details the development of the Black Muslim Movement in the United States. It covers the leadership of Elijah Muhammad as well that of Louis Farrakhan.

Standley, Fred L., and Louis H. Pratt, eds., *Conversations with James Baldwin,* University Press of Mississippi, 1989.
   This collection of interviews with Baldwin includes one by Studs Terkel in 1961 and another in which Henry Louis Gates Jr. asked Josephine Baker to join Baldwin in 1985. From the height of his fame to the last moments of his death, these interviews offer a different, more personal insight into this great author.

X, Malcolm, *Malcolm X Speaks: Selected Speeches and Statements,* edited by George Breitman, Grove Press, 1990.
   This book follows the development of Malcolm X's evolution as a minister of Islam, from his time under the supervision of Elijah Mohammad to his break with the Nation of Islam. Many scholars try to explain Malcolm X's philosophy. This book offers his beliefs in his own words.

Reunion

DAVID MAMET

1976

David Mamet is one of the most celebrated American playwrights of the twentieth century. Mamet, who has won numerous prestigious awards for his plays, is best known for his use of dialogue that captures the rhythms and idiom of colloquial American speech and powerfully expresses the struggles of his characters to express themselves to one another.

Reunion is a one-act play that dramatizes bits and pieces of one long conversation between Carol, a twenty-four-year old woman, and her father, Bernie, whom she hasn't seen since her parents divorced twenty years earlier. Bernie is a recovering alcoholic and has spent much of his life intoxicated, traveling around, and moving from job to job. Carol tells Bernie that she has contacted him because, although she is married, she is lonely. Father and daughter try to reestablish a relationship with one another by asking each other questions and attempting to explain their lives.

In *Reunion*, Mamet explores the delicate dynamics of communication between a parent and child who have been separated by divorce. The struggle to establish a genuine sense of connection between two family members is poignantly rendered through Mamet's characteristic skill at creating dialogue that expresses the difficult, sometimes painful, often unsuccessful, efforts of human beings to communicate with one another.

AUTHOR BIOGRAPHY

David Alan Mamet was born November 30, 1947. His parents were of Polish-Russian descent, and Mamet grew up in a Jewish neighborhood on the south side of Chicago. His mother was a teacher and his father a labor lawyer. After his parents divorced, Mamet moved with his mother and sister to the suburbs of Chicago but later lived with his father. He began his association with live theater in high school when he worked as a busboy at Second City, a comedy club, and as a stagehand at Hull House Theater. From 1965 to 1969, Mamet attended Goddard College in Vermont, where he majored in literature. His play *Camel* was performed at Goddard College while he was still an undergraduate.

After graduating from college, Mamet taught drama for a year at Marlboro College in Vermont, where his play *Lakeboat* was performed by the Marlboro Theater Workshop. From 1971 to 1973, he served as artist-in-residence and acting instructor at Goddard College, and helped found the Nicholas Theater Company and served as its artistic director. In 1974, Mamet was back in Chicago, having brought the St. Nicholas Theater Company with him. Over the next two years, his plays opened primarily in Chicago. He first gained significant critical attention as a playwright when his *Sexual Perversity in Chicago* was performed in 1974 and won the Jefferson Award for Best New Chicago Play. From 1975 to 1976 he taught as a visiting lecturer at the University of Chicago. *Reunion*, a one-act play, premiered in 1976, and was later performed as a triptych with *Dark Pony* (1977) and *The Sanctity of Marriage* (1979).

In 1976, Mamet moved to New York, where small theater companies were beginning to produce some of his plays. That year he received an Obie Award for Best New American Play for *Sexual Perversity in Chicago* (which was adapted to the screen in the 1986 film *About Last Night*). Mamet first rose to national prominence as a major playwright of his generation in 1977, when *American Buffalo* (1975) opened on Broadway at the Barrymore Theater, garnering Mamet the New York Drama Critics Circle Award for best American play. (Mamet also won an Obie for Best American Play for *American Buffalo* in 1983.) Many of Mamet's plays were produced in various theaters in New York, Chicago, New Haven, and London.

Mamet's international reputation as an outstanding playwright reached its pinnacle in 1983, when his most celebrated play, *Glengarry Glen*

Ross, premiered in London. *Glengarry Glen Ross* concerns the internal competition and shady dealings among several men working in a real estate agency. In 1984, Mamet was awarded the Pulitzer Prize and the Drama Critics' Circle Award for Best American Play, for *Glengarry Glen Ross*. *Glengarry Glen Ross* was adapted by Mamet to the screen in a critically acclaimed 1992 film.

Mamet's career as a Hollywood screenwriter began in 1981 with the remake of the classic *The Postman Always Rings Twice*. Other screenplays by Mamet include *The Verdict* (1982), *House of Games* (1987; also Mamet's debut as a film director), *The Untouchables* (1987), *We're No Angels* (1990), *Homicide* (1992), *Hoffa* (1992), *Oleana* (1994), *American Buffalo* (1996), *The Spanish Prisoner* (1997), *The Edge* (1997), *Wag the Dog* (1997), *Ronin* (1998), *The Winslow Boy* (1999), and *State and Maine* (2000), among many others.

PLOT SUMMARY

Reunion takes place in the apartment of fifty-three-year-old Bernie Cary. Carol Mindler, Bernie's twenty-four-year-old daughter, has come to visit him. She hasn't seen her father in twenty years, since he and her mother divorced. The play takes place in a series of fourteen short scenes, each of which represents a segment of one long conversation between father and daughter.

Scene 1

As the play opens, Carol has just arrived at Bernie's apartment on a Sunday afternoon in early March. Bernie comments, "This is a very important moment." He's relieved that she calls him Bernie, rather than "Dad." He explains that he has quit drinking and has been doing better lately than he had been in the past.

Scene 2

Carol tells Bernie his apartment looks nice, and he explains that he's been living there two years. Carol tells him the apartment she lives in with her husband, Gerry, is very nice and comfortable, although it gets a little cramped when Gerry's two sons (from a previous marriage) are staying there.

Scene 3

Carol sees a picture of Bernie with a group of Army Air Corps bombers and asks him about his military duty in World War II. He explains that he was a tail gunner in a B-17. Carol tells Bernie she wants to know more about him. He describes himself as: "Fifty-three years old. Ex-alcoholic. Ex-this. Ex-that. Democrat." Bernie asks Carol a little about her husband Gerry, and her marriage. Bernie explains to Carol that he had wanted to see her again after he and her mother were separated, but that her mother had initiated a court order in 1951, forbidding him from seeing his daughter. Carol tells Bernie she has been married to Gerry for two years, and that his sons are eight and twelve years old. Bernie tells Carol he almost burst into tears when Gerry showed up at the restaurant where he works to say Carol wanted to see him.

Scene 4

Bernie tells Carol she has a half-brother, Marty, who is three years younger than she, from his second marriage to a woman named Ruth. Bernie hasn't heard from Marty in several years, but says that, last he heard, Marty wasn't doing anything with his life. Carol also has a half-sister, Barbara, from her mother's second marriage. Bernie reminisces about the last year he saw Carol, when she was four years old, and he used to take her to the zoo and to the science museum. He tells Carol, "You were a beautiful kid." Bernie says he has some pictures of Carol from that time, which he looks at every day, but then he is unable to find them to show her. He mentions that he's thinking of marrying a woman named Leslie, whom he works with at the restaurant.

Scene 5

Bernie says that he is happy now, that he has stopped drinking, likes his job at the restaurant, and is even starting to save some money. He explains to Carol his current attitude about life, that "You got to take your chance for happiness."

Scene 6

Bernie states that the main things on his mind at the moment are getting to know Carol and possibly getting married again. Carol tells him she used to think he was Tonto (the Native American friend of the television cowboy hero The Lone Ranger), and that she was upset when he told her he wasn't Tonto. He says that "the only two worthwhile things I ever

David Mamet

did in my life" were working for the phone company and firing a machine gun during World War II.

Scene 7

Bernie admits to Carol that he was scared about meeting her again. Carol tells him she works at her husband's office, and Bernie can see that she's not really happy with the job. She then admits to Bernie that she and her husband aren't sleeping together any more, and that her husband is not a good lover. Bernie points out that Gerry seems like a nice guy and seems to be fond of her.

Scene 8

Carol points out that she is from a broken home because of her parents' divorce and that so many people are divorced these days, it is no longer considered a big deal. However, she thinks it must have affected her in some way. Bernie explains that he did feel guilty about the divorce but that he was also angry with her mother and even angry with her. He goes on to say that he was angry with the government for how he was treated in the war and as a war veteran. Carol tells him that her husband, Gerry, fought in the Korean War, but that he never talks about it.

Scene 9

Bernie tells Carol a story about something that happened to him when he was working for the phone company. He had driven to a friend's place on New Year's Eve and gotten drunk. He had paid a young man to drive him home afterward, but the young man disappeared, so he drove himself home while still drunk. As a result, he got into an accident and crashed his car into a telephone pole. A police officer found him and drove him home without arresting him or giving him a ticket for the accident. However, as soon as he got home, the phone company called him to come out and repair a telephone pole that had been knocked down in a car accident. So, he ended up getting paid to repair the telephone pole he himself had crashed into.

Scene 10

Bernie explains that he was fired from the phone company, where he had worked for ten years, after he accidentally hit a police car and his driver's license was revoked. He says his driver's license will probably be reinstated in about a year. Carol mentions that she worked as a sixth-grade teacher for a year-and-a-half. They realize that, since they've both been living in Boston for years, they probably passed each other on the street, or in a restaurant or store, many times without knowing it.

Scene 11

Bernie recalls that he had considered calling her on her twenty-first birthday, in 1968. She states that she wants to get to know him, and he assures her that he wants to get to know her. He adds, ''let's get up, go out, do this'' because ''what's between us isn't going nowhere, and the rest of it doesn't exist.''

Scene 12

Bernie asks Carol why, after all these years, she decided to seek him out and see him at this point in her life. She responds that she wanted to see him because she felt lonely. She adds, ''You're my father.''

Scene 13

Carol says she feels lonely, and that she feels cheated because she never had a father. She tells

Bernie she doesn't want to be his pal or his buddy, but wants him to be a father to her. She insists that she is entitled to have a father. Bernie agrees but states that the important thing is for them to be together. Carol asks if he'd like to go out to dinner with her and her husband, Gerry, that night. Bernie responds that he would like that. Carol then suggests that just the two of them could go out to dinner, without Gerry. Bernie tells her whatever she'd like to do is fine.

Scene 14

Bernie gives Carol a gold bracelet with the inscription ''To Carol from her Father. March eighth, 1973.'' He explains that it should say March third, but that his threes look like eights. They get ready to call Gerry and go out to dinner. Carol tells Bernie the bracelet is lovely, and he thanks her.

CHARACTERS

Bernie Cary

Bernie Cary is a fifty-three-year-old recovering alcoholic. He is the father of Carol, whom he hasn't seen since he divorced Carol's mother twenty years earlier. He tells Carol he had wanted to see her all those years, but that her mother initiated a court order forbidding him from seeing Carol. He mentions that he considered contacting Carol when she turned twenty-one, but did not do so. Bernie admits that he was scared by the prospect of meeting Carol at this point, but he seems pleased that she is there. Bernie spent most of his adult life as an alcoholic, and has only quit drinking in the last couple of years. Before that, he worked for the telephone company for ten years, until he was fired for driving drunk and smashing into a police car. He is divorced from his second wife, Ruth, with whom he has a son, Marty, whom he hasn't heard from in several years. Bernie says that he hasn't done very well for most of his life, but has been feeling much better in the last couple of years. He likes his job working at a restaurant, is saving some money, and is thinking of marrying a woman named Leslie, who works with him at the restaurant. It is clear that Bernie very much wants to reestablish a relationship with Carol.

In the final scene of the play, he gives Carol an engraved gold bracelet as they get ready to go out to dinner together.

Carol Mindler

Carol Mindler is a twenty-four-year-old woman, the daughter of Bernie. She has come to visit her father whom she hasn't seen since she was four years old, when her parents divorced. Carol repeatedly tells Bernie that she wants to get to know him, and that she wants him to be a father to her. She feels ''cheated'' because she did not have a father when she was growing up. She says she wanted to see him now because she is lonely. She is married to a man named Gerry, who has two sons from a previous marriage. Carol implies that she and Gerry's sons don't particularly like each other, although they get along. She works as an assistant in Gerry's office, a job that doesn't seem to challenge or interest her. She tells Bernie that she and her husband don't make love any more, and that he is a ''lousy'' lover anyway. Toward the end of the play, Carol tentatively asks Bernie if he will go out to dinner with her and her husband. Bernie gives her a gold bracelet with a note to her engraved on it and Carol seems very pleased to receive such a gift from her father.

THEMES

Marriage, Divorce, and Family

A central theme of *Reunion* is marriage, divorce, and family. Carol's relationship with her father was broken off when she was four years old because of her parents' divorce. Carol's mother is now remarried, and she has a half-sister from this union. Bernie remarried after divorcing Carol's mother and was divorced a second time. As a result of Bernie's second marriage, Carol has a half-brother. Now Bernie is considering a third marriage to a woman he works with at the restaurant who has already been divorced once. The marriage he is considering, however, does not sound entirely promising because his reason for wanting to remarry is for ''companionship,'' and there is no suggestion that he feels a strong or deep connection to the woman he plans on marrying.

Carol's husband, Gerry, is divorced from his first wife, with whom he had two sons. Carol indicates that she is not entirely happy in her marriage to Gerry, that she is lonely, and that they don't make love any more, so it's possible she may end up divorced from him. Carol refers to herself as being from a ''broken home.'' She points out that everyone is getting divorced and remarried these days, and that ''every child has three sets of parents.'' Carol complains that because divorce has become so common, people no longer speak of children as being from a ''broken home,'' and the effect of divorce on children is no longer considered to be a major concern. Carol seems to resent this because she herself feels that her life has been deeply scarred by her parents' divorce and the absence of her father from her life. She ironically refers to divorce as the ''Great American Institution.'' This comment implies that divorce has become commonplace in the United States, and that, according to Mamet, it is damaging to the lives of children.

Communication and Personal Connection

In *Reunion*, as in many of his plays, Mamet explores the difficulties people have in communicating with one another about their feelings and what is important to them. Mamet focuses on communication as a means by which human beings ought to be able to develop a sense of personal connection with each other. However, his characters find that conversation often has the opposite effect and ends up getting in the way of real personal connection when it should be facilitating connection. A major irony in Bernie's life is that he worked for the telephone company for ten years, and yet never once called his daughter on the phone. The telephone is clearly a symbol for verbal communication, and yet Bernie, although an expert telephone repairman, was, for most of his life, a failure at communicating with the people who are important to him.

In *Reunion*, though, Mamet ultimately expresses a more hopeful attitude about the possibilities of forming personal connections through verbal communication. Both father and daughter try very hard to make up for twenty years of separation in the space of one conversation, and they do not always succeed. However, over the course of their conversation, the two do manage to communicate mean-

TOPICS FOR FURTHER STUDY

- Mamet is ranked among the major American playwrights of the twentieth century, alongside Eugene O'Neill, Arthur Miller, Tennessee Williams, Edward Albee, Amiri Baraka, Ntozake Shange, Lanford Wilson, and August Wilson. Learn more about one of these playwrights and his or her major works. What makes this author's style unique? What major themes does this author address in her or his works? Perform one scene from a play by this author with other students and discuss the author's use of dialogue in the scene.

- Mamet is best known for his use of colloquial spoken American English in dramatic dialogue. To get a better sense of how Mamet's dialogue works in spoken form, perform one scene from *Reunion*. Does the dialogue of the characters sound natural to you? What does this style of dialogue convey when spoken aloud that you may not have noticed when reading it silently to yourself? How does this style of dialogue help to convey information about each character, and their relationship to one another?

- *Reunion* is primarily a dramatic dialogue between a young woman and her father. Write your own dramatic dialogue of a conversation between two family members, such as a son and mother, brother and sister, mother and daughter, grandchild and grandparent, etc. As much as possible, work on writing your dialogue so that it sounds natural to your ear. Perform your scene with another student.

- Mamet's theatrical career developed over time through his involvement with small, local, and regional theaters. Learn more about the local theaters in your area and describe them. For each theater, answer the questions: Is it a professional theater, a community theater, a repertory theater, or a theater affiliated with a larger institution (such as a college or university)? What plays have been performed by this theater over the past year? What plays are currently being produced by this theater? How is this theater funded? If possible, interview the artistic director about the approach this theater takes to acting, type of production, and type of plays they produce. Ask if you can sit in on a rehearsal to get a better sense of what goes into the production of a play.

- Mamet has written many screen adaptations of his plays, as well as original screenplays. Watch one film for which Mamet has written, or co-written, the screenplay, such as: *The Postman Always Rings Twice*, *The Verdict*, *House of Games*, *The Untouchables*, *We're No Angels*, *Homicide*, *Hoffa*, *Oleana*, *American Buffalo*, *The Spanish Prisoner*, *The Edge*, *Wag the Dog*, *Ronin*, *The Winslow Boy*, or *State and Maine*. Pay particular attention to the dialogue in the film you choose. In what ways is the dialogue characteristic of Mamet's style? How does his use of dialogue work differently in the cinematic medium from the medium of live performance? If you are familiar with any of the actors in this film, how do your associations or knowledge of that actor affect your experience of the dialogue, or the film as a whole? What major themes are addressed in this film?

ingful information and feelings to one another, despite the difficulties they face in trying to do so.

Storytelling

In their efforts to communicate with one another, and to explain the past twenty years of their lives to each other, Bernie and Carol engage in a certain amount of storytelling. Bernie, in particular, at several points informs Carol that he is going to tell her a story about his past. Bernie resorts to storytelling to make a connection with his estranged daughter, in a way that suggests a parent telling stories to a small child as a means of teaching the child a lesson or helping her to make sense of the world.

The importance of storytelling in parent-child relationships is explored in Mamet's short play *Dark Pony*, which is usually performed as a companion piece to *Reunion*. In *Dark Pony*, a father tells a story of Native American legend to his four-year-old daughter while they are driving home one night. In *Reunion*, however, Bernie's stories are not drawn from traditional legends or folktales, and do not contain any particular moral lesson or impart any wisdom. Instead, his stories merely recount the exploits and foibles of a severe alcoholic. The longest story Bernie tells Carol, for instance, is about driving drunk, running into a telephone pole, and then getting paid by the telephone company as part of his job to repair the pole he damaged. Bernie thus attempts to use storytelling as a means of reestablishing a father-daughter relationship with Carol; but his efforts in this direction only serve to highlight the fact that, throughout most of his life, Bernie has evaded his responsibilities as a father and lived a reckless, meaningless, existence devoid of any real personal connections or genuine relationships.

STYLE

Dialogue

Mamet is best known and most widely celebrated for his skillful use of dialogue, which conveys the natural rhythms of the American idiom. Mamet's characteristic use of dialogue is showcased in *Reunion*, as the entire play consists of bits and pieces from one long conversation. The characters speak in fits and starts, often not completing their sentences, repeating themselves, hesitating, and jumping from one thought to the next without a logical flow of ideas. This naturalistic dialogue perfectly expresses the awkwardness and discomfort experienced by Carol and her father. The dialogue indicates that these two people are essentially groping in the dark to find some form of meaningful communication.

Dramatic Structure

Reunion is a one-act play, divided into fourteen short scenes, which represent snippets of one long conversation between two people. This series of scenes has often been described as short bursts of dialogue. The effect of Mamet's choice of dramatic structure is, in part, to emphasize the fact that this conversation is not flowing smoothly and to highlight the awkwardness felt by the two characters, who don't know each other and often aren't sure what to say to one another. It is clear to both characters that this is a momentous occasion and many meaningful things are said, but the conversation does not, on the surface, seem to develop along clear lines or go in any particular direction. The characters jump incongruously from one topic to the next in their efforts to establish a rapport, and the short scenes accentuate this disjointed feeling throughout their conversation.

Setting and Stage Direction: Minimalism

The settings and stage directions in Mamet's plays are often described as minimalist. That is, they are stripped down to the bare essentials. For instance, the stage directions indicate that *Reunion* is set in Bernie's apartment, on a Sunday afternoon in early March. Whereas most playwrights would probably include some detail regarding the décor, furnishings, and various objects in Bernie's apartment, Mamet leaves such specifications up to the discretion of whoever stages the play. From the perspective of someone reading the play, such details are left to the imagination, or may be considered irrelevant. Similarly, Mamet provides no stage directions to describe the actions or movements of the two characters during the conversation. Mamet's minimalism has been interpreted as, in part, a device that emphasizes the dialogue as the most important element of the play and allows for those who wish to produce the play maximum freedom of interpretation, as far as set design and staging.

HISTORICAL CONTEXT

American Theater

Mamet is ranked among the greatest American playwrights of the twentieth century. Before World War II, the only American playwright of note was Eugene O'Neill, whose most celebrated works include the autobiographical *Long Day's Journey into Night* (1941). In the post-World War II era, several notable American playwrights began to emerge. Arthur Miller is best known for *Death of a Salesman* (1949), about an aging salesman and his relationship with his sons. Miller is also known for *The Crucible* (1953), which uses the historical setting of

COMPARE
&
CONTRAST

- **1970s:** Beginning in the 1960s, regional theaters and theaters associated with colleges and universities become an important testing ground for innovative playwrights such as Mamet. The increasing popularity of off-Broadway and off-off-Broadway theater venues offers a forum for avant-garde playwrights. Some of these serious and innovative plays are eventually performed on Broadway, once they have been proven on the smaller stage.

    Today: Because of the perceived need for greater and greater profits, Broadway productions focus almost exclusively on flashy, highly entertaining, big-budget musicals, such as stage adaptations of the animated Disney film *The Lion King*. Some serious dramatic works still see Broadway production, but these are exceptions. Thus, regional theater, off-Broadway, and off-off-Broadway are important as the primary venues for serious and innovative dramatic productions.

- **1970s:** The Women's Liberation Movement, also known as Second Wave Feminism, begun in the late 1960s, advocates greater freedoms and opportunities for women, both in the professional world and in the private realm of marriage, family, and home life. The liberalization of many divorce laws becomes an important means by which women can extract themselves from abusive or oppressive marital circumstances. Greater economic opportunities for women make it easier for women to secure the financial means to support themselves without economic dependence on men.

    Today: Most younger women do not identify themselves as "feminist," although most do agree with feminist principles and goals. Many young women, however, consider themselves as part of Third Wave Feminism, a new generation of women with different concerns from those of their mothers' generation. Divorce and remarriage, single-parent families, step-parents, and joint custody of children has become a norm in American society.

the Salem witch trials as a vehicle for social and political commentary on America in the 1950s. Tennessee Williams was another great American playwright during this era, known for his stories of sensitive personalities in the context of a Southern aristocratic society in decay. His most celebrated works include *The Glass Menagerie* (1944) and *A Streetcar Named Desire* (1947).

In the 1960s, Edward Albee emerged as a great American playwright, most notably for his *Who's Afraid of Virginia Woolf?* (1962), about the relationship of a married couple, both of whom are alcoholics. In the 1970s, alongside the rising reputation of David Mamet, Sam Shepard won critical acclaim for his *Buried Child* (1979). After the popular and critical success of Lorraine Hansberry's *A Raisin In The Sun* brought African-American playwrights and actors to the mainstream, several notable African-American playwrights emerged during the 1960s and 1970s, including Amiri Baraka (*The Slave* and *The Dutchman,* both 1964) and Ntozake Shange (*for colored girls who have considered suicide, when the rainbow is enuf,* 1976). During the 1980s, when Mamet's reputation was augmented by the success of *Glengarry Glen Ross* (1984), American playwrights Lanford Wilson (*Talley's Folly;* 1980) and August Wilson (*Ma Rainey's Black Bottom;* 1984) also gained national recognition.

Alcoholism and Alcoholics Anonymous

In *Reunion*, Bernie refers to himself as an "ex-drunk," and frequently mentions the fact that quitting drinking has completely changed his life for the better, making him a happier, more responsible, more financially stable person. There are an estimated five million alcoholics in the United States, and another four million "problem drinkers" who may eventually become alcoholics. Thus, some four percent of the adult population of the United States are alcoholics—one of every twenty-five adults.

The organization Alcoholics Anonymous (AA), devoted to helping alcoholics quit drinking and stay sober, originated in 1935 when two friends, William Griffith Wilson, a stockbroker, and Robert Holbrook Smith, a surgeon, got together to help each other quit drinking. They published the book *Alcoholics Anonymous* in 1939, which put forth the program they had devised. There are now approximately two million members of AA throughout the world. Alcoholics Anonymous programs are also known as twelve-step programs, because of the twelve steps toward achieving sobriety on which the programs are based. Alcoholics Anonymous places great emphasis on the idea that alcoholism is a disease and that people who suffer from alcoholism can only recover by practicing complete abstinence from the consumption of alcohol. Alcoholics who have successfully quit drinking are referred to in AA as "recovering alcoholics."

War

Throughout *Reunion*, Bernie makes reference to his tour of duty as a tail gunner for the American Air Corps, shooting a machine gun out of a B-17, during World War II. World War II was fought between the Allies (including the United States, Britain, and the Soviet Union) and the Axis Powers (including Germany, Italy, and Japan) from 1939 to 1945. The United States, however, did not enter the war until late in 1941, after the Japanese bombing of Pearl Harbor. Bernie takes a certain amount of pride in his position during the war, primarily, it seems, because of the high level of risk involved. He tells Carol most soldiers did not live through more than three missions. He also mentions that he was at one time mad at the government for, as he says, treating him like a kid when he was in the military.

Mamet originally wrote *Reunion* in 1973, during the tail end of the Vietnam War, and the play was first produced in 1976, just after the end of the Vietnam War. In the Vietnam War, the United States fought on the side of South Vietnam against the communist forces in North Vietnam, beginning in the mid-1960s. By 1968, the Vietnam War was becoming increasingly unpopular among many Americans, particularly young Americans, who thought the war was unjust to both the Vietnamese people and the American soldiers who were drafted to fight. Thus, Mamet's references to World War II would have been significant to the original audiences of the play as a commentary on the Vietnam

War. Bernie denies that fighting in the war was an act of heroism, asserting rather that he essentially didn't have a choice. Further, Bernie expresses anger toward the United States government for how he was treated in the military. These sentiments resonate with the sentiments of many Americans about the Vietnam War during the 1970s.

CRITICAL OVERVIEW

Mamet first gained national recognition as a major playwright with the 1977 Broadway production of *American Buffalo* (1975). He rose to international prominence as one of the greatest playwrights of the twentieth century with the production of the prestigious Pulitzer Prize-winning *Glengarry Glen Ross* in 1984. Mamet is widely celebrated for his skillful rendering of American vernacular English and the rhythms of spoken language. C. W. E. Bigsby, in *David Mamet* (1985), echoed many reviewers and drama critics in his assertion that Mamet expresses "a sensitivity to the American vernacular unequalled by any other playwright."

Summing up the extent of Mamet's status as a major American dramatist, Leslie Kane, in *David Mamet: A Casebook* (1992), explained:

> Mamet is widely considered to be one of the most prolific and powerful voices in contemporary American theater. His sensitivity to language, precision of social observation, concern for metaphor and its dramatic force, theatrical imagination and inventiveness, images of alienation, striking tone poems of betrayal and loss, brilliant use of comedy, and continuing productivity account in large part for his staying power and critical respect.

However, Mamet has also been criticized for extensive use of offensive language in his plays, and for the treatment of women in his male dialogue, which some consider degrading and sexist.

Reunion was first performed in 1976, later performed with the short companion piece *Dark Pony* (1977), and ultimately performed as part of a triptych including *The Sanctity of Marriage* (1979), also a short piece. Critics have praised *Reunion* for its minimalist plot, setting, and stage directions, which leave the viewer to focus on the dialogue and the relationship between the characters. Mamet is also praised for his creation of nuanced characters and his delicate rendering of the relationship between father and daughter in *Reunion*. Patricia Lewis, in the *Dictionary of Literary Biography,* asserted,

Showbill cover from the 1979 theatrical production of Reunion, *written by David Mamet*

''*Reunion* suggests the real and deep characters Mamet is capable of creating.'' Lewis observed, ''The relationship in this vignette is probably the strongest manifestation of character interaction and interdependency yet evidenced in [Mamet's] writing.'' Nesta Jones and Steven Dykes, in *File on Mamet* (1991) described *Reunion* as ''a good minor play in a strong minor key.'' Harold Clurman, in a 1979 review of *Reunion* in The *Nation,* stated:

> David Mamet has written more original and striking plays than *Reunion* . . . but none I have found more touching. . . . Mamet's writing here is marked by an honest sensibility and a humanity of perception which strike home. . . . It is in this play and this vein . . . that Mamet's most telling qualities are revealed.

Michael Billington, in a 1981 review of *Reunion* in the *Guardian,* commented, ''It would be hard to over-praise the way Mr. Mamet suggests behind the probing, joshing family chat an extraordinary sense of pain and loss.'' Stephen H. Gale, in *Essays on Contemporary American Drama* (1981), noted of *Reunion*, ''Mamet's drama beautifully depicts the touching way in which [the two characters] communicate, hesitatingly, as a renewed bond is formed.''

In a career spanning some three decades, Mamet's reputation as a playwright, screenwriter, and director continues to grow. In the 1990s, he also published several books of essays and memoirs, books on acting and film directing, and a novel.

CRITICISM

Liz Brent

Brent has a Ph.D. in American Culture, specializing in film studies, from the University of Michigan. She is a freelance writer and teaches courses on the history of American cinema. In the following essay, Brent discusses Bernie's personal philosophy in Mamet's play.

In *Reunion*, Bernie is a recovering alcoholic who has not seen his daughter Carol since he divorced her mother twenty years earlier. Throughout his long conversation with Carol, Bernie expresses key points in his personal philosophy on life, developed as a result of his struggles to recover from alcoholism. Bernie applies this philosophy to his relationship with Carol, as he tries to develop a renewed personal connection with his adult daughter. In addition, Bernie attempts to provide Carol with some form of parental guidance by offering her his personal wisdom about life and relationships, gained from his own experiences, both good and bad.

In the course of his conversation with Carol, Bernie repeatedly refers to his alcoholism, an addiction he has only been able to resist over the past three years. A major characteristic of Bernie's alcoholism was his refusal to take responsibility for his life, particularly in terms of his relationships with members of his family. Although he did work for the telephone company in Boston for ten years, he also drifted around the country and moved from job to job for a number of years after he divorced Carol's mother. Because of his alcoholism, he eventually crashed his car into a police car, after which his driver's license was revoked. As a result, he was fired from the phone company. Bernie even missed the funeral of his own brother, partly because he was drifting around and out of touch with his family, but also as a result of his drinking. Because he missed his brother's funeral, his brother's wife refuses to speak to him ever again. Bernie also mentions that, while he was drinking, he was always in debt. He points out that there was no good reason for him to

WHAT DO I READ NEXT?

- *Death of a Salesman* (1949), by Arthur Miller, is one of the most celebrated American plays of the twentieth century. Mamet is often compared to Miller, as both write about male ambitions and frustrations in chasing the American dream. *Death of a Salesman* concerns an aging salesman whose life has been wasted in the pursuit of unrealistic ambitions, with which he has also burdened his sons.

- *Waiting for Godot* (1953), by Irish playwright Samuel Beckett, is a classic play of the Theater of the Absurd, and a major influence on Mamet. It focuses on the dialogue between three characters who are waiting for an enigmatic man named Godot.

- *Who's Afraid of Virginia Woolf?* (1962), by the celebrated American playwright Edward Albee, is about the relationships between two couples, focusing on the professional ambitions and twisted emotional dynamics that characterize each marriage.

- *American Buffalo* (1975) is one of Mamet's most celebrated plays. It takes place in a pawn shop and concerns two men and a boy who plan to steal a valuable collector's coin from one of their customers.

- *Glengarry Glen Ross* (1982) is Mamet's most highly acclaimed play. It takes place in a real estate agency and concerns the shady deals and fierce competition in which the real estate agents engage.

---

be in debt all those years, except that he was irresponsible about work and money.

One of the most significant consequences of Bernie's alcoholism and avoidance of personal responsibility is that he never tried to contact his daughter, even after she turned twenty-one and there was no legal restriction on his relationship with her. Further, even the fact that Carol's mother was able to obtain a court order forbidding Bernie to see Carol was probably made possible on the evidence of his alcoholism—that is, Carol's mother probably informed the court that Bernie was an alcoholic, and therefore unfit to see his daughter.

In the present, however, Bernie is much more concerned about the consequences of his actions, particularly in terms of how his decisions may affect his relationship with Carol. He mentions to her that he is thinking of remarrying, but makes a point of asking how that would affect her. He tentatively asks, "How would you, you know . . . feel if I got married again? Would that . . . do anything to you?" Even after she responds that she thinks it would be good for him, Bernie assures her, "Of course it

wouldn't get in the way of our getting to know each other." Thus, although he can't change his past, and the effect of his past actions on his relationship with Carol, he is very aware of weighing the possible consequences of his present and future actions on their relationship.

Bernie understands that, for him, drinking was a way of "looking for a way around" life's challenges and difficulties, of avoiding his responsibilities and the consequences of his actions. His personal philosophy in the present, however, is grounded in the understanding that choices in life must be made based on the idea that one must be willing to face the consequences of one's actions. As Bernie says, "pay the price" for one's decisions in life, whether they be good or bad." He explains,

> You wanna drink? Go drink. You wanna do *this*? Pay the price. Always the price. Whatever it is. And you gotta know it and be prepared to pay it if you don't want it to pass you by.

By this statement, Bernie is not advocating that Carol, or anyone else, go ahead and drink; rather, he is pointing out that, if one chooses to drink exces-

> BERNIE UNDERSTANDS THAT, FOR HIM, DRINKING WAS A WAY OF 'LOOKING FOR A WAY AROUND' LIFE'S CHALLENGES AND DIFFICULTIES, OF AVOIDING HIS RESPONSIBILITIES AND THE CONSEQUENCES OF HIS ACTIONS."

sively, one must be aware of, and willing to accept, the consequences of that decision, to "pay the price" for one's actions.

Bernie has only quit drinking over the past three years, and is trying to be a more stable, responsible person. He has clearly made progress in taking responsibility for his life, since he stopped drinking. He has had the same job for two years, has his own apartment, and has even begun to save money. Although Carol was the one to contact him, after so many years, Bernie clearly seems ready to take responsibility for trying his best to reestablish a relationship with his daughter.

Throughout his conversation with Carol, Bernie tries to admit candidly what kind of person he was in the past and what kind of person he is today. He understands that he can neither deny nor change his past. He also understands that it's important not to have illusions about himself. While Carol clings to her childhood image of him as an idealized hero, Bernie repeatedly insists that he is "no hero," that he is simply an "ex-drunk," and that the only way for him to be happy is to accept himself as he truly is. He tells Carol, "I'm a happy man now," but that he in no way takes happiness for granted, that "I don't use the term loosely." Although his life has become simple, Bernie expresses genuine contentment with himself. He tells Carol, "For the first time in a long time I get a kick out of what I'm doing."

Carol tells Bernie she used to think of him as a hero, in the person of Tonto, the Native American sidekick of the television cowboy hero The Lone Ranger. She tells him she was very upset after, when she was four years old, he told her that he was not

Tonto. Bernie responds by insisting that he is not a hero. He even asserts that, although he was given a medal for his service in World War II, he was no hero in the war, but was simply doing what he did out of necessity. He explains, "They put you in a plane with a gun, it pays to shoot at the guys who are trying to kill you. Where's the courage in that." He tries to impress upon Carol that she needs to let go of her childhood ideals about her father and accept him for the flawed man that he is.

Bernie himself does not shy away from admitting his many faults and his mistakes in the past. At one point, he states, "I've spent the majority of my life drinking and, when you come right down to it, being a hateful sonofa[b——]." Yet he is willing to accept himself for who he is, and who he has been in the past. He explains that "I am what I am and that's what happiness comes from . . . being just that." In other words, happiness comes from accepting that he is no more nor less than who he really is. Carol at one point tells Bernie he is wasting his life working in a restaurant. He responds that he is not the hero Tonto, but only himself, an "ex-drunk." Further, Bernie asserts that he likes who he is today, and likes his life as he is living it in the present, that "I like it like I am," and "I like it at the restaurant. I love it at the restaurant," regardless of whether or not he lives up to other people's ideas about what he should be doing with his life.

As part of his philosophy of self-acceptance, Bernie tries to be honest with Carol about his feelings, expressing at various points anger, fear, and sadness. He tells her that he almost burst into tears when her husband, Gerry, informed him that Carol wanted to see him, and that he was scared by the prospect of seeing her after all of these years. Bernie is also honest with Carol about his feelings during the period after he and her mother were divorced. He admits that he felt guilty about not seeing Carol, but that he also felt angry with her mother, and even angry with her. On the positive side, Bernie expresses the feeling that he wants to get to know his daughter, and that their meeting after all these years is "a very important moment." Through such honest expression of his feelings, Bernie does his best not to shy away from his past, and to be honest with himself and others about who he is and how he feels in the present. Bernie thus makes a point of taking responsibility for his feelings in both the past and the present, without dwelling unrealistically on a past that he has no power to change.

Bernie ultimately tries to impress upon Carol that he is not a hero, and that she cannot continue to idealize him in the way that she did as a little girl. He tries to explain that he is no more nor less than what he is, a recovering alcoholic who has made many mistakes in life but is happy with who he is in the present.

Bernie admits to Carol that he felt guilty about abandoning her, but he also makes it clear to her that he cannot undo the past. He tries to explain to Carol that their relationship as father and daughter at this point cannot be based on what's gone on in the past, that he'll never be able to make up for the fatherless childhood Carol suffered. He explains that wanting to get to know each other in the present is still "not going to magically wipe out twenty years . . . in which you were growing up, which you had to do anyway, and I was drunk." He adds, "What's past is in the past . . . it's gone," and that, "I can't make it up to you." Bernie understands that the best he can do is to accept the consequences of his past actions, to accept his own personal limitations in the present, and to make better, more responsible, choices in the future.

Bernie tells Carol he spent a couple of days in jail once, where he learned, "you've gotta be where you are. . . . While you're there." He also states, "The actions are important. The present is important," in relation to his and Carol's relationship to each other. He seems to be saying that they cannot have a relationship by dwelling on a past that cannot be altered, or trying to recapture the years they have lost, but must forge their relationship based on who both of them are at this point in their lives, by spending time together and doing things in the present. He suggests, "let's get up, go out, do this," because "what's between us isn't going nowhere, and the rest of it doesn't exist." While this last statement is a bit enigmatic, it seems that Bernie is trying to say the past cannot be altered, that it is "going nowhere," and that the future does not yet exist. Their only choice is to develop a relationship with one another in the present by choosing to be together and do things together in the here and now. Bernie takes positive steps toward this end by giving Carol an engraved bracelet "from your father," and letting her know that he is willing to do "whatever you want" as far as how they spend their time together from that point on.

Although he does not make direct reference to it, Bernie's newfound attitude about life resonates with the "serenity prayer," recited regularly at meetings of Alcoholics Anonymous: "God, grant me the serenity to accept the things I cannot change, the courage to change the things I can, and the wisdom to know the difference." Bernie seems to have found personal serenity by quitting drinking and developing the wisdom to know the difference between what he can and cannot change. He is eager to change the things he can in the present, such as taking positive action to develop his relationship with Carol from one of two strangers into one of close interpersonal connection.

Source: Liz Brent, Critical Essay on *Reunion,* in *Drama for Students,* The Gale Group, 2002.

Kevin O'Sullivan

O'Sullivan is a writer of fiction, feature articles, and criticism. In this essay, O'Sullivan considers the economy of language and indirection in Mamet's play.

Reunion is the story of a father and daughter coming together after a separation of many years. It is a quiet play, using Mamet's trademark terse, cryptic dialogue; yet there is a degree of melancholy that distinguishes it from the playwright's other, more noisy work. The play demonstrates how language can mark the distance between two people as well as draw them together and manages to convey a sense of festering bitterness, betrayal, and recrimination without ever addressing them head on. Silences are as pregnant with meaning as the verbal exchanges.

Like the plays of the British playwright Harold Pinter, to whom he is most often compared, Mamet's plays often proceed in the form of "dramatized conversation." This conversational tone, often constituting superficial or anecdotal exchanges, conceals stresses just beneath the surface, tensions that threaten to erupt violently. Like Pinter, Mamet is sparing in his use of directions. It can be argued that they are contained in the language itself, the way it is written on the page, for example, when Carol is looking at a photograph of Bernie's bomber group. Language itself is the vehicle of dramatic action.

As with Pinter, Mamet employs silence, the space between words, as a kind of punctuation. This includes both the ways in which he organizes the individual speeches of his characters, often starting a new line with each sentence, as well as the indication of pauses written into the stage directions. This breaking up of the speeches places an emphasis on both what is said and left unsaid. In these gaps between words lie hidden meanings. It is

" THE PLAY DEMONSTRATES HOW LANGUAGE CAN MARK THE DISTANCE BETWEEN TWO PEOPLE AS WELL AS DRAW THEM TOGETHER. . . ."

no accident that both Mamet and Pinter began their careers as actors on the stage; their works are written to be performed. Mamet's famous use of profanity serves a similar purpose; it is used as a rhythmic device, linking syllables while also creating an aura of authenticity. The effect is a kind of street language that is actually highly stylized and poetic.

Reunion is one of Mamet's earliest produced plays but it already contains the elements of what is now recognized as "Mametspeak"; the clipped, authentic-sounding, yet highly stylized economy of language that in its use of compression and indirection most resembles poetry. C. W. E. Bigsby, in his study *David Mamet,* has remarked upon how Mamet's plays often proceed through the use of "parallel monologues." His characters address one another indirectly, appearing to be only half listening, or incapable of following a line of thought. Exchanges threaten, at times, to break into incoherence. A monologue may be broken, in mid-sentence, and go off on a tangent.

There is something poignant as well as comical in these digressions. What is shown is a struggle for coherence. Assertions are made, then quickly contradicted, undermining the authority of the statements. There is a built-in instability to each utterance and the truthfulness of the speaker is constantly called into question. Bigsby notes that "the inarticulate sounds made by his characters are themselves shaped into effective harmonies." This is certainly the case in *Reunion* where father and daughter, in an attempt to communicate with one another, speak half-truths, tell white lies, and construct self-serving or exculpatory narratives that allow them to finally approach a point where they can engage one another, directly and without pretense.

The play opens with uncertainty, when Bernie, a fifty-three-year-old "ex-drunk" remarks to the twenty-four-year-old daughter he has not seen in twenty years that "I would of recognized you anywhere. It is you. Isn't it? Carol. Is that you? You haven't changed a bit." This confusion, assertion of certainty, then doubt, followed by blatant dissimulation sets the tone for the piece. Assertions by either character are not to be taken at face value, even if the motives for dissembling are benevolent.

This meeting between father and daughter, fraught with tension, proceeds through a series of indirect exchanges that define, obliquely, the characters and their needs. Carol is the more reticent of the two, with Bernie evidently having more to answer for. Bernie is suspicious of her motives for seeking him out after all these years and has constructed, out of habit or a bad conscience, a well-rehearsed narrative of his life that is meant to be both an admission of his failings and exculpatory. Bernie describes himself as "ex-this, ex-that," in particular, ex-drunk. He speaks the language of recovery, with an ex-tail-gunner's reserve. This emphasis on what he once was, is a way of separating himself from his past, appealing to Carol as who he is now. The inadequacy of this approach should be apparent; Bernie cannot describe himself except as something other than he was. He exists, in the present, only vaguely. As Bigsby points out, "Unlike the present relationship, which is fraught with danger, accusations, potential embarrassments and emotional traps, the past, once reshaped by memory and imaginations, is an object that can be handled with relative safety."

Just as Bernie falls back on platitudes and anecdotes as a way of steeling himself against any true communication, Carol constructs her own fictional narrative of a happy marriage and loving husband. The truth leaks through, as fissures open up revealing the depth of her despair and the real reason for this rapprochement with Bernie. The two of them attempt to find common ground in shared memories. They try to connect, weave fictions, half-lies, and attempt to connect memories that don't correspond. Both offer stories in the hopes that they will elicit recognition in the other. "Do you remember that?" is asked hopefully but is never answered. Carol tells how she thought her father was Tonto. She recounts how she asked him if it were true and he answered in the negative. "I didn't understand why you were lying to me." Later, Bernie responds angrily "This is not Tonto the Indian but Butch Cary, ex-drunk." This self-identification seems no less a fiction, constructed out of need and convenience.

Through an accretion of details, one may draw conclusions as to why Carol chose an older man for a husband, although she does not seem conscious of what they may be. The failure of this union seems directly tied to her desire to look up her actual father. That she is unable or unwilling to address him as 'father' is revealed in their earliest exchange. At a moment when Bernie who has ventured some paternal advice to his daughter without having earned the right, Carol responds "He's my husband, Bernie, not my father." Bernie has not earned the right to patronize her, to play the paternal role. It is uncertain that it would be possible.

As the play progresses, Carol seems to hover on the brink of recognition. She speaks of coming from a broken home: "The most important institution in America." "It's got to have affected my marriage," she says. Bernie once again falls back on a platitude: life goes on. Bernie seems to intuit that Carol's admission of unhappiness in her marriage is an indirect reproach of him. He takes the offensive, admitting his own anger and hostility. He returns to the theme of ex-soldier, which he first said was "no big deal," and rails against the Veterans Administration. He plays the victim in order to release himself from responsibility. The way that Mamet handles this scene is subtle, but effective.

> Bernie: I mean, understand: I'm not asking you to understand me, Carol, because we've both been through enough.
> Am I right?
> *Pause.*
> Carol: Gerry was in Korea.
> Bernie: Yes? And what does he say about it?
> Carol: Nothing.

The failures to find a shared memory lead them to search for common ground; Bernie becomes excited when Carol tells him she taught at the Horace Mann School in Newton. Bernie used to frequent a garage across the street when he was a phone company employee. When Carol tells him she worked there in 1969, Bernie's hopes are deflated; he tells her he has not "worked for the phone company since '55." Once again, there is a disconnect, but they keep foraging, searching out a patch of shared experience:

> Bernie: I'll bet I saw you around. Boylston Street . . .
> Carol: We must've seen each other . . . in the Common . . . A hundred times.

A common past seems irretrievably lost to both of them, yet they persist in their attempts to create a linkage. Bernie tells his daughter that he was in jail once. "What it taught me," he says, "you've got to be where you are . . . While you're there. Or you're

nowhere. Do you know what I mean? As it pertains to you and me?" Carol responds: "I want to get to know you." The play has now shifted, so to speak, from the past tense to the present. Nothing can "wipe out twenty years," the years of Bernie's absence from Carol's life. Finally, Bernie asks Carol directly why she came looking for him, now. "I felt lonely," she replies. "You're my father."

The penultimate scene opens with Carol stating "I feel lonely," shifting from the past to the present tense. This gives her remarks immediacy, placing them in the moment. Finally, they are able to communicate in a direct, unambiguous fashion, yet this seems to discomfit Bernie. Out of the silence, Bernie remarks: "Who doesn't?" As Bernie appears to back away, Carol presses forward. She tells him that she feels cheated that she never had a father.

> Carol: And I don't want to be pals and buddies; I want you to be my father.
> *Pause*
> And to hear your . . . war stories and the whole thing. And that's why now because that's how I feel.
> *Pause*
> I'm entitled to it.
> Am I?
> Am I?

At the play's end, Bernie makes an offering to Carol. He presents her with a bracelet that he found on a bus, but has taken the trouble to have it inscribed to her. Even here the narrative is fouled up: in an ironic twist, the date of the inscription is wrong. "It's my fault. It's not their fault. My threes looks like eights. It's only five days off." This symbolic exchange binds one to the other in a way that their memories cannot. As Bigsby remarks, "This is a reunion only in the sense that they reencounter one another. The intimate relationship of father and daughter is no longer recoverable; they come together out of simple need."

Source: Kevin O'Sullivan, Critical Essay on *Reunion,* in *Drama for Students,* The Gale Group, 2002.

Josh Ozersky

Ozersky is a critic, essayist, and cultural historian. In this essay, Ozersky describes some of the ways in which Mamet's play is truly "Mametesque," even though it doesn't appear so at first glance.

David Mamet is one of the most famous of American writers: he has won a Pulitzer Prize, has an international reputation, and is equally at home on the Broadway stage, in independent theater, and in Hollywood, where his screenplays have been nominated for Academy Awards on two occasions. But Mamet has also suffered from being so identified with a particular genre, which he more or less invented: that of all-male workplaces bursting with an inventive and poetic dialect of American profanity. In his best-known plays, such as *Glengarry Glen Ross* and *American Buffalo*, this language takes the place of plot in advancing an understanding of the world the characters inhabit. But it is a mistake to think that this only happens in Mamet's ''male workplace'' plays.

In *Reunion*, one of Mamet's early works, the language is neither profane nor stylized. There are only two characters, Bernie and Carol. They speak in a natural, realistic way. Neither person ever gets angry or agitated. It seems uncharacteristic of Mamet; but, a closer look reveals that the author's method and preoccupations are present here as much as in his more famous plays, and in those works for which he is best known. *Reunion* is a short work in which a long-separated father and daughter meet in a series of scenes set on a single winter afternoon. Bernie ''Butch'' Cary has the vast majority of the dialog. Carol Mindler, a married woman in her early twenties, mostly listens. But in that dialog, we learn a lot more about the two people than may at first be apparent.

Take Carol, for example. Carol at first seems to be a passive figure, merely agreeable. Bernie does all the talking, and Carol seems to be content merely to provide cues for Bernie:

Carol: Bernie Cary. Army Air Corps.
Bernie: Butch. They called me Butch then.
Carol: Why?
Bernie: . . . I couldn't tell you that to save my life.
    Those were strange times.
Carol: What's this?

Bernie is a bore, the kind of middle-aged man who gasses on about his wartime experiences, his drinking days, his recovery from alcoholism and so forth, without ever seeming to notice that he is monopolizing the conversation. In the context of *Reunion*, it seems doubly obtuse. He has not seen Carol, his own daughter, in twenty years. And yet he asks her only the most perfunctory questions: ''You still go to church?'' ''Tell me about your new husband.'' ''You got any kids?''

But in fact, it is Carol who is in control of the conversation. Both people are in an awkward position; Bernie's answer is to simply spill forth with everything that comes to mind. Carol is far more conscientious in what she tells Bernie; she doesn't begin to open up to him until mid-way through the

play. By asking Bernie questions, she learns much more about him than he does about her.

But if Carol's very short, probing questions reveal something about her character, Bernie's unguarded, loquacious speeches make his character fairly transparent. We feel that we know Bernie very well by the time *Reunion* is finished. And the way we know him is only to a limited extent the result of what he actually says. Bernie lets us know that he was a drunk, a bad husband and father, a veteran. But it's in his asides that we really get a sense of how his mind works.

Bernie: . . . I mean, I'm fifty-three years old. I've spent the majority of my life drinking and, when you come right down to it, being a hateful sonofa[b——] . . . But you, married, living well. You live well. A nice guy. A fine guy for a husband. Going to have . . . maybe . . . kids. You shouldn't let it bother you, but you have a lot of possibilities.

This kind of language is very characteristic of Mamet's work. In many plays, the characters reveal themselves through finished speeches created and polished by the playwright; Mamet's characters often speak semi-incoherently, struggling to get thoughts out. Because of that struggle, the audience can get a sense of not just the way they talk, but the way they think. Bernie, as a failure, sees anyone who has any kind of stability in their life as a fitting neatly into a category. He says, ''married, living well'' as if it were a kind of blue ribbon to stamp on Carol's life—despite the fact that he knows almost nothing about her life. ''A nice guy. A fine guy for a husband.'' In fact, Carol will later tell Bernie a fairly intimate detail about her marriage, but its doubtful if even that will change Bernie's way of looking at things. Carol's life still has ''a lot of possibilities,'' whereas of course Bernie's life is almost out of possibilities. One of the most interesting, almost poignant aspects of *Reunion* is the way the two characters use their own unhappiness as a way to try to open dialog with a long-lost, and badly-needed, relative.

One of Mamet's quintessential themes is the search for a home; and both Bernie and Carol, despite the frequent triteness of their conversation, clearly both have a lot at stake. Although *Reunion* was originally written to be performed by itself, and often is, Mamet has written a very short companion piece, *Dark Pony*, which was performed as an epilogue to *Reunion* at the Yale Repertory Theater in 1977. In *Dark Pony*, the same actors who played Bernie and Carol play a father and daughter, twenty years earlier, riding home from a day in the country. The father, who is described as being "in his early 30s" (or Bernie's age twenty years earlier) tells a tall tale to the daughter, who is described as being "dressed as if 5–8 years old." Coming as it does after reunion, *Dark Pony* is intensely affecting, and the last line sums up the essence of what *Reunion* is really about: "We are almost home."

Given how emotional *Dark Pony* is for an audience who has just seen *Reunion*, one might be tempted to ask why Mamet didn't write both scenarios as one play. One answer may lie in the fact that Mamet doesn't like to give away too much. His characters don't "express themselves" and if they do, it's usually in the things they don't say. *Reunion* is an extremely restrained work, and Mamet never once gives in to the temptation to let a little bit of explicit emotion break through. The last scene of *Reunion* consists of Bernie, in a characteristically awkward moment, giving a gold bracelet to Carol. He has had the date of their reunion engraved on it, he explains, but because his threes look like eights, the date is wrong. There would be ample opportunity for a less disciplined playwright to become mawkish here, in which Carol would say something along the lines of "it's not perfect . . . nobody's perfect . . . we just have to love each other as we are." Instead, the close of the play is as follows:

> Bernie: I'm not going to tell you that you don't have to wear it if you don't like it. I hope you do like it.
> Carol: I do like it . . .
> Bernie: So what's the weather like out there?
> Carol: It's fine. Just a little chilly.
> Bernie: We should be getting ready, no? Shouldn't you call Gerry?
> Carol: Yes.
> Bernie: So you do that and I'll put away the things and we'll go.
> Carol: The bracelet's lovely, Bernie.
> Bernie: Thank you.

As with so many other Mamet works, this exchange tell so much about both characters without really seeming to tell anything. Mamet's men tend to talk too much, and his women hardy at all; but in between what they say, and why they say it, lies a world of feeling. It's just a matter of the audience being sensitive to it. The feeling is real, but not rich; *Reunion* is not the kind of play that many people find easy to warm up to. Without *Dark Pony* as a payoff afterward, the audience might feel frustrated at having spent so much time with Bernie and Carol, and seen so little understanding or even relaxation between the two. They remain in the end as awkward and ill-at-ease as two strangers.

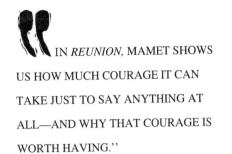

IN *REUNION*, MAMET SHOWS US HOW MUCH COURAGE IT CAN TAKE JUST TO SAY ANYTHING AT ALL—AND WHY THAT COURAGE IS WORTH HAVING."

And two strangers they will almost certainly remain. Mamet doesn't give much hope that Bernie and Carol will break down and open up to each other, after the fashion of TV movies. Bernie will remain a self-absorbed heel; Carol, like nearly all Mamet women, will continue to carry vast reservoirs of silent resentment around with her, and will have trouble connecting. But they both want badly to be father and daughter again. And that, more than anything else, is the driving force behind all their dialog, however stilted, indirect, or laconic. As the audience watches them try so hard to connect with each other, they begin to feel connected themselves. And not just with Bernie and Carol, but with all the things they have tried, and failed, to say. In *Reunion*, Mamet shows us how much courage it can take just to say anything at all—and why that courage is worth having.

Source: Josh Ozersky, Critical Essay on *Reunion,* in *Drama for Students,* The Gale Group, 2002.

SOURCES

Bigsby, C. W. E., *David Mamet,* Methuen, 1985, p. 20.

Billington, Michael, Review of *Reunion,* in *Guardian,* February 25, 1981.

Clurman, Harold, Review of *Reunion,* in *Nation,* December 1, 1979, quoted in *File on Mamet,* edited by Nestor Jones and Steven Dykes, Metheun, 1991, p. 30.

Gale, Stephen H., "David Mamet: The Plays, 1972–1980," in *Essays on Contemporary American Drama,* edited by Hedwig Bock and Albert Wertheim, Max Huber Publishers, 1981, pp. 207–23.

Jones, Nesta, and Steven Dykes, eds., *File on Mamet,* Metheun, 1991, p. 29.

Kane, Leslie, ed., *David Mamet: A Casebook,* Garland Publishing, 1992, p. xiv.

Lewis, Patricia, and Terry Browne, ''David Mamet,'' *Dictionary of Literary Biography,* Volume 7: *Twentieth-Century American Dramatists,* edited by John MacNicholas, Gale Research, 1981, pp. 63–70.

Mamet, David, *Reunion and Dark Pony: Two Plays by David Mamet,* Grove Press, 1979.

———, *Two Plays by David Mamet: Reunion, Dark Pony,* Grove Press, 1986.

FURTHER READING

Bryer, Jackson R., ed., *The Playwright's Art: Conversations with Contemporary American Dramatists,* Rutgers University Press, 1995.
    Bryer provides a selection of interviews with major contemporary American playwrights.

Jones, Nesta, and Steven Dykes, eds., *File on Mamet,* Metheun, 1991.
    Nesta and Dykes provide a general overview of Mamet's career, including a brief chronology, general synopsis of his major works, and quotes from reviews by a variety of critics on each major work.

Kane, Leslie, ed., *David Mamet: A Casebook,* Garland Publishing, 1992.
    Kane offers a selection of articles by a variety of writers on Mamet's major works. Kane includes a brief chronology of Mamet's life and career, and interviews with actors and others who have worked with Mamet.

McDonough, Carla J., *Staging Masculinity: Male Identity in Contemporary American Drama,* McFarland & Co., 1997.
    McDonough gives a critical analysis of the representations of masculinity in four major American playwrights: Sam Shepard, David Mamet, David Rabe, and August Wilson.

Rites

MAUREEN DUFFY
1969

Rites, by British playwright Maureen Duffy, was first performed in 1969, at the National Theatre Repertory Company in London. The play takes place in a woman's public restroom, and has an all-female cast. The characters are representative working class women of London, including the restroom manager and attendant, three office workers, and two widows in their sixties. The action and dialogue of the play reveal the anger and resentment the women feel toward men in their romantic and sexual relationships, and at work. The play finally erupts in a few moments of frenzied violence in which the women kill someone they believe to be a male spy, only to find that their victim is a woman.

Rites is very loosely based on *The Bacchae,* a play by the ancient Greek dramatist, Euripides, which describes the conflict between the largely female worshipers of the god Dionysus and the male representatives of law and order in the city of Thebes. Like *Rites*, *The Bacchae* culminates in a frenzied killing by a group of women.

Rites was written at a time when the women's liberation movement of the 1960s and 1970s was gathering strength. Like the women's movement, the play exposes the stifling effects on women of gender stereotypes at many levels of society.

AUTHOR BIOGRAPHY

Maureen Duffy was born on October 21, 1933, in Worthing, Sussex, England, the daughter of Cahia Patrick Duffy and Grace Rose Wright. She grew up in an impoverished environment, and at age six, when World War II broke out, she was evacuated with her mother to Trowbridge in Wiltshire. When she was fourteen, she returned to the family home in Stratford, London. After leaving grammar school, Duffy taught for two years at the City Literary Institute, Drury Lane, London, before going to King's College, London. After graduating with a bachelor of arts degree in English, Duffy taught creative writing for five years in state schools.

Since the 1960s, Duffy has distinguished herself as a poet, playwright, novelist, and biographer. Her first play, *The Lay-Off*, was produced at the City of London Festival, 1961, and her first novel, the autobiographical *That's How It Was*, followed in 1962. Her first poetry collection was *Lyrics for the Dog Hour* (1968). This was the first of five volumes of poetry; her *Collected Poems* was published in 1985. Duffy's second play, *The Silk Room*, was produced in England at Watford Civic Theatre in 1966, and *Rites* was produced by the National Theatre Repertory Company in London in 1969. Later plays include *A Nightingale in Bloomsbury Square*, produced at Hampstead Theatre in 1974.

Duffy's novels have won critical praise in the United States as well as Great Britain. Among her major novels are *Wounds* (1969), about two lovers and the emotional pain they experience; *Love Child* (1971), set in Italy with a child narrator; *Housespy*, an espionage thriller (1978); and *Gor Saga* (1981), a fable set in the near future, which critics compared favorably to works by George Orwell and Aldous Huxley. Other novels include *The Microcosm* (1966), about lesbianism; *All Heaven in a Rage* (1973), about animal rights; and *The Paradox Players* (1967), about a writer who seeks isolation on a houseboat on the Thames during a winter in the 1960s.

More recent work includes the novels *Illuminations* (1991), which follows a retired female history lecturer to newly reunified Germany, where she acquires a lesbian lover; and *Occam's Razor* (1993), in which Duffy juxtaposes the history of the terrorist group, the Irish Republican Army, with the activities of the Italian Mafia. Her most recent novel is *Restitution* (1998).

Duffy has also written a work of literary criticism, *The Erotic World of Faery* (1989), and a biography, *The Passionate Shepherdess: The Life of Aphra Behn, 1640–1689* (2000).

Her awards include the City of London Festival Playwright's Award, 1962, for *The Lay-Off*; and a Society of Authors travelling scholarship in 1976. She was a fellow of the Royal Society of Literature in 1985.

Duffy has been active in the causes in which she believes. In 1972, she co-founded the Writers Action Group, which successfully lobbied for the passage of the Public Lending Right, under which authors received royalties from a public fund whenever their work was borrowed from public libraries. Duffy has also been active in animal rights causes.

PLOT SUMMARY

Rites begins with a procession of workmen dressed in white overalls, who construct the walls and cubicles of a public lavatory (the British term for restroom). They then bring in a large mirror, toilet bowls, and cisterns. They bang and hammer away, and this is followed by a sound of simultaneous flushing. The workmen then bring two large chairs, a notice about venereal disease clinics, a sanitary towel machine, and a perfume spray.

Two women enter. Meg begins cleaning, while Ada, the manager of the facility, sits at the mirror and begins putting on her make-up, admiring the results.

As she cleans, Meg complains about her job. She hopes that Ada will get her expected promotion and take her with her, but Ada refuses to promise anything. Ada discusses the man she was with the previous night; it becomes clear that by night she is a prostitute. She spends so much time at the mirror because she wants to make the best of what she has, so that she can charge a higher price.

Meg and Ada turn away an old woman who normally eats her breakfast in one of the cubicles because the woman is too early and they are not yet open. Meg admires Ada for being clever and Ada says she learns what she knows from the financial pages of the newspaper. Meg, however, is more interested in the daily horoscopes and persuades Ada to read some of them to her.

After the old woman returns and goes to the first cubicle to eat, three office girls enter, chattering about the date one of them had the previous night. After using the toilets, the second office girl and Norma complain to Ada about obscene graffiti on the walls. The three girls claim to be shocked and say that only men could have done it.

Meg takes up her knitting; the finished product will be a Christmas gift for a man, and Ada chides her for taking so long to complete it. The conversations continue in a disjointed kind of way. Norma announces that she wants to take the day off work; Ada reads some financial news out loud; Norma recites something from a romance novel she memorized, and Ada responds by talking to Norma about relations between the sexes in terms of assets and takeover bids. The office girls discuss a newspaper advice column and one girl cracks a joke that makes them all scream with laughter.

Nellie and Dot, two respectably dressed women in their sixties, enter. Nellie remarks how she used to clean her husband's shoes every day of their life together. The office girls say they would never do that, but acknowledge how different things were for women of that generation. Norma remarks how terrible it must be to be old. Nellie continues to describe the dull routine she shared with her late husband. As the women talk about baldness, hair and wigs, the office girls get Elizabeth I (who wore a wig) mixed up with another historical figure, Mary Queen of Scots, who was beheaded.

Norma complains about being at the beck and call of her boss, and Ada says she wouldn't stand for it. But the girls say their office jobs are better than being on a factory production line or in the typing pool. Ada proudly says that she works for no man, and Nellie comments that her husband would not allow her to work. Now she and Dot are widowed, but they manage to keep themselves occupied with shopping and other trips. They have their pensions so do not have financial worries, which prompts Norma to remark that it sounds as if they are better off without their husbands. Taking up the topic of men, the first office girl complains that you cannot talk to them, unless they are married.

After more conversation, a girl comes in, buys a towel from the machine and goes to the second cubicle. The women discuss the matter of privacy, and Dot explains that there is more privacy than in the "gents" lavatory and describes how she once went to one.

Maureen Duffy

Two women enter, leading in a toddler boy (who is represented by a realistic doll). The first woman picks him up and makes a fuss of him, while the other women make some observations: Nellie says they grow up too fast, while Ada thinks that some of them never do, and tells the woman that the toddler is too old to be brought into the women's restroom. Meg wonders how Ada knows the toddler is a boy, since according to Nellie he looks more like a girl. They decide to find out. Ada takes down the boy's trousers and his loose, long-legged pants. The women make remarks about his penis, and Ada even alludes to castration, but then they say they mean no harm and are only looking. The two women dress the boy, and Ada bitterly criticizes the others' attitudes toward love and relationships.

There is a crash from the second cubicle. The women ask the girl inside if she is all right, but there is no answer. The third office girl crouches down and looks under the door. The girl inside has her head in the pan, and blood is visible. After some discussion of what they should do, the third office girl climbs up and gets into the cubicle and opens it from the inside. The women haul the girl out and discover that she has cut her wrists, but the damage appears to be superficial. The girl calls out the name of a man and then cries. She has obviously been jilted. Ada shouts "B——men!" and the others follow with their bitter complaints about men.

Except for Ada and the stricken girl, the women then begin to dance the latest version of a dance called the shake. They chant that they do not need men. As they dance, the derelict old woman who has been eating her breakfast in the first cubicle, emerges. The women encircle her and aggressively sing a song called "Knees up Mother Brown." This is repeated until it reaches a frenzy, and the old woman cowers in fear.

Then another figure, dressed like a man, emerges from one of the cubicles and tries to run to the exit. Ada calls him a spy, and all the women, including the old woman who has just been tormented, fall upon the figure. During a violent scuffle, there is a scream and then another cry. The crowd of women breaks apart, revealing a tattered figure wrapped in bloody clothing. Horrified, Norma announces that it was a woman, not a man. The other women are shocked. They decide to stuff the body down the incinerator.

The lavatory gradually empties. The office girls help the injured girl to her feet and leave. Nellie and Dot go back to discussing their hats, and then they leave also. Ada tells the two women with the toddler to leave. Ada then shoos the old woman away and goes back to the mirror and retouches her make-up. Meg resumes her cleaning, and she and Ada continue the kind of conversation they were having when the play began.

CHARACTERS

Ada

Ada is the manager of the public lavatory. She is much concerned with her own appearance, spending a lot of time in front of the mirror putting on make-up. By night she works as a prostitute, and she reasons that the more attractively she can present herself, the higher the price she will be able to charge. She prides herself on her independence, and could not stand to be at the beck and call of a man. She deals with men on her own terms and is contemptuous of them. Ada is worldly wise and well informed. She always studies the financial page of the newspaper and applies to her own profession the marketing advice it provides. She reads a lot and possesses enough general knowledge to correct the office girls when they get Queen Elizabeth I mixed up with Mary Queen of Scots. Ada is also the strongest character in the play, by virtue both of her position as manager and her leadership qualities. It is Ada who initiates the attack on the woman who looks like a man, at which point she reveals the full force of her hatred of men. After the killing, Ada blames the victim for looking like a man. She takes charge of the situation, telling the other women how to dispose of the body and shooing the women out. She then sits down at the table and goes back to doing her make-up.

Dot

Dot is a respectably dressed woman in her sixties. She can hardly be distinguished from her friend Nellie, although Dot speaks much less frequently. Like Nellie, Dot is a widow, but she and Nellie find ways to pass the time and make the best of things. Being a widow has its advantages, since there is no husband around to ask her where all the money has gone. Dot's longest speech is when she describes in detail the occasion she used a men's lavatory. Like Nellie, her marriage followed a traditional pattern. The wife was expected to look after her husband, to minister to him. But it is clear that this was not very fulfilling for Dot, since she says that what makes marriage worthwhile is not the marriage itself but the children.

First Office Girl

First Office Girl is the one with the sense of humor. Several times she makes jokes that produce screams of laughter from the other office girls. Other than that, she is not much different from the others. She shares their disdain for men, believing that it must have been a man who wrote the graffiti on the wall of the cubicle because no woman would do so. She also says you cannot talk to men unless they are married. She likes to think she is independent, saying that, unlike Nellie, no one would catch her cleaning anyone else's boots like Nellie did for her husband. Like the others, she does not like her job but thinks it is better than the alternatives.

First Woman

First Woman is one of two women who enter the lavatory with the toddler boy. She is his mother and dotes on him. She thinks it is a pity he has to grow up. After the women have partially undressed the toddler and examined him, First Woman dresses him. After this, she leaves the boy (represented by a doll) on a chair and joins the group.

Girl

The Girl enters one of the cubicles and slashes her wrists. She is unconscious and bleeding as the other women haul her out. She comes to and calls out the name Desmond, and then cries incoherently. At the end, she is helped out of the lavatory by the three office girls.

Meg

Meg works as a cleaner in the public lavatory. She does not like her job, although she works hard at it and is proud of how clean the place is. She admires and looks up to Ada, who is younger than she, and also her supervisor. She hopes that when Ada gets a promotion, Ada will be able to offer her a new job. Like the other women, Meg does not have a high opinion of men. She says of the toddler, "It's a pity they have to grow up." Meg's marital status is unclear. She may be a widow or divorcee, since she says, cryptically, "I was better off without him." She also says that no one ever wanted her, "except one night behind the gas works and he was a bit simple." Meg is not as sophisticated as Ada; she likes to read the horoscopes in the newspaper and never bothers with the financial news.

Nellie

Nellie, like her friend Dot, is a respectably dressed widow in her sixties. She describes in some detail the predictable routine of her thirty-six-year marriage. She cleaned her husband's shoes every day, always bought him fish on a Friday and cooked it exactly the way he liked it. He would not let her work outside the home, saying he would sooner die than not be able to keep her. Every day she would wait all day at home for him to return from work. Nellie and Dot have adapted well to widowhood, although when Norma suggests they are better off than when they were married, Nellie and Dot both react with horror. Nellie does not care for some things in the modern world, such as the way young people dress, or the fact that young mothers go out to work and put their children in nursery schools. Nellie says that her generation of women were happy to have their children around for as long as possible.

Norma

See Second Office Girl

Old Woman

The Old Woman is a derelict who likes to go to the public lavatory to eat her breakfast. When she comes out of the cubicle, the other women call her Old Mother Brown, and dance around her. She is frightened and holds her bag to her head to protect herself. But when the women attack the figure that looks like a man, the Old Woman also joins in.

Second Office Girl

Norma appears not to share the hostile attitudes to men that most of the other characters have. She is the only one of the office girls to have a regular boyfriend, Eddy. Norma is a romantic, and can quote passages from romance novels, and recite romantic verses she learned at school. She is not wildly in love with Eddy, referring to him as merely "all right," but she appears to have a high level of tolerance for his idiosyncrasies. Norma has a sharp temper, and threatens to scratch Ada's eyes out if Ada speaks to her the way she spoke to one of the other girls. Norma is also squeamish, and the sight of the girl with the bloody wrists makes her feel ill. Like the other girls, she does secretarial work, but is fed up with always having to do what her boss wants.

Second Woman

Second Woman enters with First Woman and the toddler boy. She says little but her negative view of men is clear: she regards them all as babies.

Third Office Girl

Third Office Girl used to work on a factory production line. She prefers her current office job and seems to like it more than the other girls do. She likes the view from the window and the chances they get to laugh and chat when their male boss leaves the room. It is she who climbs into the cubicle where the bleeding girl is, spraining her ankle in the process. She also complains that she got her shoes and her stockings wet. Third Office Girl is the one who near the end of the play sets up the chant "We don't need them," about men.

Third Woman

Third Woman appears only at the end of the play. She emerges from one of the cubicles and rushes to the exit. She has short hair, wears a suit and a coat, and looks like a man. The other women fall on her and kill her.

TOPICS FOR FURTHER STUDY

- Times have changed since Duffy wrote *Rites* in 1969. But how much have they changed? Is there still discrimination against women in employment? If so, what industries or occupations are most affected and what can be done to remedy the situation? (You might want to discuss the concept of the ''glass ceiling,'' which is a more subtle form of discrimination.)

- Does liberation for women mean liberation for men too? In what sense? How have men been changed by the women's movement over the last few decades?

- Ada's opinion about love and marriage is, ''A few moments pleasure and then a lifetime kidding yourself. Caught, bound, even if you don't know it.'' Does this cynical view have a grain of truth in it, from the woman's point of view? Or does Ada's cynicism distort the reality? What would be a succinct, two-sentence formulation that would offer a completely different view of love and marriage? How would such a formulation avoid the sentimental, clichéd view of love that rests on the stereotyping of gender roles?

- As a result of the women's movement, the roles of the sexes have become much more flexible. Has that made it more or less easy to have a successful relationship? In what ways has it made it easier, and in what ways more difficult?

- Is *Rites* a depressing play because the lives depicted seem so sterile and hopeless? Or is it an inspiring play because Duffy has the courage to depict the lives of the women of a certain social class as they are, without sentimentality or false optimism?

THEMES

Feminism and Gender Stereotypes

At the heart of the play is the idea of gender stereotyping, in which the roles and attitudes of the sexes follow highly predictable patterns. Since it is men who set the rules and design them for their own advantage, this breeds frustration, resentment, and ultimately murderous rage in the women who congregate at the public lavatory. The negative picture presented of men is almost unrelenting, and includes the world of work, sex, relationships, and the home.

The office girls, for example, have dull, repetitive jobs in which they are at the beck and call of male bosses. But their minds are so impoverished, so crushed by the accepted notions of what women can do, that they have no ideas about what else they might aspire to. All they know is that the jobs they do have are better than the available alternatives, such as working on a factory production line. Being aware of one's dissatisfaction but lacking the capacity to imagine anything better is a recipe for frustration and a stunted life.

Norma's best solution, inspired by television advertising, is simply to take the day off and go to the beach. She and the other girls are lulled by the sentimental clichés fed to them by the male-dominated culture and also by the harmless diversions they are offered. Norma soaks up the soft pornography of romance novels that are aimed at women by the publishing industry, and the girls also lap up the conventional, moralistic advice about relationships with men that are offered to them by newspaper advice columns. The treachery of men is somehow enshrined and made harmless in little romantic rhymes that Norma learned at school. That is, until one of the office girls describes the reality of a man's attitude to her as a young, single woman: ''You're all right till you're stuck with a kid then they don't want to know.''

Men are presented through the eyes of the women as nothing more than big babies who are obsessed with sex. Pornography and sexual perversions are the realm of men. "Only men, only men, only men do that," chant the office girls in unison. And when the first office girl discovers the obscene graffiti on the cubicle walls, she assumes it must have been written by a man because no decent woman would write such things. The stereotypes conveyed are that men just want sex, whereas women want romance and family.

From the point of view of the females in this play, men are selfish when it comes to sex, and their performance also leaves much to be desired. "Eddy always falls dead asleep after," says Norma, and Dot thinks of the male orgasm as "only like a sneeze, when all's said and done."

Men in their turn have a low opinion of women's intelligence, at least according to Ada, who, as she studies the financial pages of the newspaper, says contemptuously, "They think we don't read that far." The "they" in question are the men who produce the newspapers. The underlying stereotype is that the realm of business and finance belongs to men; women are content with the "women's pages" that discuss clothes, recipes, relationships, and the like.

The gender roles of the older generation, as represented by Nellie and Dot, are similarly fixed in stone. Men go to work; women wait all day for them to come home, occupying themselves, in the opinion of one of the office girls, sweeping and tidying and washing. The role of the wife is simply to make her husband comfortable, never to point out his faults or hurt his pride. Everything follows a predictable routine. Now widowed, Nellie and Dot seem in some respects to have more rewarding lives than they did when they were married. Although they do not have any directly unkind words to say about their dead husbands, they do let slip the fact that now there is no one to dock their housekeeping money after a bad week, or to ask where all the money has gone.

The younger generation of women feel the same pressure to conform to long-established roles. Women must defer to men. If a man steps on a woman's feet as they dance, says one office girl, she is the one who apologizes. The man's masculine pride must not be threatened.

Gender stereotypes emerge again when the girl with the slashed wrists is discovered. Nellie immediately says they must call a man because a man will be able to break the door down. Second Woman wants to get a policeman. The underlying stereotype is that in a crisis, you need a man. But Ada will not hear of this, and the women manage to solve the problem well enough on their own; brute strength is not always needed.

The gender stereotypes permeate society at all levels and are constantly reinforced. They can be found, for example, in the words of the nineteenth-century nursery rhyme that the women quote: little girls are made of "Sugar and spice and all things nice," whereas little boys are made of "Sni ps and snails and puppy dogs' tails."

Everything points to a rigid segregation of society along gender lines, and the relationship between the sexes is one of antagonism. This is learned in childhood, as the first office girl makes clear: "Like in the playground, boys against girls. Them onto us."

The segregated public lavatories, in which the men's lavatory is an unknown, mysterious place to the women, thus becomes a metaphor for the basic divisions in society. "It's time he stuck to his own side of the fence," says Meg of the toddler boy who has been brought by his mother to the lavatory.

Given the resentment that women in the play feel toward men—which is most exemplified in Ada—the outrage and madness that takes hold of them when they see what they think is a man emerging from one of the cubicles is not so surprising. The women's lavatory is their domain; it is one of the few places where women can be in control. The invasion of their private space is likely to provoke a violent response.

But the play does not endorse the women's violence. Since their victim turns out to be a woman, this suggests that mindlessly attacking men, or what men represent, will only hurt women, too. Duffy says as much in her introduction to the play:

> In the very moment when the women have got their own back on men for their type-casting in an orgasm of violence they find they have destroyed themselves and in death there is certainly no difference.

STYLE

Language

The language of the play reveals the characters to be working class women from London or the

London suburbs. This is apparent from a number of ungrammatical expressions. The clearest example is Ada, who says, "I've stuck me pencil in me eye"; the "me" is a nonstandard version of "my." The characters use many slang expressions, some of which may be unfamiliar to American ears. "Copped," as in "copped the whole roll" means seized or stolen. "French letter" is British slang for a condom; a "conker," as in Nellie's comment that her husband's shoes "shone like conkers" is the fruit of the horse chestnut tree. In the fall, British schoolchildren play a game called conkers with these fruits. "Bloke" is working class slang for man, the equivalent of the American use of "guy." It is more common in southern than northern England.

Realism and Fantasy

Duffy commented in her introduction that the play was deliberately "pitched between fantasy and naturalism." The public lavatory in which the play is set is "as real as in a vivid dream."

The realistic elements in the play are many and include the setting. This kind of public lavatory, with its malfunctioning toilets, graffiti-covered walls, and lingering derelict, can be found in most cities. The relationships between the characters, such as Ada and Meg (Meg's admiration of Ada; Ada's slightly amused tolerance of Meg), form another realistic element. The three office girls, with their superficial banter, will be familiar to anyone who has worked in a London office. There is realism too in the mundane things the characters discuss, the clichés they use, and the fully believable kinds of lives they describe. The incident in which the girl slashes her wrists is also grimly realistic.

To that naturalism, Duffy adds some fantastic elements: the incinerator for the sanitary towels, for example, which Meg imagines she can hear roaring like a "great furnace, a wild beast." Fantastic too is how the women dispose of the body of the woman they have killed by cramming it into the steel flap that opens into the incinerator.

Another fantastic element is the toddler boy represented by a doll, the masculine-looking woman who is attacked and killed, and the wild frenzy that takes hold of these otherwise very ordinary women as they commit their deadly act.

The result of the skillful combination of fantasy and naturalism is an unusual concoction that serves as an example of Aristotle's remark, quoted by Duffy in her introduction: "For poetic (i.e., artistic) effect a convincing impossibility is preferable to that which is unconvincing though possible."

HISTORICAL CONTEXT

The Women's Movement in Britain

When Duffy wrote *Rites* in 1969, the modern women's movement in Britain was just beginning to make an impact. This was a period of rapid social change; economic growth meant that women were entering the workforce in increasing numbers, and there was an expansion in higher education that led to increased job opportunities and higher expectations on the part of women. The emerging women's liberation movement, as it was known, campaigned for equal pay and equal opportunity in education and employment; abortion rights; day care; free contraception (through what was popularly known as "the pill"); and an end to sexism, gender stereotyping, domestic violence, and discrimination against lesbians.

Much of the women's movement was organized in local, women-only groups that linked with others through newsletters and national conferences. The First National Women's Liberation Conference was held in Oxford in 1970. In 1971, the biggest ever women's march took place in London.

The emphasis in the women's movement was on "consciousness-raising" (sharing ideas about women's experiences), direct action in support of causes, and women's self-help. In keeping with the popular feminist slogan, "the personal is the political," women examined their own private lives, including attitudes about reproduction and sexual expression, since many believed that the root of the subordination of women was in these areas of personal life.

In 1970, Germaine Greer, an Australian feminist living in England, published *The Female Eunuch,* which argued that patriarchal social structures, in alliance with capitalism, had forced women into stereotypical, subordinate roles. Greer advocated sexual liberation as a way for women to break out of this male-imposed straitjacket. The book became a highly influential best-seller.

The women's movement had some quick successes in Britain. In 1967, abortion was legalized under certain conditions. The Equal Pay Act of 1970 established the principle of equal pay for equal

COMPARE
&
CONTRAST

- **1960s:** In the United States, median female earnings relative to median male earnings is about sixty percent. In Britain in 1970, the figure is about sixty-five percent. However, the passing of equal opportunity laws in the mid-1960s lays the basis for an improvement in women's earnings and the widening of their career opportunities. The effects of these developments, in both Britain and the United States, will not be felt until the mid-1970s.

  Today: Economic inequalities relating to gender remain significant. According to the U.S. Census Bureau, the median earnings of women fifteen years and over who worked full-time in 1999 is $26,300, which is seventy-two percent of the median earnings of men ($36,500). In Britain, women's earnings are eighty-one percent of men's, but women working part-time (which amounts to over half of the women in paid employment) earn less than sixty percent of what men earn.

- **1960s:** In the United States in the late 1960s, eighteen percent of female high school graduates are completing at least four years of college, compared to twenty-six percent of men. In Britain in 1963, only a quarter of the undergraduates are female.

  Today: In Britain, more than half of the undergraduates are female. Similarly, in the United

States, women now make up the majority of students in colleges and universities. Women also receive more master's degrees than men and are entering business and law schools in record numbers.

- **1960s:** In the early 1960s, on both sides of the Atlantic, the image of women presented in the media and accepted in the culture as a whole is that they are passive and noncompetitive. Women are considered best suited to domestic work and caring for a family, or being in one of the caring professions such as nursing or school teaching. There are also fewer opportunities for women to play sports, particularly sports that are traditionally practiced only by men. Strength and athletic skill in women are regarded by some as unfeminine.

  Today: New definitions of femininity include physical strength and fitness. Women take up sports such as weightlifting in increasing numbers, for fitness and competition. They also compete in aggressive contact sports such as boxing, wrestling, and the martial arts. In the United States, for example, in 1999, 2,361 girls compete in high school wrestling, up from 132 in 1991. In 2001, the International Olympic Committee gives its approval for adding women's wrestling to the 2004 Olympics. In Britain in 1998, the British Boxing Board sanctions professional women's boxing for the first time.

---

work. In 1975, the Sex Discrimination Act outlawed discrimination on the grounds of sex or marital status and established the Equal Opportunities Commission. Women also gained the right to maternity leave.

The women's movement also had an impact in the arts. One of the reasons Duffy wrote *Rites* was to provide more opportunities for women in the theatre. She was encouraged by the eminent actress, Dame Joan Plowright, who was aware of the

lack of contemporary roles for actresses. Duffy's groundbreaking work was followed by that of Caryl Churchill. Churchill began writing radio plays with socialist and feminist themes in the 1960s. Her first professional stage production was *The Owners,* produced at the Royal Court Theatre in 1972, and she went on to become Britain's leading contemporary woman playwright. Other developments that provided more opportunities for women in the writing and performing of contemporary drama were the formation of the Joint Stock Theatre Group in

1974, and Monstrous Regiment, a theater collective, in 1975.

CRITICAL OVERVIEW

Rites received less attention from reviewers than Duffy's novels from the same period, such as *Wounds* (1969) and *Love Child* (1971). In general, Duffy's work in the theatre has been overshadowed by her achievements in other forms, including nonfiction as well as fiction. However, *Rites* has attracted attention from a number of feminist scholars. In her collection of essays on lesbian writers, Jane Rule's judgment of *Rites* is somewhat negative. She argues that the play "reduces people to objects, stereotypes of all the ugliness of heterosexual women whose revenge is ultimately self-destruction. . . . It is hard to escape feeling an indictment against women, rather than simply against labels."

Elizabeth Hale Winkler, in "Three Recent Versions of the *Bacchae*," discusses *Rites* in terms of the play that inspired it, Euripides's *The Bacchae*. She reaches the conclusion that Duffy's "overall conclusions are decidedly negative." Winkler points out that although Duffy critiques the stereotyping of gender roles, she does not point to any positive alternative. There are no female role models in the play. This is in contrast, Winkler argues, to another modern play that also revises *The Bacchae, A Mouthful of Birds* (1986) by Caryl Churchill and David Lan. That play, in addition to portraying the insanity and violence, also looks at the "more positive possibilities of solidarity, possessive madness, pleasure, and even ecstasy" that are suggested by *The Bacchae*.

Lynda Hart, in "Introduction: Performing Feminism" (in *Making a Spectacle: Feminist Essays on Contemporary Women's Theatre*) draws attention to the beginning of the play, in which workmen silently construct the set that is to represent the women's lavatory. She calls this a "slow and deliberate pantomime," and likens it to the theatrical convention of the dumb-show. She argues that the dumb-show device reminds the audience that the space within which the all-female cast act out their drama is created by men: "The ladies room is far from being a liberated space; on the contrary, it is a privilege designed to distort women's action."

CRITICISM

Bryan Aubrey

Aubrey holds a Ph.D. in English and has published many articles on twentieth-century literature. In this essay, Aubrey discusses Rites *as a creative reworking of* The Bacchae, *a play by the ancient Greek dramatist, Euripides.*

The title of *Rites* is taken from the play *The Bacchae,* written shortly before 406 B.C.E. by the ancient Greek dramatist Euripides. In addition to the title, there are parallels in plot and theme between *Rites* and *The Bacchae,* as well as some allusions and reversals. Duffy takes care to point out in her introduction to the play that *Rites* is not a version of *The Bacchae,* and that "no attempt was made to make it conform to that play." But she adds that the ancient text does add another layer of meaning to her own play, and makes it less likely that people will dismiss *Rites* as merely shocking or no more consequential than a dream.

The Bacchae revolves around a conflict between Dionysus, the god of wine, revelry and ecstasy, and Pentheus, the king of Thebes. When Dionysus begins to attract many followers in Thebes, Pentheus tries to stamp out the worship of this new god. He imprisons all the women whom he catches carrying the symbols of the god: wine, an ivy wreath, and a staff. Pentheus also captures Dionysus, who takes human form as a handsome young man. Miraculously, all the women who had been imprisoned suddenly find themselves free, and they continue their Bacchic worship in a glen just outside the city.

Pentheus then imprisons Dionysus, who warns the king that he will bring destruction on himself. Soon after his imprisonment, Dionysus conjures up an earthquake, and Pentheus's palace is reduced to ruins. Astonished, Pentheus interrogates the freed Dionysus, but a herdsman interrupts him. The herdsman tells Pentheus that Agave, Pentheus's mother, and a group of her fellow bacchantes are on a nearby mountain, celebrating the god. Dionysus, who seeks revenge on Pentheus, asks the king if he wishes to see the women at their secret rites. When Pentheus says that he does, Dionysus takes control of his mind and tricks him into disguising himself by dressing in women's clothes.

On the mountain, Pentheus sits in a tall tree to observe the women, but he is easily spotted by the bacchantes, who have been warned by Dionysus

WHAT DO I READ NEXT?

- Duffy's first novel, the autobiographical *That's How It Was* (1962), has been called one of the few authentic accounts in British fiction of a working class childhood. The novel focuses on the relationships between the protagonist and her mother, stepbrothers, school friends, and a schoolteacher.

- Betty Friedan's *The Feminine Mystique* (1963) was one of the seminal works of 1960s feminism, awakening a whole generation of women to new insights into themselves and their roles in society.

- Sylvia Plath's autobiographical novel *The Bell Jar* (1963) describes the stereotyping of women's roles as discovered by a young woman who works as an intern at a magazine in New York City in the early 1950s. The focus of the story is the woman's mental breakdown that results in a suicide attempt.

- *The Awakening* (1899), by Kate Chopin, is an early example of an emerging feminist consciousness. Set in New Orleans, it tells the story of a young woman as she awakens to psychological and sexual consciousness.

- Like *Rites, A Mouthful of Birds* (1986), a play by Caryl Churchill and David Lan, is a revision of Euripides's *The Bacchae* in a modern setting. The playwrights set out to examine issues of possession, violence, and ecstasy.

that an enemy is at hand. Led by Agave, the women attack Pentheus in a wild frenzy, tearing him limb from limb. Agave is so blinded by her frenzy that she thinks Pentheus is a mountain lion. After Pentheus's dismembered body is returned to Thebes, Agave recovers from her mad frenzy and is horrified at her murderous deed. Dionysus returns and exiles Agave and her sisters from the city.

The central conflict in *The Bacchae* is between two aspects of human nature. On the one side is the desire for order, rationality, law, decorum, restraint, and morality. All these qualities are represented by Pentheus, the king of Thebes. He feels that it is his duty to preserve the city from what he sees as the disruptive influence of the bacchantes. The other side of human nature is the nonrational dimension. It includes sensuality, the abandonment of limits, a sense of oneness with nature, spontaneity, joy, celebration, and intoxication through wine and dance. This is represented by Dionysus.

The Bacchae shows what happens when this primordial, ecstatic Dionysian energy, which is an essential component of the human condition, is ignored or suppressed. The play also shows the harm that results when it is pursued to excess. In *The Bacchae,* there is no happy medium, no path of moderation.

In *Rites,* the equivalent of the Bacchic rites of the women of Thebes are the activities of the women in the public lavatory. The lavatory is a female space that men are not allowed to penetrate, just as the bacchantes act out their ritual worship of Dionysus in an exclusively female group on the mountain. In *Rites,* the equivalent of Pentheus, who claims to abhor what the women are doing but nonetheless jumps at the chance to see their secret rites for himself, is not any of the characters but rather the audience. There is, as Duffy points out in her introduction, a voyeur in everyone: "We should all like to be able to eavesdrop, to know how people behave alone or in groups when they can really be themselves. . . . Like Pentheus, we want to be shocked and pained."

There is, needless to say, a marked contrast between the rites of the bacchantes and the rites of this group of working class women in 1960s Britain. As Elizabeth Hale Winkler, in "Three Recent Versions of the *Bacchae*," comments:

> ADA ESCAPES THE FATE OF AGAVE, WHO IS EXILED FOR HER CRIME, BUT THERE IS NO DOUBT THAT SHE IS CULPABLE. HER HATRED AND RAGE LEAD HER INTO THE KILLING OF AN INNOCENT."

Instead of the ecstatic night-time dances on the mountains ... we find only women engaging in empty, trivial secular rituals such as putting on their make-up in the morning, gossiping about unsatisfactory sex with their boyfriends and singing snatches of banal popular love songs.

If the bacchantes are full of life and a kind of divine madness (not all of which is destructive), the women in *Rites* are condemned to live stunted lives in settings that are defined for them by men. Their "rites" are exemplified at the beginning and end of the play, when Ada engages in her daily ritual of putting on her make-up with great vulgarity—she repeatedly spits into her pot of mascara and then puts her finger in it—and vainly admiring herself.

It is Ada who is the central figure in *Rites*; she is the equivalent of Agave in *The Bacchae* (although in that play Pentheus and Dionysus are the central characters; Agave does not appear directly until near the end). Just as Agave is the priestess of the bacchantes, so the strong-minded Ada is the "priestess" of the public lavatory. As the manager of the facility, she is the one in charge; she decides what is permitted there and what is not. Meg, the attendant and cleaner, treats her with deference.

In *The Bacchae,* it is Agave who initiates the murderous attack on Pentheus, and so in *Rites* it is Ada who incites the women in the lavatory to kill the masculine-looking person they assume is a male spy. Of course, there are differences between the two incidents. In *The Bacchae,* Pentheus really does intend to spy on the women, but the figure who is killed in *Rites* has no such intention. In *The Bacchae,* a man is dressed as a woman; in the ironic reversal in *Rites*, the victim is a woman who dresses like a man. In both cases, however, the situation is one of mistaken identity, and the result is a crazed mob killing. Ada is blinded by her own hatred of men,

just as Agave and the bacchantes are blinded by their mad, reason-obliterating frenzy.

There is another parallel between Agave and Ada that goes to the heart of Duffy's purpose. They are both, as Duffy points out in her introduction, deniers of life. Although Agave is a reveling bacchante, celebrating the god, she has been made so by Dionysus as a punishment for her earlier refusal to acknowledge him as a god. Agave refused to accept that Semele, her sister, had conceived Dionysus as a result of a visitation by the god Zeus. Seen in this light, Pentheus, who also denies that Dionysus is a god, is only repeating an attitude that at first was shared by his mother.

Ada, who is a more developed character than Agave, denies life by reducing sex, the life force itself, to a matter of money. Her contempt for men (whatever men may do to deserve it notwithstanding) has distorted her perceptions and given her a desire for revenge. During the course of the play, her statements about men become increasingly savage and cynical, and her anger is also directed at the women who accept the unacceptable: "I'll tell you about your kind of love: a few moments pleasure and then a lifetime kidding yourself. Caught, bound, even if you don't know it." After the girl who has cut her wrists breaks down in tears, Ada shouts with venom "B———men!" a cry she will repeat twice more before the end of the play, and launches into her bitterest tirade yet. At this point, Ada is boiling with a rage that makes her, like Agave, quite mad. She is like a volcano about to explode, and her words after the murder, as she gazes at the corpse, are chilling: "Look at it! I've seen prettier in the butcher's shop. Animals. B———men."

Ada escapes the fate of Agave, who is exiled for her crime, but there is no doubt that she is culpable. Her hatred and rage lead her into the killing of an innocent. But this is not to deny that the play is also an indictment of a patriarchal society that oppresses women, pushing them into a limited range of roles, and so creating the kind of frustration which builds up until violence results.

This pervasive sense of female oppression by men finds a parallel in *The Bacchae.* The bacchantes are mostly women. Their actions in leaving the city and celebrating Dionysus in the forests and mountains are acts of freedom committed in rebellion against a male-dominated society. This society is exemplified by Pentheus. Not only is he intolerant, authoritarian, and dictatorial, he is also a misogynist. His reaction to anyone who opposes him is to imprison them. He has already imprisoned many women, literally tying their hands. He threatens that when he catches the other bacchantes who are threatening his idea of ideal social order (and his power), he will sell them into slavery or make them work the looms in his palace.

In *Rites*, this is translated into modern terms. Women such as Nellie and Dot tell how they were confined to domestic chores throughout their marriage, and the other women are in a prison of limited opportunities that confines them to low-status jobs that amount to a kind of slavery. On the evidence of the play, the only freedom available for a woman of their social class is to transgress commonly accepted sexual mores and become a prostitute, like Ada. Ada claims that she is independent and free, largely because she ensures that it is she, not the man, who sets the terms of their sexual encounters. But by anyone's standards, that is a poor definition of freedom, not even coming close to the liberating joy of the bacchantes in the positive aspects of their Dionysian celebrations.

There is one more parallel between *Rites* and *The Bacchae* and one significant departure. Dionysus, who plays such a large role in *The Bacchae*, appears in *Rites* only as the toddler doll. Duffy explains in her introduction: "I would not have used a real child for Dionysus if I could have had one. A doll is at once more terrifying, more enigmatic and more appropriate, artistically, to the dream idiom." Dionysus in *The Bacchae* has long curly hair and an androgynous appearance, and this is also true of the doll in *Rites*. The women cannot tell whether he is a boy or a girl until they undress him and examine his genitals.

Finally, in ancient Greek drama violence is never shown on stage. The conclusion of *The Bacchae* is therefore reported by a character who witnessed it. The audience does not see it directly. However, dramatic conventions have changed since that time, and Duffy presents the violence in full view of the audience. It is meant to be disturbing, as the stage directions, referring to a "tattered and broken figure wrapped in bloody clothing," clearly suggest. *Rites*, then, may be more shocking than its ancient original, and not only for its violence. It presents an indictment of patriarchy but offers no way beyond it, pointing only to the resulting female rage that harms women and accomplishes nothing. Significantly, the play ends where it began, the mundane "rites" go on—but something terrible has hap-

pened in the meantime, and who is to say that it may not happen again?

Source: Bryan Aubrey, Critical Essay on *Rites,* in *Drama for Students,* The Gale Group, 2002.

SOURCES

Duffy, Maureen, *Rites,* in *Plays by and about Women,* edited by Victoria Sullivan and James Hatch, Vintage Books, 1974.

Hart, Lynda, ed., *Making a Spectacle: Feminist Essays on Contemporary Women's Theatre,* University of Michigan Press, 1988, pp. 9–10.

Rule, Jane, *Lesbian Images,* Crossing Press, 1982, pp. 175–82.

Winkler, Elizabeth Hale, "Three Recent Versions of the *Bacchae,*" in *Madness in Drama,* edited by James Redmond, Cambridge University Press, 1993, pp. 217–28.

FURTHER READING

Brater, Enoch, ed., *Feminine Focus: The New Women Playwrights,* Oxford University Press, 1989.
    The sixteen essays in this collection examine the work of contemporary women playwrights from a variety of angles. Katherine Worth, in "Images of Women in Modern English Theater," comments on Duffy's *Rites*.

Hennegan, Alison, "Maureen Duffy," in *New Statesman,* April 17, 1987, pp. 20–21.
    This is an interview with Duffy in which she discusses her novel, *Change* (1987). She also mentions that she started to write novels only because of the difficulty she encountered getting her plays produced.

Hersh, Allison, "'How Sweet the Kill': Orgiastic Female Violence in Contemporary Re-Visions of Euripides's *The Bacchae,*" in *Modern Drama,* Vol. 35, No. 3, September 1992, pp. 409–23.
    Hersh examines *Rites* and Caryl Churchill's *A Mouthful of Birds* in terms of how they re-present Euripides's *The Bacchae* in a different historical context.

Itzen, Catherine, *Stages in the Revolution: Political Theatre in Britain Since 1968,* Methuen, 1980.
    Itzen examines the history of alternative theatre in Britain since 1968. Alternative theatre refers to small groups that perform in community theatres rather than large commercial ones. Plays performed often have a left-wing political orientation.

Rieger, Branimir, ed., *Dionysus in Literature: Essays on Literary Madness,* Bowling Green State University Popular Press, 1994.
    This is a collection of sixteen essays that examine madness in literature from a wide variety of critical approaches.

Wandor, Michelene, *Carry on Understudies: Theatre and Sexual Politics,* Routledge and Kegan Paul, 1986.

This is a study of British women's theatre from a feminist perspective. Wandor discusses the difficulties faced by women directors, given the fact that authority and leadership have usually been seen as male characteristics.

The Rivals

RICHARD BRINSLEY SHERIDAN

1775

The Rivals, a comedy in five acts, established Richard Brinsley Sheridan's reputation in the London theatre in 1775. When the first performance was not well received, Sheridan cut it by an hour, strengthened the idiosyncratic characters, and produced the new version in a highly successful second performance that proved his merit as a great comic playwright. *The Rivals* is one of a small handful of eighteenth-century plays that continues to be produced to this day. While the plot is complex, the characters are stock comic caricatures of human folly, aptly named.

A Comedy of Manners, the play satirizes sentimentalism and sophisticated pretensions, without the typical eighteenth-century moralizing. The dialogue crackles with wit even today, over two hundred years after it was first penned. This play is the source of the term ''malapropism,'' named for Mrs. Malaprop, whose delightful ''derangement of epitaphs'' consists of using sophisticated-sounding words incorrectly. *The Rivals* is an example of what Oliver Goldsmith called in his 1773 ''An Essay on the Theatre,'' ''laughing comedy,'' in contrast with the ''weeping sentimental comedy'' that dished out heavy handed moralizing in every act. Sheridan wrote his most theatrical works, including the more well-known *The School for Scandal* during the five-year period at the beginning of his career. He went on to manage the Drury Lane Theatre for nearly thirty years and to pursue a successful career in politics, becoming famous for his oratorical abilities.

AUTHOR BIOGRAPHY

Richard Brinsley Sheridan was born in Dublin, Ireland, on January 25, 1751. His father was an actor and teacher of elocution, while his mother was a writer with several novels published. Richard studied at Harrow, an elite private school in Dublin, where he was initially looked down upon as a ''player's son'' (at the time, actors, or players, were generally held in low esteem). When Richard was twenty-one, his father took the family to the resort town of Bath, where the would-be playwright fell in love. He fought two duels over the young and beautiful Elizabeth Linley, ''the siren of Bath,'' a singer and daughter of a composer who organized concerts. The couple eloped and moved to London so that Richard could pursue a career in playwriting. He would remain in London the rest of his life, but his marriage would suffer from many infidelities.

The Rivals, his first work of any note, was first produced on January 17, 1775, at the London Theatre in Covent Garden. The story contains stock characters, and is based roughly on his elopement with and duels over Miss Linley. After a major revision to correct serious flaws, the second performance, on January 28, of *The Rivals* proved a hit, establishing Sheridan's career. Riding on this success, he, his father-in-law, and two other investors, purchased a half-ownership in the Drury Lane Theatre in 1776, which they turned into a full ownership in 1778. Sheridan produced *The School for Scandal* and became manager of the Drury in 1777, a position he held until the theater burned down in 1809. Drury Lane thrived under Sheridan's direction, despite his dissolute habits and inability to manage the financial side of the business. Sheridan preferred spending time with members of the Literary Club (established 1764), including Samuel Johnson who was the author of the 1755 English dictionary, theatre actor/director David Garrick, and statesman Edmund Burke, as well as fellow playwright Oliver Goldsmith.

In 1780, Sheridan decided to enter into politics, establishing a career in Parliament that would span thirty years until 1812 and earn him immense respect. However, his beginning was inauspicious; he essentially bought his way into a position as a Whig M. P., and then had to defend himself of the charge of bribery as his first order of business. His skills in oratory acquitted him of dishonor, and over the years, he earned a reputation as the finest orator of his time. His political interests lay in defending the French Revolution and the cause of American Colonists, trying in vain to prevent the Revolutionary War in America. A grateful American Congress awarded him 20,000 pounds for his support, but he refused it, even though he was deeply in debt.

In 1792, Elizabeth died of tuberculosis. Three years later, Sheridan married Esther Hecca, whose spendthrift ways along with his own feckless habits put him further into debt. The burning of the Drury Lane Theatre pushed him beyond the point of recovery. He was imprisoned for debt in 1813 and died destitute in 1816, although his wealthy friends gave him an extravagant funeral.

PLOT SUMMARY

Act 1

The Rivals opens with two old friends happening upon each other in Bath. Fag, servant to Captain Jack Absolute (who is masquerading as Ensign Beverley for the sake of a love affair) catches up with David, coachman to Sir Anthony Absolute, Jack's father, thus introducing some of the characters to come. In the next scene, Lucy returns from a trip to the local circulating libraries laden with romantic novels for her mistress, Lydia Languish. It is because Lydia wants a love affair like those in her romance stories that Jack Absolute has adopted a reduced title and new name.

Lydia reveals to her friend Julia Melville that her aunt, Mrs. Malaprop, has confined her to her rooms after discovering Lydia's secret passion for Beverley. Julia is in love with Faulkland, whom Lydia calls jealous, for his possessiveness of Julia. Mrs. Malaprop and Sir Anthony Absolute enter and chide Lydia to forget Beverley. When she refuses, Mrs. Malaprop sends her to her room, whereupon the pair agree that severity is the best method of childrearing. Sir Anthony wants his son to marry Lydia, and he suggests locking Lydia in her room and withholding her dinner for a few days to obtain her compliance. Mrs. Malaprop, her speeches thick with misused, pretentious words, agrees to an initial visit, for she would like to be freed of her niece so she can pursue her own affair with Sir Lucius O'Trigger. Act 1 ends with Lucy, Julia's maid, tallying up the many trifles she has earned by acting as a go-between and informer for all of the lovers.

Act 2

In parallel to Lydia and Julia, now Jack Absolute and Faulkland discuss their love affairs. Jack accuses Faulkland of being a "teasing, captious, incorrigible lover" for constantly doubting Julia's loyalty and love. Bob Acres, spurned suitor to Lydia, enters and pitches Faulkland into yet another fit of jealous despair by relating how Julia has entertained the Bath social circle with her singing of "My heart's my own, my will is free" and with her carefree country dancing. Acres, a provincial country bumpkin, brags to Jack and Faulkland that he shall win Lydia back from Ensign Beverley with his improved dress and hairstyle. He also takes pride in a "genteel" style of "sentimental swearing" that marks him as an oaf. Servant Fag announces the arrival of Jack's preemptory father, Sir Anthony, who informs Jack that he intends to confer a sizeable estate upon him, conditional to accepting an arranged marriage. Jack demurs politely, saying that his "heart is engaged to an angel." Sir Anthony leaves fuming. In a brief scene, Lucy delivers a love letter to Sir Lucius O'Trigger. She does not inform him that its real author is Mrs. Malaprop, not her niece Lydia. Before going, Sir Lucius makes a pass at Lucy. Moments later, she tells Fag of Sir Anthony's choice of a wife for Jack: Lydia Languish. Fag goes off gleefully to inform his master of the good news.

Act 3

Now that Jack knows he is being forced to marry the girl he loves, he plays repentance and wins his father's shocked approval. Faulkland confronts Julia with his paranoid fears and after several attempts at reassurance, she exits in tears. Too late, Faulkland recognizes his folly. Captain Absolute presents himself to Mrs. Malaprop, who does not guess his dual identity with Ensign Beverley. In a comic scene, she shows him his own letter to Lydia, and he feigns disgust at Beverley's rude remarks about the vigilant aunt. When she then spies on his supposed first meeting with Lydia, she fails to recognize Lydia's delight at seeing her lover in the "disguise" of his true identity. Lydia infuriates her aunt by continuing to profess her love for Beverley, in plain hearing of Jack Absolute, who calmly pretends not to be jealous of his other self.

In another scene, Sir Lucius interrupts Acres capering about in new clothes, practicing his dance lessons. Sir Lucius manages to convince Acres to challenge Absolute to a duel, to defend his honor and vaguely, to "prevent any misunderstanding." Sir Lucius has to help Acres write the challenge, but

Richard Brinsley Sheridan

claims to have another duel to fight and so cannot attend Acres's battle.

Act 4

Bob's servant David tries to deflate his master's enthusiasm for the fight with a healthy dose of reality, but Acres remains steadfast. Absolute offers his support but pleads out of acting as Bob's second, which, of course, would be impossible since he is also Bob's opponent, Beverley. Jack promises to warn Beverley that "Fighting Bob" is in a "devouring rage." In another short scene, Lydia assures Mrs. Malaprop that she will give no encouragement to Captain Absolute, hoping to prolong the charade of Beverley's "true" identity. Now the recognition scene takes place, as suddenly, Sir Anthony arrives with Jack Absolute in tow. His arrival is a volatile situation since Lydia still does not know that Absolute *is* Beverley. Jack approaches Lydia, who luckily sits with her face averted in an attempt to rebuff him. At first he cannot speak, then he modifies his voice to an awkward croak, which infuriates his father. Finally, he reveals himself to a shocked Lydia. At first, Mrs. Malaprop and Sir Anthony consider Lydia mad for insisting that this is Beverley, then in a hilarious moment, Sir Anthony accuses Jack of not being his son. Lydia sulks in realization that the two are one man, and that means—no elopement; her romantic bubble has burst. Jack's bubble has burst as well, since Mrs. Malaprop realizes that it was Jack who called her an ''old weather-beaten she dragon'' and Sir Anthony marvels at his son's roguish ingenuity. He sings and dances in delight, promoting forgiveness.

Jack realizes that Lydia has not joined in the general celebration, still brooding over the death of her romantic dream. When she lashes out at him for his role in the ruse, he praises her spirit, and she begins to sob. Mrs. Malaprop thinks the couple is ''billing and cooing'' and Sir Anthony mistakes Lydia's tears as evidence of his son's impatient blood, a trait, he proudly says, runs in his family. Sir Lucius provokes a quarrel with Jack and they arrange to duel at the same location that Acres plans to meet with Jack. Faulkland receives a letter from Julia asking to meet right away, and Jack upbraids his friend for failing to understand he's been given a second chance. Jack is correct: Faulkland decides to test her sincerity yet again, using the duel as a ruse.

Act 5

In the first scene of the final act, Julia is confronted by Faulkland claiming the necessity to leave the country for his life. True to her nature, Julia commits to accompany him, not even knowing the nature of the threat. Overwhelmed by her response, Faulkland forgets to depart, admits the ruse, and enrages Julia for trifling with her sincerity. She now sees that he will never be capable of confidence in love, so she leaves him, professing never to love again. Now, Faulkland truly understands the error of his constant doubts, and he sinks in remorse. In the meantime, Lydia's heart has softened, and when Julia tells her sad story, Lydia seems ready to accept the new, less romantic, terms of her love affair with Absolute. Suddenly, Mrs. Malaprop and the two servants David and Fag arrive, hoping to interrupt the duel in time, although Mrs. Malaprop's circuitous style of speaking delays their message being understood by the two young ladies. Eventually, all is clear, and they exit to find the field of battle.

In the meantime, Jack bumps into Sir Anthony, the last person he wants to see when he is on his way to a duel. His nervousness nearly gives him away, but when his sword falls from under his coat, Jack manages to convince his father that he intends to scare Lydia with a romantic threat of suicide if she will not accept him. Jack escapes, just as the others arrive and tell his father his real objective with the sword. Everyone is now on the way to King's Mead-Fields. After a comic scene between Acres and Sir Lucius about the best shooting distances and stance, Faulkland and Absolute arrive, and Sir Lucius assumes that Faulkland is Beverley, since, of course, he already knows Jack as Absolute. Acres, in great relief, promises to bear [his] ''disappointment like a Christian,'' while Sir Lucius and Absolute nearly come to blows before the group of concerned ladies and parents appear. The mystery of Beverley's true identity now disclosed, the couples all patch up their differences: Jack with Lydia, Faulkland with Julia, and Sir Lucius with Mrs. Malaprop.

Epilogue

A woman recites a poetic epilogue in the rhyming couplets common in the eighteenth century, reminding the audience that despite man's presumptions to the contrary, women are the true arbiters of love, and that even the strongest soldier ''droops on a sigh'' because love commands him. Even knowledge, she adds, is nothing without the ''Torch of Love.''

CHARACTERS

Sir Anthony Absolute

This spluttering, domineering baronet rules his son (Jack Absolute), and anyone else who gets in his way, with an iron fist. As Fag describes him at the very beginning of the play, Sir Anthony is ''hasty in everything.'' His method of raising Jack has consisted of issuing commands to the boy—''Jack do this''—and if Jack demurred, Anthony ''knocked him down.'' Now that Jack is a grown man, Sir Anthony announces his intention to bestow his £3,000 annual income on his son, *only* on the condition that Jack accept the bride of Anthony's choice, prior to meeting her. His ultimatum is a test of his son's obedience to his will. Sir Anthony gives the young man a mere six and one-half hours to decide. When Jack balks, Sir Anthony insists that his son not only must marry the woman, who is hideously ugly, but also that Jack will be forced to ''ogle her all day'' and ''write sonnets to her beauty.'' If Jack disobeys, Sir Anthony will strip him of his commission. Confident in his methods and oblivious to their actual effect, Sir Anthony advises Mrs. Malaprop to lock Lydia in her room and withhold her supper until she accepts the arranged marriage. Of course, things were different when Sir Anthony courted—he eloped with his beloved. Sir Absolute is a comic figure in the play.

His blustering anger is offset by the ridiculousness of some of his commands and assertions, the irony of which he fails to see; he assures Jack, "I am compliance itself, when I am not thwarted." At the end of the play, however, he has mellowed, becoming a more considerate father.

Captain Jack Absolute

Jack is Sir Anthony's son, and a captain in the army. His father had prepared him for this career by enlisting him into a marching regiment at age twelve. Jack resents his father's manner with him, but dares not resist the forceful old man. Instead, he vents his frustration on his servant, Fag. The rank of captain carries with it a reasonable commission (pay) and a great deal of prestige. It is precisely this prestige that gets in the way of his amorous intentions with Lydia, whose romantic dream is to fall in love with someone beneath her class. Therefore, Jack, a practical man at heart, woos her as Ensign Beverley, masquerading as someone with half the pay and prestige he actually has. When Lydia falls for his ruse, Jack is delighted. But he is calculating, too. He realizes that he will have to let her in on the trick gradually, so that he will win both the girl and the fortune she seems so intent on giving up for love. Jack is sophisticated in the ways of love, as compared to his friend Faulkland. Jack assures him that although he is a romantic, he does not fall victim to the "doubts, fears, hopes, wishes, and all the flimsy furniture of a country miss's brains." His friend Faulkland accuses Jack of treating love as a game, of having no particular stake in whether he wins Lydia or loses her. Just as he might recover from losing at dice, Faulkland suggests, Jack would merely, "throw again" and find another lover. However, once faced with the real prospect of losing Lydia, who becomes incensed when his charade is exposed, Jack falls properly in love with her.

Bob Acres

Bob Acres is a country squire who has been wooing Lydia without success. At the beginning of the play, Acres has just been rebuffed, told by Mrs. Malaprop to discontinue his attentions to Lydia. Acres is an oddball and simpleton who has invented his own form of swearing oaths that are "an echo to the sense," an idea he seems to have picked up from the Shakespeare line in *Hamlet*, to "suit the action to the word, the word to the action." To make himself more attractive to women, Acres takes dancing lessons from a Mr. DeLaGrace, and foolishly prances around the stage practicing his moves.

MEDIA ADAPTATIONS

- In 1961, *The Rivals* was transformed into a musical with words by Bruce Geller and music by Jacques Urbont. The show starred a then new and unknown actor named Dom Deluise. The musical script is available from Music Theatre International in New York City. A 1962 sound recording of the production is available from Mercury records.

Innocent and easily influenced, he is persuaded, against his fears and better judgment, to challenge Beverley to a duel over Lydia. Sir Lucius rouses his "valor" and courage to the point where he relishes the battle. However, with the duel close at hand, he feels his valor "oozing out." Wavering between false hopes and dismal fear, he hopes to be able to prove his "honor" before a shot is fired, so that he will not be hurt. When he realizes that his opponent is in actuality his good friend Jack Absolute, he declines to fight and says he will "bear his disappointment like a Christian."

Ensign Beverley

See Captain Jack Absolute

David

Servant to Acres, David values life over honor and tries to dissuade his master from going forward with the duel. David's homespun language is atrocious, indicating his lack of education; however, he has far more common sense than his master. David refuses even to touch the challenge letter, and he whimpers at the thought of Acres dying at the hand of his opponent.

Fag

Fag is Captain Jack Absolute's servant. Lucy, Julia's maid, knows him as Ensign Beverley's servant. Fag boasts about his master to his friend and fellow servant, David, Sir Anthony's coachman. Jack treats Fag nearly as an equal, confiding in him about his double identity and allowing Fag to make up the lies explaining his presence in Bath. Fag is like a member of the Absolute family; when Jack vents his anger at his father upon Fag, Fag in turn vents his upon an errand-boy. As a trusted manservant, Fag has a secure spot in the elaborate social caste system of the British upper class.

Faulkland

Faulkland, with his overanxious heart, is a foil for Jack Absolute. Faulkland is in love with Julia, but his worries about her constancy nearly ruin their relationship. First he fears for her life and health, then when told that she is well, he grows petulant at the fact that he has worried in vain. He resents her ''robust health'' and calls her ''unkind'' and ''unfeeling'' as though she should have made herself ill with missing him. When in fact he learns that she has been happy enough to sing at a party, he grows jealous. And when he hears she has also participated in country dances, where he insists she must have ''run the gauntlet through a string of amorous palming puppies,'' he is beside himself. However, his fears are completely unfounded; he is projecting his own fickleness onto her. Jack Absolute calls him a ''teasing, captious, incorrigible lover'' and a ''slave to fretfulness and whim'' because Faulkland cannot accept that he has found a true love. Only when Julia gives up trying to reassure him, and in frustration leaves him, does Faulkland realize his grave error of judgment. Given one last chance, he is ready to embrace a trusting love.

Lydia Languish

Lydia is a provincial young lady who lives in the fantasy world of romance novels. The titles that she lists out for Lucy to procure for her at the lending library are actual titles of popular romances of the period. While enamored of the works of fancy, however, Lydia realizes that society disapproves of them, so she ferrets away the novels when she has visitors, and poses with Lady Chesterfield's Letters. Having fallen under the influence of fictional love stories, she has taken a fancy to marrying beneath her station, a deliciously forbidden act that her aunt will not approve. She does not care that without Mrs. Malaprop's approval she will lose her inheritance of 30,000 pounds. In fact, she enjoys going against her aunt's wishes, and she disdains money as ''that burden on the wings of love.'' Lydia wants love in the most romantic terms, passionate scenes like the ones in her novels. To that end, she

hopes to intensify her romance with Beverley, which has seen no quarrels, with a bit of subterfuge.

She sends a false letter to herself exposing Beverley's involvement with another woman. Lydia confronts Beverley with his supposed falsehood to start a fight, just so that they can make up, and thereby keep their love at the fever pitch portrayed by romance novels. Her ruse fails, since Beverley does not rush to her side for forgiveness, but waits to be recalled by her. Beverley/Jack probably would have run away with her, but his father intervenes with a plot to force him to marry the wealthy young lady. Lydia is the last to know that Jack and Beverley are one and the same man. When his masquerade is exposed, and she learns that their affair is not only accepted but promoted by both Sir Anthony and Mrs. Malaprop, her ardor diminishes. She grows as sullen as a spoiled child and rebuffs Jack's avowals of love. Finally, though, Lydia comes to her senses when she sees Jack in danger of being killed in the duel. Her romantic notions are stripped away in the face of losing her lover, and she finds true love with him, presumably dropping her infatuation with sentimental love.

Lucy

Lucy is Julia's maid, and her opposite in every respect. Lucy serves as the go-between for Mrs. Malaprop (posing as Delia) and Sir Lucius O'Trigger, between Acres and Lydia, and between Beverley and Lydia. In every case, she plays upon the sweetheart's anxieties to increase the number of letters she can deliver—into the wrong hands. In her very first scene, she cites a long list of tangible rewards she has earned for her duplicity: money, hats, ruffles, caps, buckles, snuff boxes, and so on. Lucy represents the worst of the stereotype of the clever, acquisitive servant, who betrays her master's confidences for personal gain.

Mrs. Malaprop

Mrs. Malaprop was probably based on Henry Fielding's Mrs. Slipslop from his 1742 novel Joseph Andrews. Mrs. Slipslop, in turn, may have roots in the character Dogberry in Shakespeare's Much Ado About Nothing. Her literary pedigree aside, Mrs. Malaprop is one of the most memorable characters in the play, if not in eighteenth-century drama. She is the epitome of middle-class longing to be acceptable amongst the upper class, and her means of achieving this status is through language. She criticizes the improper language and protocol of her niece and other sentimental girls, yet she herself presents a comic representation of a failed attempt to adopt a sophisticated style of speaking. Her "nice derangement of epitaphs" reveals that she may have a passing knowledge of high-sounding words, but no idea of how to use them. Thus her name has evolved to mean words that are misused or as Julia aptly says, "select words . . . ingeniously *misapplied* without being *mispronounced.*" Some of her malapropisms take on an ironic second meaning due to her innocent misuse. For example, Mrs. Malaprop assures Sir Anthony that girls "should have a supercilious knowledge in accounts," which subtly implies the kind of snobbery Mrs. Malaprop desires, and she agrees with him, too, that in child-rearing, there is "nothing so conciliating to young people as severity." In the latter utterance, she inadvertently underscores the fact that severity often has little effect. Mrs. Malaprop tries to dissuade Lydia from her affair with Captain Beverley, and she joins with Sir Anthony to arrange a marriage for her niece with Jack Absolute instead. She is partly motivated by her own budding relationship with Sir Lucius O'Trigger, who has been corresponding with her, foolishly thinking her letters are from the niece.

Julia Melville

Julia plays the role of the ideal female lover. She remains true, tender, and steadfast to Faulkland, despite his ridiculous and unfounded fears that she does not love him adequately or for the right reasons. Her language, fitting to her quality, is precise, fluent, and rich. In each of her speeches, Julia demonstrates patient thoughtfulness and intelligence, taking a balanced viewpoint. She chides Lydia against treating Beverley capriciously, and she patiently protests that she loves Faulkland, in spite of himself. She even defends his poor behavior as stemming from his lack of experience in love; she overlooks his faults, not naively but with a true generosity of spirit. When she finally loses her confidence in him, her eloquent speech requesting that he reflect upon his "infirmity" and realize what he has lost, finally breaks through to him, making him realize the effect of his own lack of faith. She further adds to her credibility and dignity when she warmly takes him back, once he expresses true penitence.

Sir Lucius O'Trigger

Sir Lucius is an older Irish gentleman, and a devious fop and trigger-happy ex-soldier who fool-

ishly believes his letters are going to Lydia, and that it is this seventeen-year-old beauty who writes back lovingly, not her aging aunt. He knows his correspondent as "Delia," whose imprecision in language only endears her to him as his "queen of the dictionary." He is too old to be playing love games. While waiting for Lucy to deliver a letter, he falls asleep in a coffeehouse and nearly misses her. He is also ridiculous in his amorous overtures with Lucy, with whom he flirts openly, not realizing that she encourages this behavior simply to increase his generosity. Sir Lucius was also a soldier, and it is his Irish propensity for quarrelling that leads him to pressure Acres into dueling Absolute. Taking no risk upon himself (for he claims to have other duties that evening), he has no compunctions against putting Acres at risk. It is he who has to tell Acres how to pace out the dueling field, and he patiently explains why Acres should not stand sideways (because of the greater likelihood that a bullet would hit his internal organs), but should face his opponent squarely. Despite, or because of, his common sense about the physics of dueling, Sir Lucius skillfully avoids having a duel with Acres by muttering, "Pho! You are beneath my notice." Then, when a duel with Jack seems unavoidable, he rises to the occasion, but leaps at the chance of reconciliation the moment Jack makes a gesture of apology.

Thomas

Thomas is Sir Anthony Absolute's coachman. He sports a wig, hoping to look like a lawyer or doctor. Thomas has the same odd manner of talking as the country squire, Bob Acres; he uses oaths such as "odds life" and "odds rabbit it," which belie his pretensions and reveal his humble social standing.

THEMES

Artifice

With the exception of Julia, each of the characters in *The Rivals* practices artifice, or lying, to get what he or she wants from the other characters. Beginning with David's wig, his vain attempt to pass as a member of a higher society that has already dropped the wig from fashionable dress, and ending with Faulkland's last attempt to trick Julia into admitting base motives for loving him, no one

TOPICS FOR FURTHER STUDY

- Read one of the sentimental novels of the eighteenth century, such as Laurence Sterne's *Sentimental Journal through France and Italy.* After reading it, identify several defining aspects of the sentimental man. You might also consider contrasting the qualities of the sentimental man with those of a sentimental woman, as portrayed in Charlotte Lennox's *The Female Quixote.*

- At the end of the play, Lydia decides to marry Jack. Do you agree with her assessment of him as a marriage prospect?

- What special considerations of the status of women in the eighteenth century, as opposed to that of women in the twenty-first century, might affect the female protagonist's choices of suitable marriage partners?

- What roles do Mrs. Malaprop and Bob Acres play in this comedy? How do their language difficulties reflect on the issues that cause conflict between the lovers?

- Read Oliver Goldsmith's "An Essay on the Theatre; Or, A Comparison Between Laughing and Sentimental Comedy" (1773). Define "Laughing Comedy," and then, find evidence in Sheridan's play that supports the interpretation that *The Rivals* is a "laughing comedy."

---

willingly presents things as they really are. In fact, many of the characters lie outright. Fag lies to Sir Anthony for Jack about the son's reasons for being in Bath, and Lucy lies to Sir Lucius about who is writing love letters to him. Other characters simply misrepresent themselves. Jack masquerades as Ensign Beverley in order to win Lydia's love, while Mrs. Malaprop tries to appear more sophisticated by peppering her speech with fancy vocabulary that she neither understands nor can pronounce.

Of all the characters, Lucy stands to profit the most from her artifice, and that is because she serves as a go-between for the intrigues of the others. She tells the audience in a soliloquy, "commend me to a mask of *silliness* and a pair of sharp eyes for my own interest under it." Her comment amounts to a definition of artifice: appearing innocent enough to fool others, while actively seeking one's own selfish interests through their trust.

Courtship

The Rivals puts the two common avenues to courtship—arranged marriage and falling in love—into opposition. Marriages were one important means for wealthy families to maintain or increase their dynastic power. For ambitious members of the middle class, an "advantageous" marriage of a daughter offered a means of securing a foothold into the next level of society. Girls were protected, therefore, as a kind of investment, and thus were not allowed to choose their own mates, and their public appearances were carefully planned and guarded. Places like Bath and certain public areas of London as well as parlor gatherings offered arenas for young people to view and parlay with the opposite sex without the risk of commitment on either side. The actual marriage arrangements were made by parents (usually the father) or by a legal guardian, in the case of orphans. Inevitably, young men and women disagreed with their parents, who often were motivated by other interests than those of their children. The many novels, poems, and plays concerning such conflicts attests to the centrality of courtship issues to eighteenth-century culture.

Sentimentality and Sentimental Novels

Sentiment, or the ability to "feel," was valued greatly during the eighteenth century. The genre that responded to a rampant interest in feelings—what inspired them and how to control them—was the novel. The European novel was "invented" in Spain during the seventeenth century and, as the newcomer to literary genres, it was looked upon

---

with circumspection if not downright disfavor. In an age that favored formality such that much of the poetry consisted of rhyming couplets, the less structured format of a novel was seen as aimless and prone to corrupt its mostly female readers. Novels rose out of a rich precedent of conduct manuals and travel literature and ultimately grew into the chronicle of a protagonist's psychological "coming of age."

Sentimental novels were the most popular novel type favored by women. These works described romantic intrigues with bold lovers and winsome, virtuous women who epitomize the feeling heart. When Lydia Languish recites the list of novels she wanted Lucy to procure for her, the titles represent actual works available at the time. Lydia does not buy these books but sends Lucy to borrow them from the lending library, to which its patrons could subscribe for a reasonably small annual fee. The lending library was another new phenomenon, one that put books within reach of every young lady anxious to script her life according to these fictional models. The reading of novels by young, impressionable girls was condemned by the male patriarchy on one hand, and lauded by them as a viable alternative to education on the other.

Education and Language

One of the means to social advancement is education, and the social measure of this education is spoken language. Thus, in *The Rivals*, it is not the content of the verbal wit that matters, but the relative quality of the rhetoric employed by each of the characters. Oratorical ability is a sign of social competence, and rhetorical blunders symbolize a character's social inadequacies. Thus, Julia's formal and intellectually wrought speeches stand in stark contrast to the verbal blunderings of provincial Bob Acres, whose speech is peppered with phrases such as "odds swimmings" and "odds frogs and tambours."

At the same time, those who feign sophistication are brutally satirized. Mrs. Malaprop is a target of ridicule because her sophisticated-sounding words, used in the wrong context, expose her failure to achieve her goal of self-education. A good education would allow her to pass unnoticed among the social class she wishes to enter. Many among the audience would identify with her desire, at the same time that they mocked her inability to satisfy it.

STYLE

The Comedy of Manners

The Comedy of Manners hails from the Restoration period (1660–1700), but was revived a hundred years later toward the end of the eighteenth century by Richard Sheridan and his contemporary Oliver Goldsmith. While Restoration comedy was bawdy and playfully lewd, the eighteenth-century version is refined and genteel. Both satirize the affected manners of sophisticated society. Often the plot revolves around a love affair, which takes the form of a pitched battle with words as weapons. The dialogue is witty and characters are distinguished by their ability to match wits with their partners. Characters are usually thinly drawn, representing types rather than individual personalities. Emphasis is placed on the language, such as wit and clever double-entendres, rather than the characters' motives or actions.

The Comedy of Manners of the eighteenth century served a different audience than that of the Restoration period. Whereas the early Comedy of Manners was designed to entertain those it ridiculed—the social elite—later variations of this form of comedy served a more diverse audience, which included a growing middle class hungry to acquire the social mannerisms necessary to move up the social ladder.

Sheridan and Goldsmith revived the Comedy of Manner as a protest to the plays of sentimental comedy that predominated in the middle eighteenth century. Didactic and moralizing, sentimental comedies with titles such as *False Delicacy, The Clandestine Marriage,* and *The Fashionable Lover* portrayed tender lovers who make huge social mistakes and pay dearly for them by the last curtain. Sentimental comedies thus predicted the social reformist drama of the nineteenth century.

In the late eighteenth-century climate of puritanical conservatism, Sheridan revived the satiric bite of the true Comedy of Manners, yet in a more subdued and less bawdy form. In *The Rivals*, Sheridan satirized popular sentimental comedy by ridiculing his heroine's misguided sentimental ideas instead of presenting them as caused by society's unfairness. Lydia Languish is not to be pitied, but to be mocked. Her very name reveals the playwright's attitude toward her mawkish desire to fulfill the fantasies of sentimental novels. Her return to her senses at the end of the play as she lets go of her foolish whimsies is Sheridan's subtle attack on mawkish sentimentality.

HISTORICAL CONTEXT

High Georgian Theater

Theater in Sheridan's time appealed to everyone who could afford to attend. Prices ranged from one to five shillings, which amounts to roughly five to twenty-five American dollars in today's monetary terms. After the license of Restoration Theater, Georgian Theater must have seemed almost prudish. Gone were the bawdy burlesques, with their ribald humor. Instead, the plays would be drawn from the new Comedy of Manners, as well as well-known stock pieces from the Shakespeare repertoire, the latter usually representing half of the season's offerings.

The newly revived and adapted Comedy of Manners plays contained a moral embedded in highly sentimentalized drama or comedy. It is this genre of sentimental comedy, also known as the *comédie larmoyante* (''crying comedy'') that Sheridan adapted and satirized in *The Rivals* and *The School for Scandal*. For this reason, his comedies, and those of Oliver Goldsmith, were known as ''laughing comedies,'' a term coined by Goldsmith in an essay on the theater.

The reason for the shift away from court humor to moralizing humor lay in the interests of the new middle class, hungry to gain respectability and to learn how to advance in society. Theater became a vehicle of knowledge as well as a badge of status in itself. The novel as a popular genre was born during this time to reach the same audience, who had the leisure time to read these life scripts. Theaters were expanded to accommodate the larger audiences of approximately 2,300 people, with members of the merchant class literally rubbing shoulders with landed gentry as they sat on the backless benches. Only the very wealthy sat in the raised boxes, once again on backless benches.

The theater itself was brightly lit by oil lamps and candles throughout the performance, and the audience sat close to the stage, creating an intimate acting environment. Elaborately painted scenery panels slid into place on tongue-and-groove slots. The Covent Gardens Theatre owned one such panel representing a scene of the South Parade at Bath, which was used during act five of *The Rivals*. The evening would last a long time, at least four hours, since besides the featured play, there would be introductory music, oratories, singing and/or dancing between the acts, and an afterpiece.

David Garrick, probably the greatest actor in British theatrical history, reigned as king of theater during the years when Sheridan was still finding his way in his chosen field. Garrick managed the Drury Lane Theatre up until the time that Sheridan and his partners took over, effecting several useful changes, such as removing the ''stage loungers'' who took their seats right on the stage, and encouraging actors to work together as an ensemble to portray more life-like scenes.

James Boswell attested to Garrick's status as ''the undisputed monarch of the British stage'' and he hailed him as ''probably in fact the greatest actor who has ever lived.'' Garrick had been one of Samuel Johnson's students; together, they had moved to London to find their fortune, Johnson in writing and Garrick in the theater. Garrick was the first to find success, and that success was stupendous. Sheridan knew Garrick, but did not revere him as did the rest of London. Boswell records Sheridan as constantly denigrating Garrick's acting ability as shallow, contrary to popular opinion. Garrick died three years after Sheridan produced *The Rivals*, leaving a powerful legacy to Georgian theater.

Late Eighteenth-Century Fashion in Bath

Wigs were the height of fashion for men and women alike up until the 1770s, with special kinds of wigs worn only by physicians and judges. At the time when *The Rivals* was first produced, however, the wearing of wigs had gone completely out of style. Thus, the fact that Sir Anthony's servant Thomas sports a wig marks him as a provincial, as does his countrified speech.

Swearing also became unfashionable, suggesting unwanted vulgarity; thus Bob Acres practices ''sentimental swearing,'' a form designed not to offend the ears. The late eighteenth century saw the beginning of the Rococo period, where art and

COMPARE & CONTRAST

- **Eighteenth Century:** A small group of women intellectuals, nicknamed "bluestockings," claims to be the equal of male intellectuals, but they are both rare and resented. Samuel Johnson expresses a typical sentiment when he remarks about a female preacher, "A woman's preaching is like a dog walking on his hinder legs. It is not well done; but you are surprised to find it done at all."

  Today: While women professionals and intellectuals no longer suffer such ridicule for their accomplishments, they do not necessarily command equal pay or respect compared to their male counterparts.

- **Eighteenth Century:** Formal education is available only for men, and being costly, only for landed or wealthy men. A handful of daughters of enlightened fathers enjoy home tutoring, and a few philanthropists try to provide education for less affluent young men. For the middle class, an education is the marker and the passkey for entry to high society. This class of ambitious young men becomes a willing market for tutors, conduct guides, and newspaper columns aimed at educating them.

  Today: Public education is available for men and women of all socioeconomic groups. However, a growing number of non-English-speaking immigrants presents challenges to school systems to offer this group equal access to society through equal education.

- **Eighteenth Century:** Going to the theater is popular and fashionable. Theatergoers have favorite actors and plays, and they pay dearly for their seats on backless benches. The tickets range from one to five shillings, which equates roughly to $25 to $50 in today's currency.

  Today: Although the theater still thrives, it has been largely overshadowed by film and video technology. A handful of dedicated theatergoers still are willing to spend substantial amounts to experience live theater in houses that are often ten times the size of their eighteenth-century counterparts. In addition, today's audience is both further from the stage and also separated from the action by the dimming of the house lights, which makes it possible to view the scenes on stage without being visible in return.

- **Eighteenth Century:** In the later part of this century, England is entering a period of increased propriety and temperance after the bawdiness of the Restoration period. Self-restraint is a considerable virtue, a mark of men who would place themselves above the mob. Accordingly, Bob Acres in *The Rivals* has formulated a new manner of swearing, since "the damns have had their day."

  Today: After a period of liberalism during the second half of the last century, the new millennium may be seeing a move toward conservatism, such that prayer in school is again under consideration, and television and film industries are anxious to serve both the conservative and liberal public by clearly announcing the level of sexual and language-related offensiveness of their products.

---

music departed from the heavy ornate style of the Baroque to styles that portrayed more refinement and elegance, yet were quite playful at the same time. Clothing and speaking fashions began in London and Paris, and traveled quickly to provincial towns via coach. It became fashionable to mock the provincials' attempts to copy urbane fashions.

Swords, that marker of the gentlemen, were discouraged in the resort town of Bath. Jack mutters as he hides his sword under his coat, "A sword seen in the streets of Bath would raise as great an alarm as a mad-dog." In addition, shops, coffee houses, and drinking establishments closed early to discourage misconduct there. Bath had been quite a sleepy town before the eighteenth century, visited only by those who wanted to partake of its medicinal waters. But more leisure time and a growing class of successful merchants combined to turn Bath into a resort town, where visitors came to ogle one another and parade their own elegance.

The quiet town of Bath grew quickly after it became the haunt of the fashionable. On the North Parade of Bath, visitors would take an afternoon stroll to show off their finery, to see what others were wearing, and to socialize. Sir Lucius reveals his lack of decorum and his obtuseness to high society when he falls asleep at this social hot spot while waiting for Lucy to bring him a letter from "Delia," or Mrs. Malaprop. Of course, the truly fashionable elite avoided the crowds. Sir Anthony, with his coarse manners, is clearly one of the newly rich who visits Bath to rub shoulders with his betters.

Age of Johnson

Prior to the five-year period when Sheridan was managing the Drury Lane Theatre and writing plays, he befriended some of the London's literary lions. These included Samuel Johnson, when the older man was at the height of his literary fame, James Boswell, Johnson's biographer, and Johnson's circle of literary lions. In 1762, Sheridan missed the witty and intelligent conversation that had been a part of his shabby genteel life in Ireland. He had spent a decade writing his famous *Dictionary of the English Language* (1755), and had spent approximately two years with James Boswell, who would soon produce Johnson's biography, published in 1791.

CRITICAL OVERVIEW

Samuel Johnson called *The Rivals* and Sheridan's *The Duenna* "the two best comedies of the age." Indeed, as reported in Walter Sichel's 1909 biography of Sheridan, *Sheridan: From New and Original Material,* the play "never left the stage" from its inception until a slowdown in the latter nineteenth century. In the twentieth century, revivals have been sporadic, but successful. The first night, however, was a disaster. The theater was packed; the *London Chronicle* of January 21–24, 1775, as noted in Sichel, proclaimed "there had not been seen so

many ladies and people of fashion at a first night's representation for a long time." Most of the audience abhorred the play. Sichel summarizes the effect: "A whole chorus hissed disapproval. . . . The play itself was damned. Its blemishes—length, exuberance, and drawn-out sentiment."

As quoted in Sichel, the *Morning Post* of January 20, 1775, called it "the gulph of malevolence," while the next day's *Morning Chronicle,* recalled in Richard C. Taylor's "Rereading Sheridan's Reviewers," in *Sheridan Studies,* pronounced it too long: "insufferably tedious." A scant number of reviewers approved of some aspects, such as the reviewer on January 27, 1775, (before the revised version; also in Taylor) who saw "some of the most affecting sentimental scenes" he could remember.

Sheridan's satire was lost on his audience. Few of the reviewers understood his linguistic jokes: the January 18, 1775, *Public Ledger* found the language "defective to an extreme" with "shameful absurdities" and the same day's *Morning Chronicle* pronounced Mrs. Malaprop's lines not "copied from nature" (both reviews in Taylor). The press approved of Sheridan's decision to withdraw the play for revisions. The overhauled play appearing on January 28, 1775, met with a completely different reaction. Although some reviewers bridled at the attack on libraries, the *Morning Post* of January 30, 1775, printed a verse in rhyming couplets pronouncing the play a "perfect piece," joining a general chorus of praise (Sichel). The success was complete. Years later, when Sheridan was an old man, his son Tom arranged for a special production of *The Rivals* with an old flame of Sheridan's and Tom and his wife playing key roles. Sheridan loved it.

The Rivals enjoyed consistent play during the nineteenth century, but interest in it dwindled during the twentieth century. It became a "period piece," one that was exhumed occasionally in theaters, and more occasionally served as fodder for academic research into the eighteenth-century theater. During the 1970s, critics looked at the play through the lens of social justice, John Loftis proclaiming in 1975 that it represents a world "of social and financial practicality . . . in which a rich and repulsive suitor such as Bob Acres might be rejected in favor of a rich and attractive suitor such as Jack Absolute." Twenty years later, in 1995, Jack Durant drew parallels between Sheridan's obsession with proper language in his letters, and the valuation of "well-governed language" in his plays,

Engraving of the North Parade from the 1909 book Sheridan: From New and Original Material, *written by Walter Sichel. The city of Bath became known as a resort town for individuals to parade their own elegance, as portrayed in* The Rivals

including *The Rivals*. Today, *The Rivals* still enjoys occasional production and respectable reviews.

CRITICISM

Carole Hamilton

Hamilton is an English teacher at Cary Academy, an innovative private college preparatory school in Cary, North Carolina. In this essay, Hamilton examines the construction of ethos as a central theme of the play and as a key issue in eighteenth-century British society.

In 1780, Richard Brinsley Sheridan's father, Thomas Sheridan, saw his much-awaited pronouncing dictionary, ten years in the making, come to print. The idea had come from Thomas Sheridan's godfather, the satirist Jonathan Swift, who had dreamt of a British counterpart to the language standards of the French Academy. After Swift died, Thomas took on the task. As Swift had anticipated, this work found an immediate audience, and ran to eleven printings in its first year. Buyers wanted a reliable pronuncia-

tion guide that would help them move into a higher social class, by adopting an ethos of intellectual prowess. Ethos is the Greek term for "character."

Aristotle had written that to be a credible person, one essentially must *create* the person others will see, in order to earn their respect and trust, through a combination of ethos (character), logos (vocabulary), and pathos (emotional appeal). Sheridan, a talented orator who would pursue a thirty-year career in the British Parliament, knew the importance of a person's way of speaking in establishing credibility.

One of the most hilarious characters in *The Rivals* is Mrs. Malaprop, whose name has become synonymous with failed attempts at using big words correctly. The character of Mrs. Malaprop is a showcase role for talented actresses with a flair for oratory and style. Mark Auburn in his 1977 *Sheridan's Comedies* recommends that "[t]he actress playing Malaprop is well-advised to emphasize each malapropism with self-satisfaction, vain pluming and preening, and conscious stress: in this way the incredible vanity will provide absurd contrast to [her] learned ignorance." Despite her protestations that she would not want her daughter to be a

WHAT DO I READ NEXT?

- In Samuel Richardson's 1740–1741 *Pamela, Or Virtue Rewarded,* a young servant girl fights to repulse the advances of her master, eventually forcing him to legitimize his desire through marriage.

- Frances Burney's *Evalina; Or, The History of a Young Lady's Entrance into the World* (1778) is the story of a witty and plucky young girl who selects her mate from a host of admirers.

- Elizabeth Inchbald's *A Simple Story* (1791) relates the plight of a young girl who falls in love with her protector, who inconveniently happens to be a priest.

- In Charlotte Lennox's *The Female Quixote* (1752), a naïve female protagonist—influenced by reading too many romantic novels—persists in being completely honest, no matter what the circumstances, to the bafflement of her friends and would-be lovers.

- *London Assurance* (1841), by Dion Boucicault, is a drawing room farce with aptly metaphorical character names, and it also portrays the plight of a son whose father wants to marry him off to the very girl with whom he has already fallen in love.

- Oscar Wilde's Comedy of Manners *The Importance of Being Earnest* (1895) is a spectacularly witty take on the theme of the mistaken identity of a lover.

"progeny of learning," or to study the "inflammatory branches of learning" such as "Greek, Hebrew, or Algebra," Mrs. Malaprop herself takes pride in her "oracular tongue," her ability to speak in what she comically refers to as "a nice derangement of epitaphs."

Mrs. Malaprop professes to Sir Anthony that a young girl should strive to be what she calls "mistress of orthodoxy" so that she will not "miss-spell and mis-pronounce words so shamefully as girls usually do." She does not want them to learn too much, so she disapproves of their reading novels, which she and Sir Anthony agree would corrupt them, as it has Lydia. Therefore, Mrs. Malaprop asserts, a girl's education should be limited: "the extent of her erudition should consist in her knowing her simple letters, without their mischievous combinations." Her own endeavor to appear educated is compromised by the very method she proposes, for her education is incomplete: she knows only enough to pronounce big words, not how to use them correctly. Her mistakes are comic, and her ethos is comic because her desires are fueled by vanity. Vanity prevents her from recognizing that Jack Absolute is reading his own letter aloud to her,

and that he authored its numerous insults aimed at her "ridiculous vanity which makes her dress up her course features, and deck her dull chat with hard words—which she don't understand."

The letter goes on to state outright that her blindness "does lay her open to the grossest deceptions from flattery and pretended admiration." She is duped by her own ego, and she is the only one who fails to get the joke. Mrs. Malaprop thinks that girls should attend school only to acquire "a little ingenuity and artifice," but her own artifice is as shallow as make-up. Her attempted ethos fails because she does not fully understand the power of oration, as though she has bought the pronouncing dictionary and stopped there. She tries to get by with the surface features, never comprehending what she lacks, yet all-too-ready to prescribe her method to others. The ironies of her absurd linguistic errors and her blindness to the impression she makes is a powerful reminder of the importance of verbal skills in establishing credibility.

Bob Acres offers another role for talented comic actors. Bob exhausts every opportunity to create for himself the ethos of the country gentleman. However, it is apparent to everyone from his valet to his dueling partner that no gentrified silk purse will emerge from this country sow's ear. From "training" his hair for the latest style and capering ridiculously across the stage as he rehearses fencing moves, to practicing his own style of "referential oaths," Bob cuts not a suave figure, but a ridiculous and pathetic one. He rues his gracelessness, saying that although he can dance a country dance well enough, his English legs "don't understand their curst French lingo!"

Of course, dancing is a form of communication, and one that his country bumpkin body cannot speak. Sir Lucius O'Trigger easily feeds into Bob's pretensions and persuades him to challenge his rival for Lydia's hand to a duel. But O'Trigger has to dictate the letter for him, because Bob lacks the decorum necessary to set the right tone of self-righteous politeness. Bob knows that words can help create an external ethos of ruthlessness to frighten his opponent. Therefore, he asks his friend Captain Absolute—actually Bob's would-be opponent in the guise of Ensign Beverley—to refer to him as "Fighting Bob," a ruthless opponent who "generally kills a man a week" and now is in "a devouring rage." Bob supplies the epitaphs, but out of cowardice, he asks Jack to deliver them. Bob doesn't trust himself to project his new ethos in person.

Bob's valet David provides a useful foil to his master. David refuses to join in Bob's mania, instead reminding his master that honor holds no value in the grave. David's speech, in contrast to that of Bob Acres or Mrs. Malaprop, is simple and lacks artifice. He represents the sober voice of reason in this play of inflated egos, providing a sane view of the characters's folly that the audience can use as a measure.

Bob desires the status of the gentry, but his ethos lacks depth, just like Mrs. Malaprop's, because his adopted style of speech cannot mask his true state of mind at the time—fear, just as Mrs. Malaprop cannot mask her lack of education. Because they speak from a fantasy idea of themselves and not from the heart, their projects of ethos-creation fail, making them comic figures.

Unlike Mrs. Malaprop and Bob Acres, Julia always speaks from her heart. There is no disconnect between her words and her essential person, therefore, she has no need to manufacture an external ethos. Not surprisingly, Julia is a good orator. She chooses her words with care, in order to represent the truth as she sees it, not the fantasy she

> " SHERIDAN, A TALENTED ORATOR WHO WOULD PURSUE A THIRTY-YEAR CAREER IN THE BRITISH PARLIAMENT, KNEW THE IMPORTANCE OF A PERSON'S WAY OF SPEAKING IN ESTABLISHING CREDIBILITY."

wishes were true. She patiently explains to Lydia that Faulkland's lack of trust stems from his inexperience at love. Her speech, a sermon on the topic of honest love, rings with truth. Her diction and wording portray her natural ethos of impeccable moral character. Furthermore, never do her words contradict her true feelings. Her true character shines through, and she is credible to everyone—except for Faulkland. Faulkland suffers from a "fear of ethos" engendered by living in a world full of social climbers who present an artificial exterior. Faulkland wrongly accuses Julia of not loving him but merely esteeming him, of not feeling sad enough when he is away. Not until he has tested her beyond the limits of her patient endurance does Faulkland realize his mistake. His failure to recognize a true character when he sees one is understandable, given that he is surrounded by those who present a false ethos whenever they can.

In *The Rivals* as in eighteenth-century society, ethos-creation goes on amongst the servant class as well, although they focus mostly on matters of dress. They seem to forget, as the audience cannot fail to do, that their language gives them away. The fashion façade of Sir Anthony's coachman Thomas is as transparent as Bob Acres's heroic ethos. Thomas sports a wig, that symbol of strained image construction, but as Fag quickly points out, wigs are now hopelessly passé.

With or without the wig, the audience recognizes Thomas's lower-class status as soon as they hear his heavy brogue, filled with such linguistic giveaways as "look'ee" and "Odd rabbit it." They appear in the first act in the play, setting the stage for the series of ethos-manufacturing characters to come, whose fragile constructions also will be rent asunder as the plot unfolds. Fag dons gloves like a nobleman and generally dresses better than does Thomas, but, it is his more formal speech, and his ability to control his language when surprised, that marks him as higher in the servant pecking order than Thomas. Fag maintains his cool with a "hold—mark! mark!" in contrast to Thomas's simplistic outburst, "Zooks!" Like their masters, these servants wish to convey an ethos of social superiority, but their failure to change their style of speaking makes it impossible for them to rise above the level of the servant class.

Not all of the characters gear their ethos toward social advancement. Lydia and Jack have an entirely different purpose in mind—they seek the higher purpose of love. Lydia's purpose adopts the ethos of the woman who falls in love beneath her class, an idea she has gleaned from the sentimental novels that she consumes by the dozens. She also dreams of marrying against her aunt's wishes and being forced to relinquish her 30,000 pound annuity, thus ridding herself of "burden on the wings of love."

Unfortunately, her ethos becomes as static and fixed in her mind and heart as the print from which it derives. She is trapped in a rigid fantasy and therefore unable to respond spontaneously when Jack deviates from the script. Instead of being happy that Ensign Beverley and Captain Absolute are the same man, *and* that he has her aunt's approval, Lydia sulks. In her frustration, she cannot even reply to him, but instead seems to address her internal life script when she says, "So!—there will be no elopement after all!" Mrs. Malaprop declares that "her brain's turned by reading," expressing a concern common in eighteenth-century society. As the reviewer for the January 27, 1775, *Morning Chronicle* of London exclaimed, "almost every genteel family now presents us a Lydia Languish!" The fear was growing that sentimental novels would transform impressionable young ladies into weepy maidens *languishing* for love.

Jack Absolute is the hero because he portrays someone who can convert a lost young lady back to proper behavior. He does so by pretending to go along with her sentimental script, masquerading as Ensign Beverley, who fits Lydia's bill for an impoverished lover. Jack does not share Lydia's fantasy, but he constructs an ethos that fits the mold. Of course, the imposter Beverley excels at oratory, speaking sentimental language even better than the lovers in her books. He waxes poetic as he assures Lydia that the "gloom of adversity shall make the flame of [their] pure love show doubly bright."

He intends eventually to tell her the truth, but his plans go awry when he must appear as a "new" suitor, Jack Absolute. After calling upon "Ye Powers of Impudence"—an apostrophe to the god of imposters—he can barely croak out a few words in a froggy voice. It is an ethos crisis, and his oratorical skills desert him. He cannot utter words that will undo the damage his masquerade has caused. Jack's ethos fails under pressure because his constructed ethos cannot adapt to the changing situation and because it does not represent his true heart.

Julia alone can speak intelligently and effectively under the pressure of changing situations. It is no coincidence that the character with the truest heart also has the best oratorical skill. Each of her speeches is an oratory worthy of a British Parliamentarian, which her creator would soon become. A good orator not only projects a credible character and speaks with eloquence, he or she also can do so spontaneously, responding to the new information while drawing on a storehouse of knowledge and wisdom. Those who masquerade under a manufactured ethos cannot do so, skewed as they are by their blind faith in their inflated, false egos.

Sheridan seems to have created Julia and her comic peers as an experiment to explore how best to create a credible ethos. Sheridan himself was a newcomer to the London theatrical world, with no credibility as of yet, but with a remarkable eye for identifying imposters around him. His success lay in his ability to hold a mirror up to the society that he wanted to join, and to convince it of his own credible ethos in the process.

Source: Carole Hamilton, Critical Essay on *The Rivals,* in *Drama for Students,* The Gale Group, 2002.

Anne Parker

In the following essay, Parker examines Sheridan's practice of "'absolute sense,' common sense tempered by mirth and softened by good nature," and it's place within eighteenth-century theater.

Sheridan has frequently been accused of trying to revive a moribund dramatic tradition, namely Restoration comedy. In these terms, he becomes a kind of second-hand Congreve, and not a very good one at that. Other critics, pointing to the sentiment in his plays, accuse him of being the very thing he supposedly ridicules, a sentimentalist. Neither of these accusations, which in effect try to put Sheridan's

A scene from the 2000 theatrical production of The Rivals, *featuring Wendy Craig, as Mrs. Malaprop, and Benjamin Whitrow, as Sir Anthony Absolute*

comedies snugly into one of two camps, takes into account what is now starting to become a critical commonplace: the Georgian period had its own view of comedy and, in its own way, developed the laughing tradition. Sheridan is no exception. At his best, he adapted the conventions of the past to his own comic ends.

Unlike what the Scotchman (in Sheridan's fragment of the same name) calls "Grave Comedy", which strives to inculcate a serious moral, Sheridan's plays reflect folly and seek to mend it. More than that, like the Restoration comedies of the past,

his plays deal with artifice, though in Sheridan's case the artifice is the sentimental pose. Comedy for Sheridan has a corrective function, directed not just at folly, which takes many forms, but also at sentimental excess. Those "things that shadow and conceal" man's true nature can, in Sheridan's terms, as easily be "witty" as they can be "sentimental."

What Sheridan attempts to do in his plays is to create a balance between mirth and sentiment; he is at once benevolent and critical. What to the Restoration dramatist is a tension between the private and the public self, between appearance and reality,

> IN *THE RIVALS,* THEN, SHERIDAN DOES INDEED MOCK THE ASPECTS OF SENTIMENTALISM THAT LEAD TO FOLLY. TO EXPOSE THESE ABSURDITIES, SHERIDAN EFFECTIVELY EXPLOITS BOTH THE WITTY AND THE SENTIMENTAL MODES.''

becomes to the sentimental dramatist an identification. Eighteenth-century dramatists like Sheridan once again show the discrepancy between what is shown and what is concealed, but Sheridan does so by writing what Loftis calls ''benign comedies with a satirical bite.''

Sheridan achieves this balance by his introduction of ''absolute sense,'' common sense tempered by mirth and softened by good nature. In this, he is very much a part of the eighteenth-century tradition. Auburn, in his study of Sheridan's comedies, mentions the importance of common sense to Georgian comic writers in general. Shirley Strum Kenny also argues convincingly that ''the Charles Surfaces and Captain Absolutes of later eighteenth-century drama'' owe much to the good sense of earlier heroes.

Therefore, freed from both salaciousness and sententiousness, Sheridan's best comedies reflect ''flesh and blood.'' In this respect, his ''mix'd character,'' as Congreve calls such characters in his *Amendments,* is a visible mixture of faults and virtues. Sheridan thereby seeks to show man's undefaced side as well as his more knavish one. His doing so places him firmly within existing dramatic traditions and not within just one camp or another. His doing so also confirms his own stature as a comic dramatist.

In his earliest play, *The Rivals* (1775), Sheridan develops his comic theme of ''absolute sense'' and adapts the modes of the past to his own ends. Restoration playwrights dramatize the corrupting influence of the ''way of the world'' and frequently offer ambiguous resolutions to the struggle of the individual to survive the world and its ways. Sheridan offers the ''better way'' of sense at the same time that he dramatizes the excesses of the sentimental way. He mocks the absurdities of sentimental distress and delicacy of feeling. To do so, he reconciles the earlier themes of artifice and ''plain-dealing'' with his own treatment of virtue and sense. He reveals the folly of a world where a Puff's cant can dupe others and where a sentimental pose leads to absurdity.

Faulkland is one such example of absurdity, and Sheridan mocks the delicate lover in the scene where Faulkland hears of Julia's social activities in the country. Here, Faulkland claims to prize the ''sympathetic heart'' and the sentimental union of ''delicate and feeling souls.'' To be absent from his beloved is to endure an agony of mind. So, in Faulkland's terms, Julia's ''violent, robust, unfeeling health'' argues a happiness in his absence. She should be ''temperately healthy'' and ''plaintively gay.'' Such paradoxical statements point to Faulkland's own sentimental absurdity. He wishes Julia to be a pining heroine whose only true joy comes from her soulful union with him and whose absence from him should subdue her whole being.

But Faulkland fails to see the paradox of both his language and his demands. By wishing her to be temperate and plaintive, he in effect wishes her to be unhealthy and sad. But he does not stop there. A ''truly modest and delicate woman,'' Faulkland says, would engage in a lively country dance only with her sentimental counterpart. Only then, he argues, can she preserve the sanctity of her delicate soul:

> If there be but one vicious mind in the Set, 'twill spread like a contagion—the action of their pulse beats to the lascivious movement of the jigg—their quivering, warm-breath'd sighs impregnate the very air—the atmosphere becomes electrical to love, and each amorous spark darts thro' every link of the chain!

Faulkland's sexually charged speech comically undermines his role as the delicate lover.

The object of his ''sentimental'' ardor, Julia, refuses to play a similar role. Not only is her health robust, but she also seems to enjoy the ''electrical'' atmosphere of the country dance. Once branded as the ''unequivocal tribute to the sentimental formula'', Julia does possess a lively spirit which, at times, is critical of the over-refined temper. Faulkland's jealousy receives a check from Julia, who reminds him: ''If I wear a countenance of content, it is to shew that my mind holds no doubt of my Faulkland's truth.'' Unlike Lydia, Julia will not create an artificial sentimental distress.

In contrast, Lydia enjoys scenes of distress. To her, wealth is "that burthen on the wings of love," so she must create for herself an "undeserved persecution." She delights in the "dear delicious shifts" her lover must withstand for her sake. Describing one such romantic encounter with him, she uses homely, inappropriate language. Her lover is reduced to "a dripping statue," sneezing and coughing "so pathetically" as he tries to win her heart. They must exchange vows while the "freezing blast" numbs their joints. Such a scene, told in such language, merely accentuates the falsity and the folly of her pretensions.

In *The Rivals,* then, Sheridan does indeed mock the aspects of sentimentalism that lead to folly. To expose these absurdities, Sheridan effectively exploits both the witty and the sentimental modes. In contrast to the artifice practised by Lydia, and the distress experienced by Julia and Faulkland, traces of the witty comic mode appear in characters like Acres, the country fop, and Mrs. Malaprop and Sir Anthony Absolute, examples of "crabbed age." Acres, like many a fop before him, slavishly attempts to imitate the city gentleman, but captures only the trappings of true gentility and true wit. He, too, becomes a subject for diversion. And like the aging matrons of earlier comedy, Mrs. Malaprop fancies herself to be attractive and desirable, so much so that she is easily duped. The character of Sir Anthony Absolute, who attempts to bully his son into obedience, resembles another conventional character of the past, the obstinate father. At one point, he threatens to disown a son who refuses to capitulate to his wishes.

Foolish pretensions, like Bob Acres's "*sentimental swearing*," represent a comic "echo to the sense," a hollow imitation of the verbal and social mastery that Captain Absolute more truly embodies. In effect, Acres foppishly distorts both sense and sound, and applies Pope's injunction with respect to sound to a comic delivery of oaths. His swearing is also a parody of the sentiment. What should exhort others to a moral truth Acres uses to bolster his courage.

Similarly, Lydia's romantic notions lead to falsity and absurdity, mere "echoes" of the sensibility and sentimental distress that Julia more truly represents. So, too, with Faulkland. His refusal to forgo what he calls his "exquisite nicety" and to follow the more sensible tactics of Captain Absolute also exemplifies an "echo to the sense," for his nicety is soon found to be caprice. Therefore, both

wit and sentiment fall into excess and affectation, a "Voluntary Disguise" which cloaks genuine feeling and genuine wit.

Nearly every character in the play indulges in such excess: Mrs. Malaprop with her "oracular tongue," Sir Lucius O'Trigger with his distorted view of honor, Bob Acres with his gentlemanly pretensions, Julia with her excessive good nature, Lydia with her absurd romanticism, Faulkland with his captiousness, Sir Anthony Absolute with his penchant to be "hasty in every thing." These excesses are nonetheless intertwined, and their interrelationship is evident in the play's title. Contrary to the views expressed by Sen and Sherbo, the play's dual lines of action are not anomalous, but thematically linked. Here, in his first play, Sheridan does, as Auburn notes in *Sheridan's Comedies,* show himself to be a "master of comic technique."

Wit and sentiment are "rival" modes, and the rivalry is established as early as the prologue, where the figure of comedy stands in opposition to the sentimental muse. Julia's sweet-tempered nature, often regarded as sentimental, can be viewed only in its relation both to her lover's "captious, unsatisfied temper" and to her cousin's romantic caprice. As Rose Snider suggests, Julia's sobriety cannot be treated seriously in the context of her own absurdity. Julia's fundamental good nature "rivals," as it were, the more pronounced excess of the other characters.

By pairing these characters, Sheridan strikes a balance between them. Lydia's romantic indulgences lead to imagined distresses that stand in marked contrast to Julia's own trials. While Julia's "gentle nature" will "sympathize" with her cousin's fanciful torments, her prudence will offer only chastisement. Lydia realizes, too, that "one lecture from [her] grave Cousin" will persuade her to recall her banished lover. Later, Julia says: "If I were in spirits, Lydia, I should chide you only by laughing heartily at you."

Faulkland's fretfulness also taxes Julia's good nature and, for the most part, she allows her "teasing, captious, incorrigible lover" to subdue her: "but I have learn'd to think myself his debtor, for those imperfections which arise from the ardour of his attachment." In this manner, Julia herself becomes the victim of excess. Her exaggerated sense of duty to her morose lover and her belabored justifications of his treatment of her are found to be immoderate.

Even though she would, no doubt, crave just such an incident to befall her, Lydia points out the absurdity of Julia's own romantic obligation to the man who rescued her from drowning. She tells Julia: "Obligation!—Why a water-spaniel would have done as much.—Well, I should never think of giving my heart to a man because he could swim!" Once again, Lydia's homely comparison makes the incident more comic than sentimental.

Here, Lydia's clear-sightedness puts Julia's sentimental expostulations into perspective. By indulging Faulkland's every whim and by submitting to his sentimental notions of love, Julia tolerates his fretfulness and fosters her own excess. When Julia introduces the notions of gratitude and filial duty, for example, Faulkland tells her: "Again, Julia, you raise ideas that feed and justify my doubts." He yearns to be assured that she does in fact love him for himself alone; here she raises doubts even as she tries to remove his fears.

Finally, Julia must bear the consequences. Her indulgence eventually leads Faulkland into mistaking her sincerity for coquetry and hypocrisy. Intent on using the impending duel as "the touch-stone of Julia's sincerity and disinterestedness," Faulkland wrongly judges Julia's love. When she hears of the duel, Julia first responds in sentimental fashion. In terms of Sheridan's theme of rivalry, the contrast between this scene of tender self-abnegation and the scene in which Captain Absolute plays the self-sacrificing lover is worthy of note.

As Ensign Beverley, the captain makes use of Lydia's favorite sentimental notions. He will rescue her from her "undeserved persecution," and he pretends to revel in their anticipated poverty. He comically rhapsodizes: "Love shall be our idol and support! We will worship him with a monastic strictness; abjuring all worldly toys, to center every thought and action there." His "licensed warmth," which will "plead" for his "reward," echoes Julia's pledge to her fretful lover. She willingly promises to receive "a legal claim to be the partner of [his] sorrows and tenderest comforter." Jack vows to Lydia that, "proud of calamity, we will enjoy the wreck of wealth; while the surrounding gloom of adversity shall make the flame of our pure love show doubly bright." Similarly, Julia promises to Faulkland: "Then on the bosom of your wedded Julia, you may lull your keen regret to slumbering; while virtuous love, with a Cherub's hand, shall smooth the brow of upbraiding thought, and pluck the thorn from compunction."

Both Jack and Julia indicate their willingness to endure hardship for the sake of love. But Julia's sentiments, prompted by Faulkland's feigned distress, follow Jack's, and his scene with Lydia is highly comic. In him, artifice clearly predominates over sensibility. The captain is trying to trick Lydia into matrimony and, after his impassioned speech, he quips in an aside: "If she holds out now the devil is in it!" His sentiments are feigned—merely to utter oaths of devotion does not ensure a disinterested heart. Julia's sentiments are more sincere and yet, because they do follow Jack's comic ones, Sheridan here inverts the conventional technique of introducing a comic scene to parody a serious one. In *The Rivals,* the serious scene "imitates" the comic one, and Sheridan thereby undermines Julia's sentiments. Faulkland likewise would trick Julia into a confession of love, unqualified by either gratitude or filial duty. Structurally and thematically, Sheridan in this way suggests the kinship between sensibility and artifice.

Soon, Julia's sensibility itself changes. Once she learns of Faulkland's deception, she resembles earlier heroines who, in the proviso scene, defend their individuality. Her language retains the syntax of the sentiment, but the content does not deal with a moral truth. Rather, she renounces him and soundly condemns his artifice. Delicate feelings aside, she refuses to bring further distress upon herself. To make his comic point, Sheridan prolongs Julia's diatribe, which, in its anger, recalls the tirades of the castoff mistress. Nor can Faulkland interrupt the flow of her reproach.

At last, Faulkland's excess is checked, but not by Julia's language or her finer feelings. Although in the end he pays tribute to the reforming power of her "gentleness" and "candour," here the threat of forever losing her stirs his remorse. Julia, in witnessing the extremes to which her lover will go, also comes to realize the dangers of indulgence. Like Honeywood's in *The Good Natur'd Man,* Julia's indiscriminate good nature must be checked and restrained.

The character of Captain Absolute illustrates Sheridan's comic standard of moderation, the lesson that both Julia and Faulkland must learn. Durant remarks: "[Jack] is a sensible and practical young man; and the main thrust of the comedy comes of this practical young man's efforts to achieve sensible aims in an utterly illogical world." Auburn in *Sheridan's Comedies* writes that Jack is mildly clever, motivated by honest, not entirely selfish desires, and he is "warmly human." Unlike the other characters, who are "absolute" in their self-indulgent excess, the captain is "absolute" only in his sense. To Faulkland's suggestion that he immediately run away with Lydia and thus fulfill her romantic desire for a sentimental elopement, Captain Absolute retorts: "What, and lose two thirds of her fortune?" Like the Restoration hero, he is willing enough to woo a lady with a substantial inheritance, but he is equally unwilling to sacrifice himself to a life of poverty. As he tells Lydia: "Come, come, we must lay aside some of our romance—a little *wealth* and *comfort* may be endur'd after all." To live in an impoverished state may be romantic, but it is also needlessly foolish.

On another level, his moderation offsets Faulkland's sensibility. At one point, the captain urges Faulkland to "love like a man," and, at another, he chides his friend even more severely: "but a captious sceptic in loved—a slave to fretfulness and whim—who has no difficulties but of *his own* creating—is a subject more fit for ridicule than compassion!" Like the balance achieved through the relationship of Lydia and Julia, the Captain's good sense also balances Faulkland's excess.

Like Faulkland's, Lydia's folly must be mended, and by the captain. After Lydia discovers that Captain Absolute and Ensign Beverley are one and the same person, he initially appeals to her sensibility. Meeting with no success, he must then challenge her very pretensions to sensibility. He points out to Lydia how her reputation will suffer in a world where sentiment thrives only in the lending libraries or in whimsical imaginations. It is a point which, although critical of the sentimental mode, also modifies the earlier theme of artifice. Now, sentiment becomes just another form of affectation. Later, of course, in Joseph Surface, Sheridan will personify this kind of sentimental sham. Here, Sheridan indicates that the stage of the world and the world of the stage do not mutually influence each other. Captain Absolute brings into comic focus the illusory and ultimately absurd nature of Lydia's attempt to transfer the fictional realm of sentimentalism into her own life.

Yet, he is also a lover, "aye, and a romantic one too," and this aspect of his character exemplifies Sheridan's use of convention. After his breach with Lydia, the captain agrees to a duel. Indeed, this prospect proves more successful in winning him the hand of Lydia than all his tricks, a reversal of the Restoration practice and an apparent concession to

pathos. But it must be stressed that, unlike Steele's treatment of the duet in *The Lying Lover,* in *The Rivals* the duel becomes an effective comic device. For both Captain Absolute and Faulkland, the duel is a gesture of despair, and Sheridan has clearly indicated the absurdity of it by juxtaposing their motives with those of O'Trigger, who would fight "genteelly" and like a Christian over some imagined insult. The captain here momentarily forsakes sense, and he almost meets a romantic end. In a final comic twist, Lydia's romantic desires are almost realized, and art does indeed almost become life. It is enough to shock all the characters into sense, and pathos is thereby averted.

Therefore, the duel exemplifies the basic rivalry between the sentimental and the witty modes, and the dangers to which both are subject. Lucy capably wears a "mask of *silliness*" and yet, like the witty servants of the past, she possesses "a pair of sharp eyes for [her] own interest under it." It is her self-interest that has led to such serious misunderstandings. The fop, too, has contributed. Seeking to master the art of "*sentimental swearing,*" Acres hopes to prove his courage. A blustering oath, delivered with "propriety," would then achieve an effect which the cowardly "fighting Bob" could not do otherwise. But the duel shows his courage to be as suspect as his "sentimental swearing."

More important is the dual character of Ensign Beverley/Captain Absolute. His disguise also leads to misunderstandings, but he plays the key role of the man of sense. The comic excesses of the rival modes have been checked, largely through him. The rivalry between the various suitors for Lydia's hand reaches its climax at King's-Mead-Field, and the concomitant rivalry between wit and sentiment, represented by the combatants, finally ends. Out of rivalry, balance finally reigns.

The balance is reflected in Julia's concluding speech. Earlier, the actress who has played the part of Julia has delivered a prologue critical of the sentimental muse. Now, at the end of the play, she delivers a word of caution: "and while Hope pictures to us a flattering scene of future Bliss, let us deny its pencil those colours which are too bright to be lasting." Julia's caution highlights the folly of trusting to appearances, at the same time serving to warn against risible excess. Though couched in sentimental language, this final speech hints at the true nature of things. "Flesh and blood" as mankind is, he indulges himself in the extremes of hope or despair, wit or sentiment. The "squinting eye" of excess swivels either one way or the other.

Julia's speech, then, is less a testament to a sentimental reconciliation than a plea for moderation. Sheridan has at last shown that only "absolute sense," freed from excessive wit and sentiment, will ultimately triumph.

Source: Anne Parker, "'Absolute Sense' in Sheridan's *The Rivals*," in *Ball State University Forum,* Vol. 27, No. 3, Summer 1986, pp. 10–19.

SOURCES

Auburn, Mark S., *Sheridan's Comedies: Their Contexts and Achievements,* University of Nebraska Press, 1977, pp. 40–52.

Boswell, James, *Boswell's London Journal, 1762–1763,* edited by Frederick A. Pottle, 1950, reprint, Edinburgh University Press, 1991, p. 30.

Durant, Jack, "Sheridan and Language," in *Sheridan Studies,* edited by James Morwood and David Crane, Cambridge University Press, 1995, p. 101.

Loftis, John, *Sheridan and the Drama of Georgian England,* Oxford, 1976, pp. 46–47.

Reid, Christopher, "Foiling the Rival: Argument and Identity in Sheridan's Speeches," in *Sheridan Studies,* edited by James Morwood and David Crane, Cambridge University Press, 1995, p. 114.

Sichel, Walter, *Sheridan: From New and Original Material; including a Manuscript Diary by Georgiana Duchess of Devonshire,* Vol. 1, Houghton Mifflin Company, 1909, pp. 498–99, 502.

Taylor, Richard C., "Future Retrospection: Rereading Sheridan's Reviewers," in *Sheridan Studies,* edited by James Morwood and David Crane, Cambridge University Press, 1995, pp. 50–55.

FURTHER READING

Kelly, Linda, *Richard Brinsley Sheridan: A Life,* Sinclair-Stevenson, 1997.
    Kelly presents a detailed examination of the playwright's life, with a balanced portrayal of both his brilliance and his dalliance.

Morwood, James, *The Life and Works of Richard Brinskey Sheridan,* Scottish Academic Press, 1985.
    Morwood's biographical account focuses primarily on Sheridan's plays and theater management.

Morwood, James, and David Crane, eds., *Sheridan Studies,* Cambridge University Press, 1995.
    Morwood and Crane collect ten scholarly essays on Sheridan's plays, including one on producing Sheridan by director Peter Wood.

Porter, Roy, *English Society in the Eighteenth Century,* The Penguin Society History of Britain, Penguin Books, 1990.
    Porter looks at the political, social, and economic world of eighteenth-century British society.

Stone, George Winchester, Jr., ed., *The Stage and the Page: London's "Whole Show" in the Eighteenth-Century Theatre,* University of California Press, 1981.
    Acting, stage construction, song, and the various forms of comedy and drama are discussed in the context of eighteenth-century society.

Taylor, Richard C., "Future Retrospection: Rereading Sheridan's Reviewers," in *Sheridan Studies,* edited by James Morwood and David Crane, Cambridge University Press, 1995, pp. 47–57.
    Taylor presents a collection of snippets from contemporary and later reviews of *The Rivals.*

Worth, Katherine, *Sheridan and Goldsmith,* St. Martin's Press, 1992.
    Worth puts the key plays of Sheridan and Goldsmith into the context of the conventions of eighteenth-century drama and comedy, especially sentimental comedy.

The Shadow Box

MICHAEL CRISTOFER

1975

Michael Cristofer's *The Shadow Box*, directed by Gordon Davidson, premiered October 30, 1975, at the Mark Taper Forum in Los Angeles. Currently out of print, the play is still a hearty read for a contemporary audience. The work interweaves the lives of three dramatically different terminally ill patients and their loved ones to give a dynamic, well-rounded perspective of death and dying. The richness of the play is exemplified by its unity. The action takes place during the course of one day, on a hospital campus. The source for Cristofer's inspiration was his personal experience with two close friends dying of cancer. Offering varying perspectives of characters, comprising three different plots, gives the work a certain objectivity in its discussion of a sensitive subject.

Thematically, the work touches on the dehumanizing quality death imposes on Cristofer's patients. Other considerations are also explored— characters choose to be remorseful, engage in reminiscence, confront their disease or exist in a state of denial, or lash out in anger. The brilliance of the work and its success at dealing with such tender subject matter is precisely that it draws no moral conclusions, only offers various perspectives for the audience to ponder without compromising the serious nature of terminal illness. Celebrated by critics for its insight, perceptiveness, and humor in dealing with controversial subject matter, it is not surprising that the work earned Cristofer both a Pulitzer Prize and a Tony Award in 1977.

AUTHOR BIOGRAPHY

Michael Cristofer was born Michael Procaccino on January 28, 1945, in Trenton, New Jersey. He left Catholic University after three years to begin his acting career. Cristofer performed with the Arena Stage in Washington, D.C., ACT in Seattle, and the Theatre of the Living Arts in Philadelphia. In the late 1960s, he found a position with the Beirut Repertory Company in Lebanon and additionally worked to support himself by teaching English.

Cristofer produced a street theater production called "Americomedia." He also wrote several plays. His first play, *Mandala*, made its debut at the Theatre of the Living Arts and was met with very little interest or attention from critics. It was not until after his fourth play, *Plot Counter Plot*, that Cristofer would realize great recognition for his work. *The Shadow Box*, based on his own personal experiences with terminal illness, would be his crowning achievement, earning him both a Pulitzer Prize in drama and a Tony Award in 1977.

The Mark Taper Forum Theatre, a regional theatre of great repute, was where *The Shadow Box* initially appeared in 1975 before moving on to Broadway in 1977. The success of the playwright was not limited to just this production. Cristofer was frequently honored for his playwriting as well as his acting abilities. He earned major roles in Christopher Hampton's *Savages* (1974), Sam Shepard's *The Tooth of Crime* (1974), Maya Angelou's adaptation of Sophocles's *Ajax* (1974), Anton Chekov's *The Three Sisters* (1976), and David Rudkin's *Ashes* (1976). He won additional awards, including a Los Angeles Drama Critics Award in 1973 and a Theatre Award in 1977.

After the success of *The Shadow Box*, Cristofer continued to write plays—among them, *Black Angel*, a drama about a former Nazi officer who, upon being released from prison, must face certain challenges as a result of his involvement in World War II. Cristofer has also written several screenplays of note, including *The Witches of Eastwick* (1987) and *Bonfire of the Vanities*.

PLOT SUMMARY

Act 1

The Shadow Box opens with Joe's interview. Joe is a terminally ill patient vacationing on the grounds of a large hospital, a guest in one of three cabins, two of which are otherwise occupied by other patients and their families. He admits that he hasn't seen his family in six months due to excessive hospital bills and the belief that one day he will return home.

Joe shares that he has explained "the whole setup" to his wife, Maggie, and has asked her to relay the information to their young teenage son Steve. He is concerned about his wife's ability to cope with his illness, but for Maggie "it just takes her a little time." Joe explains to the interviewer his own emotional struggles with his condition, admitting his anger and fear.

Joe leaves the interview to meet up with his family back at the cottage. When Maggie arrives, she reacts defiantly, stating "I'm not coming in. You're coming out." In an effort to overcome the awkwardness of their separation and to avoid any discussion of Joe's condition, Maggie engages in small talk but eventually breaks down in Joe's arms. She is unable to accept his condition and insists on silencing Joe when he tries to explain his illness.

Brian is now in the interview area, explaining his own feelings as a patient to the interviewer: "people don't want to let go." He expresses his amazement at the denial of others, exclaiming "the trouble is most of us spend our entire lives trying to forget we're going to die . . . it's like pulling the cart without the horse." Further on in his reflection, Brian volunteers that his wife left him, demonstrating that he has come to terms with her departure.

Brian's interview is finished, and the action shifts toward the activity in Cottage Two, where Beverly, Brian's ex-wife, and Mark, Brian's gay lover, are meeting for the first time. Beverly is quick to assess a rather awkward scene, "Well, I think we've got that all straight now. He's dying. I'm drunk. And you're pissed off." Mark reports to Beverly that Brian is indeed dying, that his condition is terminal. He then goes into the details of Brian's health as if he were reciting a laundry list, inspiring Beverly's sarcasm, "All the details. You're very graphic." Mark assumes a protective posture with Beverly, causing her to antagonize him even further. The two do not approve of each other, and Mark, in frustration and disgust, is compelled to exit the cabin, leaving Beverly to wait for Brian.

The scene again shifts to Cottage One. Maggie is unwilling to enter the cabin, stating "I'll go in when I'm good and ready." As Maggie's irritation increases, Joe begins a lighthearted conversation about buying a farm to try to keep things happy and upbeat. The banter ends in a scuffle when Joe and Steve attempt to pull Maggie toward the cabin. Maggie answers with a hard slap to Steve's face. Steve retreats inside and Joe relents, confused. He discovers that Maggie has not told Steve that he [Joe] is going to die, and angrily turns to Maggie for clarification. Maggie responds "it isn't true" and runs off, leaving a stunned Joe to sit with his head in his hands.

"Piss poor . . . your attitude. It's a piss poor way to treat people," says Felicity to the interviewer. Felicity is also a patient and a resident of Cottage Three, along with her daughter Agnes. She is now in the interview area, but exhibits a decidedly more hostile attitude toward the interviewer than do the other patients. As she expresses:

> I'm the corpse. I have one lung, one plastic bag for a stomach, and two springs and a battery where my heart used to be. You cut me up and took everything that wasn't nailed down.

Felicity has confused the reality of the hospital grounds with the belief she is at home. In her lunacy, she states that her daughter Claire is "here," "at the house," but a few minutes later adds that "no, Claire isn't with me anymore . . . Agnes is with me now," and then calls out to Agnes in the darkness. Agnes arrives, and Felicity commands that she "take her back" to the cottage, but not before humiliating Agnes in the presence of the interviewer.

When Brian arrives at Cottage Two, his reunion with Beverly is a warm and friendly one. Brian updates Beverly on his life, and all of his recent accomplishments. He has liquidated his assets, put them "in a sock" and "buried" them on Staten Island, taken up painting and writing, even spent time in a Holiday Inn in Passaic, New Jersey. Brian's explanation for this flurry of activity is that he doesn't "want to leave anything unsaid, undone . . . not a word, not even a lonely, obscure, silly, worthless thought." Apart from this moment of elation, Brian tells Beverly "I'm scared to death" when he thinks about dying.

Act 1 ends in Cottage Three, with Felicity and Agnes. In a struggle to reach her mother, Agnes yells out "Mama!!!! Stop it!!" as her mother sings an unfamiliar, disturbing song. As the scene progresses, the voices of the inhabitants of all three cottages form a disjointed, confused dialogue of suffering, beginning with Felicity's childlike cries for help, and ending with Mark's reassuring words,

Michael Cristofer

"It'll all be over in a minute. It just seems to take forever."

Act 2

During a small party in Cottage Two, a disgusted Mark again threatens to walk out on Beverly's outrageous, drunken behavior, only to have Beverly carelessly pour a bottle of champagne on him. Brian responds to the conflict, "My God, it's only a jacket. Why are we wasting this time?" After a moving speech, Brian takes Beverly in his arms, "Come on, my beauty, I'll show you a dancer." But the activity is too much for him, and he collapses, then carefully exits to the bedroom.

Agnes confesses to the interviewer that she is writing letters, posing as her dead sister Claire to humor her mother, stating, "I didn't know what to do, I tried to tell her . . . I tried . . . but she wouldn't listen." Agnes believes that playing along with her mother "makes her [Felicity] happy." The subject turns to Felicity's suffering, and when Agnes pleads, "Why does she want to keep going like this?" she is shocked by the interviewer's answer, "It's what we call 'making a bargain.' She's made up her mind that she's not going to die until Claire arrives." A troubled Agnes flees the scene but not before promising she will return to speak to the interviewer again.

Mark admits to Beverly that he was at one time a male prostitute until Brian befriended him. He speaks of Brian's illness as if it were his, "It's sick and putrid and soft and rotten and it is killing me." Beverly calls Mark on his bout with self-pity, "from one whore to another," she says, "Brian happens to need you. And if that is not enough for you, then you get yourself out of his life, fast." The struggle ends with Beverly's departure. Before she leaves, she says to Mark, "Don't hurt him with your hope."

Meanwhile, Maggie and Joe have been reminiscing about their life together. The conversation is not a happy one—Joe expresses his anger because he is dying, and his life is ending without a sense of accomplishment. Maggie breaks down to Joe, stating that he should come home because their relationship isn't "finished," that "it's too fast." The scene between Maggie and Joe ends as they enter the cottage. Upon Maggie's request, Joe says, "I'm going to die, Maggie."

At the play's conclusion, Brian and Mark remain together. Agnes, in what seems like a moment of redemption, says to Felicity, "If I told you the truth now, would it matter?" Recognizing her mother's decline, Agnes forgoes telling the truth and proceeds to read the fictitious letter from Claire to Felicity.

CHARACTERS

Agnes

Agnes is described as a "middle-aged woman, very neat, very tense, very tired." According to the author, Agnes is someone who has "tried all her life to do the right thing, and the attempt has made her unsure of herself." She is Felicity's oldest daughter and her only surviving child. She shares with the interviewer that she suffers from psychosomatic headaches. They are so much a part of her that she has trouble recognizing them unless they have "gone away." Living in the shadow of her deceased sister, Claire, it appears that Agnes is consumed with pleasing her mother, with caring for her adequately during her illness, despite ongoing abuse from her mother, and the disruption Felicity's illness creates in her life. When asked about her sister or her mother, Agnes has little difficulty in relaying all of the details of their lives. But when asked what she will do when her mother dies, she looks at the

interviewer in silence. Agnes also admits that after one of her mother's hospital stays, she wrote a letter in response to her mother's own letter, posing as Claire. She has continually written such letters, claiming that it gives her mother hope, that "it makes her happy." But when the interviewer asks Agnes what "makes her happy," she is startled and immediately redirects the focus back to her mother's condition.

Beverly

Beverly is a surprise guest at Cottage Two, and much to Mark's dismay, she is his lover Brian's colorful ex-wife. Beverly is a world traveler, an adventurer, and a bit of a drunk. She enters the cottage in an expensive, though soiled and torn, evening dress decorated with "bits of jewelry" and hidden by a "yellow slicker raincoat and rubber boots." Despite her physical attractiveness, she has a rather bawdy sense of humor and throughout the play can be observed swigging from a gin bottle strategically placed in her purse. What makes Beverly an endearing character is her ability to be brutally honest or frank, yet at the same time interject humor into an otherwise grave situation. She is able to illuminate the reality of Brian's disease both to the patient and to his lover, appeasing or comforting one while alienating the other. Her ability to see Mark's true character is also apparent. She reminds Mark that Brian needs him.

Brian

Brian is the second terminally ill patient, introduced in the work as "a graceful man . . . simple, direct, straightforward," who "possesses an agile mind and a childlike joy about life." Of all of the characters, Brian seems to have taken considerably more time to ponder his life for the sake of productivity—his past relationships, his accomplishments, his hopes and dreams unfulfilled, as well as what it means to be dying. During a conversation with his ex-wife, when asked about his newfound interest in writing, Brian says, "I realized that there was a lot to do that I hadn't done yet. So I figured I better . . . start working." For Brian, "working" means liquidating or selling off all of his personal assets and burying the money in a sock on Staten Island, visiting Passaic, New Jersey, just to go, or writing an endless stream of literature. Besides being a dreamer of sorts, Brian is the philosophical voice of the work. He is resolved to forgive and forget the fact that his ex-wife walked out on him.

Brian has come to terms with his past, and in doing so, his universe has opened up.

Felicity

Described as being sixty or seventy and wheelchair bound, Felicity is surprisingly feisty, if not somewhat senile, and openly hostile to both the interviewer and her daughter Agnes. She refers to the interviewer as "you and your people" who've "all come to look at the dead people." Felicity's assessment of her daughter is not encouraging either, telling the interviewer, "She's a little slow. It's not her fault. Not too pretty and not too bright," and warns the interviewer "you have to be careful of Agnes. She's jealous." Felicity also appears to be suffering from dementia, speaking to the interviewer of life on her dairy farm as if she were still there, and of her deceased daughter Claire as if still alive. She holds onto these memories, according to her daughter, to keep herself going, to maintain a sense of hope. According to the interviewer, however, these memories may be the only thing keeping her alive.

Interviewer

The mysterious interviewer never reveals him or herself to the audience. This character definitely works for the hospital and appears to be a clinician. Whether he or she is a psychiatrist is unclear. It is also clear to the interviewer's subjects that meetings with the interviewer are research driven. More importantly, however, it is through the probing questions of the interviewer that the audience becomes privileged to information others do not have.

Joe

Act 1 opens with Joe, a terminally ill patient and resident of Cottage One, speaking to the interviewer. He is described as being a "strong, thick-set man, a little bit clumsy with moving and talking, but full of energy." It has been six months since Joe has seen his wife and son, and after a long hospital stay, he is a bit anxious about a family reunion. Although Joe reveals to the interviewer his fears about dying, he is quick to point out that it is his wife's mental state that troubles him deeply. When the interviewer tells Joe that he "seems" to be "fine," Joe responds half-heartedly, distracted by the momentary arrival of his family, saying, "Oh, me. Yeah sure, but Maggie." Joe does express his own personal feelings concerning his illness to Maggie, despite

MEDIA ADAPTATIONS

- *The Shadow Box* was adapted as a screenplay for television in 1980. It was directed by Paul Newman and starred Joanne Woodward, Christopher Plummer, and Ben Masters, among other notable actors.

her continued resistance to discuss such matters. He is a realist and faces his disease and feelings head on. Joe talks about his dreams and his anger at lost opportunity.

Maggie

Amid a "mass of bundles, shopping bags and suitcases," Maggie approaches the cottage, dressed up yet looking a mess. She is not just Joe's wife, or Steve's mother, but also the troop leader and family organizer. Despite her obvious leadership abilities, often times Maggie appears to be nervous, easily excitable, and highly agitated by her surroundings as well as by interactions with her husband. She reacts frantically to Joe and his attempts to talk to her about his disease, avoiding connection with Joe's illness by refusing to discuss it. After months of separation, she tells Joe that he "doesn't have to tell" her about his condition, that she can see Joe is "fine." More dramatically, Maggie refuses to walk into the cottage, stating "I'll go when I'm good and ready." In a tense moment, she resorts to slapping her son and fleeing from the cottage to avoid entering Joe's world.

Mark

Male companion and nurse to Brian, Mark is a somber character in the work. In contrast to Brian, he is rather serious, appears to be overly protective, and is a bit standoffish with Brian's ex-wife, Beverly. Upon meeting her, he immediately launches into an explanation of his experiences with Brian, as if the pain and suffering were his own. Mark warns her of Brian's changed appearance in graphic detail.

In revealing details of his relationship with Brian to Beverly, the audience discovers entirely different, selfish motives for Mark's devotion to his dying lover. He admits to working as a male prostitute before being invited into Brian's home. For Mark, Brian is his second chance. Now Brian's death means Mark is finished too.

Steve

Steve is Joe's son, an energetic boy of fourteen. Unaware of Joe's illness, Steve becomes the subject of controversy between his father and mother, Maggie.

THEMES

Death and Dying

The perspectives on death offered by three terminally ill patients define the plot of *The Shadow Box*. Voices of the patients and family members alike illuminate many aspects of death. Each character gives the audience a glimpse of death and dying that is different from the next. Those experiences—whether it be those of a concerned husband, fearful wife, or angry patient—come together to give the work a richness and depth unattainable in consideration of any one experience.

Joe's emotional efforts are spent trying to help his wife, Maggie, accept his approaching death, rather than on his own grief. Maggie is reluctant to face Joe's condition, refusing at first to enter the cottage, and then to acknowledge he will never be returning home, "Don't believe what they tell you. What do they know?" Mark, Brian's companion, shares with Beverly the horror he faces daily caring for a dying friend, speaking of death, "You can wipe up the mucous and the blood and the piss and the excrement, you can burn the sheets and boil his clothes, but it's still there." As a patient, Felicity is the only one to express anger toward the interviewer, "Patient? Patient, hell! I'm a corpse."

Appearances and Reality

All of the characters, either those dying or those affected by a dying loved one, must face the reality of death, that death is part of the human condition. Depending on the characters themselves, this proc-

ess of acceptance is expressed in a wide range of emotions. Brian expresses feelings of disbelief in an unguarded moment with the interviewer, confiding, "It's a bit of a shock, that's all. You always think . . . no matter what they tell you . . . you always think you have more time. And you don't." He expresses the sentiment of the overall work—he, not unlike the other characters, struggle with the idea of what it means to be in the process of dying as well as how to cope or live with such an idea.

Others choose denial as a means of coping. From the outset of the play, Maggie resists Joe and his attempts to involve her in his life on the hospital grounds, by refusing to enter the cabin and refusing to speak to Joe on the subject of death and change. "I'm telling you I don't want to talk about it," exclaims an insistent Maggie in an intimate moment with her husband. Because her husband appears to be fine, Maggie won't discuss his illness, claiming that Joe "looks fine," and is "getting stronger everyday." Maggie also says to Joe that she bought a "big red chair just for [Joe]" to surprise him. For Maggie, Joe's death will transform her life in ways she doesn't want to acknowledge or cope with. The idea of this event is impossible for her to embrace.

Dehumanization and Dignity

Terminal illness has a very dehumanizing effect on Joe, Felicity, and Brian alike, stripping them of human dignity. During the course of what seems to be lengthy medical treatment, each one has fallen victim to some form of poking, prodding, or cutting, as if each were part of an experiment. As a function of this scientific approach, the treatments these patients receive are also rather cold and mechanical, and by their very nature deprive these patients of human qualities or attributes. Joe is frustrated by his treatment, sharing that "nobody wants to hear about" how he feels, adding that "even the doctors . . . they shove a thermometer in your mouth. . . . How the hell are you supposed to say anything?"

Felicity is more daring in her protests. She too feels dehumanized by the experience, and voices this sentiment loudly to the interviewer, "I have one lung, one plastic bag for a stomach, and two springs and a battery where my heart used to be." She refers to those responsible as "butchers" stating that they "cut [her] up and took everything that wasn't nailed down." Mark's recollection of Brian's appearance after cortisone injections evoke monster-like images akin to those of Frankenstein, "the skin goes sort of white and puffy. It changed the shape of his face for awhile, and he started to get really fat.'' Outside of these treatments, Mark confides that Brian's dizzy spells are also a source of embarrassment for him.

Memory and Reminiscence

All of the characters reminisce about their lives before illness. Whether patient or family member, these memories are the connection to normalcy, to happier times, and those closest to them. Most of the time, these memories also serve to ease conflict and tension during interactions between characters. For both Maggie and Joe, fond recollections of their life together create the tonic necessary to soothe the reality of the present. These shared moments provide stability; they are calming because they are pleasing to both Maggie and Joe. They provide moments of neutrality in otherwise troubled discussions of Joe's condition.

It is unclear whether Felicity is suffering from dementia or denial in her refusal to accept her daughter's death. Agnes, another daughter and caretaker, insists that the memory of Claire "keeps [Felicity] going," explaining to the interviewer that, "It means so much to [Felicity]. . . . It's something to hope for. You have to have something. People need something to keep them going." Claire is a connection between the mother and the daughter unaffected by illness. Also, by denying Claire's death, Felicity finds a way to deny the passage of time and by extension, the inevitability of death.

But memories also form the basis for some stark realizations. Brian recalls a moment with a doctor when he asks why he is shaking so badly. When the doctor can offer no reasonable explanation, Brian recalls a time in his childhood when he was separated from his father during a train ride to Coney Island. He tells Mark that when he tried to ask for directions he "couldn't talk because he was shaking so badly . . . because he was frightened." He then realizes that he "shakes now" for the same reason, he is afraid, afraid to die.

Remorse and Regret

Taking an inventory of one's life, one's accomplishments, is an understandable response to terminal illness. What is left unsaid and undone becomes of primary importance to several of the characters during the course of the play. All share regrets

TOPICS FOR FURTHER STUDY

- Examine arguments on both sides of the Karen Anne Quinlan decision. What did medical ethicists have to say about this case? What was the religious viewpoint? Others?

- The creation of a test-tube baby or an embryo that was fertilized in-vitro, or outside the womb, led to speculation of a sinister future involving cloning and genetic breeding. How has the goal for "eternal" life been realized in stem-cell research? How do you feel about living forever?

- If suddenly you found out you were diagnosed with a fatal disease, how do you think you would react? What resources would you call upon to try and cope with the situation? What would you try to accomplish?

- Discuss the topic of homosexuality as it relates to *The Shadow Box*. Critics have applauded Cristofer's mention of the relationship between Brian and Mark. Study the subject of sexuality during the time period this play was written. How was the issue of homosexuality dealt with in the 1970s?

ranging from bitter disappointment to sadness or longing for something unsaid or undone.

Towards the end of the play, Joe tells Maggie that to have a house was something tangible, a symbol of life, a place where he could "put in one more . . . tree . . . fix up another room . . . see grandchildren," dwell in possibility. Joe feels a sense of loss or longing for opportunities long gone, those taken by the financial burden of illness. He also betrays feelings of disappointment concerning the finality of his condition: "one day, somebody walks up and tells you it's finished. And me . . . all I can say is 'what' . . . what's finished?''

Brian approaches his mortality driven to offset, or avoid, regret by personal achievement. He explains to Beverly that the moment he discovered he was going to die, he realized "that there was a lot to do that I hadn't done yet.'' Brian wants to champion death, claiming, ''the only way to beat this thing is to leave absolutely nothing behind.'' He will accomplish this by avoiding ''anything unsaid, undone,'' wishing even the loneliest ''obscure, silly, worthless thought'' be expressed in some fashion.

STYLE

Structure

The play is comprised of three different plots working together to create a sense of overall unity. Transitions in plot are indicated smoothly, at specific points in the play, during which one dialogue is faded out as another is woven in. The perspectives of characters involved in three different plots come together at the end of the play to give a fuller, richer picture of what it means to be dying, and how this condition impacts both the lives of those close to the terminally ill and the patients themselves. In Cottage One, Joe struggles to reach his wife, to share his thoughts and feelings with her about dying, but also to help her cope with his illness so that she is prepared for a future without him. In Cottage Two, Beverly and Mark struggle with each other concerning Brian's well-being. And in Cottage Three, Agnes struggles with the guilt and pain of failing to live up to her dying mother's expectations. Despite this blending of plots, the play does follow some strict patterns of dramatic structure. The action of the plot occurs in the course of a day, and the scene is limited to a single location, that is, the grounds of a hospital.

Point of View

Events of the play are presented outside of any one character's perspective, in the third person. At no time does a character address the audience or offer any special insight into his or her motivations or actions. Instead, the audience is able to draw conclusions about the characters themselves by observing them in dialogue with various other characters. The dynamic nature of such interactions gives breadth and depth to these individuals and helps the audience to better understand their motivations. For example, Agnes reveals to the interviewer that she has been writing phony letters from her deceased sister to her mother, Felicity, for two years. In later scenes with her mother, Agnes says simply, ''If I told you the truth, mama, would you listen?'' The audience is already privy to what the

truth is without actually hearing Agnes's admission to her mother.

Objectivity

The work achieves a sense of objectivity primarily because of its structure. It offers snapshots or glimpses into the lives of three different groups of individuals and their struggle to cope with terminal illness, without coming to a particular consensus as to what it means to ''die,'' or what right action that one who is affected by terminal illness should take. The characters often bounce around ideas of what terminal illness means for them, working off each other to reach their own conclusions. Upon observation, this open-ended structure allows the audience to view terminal illness from many different perspectives, creating a heightened awareness, thus opening up different emotional possibilities. For example, Beverly's way of facing her ex-husband's illness is to confront it head on, interjecting humor into her conversations as a means of coping. Contrast or compare this method to Maggie's avoidance. Maggie avoids the topic of Joe's illness altogether by insisting they continue on with their lives unchanged by Joe's hospital stay.

Foil

The various characters work as ''foils'' to one another, their psychological qualities often contrasting strongly. Such characters are either those interacting within a particular plot or on the basis of comparing actions of characters in different plots. Beverly's honest, if somewhat abrasive, or realistic, approach to dealing with Brian's illness, for example, illuminates the true nature of Mark's seemingly selfless concern and self-sacrifice as being a function of self-interest. Beverly is a drunk and a bit of a floozy, but she is able to admit to her shortcomings, that she is not a hero but a ''whore,'' unlike Mark who spends much of his time feigning insult and injury in response to Beverly's remarks. Maggie, in contrast to such boldness, such brashness, cannot process her husband's death. Unlike Beverly, she is unable to confront the situation head-on and offer a listening ear, which would provide some much-needed comfort to her husband, Joe; therefore, where Beverly seems to succeed, Maggie does not.

Climax

Both acts 1 and 2 reach a point in the rising action at which a climax is realized, apparent in the dramatic shift in dialogue. In a powerful moment at the play's conclusion, all of the characters express what is important to them, what makes them feel alive, each offering an idea, "this smell, this touch" offers Joe, "this taste" offers Beverly, and for Brian it's "this moment." This finale supports the simplicity of a moment in which all characters, despite their differences, come together in agreement, mirrored by the statement, "They tell you you're dying, and you say all right. But if I am dying . . . I must still be alive."

HISTORICAL CONTEXT

The era of the 1970s was the backdrop for Cristofer's *The Shadow Box*, an era marked by uncertainty. First, American political confidence was in crisis after Nixon's resignation from office. At no other time in history had a president violated the sanctity of public office as Nixon had. The country also had to cope with the aftermath of the Vietnam conflict and the failure it came to represent. Vietnam veterans returned home, greeted by indifference rather than applause. This climate led America to question its values, and image, on a national level.

Part of the political as well as social climate fixated or focused on issues surrounding the right to die and the nature of life. This concern is indeed reflected in Cristofer's in-depth exploration of mortality in his own work. The case of Karen Anne Quinlan, like Cristofer's play, explores questions concerning quality of life, and when life ends. Quinlan lost consciousness after allegedly combining alcohol and narcotics on April 15, 1975. She eventually fell into a coma and was sustained with artificial life support systems, such as respirators and intravenous nutrients. According to doctors, her brain was damaged beyond repair, leaving her body dependant on life support. But it was traces of electrical brain activity on an electroencephalograph, or EEG, that determined she was alive, from both a medical and legal perspective. Quinlan's parents demanded the right for their daughter to die with dignity rather than be connected to life-support systems, and they pursued this right legally. What transpired was a long courtroom discussion amongst physicians, medical ethicists, and jurists as to when life ended. Some felt life was sacred, no matter what the individual's physical state, while others sided with the Quinlans.

The 1970s was also marked by religious fanaticism. In 1978, Leo Ryan and a group of journalists and relatives of cult followers traveled to Guyana, South America, to investigate cult leader Jim Jones. The group was acting on the request of family members related to those participating in the Jonestown cult. They feared their relatives were being exploited financially, physically, and emotionally. When Ryan and his group tried to flee with fourteen defectors, Jones's assassins fired upon them. Some were killed, others narrowly escaped. Fearing the repercussions of such violence, Jim Jones staged a massive suicide, commanding his followers to drink cyanide-laced fruit punch. A total of 913 people died, and 276 of them were children.

At home, the United States in the 1970s was suffering economically from "Stagflation," a combination of high unemployment and inflation. The situation was worsened by the increasing cost of petroleum imposed by foreign countries. The Organization of Petroleum Exporting Countries (OPEC) was formed by key Middle Eastern countries who imposed an oil embargo against the United States and other nations, causing gas prices to soar.

In midst of what seemed like economic doom, the country was also undergoing great technological advancements with the advent of the personal computer. No longer a science fiction dream, the PC or personal computer could be purchased by the average American for a nominal price, allowing them access to seemingly unlimited amounts of information. Excited by this new technology, theorist Marshall McLuhan saw the PC, along with the advent of the television, as a means of creating "global village," an international community devoid of borders or political preference.

CRITICAL OVERVIEW

Jack Kroll's reaction to *The Shadow Box* in his article "Where is Thy Sting?" was "The American way of death is to domesticate it." While Kroll realized Michael Cristofer's abilities, he did not necessarily find Cristofer's brilliance exhibited in this play. The reaction on Broadway during the first weeks of the play's run was also less than favorable, but as word spread, attendance increased.

What most critics seem to converge on, or wholeheartedly agree to, is the play's ability to present life as a celebration rather than as a means to an end. In the *Washington Post,* Richard L. Coe expands on the idea, stating, "the stings of humor and irony quicken what might have been lugubrious sentimentality." Another value that critics like Coe

COMPARE
&
CONTRAST

- **1970s:** Karen Anne Quinlan's respirator is disconnected as a result of a New Jersey Supreme Court ruling.

  Today: Dr. Jack Kevorkian is found guilty of second-degree murder in 1999 for helping patient Thomas Youk, who suffered from Lou Gehrig's disease, to die.

- **1970s:** The American Psychological Association votes to remove homosexuality from its standard diagnostic manual of psychological diseases.

  Today: The U.S. Supreme Court rules that the Boy Scouts may exercise their right to association by excluding homosexuals from leadership positions.

- **1970s:** The heart of a chimpanzee is placed into the body of a fifty-nine-year-old man in Cape Town, South Africa.

  Today: Scientists discuss genetically altering pig organs with human genes for the purpose of "xenotransplant," an animal-to-human organ transplant procedure.

- **1970s:** Jimmy Carter is elected president of the United States in 1976 after enjoying much public popularity.

  Today: George W. Bush is named president of the United States in 2000, in one of the closest and most debated elections in history.

- **1970s:** Voyager, one of two United States space probes, is launched in 1977.

  Today: Built by Russia, Mir is the longest-lasting space station, orbiting Earth for fifteen years, which ended March 2001.

assign to the work is its ability to express the carelessness with which human beings approach life, and their inability to grasp on to every moment and treasure it. Instead, man, quite naturally, tends to move through life with a sense of urgency and of immediacy from day to day.

The work's unifying force is its subject matter. Although the inhabitants of Cottages One, Two, and Three are separated physically, their voices come together in the end of the play in a sort of collective resolution. These voices crescendo, and in the end, only serve to amplify the message Cristofer is communicating about the transience or temporary quality of life.

Coe, in another article for the *Washington Post*, was moved to call *The Shadow Box* the "finest play of the New York Season, a beautifully realized drama of sensitive perceptions often as funny as it is moving." The play did win both a Pulitzer Prize in drama and a Tony Award in 1977; however, Cristofer's career after this time did not measure up

to these accomplishments. Brendan Lemon, in his movie review of *Gia*, directed by Cristofer, offered a luke-warm response to the film's release in 1998.

CRITICISM

Laura Kryhoski

Kryhoski is currently working as a freelance writer. In this essay, Kryhoski considers Cristofer's commentary on the redemptive nature of death.

As a result of the play *The Shadow Box*, Michael Cristofer earned recognition for his honest, objective study of death, observed in the lives of three unrelated characters and their loved ones. The play, however, is more than just a playwright's attempt to come to terms with the mysterious. The very idea of death is a means of redemption for several characters of the play. While dying is an ending point for some of Cristofer's characters, it signifies the beginning, or rebirth, of others entering a new level of consciousness.

Maggie is perhaps the most resistant to change. It is clear at the outset of the play that she has been suppressing Joe's death, making it all the harder on herself, as well as on Joe, to reunite on a conscious level. When Joe asks Maggie, ''Aren't you ever coming in?'' the inference is not that he is literally anxious or impatient to enter the cottage, but is attempting instead to reach out to Maggie on a deeper level. When Maggie replies, a little too firmly, ''I'll go in when I'm good and ready,'' Joe's question takes on a different character. The cabin symbolically represents a world of sickness, of death, of finality for Maggie. By refusing to enter the cabin, she is, in effect, refusing to accept Joe's condition. What Joe is really asking Maggie to do is to accept his terminal condition so that they can move on in the relationship.

The tension in the play heightens as Maggie continues to resist, insisting Joe return home so that things are ''made normal.'' Finally, Maggie is jolted into the present by her dying husband, who says, ''Look at me. You want magic to happen? Is that what you want? Go ahead. Make it happen. I'm waiting. Make it happen!'' In hearing her own words, ''I can't, I can't,'' Maggie suddenly surrenders, asking Joe to tell her that he is dying. Her admission that she doesn't know what to do for Joe eases the tension between husband and wife, Joe no longer having to ''do it alone.''

Mark prides himself on his involvement with Brian and the support he gives to a terminally ill companion. He knows every aspect of Brian's condition, and is painstaking in recounting the nature of his friend's suffering to Beverly, Brian's ex-wife. It is Beverly who is quick to comment on this quality. When Mark shares that Brian ''falls down a lot and his face gets a little purple for a minute,'' Beverly quips, ''All the details. You're very graphic,'' as if she is responding to a horror film. Beverly and Mark continue to knock heads in a combative fashion, leading to Mark's hasty exit on several occasions. Annoyed and flustered by Brian's visitor, Mark excuses himself, but not before Beverly is again quick to note, ''How are we ever going to get to know each other if you keep leaving the room?'' When Beverly pushes Mark one last time, he fires back, ''We are dying here, lady. That's what it's about. We are dropping like flies. Look around you, one word after another, one life after another. . . . Zap. Gone. Dead.''

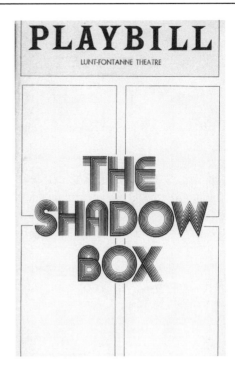

Playbill cover from the 1977 theatrical production of The Shadow Box, *performed at the Lunt-Fontanne Theatre*

Mark is dying, symbolically, because his future—supporting Brian—will be denied to him with Brian's death. Beverly exposes Mark's selfish motives for taking care of Brian. She tells Mark that he doesn't ''need to dirty'' his hands with ''that kind of rotten, putrid, filth, unless of course you need the money.'' The scene reaches its climax as Mark and Beverly exchange slaps. At this point, Mark breaks down, stating, ''I don't want him to die,'' repeatedly. The tension eases at the end of the play when the audience discovers Mark has chosen to remain with Brian, and has undergone an emotional transformation. When Brian calls himself disgusting, Mark replies, ''No you're not. Just wet.''

Finally, there is Agnes. She reveals in a conversation with the interviewer that she has actually been humoring her mother by writing letters to her. Agnes composes and signs the letters as if they are actually from Claire, who has, at this point, been dead for several years. She offers an explanation, claiming that ''it means so much to [Felicity],'' adding, ''people need something to keep them going.'' At first, it would seem Felicity was the person who needed to be humored. When asked if such letter writing makes her happy, Agnes hesitates

WHAT DO I READ NEXT?

- In *Tuesdays with Morrie: An Old Man, A Young Man, and the Last Great Lesson* (1997), Mitch Albom, a *Detroit Free Press* columnist, chronicles his visits with his dying former college professor and mentor Morrie, recalling stories of Morrie's life journey.

- *I Remain in Darkness* (1997), published in English in 1999, is Annie Ernaux's touching, troubled account of her mother's illness, decline, and eventual death in an extended care facility. The basis for the actual memoir was compiled from scraps of paper filled with Ernaux's painful scribblings.

- *Death Be Not Proud* (1949), by John Gunther, is a father's classic memoir and celebration of his son's life, who died of a brain tumor at age seventeen.

- *On Death and Dying* is a classic by Elisabeth Kübler-Ross, first published in 1969. One of the famous psychological studies of the late twentieth century, Kübler-Ross explores the five stages of death, offering sample interviews and conversations of patients and those closest to them.

---

before answering "yes." Agnes reveals a need to write letters to maintain a relationship between herself and her mother.

Failing to make a connection with Felicity, Agnes tries to reach out to her by conjuring up images of her dead sister. In engaging in this activity, Agnes is avoiding the opportunity to resolve her relationship with Felicity. The interviewer gives her pause to think, stating that Felicity is "waiting for Claire." Agnes responds, stunned, and the interviewer offers that "[Felicity's] made up her mind that she's not going to die until Claire arrives," that "it might easily be the reason, now that [Agnes] has explained about the letters." Agnes makes several feeble attempts to reconcile with her mother, by admitting the letters are forgeries, with no success. At the play's conclusion, a strong and resolute Agnes tells her mother "it's time to stop," signifying the relationship is undergoing a transformation.

Other parallels can be drawn in consideration of the regenerative powers at work in the play. The play has been identified to be built, at least structurally, by threes—there are three cottages, housing three related characters, all of whom seem to form a trinity of sorts, identical in ways that the groups consist of one terminally ill patient and two other people who are close to them. The Biblical trinity is also composed of three divine figures: God, divine Wisdom, and the Spirit of God. None preceded each other or challenge one another in power or stature. They are understood, in theological terms, to be one in substance. All share an eternal quality, all are equal. In other words, God is one nature in three persons.

Native Americans have also realized value in the process of transformation. The life-death-life cycle in some Native American cultures implies that the death of one living organism contributes to or impacts the life of something else.

Three also gives expression to the play's ultimate resolution. If the resolution of the play is death, then perhaps it is fitting that there are only two acts which comprise the play. The third, or missing act, is "death."

In *The Shadow Box*, the truth is ultimately realized through three groups of three characters, and their interactions with each other. Cristofer's truth comes out in a multitude of voices representing all of the characters in the final lines of the play. The lesson they communicate is that life should be celebrated in the moment. Brian's final realization is perhaps the most profound of all, one that captures the spirit of the work, "They tell you you're dying, and you say all right. But if I am dying . . . I must still be alive.''

Source: Laura Kryhoski, Critical Essay on *The Shadow Box,* in *Drama for Students,* The Gale Group, 2002.

Carey Wallace

Wallace's stories, poems, and essays appear in publications around the country. In this essay, Wallace considers the way in which Cristofer's characters represent different stages in the grieving process, and the progress each character makes toward acceptance of death during the course of the play.

Death, it has been said, is the one sure thing in every life. But individuals deal with the possibility, and the reality, of death in myriad ways. Some welcome it as an escape from a painful world. Some fear it so deeply they have trouble living life. Some court death, dancing to the edge of mortality, then leaping back. Some, with an eye on the grave, live life with great abandon, against the day when they will cross the mysterious border into the unknown afterlife. Some, with an eye on the afterlife, live life with great care, in hopes of receiving reward, and avoiding punishment, after they die.

But, despite the varying ways in which humanity responds to the inevitability and tragedy of death, most people deal with grief in recognizable stages. Bad news is at first unbelievable, and victims and families may respond to it with denial: ''This isn't happening.'' When reality sets in, a sense of anger often comes with it: ''This isn't fair!'' As anger wanes, people may try to cut a deal with God, or death, or the world, in a stage termed bargaining: ''If I can just do this, maybe they won't die after all.'' The final stage is termed acceptance—when victims and families finally understand the reality of their situation, and are able to face death with open eyes.

Michael Cristofer's 1975 play, *The Shadow Box*, is set in a woodland hospice, where the families and friends of three terminally ill patients come to visit them in the last days or months before their inevitable deaths. In real life, the stages of grief over death are nowhere near as clean as they may appear in psychology textbooks: the human heart is a complicated organ, and stricken victims or relatives may move back and forth between emotions over the course of the grieving process. Nevertheless, each patient and visitor represents some point on the

> THE VERY IDEA OF DEATH IS A MEANS OF REDEMPTION FOR SEVERAL CHARACTERS OF THE PLAY.''

continuum of grief, and each makes some progress toward acceptance over the course of the play.

Steve, the son of Joe, a dying patient, is at the earliest end of the grief spectrum: when he arrives, he isn't even aware of his father's condition. This is an interesting, and tragic, consequence of the stage his mother, Maggie, is in: denial. Maggie, when she arrives, is so far in denial that she has forgotten not just the fact of Joe's impending death but also everything else he has told her about the hospice. Despite the fact that Joe told her in advance that everything they needed would be available there, she has packed her suitcase with everything from a ham to canned pumpkin, in complete denial of both his death and even the substance of the place where he awaits it. Maggie's actions may also reveal some aspects of the later stage of bargaining, a sense that if she can just do enough, she can hold back her husband's death through her offerings. In any case, she has distinctly not reached acceptance. She refuses to enter Joe's cottage, which somehow represents the reality of his death to her. And when he comes down to talk, she insists on hanging on to the fiction of his eventual recovery. ''You're fine,'' she tells him. ''I can see it's all right.'' And Joe, giving in, agrees.

Interestingly, although his wife and son are among the characters who stand farthest from acceptance of the fact of death, Joe himself seems to have a simple, but profound grasp of his own passing. He's already been through several familiar grieving stages, he reveals in a conversation with the interviewer, telling him, ''You get scared at first . . . and then you get pissed off.'' But by the time his wife and son arrive, Joe has accepted his fate, saying, ''I mean, it happens to everybody, right? I ain't special.''

Brian, the patient in the cottage next door, echoes Joe's accepting sentiment. ''It's the one thing in this world you can be sure of!'' he an-

"THE HUMAN HEART IS A
COMPLICATED ORGAN, AND
STRICKEN VICTIMS OR RELATIVES
MAY MOVE BACK AND FORTH
BETWEEN EMOTIONS OVER THE
COURSE OF THE GRIEVING
PROCESS."

nounces to the interviewer. "Sooner or later, it's
going to happen. You're going to die." But as Brian
continues to speak, his bravado becomes less convincing. Instead, the audience begins to see an
intellectual who has always attempted to control life
through knowledge, and who is now attempting to
work the same trick on death, by claiming that he
can know and control it, as well. So although the
interviewer tells Brian his analysis of death is "very
helpful," Brian corrects him, saying "too much
thinking and talking," adding that his former wife,
Beverly, left him because of his tendency to intel-
lectualize everything. In reality, his "acceptance"
is a smoke screen. If it doesn't hide outright denial,
Brian's "thinking and talking" is at least a form of
bargaining: if he knows enough, he thinks, maybe
his death won't really happen. His bursts of creative
activity are transparent, attempts to achieve some
measure of immortality.

Brian's true stage is hidden below the surface,
and so are the positions of his two visitors: Beverly,
his former wife, and Mark, his current lover. At first
glance, Mark seems to be squarely in acceptance.
After all, he's the one who has been taking care of
Brian for the duration of his illness, wiping up "the
mucous and the blood and the piss and the excrement," burning the sheets and boiling the clothes,
becoming acquainted with the sights and smells of
impending death. And Beverly, who arrives already
drunk, in a blouse hung with pins and jewelry from
her former lovers, and dances in her sick ex-husband's cottage, appears to be solidly in denial.

But as the day progresses, it becomes clear that
Beverly, in fact, is the one who has accepted the fact
of her former husband's death. The acceptance
causes her pain, but the alcohol she uses to deaden it
doesn't change her essential grasp on the facts.

Beverly has come to say the things she didn't want
left unsaid, and to have the dance she and Brian
never danced in their life together. And it is Beverly
who insists to Mark that he has not really accepted
the fact of Brian's death, and points out how essentially angry Mark's position is—and that his anger
has made him self-pitying, hindering his ability to
offer Brian the help he needs.

Agnes and her ailing mother, Felicity, residents
of the final cottage, are coping with two deaths—the
death of Agnes's sister, Claire, decades earlier, and
Felicity's own imminent passing. Felicity, who has
gone senile but retains her salty tongue, fades into
and out of reality, and may not ever be able to fully
comprehend the fact of her own death. But even
when lucid, she never accepted the death of her
favorite daughter, to the extent that she has now
completely forgotten it, and believes that the fictional letters that Agnes reads to her are really from
Claire, who Felicity believes will one day be a
second visitor to her hospice cottage. Agnes, who
has never had an easy relationship with her mother,
claims to have accepted the fact of her mother's
death, and even asks the doctors why she hasn't died
yet—but her actual position is somewhat more
complicated. Although she says she writes the fictional letters from Claire simply to spare her mother
grief, her extended fiction may actually reveal her
own denial of the loss of her sister. And the death of
her mother, to whom she has devoted her life up to
this point, will leave her alone, and aimless.

The missing sister, Claire, is an interesting final
case, the only character in *The Shadow Box* who
exists beyond the farthest reaches of the grief spectrum. Although she lives in the play in the minds of
both her mother and sister and still affects their daily
lives, she has moved irretrievably beyond them, and
the human grief spectrum. Claire is the only character who has passed over into death, the only character who really knows the truth of what everyone else
is talking about—and the only character who can't
speak for herself.

As the day progresses, the residents of each of
the cottages make progress toward acceptance of
the death they must deal with. Joe and Maggie near
acceptance by navigating together the grieving process he's accomplished and she's missed. Interestingly, Maggie, who has forgotten so many details
concerning her husband's illness, complains about
the comfort of the hospice, saying, "They make
everything so nice. Why? So you forget? I can't."
Nevertheless, together, they think back on the way

things used to be. During the conversation, they admit that it's difficult to believe how things have changed, express their anger over what they've lost, then move into acceptance. Their process complete, Maggie finally agrees to enter the cottage, to break the news to Steve, so that he can begin his own grieving.

Brian, after discussing his attempts at immortality through writing with Beverly, finally attempts to dance with her the dance he never danced before. The effort proves too much for him, and he's overcome, falling to the ground. But even as he rises, he tries to insulate himself with intellectual chatter, announcing, as if describing a carnival attraction: "He walks, he talks, he falls down, he gets up." But his punch line, "Life goes on," doesn't ring true, and he stumbles off to the bedroom. In Brian's absence, Beverly reveals to Mark the truth of his attitude, and Mark sobs out the truth behind his feigned acceptance of Brian's death: "I don't want him to die." Gently, Beverly encourages Mark to move into a true acceptance, so that Brian can. "Just one favor you owe him," she says. "Don't hurt him with your hope." When Mark re-enters Brian's sickroom, some of his concern for himself seems to have faded, and he's able to help Brian negotiate his own way. When Brian, in a flash of lucidity about his condition, declares that he's "truly disgusting," Mark corrects him with reality, responding, "No, you're not. Just wet."

In the closing scenes, Agnes, like Mark, also discovers the dangers of lack of acceptance of death. In response to her question about why her own mother has not yet passed away, the doctors inform her that, perhaps, her mother is holding out for a visit from Agnes's missing sister—a visit that can never happen because Claire is already dead. Felicity's lack of acceptance of that death, and Agnes's complicity in the self-deception, has led to a situation in which Felicity is delayed indefinitely from letting go of a life she is only barely living, and in which Agnes's own life is also on hold. Ironically, if there is an afterlife in which Felicity might be reunited with Claire, Felicity's lack of acceptance of death delays Felicity from meeting her daughter again. People don't move into acceptance of a death, especially one as troubling and complicated as Claire's, over the course of one short day, and although Agnes grasps the reality of her mother's situation quickly, she doesn't bring herself to break the truth to her during the course of the play. In fact, Agnes wonders if Felicity, in her advanced senility,

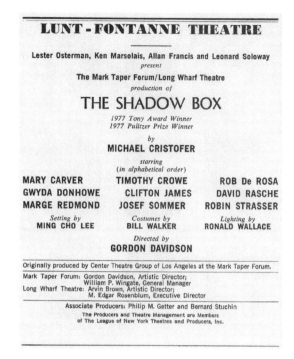

Playbill cast list from the 1977 production of The Shadow Box, *directed by Gordon Davidson*

will even believe the truth if it is told to her. But Agnes herself moves a step forward into real acceptance of both of the deaths in her family, telling her mother near the end of the play, "It's time to stop."

In some ways, Agnes's statement is a very simple definition of death. And at the close of Cristofer's *The Shadow Box*, each patient and each visitor, in their own unique way, has grappled with and grown closer to accepting it.

Source: Carey Wallace, Critical Essay on *The Shadow Box,* in *Drama for Students,* The Gale Group, 2002.

Margot A. Kelley

In the following essay excerpt, Kelley explores how characters in The Shadow Box *deal with imminent death, showing that how the characters view death defines their existence.*

During the late 1970's, a spate of plays with main characters who are dying appeared. The shift of focus in these works—from death to dying by terminal illness—substantiates one character's claim in *The Shadow Box* that "there's a huge market for

THE CHARACTERS IN *THE SHADOW BOX* DRAMATIZE THE FIVE STAGES OF DYING THAT ELISABETH KÜBLER-ROSS OUTLINED IN *ON DEATH AND DYING:* DENIAL, ANGER, BARGAINING, DEPRESSION, AND ACCEPTANCE."

dying people right now.'' This market is not only ''huge,'' but also fairly new, since progressive, long-term diseases are a comparatively recent development, ironically linked with scientific advances.

This rise of science has altered not only the way we die but also the way we approach death. Although science has replaced religion as a dominant force in Western society, it does not meet the emotional and psychological needs of either the dying person or the survivors. It does not provide a new *ars moriendi* to replace those that religions offered. Perhaps in response to this perceived lack, Bernard Pomerance, Ronald Ribman, Michael Cristofer, and several others all suggest new arts, and do so by focussing on terminal illness. By pairing the dying protagonists with at least one physically fit character in each work, the playwrights offer a newly defined art of dying, and more importantly, an art of living until the final moment, and an art of living as the survivor. These arts, as presented in *The Elephant Man, Cold Storage,* and *The Shadow Box,* are primarily individualized, secularized, and interactive processes; and they are valuable replacements for the *ars moriendi* lost when faith became subordinate to technology—the very change which heightened the need for such skills. Quite clearly these plays offer new ''mythologies of dying'' which incorporate the current fascination with death and dying, while also beginning to overcome the concurrent reluctance to discuss death with those who are imminently approaching it. . . .

The characters in *The Shadow Box* dramatize the five stages of dying that Elisabeth Kübler-Ross outlined in *On Death and Dying:* denial, anger, bargaining, depression, and acceptance. While the stages can overlap, the prevailing emotion must be acceptance in order for the individual to live fully at the end, and for the survivors to retain emotional equilibrium. Of the three characters who are dying, Joe and Brian have accepted death; the third, Felicity, is angry and still bargaining for time. Consequently, she is not able to live as the others do.

Joe is a simple, open character who explains that ''you get scared at first. Plenty. And then you get pissed off.'' But he then concludes that ''it happens to everybody, right?'' Because he has reached this point, he regards the stay in the hospice almost as a vacation, which his wife Maggie will love. The early part of their time together is marred, though, by her inability to accept his approaching death. She refuses to discuss his condition with Joe or their son, and will not even enter the cottage—as if staying outside will insure that Joe will not die. She feels abandoned and frightened, and she begs Joe to come home. When he refuses, saying that he is going inside to tell Stephen that he is dying, she makes him tell her first. Hearing it enables her to finally accept it, and she agrees to go inside, so that Joe does not have to struggle alone. Maggie is the least independent of the survivors, and needs the most guidance from the dying person. The role-reversal is carried to an extreme to show that coping is an interactive process—both parties need help, and both must be able to offer some strength.

Agnes and Felicity show a similar reluctance to confront and thereby cope with imminent death. Although Felicity realizes she is dying, she remains angry—telling the interviewer that she's a ''corpse [with] one lung, one plastic bag for a stomach, and two springs and a battery where [her] heart use to be.'' She fluctuates between this aggressive hostility and a pathetic docility, waiting for letters from her daughter Claire. Trying to give meaning to the remainder of Felicity's life, Agnes began writing letters ostensibly from Claire, who had run away as a teenager, and died shortly thereafter. However, the Interviewer attributes Felicity's unanticipated longevity to a bargain that she has probably made with herself to live until Claire comes to visit.

The result of this kind deception is an inability for either Felicity or Agnes to live. Since Felicity will not accept her death in a meaningful way, she cannot come to terms with it. Further, Agnes endures the difficult task of caring for her mother, and loses her own energy and vitality in the process. The failure to cope underscores the sadness of a death without new life.

Brian, by contrast, lives more fully in the time shortly before his death than he had up until that point. In his opening interview, he expresses not only acceptance of his approaching death, but also goes on to say that it is "a relief—if you think about it . . . if you think clearly about it." His resignation allows him to live in his last few weeks. He explains to Beverly that he is writing again because "when they told me I was on my way out . . . I realized that there was a lot to do that I hadn't done yet. So I figured I better get off my ass and start working." Approaching death intellectually, he reasons that "the only way to beat this thing is to leave absolutely nothing behind" because if it is "all used up" he can "happily leap into [his] coffin and call it a day."

While Brian explains his preparations and upcoming death sometimes calmly, and sometimes almost exuberantly, neither his lover, Mark, or his former wife, Beverly, can entirely cope with Brian's disease. Mark is horrified and disgusted by the illness itself, and frightened at the thought of Brian actually dying. He clings to "a bad case of the hopes," and Beverly is afraid that this hope will hurt Brian, realizing as Brian does that living now begins with acceptance of death. Both Mark and Beverly are frightened; and while they believe in Brian's ability to cope, they can not completely share his acceptance of the inevitable.

Even though Maggie, Beverly, and Mark have not reached the same degree of resolution about their fate that Joe and Brian have, they share in the final affirmation of life and death in the closing line of the play. These characters enumerate all that they have, and Brian observes that "they tell you you're dying, and you say all right. But if I *am* dying . . . I must still be alive." Given that, each of them affirms that what remains are "this smell, this touch," "this taste," "this breath," and lastly "this moment." The moving affirmation of the need to embrace "this moment" epitomizes the art of living that this play advocates. Only Felicity and Agnes do not participate in the affirmation; instead, Felicity repeatedly asks "what time is it?" to which Agnes replies "I don't know." because they have not reached any resolution about their fates, they remain locked in a temporal framework, unable to transcend the fear of finitude that the others are beginning to escape.

Source: Margot A. Kelley, "Life near Death: Art of Dying in Recent American Drama," in *Text and Presentation,* edited

by Karelisa Hartigan, University Press of America, 1988, pp. 117–27.

SOURCES

Axelrod, Alan, *The Complete Idiot's Guide to Twentieth Century History,* Alpha Books, 1999, pp. 377–94.

Coe, Richard L., "An Eloquent Expression of Regional Richness," in *Washington Post,* April 24, 1977.

———, Review of *The Shadow Box,* in *Washington Post,* April 1, 1977.

Cristofer, Michael, *The Shadow Box,* Drama Book Specialists, 1977.

Fretts, Bruce, Doug Brod, and Chris Willman, "The Week," in *Entertainment Weekly,* October 29, 1999.

Kroll, Jack, "Where Is Thy Sting?," in *Newsweek,* April 25, 1977.

Lemon, Brendan, Review of *Gia,* in *Advocate,* No. 752, February 3, 1998, pp. 51–52.

"Shedding Light on Life," in *Washington Post,* October 12, 1978.

Simon, John, Review *The Shadow Box,* in *Hudson Review,* Vol. 31, No.1, Spring 1978, pp. 147–48.

FURTHER READING

Carleson, James W., "Images of the Gay Male in Contemporary Drama," in *Gayspeak: Gay Male and Lesbian Communication,* Pilgrim, 1981.
    In this critical study, Carleson comments on the homosexual image in Cristofer's work.

Cristofer, Michael, *Black Angel,* Dramatists Play Service, 1984.
    This play is based on the story of a former Nazi who, upon being released from prison, must deal with the wreckage of his past.

Duclow, Donald F., "Dying on Broadway: Contemporary Drama and Mortality," in *Soundings: An Interdisciplinary Journal,* Summer 1981, pp. 197–216.
    In this work, Duclow comments on the work of Cristofer as it relates to death and dying.

Gross, Leonard, "Michael Cristofer Writes 'A Play of Questions,'" in *New York Times,* June 25, 1978.
    Gross provides an insightful review of Cristofer's play.

The Shrike

JOSEPH KRAMM

1952

When *The Shrike*, penned by Joseph Kramm, opened on Broadway on January 15, 1952, it received accolades from the public and the critics, which helped guarantee a successful run for 161 performances. Later that year, the play won the Pulitzer Prize for drama.

The Shrike chronicles the experiences of Jim Downs, a middle-aged man who has been placed in a mental hospital after a failed suicide attempt, brought on by a stalled career in the theater. His severe depression and feelings of hopelessness are alleviated, however, when an opportunity presents itself for Jim to revive his career. He insists that he is strong enough to leave the hospital and to live a productive and happy life. The doctors, however, disagree. They are convinced that his mental instability has been caused by the failure of his marriage and not because he fears that he is losing his creative energies. The play traces Jim's desperate struggle with the hospital authorities to regain his independence and retain his autonomy. His battle is complicated by his wife, Ann, who in her desperation to hold onto their marriage, becomes an effective accomplice to the hospital's autocratic system. As Kramm documents the power plays Jim must endure as he attempts to gain his release from the hospital, he presents a compelling portrait of repression and resistance.

AUTHOR BIOGRAPHY

Joseph Kramm was born September 30, 1907, in Philadelphia, Pennsylvania.

The Shrike is Kramm's ninth play and the first to be published or produced. Kramm spent most of his time working on amateur theatricals while he was a student at the University of Pennsylvania, which caused his grades to suffer. After enduring psychological intelligence tests and evaluations by psychiatrists to determine the cause of his poor grades, he came away with a critical view of the psychiatric field, a judgment that would reappear in *The Shrike*.

PLOT SUMMARY

Act 1

The first act of *The Shrike* opens at a city psychiatric hospital. Ann Downs arrives with her husband, Jim, who has just swallowed a number of pills in a suicide attempt. Eventually, Jim regains consciousness and admits what he has done. Dr. Kramer, the attending physician, tells Miss Hansen, one of the nurses, to order extra care for Jim during the next forty-eight hours. When Miss Hansen shows her concern that Ann won't be able to pay for this, Ann insists that Jim get "anything that's needed." Ann tells the doctor that she found him in his apartment and admits that they are separated.

The next morning, Miss Cardell notes that Ann has stayed by Jim's side all night and so tells her to go home, but Ann refuses. Ann discusses Jim's case with Dr. Barrow, one of the hospital's psychiatrists. She tells him that when Jim regained consciousness, he asked her, "why didn't you let me die?" Barrow tells her to get all the information she can from Jim, explaining that what he says now will express "what he really thinks and feels. As he regains consciousness, he will begin to build the walls again." In an effort to help determine Jim's motivation for the suicide, Ann notes that Jim once directed a Broadway show that got good notices, but he has not been able to get work since.

During a conversation with Dr. Barrow, Jim admits that he wants to die because he feels that he is "no good," that he has "gotten nowhere," and that

he is too old now to be a success. When Ann tells him she loves him, Jim warns her that he does not want her love. In a private conversation with Barrow, Ann insists that Jim still loves her.

Two days later, Jim is sitting up in bed, focused on getting out of the hospital as soon as possible. He asks Grosberg, an attendant, to mail a letter for him to Charlotte, his girlfriend. Ann arrives and tells Jim that he got a call about a job in the theater. The news excites him and prompts him to speed up his recovery. Ann worries that he is pushing himself too much. When Jim tells Barrow that he wants to leave in a few days so that he can interview for the position, the doctor decides to consult with the hospital's other psychiatrists.

In a private moment, Jim tells Ann that when he gets out, he will not be coming back to her, but she refuses to discuss it with him. Dr. Kramer tells him that medically, he will be well enough to leave soon and that he could not have gotten better so quickly without Ann's help. Later, when Dr. Barrow and Dr. Schlesinger discuss Jim's case with Ann, she admits that she is not sure Jim is ready to leave. She tells the doctors that Jim's eyes do not always focus and occasionally he says "something wild and incoherent," although when pressed, she does not remember exactly what. When she wonders aloud what would happen if he did not get the job, Schlesinger concludes that Jim would be in worse shape if he failed.

Schlesinger tells Ann that a woman named Charlotte has been calling and has been trying to get in to see Jim. When Ann reveals who she is, Schlesinger decides that it would be too great a strain for him to see her. Dr. Kramer tells Jim that he will be healthy enough by Monday to leave.

Ann has further conversations with Dr. Schlesinger about her relationship with Jim. Later, when Jim speaks to the doctor, he admits that he tried to kill himself because he thought his life was "hopeless." Jim tells him that he has no plans to return to Ann when he gets out. When the doctor's questions about Ann and Charlotte get too personal, Jim refuses to answer. The doctor then tells him that his release may have to be postponed and that he will be transferred to a convalescent ward for a few days. Jim becomes dazed at this news, and later, when he expresses his fears about being made to stay in the hospital, Ann tries to reassure him that it will only be for a few days. Jim, realizing that she is in agreement with the doctors, feels a chill run through him when he looks at her.

Act 2

Jim arrives in Ward One the next day and meets the other patients. During an interview with Jim, Dr. Bellman tells him that he has acquired a reputation for being "belligerent and nasty," which shocks Jim. They discuss Jim's relationship with Ann, and then Jim takes a standard psychological test, which he criticizes. When he asks when he can go home, the doctor tells him not for a while.

After two men on the ward fight, one is sent to Ward Seven, where the violent patients are kept. Miss Wingate, one of the student nurses, gives Jim a telegram from Charlotte and warns him that if he does not break off his relationship with her, he will never get out of the hospital. She explains that his release depends on Ann.

The next day, during a conversation with Ann, Jim begins to suspect that she is trying to keep him there. He asks her to contact a psychiatrist friend in an effort to get himself released. She agrees and then asks him to sign over his paycheck to her so she can pay his bills. Later, she tells Dr. Bellman that she is worried about Jim being committed and insists that she will assume responsibility for him if he is released. She admits, however, that she is not sure he is ready. Days later, when an increasingly frantic Jim explodes at the other patients, an attendant threatens him with Ward Seven.

Act 3

Two days later, Harry Downs, Jim's brother, arrives with Ann to visit the embarrassed patient. Ann admits that she has had Jim's phone disconnected and has the calls forwarded to her. She tells Jim that she tried to contact his psychiatrist friend but that he did not want to get involved. Harry explains to Jim that he has said and done things since he has been there to make the doctors think he should remain in the hospital.

In a private conversation, Harry informs Jim that the only way he can get out of the hospital is to tell the doctors what they want to hear, including that he loves Ann and wants to go back to her. He tells Jim that Ann has rented his apartment to someone else and that all of his things have been moved to Ann's. Jim suggests that he could move back with Ann only temporarily, but Harry tells him that he will be in her custody and so she could have him recommitted at any time.

Four days later, Jim has become the model patient. When he meets with the doctors, he convinces them that he loves Ann and wants to reestab-

lish their relationship. Later, Jim tells Ann and his brother that he loves Ann and is sorry for the way he has treated her. Ann insists to the doctors that Jim is telling the truth. They agree and decide to release him. When Jim is told, he calls Ann, asking her to pick him up. After he hangs up, he sobs, knowing that he is "trapped."

CHARACTERS

John Ankoritis

A patient at the hospital, John Ankoritis is proud of his Greek heritage and his intellect. He is friendly to Jim when Jim first comes to the hospital.

Dr. Barrow

Dr. Barrow, one of the psychiatrists at the hospital, discusses Jim's case at length with Ann. He allows her opinions to influence his decisions on Jim's treatment and length of stay.

Dr. Bellman

Another psychiatrist at the hospital, Dr. Bellman appears interchangeable with the other doctors in that he also tries to get Jim to conform to their notion of sanity. He tells Jim that he has acquired the reputation for being "belligerent and nasty." He, like the others, allows Ann to manipulate Jim. In his final interview with Jim, he tries to catch Jim in a lie, but when Jim calmly and passively answers questions in a way that he knows will show his submission, he decides that Jim is ready to leave the hospital.

Miss Cardell

Miss Cardell, a student nurse, works on Ward One. She maintains a tough, condescending tone toward the patients. The play opens with her chastising Mr. Fleming, one of the patients, for smoking and with her threatening to write him up. While she feels herself above running errands for the doctors, she does try to get information from the patients to give to them. As she tries to console Ann, she reveals her prejudices when she insists, "no man is worth it."

Frank Carlisle

Frank Carlisle, an elderly black patient, is "the gentlest man in the world" and expresses his desire to be left alone.

Charlotte

Charlotte never appears in the play but she plays a crucial role. She and Jim have formed a romantic relationship that impedes Jim's attempts to be released from the hospital. When he wakes from his drug induced stupor at the beginning of the play, Jim repeatedly calls her name, and she continually tries to see him at the hospital. The doctors refuse to let the two meet, insisting that their relationship is an indication of Jim's mental instability. By the end of the play, Jim reluctantly agrees to break off his relationship with Charlotte and return to Ann to gain his release from the hospital.

Ann Downs

At the beginning of the play, Ann appears to be a concerned, loving wife. She is quite worried about her husband's condition and determined to do everything she can to guarantee his recovery. Her true motives, however, emerge as the play unfolds. Ann conspires with the doctors to keep Jim in the hospital until he agrees to come back to her.

Ann reveals her manipulative nature as she discusses Jim's condition with the doctors. She insists to Dr. Barrow that it would help Jim "immensely" to get treatment for his depression and to take things slowly, and that as a result, Jim will eventually realize that leaving her was a mistake. She takes complete control of Jim's life while he is in the hospital, renting his apartment, telling his students that he will not be back in the classroom, forwarding his mail to her, and asking him to sign over his paychecks to her.

Jim explains to the doctors that the reason he left Ann was that he did not have a stable life with her. He recognizes her controlling nature, explaining that it took him a long time to "get out of her clutches." When the doctor reminds Jim what she has done for him since he has been in the hospital, Jim insists that she is an unreasonable person and is continually angered by inconsequential things.

Harry Downs

Harry Downs, a small-town businessman, becomes very uneasy at the sight of his brother at the hospital. When he warns his brother Jim that Jim's attempted suicide and stay in a state mental hospital is not good for Harry's business or his family, he reveals his self-centeredness. Harry gets defensive when Jim expresses his anger that Harry has not come to visit him sooner, insisting, "I'm not a free man. . . . I've got things to do." His lack of freedom

MEDIA ADAPTATIONS

- A film version of *The Shrike* was produced by Universal Studios in 1955. The film was directed by José Ferrer, who starred along with June Allyson.

becomes apparent during a conversation with Jim about cooperating with the doctors. Harry explains that there is nothing Jim can do to win his release unless he fully cooperates with the authority of the hospital. He instructs Jim to tell the doctors what they want to hear, just as Harry does to the police or to business clients who make passes at his wife.

While he understands that Ann has been manipulating Jim's situation and that she has made her husband completely dependent on her, Harry insists that she loves him and that Jim should decide he is in love with her to get out of the hospital. When Jim maintains that he cannot love her, Harry warns that Jim will face permanent incarceration if he does not give in to her. Harry explains, "I know it goes against the grain," and that "no man is better for selling himself," yet Harry is not strong enough to fight for Jim's, or his own, freedom, and so he suggests that Jim give up the fight.

Jim Downs

At the beginning of the play, Jim's mental condition is unstable. After his failed suicide attempt, he stays in the same depressed state that prompted him to try to take his life. He quickly finds the will to live, however, when Ann tells him of the possibility of a job in the theatre. Jim has not been able to find fulfillment in his life through his work or his marriage. Years ago, he had a successful experience directing a play, but since then, he has not been able to find work in the theatre, his first love. The teaching and odd jobs he has accepted since have not assuaged his artistic desires.

Faced with the possibility of working again in the theatre, Jim gains enough strength to try to pull himself out of his depression and begin his life again. He determines to convince the doctors that he is capable of leaving the hospital and carrying on a ''normal'' life. Jim reveals his intelligence as he patiently and thoughtfully answers the doctors' questions, often challenging their reliability and value.

Still, the doctors, with the help of Ann, thwart his attempts to leave. Jim fights nobly to gain his freedom, trying calmly and truthfully to answer all of their questions, but to no avail. At the end of the play, Jim finds no alternative but to go back to Ann. In the last scene, he is a broken man, as he recognizes that he has forever lost his autonomy.

Fleming

Fleming is the first patient Jim meets at the hospital. His opening scene with one of the student nurses reveals how little freedom the patients have there.

Don Gregory

Don Gregory is an attendant in Ward One. Most of the time, he is friendly with the men in the ward, often getting them lights for their cigarettes, but when they do not follow the rules, he threatens them with a transfer to Ward Seven, the violent ward.

Grosberg

An attendant at the hospital, Grosberg is relatively friendly with the patients, trying to soften the blow when others threaten to send them to Ward Seven. However, he, like the rest of the hospital staff, will not allow the patients any liberties. For example, when Jim gives him a letter asking him to mail it to Charlotte, he turns the letter over to the doctors.

Miss Hansen

Miss Hansen, one of the nurses at the hospital, shows her penchant for following the rules when the doctor tells her to provide extra care for Jim and she wonders where Jim will get the money to pay for it. The stage directions note that Miss Hansen ''has been soured rather than mellowed by her contact with illness.''

Dr. Kramer

Dr. Kramer, the resident physician at the hospital, appears to be more rational than the psychiatrists. While the other doctors determine to demon-

strate that everything Jim says proves that he is unstable, Dr. Kramer insists that it is normal for someone to declare that he will try to kill himself again right after he has made an attempt. He continually encourages Jim to work hard to improve his health and declares Jim physically fit to leave the hospital a few days after he gets there.

George O'Brien

George O'Brien, a young patient, shows his passivity when he admits that he came to the hospital looking for someone to give him a physical and they kept him there instead. His fragility becomes apparent in his emotional responses to the slurs Schloss throws at him. During one of these events, he threatens to break Schloss's neck; as a result, he is dragged off to Ward Seven.

Dr. Schlesinger

Dr. Schlesinger, the head psychiatrist at the hospital, deals with Jim in a cold, clinical manner. He continually pries into his personal life as he assesses his mental condition. His responses during his interviews with Jim reveal his notion that a sane person is one who conforms to society's norms.

William Schloss

William Schloss, the toughest patient at the hospital, initially appears friendly, offering to read to the others from the book he is writing. He admits that he has served time in jail for defrauding the government and that he was sent to the hospital after he hit his wife and children. More evidence of his cruelty, along with his racism, emerges in his constant taunting of O'Brien, which eventually causes O'Brien to be sent to the violent ward.

Sam Tager

Sam Tager, another patient, provides firsthand information about Ward Seven, which fills the others with fear. He explains that he was put in a straightjacket on Seven after trying to throw himself in front of a subway train and subsequently fighting with the police.

Miss Wingate

Miss Wingate, a student nurse, exercises her control over the men by continually threatening them with Ward Seven. She is the one who reports O'Brien after his fight with Schloss. She reinforces the power structure of the hospital when she informs

Jim that he will never get out of there if he tries to hold onto his girlfriend.

TOPICS FOR FURTHER STUDY

THEMES

Repression and Resistance

Throughout the play, Jim resists the hospital's attempts to dictate his morality. The doctors continually test Jim in an effort to establish his mental instability, yet he often proves himself to be keenly perceptive of their practices. On one occasion, when his psychiatrist asks him general questions about history and current events, Jim provides all the correct answers and argues that the questions prove nothing except "that institutional practice and honesty are not compatible." He adds, "we should be treated as individuals, but we're handled in categories, the same routine for everyone." Finally, he inquires whether the treatment the patients receive is due to the doctors' inexperience or lack of time. Yet, while Jim has clearly shown his mental acumen in his accurate assessment of hospital procedure, he does not win his freedom. When at the end of this session, Jim asks when he will be allowed to go home, his doctor tells him, "not for a while."

Jim also struggles to resist Ann's control over him. Before his suicide attempt, he had successfully broken off his relationship with her, but in the hospital, she regains her power under the guise of helping him to regain his sanity. She continually couches her motives in her seemingly selfless concern for his well being. During his stay in the hospital, she has in effect, taken over his life. She removes all of his belongings to her home, forwards his mail, tells his students that he will not be returning, and convinces Jim to sign his paychecks over to her so that she can pay his bills, all done in an effort, she insists, to alleviate any pressures on him. As a result, she has guaranteed that Jim has nowhere else to go when he is eventually released from the hospital.

As Jim tries to resist the hospital authority and his wife's manipulations, he becomes understandably upset. Yet his honest emotions are used to entrap him further. When Harry tells Jim that he "showed a great deal of antagonism and resentment" in their interviews, Jim wonders, "what do they expect? They probe and pry and get you upset and then expect you to behave like a normal human

- Kramm does not closely examine Ann's motivation for her treatment of Jim. Write a scene for the play in which Ann explains to Jim's brother, Harry, the reasons for her behavior.

- Read *One Flew Over the Cuckoo's Nest* and compare its themes to that of *The Shrike*.

- Research passive-aggressive behavior. How do psychiatrists treat this type of personality?

- Investigate state mental hospitals in America in the first half of the twentieth century. Does the play offer a realistic depiction of the operation of these hospitals?

- How do the minor characters reinforce the play's themes?

- One of the characters suggests that the film *The Snake Pit* presents a similar depiction of a mental institution to that in the play. View the film and either support or refute this opinion.

being." Jim sees the consequences of an honest display of emotion as George O'Brien, one of his fellow patients, is dragged off to the violent ward after his emotional, yet justifiable, response to another patient's racist taunts.

Gender Roles

In the play, the audience does not get a clear picture of Ann's motivation for her cold manipulation of Jim's predicament. Kramm does suggest a possible cause, though. During one of her interviews with Dr. Barrow, Ann admits that after she married Jim, she gave up her career in the theater. When Dr. Barrow asks her whether she regrets her decision, she pauses, and then responds with "a bitter smile, 'We all have our vanity, Doctor.'" In this scene, Ann suggests that her desperate desire to hold on to Jim, even against his will, stems from her giving up her profession. As many women did in the 1950s, Ann set aside her own independence and devoted herself to helping her husband succeed. As a result, she has become understandably "bitter," and so is not willing to give up the man who has become her entire world. Jim admits that she has nothing else in her life when he notes that she is "afraid of ending up a lonely old woman."

STYLE

Point of View

The play is written in a documentary style, focusing on the daily experiences of the main character as he tries to navigate the world of a city psychiatric hospital. Jim Down's point of view dominates the play, as he struggles to cope with the restrictive situation in which he finds himself. The audience never gains a clear look at the motivations behind the behavior of the doctors and of Ann. Kramm places the focus instead on tracing one man's complete loss of freedom and the effect that loss has on him. As a result, audiences get an in depth portrait of one man's painful resignation and ultimate defeat as his autonomy is stripped away.

Symbolism

Kramm employs symbolism in the play to illustrate and reinforce his themes. In the opening act, he uses foreshadowing to imply Jim's fate as one of the attendants searches for a bed for Jim. When Grosberg complains, "I don't know where we'll find one unless somebody dies," he suggests that death is the only escape from the hospital. In another scene, Jim is tied to the bed after he is brought into the hospital, ostensibly to ensure that he will not try to further harm himself. Eventually, Jim will in effect be prevented from exercising any free will concerning his future.

The title of the play becomes a symbol of its main action. Shrikes are robin-sized songbirds with keen eyesight and sharp beaks. Since their delicate feet prevent them from holding onto their food while they eat it, they use tools to assist their appetites. The birds skewer their prey by impaling them with thorns, barbed wire, or anything available. This habit has given them the nickname "butcher birds." Ann serves as the shrike in the play, as she impales Jim with tools provided by the psychiatric establishment. She effectively prevents him from escaping her grasp by manipulating the system to the point where she has full control over him.

HISTORICAL CONTEXT

A Woman's Place

Women's struggle for equal rights in the Western world gained slow momentum during the middle decades of the twentieth century. During World War II, women were encouraged to enter the workplace where they enjoyed a measure of independence and responsibility. After the war, they were expected (and required) to give up their jobs to the returning male troops. Hundreds of thousands of women were laid off and expected to resume their place in the home.

Training began at an early age to ensure that girls would conform to the feminine ideal—the perfect wife and mother. Women who tried to gain self-fulfillment through a career were criticized and deemed dangerous to the stability of the family. They were pressed to find fulfillment exclusively through their support of a successful husband. Television shows (such as *Ozzie and Harriet* and *Father Knows Best*), popular magazines (*Good Housekeeping*), and advertisements all encouraged the image of woman-as-housewife throughout the 1950s. The small number of women who did work outside the home often suffered discrimination and exploitation as they were relegated to low-paying clerical, service, or assembly-line positions. Women would have to wait until the 1960s and 1970s to gain meaningful social and economic advancement.

Social Realism

In the late nineteenth century, playwrights turned away from what they considered the artificiality of melodrama to a focus on the commonplace in the context of everyday contemporary life. Their work, along with much of the experimental fiction written during that period, adopts the tenets of realism, a new literary movement that took a serious look at believable characters and their sometimes problematic interactions with society. To accomplish this goal, realistic drama focuses on the commonplace and eliminates the unlikely coincidences and excessive emotionalism of melodrama. Dramatists like Henrik Ibsen discard traditional sentimental theatrical forms as they chronicle the strengths and weaknesses of ordinary people confronting difficult social problems, like the restrictive conventions under which nineteenth-century women suffered. Dramatists who embrace realism use settings and props that reflect their characters' daily lives and realistic dialogue that replicates natural speech patterns.

COMPARE
&
CONTRAST

- **1950s:** The Cold War induces anxiety among Americans, who fear both annihilation by Russians and the spread of communism at home. The fear that communism will spread to the United States leads to suspicion and paranoia, heightened by the indictment of ex-government official Alger Hiss (1950) and Julius and Ethel Rosenberg (1951) for passing defense secrets to the Russians.

   Today: The Cold War ended after communism was overthrown in the former Soviet Union, yet suspicion and paranoia are still prevalent in America due to the threat of terrorism.

- **1950s:** Wisconsin Senator Joseph McCarthy conducts hearings from 1950–1954, intended to detect communist penetration of American government and academia; for his recklessness, he is censured by the U.S. Senate in 1954.

   Today: Racial profiling is being considered as a tool to help combat the threat of terrorism.

- **1950:** David Riesman, a sociologist at the University of Chicago, and a colleague, Nathan Glazer, argue in *The Lonely Crowd* (1950) that Americans have been coerced to conform to social dictates set by politicians, religious leaders, and the media. Although this conformity often results in surface unity and serenity, it could also produce underlying feelings of alienation and frustration, thus creating the sense of being alone in a crowd.

   Today: Americans embrace diversity in religion, politics, lifestyles, and the workplace.

Realism remained a dominant form in twentieth-century drama. In the 1930s and 1940s, a group of playwrights, known as social realists, brought drama to American audiences that reflected the political and social realities of the period. Dramatists like Lillian Hellman, Sidney Howard, Sidney Kingsley, and Clifford Odets examined political institutions like capitalism, totalitarianism, and socialism along with social issues like lesbianism and poverty. This trend continued in the 1950s, as reflected in *The Shrike*'s examination of mental institutions.

CRITICAL OVERVIEW

When *The Shrike* opened on Broadway on January 15, 1952, it received praise from the public and critics alike. Most reviews focused on the compelling nature of the drama as well as the outstanding staging and performances, most notably, that of José Ferrer as Jim. *Newsweek* praised its "racking tension and suspense" while *Time* noted its "scary blend of theatricalism and truth" and proclaimed it to be a "relentless, gripping theater piece." Richard McLaughlin, writing for *Theatre Arts,* argued, "the story of a man trapped in an asylum by a carnivorous wife has its grim appeal in a time when social tensions make almost all of us potentials for the psychiatric ward." Henry Hewes in the *Saturday Review* proclaimed that one of the play's "finest moments is a stripping bare of our society's norms." Brooks Atkinson in the *New York Times* raved, "the production and performance are superb," and "Mr. Ferrer has staged it with relish, and he plays it with power and dexterity."

Some critics, however, found fault with the script. The *Time* review, for example, determined the playwriting "flawed," suggesting the improbability of hospital psychiatrists not picking up on the true relationship between Jim and Ann. McLaughlin claimed that "the writing was workmanlike and uninspired." Most reviewers, though, echoed *New York Times* critic Atkinson, who praised the play's documentary format and its "sharp and austere" story. The play received the 1952 Pulitzer Prize for drama.

Playbill cover for The Cort Thearte from the 1952 production of The Shrike

CRITICISM

Wendy Perkins

Perkins is an instructor of twentieth-century literature and film. In this essay, Perkins examines the theme of repression and conformity in Kramm's play.

Published in 1958, John Kenneth Galbraith's book *The Affluent Society* chronicles the political, cultural, and social transformations that occurred in America in the 1950s, characterizing the period as a time of unprecedented affluence. Galbraith notes that in this "age of plenty" Americans enjoyed a higher standard of living as the American economy prospered. Tensions, however, boiled beneath the successful surface of American suburbia. Galbraith noted that the rapid changes Americans were experiencing often left them confused and anxious. As a result of their eagerness to fit into the emerging community of the middle class, Americans allowed themselves to be coerced by political and religious figures to conform to social dictates instead of maintaining individual values and beliefs.

Another impetus for conformity emerged during the cold war between the Soviet Union and the

United States, which ushered in a new age of warfare and the fear of worldwide nuclear destruction. The cold war induced anxiety among Americans, leading to suspicion and paranoia that communism would spread at home. This paranoia was fed by a determined and often hysterical witch-hunt for communists, led by Senator Joe McCarthy and the House of Representatives' Un-American Activities Committee (HUAC). As a result, many Americans felt safety could be ensured only by submitting to the traditional values of church, home, and country.

In *The Shrike*, Joseph Kramm reflects this spirit of the 1950s in his focus on the pressure Americans felt to conform to conventional notions of morality. As he chronicles the experiences of one man's struggle to gain his release from a mental institution, he examines the methods employed by a repressive system to force individuals into relinquishing their freedoms.

The play opens with an illustration of the hospital's autocratic structure, which foreshadows what is in store for Jim as he struggles to retain his individuality. In the first scene, Miss Cardell, one of the authoritarian student nurses, accuses a patient of smoking, chastising him for endangering his weak heart. When Fleming refuses to admit that he has been smoking, Miss Cardell invades his privacy by looking under his covers for the cigarettes. Finally, when she tells him that she will have to call one of the attendants, he gives in. In an effort to guarantee that he will never again disobey orders, Miss Cardell tells him that she will report him.

This opening vignette presents, in miniature, what Jim will experience during his stay in the hospital. As the officials there try to get him to conform to their notion of mental health, they invade his privacy and threaten him with physical restraint, first in the hospital's violent ward, and then through transfer to a state institution from which he would have little chance of escape. His psychiatric evaluation will go on record to guarantee his compliance to their view of proper behavior.

The psychiatrists base their assessment of Jim's mental health on his willingness and ability to conform to social mores. Initially, they consider him to be a potential murderer, as they do all those who attempt suicide. Since they determine that he is a threat to himself as well as others, they tie him down in his bed, which foreshadows the complete loss of freedom he will experience by the end of the play. The doctors eventually replace the ties on his hands and feet with psychological restraints as they

WHAT DO I READ NEXT?

- *The Bell Jar* (1963), written by Sylvia Plath, focuses on a young woman's mental breakdown in New York City in the early 1950s. The novel is based on Plath's own experiences with depression and suicide attempts.

- In *Girl, Interrupted* (1993), Susanna Kaysen chronicles the author's harrowing experiences in a mental hospital in 1967. Kaysen challenges notions of sanity and insanity, concluding that the definitions of each are culturally determined.

- In the short story "The Short Happy Life of Francis Macomber" (1936), Ernest Hemingway offers a searing portrait of the power plays that can develop between a husband and wife and their destructive consequences.

- Ken Kesey's *One Flew Over the Cuckoo's Nest* (1962) explores the harsh realities of mental institutions in the 1950s and early 1960s, including the practice of lobotomies, a surgical procedure that involves severing the nerve fibers in the brain that connect the frontal lobes to the thalamus.

---

investigate Jim's past and evaluate his present emotional state.

When Jim's psychiatrists discover that he has left his wife and has become involved with another woman, they try to convince him to return to a more traditional lifestyle, suggesting that his actions have caused his present mental instability. They ignore Jim's complaints that his unrealized artistic goals prompted his suicide attempt. Jim tries to explain that he felt "hopeless" not because his marriage had broken up, but because he became convinced that he was losing his creative energies. The doctors, however, insist that his depression stems from the destruction of his relationship with Ann, a position articulated by Miss Wingate when she accuses Jim of trying "to break down the sanctity of marriage." She warns him that if he continues to try to contact Charlotte, the doctors will not let him out of the hospital. Unbeknownst to Jim, they have refused to allow Charlotte to see him, determining that a meeting with her would be too much of a strain for him.

Dr. Schlesinger's discussion with Jim about his relationship with Ann illustrates the hospital's authoritarian system. When Jim admits that he would not return to Ann if he were to be released, the doctor reminds him of Ann's love and devotion. Even after Jim explains Ann's need to control him and details evidence of her erratic temper, Dr.

Schlesinger counters that Jim's life would be more "stable" with her. Jim's rejection of this option results in the extension of his incarceration in the hospital. When he refuses to answer questions about his feelings for Charlotte, determining them to be an invasion of his privacy, the doctor tells him that he will not be released in time to attend his theatre appointment and would instead be transferred to another ward.

Ann aids hospital authorities during each step of their program to strip Jim of his autonomy in an effort to gain control over him and thus to force him to return to her. She ensures her constant presence in the hospital, and so her influence over Jim, by insisting that she remain at his bedside and thus aid in his recovery. She regularly meets with Jim's psychiatrists to discuss his past and present behavior. The doctors depend on her to provide personal information about Jim that they can use to help them assess his condition and "cure" him.

During her initial meeting with Dr. Barrow, he asks her to press Jim to divulge his inner thoughts, explaining that what he says in these early stages of recovery will express "what he really thinks and feels." In later conversations with the doctors, Ann continually misrepresents his behavior, insisting that he is "frequently wild and incoherent." She blames Charlotte for his suicide attempt and determines that he will not be ready to leave until he

ANN AIDS HOSPITAL
AUTHORITIES DURING EACH STEP
OF THEIR PROGRAM TO STRIP JIM
OF HIS AUTONOMY IN AN EFFORT
TO GAIN CONTROL OVER HIM AND
THUS TO FORCE HIM TO RETURN
TO HER."

breaks off all ties with the woman—opinions that the doctors wholeheartedly support since they reinforce their sense of normalcy.

Throughout most of the play, Jim cannot understand why he is being kept in the hospital, noting that he has expressed his true feelings to the doctors. That, however, is the crux of the problem. Jim's steadfast refusal to allow the doctors to dictate his sense of morality and to outline his future extends his incarceration.

Harry, Jim's brother, tells Jim that he will never get out of the hospital unless he tells them what they want to hear, that he has decided to return to his wife. When Jim decides that he could return to her for a short while, and then leave her and so gain his independence, Harry warns that if he is released, Jim will be in her custody and so she could have him recommitted at any time.

Seeing no way out of his dilemma, Jim takes Harry's advice and tells the doctors that he made a mistake when he left Ann. He convinces them that he is still in love with her and that he has now acquired a different set of values, the one forced on him by the hospital's psychiatric establishment. As a result, the doctors determine that he is well enough to go home under Ann's care. The play closes as Jim receives the news that he has been released. Understanding that he has been trapped into giving up his freedom and autonomy, he collapses and sobs.

John Mason Brown, in an article on the play for the *Saturday Review,* complained that Kramm's development of Ann is "hazy," and that "it is the husband's weakness rather than the wife's strength which is stressed." In Kramm's artful construction of the play, Ann's motivations for helping to strip Jim of his identity are only suggested. However,

Kramm's focus is on the effects of her machinations, as well as those of the hospital, not the causes. In his representation of the harrowing experience of Jim Downs, Kramm has created a compelling portrait of the interplay between dominance and submission and the devastating consequences that can result.

Source: Wendy Perkins, Critical Essay on *The Shrike,* in *Drama for Students,* The Gale Group, 2002.

Josh Ozersky

Ozersky is a critic, essayist, and cultural historian. In this essay, Ozersky describes some of the ways in which Kramm's play expresses the politics and fears of the early 1950s, when it was written.

Joseph Kramm's *The Shrike* is a powerful play, even nearly fifty years after it was written. It tells a familiar story: an unhappy man is institutionalized when he attempts suicide, and finds himself a prisoner of his doctors' notion of who is "sane." While this remains a compelling scenario even today, readers will understand *The Shrike* better if they look at the play in the context of the times it was written. Like Arthur Miller's *The Crucible, The Shrike* meant something very different to its cold war audience than it might to a reader encountering it for the first time today.

Contemporary readers of *The Shrike,* however, are more likely to be reminded of Ken Kesey's *One Flew Over the Cuckoo's Nest.* Although there have been many plays and movies featuring protagonists trapped in asylums, from *The Snake Pit* to *Girl, Interrupted, One Flew Over the Cuckoo's Nest* is the most famous, and parallels Kramm's play very closely. Both Jim Downs and Randall Patrick McMurphy are sane men caught under the arbitrary authority of a mental institution, and both find their primary victimizers not in their doctors, but in women.

The resemblance, though superficially strong, ends there, however. *One Flew Over the Cuckoo's Nest* was a product of the 1960s, and it identifies freedom with sex, the life force, and creativity. Authority is repressiveness, coldness, power for its own sake. McMurphy is a kind of stand-in for Kesey himself, a countercultural guru of great renown. *The Shrike,* by contrast, sees freedom as delusional, or at best conditional. Authority is a vast, forbidding force that the hero barely tries to resist.

More importantly, *The Shrike* is a product of the early 1950s—a period when American political and intellectual life was at an all time low point. This was the time of the "red scare," the communist "witch-hunt" pursued by the House of Representatives' Un-American Activities Committee (HUAC) that resulted in the Hollywood "blacklist." Worse still, it was during this period that Senator Joseph McCarthy dominated the public mind with his groundless but devastating accusations of treason. For Kramm, what is objectionable about the hospital is not its purpose or values, or the larger values of the society that created it. On the contrary, Downs only wants to get a job directing stage plays again; his major despair was his failure in his profession. Even the specific decision to kill himself is unsubversive—like *Death of a Salesman*'s Willy Loman, who wants to kill himself for the insurance money.

The fact that Downs doesn't rebel at society in no way prevents the play from reflecting the times though. Broadway audiences surely must have recognized the situation Jim finds himself in. The blacklist had ruined the careers of many directors and playwrights, a number of whom had attempted suicide. The cause of Jim's failure is that he has served his country in World War II, and returned older and out-of-touch with the times. But other possibilities could surely be inferred by the audience. Moreover, the general power of unquestioned authority, justified by a cold war that seemed to have no end in sight, made many Americans uneasy. It was a time when saying something unpopular might cause one to be branded as a "pinko" (a communist) or worse. Once Jim is inside the hospital it is up to his doctors and his wife to decide when he should be released, but neither his doctors nor his wife share his values or opinions. Jim is now in the position of having to prove to the group, which he doesn't belong to, that he shares their arbitrary values, and believes what they believe. It is the ultimate nightmare for the individual: he has no rights nor freedom except what is granted to him by society, which is represented exclusively by high-handed authority figures.

The Shrike is far from unique in positing this sinister scenario; in postwar America, it was a recurrent nightmare. Films such as *Invasion of the Body Snatchers,* sociological best sellers such as David Riesman's *The Lonely Crowd,* and popular novels like Sloan Wilson's *The Man in the Gray Flannel Suit* all look at the horrors of conformity, of

> AUTHORITY IS A VAST, FORBIDDING FORCE THAT THE HERO BARELY TRIES TO RESIST."

the individual man squashed by the tyranny of the many. For Kramm, Jim's position in the hospital was not merely analogous to the injustices suffered by a few screenwriters or intellectuals; it cut right to the heart of social life in an intensely stressful time.

Consider this speech, one of the key passages in *The Shrike*. Jim's brother, Harry Downs, visits him, and manages to get a few minutes to communicate freely with him. With the urgency of a fellow prisoner, Harry communicates to Jim the essential thing he needs to know.

> Downs: If you want to get out of here—you've got to play ball.
> Jim: How?
> Downs: Jim—I have never paid a fine in my life. Because I know that I never know more than a cop. He's the smart one—not me. And it's 'Yes, officer,' and 'No, officer' and 'I'm sorry, sir.' Don't try to know more than these people. If you want to get out of here, you'll have to swallow everything. Well—what's being proud going to get you. Don't I have to compromise every day of my life? I've got a lousy insurance business, so I get drunk with a client, watch him make passes at Helen—and flatter the hell out of him. . . . It's no different in here. It's no different out there. Try it. What can you lose?

This is not just Harry speaking: it is Miller's Willy Loman, Wilson's Tom Rath, the beleaguered men of C. Wright Mills's *White Collar,* William S. Whyte's *The Organization Man.* Kramm, and presumably his audience, understood just how representative Jim's problem really was—just as, ten years later, Ken Kesey would create a quintessential sixties hero in *One Flew Over the Cuckoo's Nest*'s McMurphy. The power of *The Shrike* comes in Kramm's ability to show how the hospital is essentially a form of social coercion—conformity at figurative gunpoint. The power of conventional morality, of social expectations, and of science are all of a piece: Miss Wingate, in letting Jim know that giving up the girl he loves will be the cost of his freedom, doesn't even bother to coat it with medical euphemism. "What are you trying to do," she asks.

"Break down the sanctity of marriage?" Jim has to renounce Charlotte, whom he truly cares about, and return to his wife to get out of the hospital. He understands, as he weeps at the final curtain, that this is merely exchanging one prison for another.

For Kramm, however, the horrors of conformity are not purely personal. He goes to some pains to show how they infect society. The small community of patients Jim comes to live with all live in fear of the horrible Ward Seven—the "snake pit" where violent psychotics are kept. Because any accusation is enough to condemn a patient to Ward Seven, every patient has the power to exile any other patient. This is a clear allegory of the witch hunt, when any accusation of disloyalty, no matter who the source, was enough to land you on the blacklist. Everyone dislikes Schloss, but has to fear him, since the weakest and most ruthless members of society are, in this topsy-turvy world, now in the positions of greatest power. O'Brien and Schloss dislike each other intensely, but there is nothing either crazy or violent in their quarrel; nonetheless, when Schloss informs on O'Brien ("He threatened me, Miss Wingate"), O'Brien must suffer the consequences. Because Schloss is utterly opportunistic, and authority, in the form of the stern and stupid Miss Wingate, so all-powerful, men like O'Brien and Jim are prisoners whether in the hospital or out of it.

Contemporary readers will underestimate the force of what Jim is up against unless they remember how nearly limitless the authority of psychologists were in the early 1950s, and how unquestioned were the moral norms of the day. Although the disruptions of the 1960s have made the cold war years ripe for nostalgia, these were not "happy days" by any means; some measure of their unhappiness can be taken from the violence of the subsequent reaction against them in the following decade. *The Shrike* speaks to some universal truths about human life, about society, about marriage and free will. But it speaks to them specifically in the language of the early 1950s. For men such as Jim and

so many other literary protagonists, the world was run by the animalistic by-laws of business, by dirty pool in politics, and by the repressive hand of female morality on the home front. A play like *The Shrike* goes much farther than some of the literary benchmarks of the 1960s in explaining how much America has changed—and why.

Source: Josh Ozersky, Critical Essay on *The Shrike,* in *Drama for Students,* The Gale Group, 2002.

SOURCES

Atkinson, Brooks, Review of *The Shrike,* in *New York Times,* Vol. 20, January 16, 1952, p. 2.

Brown, John Mason, "The Amazing Mr. Ferrer," in *Saturday Review,* Vol. 35, February 9, 1952, pp. 22–23.

Hewes, Henry, "Drama Notes," in *Saturday Review,* Vol. 35, May 17, 1952, p. 28.

McLaughlin, Richard, Review of *The Shrike,* in *Theatre Arts,* Vol. 36, July 1952, p. 4.

Review of *The Shrike,* in *Newsweek,* Vol. 39, January 28, 1952, p. 83.

Review of *The Shrike,* in *Theatre Arts,* Vol. 36, March 1952, p. 71.

Review of *The Shrike,* in *Time,* Vol. 59, January 28, 1952, p. 43.

FURTHER READING

Review of *The Shrike,* in *America,* Vol. 90, December 12, 1953, p. 306.
   This piece praises the play's thematic focus.

Review of *The Shrike,* in *Commonweal,* Vol. 55, February 1, 1952, p. 422.
   This review explores the play's themes and critiques its Broadway debut.

Review of *The Shrike,* in *New Republic,* Vol. 126, February 4, 1952, p. 23.
   This review praises the play's Broadway debut.

The Way of the World

WILLIAM CONGREVE

1700

In 1700, when *The Way of the World* was performed on the English stage at Lincoln's Inn Fields (a new theatre that William Congreve managed), it was not a popular success. This was the last play Congreve was to write, perhaps for that reason. Since that time, however, this play has come to be regarded not only as Congreve's masterpiece, but as a classic example of the Comedy of Manners. The play is aptly named for two reasons. First, its action takes place in the "present," which means it reflects the same social period during which the play was originally performed. Second, as a comedy of manners, its purpose is to expose to public scrutiny and laughter the often absurd yet very human passions and follies that characterize social behavior. It therefore transcends its time by holding a mirror to the fashionable world in all of its frivolity and confusion while posing something more precious and sensible as an antidote.

As with all comedies of this type, the principle comic material consists of sexual relations and confrontations. Marriages are made for the sake of convenience and tolerated within precise social limits. Affairs are conventional, jealousies abound, lovers are coy, and gallantry is contrived. Dowries are the coin of the marriage realm and therefore they are of central concern in all contracts and adulterous intrigues. Congreve makes clear that the general way of the world may be funny but it is not particularly nice. In the way of all romantic comedies the "marriage of true minds" is finally achieved, but

humiliation, cruelty, and villainy are the means by which the action goes forward. His comedy is not intended to remedy the world, of course, but to offer an insightful and amusing view of both its seedy and sympathetic aspects.

AUTHOR BIOGRAPHY

William Congreve was born in 1670 in Bardsey (a village near Leeds), Yorkshire. When his father was commissioned to command the garrison at Youghal four years later, the family moved to Ireland, where Congreve was enrolled at a famous school in Kilkenny. In 1686, he attended Trinity College, Dublin along with his contemporary, Jonathan Swift. In 1688, the Congreves moved back to England, where William began writing his first play, *The Old Bachelour*, as he was recovering from an illness. Although he was sent to study law at the Middle Temple in London in 1691, he was not a diligent student. He preferred writing.

The *The Old Bachelour* was an immature work and borrowed heavily from earlier seventeenth century playwrights, especially Wycherley and Etherege, but it was a popular success. Henry T. E. Perry writes in *The Comic Spirit of Restoration* that when the play first appeared on stage in 1693, with the help of John Dryden, "literary London went mad over the new author." Congreve wrote four more plays between 1693 and 1700: *The Double Dealer*, *Love for Love*, *The Mourning Bride*, and *The Way of the World*, which appeared in 1700 and is considered his masterpiece.

As Congreve's reputation grew as a dramatist, he began to enjoy the benefits of the literary establishment. He counted Swift, Dryden, and Alexander Pope among his friends. When Parson Jeremy Collier wrote his notorious attack on the English stage, Congreve answered it with *The Way of the World*. In *William Congreve*, Bonamy Dobrée conjectures that the play's lukewarm reception may have been the reason that Congreve stopped writing plays. At any rate, Congreve still maintained his connections with the stage, managing Lincoln's Inn Fields and collaborating with Vanbrugh and Walsh in writing *Squire Trelooby* in 1704. He also wrote two libretti.

As a man of letters, he also was rewarded with government sinecures. He was given a post in Customs and, in 1714, was made Secretary of Jamaica. With this patrimony, as well as revenue from theatre productions and some royalties, he made a comfortable living. Congreve never married, but he was fond of the actress, Mrs. Bracegirdle, who played leading roles in all of his plays, including the part of Mrs. Millamant in *The Way of the World*. He was also the lover of the second Duchess of Marlborough and fathered her younger daughter, Lady Mary, who became Duchess of Leeds. When he died in 1729 at the age of fifty-nine, he left most of his estate to the Duchess of Marlborough.

PLOT SUMMARY

Prologue

In ancient Greek tragedy, a prologue conventionally set forth the subject of the drama to be enacted. It still refers to the introductory material of a play that serves as a sketch of the characters or themes to appear. It also can be an explanatory speech given by one of the characters, which is the case here. Spoken by "Mr. Betterton," the actor who played the role of Fainall in 1700, the Prologue takes the form of rhyming couplets in iambic pentameter meter. Congreve adapts the classic "heroic" verse both to establish this play as a serious dramatic offering but also to add to the comic effect. The Prologue also acts as both a tongue-in-cheek apology (in advance) and a taunt or challenge to the audience to find fault.

The speech begins with a comparison between "natural" fools and fools of "fortune." Those fools, who presume themselves poets and depend upon fortune, have it the hardest because audiences are so fickle, whereas born fools are protected and even favored. Fortune is to born fools what surrogate mothers are to the offspring of cuckoo birds, known to lay their eggs in the nests of other birds. Poets, on the other hand, are like gamblers who get drawn into games with higher and higher stakes. Congreve therefore "pleads no Merit" from his past successes, a "vain Presumption" that might lose him his "Seat" in "Parnasus"—an allusion to the mountain in Greece sacred to Apollo and the Muses. He throws himself on the mercy of his audience and begs indulgence despite the "Toil" with which he "wrought the following Scenes."

However, as the Prologue progresses, the tone changes. Congreve points the finger at "peevish Wits" who insist on the value of their work despite its reception. He playfully reminds his audience not to expect a satire since everyone in ''so Reform'd a Town'' is already ''Correct'' and therefore beyond instruction. Likewise, he claims no one should take it personally if he exposes a ''Knave or Fool'' since surely no such person would be found in this audience. He ends by referring to himself as a ''Passive Poet'' who will yield to audience judgement, but clearly he believes his play to be worthy and able to please.

Act 1

The major male characters appear in the first act, set in a chocolate house in London. Two young men, Mirabell and Fainall, are playing cards, and Mirabell is losing. Fainall takes the opportunity to question Mirabell about his ''indifferent mood,'' which leads to a confession that Mirabell's ardent love, Mrs. Millamant, rebuffed him the night before in the company of others. Those others include two ''coxcombs'' or conceited fools, Witwoud and Petulant, as well as several lady friends: Lady Wishfort (Millamant's Aunt), Mrs. Marwood, and Mrs. Fainall. Fainall tells Mirabell that he must have come upon the women during one of their ''cabal-nights'' when they meet expressly to ''sit upon the murder'd Reputations of the Week'' and from which pow-wow men are deliberately excluded with the exception of the two fops mentioned above.

The following exchange reveals that half of Millamant's fortune depends upon her marrying with her Aunt's blessings. However, Lady Wishfort hates Mirabell for having pretended love to her while hiding his true designs to marry her niece. Mrs. Marwood, who, as the name intimates, is a spoiler, exposes the sham for reasons that appear later in the play. The misfortune of the lovers, the central conflict around which the action will revolve, is thus established early on.

Halfway through the act, a servant to Mirabell appears on the scene to tell him that one Waitwell is married ''and bedded.'' While it is not yet clear who Waitwell is or why this is important, Mirabell tells Fainall that he is ''engag'd in a Matter of some sort of Mirth, which is not yet ripe for discovery.'' The conversation then turns to the character of Millamant, whom Mirabell mildly criticizes for suffering fools. But in a revealing passage about the power of love, Mirabell confesses that he likes Millamant ''with all her Faults'' and even because of them. They are precious to him since he has studied them and knows them by heart. They are ''as familiar to me as my own Frailties'' he says, and ''in a little time longer I shall like 'em as well.''

William Congreve

A messenger appears next with a letter from Sir Wilfull Witwoud for his half-brother Witwoud who is in the next room playing cards. Sir Wilfull has come to London to ''Equip himself for Travel'' abroad, which Mirabell finds outrageous since the man is over forty. Again the conversation between Mirabell and Fainall reveals information about characters introduced later, in this case the bashful, obstinate, but good-natured Sir Wilfull. He is compared to Witwoud whom Mirabell describes as a meddling fool but completely undiscerning about affronts directed at him. Enter Witwoud on cue who then demonstrates the nature of his wit in an amusing exchange among the three. Cajoled into revealing the nature of his friend Petulant's faults, Witwoud reveals several, which he then turns to advantages. During the conversation, a coachman enters calling for Petulant and the audience finds that he has paid three ladies of indistinct reputations to call upon him to impress people with his own popularity. He also comes disguised in public places to call upon himself and leave messages for himself for the same reason. When he enters the room, he is affecting to be put out by the intrusion of the ladies and tells the coachman he will not come. Witwoud remarks, however, that the real reason Petulant does not go out is because there is ''no more Company here to take notice of him.''

Through Petulant and Witwoud, Mirabell learns that Lady Wishfort is hatching a plot to marry Millamant to Mirabell's uncle, who has come to London for the purpose of disinheriting Mirabell. If Millamant and the uncle marry and have a child, Mirabell will be disinherited. And he will lose his love. Throughout the exchange, Witwoud admires Petulant, but Petulant proves himself oafish and ill-bred. The men decide to walk in the ''Mall'' where they are sure to meet the ladies. Mirabell asks the two ''gallants'' to walk by themselves rather than embarrass him with their ribald remarks to women, whereby Petulant asserts that any lady who blushes deserves the shame since she has revealed in her understanding that either she is not innocent or not discreet enough to turn away. The act ends with an imputation in the form of a rhyming couplet spoken by Mirabell: the behavior that passes as fashionable wit is really thinly disguised impudence and malice.

Act 2

The action takes place in St. James's Park where Mrs. Fainall and Mrs. Marwood are first seen discussing the general depravity of men, a fashionable convention of the time; however, despite the assertions that men are ''Vipers,'' both ladies show that they are attracted to Mirabell. While they are talking, Fainall and Mirabell join them. Mr. and Mrs. Fainall seem tender toward one another, but when the two couples split, Fainall with Mrs. Marwood and Mrs. Fainall with Mirabell, it becomes plain that Fainall and Mrs. Marwood are having an affair and that Mirabell and Mrs. Fainall were once lovers. Mrs. Marwood intimates that Fainall's wife likes Mirabell, but when Fainall responds, he accuses them both of being in love with Mirabell. Mrs. Marwood is offended and they quarrel. She threatens to broadcast their affair to the world and Fainall backs down. In Fainall's ensuing attempt to make peace, Mrs. Marwood breaks into tears and to hide her face, dons a mask just as Mirabell and Mrs. Fainall enter.

Mrs. Fainall tells Mirabell how much she despises her husband. At the same time, she remarks how she once loved Mirabell ''without Bounds.'' Her marriage to Fainall, in fact, is one of convenience, made only to save her reputation. Mirabell makes Mrs. Fainall privy to his plot to have his servant, Waitwell, pretend to be his invented uncle (Sir Rowland). He has fixed it so that Waitwell has married Lady Wishfort's waiting woman, Foible, to put them in league together. The plan is to have Waitwell, in the guise of the invented uncle, profess love to Lady Wishfort. Once she is caught in a trap, she will promise her niece to Mirabell to save herself from embarrassment. The plot thickens, so to speak, when Mirabell also tells Mrs. Fainall that he deliberately directed Foible to have Lady Wishfort announce in public that she would try and make a match between this invented uncle and Mrs. Millamant, his strategy being to secretly help Lady Wishfort keep her own marriage plans to the uncle a secret.

The young lovers come together for the first time when Mrs. Millamant enters the scene with her maid, Mincing, and her gallant follower, Witwoud. Witwoud bombards the gathered friends with a barrage of witticisms that demonstrate his tedious slavery to fashion and his silliness. Millamant then playfully satirizes the convention of letter sending as she and her maid discuss how they have ''pinn'd up her hair'' with the poetry but never the prose. Mirabell cuts through the raillery by confronting Millamant about the previous night when she snubbed him. The exchange conveys a sense of the popular courting conventions that require the façade of pretense, secrets, charm, and cruelty but never the demonstration of true feeling. When Mirabell gets Millamant alone, he questions why she spends time with such fools as Witwoud and Petulant. Millamant accuses him of being tiresome and walks away, but not without first letting drop the hint that she knows all about his plot. When she exits the scene, Mirabell is left alone pondering the ''whirlwind'' of love.

As the act closes, Waitwell and Foible enter the scene, obviously enjoying their recent nuptials. Foible tells Mirabell how his plot is progressing. She has supposedly gone out to show Sir Rowland the Lady's picture in order to inflame his most ardent desires. She will then hurry back to her mistress to tell her how ''he burns with Impatience'' to see her. Mirabell is happy with the report and gives her money. He promises her that her future will be secure if all goes well. Just as Foible is about to return to her mistress, she sees Mrs. Marwood go by disguised in her mask. She suddenly panics and is in a hurry to get back lest Marwood tell her Lady she has seen her talking with Mirabell, Lady Wishfort's sworn enemy. Mirabell now encourages Waitwell to ''forget'' himself and ''transform into Sir Rowland.'' In a comic last speech, Waitwell notes that it ''will be impossible'' for him to remember his old self since he has been married and knighted all in one day. He speaks the amusing closing line (again in rhyming couplet) that feigns grief over the fact that he must lose his title and yet keep his wife.

Act 3

Finally Lady Wishfort appears. The scene is a room in her house. She is in a tizzy, asking her servant, Peg, to fetch her a "little Red." Peg mistakenly thinks she means "Ratifia," a kind of cherry brandy, but she means her make-up or "paint." However, Foible has locked up the paint and Peg can't get at it. In a fit of anxiety, Lady Wishfort tells Peg to bring the Ratifia after all. The exchange shines a light on the silly vanity and bawdy, colorful humor of the Lady. Enter Mrs. Marwood. She indeed has reached the Lady before Foible and relates what she saw in St. James Park. When the Lady hears Foible entering, she bids Marwood hide in her closet so she can sound out her maid.

Foible, however, is up to the task. She admits speaking to Mirabell, but only because he begged her. She imputes to Mirabell's character a cruelty that readily disposes the Lady to hate him even more. Lady Wishfort is especially incensed when Foible tells her that Mirabell has described her as "superannuated." Lady Wishfort is "full of the Vigour of Fifty-five," as Mirabell remarks in the first act. She has a difficult time keeping her face together and must practically lay on the paint with a trowel. The truth hurts, and the Lady is "so fretted" that she needs to repair her face before Sir Rowland comes, which Foible promises will be soon. Their exchange ends with Lady Wishfort pondering how best to receive Sir Rowland. She hopes he will be somewhat "importunate" so that she will not have to advance and "break Decorums." Clearly, while she wants to preserve conventions, she is desperate for a husband and will not be too "nice" in the observance of convention if it does not suit the purpose. Before the Lady exits the scene, Foible reassures her that Sir Rowland is a "brisk man" and will take her "by storm." The Lady is pacified.

Mrs. Fainall enters and tells Foible that she, too, is privy to the plot against her mother, Lady Wishfort. They discuss the details, not knowing that Mrs. Marwood is still hiding in the closet. Foible tells Mrs. Fainall that she is afraid Mrs. Marwood is watching her and so she must be careful. She hints at Marwood's motivations when she tells Mrs. Fainall that Marwood "has a Month's mind" (meaning she likes Mirabell), but that he "can't abide her." When they exit, Marwood enters the scene. She has overheard everything and is both angry and resolved that she will ruin Mirabell's plans. Lady Wishfort enters and Mrs. Marwood puts it into her head to match Sir Wilfull Witwoud with Lady Wishfort's niece, Millamant. The Lady thinks it a good idea and says she will "propose it." Foible enters to announce that Witwoud and Petulant have arrived to dine. The Lady and Foible exit to change for dinner.

Enter Mrs. Millamant and Mincing. The exchange between Millamant and Marwood exposes the mean-spirited jealousy of Marwood as she advises Millamant that her love of Mirabell is no longer a secret and therefore not a fit subject for "Pretence." Millamant accuses her of being "Censorious" and they trade thinly veiled insults. Millamant accuses Marwood of revealing to her aunt the secret love between her and Mirabell. Marwood taunts her, and Millamant pretends to be amused that Mirabell loves her so much that he has no use for the rest of the world, including Marwood. Marwood says she hates Mirabell and Millamant merrily agrees that she does, too, although this is just to have another go at Marwood, who is older than her and still unmarried. Marwood warns Millamant: "Your merry Note may be chang'd sooner than you think." Millamant then calls for a song that satirizes the game of love by concluding that love is measured by the ambition involved, and the only worthy conquest is the one that has been won after so many others have tried and lost. Enter Petulant and Witwoud, who strive to showcase their combined wit in an amusing sally that further proves the aptness of their names.

Millamant and Mincing exit while Sir Wilfull Witwoud, dressed in his "Country Riding Habit," along with a servant to Lady Wishfort enter. In a nod to "fashion," which disdains country breeding, Witwoud pretends not to know his half-brother. Sir Wilfull approaches the "two gallants" standing by, who still refuse to speak. He speaks first: "No Offence, I hope." Petulant and Witwoud are disgusted by his country manners and Witwoud adjures Petulant to "smoke him" or make fun of him. However, their attempts to "unman" him rebound, for Sir Wilfull is a match for them and answers them both honestly and artfully, although somewhat coarsely. "The Fashion's a Fool; and you're a Fop, dear Brother," he proclaims. He roundly berates Witwoud for leaving the service of an attorney to become a professional dandy. Mrs. Marwood inquires after Sir Wilfull's plans to travel but he says first he will "tarry" and "learn somewhat of your

Lingo.'' When Lady Wishfort and Fainall enter, the dialogue has established Sir Wilfull as somewhat buffoonish and crude but good-natured and honest.

Lady Wishfort and Fainall enter, and Lady Wishfort greets her guests. Mincing announces dinner and everyone exits except Mrs. Marwood and Fainall, who have been talking apart. Mrs. Marwood acquaints Fainall with Mirabell's plot to outwit Lady Wishfort, and Fainall is dumbfounded that he has been made a cuckold. Mrs. Marwood pragmatically suggests that they prevent the plot and thereby spoil Mirabell's chances at Millamant's fortune. She reassures Fainall that his wife had given up her affair before marriage and that he should be satisfied to stay with her as soon as he has got hold of all her money. Fainall is more outraged that his wife has out-trumped him (''put Pam in her pocket'') than that she has been unfaithful. Mrs. Marwood suggests a counter-plot: Tell Lady Wishfort that Mrs. Fainall has been unfaithful with Mirabell and Lady Wishfort will be so ''enraged'' she will do anything to save her daughter's reputation. Mrs. Marwood admits that her idea of matching Millamant and Sir Wilfull may now be an obstacle to their plan, for if they should marry, Millamant will claim her rightful fortune. However, Fainall promises to get him drunk so that he will be unable to make proper advances. Mrs. Marwood determines to write an anonymous letter to Lady Wishfort revealing all. Fainall is comforted by the notion that, in the worst case, he still has from his wife a ''deed of Settlement of the best part of her Estate; which I wheadl'd out of her.'' There is both disingenuous conceit and a premonition of truth in the closing couplet delivered by Fainall on the need for husbands to endure, to be neither too wise nor too foolish lest they suffer the consequences of pain or shame.

Act 4

The action continues in Lady Wishfort's house as the Lady and Foible discuss preparations for Sir Rowland's visit. In a moment of unself-conscious comic animation, Lady Wishfort ponders how best to effect the most ''alluring'' pose and so take Sir Rowland's breath away. As they hear his coach approaching, Foible tells the Lady that Sir Wilfull is on his way toward getting drunk and the Lady anxiously sends Foible to bring Millamant and return so that she is not left alone long with Sir Rowland. They exit and Mrs. Millamant and Fainall

enter. Foible tells Millamant that Mirabell has been waiting to see her. She hesitates coyly and then decides to receive him. All the while she is walking and repeating verses by poet John Suckling (an early seventeenth-century poet perhaps best known for his ''Ballad upon a Wedding''), which shows her to be deep in thought about the nature of sexual relationships.

Meanwhile, Sir Wilfull enters terribly drunk, and Mrs. Fainall intercepts him. She suggests that Sir Wilfull approach Millamant and ''pursue his point'' and when he hesitates, too bashful to proceed, she locks him in the room and exits. When Millamant says aloud ''Natural, easie Suckling!'' referring to the verses she has been quoting, Sir Wilfull thinks she means him and once again his inability to grasp the ''lingo'' of London makes for an amusing exchange. He is unable to make any headway with Millamant. It is clear that he is no match for her intellect or sophistication, and she sends him away somewhat frustrated as Mirabell enters.

Mirabell finishes the Suckling verse that Millamant has been quoting, which alludes to the mythical romance between Phoebus and Daphne and, by extension, the two of them. Here begins a ''dance'' of love marked by both conventional coy flirtation and true regard. They explore one another's expectations and needs by setting pre-nuptial conditions under which the marriage will be managed and tolerated. She wants to make sure of her independence and privacy before she must ''by degrees dwindle into a Wife.'' He also has his terms that must be agreed upon before he is ''enlarg'd into a Husband.'' She must, primarily, not be involved in scandals or become a slave to fashion. Millamant is outraged that he should think her capable of such behavior, and so they agree as Mrs. Fainall re-enters.

Mrs. Fainall shares in their joy but hurries Mirabell out since her mother, the Lady Wishfort is on her way in. There's danger that if he is caught there, the Lady will fly into a rage and be distracted from the business at hand; namely, Sir Rowland's pretended suit. Mirabell exits. Mrs. Foible comments on Sir Wilfull's drunkenness and mentions that he and Petulant were ready to quarrel when she came away. Millamant admits her love for Mirabell and conveys her disdain of Sir Wilfull. Enter Witwoud who tells them that Lady Wishfort broke up the ''fray'' and, soon after, a very drunk Petulant enters. He makes a rude, abrupt proposal of love to Millamant, for which Witwoud offers hyperbolic and satirical praise ("thou art an Epitomizer of words . . . a retailer of Phrases").

Petulant responds by insulting Witwoud and calling him "half of an Ass," Sir Wilfull being the other half. Witwoud finds the insult wittily endearing and asks to be kissed "for that." In the ribald dialogue that follows, Millamant learns that the would-be quarrel has been about her. Apparently, Petulant has defended her beauty and his claim to it, but moodily he relinquishes her by his next remark: "If I shall have my Reward, say so; if not, fight for your Face the next time yourself." He exits with a curt explanation that he's going home to sleep with his maid. When Mrs. Fainall asks why everyone is in such a "pickle," Witwoud explains that it is Fainall's plot to "get rid of the Knight" (Sir Wilfull).

Lady Wishfort and Sir Wilfull enter arguing over his drunkenness, but Sir Wilfull is immune to the Lady's reproaches. He is all merriment and pliability, willing and able in his drunken state to marry Millamant if that is in everyone's best interests. He is singing popular drinking songs, talking ridiculously of traveling to the "Antipodes" (the opposite poles of the earth), and making a fool of himself. Millamant and Mrs. Fainall find his smell so offensive they exit the scene. When Lady Wishfort begs him to indeed travel, to travel as far away as possible to the "Saracens or the Tartars, or the Turks" he launches into a whimsical tirade on traveling outside Christian lands. After a third round of song, Foible enters to whisper to Lady Wishfort that her suitor is impatiently awaiting her. Lady Wishfort begs Witwoud to take Sir Wilfull away and the two exit, Sir Wilfull still singing. Waitwell enters disguised as Sir Rowland and pretends to be mad with desire for her. The Lady is taken in by his advances. Goaded on by her own desperation for a husband and Sir Rowland's aspersions against "that Unnatural Viper," Mirabell, she agrees to a quick arrangement, first having secured that Sir Rowland suspects no "sinister appetite" or "scruple of Carnality" has prompted her to marry. Sir Rowland, of course, is a gallant courtier, and he reassures the Lady that her honor is not suspect. Foible enters to tell her a letter has come for her and she exits. Lady Wishfort soon reappears with the letter.

Foible recognizes Mrs. Marwoods's writing and enjoins Waitwell to get the letter from her. He

pretends to recognize the writing, and sensing his "Passion" by this show of jealousy, she has him read with her. The letter uncovers Mirabell's intrigue and Sir Rowland as an impostor. Lady Wishfort nearly faints. Waitwell, however, quick on his feet, denounces the letter as the work of Mirabell. He vows to revenge himself but Lady Wishfort pleads with him to act sensibly. He promises to give proof of his authentic intentions by bringing her the "blackbox, which Contains the Writings of my whole Estate." Lady Wishfort acquiesces, and Waitwell delivers the final couplet that promises her satisfaction and his immediate vindication. But Foible has the last word. In a final provocative pun, she suggests that the "Arrant Knight" is really an "arrant Knave."

Act 5

Lady Wishfort's house is the setting for the denouement. Lady Wishfort, in some of the most colorful language of the play, is roundly dressing down Foible for her discovered part in the humiliating charade. She threatens to send her back to the streets where she found her, and Foible is desperately trying to defend herself. But Lady Wishfort is not taken in and announces that her "Turtle" is already in custody and that she "shall Coo in the same Cage." She exits as Mrs. Fainall enters. Mrs. Fainall cheers Foible by telling her that Mirabell is releasing her husband. Foible then reveals that Mrs. Marwood and Fainall have been having an affair. She recounts that when she and Mincing caught them red-handed, she was made to swear secrecy on a "Book of Verses and Poems," an oath no one could take seriously. Mrs. Fainall is surprised but quick to understand the opportunity this discovery allows.

Mincing enters and tells them that Lady Wishfort is waiting to see Foible and that Mirabell has freed Waitwell. Mincing delivers a message from Mirabell that Foible is to hide in the closet until Lady Wishfort has calmed down. Fainall has upset her by demanding the Lady's fortune or threatening to be divorced. Mincing reports that Millamant is ready to marry Sir Wilfull to save her fortune. Mincing agrees to "vouch" for Mrs. Fainall when she calls her. Mincing and Foible exit.

Lady Wishfort and Mrs. Marwood enter. Lady Wishfort thanks Marwood for her friendship and her timely discovery of the several plots against her.

She questions her daughter's apparent fall from grace, all the more deplorable since the Lady herself was a ''Mold'' and a ''Pattern'' for her. It is of course an ironic moment since by now it is clear how little virtue plays a role in the Lady's pursuits. Mrs. Fainall protests her innocence and claims that they have both been wronged. She accuses Marwood of being a ''Friend'' to her husband and that she will prove it. Mrs. Marwood takes offense and Lady Wishfort is embarrassed for her. However, Mrs. Fainall is unfazed. She warns her mother that Marwood is ''a Leach'' who will ''drop off when she's full.'' The comic irony is obvious when Lady Wishfort then soliloquizes about the irreproachable education that her daughter has been given in the ''Rudiments of Vertue,'' taught from infancy to detest and avoid men. Indeed, she talks herself out of belief in her daughter's guilt and agrees that Fainall should prove his charges. But the clever and ambitious Mrs. Marwood regales her with scurrilous scenes of what will happen in court. The Lady shudders to think of what havoc such a course will wreck on her reputation and she backs down.

Fainall enters and details the condition under which she must surrender her estate. First, she must not marry unless, out of necessity, he chooses her husband, and second, his wife must settle her entire fortune on him and depend upon him entirely for her ''Maintenance.'' He finally demands Millamant's six thousand pounds, which ''she has forfeited . . . by her disobedience'' in contracting a marriage against the Lady's will and by refusing Sir Wilfull. The Lady asks for time to consider and Fainall grants her the amount of time needed to draw up the papers. He exits and Lady Wishfort is left to the cold comforts of Marwood who, she thinks, is still her friend. She calls Fainall a ''merciless Villain,'' a ''Barbarian'' compared to Languish, her daughter's first husband.

Millamant and Sir Wilfull then enter with the news that they will wed. Lady Wishfort is greatly comforted that Millamant has nullified her contract with Mirabell, who waits to be admitted outside. Lady Wishfort can not bear to see him, but Millamant persuades her by saying that he plans to travel with Sir Wilfull and never trouble her again. Sir Willful corroborates her statement and Marwood, who senses another plot, exits. Sir Wilfull and Mirabell enter. Mirabell apologizes and Sir Wilfull acts as his supporter. Lady Wishfort grudgingly agrees to ''stifle'' her resentment on account of Sir Wilfull if

Mirabell relinquishes any contract with her niece. Mirabell asserts that he has already done so. Despite her distrust of Mirabell, she is attracted. She says in an aside, ''his appearance rakes the Embers which have so long layn smother'd in my Breast.''

Fainall and Mrs. Marwood enter together, Fainall with the papers for the Lady to sign. She tells him of Millamant's decision to marry Sir Wilfull, which Fainall calls ''a sham.'' Sir Wilfull, his back up, threatens to draw his ''Instrument'' if Fainall does not withdraw his. But Fainall is undeterred. He insults Sir Wilfull and again warns that if the Lady doesn't sign, he will set Mrs. Fainall ''a drift, like a Leaky hulk to Sink or Swim.'' The Lady is beside herself, and when Mirabell offers advice, she accepts it. He asks for her niece in ''Compensation'' but says he is willing to help her no matter what. The Lady is overwhelmed by his generosity and agrees that he shall have Millamant if he can save her from Fainall. Enter Mrs. Fainall, Foible, and Mincing. They expose the affair between Marwood and Fainall, but Fainall still will not back down and stands on his threat to expose Mrs. Fainall's ''shame.'' Mirabell, however, has one more ace up his sleeve.

Enter Waitwell with the black box and soon after Petulant and Witwoud. The box contains Mrs. Fainall's settlement (witnessed by Witwoud and Petulant) signed over in trust to Mirabell before she married Fainall precisely in order to avoid the very treachery now being enacted. Fainall is forced to admit that the settlement he thought had been signed over to him is a fake. He tries to run at his wife with his sword but is stopped by Sir Wilfull. He exits vowing revenge. Mrs. Fainall confronts Mrs. Marwood, who also warns that she will get even. Marwood exits. Nothing remains but to celebrate the restored lovers and the truce between Lady Wishfort and Mirabell. Mirabell reveals that Sir Wilfull has been a willing accomplice in Mirabell's plans and so will suffer no pain at the loss of Millamant. The lovers embrace, and Mirabell quiets the Lady's last fears that Fainall will ''pursue some desperate Course.'' Fainall needs his marriage (and his wife's money) in order to survive, and Mirabell promises to be the mediator of peace. He restores the deed of trust to Mrs. Fainall, suggesting that ''it may be a means well manag'd to make you live Easily together.'' Her unhappy fate, then, is to continue to live with Fainall, but with new knowledge and power. The act ends with a quatrain warning against the evils of adultery.

Epilogue

Mrs. Bracegirdle, the actress who has played the part of Mrs. Millamant, speaks the closing lines of the play, which, according to comic convention, takes a satirical punch at drama critics.

CHARACTERS

Fainall

Fainall is a faithless husband who depends on his wife's inheritance for his ease and livelihood. His ''Wit and outward fair Behaviour,'' as his friendly acquaintance and rival, Mirabell, remarks, has allowed him to enjoy a good reputation ''with the Town,'' but his true nature is greedy, false, and profligate. While he is carrying on an affair with Mrs. Marwood, his wife's friend and confidante, he is plotting to wrest full control of both his wife's and his mother-in-law's estates. As his name implies, he is a pretender, but one whose talent for getting along serves him well in society. It is, in fact, this tractability that makes him a suitable man to be ''sacrificed'' to ''Arabella Languish'' (Mrs. Fainall's name by her first, deceased husband) when this widow is in need of an inoffensive second husband.

Mrs. Fainall

Mrs. Fainall is daughter to Lady Wishfort and heir to her fortune. Previously married to one ''Languish,'' she was widowed and then remarried to keep her love affair with Mirabell safe from public scrutiny. Unfortunately, her mother raised her to hate and revile men. Thus, while she can hardly bear her husband, she has warm regards still for her former lover, whom she is compelled to relinquish before she is remarried to preserve her good reputation. She is professed intimate friends with Mrs. Marwood until she learns that Mrs. Marwood is her husband's lover. Mrs. Fainall is clever and cautious, having signed over a large part of her estate in trust before her marriage because she suspected that her husband's greed would eventually force it from her. She is a loyal friend to her cousin, Mrs. Millamant, whom she helps to obtain Mirabell as a husband. In so doing, she is also generous: she not only willingly parts with her former lover, but she contrives to help Millamant, who stands to gain a portion of the moiety of her aunt's (the Lady Wishfort's) fortune when she marries.

Foible

Foible is a simple yet quick-witted, dissembling yet good-hearted waiting woman to Lady Wishfort. She nonetheless helps dupe the Lady by means of a clever yet harmless ploy hatched by Mirabell. Since her betrayal is in the cause of love, and since no one is injured (only mildly embarrassed), she is forgiven in the end. Thought to be an obedient errand girl whom her Lady uses as an emissary to procure a husband for herself, Foible guilelessly turns the tables and finds a husband for herself (Mirabell's servant, Waitwell) as well as one for her Lady's niece, Millamant. It just so happens that Millamant's choice is Mirabell, her aunt's sworn enemy, hence the necessity of Mirabell's ploy. As a servant, Foible has the means to come and go throughout her mistress's home and is therefore privy to much that other characters would like to hide. Through Foible's assistance, Fainall and Marwood's adulterous affair and their designs to steal her Lady's fortune are found out and justly brought to closure.

Mrs. Marwood

Pretended friend to Mrs. Fainall and secret lover of her husband, Mrs. Marwood schemes to spoil the happiness of others to enrich herself. She almost succeeds in foiling the hoped-for marriage between the true lovers Mirabell and Millamant by exposing their love and so inciting the rage of Lady Wishfort who scorns Mirabell because he made false advances to her. Although she pretends she hates him and all men, Marwood also likes Mirabell and is jealous of his attentions to Millamant. Of all the characters in this comedy of manners, Mrs. Marwood is perhaps the least sympathetic: in fact, she is more than once referred to as ''that devil'' by both Mrs. Fainall and Foible. Because she deliberately sets out to destroy the happiness of others, and because she is duplicitous in her friendships, she is finally despised as an adulteress and a traitor. Even the trusting Lady Wishfort, who believes Marwood's loyal friendship has saved her from the disgrace and villainy of others' machinations and plots against her comes to see her as a ''wicked accomplice.'' While she is clever, she is not nice; while she has wit, she is not funny.

Mrs. Millamant

Mrs. Millamant is a young, vivacious, pretty, and fashionable lady who loves Mirabell and, as niece to Lady Wishfort, is heir to part of her fortune should she marry with Lady Wishfort's approval. She affects a coy demeanor, as well as disdain for the opposite sex. She is often seen in the company of "fops," somewhat tiresome and affected young wits who nonetheless are entertaining enough and whom she tolerates to hide her true regard for Mirabell. She is willful and witty in her own right and adeptly manages to steer clear of the convoluted plots and schemes that pack the action and threaten to undo most of the characters by their twists and turns. Mrs. Millamant's nature is graceful, decorous, and confident; however, her tolerance for Witwoud and Petulance show her to be a creature of the world and somewhat at the mercy of the dictates of fashion. Despite her good breeding, she is not above abiding fools for her own mischievous ends.

Mincing

Mincing is a somewhat affected yet dutiful and loyal waiting woman to Mrs. Millamant. Together with her friend, Foible, Mincing witnesses and corroborates Fainall's and Marwood's adulterous affair, and so helps expose the deception of the two in plotting to exploit Mrs. Fainall and extort from Lady Wishfort her entire estate. The two servant's testimony leads to Lady Wishfort's blessing of the marriage between Mirabell and Millamant.

Mirabell

Mirabell is a clever, handsome, young, and headstrong gentleman of good manners who is the admirer of and persistent suitor to Millamant. He also is the former lover of Mrs. Fainall, and he is liked by Mrs. Marwood. While once the object of desire, he is now the sworn enemy of Lady Wishfort for pretending love to her. A man of sense, he is also a clever and effective strategist who carries out his schemes to marry Lady Wishfort's niece against her will and thereby secure his love and Millamant's dowry. While likeable, he is also ruthless in his exploitation of both servants and peers to get his own way. But since nearly everyone benefits from his schemes, no one seems to mind, except Fainall and Marwood, whom he exposes at the end as perfidious and maladroit traitors. Mirabell is a proud, artful, and generous man of the world who knows he is suffering from a love sickness from which he cannot and does not want to escape.

Petulant

This dandy and follower of Mrs. Millamant is every bit as rude and ill humored, as peevish and capricious, as the name would suggest. Friend to Witwoud, he is perceived by other characters to be the inferior wit of the two. He is illiterate and proud, boorish and vain. To give the impression that he is popular, he pays ladies of questionable virtue to call on him in public places, and he has also disguised himself precisely to call upon himself in public. He likes Mrs. Millamant but really would just as soon sleep with his maid. His raillery is pure brilliance to Witwoud, but he is barely tolerated by people of any sensibility. Petulant is endowed with a brutal tactlessness but is unable to speak a truth since everything he says and does is a performance based on his mood at the moment. As a fool, he is rather more dour than deft.

Waitwell

Servant to Mirabell, Waitwell is essential to furthering his master's marriage designs. Being loyal and eager to please, he agrees both to marry Lady Wishfort's maid, Foible, in order to better secure the plan, and also to impersonate Mirabell's uncle in order to profess love to Lady Wishfort. As Mirabell's invented uncle, Sir Rowland, Waitwell gives a delightful performance that convinces the Lady of his ardent desire and his rush to marry in order to foil Mirabell's hope for a marriage dowry. It is his gallant love act that places Lady Wishfort in the embarrassing and precarious position of being fooled once again by a suitor, and, by helping to place her at the mercy of her enemies, clears the way for Mirabell to extricate her.

Lady Wishfort

An aging grand dame, Lady Wishfort is as desperate to get a husband as she is unsuspecting of the plans afoot to rob her of her fortune and her "virtue." Mother to Mrs. Fainall and aunt to Mrs. Millamant, she holds the key to the money and the maid that will bring the action to its conclusion. Lady Wishfort's colorful language and vehement expressions of emotion cause the greatest moments of amusement and liveliness in the play. She is the dupe of nearly everyone close to her, including her own daughter, and while she is in danger of loosing her fortune, she is more worried about damaging her reputation. Her "paint" is practically laid on with a trowel to hide the wrinkles, but she fancies herself attractive to men the likes of Mirabell and the pretender, Sir Rowland. While she raises her daughter to hate men, she cannot be reconciled to life without them. And while she is at great pains to keep up appearances, her mighty constitution suffers all forms of indignities and humiliation, yet she is able to recover with some modicum of good grace and in the end forgive all.

Witwoud

A man who prides himself on his never-failing wit, raillery, and charm, this "becravated and beperriwig'd" fool (as Sir Wilfull calls him) is an admirer of Mrs. Millamant and a pretended favorite of the ladies. His chief usefulness is entertaining with his droll wit, and he is taken into the confidence of the ladies' thrice weekly "cabals" as they set about destroying reputations and professing their fashionable opinions on marriage, men, and morals. By his good-natured affectation and unself-conscious methods, he allows the other characters to disguise their true emotions; his superficial and careless remedy of jokes, similes, and puns relieves tension and unwittingly exposes the foolishness of contemporary fashion and manners. While he is foolish, he is also harmless, and he furnishes, despite his desperate attempts at wit, some very funny and insightful moments.

Sir Wilfull Witwoud

Bashful and obstinate by turns, feisty and deferential when necessary, a country bumpkin with a good nature and a will to please, Sir Wilfull Witwoud, half brother by marriage to Witwoud, would be a wit if he could. He has come to town to look around before setting out on his travels and finds he doesn't understand the "lingo" of the fashionable world. He serves as a foil to the well bred. In contrast to their studied rudeness and affectation, he is simple and matter-of-fact. Thus, he is an easy mark in the scheming game of matchmaking, but a cheerful one, especially after a long bout of drinking. In a show of generosity and an imposture of sincerity, he gladly agrees to marry Millamant as a last resort to save her fortune. However, he also dissembles well. His is

but another actor in Mirabell's clever ruse to catch Fainall and Mrs. Marwood in their deception and to lure Lady Wishfort into his harmless trap.

THEMES

Social Convention

Congreve's "comedy of manners" takes the fashionable or conventional social behavior of the time as the principle subject of satire. Conflicts that arise between and among characters are prompted by affected and artificial social mores, especially with respect to relationships between the sexes. Social pretenses and plot complications abound in *The Way of the World*. Women are compelled to act coyly and to dissemble in courtship, couples deceive one another in marriage, friends are double-dealing, and conquests have more to do with dowries and convenience than love. All moral principle is risked for the sake of reputation and money. However, what makes the action comic is the subterfuge. What one says is hardly ever what one really thinks or means. To judge by appearances, for example, no one could be happier in his marriage than Fainall, who in reality disdains his wife and is carrying on an adulterous affair with his wife's close friend. Congreve intimates that, in fashionable society at the turn of the eighteenth century, it is crucial to preserve the outer trappings of beauty, wit, and sophistication no matter how egregious one's actions and words might prove.

Dowries, Marriage, and Adultery

In the male-dominated, patriarchal society of Congreve's time, a woman was little more than property in a marriage transaction. Her dowry (money, property, and estate) was relinquished to her husband at marriage and she became, by law, his chattel. In the upper classes, women had little voice in their own fate, and marriages were usually arranged according to social status, size of fortune, and family name. In the play, Millamant's dowry is at the center of the struggle that pits Mirabell, her true lover, against Fainall and Mrs. Marwood, the two adulterers plotting to gain control of Millamant's fortune as well as Fainall's wife's. Cunningly, Mrs.

TOPICS FOR FURTHER STUDY

- The seventeenth century was a time of great political upheaval in England. Research the period dating from the Civil War in the 1640s, which led to the dissolution of the English monarchy, to the ''Restoration'' of Charles II in 1660. In what ways did political change help shape ''Restoration Drama?'' In particular, how did political realities contribute to the rise and popular appeal of the ''comedy of manners?''

- Lady Wishfort is a central comic figure in *The Way of the World*. As the aging but still amorous dowager, the capricious yet tenacious holder of the purse strings, and the twice duped lover so desperate to marry and so patently superficial in her disapproval of men, she amuses by the very nature of her naïve yet bold heart. How would you direct the pivotal opening of act 3, when we are introduced to Lady Wishfort for the first time? This will involve her interaction with Peg, Foible, and Mrs. Marwood up until her exit from the scene.

- John Dryden is a major literary figure of the seventeenth century, and he was one of the most vocal supporters of Congreve's work. It was Dryden who helped Congreve polish his wildly popular first play, *The Old Batchelour* for the London stage. Research the life of Dryden and discuss the significance of his relationship to Congreve in particular and Restoration literature in general.

- Read William Wycherley's *The Country Wife*. As an early example of Restoration comedy, how does it compare to Congreve's *The Way of the World*, written twenty-five years later? What are some common themes and comic devices? What are some essential differences?

- Choose a major character in *The Way of the World*. Say why that character is important to the theme and plot. How is that character significant in relation to other characters in the play? How does the character's role add to the overall comic effect? Refer directly to dramatic lines of the text in your analysis.

- It has been said that every good comedy contains an element of tragedy. Describe the tragic elements in *The Way of the World*. Does the play have a happy ending?

Fainall has had a large part of her estate signed over in trust before her marriage to prevent her husband from acquiring it.

While marriages are important economic contracts, they are also convenient vehicles for protecting social reputations. Mrs. Fainall has made such a marriage, which is socially acceptable and even expected, as long as the pretense of civility is maintained. However, getting caught in an adulterous relationship puts both reputation and fortune at risk. Hence when the relationship between Fainall and Mrs. Marwood is discovered, the two become social outcasts. Fainall has staked his reputation on a plot to disinherit his wife. As punishment, he will have to bear the humiliating exposure, continuing to live with his wife and depend on her for his livelihood. Mrs. Marwood's reputation is ruined, her future hopes destroyed. Congreve's intent is to reflect the way of the world in all its manifest greed. The lesson is that those who cheat get their just desserts in the end.

Decorum and Wit

Congreve invents several characters who, as fops, dandies, and fools, provide fitting foils to the romantic hero and heroine. He pits these purported ''wits'' against Mirabell and Millamant to comment on the social decline of manners. Since the play is a comedy, audiences are to take it both as serious social satire and also as an amusing romp. No one, of course, escapes Congreve's satirical pen entirely. All people are sometimes fools, Congreve suggests, or sometimes too earnest or too busy inventing counterfeit personas in order to hide their own moral turpitude. Petulant and Witwoud make good fools for they epitomize the shallowness and silliness of fashionable society, but they both also are capable of voicing through their wit the real motivations behind people's actions. They mistake fashionable behavior for decorum and good manners, but they are basically harmless. The comic hero, Mirabell, unscrupulously uses blackmail and trickery to promote his own interests, yet he also represents what is wise and decent in society, and he protects and thoughtfully provides for his friends. Millament, while she acts capriciously and spends time with fops, is inherently thoughtful and able to distinguish between fashion and principles. Lady Wishfort is perhaps the most sympathetically comic character in that, for all her desperate attempts to preserve decorum and for all the power she wields as the wealthy matriarch of the family, she is at heart a lonely widow who will do anything for a husband.

Passion and Puritanism

It has been noted that this final Congreve play was, in effect, a dramatic answer to Puritan Pastor Jeremy Collier's vilification of the theatre world, in which he publicly denounced the English stage as morally bankrupt. As comic heroes, Millamant and Mirabell represent characters who are most in touch with their own natural passions and creative spirits, free of both a fashionable sexual freedom and overwrought piety. Lady Wishfort symbolizes the tyranny and hypocrisy with which society constrains these natural, creative passions in the name of Puritanism. In contrast to the true lovers, she pretends to an elegance and pretentious demeanor at odds with the emotions and passions raging inside her. In a strict and amusingly eccentric Puritanical education in the ways of the world, she has served as a "model" by which to teach her daughter to despise men and lewd behavior, including "going to filthy Plays." It is no coincidence that, in order for the two lovers to finally come together, they must reduce Lady Wishfort's logic and principles to the transparent artifice that it has so clearly become by the end of the play.

Sexual Politics

The war between the sexes in this dramatic comedy is played with wit and artistry, treachery and complex design, tenderness and teasing, passion and charm, and, above all, precise timing. In Congreve's play, it is safe to say that in this particu-lar struggle—the high stakes of which are love, money, and social survival—men and women are equally proficient and powerful. Gender behavior is proscribed within the limits of social convention. Thus male and female attitudes and actions are expected to be very different and those differences are to be strictly maintained. The prenuptial "negotiation" scene between Mirabell and Millamant amusingly yet sincerely establishes the rules by which the couple will manage their marriage, preserving independence and privacy as well as intimacy and love. While the conditions of their agreements seem petty at first glance, it is clear that they reflect prohibitions against the "evil" tendencies of each sex. The bottom line is that Millamant will not be unduly dominated or possessed by her husband and her husband will not be vexed with the wiles of intrigue or the vain fashions of the time. It is a good exchange: it preserves the respect of each party as well as the distinctions and charms perceived to be natural and unique to men and women. Mirabell and Millamant's union is certainly intended as a corrective to the deceitful adultery of Fainall, the pathetic loneliness of Lady Wishfort, and the emptiness and debauchery of the life of the dandy.

STYLE

Restoration Comedy

Congreve's plays belong to a genre known as Restoration comedy. The Restoration refers to the reestablishment of the monarchy in England with the return of Charles II to the throne in 1660 after a period of social upheaval. In English literature, the Restoration "age" parallels the political period, covering roughly the years from 1660 to the revolution in 1688 when Parliament regained power. The genre is characterized by its satirical view of the times, with its particular focus on the relationship between conventional morality and the individual spirit. Its comic characters are often reflections of the shallow aristocrats of court society; they are peopled with libertines and wits, gallants and dandies. The hero is usually sophisticated and critical of convention and fashion: In *The Way of the World*, for example, Mirabell is able to out-rascal the other rogues and thereby wins the love and prosperity he seeks as well as the respect and admiration of the other characters. The plays of George Etherege,

William Wycherley, Sir John Vanbrugh, and George Farquhar also belong to the English tradition of Restoration comedy.

Setting

Congreve's play takes place in London, an apt setting since the play's action revolves around the ways of the fashionable world. Indeed, the play reflects the manners and customs of London life in 1700, when it was first performed. Within the play, Congreve contrasts the pretentious, artificial (and often reprehensible and barbaric) manners of "Town" life with the rough, untutored but more natural country manners reflected in the character of Sir Wilfull. The play's five acts include just three settings: a chocolate house, St. James Park, and Lady Wishfort's London house. Each setting allows a glimpse of the way in which characters comport themselves in public and private.

In the chocolate house, the major male characters meet to drink and gamble in act 1. This is the domain where men seem to rule, and Congreve orients the audience to the social dictates by which they speak and act together. In act 2, the action moves to St. James Park, a more open and public place where men and women interact. In this setting, the intrigues of plot multiply. Couples are on display in the park, to see and be seen. The park is central to the plot because it allows Congreve to show the gap between the outward appearance of good manners and the scheming dialogue between couples in which slander, deceit, and trickery hold sway and where reputations are being ruined or advanced. In the following three acts, the scenes shift to Lady Wishfort's house. Again, the setting is appropriate since it is Lady Wishfort's fortune and her central position as the matriarch of the family that drives the action of the play. The house plays an important role in the development of the action because it has both public and private spaces— closets where characters may hide and overhear, rooms that can be locked, chambers where the private habits of the characters come into sharp contrast with outward appearances. It is in the private world of the house where the management or mismanagement of domestic affairs—marriage, dowry arrangements, match-making, and sexual intrigues—most properly belong.

Five-Act Play

Congreve is following a long tradition of dramatists who, since the classical period, used a formula of dividing the play into five acts of approximately the same length and playing time. The action rises, where it climaxes in the third act, and falls to its denouement. Typically, and it is true in Congreve's play, the first act introduces the characters and sets up the plot, giving background information that helps the audience understand relationships between characters as well as thematic direction. For example, in the first act of this play, Congreve introduces the major male characters, sets up a romantic conflict, establishes the hero as antithetical to the shallow mannerisms of the times, and indicates that the dramatic action will revolve around the play of courtship. The second act complicates the action, increases the conflict, and leads the audience to the crisis of the third act, where the action reaches its most exciting turning point.

The women converge with the men in the second act where the park is the setting for intrigue, the revelation of extra-marital affairs, and the hatching of the plot to trick Lady Wishfort into agreeing to the marriage of Mirabell and Millamant. The action leads naturally to the third act where all characters meet in Lady Wishfort's house and where Fainall and Marwood plan their devious plot to exploit Lady Wishfort. It is in the third act that suspense is greatest. The action falls in the fourth act with the resolution of the various plots. The merriment is at its height here: Millamant and Mirabaell negotiate their famous pre-nuptial agreement, Sir Wilfull performs his finest drunken hour, and the fake Sir Rowland plights his troth to Lady Wishfort only to be undone by the evil machinations of Marwood and Fainall. In the fifth act, the various plots are unraveled and the final event is a happy marriage contract between the two heroes.

Dramatic Devices

Congreve uses several dramatic devices to good purpose. Of particular importance here are impersonation (and disguise), the foil, comic relief, counterplot, and hyperbole. Without these devices, the action could not go forward and the comedy would fall flat.

Impersonation is, of course, a ploy by which Mirabell plans to trick Lady Wishfort into surrendering her niece. With Waitwell disguised as Sir Rowland, Mirabell hopes to inflame Lady Wishfort's passion, persuade her to marry Sir Rowland, and then, when the hoax is revealed, to force her into agreeing to his marriage with Millamant. Disguise is also used in two other instances—when Marwood dons a mask to escape attention in the park after her quarrel with Fainall, and when she hides in the closet and overhears Mirabell's plot. Pretense and disguise are the raw materials of comedy, and they abound in this play. Everyone is pretending, from Lady Wishfort, who must wear layers of paint to hide her age and layers of self-righteousness to feign her disinterest in men, to Mrs. Fainall, who appears to be a wife at the mercy of her husband and turns out to be a shrewd businesswoman. Mirabell plays at being Lady Wishfort's lover; Fainall appears to be an honest husband; Foible is not the loyal waiting woman she seems; and Sir Wilfull good-naturedly feigns his pursuit of Millamant, who, in turn, demonstrates that the shallow and capricious "femme fatale" is in reality an intelligent, passionate, and worthy match to Mirabell.

A character may serve as foil to a protagonist or hero by representing unattractive traits or immoral behavior, thereby causing the hero to shine in a comparatively brighter, superior light. It's easy to see how Fainall, for example, acts as a foil to Mirabell. Both are gentlemen, both are scheming to achieve their own ends. However, Fainall's treachery, his willingness to sacrifice everyone to win, makes him a villain. From the shadows cast by Fainall's evil, Mirabell emerges as a true gallant, saving Mrs. Fainall and Lady Wishfort's reputation and fortune, winning his bride as a reward, and generally succeeding in bringing the action to a happy ending. A similar comparison can be made between Marwood and Millamant.

Comic relief signifies precisely what its name suggests—the introduction of laughter to break the tension over a conflict arising in the action. Paradoxically, comic relief is designed both to ease emotional intensity and to heighten the seriousness of the potential crisis or action. In Congreve's play, as in all good dramatic comedy, tragedy figures largely. It is the reverse side of the coin, the tension, that makes the comedy work. In this play, a funny remark or observation relieves many serious moments of suspense. For example, in act 5 Mirabell first enters Lady Wishfort's presence having been cast out as an object of scorn. His future depends on this moment. He must complete his scheme to liberate Lady Wishfort from her foes and win Millamant. Enter Sir Wilfull by his side, and stepping into the serious breach between them offers words of encouragement:

"Look up Man, I'll stand by you, 'sbud an she do frown, she can't kill you;—besides—Hearkee she

dare not frown desperately, because her face is none of her own; 'Sheart an she shou'd her forehead wou'd wrinkle like the Coat of a Cream-cheese."

Sir Wilfull has managed both to remind the audience of the seriousness of the undertaking and to immediately relieve any prospect of danger by alluding to Lady Wishfort's by now generally-acknowledged vanity and her desperate attempts to maintain her looks.

Using counterplots or subplots, Congreve echoes the themes being played out in the main drama. Subplots complicate the drama and are intended to further engage the audience in the action, vary the theme, and convey the sense of a real and larger world beyond the life of the heroes. Marwood and Fainall conspire in a subplot to ruin Lady Wishfort that provides a counter to Mirabell's own scheme to win the hand of her niece. Lady Wishfort also secretly plans to marry her niece to Sir Wilfull while she herself marries Sir Rowland (Mirabell's pretended uncle) hoping at one and the same time to foil Mirabell's prospects of marriage and have him disinherited.

Hyperbole (deliberate and obvious exaggeration) works together with understatement (deliberately restrained and therefore ironic expressions of reality) to make comedy potent. Such devices also serve to expose cultural stereotypes and, especially in this play, deeply held assumptions about male and female behavior. Examples of hyperbole and understatement abound in Congreve's play. The two "experts" are Witwoud and Petulant, although each character is endowed with a witty energy that is often employed to insult or outsmart a foe. In act 3, Petulant hopes to insult Sir Wilfull by remarking how obvious it is that he's been traveling. "I presume," he says, "upon the Information of your Boots." Petulant's attitude and speech are patently silly and pretentious. But Sir Wilfull is not taken aback. He matches Petulant at his own game by replying in just as exaggerated and deliberate a fashion, "If you are not satisfy'd with the Information of my Boots, Sir if you will step to the Stable, you may enquire further of my Horse, Sir." In the same act, a servant entering the scene with Sir Wilfull conveys the deliberately understated information that Lady Wishfort is growing so old that it takes her all morning to prepare herself for public examination. It is afternoon, and Sir Wilfull has asked the servant if he would even recognize the Lady since he has only been in her employ a week. The servant replies, "Why truly Sir, I cannot safely swear to her Face in a Morning, before she is dress'd. 'Tis like I may give a shrew'd guess at her by this time.''

HISTORICAL CONTEXT

The period in English history from 1670 to 1729, when Congreve lived and worked, was marked by a dramatic political event, which gave its name to the literary tradition known as Restoration drama. In 1660, Charles II came to the throne, and the monarchy, which had been in exile, once again ruled England. Although that restoration period was short-lived (Parliament regained power in 1688), it was important to western culture in that it provided a perfect milieu for the comedy of manners.

The English comedies of this time, Congreve's included, take the manners of high society and the aristocracy as material for satire, focusing their attention, as Henry T. E. Perry writes in *The Comic Spirit in Restoration Drama* ''upon the surface of a highly polished and fundamentally insecure civilization.'' The merry licentiousness that characterized the new court was itself a reaction against the civil war of the 1640s, which resulted in the dissolution of the monarchy and led to the subsequent Puritanical mood that settled over the country. As Joseph Wood Krutch observes in *Comedy and Conscience After the Restoration,* the court of Charles II

> wished to make the time to come in every way the reverse of the time that was past, and the sin of regicide of which the preceding generation had been guilty made it seem a sort of piety to reverse all that had been done; to pull down all that had been set up, and set up all that had been pulled down; to hate all that had been loved and love all that had been hated.

King Charles loved the theatre, and the Restoration comedies that flourished in this period contain ample cultural evidence of the sophisticated decadence of the times during which he ruled. In the theatres, playgoers did their best to prove the point that the dramatic characters had indeed been modeled on them. High society gentlemen were loud and lewd, more interested in the appearance of their wigs than the play itself, keen to appear witty and cruel and willing to preserve their reputations as gallants by any means necessary, be they ever so barbaric. Krutch notes that it is no wonder that language and actions that would shock modern audiences would merely amuse a seventeenth-century audience. He writes,

> ''Dramatists were not perverse creatures creating monsters to debase the auditors, but . . . were merely holding the mirror up to nature, or rather, to that part of nature which was best known to their fashionable auditors.''

Of course, not all of England was peopled by creatures of fashion or high society. Plenty of Puritans lived among the middle and lower classes, and most of the literature written in this period was either religious in nature or scientific and philosophical. John Bunyan had published ''Pilgrim's Progress'' in 1684, and John Locke published his ''Essay Concerning Humane Understanding'' in 1690. The epistemology of Locke and the religious passion of Bunyan were far cries from the London stage. It is interesting to note that critics such as the Puritan moralist Jeremy Collier—whose criticism of the stage best expresses the dogmatic protest against it—led the charge to ''reform'' the English theatre world. Collier's attack on the theatre came two years before the performance of *The Way of the World*. This play, then, can be read as an amusing retort to the criticism leveled against the stage as well as a symbolic maker at the historical juncture when Restoration comedy was giving way to the next incarnation of English drama, the so-called Sentimental comedy.

CRITICAL OVERVIEW

The Way of the World is considered one of the finest examples of late seventeenth-century Restoration drama during the period when the comedy of manners flourished in England. Congreve had written two extremely popular dramas before this, *Love for Love* (1695) and *The Mourning Bride* (1697), which received rave reviews in London and cemented his reputation as a major playwright. However, his next and final play, *The Way of the World*, was only a marginal success when it was performed in 1700. Several theories have been forwarded as to why audience reaction at the time was lukewarm. One of Congreve's biographers, Bonamy Dobráee, speculates that, while Congreve's masterpiece must be appreciated for ''depth and sympathy of its characterisation . . . together with the general sense of what is precious in life, and the magnificent

COMPARE
&
CONTRAST

- **1600s:** The patronage of a wealthy aristocrat or noble is an important source of income as well as inspiration for artists of all kinds. In his dedication of *The Way of the World* to ''The Right Honourable Ralph Earl of Mountague,'' Congreve acknowledges his gratitude and respect to the earl for his ''protection'' of the play. Congreve started work on it soon after summering with the earl and taking inspiration from the company he met at his home.

  Today: The work of artists is often supported by public grants and residencies, and young writers are often championed by older, more experienced ones. The system of patronage has been replaced by professional agents, and authors depend upon publishers to buy and promote their work.

- **1600s:** The theatre is a raucous place in Congreve's time. Prostitutes and people of questionable character jammed the ''pits,'' while fashionable ladies and gentlemen busied themselves in boxes making loud, ''witty'' observations and exchanging malicious gossip, while the actors strove to be heard above the audience.

  Today: The theatre audience is polite and attentive. Although critics still yield as uncompromising a pen as they did in Congreve's day, it is not considered either fashionable or agreeable to hiss, boo, or demonstrate obnoxious behavior at any time during the performance of a play.

- **1600s:** The theater is one of the few forms of public entertainment available, but during Congreve's time, no more than two theatres are in operation in London. Because plays are written for a general audience, the price of theatre tickets is affordable to almost everyone.

  Today: The various kinds and forms of public entertainment are numerous. While cinema has replaced the theatre as the most popular and affordable medium for drama, plays, especially in urban areas, still represent an important cultural outlet. Generally, however, they are expensive and must be booked far in advance.

- **1660s:** The Stuart courts regain power after an English civil war that temporarily dissolved the monarchy. Plays of the time reflect the restoration of the aristocracy in their comic attempt at mirroring the high society world of immorality and decadence.

  Today: Contemporary comedies also mirror the times and lives of real people. As in the late seventeenth century, popular modern comedies offer similar subject matter. Neil Simon's plays, for example, revolve around marital relationships or antagonism between the sexes.

- **1600s:** In the late seventeenth century, reform of the theater world is pursued by critics who find it too licentious. Much of the impetus for this reform comes from the fact that England is still, by and large, a Christian land with strong Calvinist leanings.

  Today: The National Endowment for the Arts, a federally-supported grant agency, comes under attack for its sponsorship of art that is perceived by the government to be pornographic and without artistic merit.

- **1600s:** Women possess few political rights and little or no economic independence. Upon marriage, women of means are obliged to relinquish their property to their husbands' control and depend upon them for their livelihood.

  Today: Women are, by law, politically equal with men and control their own property and financial affairs. In contemporary marriages, joint ownership of property and money is common, and most women work to help support the household.

handling of language,'' the play might have been ''too subtle.'' A character like Witwoud, he notes, is ''indeed a coxcomb'' but he was also ''no idiot.'' Dobráee also characterizes the resolution of the plot as ''abrupt and unlikely.''

Several studies of late seventeenth-century drama make the claim that Congreve was writing for a ''coterie'' audience (fashionable high society) that disappeared at the turn of the century. The argument is that new playgoers were middle class or bourgeois in their tastes, and they demanded a new style, hence the rise of ''sentimental'' comedy popular after 1700. As Virginia Ogden Birdsall writes in *Wild Civility, The English Comic Spirit on the Restoration Stage,* the ''conditions and circumstances in which English civilization had to grow'' led to ''a new and not inconsiderable ally in the cause of repressive sobriety—namely, an increasingly influential middle-class mentality almost invariably hostile to the comic or play spirit.''

Recent studies by such scholars as Emmett Avery, Harold Love, and Pierre Danchin have demonstrated that the late seventeenth-century London theatre-going audience (at the time only two theatres, Drury Lane and Lincoln's Inn Fields, were in operation in London) was perhaps more heterogeneous than modern audiences. Robert Hume calls the audiences of the period between 1697 and 1703 ''cranky'' and for reasons not completely understood, they ''damned'' the new plays of the Restoration while continuing to enjoy the older, stock dramas of the period that expressed similar sentiments. In the 1697–1698 season, writes Hume, ''fifteen out of seventeen new plays failed.'' Jeremy Collier's attack on the theatre and the consequent controversy over the theatre world's morality probably added to the troubles that plagued the theatre at this time, but as Hume observes, audiences were ''revolting'' prior to Collier's scathing denouncements. Here, it is worth quoting Hume at length:

> Why audiences were so difficult in the years around 1700 we frankly do not know. Authors were baffled: in prologue after prologue they lamented the fickleness of the audience, and in prefaces and dedications they tended to blame actors and managers for their misfortunes. If authors were puzzled and indignant, managers were frantic. They imported foreign singers at inflated prices, tried entr'acte dancers, animal acts, acrobats, and vaudeville turns. They cannibalized favorite scenes from plays and popular operas. They kept changing the starting time of performance.

Whatever the reasons for the minimal success of *The Way of the World* in 1700, it was revived to popular acclaim in the eighteenth century: it was performed over two hundred times in London. Professor Avery, writes Hume, concluded that Congreve's play flourished and ''gained popularity steadily over a period of some forty years, achieving his greatest share in the repertory around 1740.'' When Garrick, who was indifferent to Congreve, took over management of Drury Lane, performances of the play diminished. During the nineteenth century, as Herbert Davies notes in *The Complete Plays of William Congreve,* it was performed ''with considerable cuts and alterations to suit the taste of the times.'' It was revived in 1904 and continues to be performed today.

CRITICISM

Kathy Smith

Smith is an independent scholar and freelance writer. In this essay, Smith explores the significance of Congreve's play to Restoration drama, particularly the comedy of manners.

Western philosophers have theorized about the nature and causes of mirth at least since the time of Plato. Comedy feeds on incongruity; people laugh even when the joke is cruel because they want to feel a sense of relief that their own follies are not fatal. Indeed, comedy has the power to heighten people's sense of belonging to a common human family. Restoration playwrights understood the value of laughter as a social force, and they used the theatre as a staging ground. With an attitude of detached instruction that was still entertaining, they contrived their plots, fashioned their stock characters (the country bumpkin, the wit, the hero, the fool, etc.), and satirized familiar domestic situations and themes to reflect the ridiculous but nonetheless very human impulses of the times. No playwright was more adept at this in the late seventeeth century than Congreve. And no play better represents his mastery of the comedy of manners than his final play, *The Way of the World*.

Congreve's decision to include lines from Horace, the Roman satirist, on the title page of the printed play immediately alert the reader that his work will relate to the immorality and unscrupulousness of society. These lines, quoted in the original Latin from Horace's *Satires,* cautions adulterers and mocks the fate of those who, caught in the

James Grout, as Sir Wilfull Witwoud, and John Moffatt, as Witwoud, in a scene from the 1984 theatrical production of Way of the World, *performed at the Theatre Royal in London*

act, must relinquish their dowries. Of course, marital disharmony and sexual intrigue are not new themes. What is of interest is the way these themes are treated in Restoration comedy, where, as Joseph Wood Krutch notes in *Comedy and Conscience after the Restoration,* ''the technique of wit'' is used to great advantage in ''rationalizing debauchery into a philosophical system.''

Taking nothing away from Congreve as a master of polished dialogue and a purveyor of wit, it must be observed that this final play was written in answer to one of the most notorious Puritanical attacks on the theatre by Parson Jeremy Collier. The play therefore offers much more than a witty ''rationalization,'' however. It playfully teaches people how to find an antidote to debauchery. In Congreve's dedication of the play to the Earl of Montague, he announces the profound, if comic, intent of his art by placing himself in direct line of ancestry with Terence, ''the most correct Writer in the World'' who is himself a descendent of the masters of comedy in the classic tradition from Theophrastus to Moliére. Of this new play, he laments that it will be little understood because it is not animated by the usual characters who ''are Fools so gross, that in my

humble Opinion, they should rather disturb than divert the well-natur'd and reflecting part of an Audience. . . .'' While Congreve is no moralist, nor should his play be read as anything more doctrinal than a well-wrought fable with a moral attached, the heroes of this play nonetheless undertake a ''remarriage'' of minds that is possible only when both perversely jaded and self-righteously censorious views on marriage are rejected.

In order for the romantic heroes Mirabell and Mrs. Millamant to come together in marriage and to achieve a happy ending for the play, they must first thwart the devious intentions of their foes and character foils Fainall and Mrs. Marwood, who are carrying on an adulterous affair. Moreover, they must undermine Lady Wishfort's falsely pious pronouncements and patently disingenuous hatred of men. It is no accident that the Lady appears in the third act to take her place as the central comic figure of the play when the action reaches a climax. As the dominant matriarch in control of the purse strings, she is also the character who best reflects the sworn enemies of comedy: hypocritical and self-righteousness, with a fashionable but overdeveloped appetite for the opposite sex. Finally, by relying on

WHAT DO I READ NEXT?

- *The Mourning Bride* was Congreve's only dramatic tragedy. Performed in 1697, it was a triumphant success and ran for thirteen days at Lincoln's Inn Fields. Set in the south of Spain, it dramatizes earlier historical conflicts between Granada and Valencia and the part played in this struggle by Moorish expeditions from the north coast of Africa. But the plot is fictional and characters are drawn not from history but from earlier heroic plays.

- When *The Old Batchelour,* Congreve's first play, was printed in 1693, it was an immediate success and its author hailed as John Dryden's successor. Indeed, Dryden helped Congreve, who was only twenty-three years old at the time, prepare the play for the theatre. This first play, like his later comedies, mirrored the manners of fashionable society. It can be enjoyed for its sheer gaiety and youthful energy, but it also provides a contrast to later works where maturity affords him a more original style and a more discerning attitude to the society he evokes.

- William Wycherley's play *The Country Wife* is one of the best examples of early Restoration comedy. Born in 1640, thirty years before Congreve, Wycherley is often regarded, along with Sir George Etherege, as one of Congreve's most important literary predecessors. Although there is disagreement about when Wycherley's play was first performed, most scholars put it between 1672 and 1675. The play takes a satirical look at the jealous husband, concluding that jealousy is indeed a monster that consumes those who suffer from it most.

- More than any other English playwright, Ben Jonson probably had the most influence on the comic tradition of which Congreve is a part. He was a primary force in the rise of the comedy of "humours" during the Elizabethan period. His play *Volpone,* or *The Fox,* first performed in 1606, provides one of the best examples of comedy at work in the service of social satire.

- When Jeremy Collier's *Short View of the Immorality and Profaneness of the English Stage* was published in 1698, several playwrights of the period, including Congreve, responded to this attack. Indeed, Collier's book is one of several popular works of Puritan piety that Lady Wishfort tells Mrs. Marwood to entertain herself with when she hides in the closet in the third act of *The Way of the World.* Collier's book is considered one of the most articulate expressions of the Puritanical attempt to reform the stage and purge it from the perceived evils and corruption of the day.

---

their intelligence and thoughtful common sense, the two heroes also deflect the tiresome banter of the self-proclaimed "wits," Witwoud and Petulant. These two dandies playfully engage the audience in amusing and often sophisticated dialogues, pointing up unpleasant yet honest insights into the way of the world. But they are essentially shallow, as is the fashionable world they represent, and as such they also serve as foils to the heroes.

In the opening of the first act, when Fainall and Mirabell are gambling (a foreshadowing of the suspenseful battle they will wage for love and money), Congreve establishes the prevailing cavalier attitude toward sexual encounters. Fainall's quip to Mirabell over cards that "I'd no more play with a Man that slighted his ill Fortune, than I'd make Love to a Woman who undervalu'd the Loss of her Reputation" demonstrates the value both he and society place on conquests that will prove disastrous for the vanquished. Congreve would have the audience smile at the sentiment, to acknowledge its compelling force in the way of the world. But he also finally undermines Fainall and society's libertine attitudes toward adultery and scandal. Both

Fainall's "Inconstancy and Tyranny of temper" have led Mirabell to protect Mrs. Fainall's fortunes from her husband by deeding them over in trust to him before she was married. In the final act, this precaution proves to be Fainall's undoing, for without the deed to Mrs. Fainall's property he is without means. He cannot extort Lady Wishfort's estate by blackmail or make good on his promise to set his wife "a drift, like a Leaky hulk to Sink or Swim, as she and the Current of this Lewd Town can agree." He needs his wife's money (which he thought he had "wheadl'd out of her") to survive. Mrs. Marwood suffers a more ignominious fate for her role as a spoiler. She exits the play vowing revenge on Mrs. Fainall. My resentment, she swears, "shall have Vent, and to your Confusion, or I'll perish in the attempt." But her vow is an empty one. She has been revealed as a vicious, grasping adulteress, and she is left without husband or means. Fainall can return to his wife, and Mirabell promises to "Contribute all that in me lies to a Reunion," but Marwood has become, ironically and by her own hand, the "Leaky hulk" that risks perishing. She has exploited her wit, Congreve implies, at the expense of true feelings.

Congreve comically draws out the natural and enduring conflict between the sexes in order to make his audience laugh at human foibles and to poke fun at the posturing associated with romance and sexual intrigue. Early on, Mirabell expresses his mocking disdain of the romantic entanglements that drive the story. The night before the story begins, Millamant has rebuffed him. What can he expect, Fainall asks. The women had met on "one of their Cabal-nights . . . where they come together like the Coroner's Inquest, to sit upon the murder'd Reputations of the Week." Men are excluded from the gossip circle, and their presence (with the exception of the "coxcombs" Witwoud and Petulant) would naturally stall all conversation.

Clearly Mirabell is too grave, too love-struck, to understand that he has breached "decorum." It is further learned that he cannot win Millamant without first pacifying her aunt, whom he has angered by playing the knave and pretending love to her. Fashion has dictated the rules by which men must pay court to women, and, in the case of Lady Wishfort, Mirabell has paid them only lip service. He has indeed engaged in the "last Act of Flattery with her, and was guilty of a Song in her Commendation." He tells Fainall he even went so far as to "complement her with the Imputation of an Affair with a

> " IF CONGREVE TOOK EXCEPTION TO THE LEWDNESS AND OVER-ELABORATE ARTIFICIALITY OF THE TIMES, HE ALSO CLEARLY RESENTED THE PURITANICAL ATTACKS UPON IT."

young Fellow . . ." But his attentions have been false. Throughout the exchange of dialogue in act 1, Congreve shines the light of truth on the way things are. The none too subtle implication is that fashionable women and men are victims of their own vanities, that they delight in the weaknesses of others, and that they are blind to their own defects.

For his gravity as a lover and his knavery as a gallant, Mirabell must temporarily suffer. He will be disappointed in his expectations of Millamant until it appears that his gallant efforts to win her have been in vain. For his ability to read the corrupt nature of the world and his desire to circumvent it, even while deploying its methods, he is victorious in the end. He is able to rise above the superficial manners of his peers; furthermore, his deceptions and undisguised attempts at blackmail have been wrought in the name of love rather than greed or artificial gallantry. He is, as Virginia Birsdall has pointed out in *Wild Civility: The English Comic Spirit on the Restoration Stage,* "a promoter of marriages." The marriages he promotes and also helps to sustain suit his own interests. His arrangement of Foible and Waitwell's marriage secures him the co-conspiracy of Foible against Lady Wishfort. His arrangement of marriage between Mrs. Fainall and her husband and his consequent safeguarding of her estate enable him to foil Fainall, who wants to use his wife's fortune as leverage in the game of extortion. Yet, at the same time, Foible loves Waitwell and is made happy by the union. And Mrs. Fainall, who has been widowed and has indulged in an affair with Mirabell, protects her reputation by marrying Fainall. His ability to be both gallant and wise, both sophisticated and loving render his plots harmless and instructive. It is later left up to Millamant to teach him how to be "enlarg'd" into a proper husband.

In the famous "prenuptial agreement" scene in act 4, Millamant outlines the conditions under which she will "by degrees dwindle into a Wife." The gaiety, capriciousness, and arrogance that has characterized her behavior and conversation with Mirabell are offset by veins of gravity and intelligence, an energetic charm and a desire for profound love that culminate here in a style that reflects her power as a heroine. She has toyed with Mirabell unmercifully, snubbing and teasing him until, at the end of act 2, he can think of her only as "a Whirlwind" and himself unwittingly lodged in that whirlwind. While he allows passion to tyrannize him, she is in complete control. Her airy detachment is a challenge to the despotism of the old marriage code. Indeed, she wishes to establish a new marriage pattern that will look very much like a permanent courtship: "I'll fly and be follow'd to the last Moment," she asserts to Mirabell,

> "tho' I am upon the very Verge of Matrimony, I expect you should sollicit me as much as if I were wavering at the Grate of a Monastery, with one Foot over the Threshold. I'll be sollicited to the very last, nay and afterwards."

While she is a genius in her manipulation of other characters and while her playfulness borders on cruelty, she is intrinsically aware of her own follies, and she finally cannot deny her own natural inclinations. At the end of the scene she admits to Fainall, "Well, If Mirabell shou'd not make a good Husband, I am a lost thing; for I find I love him violently."

It is fitting to conclude with Lady Wishfort, whose declarations of piety and hatred of men have fooled no one, including herself. In act 3, Mrs. Marwood enters the Lady's house to tattle on Foible whom she has seen speaking with Mirabell in St. James Park. Lady Wishfort knows Foible has gone out with the Lady's picture to show Sir Rowland, the more to incite his passions for her. Of course, she doesn't know that Mirabell has invented the admiring uncle for his own purposes. She only fears here that her own passions will be found out and that she will lose her last chance at marriage, an unpleasant thought at the ripe old age of fifty-five. She laments to Marwood,

> "Oh, he carries Poyson in his Tongue that wou'd corrupt Integrity it self. If she has given him an Opportunity, she has as good as put her Integrity into his Hands. Ah dear Marwood, what's Integrity to an Opportunity?"

Despite her willingness to take advantage of her own opportunity, especially at the expense of

ruining Mirabell, she falsely insists on her disdain of men in general. Compare the very funny scene with Foible in act 4, during which she readies herself for Sir Rowland:

> "In what figure shall I give his Heart the first Impression? . . . Shall I sit? . . . No I won't sit . . . I'll walk . . . and then turn full upon him . . . No, that will be too sudden . . . I'll lie . . . aye, I'll lie down . . . I'll receive him in my little dressing Room . . . with one Foot a little dangling off . . . and then as soon as he appear, start, aye, start and be surpriz'd, and rise to meet him in a pretty disorder . . ."

to her soliloquy in the final act on the virtues of raising a daughter to despise men:

> "I chiefly made it my own Care to Initiate her very Infancy in the Rudiments of Vertue, and to Impress upon her tender Years, a Young *Odium* and *Aversion* to the very sight of Men . . . she never look'd a Man in the Face but her own Father, or the Chaplain, and him we made a shift to put upon her for a Woman, by the help of his long Garments, and his Sleek-face . . ."

Her unnatural parenting is not only hypocritical, it has by implication contributed to the unfortunate circumstances in which her daughter has found herself sadly married to a man she truly does hate. And it is Congreve's final "revenge" that she not only be humiliated in her romance with "Sir Rowland," but be the butt of his general joke. For while her fortune is "saved" from Fainall, her reputation as a "superannuated Frippery," a fate she fears most, has indeed come to pass. If Congreve took exception to the lewdness and over-elaborate artificiality of the times, he also clearly resented the Puritanical attacks upon it. Clearly, Lady Wishfort supplies his comic vehicle for demonstrating the weakness of both extremes. But perhaps the most unconsciously insightful remark belongs to the rude but kind-hearted country bumpkin, Sir Wilfull, who for all his misunderstandings of the "lingo" of London, speaks the great lesson of the play when he denounces Witwoud as a fop and declares that "Fashion" is indeed "a Fool."

Source: Kathy Smith, Critical Essay on *The Way of the World,* in *Drama for Students,* The Gale Group, 2002.

Deborah Kaplan

In the following essay excerpt, Kaplan studies The Way of the World *as a representative twentieth-century revival of a Restoration comedy.*

Opening in a small Greenwich Village playhouse in 1924, *The Way of the World* created a considerable stir among New York theatregoers. The play was a novelty to many, "so old," one reviewer said, "that it is new." The play, however, seemed fresh and unusual not simply because of its age but because it had not been seen and heard for a long time. Considered too bawdy for public performances, most Restoration comedies had been banished from theatres in Great Britain and the United States for several generations. The necessary prelude to their twentieth-century return to the stage—and to the attention that return generated—was literary. In the late nineteenth and early twentieth centuries, men of letters such as Algernon Charles Swinburne and Edmund Gosse rehabilitated the comedies' reputations, convincing their readers that the plays were not tasteless, obscene works but brilliant and witty classics.

Restoration comedy seemed as new to theatre workers in the 1920s as to their audiences, for the plays had no performance tradition. An authentic or "authorized" performance style for classic plays is, of course, unattainable, but there were no vital conventions on which theatre groups could draw. How, then, were the plays to be performed? This essay charts the answers provided to this question in the United States throughout the twentieth century. Although that performance history can not be isolated from twentieth-century British revivals of Restoration comedies, I have chosen to foreground the American productions because their history is generally unknown. Reviewers of the American revivals still all too frequently invoke only British productions. Indeed, they do not always seem aware, when reviewing a particular comedy, that it was revived in the United States earlier in the century. But my aim is to do more than just fill in a gap. We can not adequately understand and assess the ways that Restoration comedies are currently being performed in the U.S. unless we historicize the production and reception of these plays.

I focus on the theatrical career of one play in order to make manifest long-term trends impossible to see in an essay surveying productions of several different plays. I have chosen William Congreve's *The Way of the World* because of its prestige and prominence on twentieth-century British and American stages. Often said to be not just the greatest comedy of its period but the greatest English language comedy, it was the Restoration play first offered in modern, commercial revivals in both London and New York. And it has been performed steadily over the course of the century, travelling the route taken by many other classic plays in the

> "OFTEN SAID TO BE NOT JUST THE GREATEST COMEDY OF ITS PERIOD BUT THE GREATEST ENGLISH LANGUAGE COMEDY, IT WAS THE RESTORATION PLAY FIRST OFFERED IN MODERN, COMMERCIAL REVIVALS IN BOTH LONDON AND NEW YORK."

U.S.—from little theatres and semi-private theatrical clubs to off and off-off-Broadway and resident theatres after World War II, with an occasional British import offered on Broadway or in one of the larger resident venues. *The Way of the World* is regarded by many critics as the quintessence of Restoration comedy. Moreover, when staged, it concentrates the problems as well as the virtues of Restoration comedy. Its plot may be even more maze-like, its pyrotechnic wit somewhat more dense and topical, but these features in most Restoration comedies have challenged twentieth-century directors and theatre companies and have influenced the way Congreve's play and the other comedies of its period have been performed. It is not, to be sure, the quintessence of bawdiness. *The Way of the World* comes late—1700—in the corpus of Restoration comedies, and it is less ribald than many of its predecessors written during the reign of Charles II. But for most twentieth-century American theatre workers and theatregoers the reputed naughtiness of Restoration comedies has been more salient than the *degree* of ribaldry within any one of them.

The revival history exemplified by *The Way of the World* has at its center a single performance style. When Restoration comedies came back to American theatres in the 1920s, a period style that had recently been devised for them in Britain was imported along with the plays. It included late seventeenth-century props and costumes and acting that mixed farce, parody, and "artificial" or "high style" performance. The artificial acting, conveying the affectations and hauteur of the play's elite characters, was considered the most important and most characteristic element of this period style. In the interwar years, theatre companies appropriated the period style, but some of the most successful also adjusted it to suit the New York context. Early on, theatre workers and critics identified certain features of the style as "British" and certain as "American," and directors exploited these nationalistic constructions and comparisons to the enjoyment of their audiences. Such identifications and juxtapositions of stylistic elements expressed simultaneously a recognition of Restoration comedy as culturally prestigious drama and performance *and* an iconoclastic, nationalistic impulse—to mock British, highbrow culture and assert the superior vitality of popular American theatrical arts. By contrast, after World War II there was very little interest in adjusting or altering the 1920s period style. Theatre companies engaged in reverential conservation of the early twentieth-century style, which had come to be seen as entirely, admirably British and traditional.

These two phases in the performance of Restoration comedies we owe, of course, to theatre companies and, especially, to directors. But the institutional contexts for productions also constrain or enable performance styles or, in this case, alterations in the treatment of a single performance style. The cultural stature accorded to a theatrical production has an impact on its presentational features, and the development of diverse theatrical institutions has underwritten the creation of a hierarchy of cultural prestige. This variation in institutions has in twentieth-century America succeeded in establishing classifications of high and popular theatre, even though the boundaries between American theatrical institutions in this century have usually been weak. The type of theatre institutions, including the audiences they address, and the social and financial strains they experience have had an impact on the style of the productions.

My history of Restoration period style that follows will suggest the revivals offered in the interwar period were more interesting than those presented after World War II. Modern bodies, modern materials, and the modern mental lives of theatre workers and theatregoers make inevitable the mediating function of performance styles, suiting a play written in and for one culture to the culture in which it is staged. Between the two world wars, the period style was reproduced, but it was also challenged and altered with new "Americanized" elements. After World War II, however, the intercultural work of performance styles was denied, as directors and

companies sought again and again to recapture a style devised in the 1920s.

Those years of denial appear to be coming to an end, for the question of how to perform Restoration comedies has recently been reopened. Distancing themselves from the theatrical Anglophilism so pervasive between 1945 and 1990, some directors have consciously rejected many if not all of the elements of the period style. While they have acknowledged Restoration comedies as classics, they have not given the plays' conventional performance style the same status. In the second section of this essay, I look at three of the revivals of *The Way of the World* that have pioneered new approaches to Restoration comedy. Although these recent productions have not all been critical or box-office successes, they have been important efforts to find new and compelling performance idioms. More than aesthetic achievement is at stake in these attempts. Their directors have sought to bridge the cultural chasm between Restoration comedy and late twentieth-century audiences in the United States.

Restoration Period Style in America

During the interwar period, a handful of Restoration revivals were offered in New York. The institutional contexts for the majority of the American productions—the art theatre and the private theatre club—facilitated the inventiveness of their stylistic appropriations. The art theatre provided a venue for serious contemporary and classic European plays, new American plays, and experimental stagings. The Players' Club, in its annual spring productions, staged mostly classics. By presenting plays and productions not usually seen on Broadway, these two institutions contributed to the segmentation of theatre, to the creation of a "high" as opposed to "popular" culture. But while they helped to create these categories, they enjoyed playing with this new distinction as well. Such play was possible because culturally elite audiences in this period were notable for their broad tastes, enjoying popular as well as high art. It was also possible because the institutional boundaries between the culturally prestigious and the popular were not yet firm. That transformation occurred gradually, between 1910 and 1940. Productions done initially under the aegis of the art theatre and the Players' Club did not always play only to small, culturally elite audiences. The Restoration revivals they sponsored were most compelling precisely when they mingled high and popular elements for audiences consisting not only of "longhairs" with wide interests but also of those with less cultural capital.

An art theatre, the Cherry Lane Playhouse in Greenwich Village, first offered *The Way of the World* in twentieth-century New York. The immediate impetus for the production in the Village was a revival that had opened nine months earlier in February 1924. Directed by Nigel Playfair, Congreve's play was the first commercially produced Restoration comedy in twentieth-century London. Because of its great popularity with both critics and the theatregoing public, this and other Restoration comedies were deemed "playable" again. The performance style that Playfair developed for *The Way of the World* was subsequently emulated in the United States as well as in Great Britain because British actor and director Dennis Cleugh presented not only the comedy but also Playfair's performance style at the Cherry Lane.

What was it he appropriated? Nigel Playfair had chosen to do the play because he considered it "the greatest of all comedies of manners," but he disliked reverential, scholarly, and theatrically dull approaches to classics. He believed that "one is out . . . in reproducing old plays, not so much to give a replica (which is impossible) as to furnish a sort of review and criticism—a *parody* if you like, but a parody which expresses admiration." He mocked many aspects of Restoration period manners. Doris Zinkeisen created brightly colored, poster style sets, whose overtly artificial strokes complemented the stage business he devised. As one reviewer summed up the production, "the servants had to light the candles in quartet formation, and everybody who was not speaking had to strike attitudes with arms raised or elbow stuck out, and all the dresses were as gorgeously polychromatic as could be, and the very ladies in the orchestra wore full-bottomed wigs. In a word, the play was fantasticated." The actors were even instructed to give archaic pronunciations to certain words—"tay" for tea, for example, and "rallery" for raillery—not for the sake of historical accuracy but to give aural reminders of the "old-fashioned" character of this Restoration world.

Playfair worried that audiences would find the plot of *The Way of the World* too confusing. His response was to mock the plot as well and, in general, to draw attention away from it and to the style of the production. Some reviewers thought that he was also trying to distract spectators from the sexual content of the already lightly expurgated script. In Great Britain, Victorian prudery had not yet entirely disappeared. His mocking approach also infused the acting, which was a mix of high style, parody, and farce. In Edith Evans, as Millamant, Playfair found an actress capable of brilliant high style playing. Nineteenth-century essayist and critic Charles Lamb had insisted on the artificiality of Restoration comedy, and early twentieth-century actors attempted to make themselves as highly mannered and affected, as polished and brittle, as possible. Writing in 1963, John Gielgud remembered Evans's performance as "probably the finest stylized piece of bravura acting seen in London in the last fifty years. Her economy and grace of movement, her perfectly sustained poses, the purring, coquetry of her voice with its extraordinary subtlety of range, was inimitably captivating." As Gielgud's description suggests, high style acting could—and sometimes did—shade into the parody of camp. Playfair also encouraged farcical playing by a few of the actors. Next to Edith Evans, Margaret Yarde attracted the most attention in his production with her broad interpretation of Lady Wishfort. Some spectators objected, convinced that her performance was not in the spirit of Congreve's play, but most praised her performance.

Although a few reviewers thought that Playfair gingered up *The Way of the World* too much, this generally well-received production determined what became known as Restoration period style in early twentieth-century Britain. "The approach," according to J. L. Styan, "was not that of 'Let's put on a Restoration comedy,' but of 'Let's *pretend* to put on a Restoration comedy.'" And the playfully ridiculed, campy world produced became "the Restoration" in British revivals for many subsequent decades. Playfair's work also set the perimeters for Restoration period style and the world that it conveyed in the United States through the medium of Cleugh's production in New York.

The actors at the Cherry Lane aimed for both high style and farce, giving their performances parodic touches as well. Cleugh steered the actors to silly sounding pronunciations such as "obleeged" for obliged, for example. Playfair's style also influenced the visual look of the production: "beribboned and bewigged, flaring linings, lace cuffs, tight bodices, fans and monocles; the world of fashion did not spare color." This review in the *New York Times* suggests not just elaborate but also comically exaggerated period dress. The sets too, another reviewer noted approvingly, were "quaintly and amusingly done," no doubt, referring particularly to the scenery for act two, signifying St. James's

Park. The backdrop offered a row of townhouses, painted only one or two feet high to indicate their distance. Because perspective was only suggested and not realistically represented, the residences looked like doll houses.

The successful commercial production between the wars had 100 performances, and Cleugh's revival topped that number by twenty. So popular was it that part way through the run the production was moved uptown to the Princess Theatre near Broadway at 39th Street. *The Way of the World* was so successful at least in part because it offered theatregoers an opportunity to demonstrate their cultural sophistication. The play had high status as a British dramatic classic. But it was also known as a risqué work, and spectators could display their cultural capital by responding aesthetically rather than morally, by remaining unperturbed by what they heard. Reviewers let it be known that they were unfazed by the play's bawdiness and observed no "moral agitation" among audience members.

Moreover, culturally sophisticated New Yorkers appreciated popular and mass culture as well as high culture, and they took pleasure in comparing the ribaldry of the Restoration with homegrown, widely enjoyed versions. Critics proudly asserted that American entertainment was at least as bawdy as what had been produced long ago about a British social elite. For *Variety*'s reviewer burlesque was the relevant comparison. In the slang that writers for the weekly liked to affect, he announced: "I heard it was very 'dirty' before I cum down, but it's as tame as a Sunday night with the wife . . . if this mob think this is a peppy opera I would just like to see a flock of them long-haired guys sittin' in rail seats up at the Prospect when the "Hot Water-Bag Babies" strut bare-legged out on that runway."

It was not just the ribaldry of the play, however, but the performance as a whole to which New York theatregoers responded. Although the American production revealed small alterations in Playfair's composite of acting styles, it did not dispense with high style playing. Most reviewers thought that the actors failed to convey its polished artifice, but high style was apparently already understood to be an aspect of the Restoration period style too crucial to reject. Critics attributed the difficulties that the cast had with it to their modernity: "it is of course impossible in this year of grace," noted one, "to bring back to the stage the full flavor of aristocratic comedy. The grand air must be acquired for the occasion, and the grand air does not flourish on Broadway or even

on Shaftesbury Avenue." The actors' national identity, however, and, in particular, their location in a polyglot and poly-accented American city, was thought to be an even greater handicap, preventing the players from achieving an Anglo-Saxon standard. "The actors," he continued, "must learn to speak the English language. This is a particular difficulty in New York."

If being American was deemed a cultural liability for performing high style, it was an asset for performing farce and parody, the other components of Restoration period style acting. Americans were considered very adept at low comedy, as the vaudeville and burlesque industries were demonstrating. Sir Wilfull Witwoud was apparently the character most farcically rendered, and the critics loved him. Bruce de Lette and Lawrence Tulloch, as Witwoud and Petulant, also won praise for presenting the parody of camp. Indeed, references to the "slapstick" and "buffoonery" in the production as well as to Witwoud and Petulant as "female impersonators" suggest that the actors borrowed from vaudeville and burlesque—and perhaps from the drag balls and "Pansy" acts, popular at that time in New York—for their "low turns." *The Way of the World*'s performance style may have been appealing enough to fill the uptown Princess Theatre not only because the farcical and parodic elements compensated for the technical deficiencies of the high style playing but also because the farce and parody incorporated elements from other New York entertainments.

Cleugh's production set precedents not only by introducing Restoration comedies to the twentieth-century American stage and not only by introducing Playfair's performance style for that comedy but also by introducing acting tagged according to nationality into Restoration comedy. The propensity to treat high style acting as British and farce and parody as American shaped both the production and consumption of some of the most successful of the American revivals in the interwar period. In a more pronounced way than Cleugh's, subsequent productions exploited the hybrid of high and low, British and American. Playfair had lightly parodied the world of Restoration comedy. In the United States additional parodic effects were achieved through the juxtaposition, and by that means the creation, of "national" styles. These revivals simultaneously offered high art fare and took advantage of Playfair's parodic approach to make fun not just of the early eighteenth century but also of highbrow and British art.

To see this, we need to turn to the other institution that showcased Restoration comedy, the Players' Club. Established by Edwin Booth in the late 1880s as a men's club for actors and others interested in the theatre, the Players' began offering annual spring productions in 1922 and continued until 1940. During that time it presented three Restoration plays. Its productions can not be readily characterized as either art or commercial theatre. The club usually performed classics for an audience that contained a strong contingent of artists and others in the theatre industry. It ran productions for only one week and gave some of the profits to charity. But it also performed in Broadway theatres and used all-star casts who donated their services. Moreover, successful productions sometimes got picked up by producers who sent them on tours. The ambiguity or even liminality of the club's position in the emerging cultural hierarchy for theatrical productions could make for dramatizations of surprising, audience-pleasing incongruities.

The Players' Club's production of *The Way of the World* in 1931 was the flop that proves the rule. No one quarrelled with the look of the production. "Bewigged, becravatted, beflounced and also bedevilled with amorous intrigue," noted *New York Times* reviewer Brooks Atkinson about the characters, "they make a fine pictorial showing as they strut across the stage." "There are singers and dancers and musicians," another critic enumerated, "and no end of silks and satins and furbelows and wigs upon the players." Critics grumbled once again, however, at the high style acting. Walter Hampden, famous for his appearances in costume dramas, knew how to express elegance and artifice in his stage posturings. But he had so much difficulty with diction that it was impossible for the audiences to understand him much of the time. The other cast members too had substantial difficulties with technique, so much so that they were unable to give the impression of a common, lacquered playing style. What sunk the production, however, was not poor high style playing but a dearth of the broad, "Americanized" comedy that could offset it. Although he commended Ernest Cossart for his performance as Sir Wilfull Witwoud, Percy Hammond, writing for the *New York Herald Tribune*, thought the part "cries out for Mr. James T. Powers to play it."

Famous for hamming it up in musical comedies and comic operas, Powers had played Scrub in the Players' Club's revival of *The Beaux' Stratagem* in 1928. He and Raymond Hitchcock—star of vaude-ville, musical comedies, and revues and in *The Beaux' Stratagem* playing the role of Boniface—delighted audiences with their improvised antics. Both took liberties with the text, inventing a good deal of "horseplay." One reviewer thought the production lacked "cohesion," but most critics and the audiences in general did not care. With its combination of high style and shtick, *The Beaux' Stratagem* played to standing room only crowds.

The Players' Club's production of *The Way of the World* failed because American actors were not deemed capable of carrying a Restoration revival on the strength of their high style playing alone. But more problematic than that, the production took a reverential approach to a Restoration classic. (Playfair knew that he couldn't sell that approach even to British theatregoers, to whose national dramatic heritage the play belonged.) New York theatregoers were ready to acknowledge the cultural prestige of the play as long as they weren't asked to attend exclusively to its performance metaphor—high style playing—or to watch American actors defeated by that playing. The other Players' Club revivals of Restoration comedies succeeded not just because they included irreverent acting but because they relied on indigenous versions of irreverence.

Theatre workers and audiences understood and enjoyed the incongruities of putting twentieth-century vaudevillians and musical comedy stars into Restoration comedy. Funnier still were productions in which the encounters between high and low, British and American, old and modern did *not* seem incongruous. When Bobby Clark played Ben in the Players' Club's revival of *Love for Love* in 1940, he brought his well known vaudeville and burlesque routines to Congreve's comedy. As one reviewer explained, he "abandoned the painted spectacles and immense cigar, which are his trademarks, but he played the part with all the abundant spirit of burlesque, the lusty, gusty, leering magnificence that makes his modern clowning supreme in its field." The play had become an exhilarating showcase for American popular culture. "All those years ago William Congreve was really writing a vehicle for Bobby Clark," declared one amused—and gratified—reviewer.

After World War II, with the exception of an occasional British production imported to Broadway, Restoration comedies were performed in the U.S. by off-Broadway and resident theatres and, only in more recent years, by off-off-Broadways. The impetus for off-Broadway originally was "more economic than artistic.'' It provided outlets for plays produced more cheaply than they could be on Broadway, though a few off-Broadway companies, such as Proscenium Productions, which performed *The Way of the World* in Greenwich Village in 1954, were dedicated to classic revivals or to new plays without commercial appeal. By contrast, the not-for-profit resident theatres, in general, did aim at least originally ''to be an independent channel for presentations of a more adventurous, if usually less popular, nature.'' But they and an increasing pool of non-profit off-Broadways, while supposedly protected from the whims of the marketplace, needed to take into account the tastes of their subscribers, their boards of trustees, and the private foundations and government agencies that began providing financial support in the late 1950s and mid-1960s respectively. The regional and many of the off-Broadway theatres settled on a repertoire of culturally prestigious high art mixed with some entertaining Broadway-like and, beginning in the late 1960s, Broadway-bound fare.

Resident and off-Broadway productions throughout this period had to please audiences that were notably homogeneous—white, affluent, and well-educated. Theatre historians and critics were lamenting the absence of multi-class audiences by the mid-1960s, and though some theatres, often with the help of government and foundation support, sought out new, more diverse audiences in that and subsequent decades, they had little success. Audiences did become somewhat more racially diverse over the course of the 1980s, but the multi-class audience remained an unattainable goal. In 1965 Richard Schechner enumerated the stultifying effects that resulted from resident theatres addressing the interests of middle-class subscribers—''little truly adventurous drama'' and productions that ''have a museum quality.'' ''A resident theatre that has systematically retreated into the middleclass is doomed to a monotony equivalent to an Ohio highway,'' he complained. It was a monotony that Jack Poggi found particularly in the major resident theatres. In their schedules, he observed, ''the same plays crop up over and over again. The directors, the managers, and the actors can move easily from one company to another—an indication that there really is not much difference in style among the theaters.'' The predominance of an upper middle- and middle-class audience, and the consequently monotonous fare of the theatres that catered to them, help to explain why the style of Restoration revivals was so unvarying in this period.

And yet, within these staid off-Broadway and resident venues, the revivals were *more* unvarying than productions of other classic plays. These institutions did make excursions off the bland Ohio highway, choosing unusual plays or performance styles. Off-off-Broadway, which emerged in the 1960s, was a likely source of their experiments with style. Conceptual directors working in unconventional performance spaces were occasionally invited into off-Broadway or resident theatres to essay boldly avant-garde productions of plays by, for example, Euripides, Shakespeare, and Molière. The plays of Congreve and other Restoration writers, however, did not receive similarly innovative treatments.

In addition, even the alternative Restoration period style seen in London theatres by the early 1960s had little impact on the American revivals. William Gaskill, directing *The Recruiting Officer* at Britain's National Theatre in 1963, did most to transform the style of performance. He replaced high style and its camp extremes with naturalistic acting. There were bits of farce in the production, but Playfair's parodic approach to period and play was banished. Gaskill steered the actors away from ''coy archaisms'' in pronunciation and rejected ''lisps, huge wigs, canes and fans.'' He tried, as he later explained, ''to make the text sound as if it was being spoken by real people in recognizable situations.'' The result was a dark and biting vision of the period, whose cynicism seemed quite relevant to late twentieth-century audiences and critics. But while that performance style quickly spread to most subsequent Restoration revivals in Great Britain, including most of the major productions of *The Way of the World,* only one American production in this period, staged at New Haven's Long Wharf Theater in 1972 by British director Malcolm Black, adopted a naturalistic style.

The lack of change can be explained by considering the function of Restoration revivals within resident and off-Broadway theatres. These institutions justified their non-profit status and established themselves more firmly through the interwoven public services of cultural conservation and instruction. They helped to maintain dramatic canons through productions, educating theatregoers and theatre workers in older plays. And they were sometimes able to win government and foundation grants specifically earmarked for gathering student audiences or improving the skills of their companies. Such public service extended to performance styles as well as to play—when possible. Many artistic directors included a Restoration comedy in their seasonal offerings in order to introduce audiences and actors not just to a dramatic classic but also to that classic's "classic" performance style. And it was the 1920s version of period style, rather than the alternative devised by the early 1960s, that reigned in the non-profits. It was older, of course. But, ironically, it also had the stature of a tradition precisely because of its strangeness and greater difficulty for those used to naturalistic acting.

Some directors with reputations as specialists in Restoration period style were invited in those years to train American theatre companies. Norman Ayrton and Anthony Cornish, for example, both known for that expertise, staged two of the resident theatre revivals of *The Way of the World* in the postwar period, Ayrton for the Acting Company and Cornish for the Intiman Theater Company. Ayrton acknowledged in a newspaper interview, just before the Acting Company's production opened in 1976: "I'm very often called upon for Restoration drama . . . I don't like to be typed any more than an actor does. But I feel compelled to accept Restoration assignments to help keep the style alive and well."

Within institutions that needed to offer culturally prestigious as well as popular art, Playfair's performance style became highbrow not only because it was supposedly traditional but also because it was British. That national identity was encoded now not just in high style acting but in the composite of acting styles and in late seventeenth-century costume. It was expressed in the impression produced by these period elements: at best "brightly quaint figures flitting about, sparkling and remote, in an unfamiliar world." And it was reinforced through publicity that stressed the nationality of the director/specialists. "London Expert Here for 'Way of the World,'" was the title of a local newspaper article featuring Cornish, a few days before the Intiman Theater Company began its run of Congreve's play.

Directors who viewed the preservation of Restoration period style as a cultural mission found support among theatergoers. "Ever since the end of World War II," Robert Brustein has observed, "American audiences have been in thrall to the theatre emanating from Great Britain. . . . Our admiration for British playwriting, directing, composing—and particularly acting—has begun to resemble something of a national inferiority complex." Those who disliked sacralized and Anglo-identified styles, however, were, no doubt, repelled by the style and the silly, self-mocking—and irrelevant—world it constructed. The wonder is that the dominance of this reified period style in the postwar era did not permanently inhibit new approaches. In the early 1990s some directors did finally begin to see in late seventeenth-century comedies possibilities for innovative performance styles and new Restorations.

Source: Deborah Kaplan, "Learning 'to Speak the English Language': *The Way of the World* on the Twentieth-Century American Stage," in *Theatre Journal,* Vol. 49, No. 3, October 1997, pp. 301–21.

Sue L. Kimball

In the following essay excerpt, Kimball examines the theme of gaming in The Way of the World, *including the "idea that life is a game in the world of play and elsewhere."*

The opening chocolate house scene of Congreve's last comedy, *The Way of the World*, informs the rest of the play, establishing gaming as the playwright's metaphor for life and love. The comedy's prolific gaming imagery provides a thematic and structural emphasis on gaming as the world's way, and, finally, every character is at one time or another playing a game that may be a singles or doubles match, but that is usually part of a team effort. The audience of *The Way of the World* would, of course, have been familiar with the circumstances of the scene that begins with Mirabell and Fainall "rising from cards." We learn that Mirabell, though he has lost to Fainall, will "play on" if his competitor insists on further entertainment. Fainall demurs:

> No, I'll give you your revenge another time, when you are not so indifferent; you are thinking of something else now, and play too negligently. The coldness of a losing gamester lessens the pleasure of the winner. I'd no more play with a man that slighted his ill fortune than I'd make love to a woman who undervalued the loss of her reputation.

This speech of Fainall's is a most significant passage, not only because it is pregnant with dramatic irony, for reasons to be discussed later, but also because it establishes the motif on which the play's structure, theme, and much of its language build and introduces the idea that life is a game in the world of the play and elsewhere, with love, money, and their concomitant pleasures as reward to the winners.

Congreve introduces his gaming imagery in the Prologue, first describing poets as the unluckiest of fools, and then as

*A scene from the 1953 theatrical
production of* Way of the World,
*featuring Margaret Rutherford, as Lady
Wishfort*

. . . bubbles, by the town drawn in,
Suffered at first some trifling stakes to win;
But what unequal hazards do they run!
Each time they write they venture all they've won.

The word "bubble" acquired in the seventeenth century the meaning of "dupe" or "gull" and was frequently used to describe one easily victimized at cards. An attaché at the British Embassy in Paris had warned his countrymen against gaming with the French because "Even the ladies do not want tricks to strip a Bubble." About 1700, English manufacturers of cards began issuing decks with propaganda depicted on the backs; one such set entitled "All the Bubbles" warns against investing in spurious business ventures. Congreve intimates in the Prologue that poets are gulled into writing plays by some "trifling stakes," despite the "hazards." The word "hazard," as it is used in two prologues by Congreve, would have been a gaming pun familiar to the audience, as the game of hazard is described in *The Compleat Gamester* as the "most bewitching game that is plaid on the dice." Congreve's suggestion that poets "venture all they've won" is perhaps an oblique reference to Jeremy Collier's celebrated *Short View of the Immorality*

and Profaneness of the English Stage, a pamphlet that appeared in 1698, the year before the actual writing of *The Way of the World*, and to which Congreve later wrote a "vindication." Undoubtedly, the playwright found the Puritan divine a threat to his security in the dramatic world, and much of the criticism of the play contains conjectures about the effect of Collier's attack on Congreve's decision to retire from the stage world after 1700. Interestingly, Collier fired a later salvo in 1713, entitled "Essay on Gaming," in which he deplored the bloodthirsty instincts fed by gaming: "When your bubbles are going down the hill, you lend them a push, though their bones are broken at the bottom."

The Prologue continues with another gaming pun: "Should he [the poet] by chance a knave or fool expose, / That hurts none here, sure here are none of those." The word "knave" by the sixteenth century carried a double meaning—an "unprincipled man given to dishonourable and deceitful practices," and also the "name given to the lowest court card in the deck, bearing the picture of a soldier or a servant." "Expose" is a gaming term used to describe an inadvertently overturned card; an exposed knave in a whist game, for example, would result in a redeal, or if the exposure occurred during play, a penalty.

In Act I of *The Way of the World*, Witwoud relates that he has lost money to his fellow gamester Petulant, but Fainall consoles Witwoud with the remark:

You may allow him to win of you at play, for you are sure to be hard of him at repartee; since you monopolize the wit that is between you, the fortune must be his of course

To Mirabell, Witwoud explains,

Petulant's my friend, and a very honest fellow, and a very pretty fellow, and has a smattering—faith and troth a pretty deal of an odd sort of a small wit.

Witwoud continues the gaming motif with his pun on the word "deal": Petulant has been "dealt" a small amount of wit, or he has a great "deal" of it. Cotton describes a card game called plain-dealing as being "a pastime not noted for its ingenuity." Mirabell later remarks to Millamant,

I say that a man may as soon make a friend by his wit, or a fortune by his honesty, as win a woman with plain dealing and sincerity.

The delightful ambiguity here allows the choice between the card game or a straightforward manner as a means of winning the lady and is also a commentary on the times: devious means seem to be required for almost any undertaking, Millamant, well aware of her value as the prize in their game, urges him, ''Well, Mirabell, if ever you will win me, woo me now.''

Also in Act I, Petulant ''calls for himself'' at the chocolate house, and then refuses to go, with the words, ''Let it pass,'' and ''pass on,'' phrases that he might have used at the whist table. When Mirabell threatens him, Petulant replies, ''Let that pass. There are other throats to be cut.'' He is so casual in his suggestion that he might be offering a deck of cards to be cut, but what he is actually offering is information, which is Petulant's only contribution to the game of intrigue. Petulant, who is the witless fop, repeats the word ''pass'' so frequently that it seems to be a refrain associated with him, and he inquires ''whose hand's out?'' when Waitwell arrives with the black box.

In Act II Witwoud, who has been observing the game of wit in which Millamant and Mirabell are engaged, observes to the lady, ''Very pretty. Why, you make no more of making of lovers, madam, than of making so many card-matches,'' an expression that carries the dual meaning of cardboard matches and the holding of a pair or three of a kind in a game like gleek or picket. Witwoud later compares himself and Petulant to two battledores— or to participants in an early eighteenth-century version of badminton; what they bandy back and forth is witless banter instead of shuttlecocks. Shortly afterwards, Mrs. Marwood, in speaking to Fainall about his wife's virtue, remarks, ''I dare swear she had given up her game before she was married,'' to which Fainall replies, ''Hum! That may be. She might throw up her cards; but I'll be hanged if she did not put Pam in her pocket.'' The imagery here is that of the then popular gambling game of loo, or lanterloo, in which the Pam is the jack of clubs. Lynch's note indicates that ''Fainall implies that although his wife might have given up other lovers, she has an 'ace' up her sleeve—Mirabell.''

Fainall tells Mrs. Marwood how he will dispose of Sir Wilfull: ''He will drink like a Dane; after dinner I'll set his hand in.'' Here Fainall may mean ''I'll start him in his drinking,'' or ''I'll take his 'hand' in whatever game comes up.'' And in referring to his wife's reputation, Fainall muses, ''Bringing none to me, she can take none from me. 'Tis against all rule of play that I should lose to one who has not wherewithal to stake.'' In this instance,

THE COMEDY'S PROLIFIC GAMING IMAGERY PROVIDES A THEMATIC AND STRUCTURAL EMPHASIS ON GAMING AS THE WORLD'S WAY, AND, FINALLY, EVERY CHARACTER IS AT ONE TIME OR ANOTHER PLAYING A GAME. . . .''

Fainall cruelly notes that his wife has nothing in the way of a good reputation to lose; therefore convention decrees that he should not allow her in the game. In the parlance of poker, or its four-hundred-year-old antecedent, brag, she has no ante to put up, so she cannot play. This statement recalls Fainall's line from the chocolate house scene in which he indicates he will not ''make love to a woman who undervalues the loss of her reputation.''

In addition to its language, a further indication that *The Way of the World* is a consciously devised metaphor for gaming is Congreve's choice of quotations from the poets Waller and Suckling. First of all, the two poets represent opposing views about how to play the game of love and life—one arguing against, the other for, premarital or extramarital fruition. Millamant uses their poems, which deal with inconstancy in love, to prove that Sir Willful is incapable of playing any of the sophisticated games of wit that she enjoys; he not only cannot complete the couplet she offers him but does not even recognize it as poetry. Suckling, a writer for whom, according to Lynch, Congreve had a ''more than casual esteem,'' had established a dialogue pattern in his play *Agalaura* that was much like a conversational game. In the play, Agalaura's lover, at her request, and without knowing her reasons, agrees to give up his favorite diversion of gaming; yet she is required to assign him a new sin to replace this one. The poet Suckling himself, known as ''the most skillful and reckless player of his time'' is the only man credited with singly inventing a major card game—cribbage. He was a gambler who, according to rumors, arranged for the importation from France of specially marked decks for his own personal use and advantage. Waller, who may have been present when Queen Catherine tore the celebrated card at ombre, wrote a delightful little epigram to celebrate that occasion:

> The cards you tear in value rise;
> So do the wounded by your eyes.
> Who to celestial things aspire
> Are by that passion raised the higher.

Interestingly enough, the lines Sir Willful fails to recognize are those of the inconstant lover, Suckling, while Mirabell completes a couplet by Waller, the more idealistic poet.

In order to observe the structure of the play as a game, it is helpful to determine the kinds of partnerships involved. Millamant and Mirabell are silent partners who work toward the same end, have the same desire, and have the same reluctance to acknowledge their desires publicly. Mr. Fainall's ostensible partner is Mrs. Fainall, who is actually allied in sympathy with Mirabell and Millamant. Mrs. Marwood is Mr. Fainall's actual confederate, and the one for whom he is scheming; at one point, Marwood intimates to Lady Wishfort that they (the two ladies) might escape to some rural, idyllic spot, but Marwood actually continues to work with Mr. Fainall because of their common aim, which is the frustration of all of Mirabell's plans. The Marwood-Fainall relationship should parallel that of Mirabell and Millamant but cannot, because it is extramarital and because Fainall and Marwood are selfish and completely unscrupulous. While there is some evidence that Mirabell abides by the rules in the game of life in this world, there is no rule that Fainall will not break if he can advance himself by doing so. Witwoud and Petulant are partners of a sort. They complement, but do not compliment, one another, and there is definite evidence that the pair of them would represent but a single entry in any game. They are habitual, ineffective, halfhearted competitors for the game prize of Millamant and her fortune. Lady Wishfort wants a marital partner and refuses to admit that she has nothing to contribute to a connubial relationship. Even her fortune cannot outweigh the fact that she is no longer attractive as a marriage prospect; she is so blind to reality that she for a time has accepted Mirabell's advances as proof of her desirability. Foible and Waitwell appear to be a minor partnership—the second team necessary to support Mirabell in his game plan—but Foible, when examined carefully, is indeed, as Marwood calls her, the *passe-partout.* Sir Willful, a loner who serves as bumpkinlike contrast for his half brother, and an involuntary contestant for the first prize, willingly relinquishes it once Millamant is within

his grasp, so that he can travel to find for himself ''another way of the world.''

Partnership understandings vary, as do audience understandings of partnerships. In the chocolate house scene, the audience impression is that Fainall is a good sport who is willing to terminate his game during a winning streak in order to give his opponent a chance on a luckier day. Later developments show, however, that although Fainall never acts from benevolent motives, he speaks the truth when he says, ''The coldness of a losing gamester lessens the pleasure of the winner.'' He enjoys the winning more when his victim writhes; a listless Mirabell affords Fainall no joy. The irony of Fainall's statement lies in the fact that he is actually expressing the sentiments of Mirabell, who is the same kind of competitor. Several critics have wondered why Mirabell holds for so long his ace-in-the-hole in the form of Mrs. Fainall's deed, when he could have produced it earlier. The reason is that, like Fainall, Mirabell finds no thrill in competing with a ''cold gamester,'' or one who ''slights his ill fortune,'' and he does enjoy toying with an overconfident Fainall. He wants to let Fainall believe himself to have won Millamant's fortune and then stymie the villain with one master stroke. Doubtless, Mirabell had dreamed early in the game of having everyone present for his revelation, as proves to be the case. The idea of delight in resistance is also reiterated in the song requested by Millamant in Act III:

> Then I alone the conquest prize,
> When I insult a rival's eyes;
> If there's delight in love, 'tis when I see
> That heart, which others bleed for, bleed for me.

As do Fainall and Mirabell, Millamant thrives on spirited competition.

Source: Sue L. Kimball, ''Games People Play in Congreve's *The Way of the World,''* in *A Provision of Human Nature: Essays on Fielding and Others in Honor of Miriam Austin Locke,* edited by Donald Kay, University of Alabama Press, 1977, pp. 191–207.

SOURCES

Birdsall, Virginia Ogden, *Wild Civility: The English Comic Spirit on the Restoration Stage,* Indiana University Press, 1970, pp. 227–52.

Congreve, William, *The Complete Plays of William Congreve,* edited by Herbert Davis, University of Chicago Press, 1967, pp. 386–479.

Dobráee, Bonamy, *William Congreve,* Longmans, Green & Co., 1963.

Hume, Robert, *The Rakish Stage: Studies in English Drama, 1660–1800,* Southern Illinois University Press, 1983.

Krutch, Joseph Wood, *Comedy and Conscience after the Restoration,* Columbia University Press, 1949.

Perry, Henry Ten Eyck, *The Comic Spirit in Restoration Drama,* Russell & Russell, Inc., 1962, pp. 56–81.

Wilcox, John, *The Relation of Moliére to Restoration Comedy,* Benjamin Blom, 1964, pp. 154–201.

FURTHER READING

Gardiner, Samuel R., *History of the Great Civil War, 1642–1649,* London, 1886–1891.

>   Gardiner discusses the Civil War that temporarily ended the reign of the monarchy in England and replaced it with a parliamentary form of government. The "Restoration" of the monarchy took place when Charles II came to the throne in 1660.

Holland, Norman, *The First Modern Comedies: The Significance of Etherege, Wycherley, and Congreve,* Harvard University Press, 1959.

>   Holland provides a thorough study of the three Restoration playwrights, their influences, and their heirs.

Johnson, Samuel, "Preface to William Congreve" in *Lives of the English Poets,* 1781.

>   It is a token of Johnson's eminence that the later eighteenth century is often called the "Age of Johnson." His collection of biographies on the lives of the poets from Cowley to Gray are amusing, often disparaging, but always insightful glosses on the literary giants of the age. The language of the "Preface" is singularly witty, urbane, and acerbic. He outlines the life and work of Congreve from his vantage point only fifty years after Congreve's death.

Loftis, John, *Comedy and Society from Congreve to Fielding,* Stanford University Press, 1959.

>   As its title would suggest, this critical work reviews the relationship between social history and culture in the seventeenth and eighteenth centuries. The book is particularly appropriate in its study of moral matters, social customs, and theater values.

Glossary of Literary Terms

A

Abstract: Used as a noun, the term refers to a short summary or outline of a longer work. As an adjective applied to writing or literary works, abstract refers to words or phrases that name things not knowable through the five senses. Examples of abstracts include the *Cliffs Notes* summaries of major literary works. Examples of abstract terms or concepts include "idea," "guilt" "honesty," and "loyalty."

Absurd, Theater of the: See *Theater of the Absurd*

Absurdism: See *Theater of the Absurd*

Act: A major section of a play. Acts are divided into varying numbers of shorter scenes. From ancient times to the nineteenth century plays were generally constructed of five acts, but modern works typically consist of one, two, or three acts. Examples of five-act plays include the works of Sophocles and Shakespeare, while the plays of Arthur Miller commonly have a three-act structure.

Acto: A one-act Chicano theater piece developed out of collective improvisation. *Actos* were performed by members of Luis Valdez's Teatro Campesino in California during the mid-1960s.

Aestheticism: A literary and artistic movement of the nineteenth century. Followers of the movement believed that art should not be mixed with social, political, or moral teaching. The statement "art for art's sake" is a good summary of aestheticism. The movement had its roots in France, but it gained widespread importance in England in the last half of the nineteenth century, where it helped change the Victorian practice of including moral lessons in literature. Oscar Wilde is one of the best-known "aesthetes" of the late nineteenth century.

Age of Johnson: The period in English literature between 1750 and 1798, named after the most prominent literary figure of the age, Samuel Johnson. Works written during this time are noted for their emphasis on "sensibility," or emotional quality. These works formed a transition between the rational works of the Age of Reason, or Neoclassical period, and the emphasis on individual feelings and responses of the Romantic period. Significant writers during the Age of Johnson included the novelists Ann Radcliffe and Henry Mackenzie, dramatists Richard Sheridan and Oliver Goldsmith, and poets William Collins and Thomas Gray. Also known as Age of Sensibility

Age of Reason: See *Neoclassicism*

Age of Sensibility: See *Age of Johnson*

Alexandrine Meter: See *Meter*

Allegory: A narrative technique in which characters representing things or abstract ideas are used to convey a message or teach a lesson. Allegory is typically used to teach moral, ethical, or religious lessons but is sometimes used for satiric or political purposes. Examples of allegorical works include Edmund Spenser's *The Faerie Queene* and John Bunyan's *The Pilgrim's Progress.*

Allusion: A reference to a familiar literary or historical person or event, used to make an idea more easily understood. For example, describing someone as a ''Romeo'' makes an allusion to William Shakespeare's famous young lover in *Romeo and Juliet.*

Amerind Literature: The writing and oral traditions of Native Americans. Native American literature was originally passed on by word of mouth, so it consisted largely of stories and events that were easily memorized. Amerind prose is often rhythmic like poetry because it was recited to the beat of a ceremonial drum. Examples of Amerind literature include the autobiographical *Black Elk Speaks,* the works of N. Scott Momaday, James Welch, and Craig Lee Strete, and the poetry of Luci Tapahonso.

Analogy: A comparison of two things made to explain something unfamiliar through its similarities to something familiar, or to prove one point based on the acceptedness of another. Similes and metaphors are types of analogies. Analogies often take the form of an extended simile, as in William Blake's aphorism: ''As the caterpillar chooses the fairest leaves to lay her eggs on, so the priest lays his curse on the fairest joys.''

Angry Young Men: A group of British writers of the 1950s whose work expressed bitterness and disillusionment with society. Common to their work is an anti-hero who rebels against a corrupt social order and strives for personal integrity. The term has been used to describe Kingsley Amis, John Osborne, Colin Wilson, John Wain, and others.

Antagonist: The major character in a narrative or drama who works against the hero or protagonist. An example of an evil antagonist is Richard Lovelace in Samuel Richardson's *Clarissa,* while a virtuous antagonist is Macduff in William Shakespeare's *Macbeth.*

Anthropomorphism: The presentation of animals or objects in human shape or with human characteristics. The term is derived from the Greek word for ''human form.'' The fables of Aesop, the animated films of Walt Disney, and Richard Adams's *Watership Down* feature anthropomorphic characters.

Anti-hero: A central character in a work of literature who lacks traditional heroic qualities such as courage, physical prowess, and fortitude. Anti-heros typically distrust conventional values and are unable to commit themselves to any ideals. They generally feel helpless in a world over which they have no control. Anti-heroes usually accept, and often celebrate, their positions as social outcasts. A well-known anti-hero is Yossarian in Joseph Heller's novel *Catch-22.*

Antimasque: See *Masque*

Antithesis: The antithesis of something is its direct opposite. In literature, the use of antithesis as a figure of speech results in two statements that show a contrast through the balancing of two opposite ideas. Technically, it is the second portion of the statement that is defined as the ''antithesis''; the first portion is the ''thesis.'' An example of antithesis is found in the following portion of Abraham Lincoln's ''Gettysburg Address''; notice the opposition between the verbs ''remember'' and ''forget'' and the phrases ''what we say'' and ''what they did'': ''The world will little note nor long remember what we say here, but it can never forget what they did here.''

Apocrypha: Writings tentatively attributed to an author but not proven or universally accepted to be their works. The term was originally applied to certain books of the Bible that were not considered inspired and so were not included in the ''sacred canon.'' Geoffrey Chaucer, William Shakespeare, Thomas Kyd, Thomas Middleton, and John Marston all have apocrypha. Apocryphal books of the Bible include the Old Testament's Book of Enoch and New Testament's Gospel of Peter.

Apollonian and Dionysian: The two impulses believed to guide authors of dramatic tragedy. The Apollonian impulse is named after Apollo, the Greek god of light and beauty and the symbol of intellectual order. The Dionysian impulse is named after Dionysus, the Greek god of wine and the symbol of the unrestrained forces of nature. The Apollonian impulse is to create a rational, harmonious world, while the Dionysian is to express the irrational forces of personality. Friedrich Nietzche uses these terms in *The Birth of Tragedy* to designate contrasting elements in Greek tragedy.

Apostrophe: A statement, question, or request addressed to an inanimate object or concept or to a nonexistent or absent person. Requests for inspiration from the muses in poetry are examples of apostrophe, as is Marc Antony's address to Caesar's corpse in William Shakespeare's *Julius Caesar*: ''O, pardon me, thou bleeding piece of earth, That I am meek and gentle with these butchers!. . . Woe to the hand that shed this costly blood!. . .''

Archetype: The word archetype is commonly used to describe an original pattern or model from which all other things of the same kind are made. This term was introduced to literary criticism from the psychology of Carl Jung. It expresses Jung's theory that behind every person's ''unconscious,'' or repressed memories of the past, lies the ''collective unconscious'' of the human race: memories of the countless typical experiences of our ancestors. These memories are said to prompt illogical associations that trigger powerful emotions in the reader. Often, the emotional process is primitive, even primordial. Archetypes are the literary images that grow out of the ''collective unconscious.'' They appear in literature as incidents and plots that repeat basic patterns of life. They may also appear as stereotyped characters. Examples of literary archetypes include themes such as birth and death and characters such as the Earth Mother.

Argument: The argument of a work is the author's subject matter or principal idea. Examples of defined ''argument'' portions of works include John Milton's *Arguments* to each of the books of *Paradise Lost* and the ''Argument'' to Robert Herrick's *Hesperides.*

Aristotelian Criticism: Specifically, the method of evaluating and analyzing tragedy formulated by the Greek philosopher Aristotle in his *Poetics.* More generally, the term indicates any form of criticism that follows Aristotle's views. Aristotelian criticism focuses on the form and logical structure of a work, apart from its historical or social context, in contrast to ''Platonic Criticism,'' which stresses the usefulness of art. Adherents of New Criticism including John Crowe Ransom and Cleanth Brooks utilize and value the basic ideas of Aristotelian criticism for textual analysis.

Art for Art's Sake: See *Aestheticism*

Aside: A comment made by a stage performer that is intended to be heard by the audience but supposedly not by other characters. Eugene O'Neill's *Strange Interlude* is an extended use of the aside in modern theater.

Audience: The people for whom a piece of literature is written. Authors usually write with a certain audience in mind, for example, children, members of a religious or ethnic group, or colleagues in a professional field. The term ''audience'' also applies to the people who gather to see or hear any

performance, including plays, poetry readings, speeches, and concerts. Jane Austen's parody of the gothic novel, *Northanger Abbey,* was originally intended for (and also pokes fun at) an audience of young and avid female gothic novel readers.

Avant-garde: A French term meaning ''vanguard.'' It is used in literary criticism to describe new writing that rejects traditional approaches to literature in favor of innovations in style or content. Twentieth-century examples of the literary *avant-garde* include the Black Mountain School of poets, the Bloomsbury Group, and the Beat Movement.

B

Ballad: A short poem that tells a simple story and has a repeated refrain. Ballads were originally intended to be sung. Early ballads, known as folk ballads, were passed down through generations, so their authors are often unknown. Later ballads composed by known authors are called literary ballads. An example of an anonymous folk ballad is ''Edward,'' which dates from the Middle Ages. Samuel Taylor Coleridge's ''The Rime of the Ancient Mariner'' and John Keats's ''La Belle Dame sans Merci'' are examples of literary ballads.

Baroque: A term used in literary criticism to describe literature that is complex or ornate in style or diction. Baroque works typically express tension, anxiety, and violent emotion. The term ''Baroque Age'' designates a period in Western European literature beginning in the late sixteenth century and ending about one hundred years later. Works of this period often mirror the qualities of works more generally associated with the label ''baroque'' and sometimes feature elaborate conceits. Examples of Baroque works include John Lyly's *Euphues: The Anatomy of Wit,* Luis de Gongora's *Soledads,* and William Shakespeare's *As You Like It.*

Baroque Age: See *Baroque*

Baroque Period: See *Baroque*

Beat Generation: See *Beat Movement*

Beat Movement: A period featuring a group of American poets and novelists of the 1950s and 1960s—including Jack Kerouac, Allen Ginsberg, Gregory Corso, William S. Burroughs, and Lawrence Ferlinghetti—who rejected established social and literary values. Using such techniques as stream of consciousness writing and jazz-influenced free verse and focusing on unusual or abnormal states of mind—generated by religious ecstasy or the use of drugs—the Beat writers aimed to create works that were unconventional in both form and subject matter. Kerouac's *On the Road* is perhaps the best-known example of a Beat Generation novel, and Ginsberg's *Howl* is a famous collection of Beat poetry.

Black Aesthetic Movement: A period of artistic and literary development among African Americans in the 1960s and early 1970s. This was the first major African-American artistic movement since the Harlem Renaissance and was closely paralleled by the civil rights and black power movements. The black aesthetic writers attempted to produce works of art that would be meaningful to the black masses. Key figures in black aesthetics included one of its founders, poet and playwright Amiri Baraka, formerly known as LeRoi Jones; poet and essayist Haki R. Madhubuti, formerly Don L. Lee; poet and playwright Sonia Sanchez; and dramatist Ed Bullins. Works representative of the Black Aesthetic Movement include Amiri Baraka's play *Dutchman,* a 1964 Obie award-winner; *Black Fire: An Anthology of Afro-American Writing,* edited by Baraka and playwright Larry Neal and published in 1968; and Sonia Sanchez's poetry collection *We a BaddDDD People,* published in 1970. Also known as Black Arts Movement.

Black Arts Movement: See *Black Aesthetic Movement*

Black Comedy: See *Black Humor*

Black Humor: Writing that places grotesque elements side by side with humorous ones in an attempt to shock the reader, forcing him or her to laugh at the horrifying reality of a disordered world. Joseph Heller's novel *Catch-22* is considered a superb example of the use of black humor. Other well-known authors who use black humor include Kurt Vonnegut, Edward Albee, Eugene Ionesco, and Harold Pinter. Also known as Black Comedy.

Blank Verse: Loosely, any unrhymed poetry, but more generally, unrhymed iambic pentameter verse (composed of lines of five two-syllable feet with the first syllable accented, the second unaccented). Blank verse has been used by poets since the Renaissance for its flexibility and its graceful, dignified tone. John Milton's *Paradise Lost* is in blank verse, as are most of William Shakespeare's plays.

Bloomsbury Group: A group of English writers, artists, and intellectuals who held informal artistic and philosophical discussions in Bloomsbury, a district of London, from around 1907 to the early 1930s. The Bloomsbury Group held no uniform philosophical beliefs but did commonly express an aversion to moral prudery and a desire for greater social tolerance. At various times the circle included Virginia Woolf, E. M. Forster, Clive Bell, Lytton Strachey, and John Maynard Keynes.

Bon Mot: A French term meaning "good word." A *bon mot* is a witty remark or clever observation. Charles Lamb and Oscar Wilde are celebrated for their witty *bon mots.* Two examples by Oscar Wilde stand out: (1) "All women become their mothers. That is their tragedy. No man does. That's his." (2) "A man cannot be too careful in the choice of his enemies."

Breath Verse: See *Projective Verse*

Burlesque: Any literary work that uses exaggeration to make its subject appear ridiculous, either by treating a trivial subject with profound seriousness or by treating a dignified subject frivolously. The word "burlesque" may also be used as an adjective, as in "burlesque show," to mean "striptease act." Examples of literary burlesque include the comedies of Aristophanes, Miguel de Cervantes's *Don Quixote,*, Samuel Butler's poem "Hudibras," and John Gay's play *The Beggar's Opera.*

C

Cadence: The natural rhythm of language caused by the alternation of accented and unaccented syllables. Much modern poetry—notably free verse—deliberately manipulates cadence to create complex rhythmic effects. James Macpherson's "Ossian poems" are richly cadenced, as is the poetry of the Symbolists, Walt Whitman, and Amy Lowell.

Caesura: A pause in a line of poetry, usually occurring near the middle. It typically corresponds to a break in the natural rhythm or sense of the line but is sometimes shifted to create special meanings or rhythmic effects. The opening line of Edgar Allan Poe's "The Raven" contains a caesura following "dreary": "Once upon a midnight dreary, while I pondered weak and weary. . . . "

Canzone: A short Italian or Provencal lyric poem, commonly about love and often set to music. The *canzone* has no set form but typically contains five or six stanzas made up of seven to twenty lines of eleven syllables each. A shorter, five- to ten-line "envoy," or concluding stanza, completes the poem.

Masters of the *canzone* form include Petrarch, Dante Alighieri, Torquato Tasso, and Guido Cavalcanti.

Carpe Diem: A Latin term meaning "seize the day." This is a traditional theme of poetry, especially lyrics. A *carpe diem* poem advises the reader or the person it addresses to live for today and enjoy the pleasures of the moment. Two celebrated *carpe diem* poems are Andrew Marvell's "To His Coy Mistress" and Robert Herrick's poem beginning "Gather ye rosebuds while ye may. . . ."

Catharsis: The release or purging of unwanted emotions— specifically fear and pity—brought about by exposure to art. The term was first used by the Greek philosopher Aristotle in his *Poetics* to refer to the desired effect of tragedy on spectators. A famous example of catharsis is realized in Sophocles' *Oedipus Rex,* when Oedipus discovers that his wife, Jacosta, is his own mother and that the stranger he killed on the road was his own father.

Celtic Renaissance: A period of Irish literary and cultural history at the end of the nineteenth century. Followers of the movement aimed to create a romantic vision of Celtic myth and legend. The most significant works of the Celtic Renaissance typically present a dreamy, unreal world, usually in reaction against the reality of contemporary problems. William Butler Yeats's *The Wanderings of Oisin* is among the most significant works of the Celtic Renaissance. Also known as Celtic Twilight.

Celtic Twilight: See *Celtic Renaissance*

Character: Broadly speaking, a person in a literary work. The actions of characters are what constitute the plot of a story, novel, or poem. There are numerous types of characters, ranging from simple, stereotypical figures to intricate, multifaceted ones. In the techniques of anthropomorphism and personification, animals—and even places or things—can assume aspects of character. "Characterization" is the process by which an author creates vivid, believable characters in a work of art. This may be done in a variety of ways, including (1) direct description of the character by the narrator; (2) the direct presentation of the speech, thoughts, or actions of the character; and (3) the responses of other characters to the character. The term "character" also refers to a form originated by the ancient Greek writer Theophrastus that later became popular in the seventeenth and eighteenth centuries. It is a short essay or sketch of a person who prominently displays a specific attribute or quality, such as miserliness or ambition. Notable characters in lit-

erature include Oedipus Rex, Don Quixote de la Mancha, Macbeth, Candide, Hester Prynne, Ebenezer Scrooge, Huckleberry Finn, Jay Gatsby, Scarlett O'Hara, James Bond, and Kunta Kinte.

Characterization: See *Character*

Chorus: In ancient Greek drama, a group of actors who commented on and interpreted the unfolding action on the stage. Initially the chorus was a major component of the presentation, but over time it became less significant, with its numbers reduced and its role eventually limited to commentary between acts. By the sixteenth century the chorus—if employed at all—was typically a single person who provided a prologue and an epilogue and occasionally appeared between acts to introduce or underscore an important event. The chorus in William Shakespeare's *Henry V* functions in this way. Modern dramas rarely feature a chorus, but T. S. Eliot's *Murder in the Cathedral* and Arthur Miller's *A View from the Bridge* are notable exceptions. The Stage Manager in Thornton Wilder's *Our Town* performs a role similar to that of the chorus.

Chronicle: A record of events presented in chronological order. Although the scope and level of detail provided varies greatly among the chronicles surviving from ancient times, some, such as the *Anglo-Saxon Chronicle,* feature vivid descriptions and a lively recounting of events. During the Elizabethan Age, many dramas— appropriately called "chronicle plays"—were based on material from chronicles. Many of William Shakespeare's dramas of English history as well as Christopher Marlowe's *Edward II* are based in part on Raphael Holinshead's *Chronicles of England, Scotland, and Ireland.*

Classical: In its strictest definition in literary criticism, classicism refers to works of ancient Greek or Roman literature. The term may also be used to describe a literary work of recognized importance (a "classic") from any time period or literature that exhibits the traits of classicism. Classical authors from ancient Greek and Roman times include Juvenal and Homer. Examples of later works and authors now described as classical include French literature of the seventeenth century, Western novels of the nineteenth century, and American fiction of the mid-nineteenth century such as that written by James Fenimore Cooper and Mark Twain.

Classicism: A term used in literary criticism to describe critical doctrines that have their roots in ancient Greek and Roman literature, philosophy, and art. Works associated with classicism typically exhibit restraint on the part of the author, unity of design and purpose, clarity, simplicity, logical organization, and respect for tradition. Examples of literary classicism include Cicero's prose, the dramas of Pierre Corneille and Jean Racine, the poetry of John Dryden and Alexander Pope, and the writings of J. W. von Goethe, G. E. Lessing, and T. S. Eliot.

Climax: The turning point in a narrative, the moment when the conflict is at its most intense. Typically, the structure of stories, novels, and plays is one of rising action, in which tension builds to the climax, followed by falling action, in which tension lessens as the story moves to its conclusion. The climax in James Fenimore Cooper's *The Last of the Mohicans* occurs when Magua and his captive Cora are pursued to the edge of a cliff by Uncas. Magua kills Uncas but is subsequently killed by Hawkeye.

Colloquialism: A word, phrase, or form of pronunciation that is acceptable in casual conversation but not in formal, written communication. It is considered more acceptable than slang. An example of colloquialism can be found in Rudyard Kipling's *Barrack-room Ballads:* When 'Omer smote 'is bloomin' lyre He'd 'eard men sing by land and sea; An' what he thought 'e might require 'E went an' took—the same as me!

Comedy: One of two major types of drama, the other being tragedy. Its aim is to amuse, and it typically ends happily. Comedy assumes many forms, such as farce and burlesque, and uses a variety of techniques, from parody to satire. In a restricted sense the term comedy refers only to dramatic presentations, but in general usage it is commonly applied to nondramatic works as well. Examples of comedies range from the plays of Aristophanes, Terrence, and Plautus, Dante Alighieri's *The Divine Comedy,* Francois Rabelais's *Pantagruel* and *Gargantua,* and some of Geoffrey Chaucer's tales and William Shakespeare's plays to Noel Coward's play *Private Lives* and James Thurber's short story "The Secret Life of Walter Mitty."

Comedy of Manners: A play about the manners and conventions of an aristocratic, highly sophisticated society. The characters are usually types rather than individualized personalities, and plot is less important than atmosphere. Such plays were an important aspect of late seventeenth-century English comedy. The comedy of manners was revived in the eighteenth century by Oliver Goldsmith and Richard Brinsley Sheridan, enjoyed a second revival in the late nineteenth century, and has endured

into the twentieth century. Examples of comedies of manners include William Congreve's *The Way of the World* in the late seventeenth century, Oliver Goldsmith's *She Stoops to Conquer* and Richard Brinsley Sheridan's *The School for Scandal* in the eighteenth century, Oscar Wilde's *The Importance of Being Earnest* in the nineteenth century, and W. Somerset Maugham's *The Circle* in the twentieth century.

Comic Relief: The use of humor to lighten the mood of a serious or tragic story, especially in plays. The technique is very common in Elizabethan works, and can be an integral part of the plot or simply a brief event designed to break the tension of the scene. The Gravediggers' scene in William Shakespeare's *Hamlet* is a frequently cited example of comic relief.

Commedia dell'arte: An Italian term meaning "the comedy of guilds" or "the comedy of professional actors." This form of dramatic comedy was popular in Italy during the sixteenth century. Actors were assigned stock roles (such as Pulcinella, the stupid servant, or Pantalone, the old merchant) and given a basic plot to follow, but all dialogue was improvised. The roles were rigidly typed and the plots were formulaic, usually revolving around young lovers who thwarted their elders and attained wealth and happiness. A rigid convention of the *commedia dell'arte* is the periodic intrusion of Harlequin, who interrupts the play with low buffoonery. Peppino de Filippo's *Metamorphoses of a Wandering Minstrel* gave modern audiences an idea of what *commedia dell'arte* may have been like. Various scenarios for *commedia dell'arte* were compiled in Petraccone's *La commedia dell'arte, storia, technica, scenari,* published in 1927.

Complaint: A lyric poem, popular in the Renaissance, in which the speaker expresses sorrow about his or her condition. Typically, the speaker's sadness is caused by an unresponsive lover, but some complaints cite other sources of unhappiness, such as poverty or fate. A commonly cited example is "A Complaint by Night of the Lover Not Beloved" by Henry Howard, Earl of Surrey. Thomas Sackville's "Complaint of Henry, Duke of Buckingham" traces the duke's unhappiness to his ruthless ambition.

Conceit: A clever and fanciful metaphor, usually expressed through elaborate and extended comparison, that presents a striking parallel between two seemingly dissimilar things—for example, elaborately comparing a beautiful woman to an object like a garden or the sun. The conceit was a popular device throughout the Elizabethan Age and Baroque Age and was the principal technique of the seventeenth-century English metaphysical poets. This usage of the word conceit is unrelated to the best-known definition of conceit as an arrogant attitude or behavior. The conceit figures prominently in the works of John Donne, Emily Dickinson, and T. S. Eliot.

Concrete: Concrete is the opposite of abstract, and refers to a thing that actually exists or a description that allows the reader to experience an object or concept with the senses. Henry David Thoreau's *Walden* contains much concrete description of nature and wildlife.

Concrete Poetry: Poetry in which visual elements play a large part in the poetic effect. Punctuation marks, letters, or words are arranged on a page to form a visual design: a cross, for example, or a bumblebee. Max Bill and Eugene Gomringer were among the early practitioners of concrete poetry; Haroldo de Campos and Augusto de Campos are among contemporary authors of concrete poetry.

Confessional Poetry: A form of poetry in which the poet reveals very personal, intimate, sometimes shocking information about himself or herself. Anne Sexton, Sylvia Plath, Robert Lowell, and John Berryman wrote poetry in the confessional vein.

Conflict: The conflict in a work of fiction is the issue to be resolved in the story. It usually occurs between two characters, the protagonist and the antagonist, or between the protagonist and society or the protagonist and himself or herself. Conflict in Theodore Dreiser's novel *Sister Carrie* comes as a result of urban society, while Jack London's short story "To Build a Fire" concerns the protagonist's battle against the cold and himself.

Connotation: The impression that a word gives beyond its defined meaning. Connotations may be universally understood or may be significant only to a certain group. Both "horse" and "steed" denote the same animal, but "steed" has a different connotation, deriving from the chivalrous or romantic narratives in which the word was once often used.

Consonance: Consonance occurs in poetry when words appearing at the ends of two or more verses have similar final consonant sounds but have final vowel sounds that differ, as with "stuff" and "off." Consonance is found in "The curfew tolls the knells of parting day" from Thomas Grey's "An Elegy Written in a Country Church Yard." Also known as Half Rhyme or Slant Rhyme.

Convention: Any widely accepted literary device, style, or form. A soliloquy, in which a character reveals to the audience his or her private thoughts, is an example of a dramatic convention.

Corrido: A Mexican ballad. Examples of *corridos* include "Muerte del afamado Bilito," "La voz de mi conciencia," "Lucio Perez," "La juida," and "Los presos."

Couplet: Two lines of poetry with the same rhyme and meter, often expressing a complete and self-contained thought. The following couplet is from Alexander Pope's "Elegy to the Memory of an Unfortunate Lady": 'Tis Use alone that sanctifies Expense, And Splendour borrows all her rays from Sense.

Criticism: The systematic study and evaluation of literary works, usually based on a specific method or set of principles. An important part of literary studies since ancient times, the practice of criticism has given rise to numerous theories, methods, and "schools," sometimes producing conflicting, even contradictory, interpretations of literature in general as well as of individual works. Even such basic issues as what constitutes a poem or a novel have been the subject of much criticism over the centuries. Seminal texts of literary criticism include Plato's *Republic,* Aristotle's *Poetics,* Sir Philip Sidney's *The Defence of Poesie,* John Dryden's *Of Dramatic Poesie,* and William Wordsworth's "Preface" to the second edition of his *Lyrical Ballads.* Contemporary schools of criticism include deconstruction, feminist, psychoanalytic, poststructuralist, new historicist, postcolonialist, and reader-response.

D

Dactyl: See *Foot*

Dadaism: A protest movement in art and literature founded by Tristan Tzara in 1916. Followers of the movement expressed their outrage at the destruction brought about by World War I by revolting against numerous forms of social convention. The Dadaists presented works marked by calculated madness and flamboyant nonsense. They stressed total freedom of expression, commonly through primitive displays of emotion and illogical, often senseless, poetry. The movement ended shortly after the war, when it was replaced by surrealism. Proponents of Dadaism include Andre Breton, Louis Aragon, Philippe Soupault, and Paul Eluard.

Decadent: See *Decadents*

Decadents: The followers of a nineteenth-century literary movement that had its beginnings in French aestheticism. Decadent literature displays a fascination with perverse and morbid states; a search for novelty and sensation—the "new thrill"; a preoccupation with mysticism; and a belief in the senselessness of human existence. The movement is closely associated with the doctrine Art for Art's Sake. The term "decadence" is sometimes used to denote a decline in the quality of art or literature following a period of greatness. Major French decadents are Charles Baudelaire and Arthur Rimbaud. English decadents include Oscar Wilde, Ernest Dowson, and Frank Harris.

Deconstruction: A method of literary criticism developed by Jacques Derrida and characterized by multiple conflicting interpretations of a given work. Deconstructionists consider the impact of the language of a work and suggest that the true meaning of the work is not necessarily the meaning that the author intended. Jacques Derrida's *De la grammatologie* is the seminal text on deconstructive strategies; among American practitioners of this method of criticism are Paul de Man and J. Hillis Miller.

Deduction: The process of reaching a conclusion through reasoning from general premises to a specific premise. An example of deduction is present in the following syllogism: Premise: All mammals are animals. Premise: All whales are mammals. Conclusion: Therefore, all whales are animals.

Denotation: The definition of a word, apart from the impressions or feelings it creates in the reader. The word "apartheid" denotes a political and economic policy of segregation by race, but its connotations— oppression, slavery, inequality—are numerous.

Denouement: A French word meaning "the unknotting." In literary criticism, it denotes the resolution of conflict in fiction or drama. The *denouement* follows the climax and provides an outcome to the primary plot situation as well as an explanation of secondary plot complications. The *denouement* often involves a character's recognition of his or her state of mind or moral condition. A well-known example of *denouement* is the last scene of the play *As You Like It* by William Shakespeare, in which couples are married, an evildoer repents, the identities of two disguised characters are revealed, and a ruler is restored to power. Also known as Falling Action.

Description: Descriptive writing is intended to allow a reader to picture the scene or setting in which the action of a story takes place. The form this description takes often evokes an intended emotional response—a dark, spooky graveyard will evoke fear, and a peaceful, sunny meadow will evoke calmness. An example of a descriptive story is Edgar Allan Poe's *Landor's Cottage,* which offers a detailed depiction of a New York country estate.

Detective Story: A narrative about the solution of a mystery or the identification of a criminal. The conventions of the detective story include the detective's scrupulous use of logic in solving the mystery; incompetent or ineffectual police; a suspect who appears guilty at first but is later proved innocent; and the detective's friend or confidant— often the narrator—whose slowness in interpreting clues emphasizes by contrast the detective's brilliance. Edgar Allan Poe's "Murders in the Rue Morgue" is commonly regarded as the earliest example of this type of story. With this work, Poe established many of the conventions of the detective story genre, which are still in practice. Other practitioners of this vast and extremely popular genre include Arthur Conan Doyle, Dashiell Hammett, and Agatha Christie.

Deus ex machina: A Latin term meaning "god out of a machine." In Greek drama, a god was often lowered onto the stage by a mechanism of some kind to rescue the hero or untangle the plot. By extension, the term refers to any artificial device or coincidence used to bring about a convenient and simple solution to a plot. This is a common device in melodramas and includes such fortunate circumstances as the sudden receipt of a legacy to save the family farm or a last-minute stay of execution. The *deus ex machina* invariably rewards the virtuous and punishes evildoers. Examples of *deus ex machina* include King Louis XIV in Jean-Baptiste Moliere's *Tartuffe* and Queen Victoria in *The Pirates of Penzance* by William Gilbert and Arthur Sullivan. Bertolt Brecht parodies the abuse of such devices in the conclusion of his *Threepenny Opera.*

Dialogue: In its widest sense, dialogue is simply conversation between people in a literary work; in its most restricted sense, it refers specifically to the speech of characters in a drama. As a specific literary genre, a "dialogue" is a composition in which characters debate an issue or idea. The Greek philosopher Plato frequently expounded his theories in the form of dialogues.

Diction: The selection and arrangement of words in a literary work. Either or both may vary depending on the desired effect. There are four general types of diction: ''formal,'' used in scholarly or lofty writing; ''informal,'' used in relaxed but educated conversation; ''colloquial,'' used in everyday speech; and ''slang,'' containing newly coined words and other terms not accepted in formal usage.

Didactic: A term used to describe works of literature that aim to teach some moral, religious, political, or practical lesson. Although didactic elements are often found in artistically pleasing works, the term ''didactic'' usually refers to literature in which the message is more important than the form. The term may also be used to criticize a work that the critic finds ''overly didactic,'' that is, heavy-handed in its delivery of a lesson. Examples of didactic literature include John Bunyan's *Pilgrim's Progress,* Alexander Pope's *Essay on Criticism,* Jean-Jacques Rousseau's *Emile,* and Elizabeth Inchbald's *Simple Story.*

Dimeter: See *Meter*

Dionysian: See *Apollonian and Dionysian*

Discordia concours: A Latin phrase meaning ''discord in harmony.'' The term was coined by the eighteenth-century English writer Samuel Johnson to describe ''a combination of dissimilar images or discovery of occult resemblances in things apparently unlike.'' Johnson created the expression by reversing a phrase by the Latin poet Horace. The metaphysical poetry of John Donne, Richard Crashaw, Abraham Cowley, George Herbert, and Edward Taylor among others, contains many examples of *discordia concours.* In Donne's ''A Valediction: Forbidding Mourning,'' the poet compares the union of himself with his lover to a draftsman's compass: If they be two, they are two so, As stiff twin compasses are two: Thy soul, the fixed foot, makes no show To move, but doth, if the other do; And though it in the center sit, Yet when the other far doth roam, It leans, and hearkens after it, And grows erect, as that comes home.

Dissonance: A combination of harsh or jarring sounds, especially in poetry. Although such combinations may be accidental, poets sometimes intentionally make them to achieve particular effects. Dissonance is also sometimes used to refer to close but not identical rhymes. When this is the case, the word functions as a synonym for consonance. Robert Browning, Gerard Manley Hopkins, and many other poets have made deliberate use of dissonance.

Doppelganger: A literary technique by which a character is duplicated (usually in the form of an alter ego, though sometimes as a ghostly counterpart) or divided into two distinct, usually opposite personalities. The use of this character device is widespread in nineteenth- and twentieth-century literature, and indicates a growing awareness among authors that the ''self'' is really a composite of many ''selves.'' A well-known story containing a *doppelganger* character is Robert Louis Stevenson's *Dr. Jekyll and Mr. Hyde,* which dramatizes an internal struggle between good and evil. Also known as The Double.

Double Entendre: A corruption of a French phrase meaning ''double meaning.'' The term is used to indicate a word or phrase that is deliberately ambiguous, especially when one of the meanings is risque or improper. An example of a *double entendre* is the Elizabethan usage of the verb ''die,'' which refers both to death and to orgasm.

Double, The: See *Doppelganger*

Draft: Any preliminary version of a written work. An author may write dozens of drafts which are revised to form the final work, or he or she may write only one, with few or no revisions. Dorothy Parker's observation that ''I can't write five words but that I change seven'' humorously indicates the purpose of the draft.

Drama: In its widest sense, a drama is any work designed to be presented by actors on a stage. Similarly, ''drama'' denotes a broad literary genre that includes a variety of forms, from pageant and spectacle to tragedy and comedy, as well as countless types and subtypes. More commonly in modern usage, however, a drama is a work that treats serious subjects and themes but does not aim at the grandeur of tragedy. This use of the term originated with the eighteenth-century French writer Denis Diderot, who used the word *drame* to designate his plays about middle-class life; thus ''drama'' typically features characters of a less exalted stature than those of tragedy. Examples of classical dramas include Menander's comedy *Dyscolus* and Sophocles' tragedy *Oedipus Rex.* Contemporary dramas include Eugene O'Neill's *The Iceman Cometh,* Lillian Hellman's *Little Foxes,* and August Wilson's *Ma Rainey's Black Bottom.*

Dramatic Irony: Occurs when the audience of a play or the reader of a work of literature knows something that a character in the work itself does not know. The irony is in the contrast between the intended meaning of the statements or actions of a character and the additional information understood by the audience. A celebrated example of dramatic irony is in Act V of William Shakespeare's *Romeo and Juliet,* where two young lovers meet their end as a result of a tragic misunderstanding. Here, the audience has full knowledge that Juliet's apparent ''death'' is merely temporary; she will regain her senses when the mysterious ''sleeping potion'' she has taken wears off. But Romeo, mistaking Juliet's drug-induced trance for true death, kills himself in grief. Upon awakening, Juliet discovers Romeo's corpse and, in despair, slays herself.

Dramatic Monologue: See *Monologue*

Dramatic Poetry: Any lyric work that employs elements of drama such as dialogue, conflict, or characterization, but excluding works that are intended for stage presentation. A monologue is a form of dramatic poetry.

Dramatis Personae: The characters in a work of literature, particularly a drama. The list of characters printed before the main text of a play or in the program is the *dramatis personae.*

Dream Allegory: See *Dream Vision*

Dream Vision: A literary convention, chiefly of the Middle Ages. In a dream vision a story is presented as a literal dream of the narrator. This device was commonly used to teach moral and religious lessons. Important works of this type are *The Divine Comedy* by Dante Alighieri, *Piers Plowman* by William Langland, and *The Pilgrim's Progress* by John Bunyan. Also known as Dream Allegory.

Dystopia: An imaginary place in a work of fiction where the characters lead dehumanized, fearful lives. Jack London's *The Iron Heel,* Yevgeny Zamyatin's *My,* Aldous Huxley's *Brave New World,* George Orwell's *Nineteen Eighty-four,* and Margaret Atwood's *Handmaid's Tale* portray versions of dystopia.

E

Eclogue: In classical literature, a poem featuring rural themes and structured as a dialogue among shepherds. Eclogues often took specific poetic forms, such as elegies or love poems. Some were written as the soliloquy of a shepherd. In later centuries, ''eclogue'' came to refer to any poem that was in the pastoral tradition or that had a dialogue or monologue structure. A classical example of an eclogue is Virgil's *Eclogues,* also known as *Bucolics.* Giovanni

Boccaccio, Edmund Spenser, Andrew Marvell, Jonathan Swift, and Louis MacNeice also wrote eclogues.

Edwardian: Describes cultural conventions identified with the period of the reign of Edward VII of England (1901–1910). Writers of the Edwardian Age typically displayed a strong reaction against the propriety and conservatism of the Victorian Age. Their work often exhibits distrust of authority in religion, politics, and art and expresses strong doubts about the soundness of conventional values. Writers of this era include George Bernard Shaw, H. G. Wells, and Joseph Conrad.

Edwardian Age: See *Edwardian*

Electra Complex: A daughter's amorous obsession with her father. The term Electra complex comes from the plays of Euripides and Sophocles entitled *Electra,* in which the character Electra drives her brother Orestes to kill their mother and her lover in revenge for the murder of their father.

Elegy: A lyric poem that laments the death of a person or the eventual death of all people. In a conventional elegy, set in a classical world, the poet and subject are spoken of as shepherds. In modern criticism, the word elegy is often used to refer to a poem that is melancholy or mournfully contemplative. John Milton's ''Lycidas'' and Percy Bysshe Shelley's ''Adonais'' are two examples of this form.

Elizabethan Age: A period of great economic growth, religious controversy, and nationalism closely associated with the reign of Elizabeth I of England (1558–1603). The Elizabethan Age is considered a part of the general renaissance—that is, the flowering of arts and literature—that took place in Europe during the fourteenth through sixteenth centuries. The era is considered the golden age of English literature. The most important dramas in English and a great deal of lyric poetry were produced during this period, and modern English criticism began around this time. The notable authors of the period—Philip Sidney, Edmund Spenser, Christopher Marlowe, William Shakespeare, Ben Jonson, Francis Bacon, and John Donne—are among the best in all of English literature.

Elizabethan Drama: English comic and tragic plays produced during the Renaissance, or more narrowly, those plays written during the last years of and few years after Queen Elizabeth's reign. William Shakespeare is considered an Elizabethan dramatist in the broader sense, although most of his work was produced during the reign of James I. Examples of Elizabethan comedies include John

Lyly's *The Woman in the Moone,* Thomas Dekker's *The Roaring Girl, or, Moll Cut Purse,* and William Shakespeare's *Twelfth Night.* Examples of Elizabethan tragedies include William Shakespeare's *Antony and Cleopatra,* Thomas Kyd's *The Spanish Tragedy,* and John Webster's *The Tragedy of the Duchess of Malfi.*

Empathy: A sense of shared experience, including emotional and physical feelings, with someone or something other than oneself. Empathy is often used to describe the response of a reader to a literary character. An example of an empathic passage is William Shakespeare's description in his narrative poem *Venus and Adonis* of: the snail, whose tender horns being hit, Shrinks backward in his shelly cave with pain. Readers of Gerard Manley Hopkins's *The Windhover* may experience some of the physical sensations evoked in the description of the movement of the falcon.

English Sonnet: See *Sonnet*

Enjambment: The running over of the sense and structure of a line of verse or a couplet into the following verse or couplet. Andrew Marvell's "To His Coy Mistress" is structured as a series of enjambments, as in lines 11–12: "My vegetable love should grow/Vaster than empires and more slow."

Enlightenment, The: An eighteenth-century philosophical movement. It began in France but had a wide impact throughout Europe and America. Thinkers of the Enlightenment valued reason and believed that both the individual and society could achieve a state of perfection. Corresponding to this essentially humanist vision was a resistance to religious authority. Important figures of the Enlightenment were Denis Diderot and Voltaire in France, Edward Gibbon and David Hume in England, and Thomas Paine and Thomas Jefferson in the United States.

Epic: A long narrative poem about the adventures of a hero of great historic or legendary importance. The setting is vast and the action is often given cosmic significance through the intervention of supernatural forces such as gods, angels, or demons. Epics are typically written in a classical style of grand simplicity with elaborate metaphors and allusions that enhance the symbolic importance of a hero's adventures. Some well-known epics are Homer's *Iliad* and *Odyssey,* Virgil's *Aeneid,* and John Milton's *Paradise Lost.*

Epic Simile: See *Homeric Simile*

Epic Theater: A theory of theatrical presentation developed by twentieth-century German playwright Bertolt Brecht. Brecht created a type of drama that the audience could view with complete detachment. He used what he termed "alienation effects" to create an emotional distance between the audience and the action on stage. Among these effects are: short, self-contained scenes that keep the play from building to a cathartic climax; songs that comment on the action; and techniques of acting that prevent the actor from developing an emotional identity with his role. Besides the plays of Bertolt Brecht, other plays that utilize epic theater conventions include those of Georg Buchner, Frank Wedekind, Erwin Piscator, and Leopold Jessner.

Epigram: A saying that makes the speaker's point quickly and concisely. Samuel Taylor Coleridge wrote an epigram that neatly sums up the form: What is an Epigram? A Dwarfish whole, Its body brevity, and wit its soul.

Epilogue: A concluding statement or section of a literary work. In dramas, particularly those of the seventeenth and eighteenth centuries, the epilogue is a closing speech, often in verse, delivered by an actor at the end of a play and spoken directly to the audience. A famous epilogue is Puck's speech at the end of William Shakespeare's *A Midsummer Night's Dream.*

Epiphany: A sudden revelation of truth inspired by a seemingly trivial incident. The term was widely used by James Joyce in his critical writings, and the stories in Joyce's *Dubliners* are commonly called "epiphanies."

Episode: An incident that forms part of a story and is significantly related to it. Episodes may be either self-contained narratives or events that depend on a larger context for their sense and importance. Examples of episodes include the founding of Wilmington, Delaware in Charles Reade's *The Disinherited Heir* and the individual events comprising the picaresque novels and medieval romances.

Episodic Plot: See *Plot*

Epitaph: An inscription on a tomb or tombstone, or a verse written on the occasion of a person's death. Epitaphs may be serious or humorous. Dorothy Parker's epitaph reads, "I told you I was sick."

Epithalamion: A song or poem written to honor and commemorate a marriage ceremony. Famous examples include Edmund Spenser's

"Epithalamion" and e. e. cummings's "Epithalamion." Also spelled Epithalamium.

Epithalamium: See *Epithalamion*

Epithet: A word or phrase, often disparaging or abusive, that expresses a character trait of someone or something. "The Napoleon of crime" is an epithet applied to Professor Moriarty, arch-rival of Sherlock Holmes in Arthur Conan Doyle's series of detective stories.

Exempla: See *Exemplum*

Exemplum: A tale with a moral message. This form of literary sermonizing flourished during the Middle Ages, when *exempla* appeared in collections known as "example-books." The works of Geoffrey Chaucer are full of *exempla*.

Existentialism: A predominantly twentieth-century philosophy concerned with the nature and perception of human existence. There are two major strains of existentialist thought: atheistic and Christian. Followers of atheistic existentialism believe that the individual is alone in a godless universe and that the basic human condition is one of suffering and loneliness. Nevertheless, because there are no fixed values, individuals can create their own characters—indeed, they can shape themselves—through the exercise of free will. The atheistic strain culminates in and is popularly associated with the works of Jean-Paul Sartre. The Christian existentialists, on the other hand, believe that only in God may people find freedom from life's anguish. The two strains hold certain beliefs in common: that existence cannot be fully understood or described through empirical effort; that anguish is a universal element of life; that individuals must bear responsibility for their actions; and that there is no common standard of behavior or perception for religious and ethical matters. Existentialist thought figures prominently in the works of such authors as Eugene Ionesco, Franz Kafka, Fyodor Dostoyevsky, Simone de Beauvoir, Samuel Beckett, and Albert Camus.

Expatriates: See *Expatriatism*

Expatriatism: The practice of leaving one's country to live for an extended period in another country. Literary expatriates include English poets Percy Bysshe Shelley and John Keats in Italy, Polish novelist Joseph Conrad in England, American writers Richard Wright, James Baldwin, Gertrude Stein, and Ernest Hemingway in France, and Trinidadian author Neil Bissondath in Canada.

Exposition: Writing intended to explain the nature of an idea, thing, or theme. Expository writing is often combined with description, narration, or argument. In dramatic writing, the exposition is the introductory material which presents the characters, setting, and tone of the play. An example of dramatic exposition occurs in many nineteenth-century drawing-room comedies in which the butler and the maid open the play with relevant talk about their master and mistress; in composition, exposition relays factual information, as in encyclopedia entries.

Expressionism: An indistinct literary term, originally used to describe an early twentieth-century school of German painting. The term applies to almost any mode of unconventional, highly subjective writing that distorts reality in some way. Advocates of Expressionism include dramatists George Kaiser, Ernst Toller, Luigi Pirandello, Federico Garcia Lorca, Eugene O'Neill, and Elmer Rice; poets George Heym, Ernst Stadler, August Stramm, Gottfried Benn, and Georg Trakl; and novelists Franz Kafka and James Joyce.

Extended Monologue: See *Monologue*

F

Fable: A prose or verse narrative intended to convey a moral. Animals or inanimate objects with human characteristics often serve as characters in fables. A famous fable is Aesop's "The Tortoise and the Hare."

Fairy Tales: Short narratives featuring mythical beings such as fairies, elves, and sprites. These tales originally belonged to the folklore of a particular nation or region, such as those collected in Germany by Jacob and Wilhelm Grimm. Two other celebrated writers of fairy tales are Hans Christian Andersen and Rudyard Kipling.

Falling Action: See *Denouement*

Fantasy: A literary form related to mythology and folklore. Fantasy literature is typically set in non-existent realms and features supernatural beings. Notable examples of fantasy literature are *The Lord of the Rings* by J. R. R. Tolkien and the Gormenghast trilogy by Mervyn Peake.

Farce: A type of comedy characterized by broad humor, outlandish incidents, and often vulgar subject matter. Much of the "comedy" in film and television could more accurately be described as farce.

Feet: See *Foot*

Feminine Rhyme: See *Rhyme*

Femme fatale: A French phrase with the literal translation "fatal woman." A *femme fatale* is a sensuous, alluring woman who often leads men into danger or trouble. A classic example of the *femme fatale* is the nameless character in Billy Wilder's *The Seven Year Itch,* portrayed by Marilyn Monroe in the film adaptation.

Fiction: Any story that is the product of imagination rather than a documentation of fact. characters and events in such narratives may be based in real life but their ultimate form and configuration is a creation of the author. Geoffrey Chaucer's *The Canterbury Tales,* Laurence Sterne's *Tristram Shandy,* and Margaret Mitchell's *Gone with the Wind* are examples of fiction.

Figurative Language: A technique in writing in which the author temporarily interrupts the order, construction, or meaning of the writing for a particular effect. This interruption takes the form of one or more figures of speech such as hyperbole, irony, or simile. Figurative language is the opposite of literal language, in which every word is truthful, accurate, and free of exaggeration or embellishment. Examples of figurative language are tropes such as metaphor and rhetorical figures such as apostrophe.

Figures of Speech: Writing that differs from customary conventions for construction, meaning, order, or significance for the purpose of a special meaning or effect. There are two major types of figures of speech: rhetorical figures, which do not make changes in the meaning of the words, and tropes, which do. Types of figures of speech include simile, hyperbole, alliteration, and pun, among many others.

Fin de siecle: A French term meaning "end of the century." The term is used to denote the last decade of the nineteenth century, a transition period when writers and other artists abandoned old conventions and looked for new techniques and objectives. Two writers commonly associated with the *fin de siecle* mindset are Oscar Wilde and George Bernard Shaw.

First Person: See *Point of View*

Flashback: A device used in literature to present action that occurred before the beginning of the story. Flashbacks are often introduced as the dreams or recollections of one or more characters. Flashback techniques are often used in films, where they are typically set off by a gradual changing of one picture to another.

Foil: A character in a work of literature whose physical or psychological qualities contrast strongly with, and therefore highlight, the corresponding qualities of another character. In his Sherlock Holmes stories, Arthur Conan Doyle portrayed Dr. Watson as a man of normal habits and intelligence, making him a foil for the eccentric and wonderfully perceptive Sherlock Holmes.

Folk Ballad: See *Ballad*

Folklore: Traditions and myths preserved in a culture or group of people. Typically, these are passed on by word of mouth in various forms—such as legends, songs, and proverbs— or preserved in customs and ceremonies. This term was first used by W. J. Thoms in 1846. Sir James Frazer's *The Golden Bough* is the record of English folklore; myths about the frontier and the Old South exemplify American folklore.

Folktale: A story originating in oral tradition. Folktales fall into a variety of categories, including legends, ghost stories, fairy tales, fables, and anecdotes based on historical figures and events. Examples of folktales include Giambattista Basile's *The Pentamerone,* which contains the tales of Puss in Boots, Rapunzel, Cinderella, and Beauty and the Beast, and Joel Chandler Harris's Uncle Remus stories, which represent transplanted African folktales and American tales about the characters Mike Fink, Johnny Appleseed, Paul Bunyan, and Pecos Bill.

Foot: The smallest unit of rhythm in a line of poetry. In English-language poetry, a foot is typically one accented syllable combined with one or two unaccented syllables. There are many different types of feet. When the accent is on the second syllable of a two syllable word (con-*tort*), the foot is an "iamb"; the reverse accentual pattern (*tor* -ture) is a "trochee." Other feet that commonly occur in poetry in English are "anapest", two unaccented syllables followed by an accented syllable as in inter-*cept*, and "dactyl", an accented syllable followed by two unaccented syllables as in *su*-i-cide.

Foreshadowing: A device used in literature to create expectation or to set up an explanation of later developments. In Charles Dickens's *Great Expectations,* the graveyard encounter at the beginning of the novel between Pip and the escaped convict Magwitch foreshadows the baleful atmosphere and events that comprise much of the narrative.

Form: The pattern or construction of a work which identifies its genre and distinguishes it from other genres. Examples of forms include the different genres, such as the lyric form or the short story form, and various patterns for poetry, such as the verse form or the stanza form.

Formalism: In literary criticism, the belief that literature should follow prescribed rules of construction, such as those that govern the sonnet form. Examples of formalism are found in the work of the New Critics and structuralists.

Fourteener Meter: See *Meter*

Free Verse: Poetry that lacks regular metrical and rhyme patterns but that tries to capture the cadences of everyday speech. The form allows a poet to exploit a variety of rhythmical effects within a single poem. Free-verse techniques have been widely used in the twentieth century by such writers as Ezra Pound, T. S. Eliot, Carl Sandburg, and William Carlos Williams. Also known as *Vers libre.*

Futurism: A flamboyant literary and artistic movement that developed in France, Italy, and Russia from 1908 through the 1920s. Futurist theater and poetry abandoned traditional literary forms. In their place, followers of the movement attempted to achieve total freedom of expression through bizarre imagery and deformed or newly invented words. The Futurists were self-consciously modern artists who attempted to incorporate the appearances and sounds of modern life into their work. Futurist writers include Filippo Tommaso Marinetti, Wyndham Lewis, Guillaume Apollinaire, Velimir Khlebnikov, and Vladimir Mayakovsky.

G

Genre: A category of literary work. In critical theory, genre may refer to both the content of a given work—tragedy, comedy, pastoral—and to its form, such as poetry, novel, or drama. This term also refers to types of popular literature, as in the genres of science fiction or the detective story.

Genteel Tradition: A term coined by critic George Santayana to describe the literary practice of certain late nineteenth-century American writers, especially New Englanders. Followers of the Genteel Tradition emphasized conventionality in social, religious, moral, and literary standards. Some of the best-known writers of the Genteel Tradition are R. H. Stoddard and Bayard Taylor.

Gilded Age: A period in American history during the 1870s characterized by political corruption and materialism. A number of important novels of social and political criticism were written during this time. Examples of Gilded Age literature include Henry Adams's *Democracy* and F. Marion Crawford's *An American Politician.*

Gothic: See *Gothicism*

Gothicism: In literary criticism, works characterized by a taste for the medieval or morbidly attractive. A gothic novel prominently features elements of horror, the supernatural, gloom, and violence: clanking chains, terror, charnel houses, ghosts, medieval castles, and mysteriously slamming doors. The term ''gothic novel'' is also applied to novels that lack elements of the traditional Gothic setting but that create a similar atmosphere of terror or dread. Mary Shelley's *Frankenstein* is perhaps the best-known English work of this kind.

Gothic Novel: See *Gothicism*

Great Chain of Being: The belief that all things and creatures in nature are organized in a hierarchy from inanimate objects at the bottom to God at the top. This system of belief was popular in the seventeenth and eighteenth centuries. A summary of the concept of the great chain of being can be found in the first epistle of Alexander Pope's *An Essay on Man,* and more recently in Arthur O. Lovejoy's *The Great Chain of Being: A Study of the History of an Idea.*

Grotesque: In literary criticism, the subject matter of a work or a style of expression characterized by exaggeration, deformity, freakishness, and disorder. The grotesque often includes an element of comic absurdity. Early examples of literary grotesque include Francois Rabelais's *Pantagruel* and *Gargantua* and Thomas Nashe's *The Unfortunate Traveller,* while more recent examples can be found in the works of Edgar Allan Poe, Evelyn Waugh, Eudora Welty, Flannery O'Connor, Eugene Ionesco, Gunter Grass, Thomas Mann, Mervyn Peake, and Joseph Heller, among many others.

H

Haiku: The shortest form of Japanese poetry, constructed in three lines of five, seven, and five syllables respectively. The message of a *haiku* poem usually centers on some aspect of spirituality and provokes an emotional response in the reader. Early masters of *haiku* include Basho, Buson, Kobayashi

Issa, and Masaoka Shiki. English writers of *haiku* include the Imagists, notably Ezra Pound, H. D., Amy Lowell, Carl Sandburg, and William Carlos Williams. Also known as *Hokku.*

Half Rhyme: See *Consonance*

Hamartia: In tragedy, the event or act that leads to the hero's or heroine's downfall. This term is often incorrectly used as a synonym for tragic flaw. In Richard Wright's *Native Son,* the act that seals Bigger Thomas's fate is his first impulsive murder.

Harlem Renaissance: The Harlem Renaissance of the 1920s is generally considered the first significant movement of black writers and artists in the United States. During this period, new and established black writers published more fiction and poetry than ever before, the first influential black literary journals were established, and black authors and artists received their first widespread recognition and serious critical appraisal. Among the major writers associated with this period are Claude McKay, Jean Toomer, Countee Cullen, Langston Hughes, Arna Bontemps, Nella Larsen, and Zora Neale Hurston. Works representative of the Harlem Renaissance include Arna Bontemps's poems ''The Return'' and ''Golgotha Is a Mountain,'' Claude McKay's novel *Home to Harlem,* Nella Larsen's novel *Passing,* Langston Hughes's poem ''The Negro Speaks of Rivers,'' and the journals *Crisis* and *Opportunity,* both founded during this period. Also known as Negro Renaissance and New Negro Movement.

Harlequin: A stock character of the *commedia dell'arte* who occasionally interrupted the action with silly antics. Harlequin first appeared on the English stage in John Day's *The Travailes of the Three English Brothers.* The San Francisco Mime Troupe is one of the few modern groups to adapt Harlequin to the needs of contemporary satire.

Hellenism: Imitation of ancient Greek thought or styles. Also, an approach to life that focuses on the growth and development of the intellect. ''Hellenism'' is sometimes used to refer to the belief that reason can be applied to examine all human experience. A cogent discussion of Hellenism can be found in Matthew Arnold's *Culture and Anarchy.*

Heptameter: See *Meter*

Hero/Heroine: The principal sympathetic character (male or female) in a literary work. Heroes and heroines typically exhibit admirable traits: idealism, courage, and integrity, for example. Famous heroes and heroines include Pip in Charles Dickens's *Great Expectations,* the anonymous narrator in Ralph Ellison's *Invisible Man,* and Sethe in Toni Morrison's *Beloved.*

Heroic Couplet: A rhyming couplet written in iambic pentameter (a verse with five iambic feet). The following lines by Alexander Pope are an example: ''Truth guards the Poet, sanctifies the line,/ And makes Immortal, Verse as mean as mine.''

Heroic Line: The meter and length of a line of verse in epic or heroic poetry. This varies by language and time period. For example, in English poetry, the heroic line is iambic pentameter (a verse with five iambic feet); in French, the alexandrine (a verse with six iambic feet); in classical literature, dactylic hexameter (a verse with six dactylic feet).

Heroine: See *Hero/Heroine*

Hexameter: See *Meter*

Historical Criticism: The study of a work based on its impact on the world of the time period in which it was written. Examples of postmodern historical criticism can be found in the work of Michel Foucault, Hayden White, Stephen Greenblatt, and Jonathan Goldberg.

Hokku: See *Haiku*

Holocaust: See *Holocaust Literature*

Holocaust Literature: Literature influenced by or written about the Holocaust of World War II. Such literature includes true stories of survival in concentration camps, escape, and life after the war, as well as fictional works and poetry. Representative works of Holocaust literature include Saul Bellow's *Mr. Sammler's Planet,* Anne Frank's *The Diary of a Young Girl,* Jerzy Kosinski's *The Painted Bird,* Arthur Miller's *Incident at Vichy,* Czeslaw Milosz's *Collected Poems,* William Styron's *Sophie's Choice,* and Art Spiegelman's *Maus.*

Homeric Simile: An elaborate, detailed comparison written as a simile many lines in length. An example of an epic simile from John Milton's *Paradise Lost* follows: Angel Forms, who lay entranced Thick as autumnal leaves that strow the brooks In Vallombrosa, where the Etrurian shades High over-arched embower; or scattered sedge Afloat, when with fierce winds Orion armed Hath vexed the Red-Sea coast, whose waves o'erthrew Busiris and his Memphian chivalry, While with perfidious hatred they pursued The sojourners of

Goshen, who beheld From the safe shore their floating carcasses And broken chariot-wheels. Also known as Epic Simile.

Horatian Satire: See *Satire*

Humanism: A philosophy that places faith in the dignity of humankind and rejects the medieval perception of the individual as a weak, fallen creature. "Humanists" typically believe in the perfectibility of human nature and view reason and education as the means to that end. Humanist thought is represented in the works of Marsilio Ficino, Ludovico Castelvetro, Edmund Spenser, John Milton, Dean John Colet, Desiderius Erasmus, John Dryden, Alexander Pope, Matthew Arnold, and Irving Babbitt.

Humors: Mentions of the humors refer to the ancient Greek theory that a person's health and personality were determined by the balance of four basic fluids in the body: blood, phlegm, yellow bile, and black bile. A dominance of any fluid would cause extremes in behavior. An excess of blood created a sanguine person who was joyful, aggressive, and passionate; a phlegmatic person was shy, fearful, and sluggish; too much yellow bile led to a choleric temperament characterized by impatience, anger, bitterness, and stubbornness; and excessive black bile created melancholy, a state of laziness, gluttony, and lack of motivation. Literary treatment of the humors is exemplified by several characters in Ben Jonson's plays *Every Man in His Humour* and *Every Man out of His Humour.* Also spelled Humours.

Humours: See *Humors*

Hyperbole: In literary criticism, deliberate exaggeration used to achieve an effect. In William Shakespeare's *Macbeth,* Lady Macbeth hyperbolizes when she says, "All the perfumes of Arabia could not sweeten this little hand."

I

Iamb: See *Foot*

Idiom: A word construction or verbal expression closely associated with a given language. For example, in colloquial English the construction "how come" can be used instead of "why" to introduce a question. Similarly, "a piece of cake" is sometimes used to describe a task that is easily done.

Image: A concrete representation of an object or sensory experience. Typically, such a representation helps evoke the feelings associated with the object or experience itself. Images are either "literal" or "figurative." Literal images are especially concrete and involve little or no extension of the obvious meaning of the words used to express them. Figurative images do not follow the literal meaning of the words exactly. Images in literature are usually visual, but the term "image" can also refer to the representation of any sensory experience. In his poem "The Shepherd's Hour," Paul Verlaine presents the following image: "The Moon is red through horizon's fog;/ In a dancing mist the hazy meadow sleeps." The first line is broadly literal, while the second line involves turns of meaning associated with dancing and sleeping.

Imagery: The array of images in a literary work. Also, figurative language. William Butler Yeats's "The Second Coming" offers a powerful image of encroaching anarchy: Turning and turning in the widening gyre The falcon cannot hear the falconer; Things fall apart. . . .

Imagism: An English and American poetry movement that flourished between 1908 and 1917. The Imagists used precise, clearly presented images in their works. They also used common, everyday speech and aimed for conciseness, concrete imagery, and the creation of new rhythms. Participants in the Imagist movement included Ezra Pound, H. D. (Hilda Doolittle), and Amy Lowell, among others.

In medias res: A Latin term meaning "in the middle of things." It refers to the technique of beginning a story at its midpoint and then using various flashback devices to reveal previous action. This technique originated in such epics as Virgil's *Aeneid.*

Induction: The process of reaching a conclusion by reasoning from specific premises to form a general premise. Also, an introductory portion of a work of literature, especially a play. Geoffrey Chaucer's "Prologue" to the *Canterbury Tales,* Thomas Sackville's "Induction" to *The Mirror of Magistrates,* and the opening scene in William Shakespeare's *The Taming of the Shrew* are examples of inductions to literary works.

Intentional Fallacy: The belief that judgments of a literary work based solely on an author's stated or implied intentions are false and misleading. Critics who believe in the concept of the intentional fallacy typically argue that the work itself is sufficient matter for interpretation, even though they may concede that an author's statement of purpose can be useful. Analysis of William Wordsworth's *Lyrical Ballads* based on the observations about poetry he makes in his "Preface" to the second edition of that work is an example of the intentional fallacy.

Interior Monologue: A narrative technique in which characters' thoughts are revealed in a way that appears to be uncontrolled by the author. The interior monologue typically aims to reveal the inner self of a character. It portrays emotional experiences as they occur at both a conscious and unconscious level. images are often used to represent sensations or emotions. One of the best-known interior monologues in English is the Molly Bloom section at the close of James Joyce's *Ulysses.* The interior monologue is also common in the works of Virginia Woolf.

Internal Rhyme: Rhyme that occurs within a single line of verse. An example is in the opening line of Edgar Allan Poe's "The Raven": "Once upon a midnight dreary, while I pondered weak and weary." Here, "dreary" and "weary" make an internal rhyme.

Irish Literary Renaissance: A late nineteenth- and early twentieth-century movement in Irish literature. Members of the movement aimed to reduce the influence of British culture in Ireland and create an Irish national literature. William Butler Yeats, George Moore, and Sean O'Casey are three of the best-known figures of the movement.

Irony: In literary criticism, the effect of language in which the intended meaning is the opposite of what is stated. The title of Jonathan Swift's "A Modest Proposal" is ironic because what Swift proposes in this essay is cannibalism—hardly "modest."

Italian Sonnet: See *Sonnet*

J

Jacobean Age: The period of the reign of James I of England (1603–1625). The early literature of this period reflected the worldview of the Elizabethan Age, but a darker, more cynical attitude steadily grew in the art and literature of the Jacobean Age. This was an important time for English drama and poetry. Milestones include William Shakespeare's tragedies, tragi-comedies, and sonnets; Ben Jonson's various dramas; and John Donne's metaphysical poetry.

Jargon: Language that is used or understood only by a select group of people. Jargon may refer to terminology used in a certain profession, such as

computer jargon, or it may refer to any nonsensical language that is not understood by most people. Literary examples of jargon are Francois Villon's *Ballades en jargon,* which is composed in the secret language of the *coquillards,* and Anthony Burgess's *A Clockwork Orange,* narrated in the fictional characters' language of "Nadsat."

Juvenalian Satire: See *Satire*

K

Knickerbocker Group: A somewhat indistinct group of New York writers of the first half of the nineteenth century. Members of the group were linked only by location and a common theme: New York life. Two famous members of the Knickerbocker Group were Washington Irving and William Cullen Bryant. The group's name derives from Irving's *Knickerbocker's History of New York.*

L

Lais: See *Lay*

Lay: A song or simple narrative poem. The form originated in medieval France. Early French *lais* were often based on the Celtic legends and other tales sung by Breton minstrels—thus the name of the "Breton lay." In fourteenth-century England, the term "lay" was used to describe short narratives written in imitation of the Breton lays. The most notable of these is Geoffrey Chaucer's "The Minstrel's Tale."

Leitmotiv: See *Motif*

Literal Language: An author uses literal language when he or she writes without exaggerating or embellishing the subject matter and without any tools of figurative language. To say "He ran very quickly down the street" is to use literal language, whereas to say "He ran like a hare down the street" would be using figurative language.

Literary Ballad: See *Ballad*

Literature: Literature is broadly defined as any written or spoken material, but the term most often refers to creative works. Literature includes poetry, drama, fiction, and many kinds of nonfiction writing, as well as oral, dramatic, and broadcast compositions not necessarily preserved in a written format, such as films and television programs.

Lost Generation: A term first used by Gertrude Stein to describe the post-World War I generation of

American writers: men and women haunted by a sense of betrayal and emptiness brought about by the destructiveness of the war. The term is commonly applied to Hart Crane, Ernest Hemingway, F. Scott Fitzgerald, and others.

Lyric Poetry: A poem expressing the subjective feelings and personal emotions of the poet. Such poetry is melodic, since it was originally accompanied by a lyre in recitals. Most Western poetry in the twentieth century may be classified as lyrical. Examples of lyric poetry include A. E. Housman's elegy "To an Athlete Dying Young," the odes of Pindar and Horace, Thomas Gray and William Collins, the sonnets of Sir Thomas Wyatt and Sir Philip Sidney, Elizabeth Barrett Browning and Rainer Maria Rilke, and a host of other forms in the poetry of William Blake and Christina Rossetti, among many others.

M

Mannerism: Exaggerated, artificial adherence to a literary manner or style. Also, a popular style of the visual arts of late sixteenth-century Europe that was marked by elongation of the human form and by intentional spatial distortion. Literary works that are self-consciously high-toned and artistic are often said to be "mannered." Authors of such works include Henry James and Gertrude Stein.

Masculine Rhyme: See *Rhyme*

Masque: A lavish and elaborate form of entertainment, often performed in royal courts, that emphasizes song, dance, and costumery. The Renaissance form of the masque grew out of the spectacles of masked figures common in medieval England and Europe. The masque reached its peak of popularity and development in seventeenth-century England, during the reigns of James I and, especially, of Charles I. Ben Jonson, the most significant masque writer, also created the "antimasque," which incorporates elements of humor and the grotesque into the traditional masque and achieved greater dramatic quality. Masque-like interludes appear in Edmund Spenser's *The Faerie Queene* and in William Shakespeare's *The Tempest.* One of the best-known English masques is John Milton's *Comus.*

Measure: The foot, verse, or time sequence used in a literary work, especially a poem. Measure is often used somewhat incorrectly as a synonym for meter.

Melodrama: A play in which the typical plot is a conflict between characters who personify extreme good and evil. Melodramas usually end happily and

emphasize sensationalism. Other literary forms that use the same techniques are often labeled "melodramatic." The term was formerly used to describe a combination of drama and music; as such, it was synonymous with "opera." Augustin Daly's *Under the Gaslight* and Dion Boucicault's *The Octoroon, The Colleen Bawn,* and *The Poor of New York* are examples of melodramas. The most popular media for twentieth-century melodramas are motion pictures and television.

Metaphor: A figure of speech that expresses an idea through the image of another object. Metaphors suggest the essence of the first object by identifying it with certain qualities of the second object. An example is "But soft, what light through yonder window breaks?/ It is the east, and Juliet is the sun" in William Shakespeare's *Romeo and Juliet.* Here, Juliet, the first object, is identified with qualities of the second object, the sun.

Metaphysical Conceit: See *Conceit*

Metaphysical Poetry: The body of poetry produced by a group of seventeenth-century English writers called the "Metaphysical Poets." The group includes John Donne and Andrew Marvell. The Metaphysical Poets made use of everyday speech, intellectual analysis, and unique imagery. They aimed to portray the ordinary conflicts and contradictions of life. Their poems often took the form of an argument, and many of them emphasize physical and religious love as well as the fleeting nature of life. Elaborate conceits are typical in metaphysical poetry. Marvell's "To His Coy Mistress" is a well-known example of a metaphysical poem.

Metaphysical Poets: See *Metaphysical Poetry*

Meter: In literary criticism, the repetition of sound patterns that creates a rhythm in poetry. The patterns are based on the number of syllables and the presence and absence of accents. The unit of rhythm in a line is called a foot. Types of meter are classified according to the number of feet in a line. These are the standard English lines: Monometer, one foot; Dimeter, two feet; Trimeter, three feet; Tetrameter, four feet; Pentameter, five feet; Hexameter, six feet (also called the Alexandrine); Heptameter, seven feet (also called the "Fourteener" when the feet are iambic). The most common English meter is the iambic pentameter, in which each line contains ten syllables, or five iambic feet, which individually are composed of an unstressed syllable followed by an accented syllable. Both of the following lines from Alfred, Lord Tennyson's

"Ulysses" are written in iambic pentameter: Made weak by time and fate, but strong in will To strive, to seek, to find, and not to yield.

Mise en scene: The costumes, scenery, and other properties of a drama. Herbert Beerbohm Tree was renowned for the elaborate *mises en scene* of his lavish Shakespearean productions at His Majesty's Theatre between 1897 and 1915.

Modernism: Modern literary practices. Also, the principles of a literary school that lasted from roughly the beginning of the twentieth century until the end of World War II. Modernism is defined by its rejection of the literary conventions of the nineteenth century and by its opposition to conventional morality, taste, traditions, and economic values. Many writers are associated with the concepts of Modernism, including Albert Camus, Marcel Proust, D. H. Lawrence, W. H. Auden, Ernest Hemingway, William Faulkner, William Butler Yeats, Thomas Mann, Tennessee Williams, Eugene O'Neill, and James Joyce.

Monologue: A composition, written or oral, by a single individual. More specifically, a speech given by a single individual in a drama or other public entertainment. It has no set length, although it is usually several or more lines long. An example of an "extended monologue"—that is, a monologue of great length and seriousness—occurs in the one-act, one-character play *The Stronger* by August Strindberg.

Monometer: See *Meter*

Mood: The prevailing emotions of a work or of the author in his or her creation of the work. The mood of a work is not always what might be expected based on its subject matter. The poem "Dover Beach" by Matthew Arnold offers examples of two different moods originating from the same experience: watching the ocean at night. The mood of the first three lines— The sea is calm tonight The tide is full, the moon lies fair Upon the straights. . . . is in sharp contrast to the mood of the last three lines— And we are here as on a darkling plain Swept with confused alarms of struggle and flight, Where ignorant armies clash by night.

Motif: A theme, character type, image, metaphor, or other verbal element that recurs throughout a single work of literature or occurs in a number of different works over a period of time. For example, the various manifestations of the color white in Herman Melville's *Moby Dick* is a "specific" *motif,* while the trials of star-crossed lovers is a "conventional"

motif from the literature of all periods. Also known as *Motiv* or *Leitmotiv.*

Motiv: See *Motif*

Muckrakers: An early twentieth-century group of American writers. Typically, their works exposed the wrongdoings of big business and government in the United States. Upton Sinclair's *The Jungle* exemplifies the muckraking novel.

Muses: Nine Greek mythological goddesses, the daughters of Zeus and Mnemosyne (Memory). Each muse patronized a specific area of the liberal arts and sciences. Calliope presided over epic poetry, Clio over history, Erato over love poetry, Euterpe over music or lyric poetry, Melpomene over tragedy, Polyhymnia over hymns to the gods, Terpsichore over dance, Thalia over comedy, and Urania over astronomy. Poets and writers traditionally made appeals to the Muses for inspiration in their work. John Milton invokes the aid of a muse at the beginning of the first book of his *Paradise Lost:* Of Man's First disobedience, and the Fruit of the Forbidden Tree, whose mortal taste Brought Death into the World, and all our woe, With loss of Eden, till one greater Man Restore us, and regain the blissful Seat, Sing Heav'nly Muse, that on the secret top of Oreb, or of Sinai, didst inspire That Shepherd, who first taught the chosen Seed, In the Beginning how the Heav'ns and Earth Rose out of Chaos. . . .

Mystery: See *Suspense*

Myth: An anonymous tale emerging from the traditional beliefs of a culture or social unit. Myths use supernatural explanations for natural phenomena. They may also explain cosmic issues like creation and death. Collections of myths, known as mythologies, are common to all cultures and nations, but the best-known myths belong to the Norse, Roman, and Greek mythologies. A famous myth is the story of Arachne, an arrogant young girl who challenged a goddess, Athena, to a weaving contest; when the girl won, Athena was enraged and turned Arachne into a spider, thus explaining the existence of spiders.

N

Narration: The telling of a series of events, real or invented. A narration may be either a simple narrative, in which the events are recounted chronologically, or a narrative with a plot, in which the account is given in a style reflecting the author's artistic concept of the story. Narration is sometimes used as a synonym for "storyline." The recounting of scary stories around a campfire is a form of narration.

Narrative: A verse or prose accounting of an event or sequence of events, real or invented. The term is also used as an adjective in the sense "method of narration." For example, in literary criticism, the expression "narrative technique" usually refers to the way the author structures and presents his or her story. Narratives range from the shortest accounts of events, as in Julius Caesar's remark, "I came, I saw, I conquered," to the longest historical or biographical works, as in Edward Gibbon's *The Decline and Fall of the Roman Empire,* as well as diaries, travelogues, novels, ballads, epics, short stories, and other fictional forms.

Narrative Poetry: A nondramatic poem in which the author tells a story. Such poems may be of any length or level of complexity. Epics such as *Beowulf* and ballads are forms of narrative poetry.

Narrator: The teller of a story. The narrator may be the author or a character in the story through whom the author speaks. Huckleberry Finn is the narrator of Mark Twain's *The Adventures of Huckleberry Finn.*

Naturalism: A literary movement of the late nineteenth and early twentieth centuries. The movement's major theorist, French novelist Emile Zola, envisioned a type of fiction that would examine human life with the objectivity of scientific inquiry. The Naturalists typically viewed human beings as either the products of "biological determinism," ruled by hereditary instincts and engaged in an endless struggle for survival, or as the products of "socioeconomic determinism," ruled by social and economic forces beyond their control. In their works, the Naturalists generally ignored the highest levels of society and focused on degradation: poverty, alcoholism, prostitution, insanity, and disease. Naturalism influenced authors throughout the world, including Henrik Ibsen and Thomas Hardy. In the United States, in particular, Naturalism had a profound impact. Among the authors who embraced its principles are Theodore Dreiser, Eugene O'Neill, Stephen Crane, Jack London, and Frank Norris.

Negritude: A literary movement based on the concept of a shared cultural bond on the part of black Africans, wherever they may be in the world. It traces its origins to the former French colonies of Africa and the Caribbean. Negritude poets, novelists, and essayists generally stress four points in their writings: One, black alienation from tradi-

tional African culture can lead to feelings of inferiority. Two, European colonialism and Western education should be resisted. Three, black Africans should seek to affirm and define their own identity. Four, African culture can and should be reclaimed. Many Negritude writers also claim that blacks can make unique contributions to the world, based on a heightened appreciation of nature, rhythm, and human emotions—aspects of life they say are not so highly valued in the materialistic and rationalistic West. Examples of Negritude literature include the poetry of both Senegalese Leopold Senghor in *Hosties noires* and Martiniquais Aime-Fernand Cesaire in *Return to My Native Land.*

Negro Renaissance: See *Harlem Renaissance*

Neoclassical Period: See *Neoclassicism*

Neoclassicism: In literary criticism, this term refers to the revival of the attitudes and styles of expression of classical literature. It is generally used to describe a period in European history beginning in the late seventeenth century and lasting until about 1800. In its purest form, Neoclassicism marked a return to order, proportion, restraint, logic, accuracy, and decorum. In England, where Neoclassicism perhaps was most popular, it reflected the influence of seventeenth-century French writers, especially dramatists. Neoclassical writers typically reacted against the intensity and enthusiasm of the Renaissance period. They wrote works that appealed to the intellect, using elevated language and classical literary forms such as satire and the ode. Neoclassical works were often governed by the classical goal of instruction. English neoclassicists included Alexander Pope, Jonathan Swift, Joseph Addison, Sir Richard Steele, John Gay, and Matthew Prior; French neoclassicists included Pierre Corneille and Jean-Baptiste Moliere. Also known as Age of Reason.

Neoclassicists: See *Neoclassicism*

New Criticism: A movement in literary criticism, dating from the late 1920s, that stressed close textual analysis in the interpretation of works of literature. The New Critics saw little merit in historical and biographical analysis. Rather, they aimed to examine the text alone, free from the question of how external events—biographical or otherwise—may have helped shape it. This predominantly American school was named "New Criticism" by one of its practitioners, John Crowe Ransom. Other important New Critics included Allen Tate, R. P. Blackmur, Robert Penn Warren, and Cleanth Brooks.

New Negro Movement: See *Harlem Renaissance*

Noble Savage: The idea that primitive man is noble and good but becomes evil and corrupted as he becomes civilized. The concept of the noble savage originated in the Renaissance period but is more closely identified with such later writers as Jean-Jacques Rousseau and Aphra Behn. First described in John Dryden's play *The Conquest of Granada,* the noble savage is portrayed by the various Native Americans in James Fenimore Cooper's ''Leatherstocking Tales,'' by Queequeg, Daggoo, and Tashtego in Herman Melville's *Moby Dick,* and by John the Savage in Aldous Huxley's *Brave New World.*

O

Objective Correlative: An outward set of objects, a situation, or a chain of events corresponding to an inward experience and evoking this experience in the reader. The term frequently appears in modern criticism in discussions of authors' intended effects on the emotional responses of readers. This term was originally used by T. S. Eliot in his 1919 essay ''Hamlet.''

Objectivity: A quality in writing characterized by the absence of the author's opinion or feeling about the subject matter. Objectivity is an important factor in criticism. The novels of Henry James and, to a certain extent, the poems of John Larkin demonstrate objectivity, and it is central to John Keats's concept of ''negative capability.'' Critical and journalistic writing usually are or attempt to be objective.

Occasional Verse: poetry written on the occasion of a significant historical or personal event. *Vers de societe* is sometimes called occasional verse although it is of a less serious nature. Famous examples of occasional verse include Andrew Marvell's ''Horatian Ode upon Cromwell's Return from England,'' Walt Whitman's ''When Lilacs Last in the Dooryard Bloom'd''— written upon the death of Abraham Lincoln—and Edmund Spenser's commemoration of his wedding, ''Epithalamion.''

Octave: A poem or stanza composed of eight lines. The term octave most often represents the first eight lines of a Petrarchan sonnet. An example of an octave is taken from a translation of a Petrarchan sonnet by Sir Thomas Wyatt: The pillar perisht is whereto I leant, The strongest stay of mine unquiet mind; The like of it no man again can find, From East to West Still seeking though he went. To mind unhap! for hap away hath rent Of all my joy the very

bark and rind; And I, alas, by chance am thus assigned Daily to mourn till death do it relent.

Ode: Name given to an extended lyric poem characterized by exalted emotion and dignified style. An ode usually concerns a single, serious theme. Most odes, but not all, are addressed to an object or individual. Odes are distinguished from other lyric poetic forms by their complex rhythmic and stanzaic patterns. An example of this form is John Keats's ''Ode to a Nightingale.''

Oedipus Complex: A son's amorous obsession with his mother. The phrase is derived from the story of the ancient Theban hero Oedipus, who unknowingly killed his father and married his mother. Literary occurrences of the Oedipus complex include Andre Gide's *Oedipe* and Jean Cocteau's *La Machine infernale,* as well as the most famous, Sophocles' *Oedipus Rex.*

Omniscience: See *Point of View*

Onomatopoeia: The use of words whose sounds express or suggest their meaning. In its simplest sense, onomatopoeia may be represented by words that mimic the sounds they denote such as ''hiss'' or ''meow.'' At a more subtle level, the pattern and rhythm of sounds and rhymes of a line or poem may be onomatopoeic. A celebrated example of onomatopoeia is the repetition of the word ''bells'' in Edgar Allan Poe's poem ''The Bells.''

Opera: A type of stage performance, usually a drama, in which the dialogue is sung. Classic examples of opera include Giuseppi Verdi's *La traviata,* Giacomo Puccini's *La Boheme,* and Richard Wagner's *Tristan und Isolde.* Major twentieth-century contributors to the form include Richard Strauss and Alban Berg.

Operetta: A usually romantic comic opera. John Gay's *The Beggar's Opera,* Richard Sheridan's *The Duenna,* and numerous works by William Gilbert and Arthur Sullivan are examples of operettas.

Oral Tradition: See *Oral Transmission*

Oral Transmission: A process by which songs, ballads, folklore, and other material are transmitted by word of mouth. The tradition of oral transmission predates the written record systems of literate society. Oral transmission preserves material sometimes over generations, although often with variations. Memory plays a large part in the recitation and preservation of orally transmitted material. Breton lays, French *fabliaux,* national epics (including the Anglo-Saxon *Beowulf,* the Spanish *El Cid,* and the Finnish *Kalevala*), Native American myths and legends, and African folktales told by plantation slaves are examples of orally transmitted literature.

Oration: Formal speaking intended to motivate the listeners to some action or feeling. Such public speaking was much more common before the development of timely printed communication such as newspapers. Famous examples of oration include Abraham Lincoln's "Gettysburg Address" and Dr. Martin Luther King Jr.'s "I Have a Dream" speech.

Ottava Rima: An eight-line stanza of poetry composed in iambic pentameter (a five-foot line in which each foot consists of an unaccented syllable followed by an accented syllable), following the abababcc rhyme scheme. This form has been prominently used by such important English writers as Lord Byron, Henry Wadsworth Longfellow, and W. B. Yeats.

Oxymoron: A phrase combining two contradictory terms. Oxymorons may be intentional or unintentional. The following speech from William Shakespeare's *Romeo and Juliet* uses several oxymorons: Why, then, O brawling love! O loving hate! O anything, of nothing first create! O heavy lightness! serious vanity! Mis-shapen chaos of well-seeming forms! Feather of lead, bright smoke, cold fire, sick health! This love feel I, that feel no love in this.

P

Pantheism: The idea that all things are both a manifestation or revelation of God and a part of God at the same time. Pantheism was a common attitude in the early societies of Egypt, India, and Greece—the term derives from the Greek *pan* meaning "all" and *theos* meaning "deity." It later became a significant part of the Christian faith. William Wordsworth and Ralph Waldo Emerson are among the many writers who have expressed the pantheistic attitude in their works.

Parable: A story intended to teach a moral lesson or answer an ethical question. In the West, the best examples of parables are those of Jesus Christ in the New Testament, notably "The Prodigal Son," but parables also are used in Sufism, rabbinic literature, Hasidism, and Zen Buddhism.

Paradox: A statement that appears illogical or contradictory at first, but may actually point to an underlying truth. "Less is more" is an example of a paradox. Literary examples include Francis Bacon's statement, "The most corrected copies are commonly the least correct," and "All animals are equal, but some animals are more equal than others" from George Orwell's *Animal Farm*.

Parallelism: A method of comparison of two ideas in which each is developed in the same grammatical structure. Ralph Waldo Emerson's "Civilization" contains this example of parallelism: Raphael paints wisdom; Handel sings it, Phidias carves it, Shakespeare writes it, Wren builds it, Columbus sails it, Luther preaches it, Washington arms it, Watt mechanizes it.

Parnassianism: A mid nineteenth-century movement in French literature. Followers of the movement stressed adherence to well-defined artistic forms as a reaction against the often chaotic expression of the artist's ego that dominated the work of the Romantics. The Parnassians also rejected the moral, ethical, and social themes exhibited in the works of French Romantics such as Victor Hugo. The aesthetic doctrines of the Parnassians strongly influenced the later symbolist and decadent movements. Members of the Parnassian school include Leconte de Lisle, Sully Prudhomme, Albert Glatigny, Francois Coppee, and Theodore de Banville.

Parody: In literary criticism, this term refers to an imitation of a serious literary work or the signature style of a particular author in a ridiculous manner. A typical parody adopts the style of the original and applies it to an inappropriate subject for humorous effect. Parody is a form of satire and could be considered the literary equivalent of a caricature or cartoon. Henry Fielding's *Shamela* is a parody of Samuel Richardson's *Pamela*.

Pastoral: A term derived from the Latin word "pastor," meaning shepherd. A pastoral is a literary composition on a rural theme. The conventions of the pastoral were originated by the third-century Greek poet Theocritus, who wrote about the experiences, love affairs, and pastimes of Sicilian shepherds. In a pastoral, characters and language of a courtly nature are often placed in a simple setting. The term pastoral is also used to classify dramas, elegies, and lyrics that exhibit the use of country settings and shepherd characters. Percy Bysshe Shelley's "Adonais" and John Milton's "Lycidas" are two famous examples of pastorals.

Pastorela: The Spanish name for the shepherds play, a folk drama reenacted during the Christmas season. Examples of *pastorelas* include Gomez

Manrique's *Representacion del nacimiento* and the dramas of Lucas Fernandez and Juan del Encina.

Pathetic Fallacy: A term coined by English critic John Ruskin to identify writing that falsely endows nonhuman things with human intentions and feelings, such as "angry clouds" and "sad trees." The pathetic fallacy is a required convention in the classical poetic form of the pastoral elegy, and it is used in the modern poetry of T. S. Eliot, Ezra Pound, and the Imagists. Also known as Poetic Fallacy.

Pelado: Literally the "skinned one" or shirtless one, he was the stock underdog, sharp-witted picaresque character of Mexican vaudeville and tent shows. The *pelado* is found in such works as Don Catarino's *Los effectos de la crisis* and *Regreso a mi tierra*.

Pen Name: See *Pseudonym*

Pentameter: See *Meter*

Persona: A Latin term meaning "mask." *Personae* are the characters in a fictional work of literature. The *persona* generally functions as a mask through which the author tells a story in a voice other than his or her own. A *persona* is usually either a character in a story who acts as a narrator or an "implied author," a voice created by the author to act as the narrator for himself or herself. *Personae* include the narrator of Geoffrey Chaucer's *Canterbury Tales* and Marlow in Joseph Conrad's *Heart of Darkness*.

Personae: See *Persona*

Personal Point of View: See *Point of View*

Personification: A figure of speech that gives human qualities to abstract ideas, animals, and inanimate objects. William Shakespeare used personification in *Romeo and Juliet* in the lines "Arise, fair sun, and kill the envious moon,/ Who is already sick and pale with grief." Here, the moon is portrayed as being envious, sick, and pale with grief—all markedly human qualities. Also known as *Prosopopoeia*.

Petrarchan Sonnet: See *Sonnet*

Phenomenology: A method of literary criticism based on the belief that things have no existence outside of human consciousness or awareness. Proponents of this theory believe that art is a process that takes place in the mind of the observer as he or she contemplates an object rather than a quality of the object itself. Among phenomenological critics

are Edmund Husserl, George Poulet, Marcel Raymond, and Roman Ingarden.

Picaresque Novel: Episodic fiction depicting the adventures of a roguish central character ("picaro" is Spanish for "rogue"). The picaresque hero is commonly a low-born but clever individual who wanders into and out of various affairs of love, danger, and farcical intrigue. These involvements may take place at all social levels and typically present a humorous and wide-ranging satire of a given society. Prominent examples of the picaresque novel are *Don Quixote* by Miguel de Cervantes, *Tom Jones* by Henry Fielding, and *Moll Flanders* by Daniel Defoe.

Plagiarism: Claiming another person's written material as one's own. Plagiarism can take the form of direct, word-for-word copying or the theft of the substance or idea of the work. A student who copies an encyclopedia entry and turns it in as a report for school is guilty of plagiarism.

Platonic Criticism: A form of criticism that stresses an artistic work's usefulness as an agent of social engineering rather than any quality or value of the work itself. Platonic criticism takes as its starting point the ancient Greek philosopher Plato's comments on art in his *Republic*.

Platonism: The embracing of the doctrines of the philosopher Plato, popular among the poets of the Renaissance and the Romantic period. Platonism is more flexible than Aristotelian Criticism and places more emphasis on the supernatural and unknown aspects of life. Platonism is expressed in the love poetry of the Renaissance, the fourth book of Baldassare Castiglione's *The Book of the Courtier*, and the poetry of William Blake, William Wordsworth, Percy Bysshe Shelley, Friedrich Holderlin, William Butler Yeats, and Wallace Stevens.

Play: See *Drama*

Plot: In literary criticism, this term refers to the pattern of events in a narrative or drama. In its simplest sense, the plot guides the author in composing the work and helps the reader follow the work. Typically, plots exhibit causality and unity and have a beginning, a middle, and an end. Sometimes, however, a plot may consist of a series of disconnected events, in which case it is known as an "episodic plot." In his *Aspects of the Novel*, E. M. Forster distinguishes between a story, defined as a "narrative of events arranged in their time-sequence," and plot, which organizes the events to a "sense of causality." This definition closely mirrors Aristotle's discussion of plot in his *Poetics*.

Poem: In its broadest sense, a composition utilizing rhyme, meter, concrete detail, and expressive language to create a literary experience with emotional and aesthetic appeal. Typical poems include sonnets, odes, elegies, *haiku*, ballads, and free verse.

Poet: An author who writes poetry or verse. The term is also used to refer to an artist or writer who has an exceptional gift for expression, imagination, and energy in the making of art in any form. Well-known poets include Horace, Basho, Sir Philip Sidney, Sir Edmund Spenser, John Donne, Andrew Marvell, Alexander Pope, Jonathan Swift, George Gordon, Lord Byron, John Keats, Christina Rossetti, W. H. Auden, Stevie Smith, and Sylvia Plath.

Poetic Fallacy: See *Pathetic Fallacy*

Poetic Justice: An outcome in a literary work, not necessarily a poem, in which the good are rewarded and the evil are punished, especially in ways that particularly fit their virtues or crimes. For example, a murderer may himself be murdered, or a thief will find himself penniless.

Poetic License: Distortions of fact and literary convention made by a writer—not always a poet—for the sake of the effect gained. Poetic license is closely related to the concept of "artistic freedom." An author exercises poetic license by saying that a pile of money "reaches as high as a mountain" when the pile is actually only a foot or two high.

Poetics: This term has two closely related meanings. It denotes (1) an aesthetic theory in literary criticism about the essence of poetry or (2) rules prescribing the proper methods, content, style, or diction of poetry. The term poetics may also refer to theories about literature in general, not just poetry.

Poetry: In its broadest sense, writing that aims to present ideas and evoke an emotional experience in the reader through the use of meter, imagery, connotative and concrete words, and a carefully constructed structure based on rhythmic patterns. Poetry typically relies on words and expressions that have several layers of meaning. It also makes use of the effects of regular rhythm on the ear and may make a strong appeal to the senses through the use of imagery. Edgar Allan Poe's "Annabel Lee" and Walt Whitman's *Leaves of Grass* are famous examples of poetry.

Point of View: The narrative perspective from which a literary work is presented to the reader.

There are four traditional points of view. The "third person omniscient" gives the reader a "godlike" perspective, unrestricted by time or place, from which to see actions and look into the minds of characters. This allows the author to comment openly on characters and events in the work. The "third person" point of view presents the events of the story from outside of any single character's perception, much like the omniscient point of view, but the reader must understand the action as it takes place and without any special insight into characters' minds or motivations. The "first person" or "personal" point of view relates events as they are perceived by a single character. The main character "tells" the story and may offer opinions about the action and characters which differ from those of the author. Much less common than omniscient, third person, and first person is the "second person" point of view, wherein the author tells the story as if it is happening to the reader. James Thurber employs the omniscient point of view in his short story "The Secret Life of Walter Mitty." Ernest Hemingway's "A Clean, Well-Lighted Place" is a short story told from the third person point of view. Mark Twain's novel *Huck Finn* is presented from the first person viewpoint. Jay McInerney's *Bright Lights, Big City* is an example of a novel which uses the second person point of view.

Polemic: A work in which the author takes a stand on a controversial subject, such as abortion or religion. Such works are often extremely argumentative or provocative. Classic examples of polemics include John Milton's *Aeropagitica* and Thomas Paine's *The American Crisis*.

Pornography: Writing intended to provoke feelings of lust in the reader. Such works are often condemned by critics and teachers, but those which can be shown to have literary value are viewed less harshly. Literary works that have been described as pornographic include Ovid's *The Art of Love*, Margaret of Angouleme's *Heptameron*, John Cleland's *Memoirs of a Woman of Pleasure; or, the Life of Fanny Hill*, the anonymous *My Secret Life*, D. H. Lawrence's *Lady Chatterley's Lover*, and Vladimir Nabokov's *Lolita*.

Post-Aesthetic Movement: An artistic response made by African Americans to the black aesthetic movement of the 1960s and early '70s. Writers since that time have adopted a somewhat different tone in their work, with less emphasis placed on the disparity between black and white in the United States. In the words of post-aesthetic authors such as Toni Morrison, John Edgar Wideman, and Kristin Hunter, African Americans are portrayed as looking inward for answers to their own questions, rather than always looking to the outside world. Two well-known examples of works produced as part of the post-aesthetic movement are the Pulitzer Prize-winning novels *The Color Purple* by Alice Walker and *Beloved* by Toni Morrison.

Postmodernism: Writing from the 1960s forward characterized by experimentation and continuing to apply some of the fundamentals of modernism, which included existentialism and alienation. Postmodernists have gone a step further in the rejection of tradition begun with the modernists by also rejecting traditional forms, preferring the anti-novel over the novel and the anti-hero over the hero. Postmodern writers include Alain Robbe-Grillet, Thomas Pynchon, Margaret Drabble, John Fowles, Adolfo Bioy-Casares, and Gabriel Garcia Marquez.

Pre-Raphaelites: A circle of writers and artists in mid nineteenth-century England. Valuing the pre-Renaissance artistic qualities of religious symbolism, lavish pictorialism, and natural sensuousness, the Pre-Raphaelites cultivated a sense of mystery and melancholy that influenced later writers associated with the Symbolist and Decadent movements. The major members of the group include Dante Gabriel Rossetti, Christina Rossetti, Algernon Swinburne, and Walter Pater.

Primitivism: The belief that primitive peoples were nobler and less flawed than civilized peoples because they had not been subjected to the tainting influence of society. Examples of literature espousing primitivism include Aphra Behn's *Oroonoko: Or, The History of the Royal Slave,* Jean-Jacques Rousseau's *Julie ou la Nouvelle Heloise,* Oliver Goldsmith's *The Deserted Village,* the poems of Robert Burns, Herman Melville's stories *Typee, Omoo,* and *Mardi,* many poems of William Butler Yeats and Robert Frost, and William Golding's novel *Lord of the Flies.*

Projective Verse: A form of free verse in which the poet's breathing pattern determines the lines of the poem. Poets who advocate projective verse are against all formal structures in writing, including meter and form. Besides its creators, Robert Creeley, Robert Duncan, and Charles Olson, two other well-known projective verse poets are Denise Levertov and LeRoi Jones (Amiri Baraka). Also known as Breath Verse.

Prologue: An introductory section of a literary work. It often contains information establishing the situation of the characters or presents information about the setting, time period, or action. In drama, the prologue is spoken by a chorus or by one of the principal characters. In the ''General Prologue'' of *The Canterbury Tales,* Geoffrey Chaucer describes the main characters and establishes the setting and purpose of the work.

Prose: A literary medium that attempts to mirror the language of everyday speech. It is distinguished from poetry by its use of unmetered, unrhymed language consisting of logically related sentences. Prose is usually grouped into paragraphs that form a cohesive whole such as an essay or a novel. Recognized masters of English prose writing include Sir Thomas Malory, William Caxton, Raphael Holinshed, Joseph Addison, Mark Twain, and Ernest Hemingway.

Prosopopoeia: See *Personification*

Protagonist: The central character of a story who serves as a focus for its themes and incidents and as the principal rationale for its development. The protagonist is sometimes referred to in discussions of modern literature as the hero or anti-hero. Well-known protagonists are Hamlet in William Shakespeare's *Hamlet* and Jay Gatsby in F. Scott Fitzgerald's *The Great Gatsby.*

Protest Fiction: Protest fiction has as its primary purpose the protesting of some social injustice, such as racism or discrimination. One example of protest fiction is a series of five novels by Chester Himes, beginning in 1945 with *If He Hollers Let Him Go* and ending in 1955 with *The Primitive.* These works depict the destructive effects of race and gender stereotyping in the context of interracial relationships. Another African American author whose works often revolve around themes of social protest is John Oliver Killens. James Baldwin's essay ''Everybody's Protest Novel'' generated controversy by attacking the authors of protest fiction.

Proverb: A brief, sage saying that expresses a truth about life in a striking manner. ''They are not all cooks who carry long knives'' is an example of a proverb.

Pseudonym: A name assumed by a writer, most often intended to prevent his or her identification as the author of a work. Two or more authors may work together under one pseudonym, or an author may use a different name for each genre he or she publishes in. Some publishing companies maintain "house pseudonyms," under which any number of authors may write installations in a series. Some authors also choose a pseudonym over their real names the way an actor may use a stage name. Examples of pseudonyms (with the author's real name in parentheses) include Voltaire (Francois-Marie Arouet), Novalis (Friedrich von Hardenberg), Currer Bell (Charlotte Bronte), Ellis Bell (Emily Bronte), George Eliot (Maryann Evans), Honorio Bustos Donmecq (Adolfo Bioy-Casares and Jorge Luis Borges), and Richard Bachman (Stephen King).

Pun: A play on words that have similar sounds but different meanings. A serious example of the pun is from John Donne's "A Hymne to God the Father": Sweare by thyself, that at my death thy sonne Shall shine as he shines now, and hereto fore; And, having done that, Thou haste done; I fear no more.

Pure Poetry: poetry written without instructional intent or moral purpose that aims only to please a reader by its imagery or musical flow. The term pure poetry is used as the antonym of the term "didacticism." The poetry of Edgar Allan Poe, Stephane Mallarme, Paul Verlaine, Paul Valery, Juan Ramoz Jimenez, and Jorge Guillen offer examples of pure poetry.

Q

Quatrain: A four-line stanza of a poem or an entire poem consisting of four lines. The following quatrain is from Robert Herrick's "To Live Merrily, and to Trust to Good Verses": Round, round, the root do's run; And being ravisht thus, Come, I will drink a Tun To my *Propertius.*

R

Raisonneur: A character in a drama who functions as a spokesperson for the dramatist's views. The *raisonneur* typically observes the play without becoming central to its action. *Raisonneurs* were very common in plays of the nineteenth century.

Realism: A nineteenth-century European literary movement that sought to portray familiar characters, situations, and settings in a realistic manner. This was done primarily by using an objective narrative point of view and through the buildup of accurate detail. The standard for success of any realistic work depends on how faithfully it transfers common experience into fictional forms. The realistic method may be altered or extended, as in stream of consciousness writing, to record highly subjec-

tive experience. Seminal authors in the tradition of Realism include Honore de Balzac, Gustave Flaubert, and Henry James.

Refrain: A phrase repeated at intervals throughout a poem. A refrain may appear at the end of each stanza or at less regular intervals. It may be altered slightly at each appearance. Some refrains are nonsense expressions—as with "Nevermore" in Edgar Allan Poe's "The Raven"—that seem to take on a different significance with each use.

Renaissance: The period in European history that marked the end of the Middle Ages. It began in Italy in the late fourteenth century. In broad terms, it is usually seen as spanning the fourteenth, fifteenth, and sixteenth centuries, although it did not reach Great Britain, for example, until the 1480s or so. The Renaissance saw an awakening in almost every sphere of human activity, especially science, philosophy, and the arts. The period is best defined by the emergence of a general philosophy that emphasized the importance of the intellect, the individual, and world affairs. It contrasts strongly with the medieval worldview, characterized by the dominant concerns of faith, the social collective, and spiritual salvation. Prominent writers during the Renaissance include Niccolo Machiavelli and Baldassare Castiglione in Italy, Miguel de Cervantes and Lope de Vega in Spain, Jean Froissart and Francois Rabelais in France, Sir Thomas More and Sir Philip Sidney in England, and Desiderius Erasmus in Holland.

Repartee: Conversation featuring snappy retorts and witticisms. Masters of *repartee* include Sydney Smith, Charles Lamb, and Oscar Wilde. An example is recorded in the meeting of "Beau" Nash and John Wesley: Nash said, "I never make way for a fool," to which Wesley responded, "Don't you? I always do," and stepped aside.

Resolution: The portion of a story following the climax, in which the conflict is resolved. The resolution of Jane Austen's *Northanger Abbey* is neatly summed up in the following sentence: "Henry and Catherine were married, the bells rang and every body smiled."

Restoration: See *Restoration Age*

Restoration Age: A period in English literature beginning with the crowning of Charles II in 1660 and running to about 1700. The era, which was characterized by a reaction against Puritanism, was the first great age of the comedy of manners. The finest literature of the era is typically witty and urbane, and often lewd. Prominent Restoration Age writers include William Congreve, Samuel Pepys, John Dryden, and John Milton.

Revenge Tragedy: A dramatic form popular during the Elizabethan Age, in which the protagonist, directed by the ghost of his murdered father or son, inflicts retaliation upon a powerful villain. Notable features of the revenge tragedy include violence, bizarre criminal acts, intrigue, insanity, a hesitant protagonist, and the use of soliloquy. Thomas Kyd's *Spanish Tragedy* is the first example of revenge tragedy in English, and William Shakespeare's *Hamlet* is perhaps the best. Extreme examples of revenge tragedy, such as John Webster's *The Duchess of Malfi,* are labeled "tragedies of blood." Also known as Tragedy of Blood.

Revista: The Spanish term for a vaudeville musical revue. Examples of *revistas* include Antonio Guzman Aguilera's *Mexico para los mexicanos,* Daniel Vanegas's *Maldito jazz,* and Don Catarino's *Whiskey, morfina y marihuana* and *El desterrado.*

Rhetoric: In literary criticism, this term denotes the art of ethical persuasion. In its strictest sense, rhetoric adheres to various principles developed since classical times for arranging facts and ideas in a clear, persuasive, appealing manner. The term is also used to refer to effective prose in general and theories of or methods for composing effective prose. Classical examples of rhetorics include *The Rhetoric of Aristotle,* Quintillian's *Institutio Oratoria,* and Cicero's *Ad Herennium.*

Rhetorical Question: A question intended to provoke thought, but not an expressed answer, in the reader. It is most commonly used in oratory and other persuasive genres. The following lines from Thomas Gray's "Elegy Written in a Country Churchyard" ask rhetorical questions: Can storied urn or animated bust Back to its mansion call the fleeting breath? Can Honour's voice provoke the silent dust, Or Flattery soothe the dull cold ear of Death?

Rhyme: When used as a noun in literary criticism, this term generally refers to a poem in which words sound identical or very similar and appear in parallel positions in two or more lines. Rhymes are classified into different types according to where they fall in a line or stanza or according to the degree of similarity they exhibit in their spellings and sounds. Some major types of rhyme are "masculine" rhyme, "feminine" rhyme, and "triple" rhyme. In a masculine rhyme, the rhyming sound falls in a single accented syllable, as with "heat"

and "eat." Feminine rhyme is a rhyme of two syllables, one stressed and one unstressed, as with "merry" and "tarry." Triple rhyme matches the sound of the accented syllable and the two unaccented syllables that follow: "narrative" and "declarative." Robert Browning alternates feminine and masculine rhymes in his "Soliloquy of the Spanish Cloister": Gr-r-r—there go, my heart's abhorrence! Water your damned flower-pots, do! If hate killed men, Brother Lawrence, God's blood, would not mine kill you! What? Your myrtle-bush wants trimming? Oh, that rose has prior claims— Needs its leaden vase filled brimming? Hell dry you up with flames! Triple rhymes can be found in Thomas Hood's "Bridge of Sighs," George Gordon Byron's satirical verse, and Ogden Nash's comic poems.

Rhyme Royal: A stanza of seven lines composed in iambic pentameter and rhymed *ababbcc.* The name is said to be a tribute to King James I of Scotland, who made much use of the form in his poetry. Examples of rhyme royal include Geoffrey Chaucer's *The Parlement of Foules,* William Shakespeare's *The Rape of Lucrece,* William Morris's *The Early Paradise,* and John Masefield's *The Widow in the Bye Street.*

Rhyme Scheme: See *Rhyme*

Rhythm: A regular pattern of sound, time intervals, or events occurring in writing, most often and most discernably in poetry. Regular, reliable rhythm is known to be soothing to humans, while interrupted, unpredictable, or rapidly changing rhythm is disturbing. These effects are known to authors, who use them to produce a desired reaction in the reader. An example of a form of irregular rhythm is sprung rhythm poetry; quantitative verse, on the other hand, is very regular in its rhythm.

Rising Action: The part of a drama where the plot becomes increasingly complicated. Rising action leads up to the climax, or turning point, of a drama. The final "chase scene" of an action film is generally the rising action which culminates in the film's climax.

Rococo: A style of European architecture that flourished in the eighteenth century, especially in France. The most notable features of *rococo* are its extensive use of ornamentation and its themes of lightness, gaiety, and intimacy. In literary criticism, the term is often used disparagingly to refer to a decadent or over-ornamental style. Alexander Pope's "The Rape of the Lock" is an example of literary *rococo.*

Roman a clef: A French phrase meaning "novel with a key." It refers to a narrative in which real persons are portrayed under fictitious names. Jack Kerouac, for example, portrayed various real-life beat generation figures under fictitious names in his *On the Road.*

Romance: A broad term, usually denoting a narrative with exotic, exaggerated, often idealized characters, scenes, and themes. Nathaniel Hawthorne called his *The House of the Seven Gables* and *The Marble Faun* romances in order to distinguish them from clearly realistic works.

Romantic Age: See *Romanticism*

Romanticism: This term has two widely accepted meanings. In historical criticism, it refers to a European intellectual and artistic movement of the late eighteenth and early nineteenth centuries that sought greater freedom of personal expression than that allowed by the strict rules of literary form and logic of the eighteenth-century neoclassicists. The Romantics preferred emotional and imaginative expression to rational analysis. They considered the individual to be at the center of all experience and so placed him or her at the center of their art. The Romantics believed that the creative imagination reveals nobler truths—unique feelings and attitudes—than those that could be discovered by logic or by scientific examination. Both the natural world and the state of childhood were important sources for revelations of "eternal truths." "Romanticism" is also used as a general term to refer to a type of sensibility found in all periods of literary history and usually considered to be in opposition to the principles of classicism. In this sense, Romanticism signifies any work or philosophy in which the exotic or dreamlike figure strongly, or that is devoted to individualistic expression, self-analysis, or a pursuit of a higher realm of knowledge than can be discovered by human reason. Prominent Romantics include Jean-Jacques Rousseau, William Wordsworth, John Keats, Lord Byron, and Johann Wolfgang von Goethe.

Romantics: See *Romanticism*

Russian Symbolism: A Russian poetic movement, derived from French symbolism, that flourished between 1894 and 1910. While some Russian Symbolists continued in the French tradition, stressing aestheticism and the importance of suggestion above didactic intent, others saw their craft as a form of mystical worship, and themselves as mediators between the supernatural and the mun-

dane. Russian symbolists include Aleksandr Blok, Vyacheslav Ivanovich Ivanov, Fyodor Sologub, Andrey Bely, Nikolay Gumilyov, and Vladimir Sergeyevich Solovyov.

S

Satire: A work that uses ridicule, humor, and wit to criticize and provoke change in human nature and institutions. There are two major types of satire: "formal" or "direct" satire speaks directly to the reader or to a character in the work; "indirect" satire relies upon the ridiculous behavior of its characters to make its point. Formal satire is further divided into two manners: the "Horatian," which ridicules gently, and the "Juvenalian," which derides its subjects harshly and bitterly. Voltaire's novella *Candide* is an indirect satire. Jonathan Swift's essay "A Modest Proposal" is a Juvenalian satire.

Scansion: The analysis or "scanning" of a poem to determine its meter and often its rhyme scheme. The most common system of scansion uses accents (slanted lines drawn above syllables) to show stressed syllables, breves (curved lines drawn above syllables) to show unstressed syllables, and vertical lines to separate each foot. In the first line of John Keats's *Endymion,* "A thing of beauty is a joy forever:" the word "thing," the first syllable of "beauty," the word "joy," and the second syllable of "forever" are stressed, while the words "A" and "of," the second syllable of "beauty," the word "a," and the first and third syllables of "forever" are unstressed. In the second line: "Its loveliness increases; it will never" a pair of vertical lines separate the foot ending with "increases" and the one beginning with "it."

Scene: A subdivision of an act of a drama, consisting of continuous action taking place at a single time and in a single location. The beginnings and endings of scenes may be indicated by clearing the stage of actors and props or by the entrances and exits of important characters. The first act of William Shakespeare's *Winter's Tale* is comprised of two scenes.

Science Fiction: A type of narrative about or based upon real or imagined scientific theories and technology. Science fiction is often peopled with alien creatures and set on other planets or in different dimensions. Karel Capek's *R.U.R.* is a major work of science fiction.

Second Person: See *Point of View*

Semiotics: The study of how literary forms and conventions affect the meaning of language. Semioticians include Ferdinand de Saussure, Charles Sanders Pierce, Claude Levi-Strauss, Jacques Lacan, Michel Foucault, Jacques Derrida, Roland Barthes, and Julia Kristeva.

Sestet: Any six-line poem or stanza. Examples of the sestet include the last six lines of the Petrarchan sonnet form, the stanza form of Robert Burns's "A Poet's Welcome to his love-begotten Daughter," and the sestina form in W. H. Auden's "Paysage Moralise."

Setting: The time, place, and culture in which the action of a narrative takes place. The elements of setting may include geographic location, characters' physical and mental environments, prevailing cultural attitudes, or the historical time in which the action takes place. Examples of settings include the romanticized Scotland in Sir Walter Scott's "Waverley" novels, the French provincial setting in Gustave Flaubert's *Madame Bovary,* the fictional Wessex country of Thomas Hardy's novels, and the small towns of southern Ontario in Alice Munro's short stories.

Shakespearean Sonnet: See *Sonnet*

Signifying Monkey: A popular trickster figure in black folklore, with hundreds of tales about this character documented since the 19th century. Henry Louis Gates Jr. examines the history of the signifying monkey in *The Signifying Monkey: Towards a Theory of Afro-American Literary Criticism,* published in 1988.

Simile: A comparison, usually using "like" or "as", of two essentially dissimilar things, as in "coffee as cold as ice" or "He sounded like a broken record." The title of Ernest Hemingway's "Hills Like White Elephants" contains a simile.

Slang: A type of informal verbal communication that is generally unacceptable for formal writing. Slang words and phrases are often colorful exaggerations used to emphasize the speaker's point; they may also be shortened versions of an often-used word or phrase. Examples of American slang from the 1990s include "yuppie" (an acronym for Young Urban Professional), "awesome" (for "excellent"), wired (for "nervous" or "excited"), and "chill out" (for relax).

Slant Rhyme: See *Consonance*

Slave Narrative: Autobiographical accounts of American slave life as told by escaped slaves. These works first appeared during the abolition movement of the 1830s through the 1850s. Olaudah Equiano's *The Interesting Narrative of Olaudah Equiano, or Gustavus Vassa, The African* and Harriet Ann Jacobs's *Incidents in the Life of a Slave Girl* are examples of the slave narrative.

Social Realism: See *Socialist Realism*

Socialist Realism: The Socialist Realism school of literary theory was proposed by Maxim Gorky and established as a dogma by the first Soviet Congress of Writers. It demanded adherence to a communist worldview in works of literature. Its doctrines required an objective viewpoint comprehensible to the working classes and themes of social struggle featuring strong proletarian heroes. A successful work of socialist realism is Nikolay Ostrovsky's *Kak zakalyalas stal (How the Steel Was Tempered).* Also known as Social Realism.

Soliloquy: A monologue in a drama used to give the audience information and to develop the speaker's character. It is typically a projection of the speaker's innermost thoughts. Usually delivered while the speaker is alone on stage, a soliloquy is intended to present an illusion of unspoken reflection. A celebrated soliloquy is Hamlet's "To be or not to be" speech in William Shakespeare's *Hamlet.*

Sonnet: A fourteen-line poem, usually composed in iambic pentameter, employing one of several rhyme schemes. There are three major types of sonnets, upon which all other variations of the form are based: the "Petrarchan" or "Italian" sonnet, the "Shakespearean" or "English" sonnet, and the "Spenserian" sonnet. A Petrarchan sonnet consists of an octave rhymed *abbaabba* and a "sestet" rhymed either *cdecde, cdccdc,* or *cdedce.* The octave poses a question or problem, relates a narrative, or puts forth a proposition; the sestet presents a solution to the problem, comments upon the narrative, or applies the proposition put forth in the octave. The Shakespearean sonnet is divided into three quatrains and a couplet rhymed *abab cdcd efef gg.* The couplet provides an epigrammatic comment on the narrative or problem put forth in the quatrains. The Spenserian sonnet uses three quatrains and a couplet like the Shakespearean, but links their three rhyme schemes in this way: *abab bcbc cdcd ee.* The Spenserian sonnet develops its theme in two parts like the Petrarchan, its final six lines resolving a problem, analyzing a narrative, or applying a proposition put forth in its first eight lines. Examples of sonnets can be found in Petrarch's *Canzoniere,* Edmund Spenser's *Amoretti,* Elizabeth Barrett

Browning's *Sonnets from the Portuguese,* Rainer Maria Rilke's *Sonnets to Orpheus,* and Adrienne Rich's poem "The Insusceptibles."

Spenserian Sonnet: See *Sonnet*

Spenserian Stanza: A nine-line stanza having eight verses in iambic pentameter, its ninth verse in iambic hexameter, and the rhyme scheme ababbcbcc. This stanza form was first used by Edmund Spenser in his allegorical poem *The Faerie Queene.*

Spondee: In poetry meter, a foot consisting of two long or stressed syllables occurring together. This form is quite rare in English verse, and is usually composed of two monosyllabic words. The first foot in the following line from Robert Burns's "Green Grow the Rashes" is an example of a spondee: Green grow the rashes, O

Sprung Rhythm: Versification using a specific number of accented syllables per line but disregarding the number of unaccented syllables that fall in each line, producing an irregular rhythm in the poem. Gerard Manley Hopkins, who coined the term "sprung rhythm," is the most notable practitioner of this technique.

Stanza: A subdivision of a poem consisting of lines grouped together, often in recurring patterns of rhyme, line length, and meter. Stanzas may also serve as units of thought in a poem much like paragraphs in prose. Examples of stanza forms include the quatrain, *terza rima, ottava rima,* Spenserian, and the so-called *In Memoriam* stanza from Alfred, Lord Tennyson's poem by that title. The following is an example of the latter form: Love is and was my lord and king, And in his presence I attend To hear the tidings of my friend, Which every hour his couriers bring.

Stereotype: A stereotype was originally the name for a duplication made during the printing process; this led to its modern definition as a person or thing that is (or is assumed to be) the same as all others of its type. Common stereotypical characters include the absent-minded professor, the nagging wife, the troublemaking teenager, and the kind-hearted grandmother.

Stream of Consciousness: A narrative technique for rendering the inward experience of a character. This technique is designed to give the impression of an ever-changing series of thoughts, emotions, images, and memories in the spontaneous and seemingly illogical order that they occur in life. The

textbook example of stream of consciousness is the last section of James Joyce's *Ulysses.*

Structuralism: A twentieth-century movement in literary criticism that examines how literary texts arrive at their meanings, rather than the meanings themselves. There are two major types of structuralist analysis: one examines the way patterns of linguistic structures unify a specific text and emphasize certain elements of that text, and the other interprets the way literary forms and conventions affect the meaning of language itself. Prominent structuralists include Michel Foucault, Roman Jakobson, and Roland Barthes.

Structure: The form taken by a piece of literature. The structure may be made obvious for ease of understanding, as in nonfiction works, or may obscured for artistic purposes, as in some poetry or seemingly "unstructured" prose. Examples of common literary structures include the plot of a narrative, the acts and scenes of a drama, and such poetic forms as the Shakespearean sonnet and the Pindaric ode.

Sturm und Drang: A German term meaning "storm and stress." It refers to a German literary movement of the 1770s and 1780s that reacted against the order and rationalism of the enlightenment, focusing instead on the intense experience of extraordinary individuals. Highly romantic, works of this movement, such as Johann Wolfgang von Goethe's *Gotz von Berlichingen,* are typified by realism, rebelliousness, and intense emotionalism.

Style: A writer's distinctive manner of arranging words to suit his or her ideas and purpose in writing. The unique imprint of the author's personality upon his or her writing, style is the product of an author's way of arranging ideas and his or her use of diction, different sentence structures, rhythm, figures of speech, rhetorical principles, and other elements of composition. Styles may be classified according to period (Metaphysical, Augustan, Georgian), individual authors (Chaucerian, Miltonic, Jamesian), level (grand, middle, low, plain), or language (scientific, expository, poetic, journalistic).

Subject: The person, event, or theme at the center of a work of literature. A work may have one or more subjects of each type, with shorter works tending to have fewer and longer works tending to have more. The subjects of James Baldwin's novel *Go Tell It on the Mountain* include the themes of father-son relationships, religious conversion, black life, and sexuality. The subjects of Anne Frank's

Diary of a Young Girl include Anne and her family members as well as World War II, the Holocaust, and the themes of war, isolation, injustice, and racism.

Subjectivity: Writing that expresses the author's personal feelings about his subject, and which may or may not include factual information about the subject. Subjectivity is demonstrated in James Joyce's *Portrait of the Artist as a Young Man,* Samuel Butler's *The Way of All Flesh,* and Thomas Wolfe's *Look Homeward, Angel.*

Subplot: A secondary story in a narrative. A subplot may serve as a motivating or complicating force for the main plot of the work, or it may provide emphasis for, or relief from, the main plot. The conflict between the Capulets and the Montagues in William Shakespeare's *Romeo and Juliet* is an example of a subplot.

Surrealism: A term introduced to criticism by Guillaume Apollinaire and later adopted by Andre Breton. It refers to a French literary and artistic movement founded in the 1920s. The Surrealists sought to express unconscious thoughts and feelings in their works. The best-known technique used for achieving this aim was automatic writing— transcriptions of spontaneous outpourings from the unconscious. The Surrealists proposed to unify the contrary levels of conscious and unconscious, dream and reality, objectivity and subjectivity into a new level of "super-realism." Surrealism can be found in the poetry of Paul Eluard, Pierre Reverdy, and Louis Aragon, among others.

Suspense: A literary device in which the author maintains the audience's attention through the buildup of events, the outcome of which will soon be revealed. Suspense in William Shakespeare's *Hamlet* is sustained throughout by the question of whether or not the Prince will achieve what he has been instructed to do and of what he intends to do.

Syllogism: A method of presenting a logical argument. In its most basic form, the syllogism consists of a major premise, a minor premise, and a conclusion. An example of a syllogism is: Major premise: When it snows, the streets get wet. Minor premise: It is snowing. Conclusion: The streets are wet.

Symbol: Something that suggests or stands for something else without losing its original identity. In literature, symbols combine their literal meaning with the suggestion of an abstract concept. Literary symbols are of two types: those that carry complex associations of meaning no matter what their con-

texts, and those that derive their suggestive meaning from their functions in specific literary works. Examples of symbols are sunshine suggesting happiness, rain suggesting sorrow, and storm clouds suggesting despair.

Symbolism: This term has two widely accepted meanings. In historical criticism, it denotes an early modernist literary movement initiated in France during the nineteenth century that reacted against the prevailing standards of realism. Writers in this movement aimed to evoke, indirectly and symbolically, an order of being beyond the material world of the five senses. Poetic expression of personal emotion figured strongly in the movement, typically by means of a private set of symbols uniquely identifiable with the individual poet. The principal aim of the Symbolists was to express in words the highly complex feelings that grew out of everyday contact with the world. In a broader sense, the term "symbolism" refers to the use of one object to represent another. Early members of the Symbolist movement included the French authors Charles Baudelaire and Arthur Rimbaud; William Butler Yeats, James Joyce, and T. S. Eliot were influenced as the movement moved to Ireland, England, and the United States. Examples of the concept of symbolism include a flag that stands for a nation or movement, or an empty cupboard used to suggest hopelessness, poverty, and despair.

Symbolist: See *Symbolism*

Symbolist Movement: See *Symbolism*

Sympathetic Fallacy: See *Affective Fallacy*

T

Tale: A story told by a narrator with a simple plot and little character development. Tales are usually relatively short and often carry a simple message. Examples of tales can be found in the work of Rudyard Kipling, Somerset Maugham, Saki, Anton Chekhov, Guy de Maupassant, and Armistead Maupin.

Tall Tale: A humorous tale told in a straightforward, credible tone but relating absolutely impossible events or feats of the characters. Such tales were commonly told of frontier adventures during the settlement of the west in the United States. Tall tales have been spun around such legendary heroes as Mike Fink, Paul Bunyan, Davy Crockett, Johnny Appleseed, and Captain Stormalong as well as the real-life William F. Cody and Annie Oakley. Literary use of tall tales can be found in Washington Irving's *History of New York,* Mark Twain's *Life on the Mississippi,* and in the German R. F. Raspe's *Baron Munchausen's Narratives of His Marvellous Travels and Campaigns in Russia.*

Tanka: A form of Japanese poetry similar to *haiku.* A *tanka* is five lines long, with the lines containing five, seven, five, seven, and seven syllables respectively. Skilled *tanka* authors include Ishikawa Takuboku, Masaoka Shiki, Amy Lowell, and Adelaide Crapsey.

Teatro Grottesco: See *Theater of the Grotesque*

Terza Rima: A three-line stanza form in poetry in which the rhymes are made on the last word of each line in the following manner: the first and third lines of the first stanza, then the second line of the first stanza and the first and third lines of the second stanza, and so on with the middle line of any stanza rhyming with the first and third lines of the following stanza. An example of *terza rima* is Percy Bysshe Shelley's ''The Triumph of Love'': As in that trance of wondrous thought I lay This was the tenour of my waking dream. Methought I sate beside a public way Thick strewn with summer dust, and a great stream Of people there was hurrying to and fro Numerous as gnats upon the evening gleam,. . .

Tetrameter: See *Meter*

Textual Criticism: A branch of literary criticism that seeks to establish the authoritative text of a literary work. Textual critics typically compare all known manuscripts or printings of a single work in order to assess the meanings of differences and revisions. This procedure allows them to arrive at a definitive version that (supposedly) corresponds to the author's original intention. Textual criticism was applied during the Renaissance to salvage the classical texts of Greece and Rome, and modern works have been studied, for instance, to undo deliberate correction or censorship, as in the case of novels by Stephen Crane and Theodore Dreiser.

Theater of Cruelty: Term used to denote a group of theatrical techniques designed to eliminate the psychological and emotional distance between actors and audience. This concept, introduced in the 1930s in France, was intended to inspire a more intense theatrical experience than conventional theater allowed. The ''cruelty'' of this dramatic theory signified not sadism but heightened actor/audience involvement in the dramatic event. The theater of cruelty was theorized by Antonin Artaud in his *Le Theatre et son double* (*The Theatre and Its Double*), and also appears in the work of Jerzy Grotowski, Jean Genet, Jean Vilar, and Arthur Adamov, among others.

Theater of the Absurd: A post-World War II dramatic trend characterized by radical theatrical innovations. In works influenced by the Theater of the absurd, nontraditional, sometimes grotesque characterizations, plots, and stage sets reveal a meaningless universe in which human values are irrelevant. Existentialist themes of estrangement, absurdity, and futility link many of the works of this movement. The principal writers of the Theater of the Absurd are Samuel Beckett, Eugene Ionesco, Jean Genet, and Harold Pinter.

Theater of the Grotesque: An Italian theatrical movement characterized by plays written around the ironic and macabre aspects of daily life in the World War I era. Theater of the Grotesque was named after the play *The Mask and the Face* by Luigi Chiarelli, which was described as ''a grotesque in three acts.'' The movement influenced the work of Italian dramatist Luigi Pirandello, author of *Right You Are, If You Think You Are.* Also known as *Teatro Grottesco.*

Theme: The main point of a work of literature. The term is used interchangeably with thesis. The theme of William Shakespeare's *Othello*—jealousy—is a common one.

Thesis: A thesis is both an essay and the point argued in the essay. Thesis novels and thesis plays share the quality of containing a thesis which is supported through the action of the story. A master's thesis and a doctoral dissertation are two theses required of graduate students.

Thesis Play: See *Thesis*

Three Unities: See *Unities*

Tone: The author's attitude toward his or her audience may be deduced from the tone of the work. A formal tone may create distance or convey politeness, while an informal tone may encourage a friendly, intimate, or intrusive feeling in the reader. The author's attitude toward his or her subject matter may also be deduced from the tone of the words he or she uses in discussing it. The tone of John F. Kennedy's speech which included the appeal to ''ask not what your country can do for you'' was intended to instill feelings of camaraderie and national pride in listeners.

Tragedy: A drama in prose or poetry about a noble, courageous hero of excellent character who, because of some tragic character flaw or *hamartia*, brings ruin upon him- or herself. Tragedy treats its subjects in a dignified and serious manner, using poetic language to help evoke pity and fear and bring about catharsis, a purging of these emotions. The tragic form was practiced extensively by the ancient Greeks. In the Middle Ages, when classical works were virtually unknown, tragedy came to denote any works about the fall of persons from exalted to low conditions due to any reason: fate, vice, weakness, etc. According to the classical definition of tragedy, such works present the "pathetic"—that which evokes pity—rather than the tragic. The classical form of tragedy was revived in the sixteenth century; it flourished especially on the Elizabethan stage. In modern times, dramatists have attempted to adapt the form to the needs of modern society by drawing their heroes from the ranks of ordinary men and women and defining the nobility of these heroes in terms of spirit rather than exalted social standing. The greatest classical example of tragedy is Sophocles' *Oedipus Rex*. The "pathetic" derivation is exemplified in "The Monk's Tale" in Geoffrey Chaucer's *Canterbury Tales*. Notable works produced during the sixteenth century revival include William Shakespeare's *Hamlet, Othello,* and *King Lear*. Modern dramatists working in the tragic tradition include Henrik Ibsen, Arthur Miller, and Eugene O'Neill.

Tragedy of Blood: See *Revenge Tragedy*

Tragic Flaw: In a tragedy, the quality within the hero or heroine which leads to his or her downfall. Examples of the tragic flaw include Othello's jealousy and Hamlet's indecisiveness, although most great tragedies defy such simple interpretation.

Transcendentalism: An American philosophical and religious movement, based in New England from around 1835 until the Civil War. Transcendentalism was a form of American romanticism that had its roots abroad in the works of Thomas Carlyle, Samuel Coleridge, and Johann Wolfgang von Goethe. The Transcendentalists stressed the importance of intuition and subjective experience in communication with God. They rejected religious dogma and texts in favor of mysticism and scientific naturalism. They pursued truths that lie beyond the "colorless" realms perceived by reason and the senses and were active social reformers in public education, women's rights, and the abolition of slavery. Promi-

nent members of the group include Ralph Waldo Emerson and Henry David Thoreau.

Trickster: A character or figure common in Native American and African literature who uses his ingenuity to defeat enemies and escape difficult situations. Tricksters are most often animals, such as the spider, hare, or coyote, although they may take the form of humans as well. Examples of trickster tales include Thomas King's *A Coyote Columbus Story,* Ashley F. Bryan's *The Dancing Granny* and Ishmael Reed's *The Last Days of Louisiana Red*.

Trimeter: See *Meter*

Triple Rhyme: See *Rhyme*

Trochee: See *Foot*

U

Understatement: See *Irony*

Unities: Strict rules of dramatic structure, formulated by Italian and French critics of the Renaissance and based loosely on the principles of drama discussed by Aristotle in his *Poetics*. Foremost among these rules were the three unities of action, time, and place that compelled a dramatist to: (1) construct a single plot with a beginning, middle, and end that details the causal relationships of action and character; (2) restrict the action to the events of a single day; and (3) limit the scene to a single place or city. The unities were observed faithfully by continental European writers until the Romantic Age, but they were never regularly observed in English drama. Modern dramatists are typically more concerned with a unity of impression or emotional effect than with any of the classical unities. The unities are observed in Pierre Corneille's tragedy *Polyeuctes* and Jean-Baptiste Racine's *Phedre*. Also known as Three Unities.

Urban Realism: A branch of realist writing that attempts to accurately reflect the often harsh facts of modern urban existence. Some works by Stephen Crane, Theodore Dreiser, Charles Dickens, Fyodor Dostoyevsky, Emile Zola, Abraham Cahan, and Henry Fuller feature urban realism. Modern examples include Claude Brown's *Manchild in the Promised Land* and Ron Milner's *What the Wine Sellers Buy*.

Utopia: A fictional perfect place, such as "paradise" or "heaven." Early literary utopias were included in Plato's *Republic* and Sir Thomas More's *Utopia,* while more modern utopias can be found in

Samuel Butler's *Erewhon,* Theodor Herzka's *A Visit to Freeland,* and H. G. Wells' *A Modern Utopia.*

Utopian: See *Utopia*

Utopianism: See *Utopia*

V

Verisimilitude: Literally, the appearance of truth. In literary criticism, the term refers to aspects of a work of literature that seem true to the reader. Verisimilitude is achieved in the work of Honore de Balzac, Gustave Flaubert, and Henry James, among other late nineteenth-century realist writers.

Vers de societe: See *Occasional Verse*

Vers libre: See *Free Verse*

Verse: A line of metered language, a line of a poem, or any work written in verse. The following line of verse is from the epic poem *Don Juan* by Lord Byron: ''My way is to begin with the beginning.''

Versification: The writing of verse. Versification may also refer to the meter, rhyme, and other mechanical components of a poem. Composition of a ''Roses are red, violets are blue'' poem to suit an occasion is a common form of versification practiced by students.

Victorian: Refers broadly to the reign of Queen Victoria of England (1837–1901) and to anything with qualities typical of that era. For example, the qualities of smug narrowmindedness, bourgeois materialism, faith in social progress, and priggish morality are often considered Victorian. This stereotype is contradicted by such dramatic intellectual developments as the theories of Charles Darwin, Karl Marx, and Sigmund Freud (which stirred strong debates in England) and the critical attitudes of serious Victorian writers like Charles Dickens and George Eliot. In literature, the Victorian Period was the great age of the English novel, and the latter part of the era saw the rise of movements such as decadence and symbolism. Works of Victorian literature include the poetry of Robert Browning and Alfred, Lord Tennyson, the criticism of Matthew Arnold and John Ruskin, and the novels of Emily Bronte, William Makepeace Thackeray, and Thomas Hardy. Also known as Victorian Age and Victorian Period.

Victorian Age: See *Victorian*

Victorian Period: See *Victorian*

W

Weltanschauung: A German term referring to a person's worldview or philosophy. Examples of *weltanschauung* include Thomas Hardy's view of the human being as the victim of fate, destiny, or impersonal forces and circumstances, and the disillusioned and laconic cynicism expressed by such poets of the 1930s as W. H. Auden, Sir Stephen Spender, and Sir William Empson.

Weltschmerz: A German term meaning ''world pain.'' It describes a sense of anguish about the nature of existence, usually associated with a melancholy, pessimistic attitude. *Weltschmerz* was expressed in England by George Gordon, Lord Byron in his *Manfred* and *Childe Harold's Pilgrimage,* in France by Viscount de Chateaubriand, Alfred de Vigny, and Alfred de Musset, in Russia by Aleksandr Pushkin and Mikhail Lermontov, in Poland by Juliusz Slowacki, and in America by Nathaniel Hawthorne.

Z

Zarzuela: A type of Spanish operetta. Writers of *zarzuelas* include Lope de Vega and Pedro Calderon.

Zeitgeist: A German term meaning ''spirit of the time.'' It refers to the moral and intellectual trends of a given era. Examples of *zeitgeist* include the preoccupation with the more morbid aspects of dying and death in some Jacobean literature, especially in the works of dramatists Cyril Tourneur and John Webster, and the decadence of the French Symbolists.

Cumulative Author/Title Index

Nationality/Ethnicity Index

Native Canadian

Highway, Tomson
   The Rez Sisters: V2

Nigerian

Clark, John Pepper
   The Raft: V13
Soyinka, Wole
   *Death and the King's
      Horseman:* V10

Norwegian

Ibsen, Henrik
   A Doll's House: V1
   Ghosts: V11
   Hedda Gabler: V6
   The Master Builder: V15
   Peer Gynt: V8
   The Wild Duck: V10

Romanian

Ionesco, Eugène
   The Bald Soprano: V4
   The Chairs: V9

Russian

Chekhov, Anton
   The Cherry Orchard: V1
   The Seagull: V12
   The Three Sisters: V10
   Uncle Vanya: V5
Gogol, Nikolai
   The Government Inspector: V12
Gorki, Maxim
   The Lower Depths: V9
Turgenev, Ivan
   A Month in the Country: V6

Scottish

Barrie, J(ames) M.
   Peter Pan: V7

South African

Fugard, Athol
   *"Master Harold". . . and
      the Boys:* V3
   Boesman & Lena: V6
   Sizwe Bansi is Dead: V10

Spanish

Buero Vallejo, Antonio
   The Sleep of Reason: V11
García Lorca, Federico
   Blood Wedding: V10
   The House of Bernarda Alba: V4

Swedish

Strindberg, August
   The Ghost Sonata: V9
   Miss Julie: V4

Subject/Theme Index

Fate and Chance
Idiot's Delight: 49, 54, 57, 59
J. B.: 70, 73–74, 77,
84–85, 87–88
The Master Builder:
158, 160, 163
Fear and Terror
*The Diary of Anne
Frank:* 3–4, 7–8
The Master Builder: 158, 160,
163, 165, 170–173
The Shadow Box: 252, 256–257
Feminism and Gender Stereotypes
Rites: 220
Feminism
Rites: 222–224
Film
The Diary of Anne Frank: 15–19
The Last Night of Ballyhoo: 91,
97–98, 105–106
*One Day, When I Was Lost: A
Scenario:* 175–176, 185, 187
Free Will and Determinism
The Great White Hope: 33

G

Gender Roles
The Shrike: 273
Gender Roles
Rites: 221, 224
Ghost
Ma Rainey's Black Bottom:
143–144, 146
God
J. B.: 68–71, 73–75, 79–88
Ma Rainey's Black Bottom:
152, 154–156
The Master Builder: 167–168
Rites: 224, 226
Greed
*The Life and Adventures of
Nicholas Nickleby:*
111, 115, 117
Grief and Sorrow
J. B.: 84, 86–87
The Shadow Box: 263–265
Guilt
J. B.: 83, 86
The Master Builder: 160,
163–164, 171–173

H

Happiness and Gaiety
*The Life and Adventures of
Nicholas Nickleby:* 110–111,
117, 120, 123–124
Ma Rainey's Black Bottom: 156
Reunion: 208–209
Rites: 224–227
The Way of the World: 284,
286–287, 294–295

Harlem Renaissance
Ma Rainey's Black Bottom: 137
Hatred
The Diary of Anne Frank: 9–10
*The Great White
Hope:* 27–28, 36
J. B.: 84–87
Ma Rainey's Black Bottom: 146,
150–151, 154–155
*One Day, When I Was Lost: A
Scenario:* 179, 183, 186
Rites: 225–226
The Shadow Box: 265
The Way of the World: 284–285,
288, 295–299, 302
Heroism
The Great White Hope: 39–44
The Master Builder:
169, 171–172
Reunion: 208–209
The Rivals: 246, 248–249
The Shrike: 278–279
The Way of the World: 292–295,
298–300, 302
History
The Diary of Anne Frank: 15–20
J. B.: 75
*The Last Night of
Ballyhoo:* 96–97
*Ma Rainey's Black
Bottom:* 141–143
The Shrike: 273
The Way of the World: 296,
303–304, 308
Homosexuality
Ma Rainey's Black Bottom: 149
Honor
The Last Night of Ballyhoo: 105
The Way of the World: 287
Hope
The Diary of Anne Frank: 1, 4,
6, 8, 10, 15–16, 18–19
The Great White Hope: 26–28,
33–35, 40–41, 43–44
Idiot's Delight: 54, 56
J. B.: 68–69, 71, 73, 78
The Way of the World: 285,
292, 294–295
Hopelessness and Despair
J. B.: 73
Humiliation and Degradation
*The Last Night of
Ballyhoo:* 102–104
The Way of the World: 282, 284,
286–288, 292
Humor
The Great White Hope: 41–43
The Last Night of Ballyhoo:
90, 97, 99
*Ma Rainey's Black
Bottom:* 144–145
The Rivals: 229, 231–232, 238,
240, 242–249

The Shadow Box: 251,
253, 258–259
The Way of the World: 281–282,
284–289, 291, 293–295,
297–299, 302, 310

I

Identity
The Diary of Anne Frank: 7
Ignorance
J. B.: 86–87
Imagery and Symbolism
J. B.: 83
Ma Rainey's Black Bottom:
143–146, 150–152, 156
The Way of the World: 309, 311
Imagination
The Master Builder: 159, 164
The Way of the World:
283–287, 293, 295
Immigrants and Immigration
*The Last Night of
Ballyhoo:* 96, 98
Interracial Relationships
The Great White Hope: 32
Irony
The Great White Hope: 42
Idiot's Delight: 65–66
*Ma Rainey's Black
Bottom:* 147, 149
The Way of the World: 288, 295
Islamism
*One Day, When I Was Lost: A
Scenario:* 177–179, 182–183,
186, 189–190, 192–195

J

Judaism
The Diary of Anne Frank: 1, 3,
9–11, 16–23
The Last Night of Ballyhoo:
90–91, 93, 95–97, 99–107
Justice versus Love
J. B.: 74

K

Killers and Killing
The Diary of Anne Frank: 15, 20
J. B.: 70–71, 73,
75–77, 84–85, 87
*Ma Rainey's Black
Bottom:* 147, 155
*One Day, When I Was Lost: A
Scenario:* 178, 184
Rites: 215, 222
The Shrike: 269, 274–275
Kindness
The Rivals: 245, 247–248